Audi Alteram Partem in Criminal Proceedings

Stefano Ruggeri

Audi Alteram Partem in Criminal Proceedings

Towards a Participatory Understanding of Criminal Justice in Europe and Latin America

Springer

Stefano Ruggeri
Department of Law
University of Messina
Messina, Italy

ISBN 978-3-319-54572-1 ISBN 978-3-319-54573-8 (eBook)
DOI 10.1007/978-3-319-54573-8

Library of Congress Control Number: 2017934918

Printed on acid-free paper

This Springer imprint is published by Springer Nature
The registered company is Springer International Publishing AG
The registered company address is: Gewerbestrasse 11, 6330 Cham, Switzerland

To Figaro, who left us too soon to run back to the forest as he always loved it

Acknowledgements

This book is the result of a long period of research, and therefore, there is also a long list of institutions and people I am in debt to. This study was mainly carried out at the *Max-Planck Institute of Foreign and International Criminal Law* (Freiburg i.Br., Germany) and contains a great part of the results of research supported by the *Alexander von Humboldt Foundation*. Without the generous support of the *Humboldt Foundation* and the hospitality and assistance of *Prof. Dr. Dr. h.c. mult. Ulrich Sieber* (director of the Criminal Law Department at the *Max-Planck Institute*), this would certainly have been impossible, and it is therefore difficult for me to find the appropriate words to express the gratitude I feel towards both of them. I am also grateful to the Law Faculty at Basel University and to *Prof. Dr. Sabine Gleß*, especially for her support and hospitality in her department during the 2 months of May and June 2016. Moreover, I wish to thank the Law Department at Messina University, which organised excellent arrangements to cover my long absence from Sicily. A special thank you goes, once again, to *Springer Verlag* and especially to *Dr. Brigitte Reschke* for her patience and interest shown in this research.

A number of colleagues and friends have supported this research in various ways over the years. In particular, I wish to thank my mentor *Prof. Enrico Marzaduri*, as well as *Prof. Dr. Lorena Bachmaier Winter*, *Prof. Dr. Bernd Hecker*, *Dr. Barbara Huber*, *Prof. Dr. Serena Quattrocolo* and *Prof. Dr. Arndt Sinn*. Their advice and irreplaceable suggestions on several topics dealt with in this study were priceless for me. I am also grateful to my colleagues and researchers at the *Max-Planck Institute*, who provided me with the unique opportunity of a daily exchange of ideas on several issues. A special thank you goes to my father, *Prof. Antonio Ruggeri*, for his constant support and his advice in dealing with the constitutional law issues.

Carrying out this comparative study was a very demanding challenge for me on several grounds. Thus, I would like to apologise in advance to the reader for providing a result that will certainly have a number of deficiencies. Notwithstanding the great amount of books and materials I have read over the years, I am aware that my experience is still too limited to grasp the complexity of developments that have occurred in my own country, as well as in EU law and Strasbourg case law.

Even more limited was my knowledge to manage the difficult comparison with Brazil and Inter-American case law. Therefore, I would like to thank my colleagues at the PURCS University of Porto Alegre (Brazil), especially *Prof. Dr. Nereu Giacomolli* and *Prof. Dr. Aury Lopes Jr.*, for providing me with the necessary bibliography and for their advice. The choice of language of this book was also a demanding task. Despite my limited experience with articles in foreign languages, writing an entire book in English certainly required skills that went far beyond the command of language. I am aware of the limits of my English, and so I am very grateful to *Christopher Schuller* for providing excellent editing of this study. In the light of all this, I hope the reader will look at this research with patient eyes.

I would like to end these lines by thanking my whole family, especially my parents, who had to bear the difficulties of our absence over these years. As always, my last words are directed to my wife *Norma* and my two little girls, *Anna Lucia* and *Maria Isabel*, who have unconditionally accompanied me in this road and have constantly supported my research with their love. Moreover, my thoughts also now go to two new members of my family, *Mango* and *Cocco*, who have come to warm up our lives and daily help me cope with the loss of *Figaro*, for me a son and incomparable friend, to whom this research—with all its limitations—is dedicated.

Ganzirri, Italy Stefano Ruggeri
December 2016

Contents

Part I Introduction to the Research

1 Preliminary Issues 3
A. The Problem 3
B. Subject and Aims of the Investigation 5
C. Methodology and Structure of the Investigation 6
References 8

Part II *Audi Alteram Partem* in National Criminal Justice. The Perspective of Domestic Law

2 Participatory Rights in Italian Criminal Justice and the Developments Towards a *contradictoire*-Based Model of Criminal Proceedings 11
A. Introductory Remarks. The Long Road of Italian Law Towards a New Model of Criminal Proceedings, Based on the Contribution of Private Parties to the Administration of Justice 13
B. The Development of a Constitutional Participatory Model of Fair Criminal Justice 17
I. Participatory Rights in the 1947 Constitution 17
II. The Enactment of a *contradictoire*-Based Model of Criminal Justice Under the Increasing Influence of International Human Rights Law 19
1. The Principle of *contradictoire* as the Core Guarantee of the Constitutional Model of a Fair Trial 19
2. A Systematic Understanding of the Constitutional Model of a Fair Trial and the Need for an Overall Balance Between the Right to Confrontation and Other Constitutional Interests 21

C. The Principle of *contradictoire* and Equality of Arms 24
I. Premise. The Link Between the Requirements of *contradictoire* and Equality of Arms in the Constitutional Model of a Fair Trial 24
II. Defence and Prosecutorial Inquiries 25
D. The Role of Private Parties in the Exercise of Criminal Prosecutions 28
I. The Role of the Victim in the Institution of Criminal Proceedings. The Relationship Between Private and Public Prosecution 28
II. Parties' Involvement in the Decision Not to Institute a Criminal Prosecution or to Drop Criminal Proceedings 32
1. The Defence's Involvement in the Decision Not to Institute a Criminal Prosecution 32
2. The Need to Balance Conflicting Interests in the Decision Whether to Prosecute or to Terminate Criminal Proceedings 34
E. The Principle of *contradictoire* and the Right to Be Informed in Criminal Proceedings 39
I. The Constitutional Model of Informed Participation in Criminal Proceedings 39
II. Information on the Accusation 41
1. Information on the Charge in the Pre-Trial Inquiry 41
2. Preventive Information About the Decision to Charge 44
3. Information on the Indictment 48
III. Information on Developments of the Criminal Inquiry and the Evidence Supporting the Charging Decision 49
IV. Notice of the Institution of Court Proceedings and the Right to Know the Initiation of a Criminal Prosecution 52
F. Prosecutorial Needs and the Right of Participation in Criminal Proceedings 54
I. Premise 54
II. Prosecutorial Needs and the Right to Personally Participate in Court Proceedings. The Problem of *in absentia* Proceedings 55
1. The 1988 Rules on Default Proceedings and Developments Due to the Strasbourg Case-Law 55
2. The 2014 Reform: The Disappearance of Default Proceedings and the New Procedure for Absent Defendants 57
III. Participatory Rights in Alternative Proceedings 59
1. Premise 60
2. *Inaudito reo* Proceedings and the Problem of Criminal Conviction Without Previous Hearing. The Case of Penal Order Proceedings 61

3. Criminal Hearings *in camera* and the Right to Be Heard Fairly. The Complex Trade-Offs Required by Plea Bargaining and Abbreviated Proceedings 64
G. The Right to Have Oneself Fairly Heard 68
I. Premise 68
II. The Right to Be Fairly Heard in the Pre-Trial Phase 68
1. The 1988 Model and the Subsequent Developments in the Dynamics of the Prosecutorial Inquiry. The Progressive Re-Enhancement of the Power of the Investigative Bodies to Obtain Oral Evidence 68
2. The Weak Protection of Suspects and Victims 71
3. The Risks of the Witness Testimony of Co-Defendants Assisted by a Lawyer 74
III. The Right to Be Heard Fairly in Open Court 76
H. *Audi alteram partem* and the Collection of Evidence 80
I. Introductory Remarks. Principle of *contradictoire* in the Taking of Evidence 80
II. Participatory Rights in Evidence-Gathering in the Pre-Trial Inquiry 82
1. The Involvement of Private Parties in Prosecutorial and Police Inquiries 82
2. The Right to Confrontation in *incidente probatorio* 83
III. Participatory Rights in Evidence-Gathering at Trial 85
1. Principle of *contradictoire*, Oral Evidence and the Need for Constant Balance Among Conflicting Interests 85
2. Principle of *contradictoire* and the Collection of Expert Evidence 87
3. Principle of *contradictoire* and Documentary Evidence. Participatory Rights and the Admission of Evidence Gathered in Other Proceedings 89
4. Defendant's Consent and Evidentiary Agreements Among the Parties 91
I. Participatory Rights, the Use of Untested Evidence and the Defence's Contribution to Fact-Finding 93
I. Systematic Remarks. The High Relativism of Italian Evidence Law 93
II. Participatory Rights and Fact-Finding in the Trial Phase 96
1. Premise 96
2. Evidence Unavailable at Trial 97
3. Hearsay Evidence 100
4. Inconsistent Out-of-Court Evidence 102
III. Participatory Rights and Fact-Finding in Alternative Proceedings 109
1. Premise 109

2. Alternative Proceedings and the Waiver of the Right to Participation in Evidence-Gathering 109
3. The Impact of the Accused's Waiver on the Interests of Other Parties and on Fact-Finding 112
J. The Principle of *contradictoire* and Pre-Trial Restrictions on Freedom 113
I. Premise 113
II. Participatory Rights and Fact-Finding in the Decision on Coercive Measures. Another Endurance Test for the Distinction Between Strict and Free Assessment of Evidence 115
III. *Audi alteram partem* in the Procedure on Remand Detention and Further Restrictions on Liberty 117
1. Participatory Safeguards in the Procedure on the Application of Coercive Measures. The Inconveniences of Another Example of *inaudito reo* Proceedings 117
2. Participatory Rights in the Judicial Review Proceedings Against Coercive Measures 120
K. Provisional Conclusions 123
References 124

3 Participatory Rights in Brazilian Law and the Requirements of *contradictoire* and Full Defence in Criminal Proceedings 129
A. Premise 130
B. Participatory Safeguards in the Constitutional Model of a Fair Trial. The Right to *contradictoire* and Full Defence 130
C. *Audi alteram partem* and Equality of Arms 132
D. The Role of Private Parties in the Decision to Charge 135
I. Participatory Rights of the Victim in the Initiation of Criminal Proceedings. The Forms of Private Criminal Prosecution 135
II. The Involvement of Private Parties in the Decision Not to Institute or to Drop a Criminal Prosecution 136
E. The Principle of *contradictoire* and Right to Information in Criminal Proceedings 138
I. The Right to Information in the Pre-Trial Stage 138
II. Charging Decision and the Need for Proper Information on the Initiation of Criminal Proceedings 140
F. Prosecutorial Needs and the Right to Take Part Personally in Criminal Proceedings. The Problem of *in absentia* Procedures in Brazilian Law 141
G. Investigative Needs and the Right to Be Fairly Heard 145
I. The Right to Be Fairly Heard in the Pre-Trial Phase 145
II. The Right to Be Fairly Heard in Court Proceedings 146
H. *Audi alteram partem* and the Collection of Evidence 149
I. The Right to *contradictoire* in Obtaining Oral Evidence 149
II. The Right to *contradictoire* in the Taking of Expert Evidence . . . 151
III. The Right to *contradictoire* and Documentary Evidence 152

I. *Audi alteram partem* and the Proof of Guilt . . . 153
J. *Audi alteram partem* and the Use of Measures of Coercion . . . 155
I. Premise . . . 155
II. The Right to *contradictoire* and Restrictions on Freedom . . . 155
1. Participatory Safeguards in Remand Proceedings . . . 155
2. *Audi alteram partem* and Provisional Arrest . . . 159
3. The Right to Be fairly Heard in Cases of Temporary Detention . . . 160
III. The Right to Be fairly Heard and Investigative Interferences with Fundamental Rights . . . 161
IV. *Audi alteram partem* in *habeas corpus* Proceedings . . . 162
1. *Habeas corpus* in Brazilian Law . . . 162
2. Participatory Rights in *habeas corpus* Proceedings . . . 163
K. Interim Conclusions . . . 164
References . . . 165

Part III *Audi Alteram Partem* in Transnational Criminal Justice. The Perspective of Domestic Law

4 Participatory Rights in Transnational Criminal Justice Under Italian Law . . . 169
A. General Remarks on the Rules Governing Transnational Criminal Inquiries . . . 170
I. The Domestic Rules on Legal Assistance and the Influence of International Law Instruments . . . 170
II. The Domestication of EU Law on Legal Assistance . . . 171
B. Human Rights Developments in the Italian Law on Transnational Criminal Justice. Introductory Remarks . . . 172
C. Participatory Rights in National Cases with Transnational Features . . . 174
D. Participatory Rights, Right to Freedom and International Surrender Procedures. The Italian Law on Extradition . . . 176
I. *In absentia* Trials and International Surrender . . . 176
II. The Right to Be Fairly Heard and to Challenge the Lawfulness of the Surrender Procedure . . . 179
III. Coercive Means and the Right to a Judicial Hearing . . . 181
1. Coercive Means in Surrender Procedures . . . 181
2. The Hearing of the Person Subject to Measures of Coercion . . . 183
IV. The Role of the Judiciary in Extradition Procedures . . . 185
E. Participatory Rights and Transnational Evidence . . . 188
I. Models of Gathering Evidence Abroad . . . 188
II. Participatory Rights in the Taking of Evidence Abroad . . . 190

III. Defence Rights and the Use of Overseas Evidence 192
1. Premise 192
2. Movement of Evidence and Defence Rights in the Admission of Information already Gathered Abroad 192
3. Defence Rights and the Use of Evidence Taken Abroad in Response of an Italian Request for Legal Assistance 194
4. The Lax Approach of Italian Courts to the Use of Overseas Evidence 196
IV. Defence Rights in Gathering Evidence Requested by Other Countries 197
F. Provisional Conclusions 199
References 199

5 Participatory Safeguards in Transnational Criminal Justice Under Brazilian Law 201
A. General Remarks on the Brazilian Rules Governing Transnational Criminal Justice 201
B. Human Rights in Brazilian Transnational Inquiries 203
C. Participatory Rights in Domestic Criminal Proceedings with Transnational Features 205
D. *Audi alteram partem* and the Protection of Personal Freedom in Extradition Procedures 206
I. The Problem of *in absentia* Trials 206
II. The Right to a Fair Hearing and the Role of the Judiciary in Extradition Procedures 207
E. Participatory Rights and the Taking of Evidence in Transnational Cases 210
I. Modes of Gathering Overseas Evidence 210
II. The Right to a Defence and Equality of Arms in the Taking of Overseas Evidence 211
III. Participatory Rights in the Collection of Evidence Requested by Foreign Countries 213
F. Provisional Conclusions 215
References 215

Part IV Convergences and Divergences in the National Understanding of Participatory Rights in Domestic and Transnational Criminal Justice

6 Common Developments and Deficiencies of the Domestic Approach to Participatory Safeguards in Criminal Proceedings 219
A. Premise 220
B. The Constitutionalisation of the Principle of *contradictoire* and Its Contribution of to a Human Rights-Oriented Understanding of Criminal Justice 222

C. *Audi alteram partem* and the Principle of Equality of Arms. The Weak Role of the Judiciary and Persistent Imbalances in the Pre-trial Inquiry 225
D. Criminal Prosecution and the Role of Private Parties 227
I. The Proactive Role of the Injured Party in the Institution of Criminal Proceedings. The Problem of Private Prosecutions 227
II. The Involvement of Private Parties in the Decision Not to Institute or to Drop a Criminal Prosecution 230
E. Principle of *contradictoire* and Information in Criminal Proceedings 234
I. The Right to Information on the Charge, Right to Know Relevant Evidence and the Difficult Trade-Offs Required in the Investigative Phase 234
II. Information on the Initiation of a Criminal Law Action and Recent Legal Arrangements to Involve the Accused Personally in the Proceedings 237
F. The Right to Personal Participation in Criminal Proceedings and the Problem of *in absentia* Proceedings 239
G. Investigative Needs and the Right to Be Fairly Heard in Criminal Proceedings 241
I. The Right to a Fair Hearing, Legal Assistance and the Role of the Judiciary in the Pre-trial Examination of the Accused 241
II. The Right to a Fair Hearing of Individuals Other Than the Accused and the Lack of Comprehensive Rules on Different Informants 245
III. The Right to Silence, Defensive Choices and the Right to Be Fairly Heard in Judicial Proceedings 246
IV. Methods of Examination and the Guarantees of a Fair Hearing 248
H. *Audi alteram partem* and the Collection of Criminal Evidence 250
I. Participatory Rights in the Taking of Oral Evidence and the Role of the Judiciary 250
II. The Right to Confrontation, Documentary Evidence and the Use of Information Gathered in Other Proceedings 253
III. The Right to *contradictoire*, Technical Investigations and Expert Evidence 255
I. The Parties' Contribution to the Decision-Making and the Requirements of *contradictoire*-Based Fact-Finding 257
I. Relativism of Criminal Evidence and the Different Probative Value Depending on the Decision at Stake 257
II. Principle of *contradictoire*, the Proof of Guilt and the Principle of Free Assessment of Evidence 259

J. *Audi alteram partem* and Pre-trial Restrictions on Freedom 261
I. Premise 261
II. The Right to *contradictoire* and Short-Term Restrictions on Liberty 262
III. Pre-trial Measures and the Guarantee of a Fair Hearing of the Accused and the Victim in Remand Proceedings 265
IV. Participatory Rights in the Proceedings Activated by the Defence on Judicial Oversight of Restrictions on Freedom 267
K. Provisional Conclusions 268
References 269

7 Similarities and Shortcomings of the National Understanding of Participatory Rights in the Field of Transnational Criminal Justice 271
A. Constitutional Law Safeguards and the Slow Enhancement of Participatory Rights in Transnational Criminal Cases 272
B. Information Rights and the Conduct of a Criminal Law Action with Transnational Elements 274
C. *Audi alteram partem* and International Surrender Procedures 276
I. Premise 276
II. Participatory Rights in the Trial Country and Surrender Procedures. The Rising Influence of International and Constitutional Law, and the Enhancement of the Procedural Safeguards in the Field of *in absentia* Proceedings 276
III. Participatory Rights in the Surrender Procedure 278
1. Giving a Voice to the Sought Person 278
a) Procedural Safeguards in the Prosecutorial Hearing and the Right to be Fairly Heard by a Judge 278
b) Surrender Procedures, Coercive Means and the Right to a Fair Hearing 281
2. The Role of the Judiciary in the Surrender Procedures and the Right to Challenge the Lawfulness of the Proceeding 282
D. Participatory Rights and Transnational Evidence 284
I. Models of Gathering Transnational Evidence. The Traditional Approach of the Brazilian and Italian Law and the Rising Development of Informal Modes of International Cooperation . . . 284
II. Participatory Safeguards in the Collection of Evidence Abroad 285
1. Defence Rights in the Evidence-Gathering and the Right to Obtain Exculpatory Evidence 285
2. Participatory Safeguards and the Admissibility of Overseas Evidence 287

III. Participatory Rights in the Collection of Evidence Requested by Foreign Countries . . . 289
E. Interim Findings . . . 290
References . . . 290

Part V Evolution of a Wideranging Participatory Approach to Criminal Justice in International Human Rights Law and EU Law

8 *Audi alteram partem* in Criminal Proceedings Under the European Convention on Human Rights . . . 293
A. Introductory Issues. The Right to a Fair Hearing and the Need for Overall Balance of Conflicting Interests . . . 294
B. *Audi alteram partem* and the Principle of Equality of Arms . . . 296
C. Prosecutorial Needs and the Right to Be personally Involved in Criminal Proceedings. The Flexible Approach of the Strasbourg Case-Law . . . 297
I. The Right to Be Present in Criminal Proceedings and Individual Duties of Diligence . . . 297
1. The Right to Be Present at Trial . . . 297
2. The Right to Be Present Before a Higher Instance . . . 299
II. The Problem of *in absentia* Procedures . . . 300
III. *Inaudito reo* Proceedings and the Right of the Injured Party to Participate in Criminal Hearings . . . 302
D. Information Rights and Requirements of Effective Participation in Criminal Proceedings . . . 304
I. Premise . . . 304
II. The Right to Know and Understand the Accusation . . . 305
1. Information on the Charge . . . 305
2. Decision to Charge and Information Rights in the Pre-Trial Inquiry . . . 308
III. Information on the Evidence Gathered and the Right to Access to the Prosecutorial File . . . 310
E. The Guarantee of a Fair Hearing and the Privilege Against Self-Incrimination . . . 313
I. The Accused's Right to Be fairly Heard by an Independent Body and Qualitative Requirements of Pre-Trial Questionings . . . 313
II. Prosecutorial Needs and the Right of Individuals Other than the Accused to Make Their Voice Heard in Criminal Proceedings . . . 314
III. The Right Not to Be Heard in Criminal Justice. Developments in the Principle of *nemo tenetur se detegere* . . . 315
F. Defence's Contribution to the Evidence-Gathering and the Requirements of a Fair Decision-Making . . . 319
I. Premise . . . 319

II. Participation Rights in the Collection of Criminal Evidence 321
1. The Right to Confrontation and the Need for an Overall Balance of Conflicting Interests in Criminal Proceedings 321
2. Methods of Confrontation 321
a) Direct and Indirect Examination 321
b) Anonymous Witnesses and the Use of Alternative Means of Confrontation 323
3. The Right to Confrontation and Inconsistent Testimony 326
III. The Right to Confrontation and the Proof of Guilt 327
1. Premise 327
2. Out-of-Court Confrontations and the Use of Evidence Obtained Without the Defence's Participation in the Case of Subsequent Confrontation 327
3. Absent Witnesses and the Use of Untested Evidence 329
a) The Traditional Approach of the Strasbourg Case-Law: The Sole and Decisive Evidence Doctrine 329
b) The Developments in the European Case-Law After the *Al-Khawaja and Tahery* Judgment: The Progressive Softening of the Sole and Decisive Evidence Test 330
IV. The Contribution of Private Parties to the Decision-Making. *Audi alteram partem* Rule and Argumentation in Criminal Proceedings 331
G. *Audi alteram partem* and Measures of Coercion in Criminal Proceedings 335
I. Deprivation of Freedom and the Right to Information. The Soft Approach of the European Case-Law 335
II. The Right to a Fair Hearing and the Guarantee of Prompt Judicial Review of Arrest or Detention 337
III. Participatory Rights in *habeas corpus* Proceedings 340
H. Provisional Conclusions 343
References 343

9 Participatory Rights in Criminal Justice Under the American Convention on Human Rights 345
A. Premise. The Criminal Trial as a Listening Space with Due Guarantees and the Strong Human Rights Approach of the American Convention 345
B. The Right to Be Fairly Heard and the Overall Assessment of Human Rights Violations 347
C. The Right to Have Personal Access to Court and the Need for Comprehensive Judicial Oversight of Infringements on Human Rights 349
D. Investigative Needs and the Right to Informed Participation in Criminal Proceedings 350

E. Participatory Rights and the Taking of Criminal Evidence 353
I. The Right to Contribute to Evidence-Gathering in the Light of an Overall Human Rights Assessment 353
1. The Defence's Involvement in the Taking of Incriminating Evidence 353
2. Qualitative Conditions of Effective Confrontation, Miscarriage of Justice and Deficiencies of National Law 354
3. Anonymous Witnesses and the Use of Untested Evidence 355
II. The Right to Access to Exculpatory Evidence in Death Penalties 357
F. The Defence's Argumentative Contribution to the Decision-Making 357
G. Restrictions on Freedom, Right to Be Fairly Heard and the Enhanced Need for Overall Human Rights Oversight 359
I. The Broad Protection of Information Rights 359
II. The Right to a Prompt Judicial Hearing and the Protection Against Inhuman Treatment 362
III. *Audi alteram partem* in *habeas corpus* Proceedings 363
H. Provisional Conclusions 364
References 365

10 Harmonisation of Criminal Justice and Participatory Rights in Criminal Proceedings. New Developments in EU Law After the Lisbon Treaty 367
A. Harmonisation of Criminal Procedure Law and the Enhancement of Participatory Rights in Criminal Justice After the Lisbon Treaty 368
B. The Right to Be personally Involved in Criminal Proceedings in the EU Area 370
I. The Right to Personal Participation in Criminal Hearings. A Limited Guarantee 370
II. Exceptions to the Right to Personal Participation 372
1. *In absentia* Procedures 372
2. *Inaudito reo* Proceedings 375
a) The *Covaci* Case and the Indications of the European Court of Justice 375
b) The New Safeguards Laid Down by EU Statutory Law . . . 379
III. Towards a Victim's Right to Personally Participate in Criminal Proceedings? 380
C. Conditions of Effective Defence and the Right to Active Participation in Criminal Proceedings 381
I. Language and the Right to Effective Participation in Criminal Proceedings 381
1. Linguistic Guarantees of the Accused 381
2. Linguistic Guarantees of the Victim 383

II. Information Rights and the Guarantee of Effective Defence 386
1. Information Rights of the Accused 386
a) Premise 386
b) Information on the Charge 386
c) Information on the Investigation and the Right to Access the File 388
2. Information Rights of the Victim 389
III. The Right to Be fairly Heard in Criminal Proceedings 390
1. The Voice of the Accused 390
2. The Voice of the Victim 392
IV. The Defence's Contribution to the Gathering of Evidence 393
D. Participatory Rights and Coercive Measures in the Field of Personal Freedom 396
E. Interim Conclusions 398
References 399

Part VI Developments in International and Supranational Law Towards a Participatory Understanding of Transnational Criminal Justice

11 Participatory Rights and Transnational Criminal Justice in the European Convention 403
A. Introductory Remarks 403
B. The European Convention and the Protection of Fair Trial Rights in Transnational Cases 405
C. Information and Participatory Safeguards in National Criminal Proceedings Having Transnational Dimension 409
D. Participatory Rights in International Cooperation in Criminal Matters 412
I. Premise 412
II. The Right to Freedom and Participatory Guarantees in Surrender Procedures 412
1. Information Rights in Extradition Proceedings 412
2. Extradition Proceedings and the Right to Be Heard in Person 413
3. The Problem of *in absentia* Trials in the Field of International Surrender 414
III. Participatory Rights in Cross-Border Investigations and the Taking of Overseas Evidence 416
1. Premise 416
2. The Responsibility for Ensuring Confrontation 417
3. The Method of Confrontation 419
4. The Use of Witness Evidence Taken Abroad Without Confrontation 420
E. Provisional Conclusions 422
References 422

12 *Audi alteram partem* in Transnational Cases Under the American Convention 423
A. Introductory Remarks. The Need for a Systematic Approach to Transnational Cases Under the American Convention 423
B. A Victim-Centred Approach to International Cooperation and the Responsibility of the International Community for Avoiding the Impunity of the Perpetrators of Serious Human Rights Violations 424
C. Participatory Guarantees in International Cooperation Under the American Convention 425
I. Premise 425
II. Extradition Procedures and the Right of the Victims of Serious Human Rights Violations to Examine the Alleged Perpetrators. The Colombian Case of the Justice and Peace Process 426
III. The Right to Obtain Exculpatory Evidence, the Guarantee of Confrontation and the Use of Untested Evidence in Transborder Cases 428
D. Interim Conclusions 430
References 430

13 Defence Rights and Participatory Guarantees Acknowledged by EU Law in the International Cooperation Within the Area of Freedom, Security and Justice 431
A. Introductory Remarks 432
B. Participatory Guarantees and the Protection of Personal Freedom in International Cooperation Among Member States 432
I. Premise 432
II. The Right to Personal Participation in Criminal Proceedings and Surrender Procedures. The Protection of Absent Defendants in EAW Proceedings 433
1. The Soft Solutions of the 2002 Legislation on the European Arrest Warrant 433
2. Subsequent Developments in EU Law 434
a) The Enhancement of Information and Participatory Rights by the 2009 Legislation 434
b) The Responses of the EU Court of Justice. The '*Melloni* Doctrine' 437
III. Participatory Rights and International Procedures Involving Restrictions on Liberty 438
1. Information Rights and Guarantees of a Fair Hearing in EAW Proceedings 438
2. Defence Rights in the Proceedings on Supervision Measures 443
C. Participatory Rights and Transnational Evidence in the EU Area . . . 445
I. Premise 445

II. Participatory Rights, Transnational Evidence-Gathering and the Developments of Legal Assistance Models 446
1. The Solutions of the Brussels Convention on Transnational Evidence-Gathering 446
2. The Shift from Mutual Legal Assistance to Mutual Recognition and the Defence Rights in the Order Model 447
a) The Combined Methods of Evidence-Gathering in the Order Model and the Weak Protection of Participatory Rights in the EU Legislation on the European Evidence Warrant and the European Investigation Order 447
b) Hearings by Videoconference, Right to Be fairly Heard and the Guarantee of Confrontation in Transnational Cases 452
III. Defence Rights in Joint Criminal Inquiries 454
D. Interim Conclusions 455
References 456

Part VII Solution Models and Principles of a Participatory Approach to Criminal Justice in International Human Rights Law and EU Law

14 Principles and Common Requirements of a Participatory Model of Criminal Justice in International Human Rights Law and EU Law 461
A. Premise 462
B. The Complex Character of Criminal Proceedings and the Broad Scope of the Right to Be Fairly Heard in International Human Rights Law and EU Law 462
C. The Proactive Role of the Parties in the Exercise of Criminal Prosecution. An Irrelevant Issue Under International Human Rights Law and EU Law? 464
D. The Right to Personal Participation in Criminal Proceedings. The Flexible Approach of International Human Rights Case-Law and the New Findings of EU Law 467
I. The Right to Be personally Involved in Criminal Proceedings and the Assessment of Human Rights Violations Under the European Convention and the Pact of San José 467
II. The Problem of *in absentia* Proceedings. A Comparison Between Strasbourg's Approach and the New Arrangements of EU Law 469
III. Out-of-Court Decisions on the Merits of the Case. The Issue of *inaudito reo* Proceedings Under the European Convention and EU Law 473

IV. The Right of the Aggrieved Parties to Personally Participate in Criminal Proceedings Under the European Convention and EU Law 476
E. Conditions and Qualitative Requirements for Effective Participation in Criminal Proceedings under International and EU Law 477
I. Premise 477
II. Linguistic Guarantees 478
III. Information Safeguards 480
1. Information on the Charge 480
2. Information on the Evidence Available and the Right to Access to the Investigative File 483
F. The Right to a Fair Examination as a General Guarantee of All the Individuals Involved in Criminal Proceedings 484
I. Premise 484
II. The Conditions of a Fair Examination 485
III. *Nemo tenetur* Principle and the Right Not to Be Heard in Criminal Proceedings. The Admissibility of Incriminating Evidence Obtained Coercively 486
IV. The Right to Give Statements in One's Favour 488
G. The Defence's Contribution to Evidence-Gathering 489
I. The Right to Produce Exculpatory Evidence 489
II. The Right to Be Involved in the Taking of Incriminating Evidence. The Complex Challenges of the Right to Confrontation 490
1. Direct and Indirect Forms of Confrontation 490
2. Context of Confrontation 491
3. Conditions of Effective Confrontation 493
III. A Systematic Understanding of the Right to Confrontation. The Need to Balance the Right to Challenge Incriminating Evidence and the Protection of Other Human Rights 494
H. Participatory Rights and the Requirements of a Fair Decision-Making. The Complex Trade-Offs Among Conflicting Interests Required by International Human Rights Law 496
I. Premise 496
II. The Right to Confrontation and the Proof of Guilt 496
1. The Admissibility of Out-of-Court Evidence in Cases of Subsequent Confrontation and the Problem of Anonymous Testimony 496
2. The Conditions on Use of Untested Evidence 498
III. Argumentative Contribution to the Decision-Making 500
I. *Audi alteram partem* and Restrictions on Freedom. The Requirements of International Human Rights Case-Law and the Developments in the EU Legislation 501

I. Information Rights of Arrested and Detained Individuals 501
II. The Right to a Prompt Independent Review of the Lawfulness of Coercion and the Need for an Overall Human Rights Assessment 504
III. The Defence's Right to Challenge Unlawful Detention. Participatory Rights in *habeas corpus* Proceedings 507
J. Provisional Conclusions 508
References 509

15 Solution Models for a Participatory Approach to Transnational Criminal Justice in International and Supranational Law 511
A. International Human Rights Law and the Protection of Fair Trial Guarantees. Introductory Remarks 511
B. *Audi alteram partem* and the Specific Human Rights Challenges of Criminal Proceedings with Transnational Features 513
C. *Audi alteram partem* in the Field of Surrender Procedures 515
I. The Right to Personal Participation in the Trial Country and Procedural Guarantees in the Surrender Procedure. The Soft Approach of the Strasbourg Court and the Safeguards Set by EU Law 515
II. Participatory Safeguards and the Right to Evidence in Surrender Procedures. The Qualitative Requirements Set by International Human Rights Case-Law and the Solution Models of EU Law . . . 518
D. Participatory Rights and Transnational Evidence-Gathering 521
I. The Right to Obtain Exculpatory Evidence. A Proactive Right of the Defence in the Field of International Cooperation? 521
II. The Multiple Expressions of the Guarantee of Confrontation in the Field of Transnational Evidence-Gathering 521
1. Responsibility for Ensuring Confrontation 521
2. The Role of the Defence in the Taking of Incriminating Evidence 524
3. The Use of Untested Evidence 525
E. Interim Conclusions 526
References 527

Part VIII De-formalisation of Legal Systems and Reconstruction of a Participatory Model of Criminal Justice

16 Mutual Interaction of Systems of Human Rights Protection and the Development of a Participatory Understanding of Criminal Justice Based on Transcultural Dialogue 531
A. Introductory Remarks 533
B. The Relevance of International Human Rights Law in the Selected Countries and Its Relationship with National Law 535
I. The Long Road Towards the Enhancement of International Human Rights Law in Italy 535

1. The Traditional Approach to International Human Rights Law and the Weak Formal Status of the European Convention 535
2. The Contribution of the Constitutional Case-Law to the Enhancement of International Human Rights Law and the Legislative Reforms of the Constitution 536
3. The Shift from the Formal Perspective to the Para-Constitutional Relevance of International Human Rights Law. The Complex Relationship Between Constitutional and Strasbourg Case-Law 539
II. The Relevance of the American Convention in the Contracting States and the Relationship with National Law 540
1. The Multisided Relevance of International Human Rights Law in Brazil 540
2. The Strong Approach of the Inter-American Court to Constitutional Law, Viewed from the Perspective of Brazilian Law 542
III. Comparative Remarks 544
C. The Relevance of EU Human Rights Law and the Relationship with Constitutional Law 546
I. The Approach of the EU Court of Justice and the Reaction of Constitutional Courts in the EU Area 546
II. The Approach of the Italian Constitutional Court to EU Law and the 'Counter-Limits Doctrine' 550
D. Cross-Fertilisation of Systems of Human Rights Protection and the Enhancement of a Participatory Understanding of National Criminal Justice on the Basis of Transcultural Dialogue 553
I. Premise 553
II. Personal Participation in Criminal Proceedings and the Lawfulness of Procedures in the Absence of the Individuals Concerned. A Multilevel Approach 554
1. Right to Personal Participation, Fairness of Criminal Proceedings and *in absentia* Proceedings 554
a) The Impact of International Human Rights Law on the Developments in Criminal Proceedings *in absentia* and the Persistent Lacunas of National Law 554
b) New Perspectives of EU Law and the Room for Manoeuvre for Italian Law 560
2. The Problem of *inaudito reo* Proceedings. General Requirements of International Human Rights Law, Developments at the EU Level and the Legal Arrangements of Italian Law 562
III. Conditions of Effective Participation in Criminal Proceedings. The Incidence of International Human Rights Law on the Developments in Brazilian and Italian Criminal Justice and the Evolution of Italian Law Under the Influence of EU Legislation 564

1. Information Rights in Criminal Proceedings 564
a) Information on the Charge. A Human Rights Approach . . . 564
aa) Information Rights and the Need for a Balance Between Conflicting Interests 564
bb) Developments in Italian Criminal Justice Towards EU Law and the Persistent Deficiencies in the Light of the European Convention 567
b) Information on the Evidence Gathered and Interferences with Fundamental Rights. The Safeguards of EU and International Human Rights Law and the Weak National Arrangements 568
2. Linguistic Guarantees in Criminal Proceedings. Developments Towards International Human Rights Law and EU Law and the Shortcomings of National Criminal Justice 570
IV. *Audi alteram partem*, the Right to Be Fairly Examined and the Privilege Against Self-Incrimination 571
1. Procedural Safeguards and Conditions of a Fair Hearing in the Pre-trial Inquiry 571
2. The Right to a Fair Hearing and the Procedural Safeguards Against Coercion. The Increased Enhancement of the *nemo tenetur* Principle 575
3. Private Initiative and the Right to Make Oneself Heard by the Competent Authority 578
V. *Audi alteram partem*, Evidence-Gathering and Qualitative Requirements of a Fair Fact-Finding. The Need for Broad Balance Among Conflicting Interests 580
1. Obtaining Incriminating Evidence. The Need for Systematic Approach to the Right to Confrontation in the Light of the Overall Set of the Human Rights Challenges Posed by Each Concrete Case 580
a) The Requirements Set by International Human Rights Case-Law and the Developments in National Law 580
b) The Risks of an Enlarged View of the Guarantee of Confrontation. The Problems of Indirect Examination and of Subsequent Confrontation 582
c) Right to Confrontation and Inconsistent Evidence. The Need to Avoid an Accused-Centred Understanding of the Principle of *contradictoire* 584
2. Proof of Guilt and the Defence's Contribution to a Fair Decision-Making 586
a) Impossibility of Confrontation and the Use of Untested Evidence. The Need to Avoid Absolutist Interpretations . . . 586
b) Special Forms of Confrontation and the Use of the Information Gathered. The Problem of Anonymous Testimony 590

VI. Participatory Rights and Restrictions on Freedom 591
1. The Right to Be Fairly Heard and the Qualitative Requirements of Effective Participation in Remand Proceedings 591
a) Premise 591
b) The Guarantee of Information in International Human Rights Instruments and EU Law, and the Procedural Safeguards Provided at the Domestic Level 592
c) The Need for Comprehensive Assistance in the Remand Proceedings 594
2. The Guarantee of a Prompt Independent Review of the Deprivation of Liberty and the Voice of the Defence 595
3. Challenging Pre-trial Restrictions on Liberty. The Persistent Distance from the Standards Set Forth by International Human Rights Law and EU Law 598
E. Interaction of Legal Systems and the Strengthening of a Participatory Approach to Transnational Criminal Justice 599
I. Introductory Remarks 599
II. *Audi alteram partem*, Right to Freedom and Procedural Safeguards in the Field of International Surrender. The EU Legislation on the European Arrest Warrant and Its Influence on Italian Law 600
1. *In absentia* Trials and Surrender Procedures with EU Countries 600
2. Participatory Rights in the Executing Country and the Right to Be Fairly Heard in EAW Proceedings 602
3. Coercive Measures and the Right to a Fair Hearing in the Executing Country 604
4. The Enhanced Role of the Judiciary in EAW Proceedings . . . 607
III. Participatory Rights and Transnational Evidence-Gathering . . . 612
1. Responsibility of the Cooperating Countries for the Granting of Participatory Safeguards in Transnational Inquiries. The Feasibility of the Strasbourg Case-Law at the Domestic Level 612
2. The Right to Confrontation, the Participatory Safeguards in the Taking of Incriminating Evidence, and the Use of Untested Evidence 613
F. Conclusions 615
References 615

17 Concluding Findings. Proposals and Qualitative Requirements of a Participatory Model of Criminal Justice 619
A. *Audi alteram partem*, Fairness of Criminal Proceedings and the Reliability of the Fact-Finding: From the Fragmentary Enhancement of Individual Rights to a Balanced Relationship between Participatory Safeguards 620
B. Participatory Rights, Equality of Arms and the Guarantee of an Independent Review of the Proceedings 623
C. Towards a Participatory Model of Criminal Prosecution? 625
I. The Contribution of Private Parties to the Decision to Initiate a Public Prosecution 625
II. Participatory Safeguards in the Decision Not to Institute or to Drop a Criminal Prosecution 628
D. Personal Participation in Criminal Proceedings and the Problem of the Proceedings Held Without the Involvement of the Individuals Concerned 631
I. The Multifaceted Features of the Guarantee of Personal Participation in a Criminal Law Action. A Human Rights Perspective 631
II. Whether and Under What Conditions the Proceedings Held Without the Involvement of the Accused Can Be Made Compatible with a Participatory Model of Criminal Justice 633
1. The Problem of Trials *in absentia* or *inaudito reo* 633
2. *In absentia* Proceedings and International Surrender Procedures 635
E. Information Safeguards, Prosecutorial Efficiency and Requirements of Effective Participation in Criminal Proceedings 636
I. Decision to Charge, Information Rights and the Need for a Differentiated Approach Depending on the Role of Private Parties in Criminal Proceedings 636
II. Access to Relevant Evidence, Coercive Measures, and Defence Rights 639
F. Criminal Proceedings as a Listening Space 640
I. Premise. Right to a Fair Examination, Right to Make Oneself Heard, Right Not to Be Heard 640
II. Procedural Safeguards of a Fair Questioning and the Need for Differentiated Assistance Depending on the Person to Be Examined 640
III. Whether and How Private Parties Can Make Themselves Heard in Criminal Proceedings Without Being Questioned by the Competent Authorities 644
IV. Right Not to Be Questioned, Right Not to Give Evidence Against Oneself and Right to Be Forgotten 645

G. Active Involvement of Private Parties in Evidence-Gathering and the Defence's Contribution to Decision-Making. A Multifaceted Approach to Evidence Law . . . 647
I. Different Forms of Confrontation and the Need to Balance the Accused's Right to Participate in the Taking of Incriminating Evidence with the Protection of the Human Rights of Other Individuals Involved in Criminal Proceedings . . . 647
II. Qualitative Requirements of a Fair Confrontation . . . 648
III. Decision-Making Process in a Participatory Model of Criminal Justice . . . 649
1. The Contribution of Private Parties to the Fact-Finding . . . 649
a) The Need to Scrutinise the Probative Relevance in a Concrete Case Beyond the Rigid Conditions of Use of Out-of-Court Evidence. The Argumentative Role of the Parties in the Fact-Finding . . . 649
b) Untested Evidence and the Proof of Guilt. The Progressive Erosion of the Sole and Decisive Evidence Doctrine . . . 652
c) Variations of the Right to Confrontation and the Factual Background for the Use of Indirect Evidence. The Need for Justification *in concreto* . . . 654
2. Argumentation and the Legal Contribution of the Defence to Decision-Making . . . 655
H. Restrictions on Freedom and the Need for Enhanced Participatory Safeguards . . . 658
I. Decision-Making on Restrictions on Liberty and the Right to a Fair Hearing by an Independent Authority . . . 658
1. The Perspective of Domestic Proceedings. The Need to Involve the Individuals Against Whom Pre-Trial Measures Are Requested in the Decision-Making and to Enable Them to Contribute to Further Decisions on the Measure Applied . . . 658
2. The Perspective of International Surrender Procedures. The Need to Strengthen the Oversight of Participatory Safeguards in the Trial Country and the Right to a Fair Hearing in the Host State . . . 660
II. Qualitative Requirements of Effective Participation in the Decision on Coercive Measures. Information Safeguards and the Right to Comprehensive Assistance for the Individuals Concerned . . . 661
III. Proportionality of Restrictions on Freedom and the Guarantee of Regular Judicial Oversight . . . 664
I. Concluding Remarks . . . 665
References . . . 665

Appendix A: Format for the Comparative-Law Examination of Domestic Criminal Justice 667

Appendix B: Format for the Comparative-Law Examination of Transnational Criminal Justice 669

References 671

Table of Abbreviations

AFSJ	Area of Freedom, Security and Justice
ALA	Agreement on Legal Assistance
BVerfG	Federal Constitutional Court (*Bundesverfassungsgericht*)
CCass	Court of cassation
CConst	Constitutional court
CCP	Code of Criminal Procedure
CISA	Convention Implementing the Schengen Agreement
DirAL	Directive on the right of access to a lawyer in criminal proceedings
DirEIO	Directive on a European investigation order
DirICP	Directive on the right to information in criminal proceedings
DirIT	Directive on the right to interpretation and translation in criminal proceedings
DirLA	Directive on legal aid for suspects and accused persons in criminal proceedings and for requested persons in European arrest warrant proceedings
DirPIRPT	Directive on certain aspects on the presumption of innocence and the right to be present at trial in criminal proceedings
DirVR	Directive on the rights, support and protection of victims of crime
EAW	European Arrest Warrant
ECE	European Convention on Extradition
ECHR	European Convention on Human Rights
ECJ	Court of Justice of the European Union
ECMACM	European Convention on Mutual Legal Assistance in Criminal Matters
ECtHR	European Court of Human Rights
EEW	European Evidence Warrant
EIO	European Investigation Order
ExT	Extradition treaty
EU	European Union

EU-CMACM	Convention on Mutual Assistance in Criminal Matters Between the Member States of the European Union
EU-FRCh	Charter of Fundamental Rights of the European Union
FdEAW	Framework Decision on the European Arrest Warrant
FdEEW	Framework Decision on the European Evidence Warrant
FdJIT	Framework Decision on Joint Investigation Teams
FdSM	Framework Decision on Supervision Measures
FdVS	Framework Decision on the Standing of the Victim in Criminal Proceedings
ICCPR	International Covenant on Civil and Political Rights
JIT	Joint Investigation Teams
MLA	Mutual legal assistance
PC	Penal code
RICCP	Rules Implementing the Code of Criminal Procedure
SAP ECE	Second Additional Protocol to the European Convention on Extradition
SAP ECMACM	Second Additional Protocol to the European Convention on Mutual Legal Assistance in Criminal Matters
STC	Spanish Constitutional Tribunal
STF	Federal Supreme Tribunal (*Supremo Tribunal Federal*)
STJ	Superior Court of Justice (*Superior Tribunal de Justiça*)
TEU	Treaty on European Union
TFEU	Treaty on the Functioning of the European Union
TLA	Treaty on Legal Assistance

Part I
Introduction to the Research

Chapter 1
Preliminary Issues

Contents

A. The Problem 3
B. Subject and Aims of the Investigation 5
C. Methodology and Structure of the Investigation 6
References 8

A. The Problem

It is widely recognised that a fair criminal trial necessitates the involvement of private parties in fact-finding, since their participation in criminal proceedings not only sets the necessary conditions for the proper protection of the defence's rights but also contributes to reliable decision-making. In recent times, awareness of the decisive role of the defence has grown worldwide as a result of the increasing influence of common-law procedure. This has lead to the rise of clear adversarial tendencies even in civil-law countries, which have progressively reduced the weight of out-of-court fact-finding, typical of the inquisitorial tradition.

Italy and Brazil provide enlightening examples of the adversarial orientation, which has characterised the mixed criminal justice systems. The enshrinement of the *principe du contradictoire* at the constitutional level in both countries reveals the clear attempt to strengthen the role of the parties (including the public prosecutor) in criminal proceedings. Notwithstanding its benefits, these constitutional reforms did not however suffice to erase a rather formalistic understanding of a number of participatory safeguards even of the accused. This can explain the survival of somewhat inquisitorial procedures, which exclude any involvement of the defence prior to the decision-making,[1] as well as the long road that both Brazil and Italy had to walk to reduce the room for the proceedings held *in absentia*. On a deeper level still, the constitutionalisation of the principle of *contradictoire* did not succeed in overcoming the traditional dualistic view of criminal proceedings, which

[1]For instance, the penal order proceeding, typical of the countries of Roman-German tradition and later transposed into Italian criminal justice since the 1913 code of criminal procedure. Cf. Ruggeri (2008), p. 3ff.

S. Ruggeri, Audi Alteram Partem *in Criminal Proceedings*,
DOI 10.1007/978-3-319-54573-8_1

still largely inspires Italian and Brazilian criminal justice.[2] Doubtless, this approach does not best fit the difficult human rights challenges of modern criminal trials. Especially in the field of evidence-gathering, a rigid conception of the principle of *contradictoire* has led to the abuse of information obtained through hidden coercive means without any involvement of the individuals concerned, such as wiretapping.[3]

Over the last two decades, however, a more complex participatory understanding of criminal justice has spread inside and outside Europe, which goes far beyond the area of the defendant's rights and the safeguards for those who have the formal status of 'parties' according to domestic law. To a great extent, this phenomenon was due to the increasing influence of international human rights case-law on national criminal justice. One of the main achievements of international human rights case-law was to develop an approach to criminal proceedings, which transcends the traditional dichotomy between adversarial and inquisitorial models without aiming at a convergence towards an intermediate model. One might argue that this participatory conception of criminal proceedings is in line with the *contradictoire*-based approach to criminal justice existing in several civil-law countries. Yet this conclusion would be misleading since it would not reflect the complex developments that have led international human rights courts to redefine the scope of the participatory safeguards laid down by human rights charters for specific individuals (detained persons, defendants, etc.) in the light of an overall assessment of the challenges posed by the specific case under examination. Certainly, a fair criminal trial rules out purely unilateral solutions, which lead to the fulfilment of rights of individual parties to the extent that not only the guarantees provided to other persons protected by international law but also state-related interests acknowledged by constitutional law are unduly sacrificed. Here also, the delicate field of evidence-gathering constituted an important testing ground especially for the Strasbourg case-law, which has long called for a constant balance between the defendant's fair trial rights and the need to give a voice to people involved in criminal proceedings in different ways (no matter whether parties or not under national law), such as witnesses, co-defendants, victims, police officers and so on. Moreover, it is noteworthy that international human rights case-law has increasingly included specific duties into the *audi alteram partem* rule even on the part of the private parties by strengthening their responsibility for ensuring a fair trial.

Similar developments have characterised the Inter-American case-law, notwithstanding that the institutions of San José traditionally dealt with severe human rights abuses and were only recently called upon to examine issues concerned with due process safeguards. Here, a strongly victim-oriented approach has enabled the Inter-American Court to overcome the accused-centred view of criminal proceedings promoted by the statutory provisions of the Pact of San José.

---

[2]A clear example is provided by the Italian Constitution, which enables the legislature to depart form the principle of *contradictoire* in the field of evidence-gathering and for the purposes of the decision on the merits in the case of the consent of the accused. Cf. Art. 111(5) Const.-Italy.

[3]Kostoris (2008), p. 9; Balsamo and Lo Piparo (2008), p. 337f.

In the Inter-American case-law, moreover, the very notion of 'victim' is multisided and goes far beyond the individuals injured by criminal offences, encompassing also their next of kin and even persons subject to a criminal prosecution if by this means human rights violations were committed against them. In this light, the *audi alteram partem* rule allows the Inter-American case-law to carry out an overall assessment of human rights infringements.

In a nutshell, international human rights law provides useful models of solutions for the reconstruction of a participatory model of criminal proceedings. In Europe, alongside its direct influence on national case-law and criminal justice policies, Strasbourg case-law has also played a decisive role in the evolution that has occurred in EU law in criminal matters. Notwithstanding the failure to enact a comprehensive statute on minimum procedural safeguards in criminal matters in the last decade, the piecemeal approach of the post-Lisbon EU legislation on specific defence rights in criminal proceedings has undoubtedly drawn on the heritage of the European case-law. In spite of its scanter jurisprudence, Inter-American case-law has also contributed to broadening of domestic protection of participatory safeguards of the individuals involved in criminal proceedings. Yet the strong impact of international human rights law and EU law also has its price, entailing the risk of the weakening of the domestic standards of human rights protection by orienting national case-law towards compromise solutions aimed at applying to the overall area of the contracting states.[4]

B. Subject and Aims of the Investigation

The present study is a comparative-law examination of the development of a wide-ranging participatory conception of criminal justice that has occurred both in Europe and Latin America. The research will be carried out at the domestic level on the basis of the experience of two countries, namely Italy and Brazil. These countries were selected for two main reasons. Firstly, we have noted that both Italy and Brazil, despite the long tradition of mixed criminal justice, provide clear examples of the shift that over the last decades continental countries have had towards a common law-based model of criminal proceedings. Secondly, the developments that have taken place in the field of criminal justice in Italy and Brazil had a common starting point, since the 1930 Italian codification expressly inspired the 1941 Brazilian code of criminal procedure. Notwithstanding significantly similar steps, such as the aforementioned constitutionalisation of the principle of *contradictoire*, the two criminal justice systems have however developed in rather different ways. This result cannot solely be explained by the different structure of criminal proceedings and by the different organisation of justice in the two

[4]This risk is apparent in the field of *in absentia* trials because of the national rules on judicial service.

countries. More complex factors have also conditioned the domestic understanding of the role of private parties in fact-finding in criminal matters, particularly the cultural and social background of the two countries. Moreover, external factors have also played increasing role in the renovation of the two criminal justice systems, particularly the case-law of the Inter-American Court and the Strasbourg Court. As far as Italy is concerned, one should also take into consideration the increasing impact of EU legislation on the evolution that has occurred over the last few years in Italian procedural law, a phenomenon that as yet cannot be compared with the limited experience of Mercosur.[5]

These observations set the general framework of the present research. The comparative analysis will therefore be carried out from three main perspectives, namely from the viewpoint of domestic (procedural and constitutional) law, international human rights law and EU law. It cannot be doubted that a participatory view of criminal justice requires a multilevel analysis. This approach has already been used in various areas of criminal justice. A close examination of evidence law, in particular, has highlighted the increasing internationalisation of evidentiary processes[6] and as a result of this, the spread of a participatory conception of criminal evidence.[7] However, as anticipated, this phenomenon certainly transcends the field of evidence law, revealing complex developments that cut across the overall course of criminal proceedings.

The ultimate purpose of this study is to provide a comprehensive analysis of these developments in order to define the main qualitative requirements that should nowadays guide a participatory model of criminal justice. In fact, the spread of a wide-ranging participatory conception of criminal proceedings can today be observed in various areas of both national and transnational criminal justice, from the investigative phase to the institution of criminal prosecutions, the decision-making up to the procedures of international cooperation in criminal matters. For the sake of clarity, the analysis of the selected countries will be conducted on the basis of the issues laid down in the Appendices A and B at the end of this book. These Appendices not only provide the basis for the examination of selected countries but also for the comparative analysis as well as for the examination of the international human rights case-law and of EU law.

C. Methodology and Structure of the Investigation

It has been anticipated that the present research will be conducted with an interdisciplinary approach and through the method of comparative law. The proposed comparison pursues different aims depending on the phases of this study.

[5]For a comparison between Mercosur and European Union see Pereira and Ambos (eds) (2006).

[6]Jackson and Summers (2012).

[7]Jackson (2005), p. 740ff.; Balsamo and Lo Piparo (2008), p. 334ff.

On the first level, comparison will be carried out on the basis of domestic law with a view to analysing the convergences and divergences in the national understanding of the role of private parties in criminal proceedings and in the field of transnational criminal justice.[8] This discussion, however, does not only aim at detecting similarities and differences existing in the current legislation in Brazil and Italy. One the one hand, comparative-law examination will be combined with historical analysis, aimed at assessing how participatory safeguards have developed in the two criminal justice systems. On the other, legislative solutions will not be examined in abstract terms but in the light of the different cultural background in the two countries. To this end, special attention shall be paid to the case-law, which has played a decisive role in filling legal lacunas and particularly in updating old statutory solutions by bringing them closer to the new requirements set out by international human rights case-law.

The aim of second phase of the investigation is to examine the solution models provided by international human rights law and EU law to the issues dealt with by domestic law in both the areas of national and transnational criminal justice. This discussion will lead to second comparison aimed at analysing the models for solution and principles of a participatory approach to criminal justice, which are relevant in relation to both domestic and transnational criminal proceedings.[9] By comparing the solutions emerging from international human rights law, I will also deal with the influence of the Strasbourg jurisprudence on the Inter-American case-law, while examining how different human rights requirements were elaborated in Europe and America despite the statutory law similarities of the European Convention and the Pact of San José. As far as the European scenario is concerned, the analysis will also focus on the influence that Strasbourg case-law has had on the enhancement of participatory guarantees by EU law in the field of both international cooperation in criminal matters and domestic criminal justice.

The last phase of the research is oriented towards reconstructive goals. In particular, it aims at the assessment of the mutual interaction of systems of human rights protection and at the laying down of some qualitative requirements of a participatory understanding of criminal justice. To this end, a third comparison will be carried out in the light of the principles elaborated on the basis of the solution models provided by international human rights law and EU law.[10] The ultimate aim of this comparative analysis is to examine the influence that international human rights law (and as far as Italy is concerned, EU law also) has had, or will possibly have in the near future, on the development of a participatory understanding of criminal justice both in Italy and in Brazil. This phase of the research will follow the requirements of the so-called ‘functional comparison’.[11] The main question that will be addressed is how the effective involvement of

---

[8]Chapters 6 and 7.

[9]Chapters 14 and 15.

[10]Chapter 16.

[11]Cfr. Jescheck (1955), p. 36ff.; Sieber (2006), p. 112ff.; Gleß (2006), p. 43ff.

private parties and the achievement of proper trade-offs between conflicting interests can enhance the overall fairness of criminal proceedings as well as the reliability and the social sustainability of decision-making.

The results of this comparative-law examination will allow us to observe the increasing de-formalisation of the traditional barriers among legal systems, which calls for in-depth reflection on the meaning that should today be attached to traditional concepts, such as those of 'legal system', 'criminal procedure' and 'fundamental rights protection'. In the current complex era, these notions can no longer be understood to concern isolated and well-defined entities, but concepts whose features need be redefined by means of an integrated approach. The adoption of a multilevel approach will help us elaborate some guidelines for a participatory model of criminal justice on the basis of transcultural dialogue.[12]

References

Balsamo A, Lo Piparo A (2008) Principio del contraddittorio, utilizzabilità delle dichiarazioni predibattimentali e nozione di testimone tra giurisprudenza europea e criticità del sistema italiano. In: Balsamo A, Kostoris RE (eds) Giurisprudenza europea e processo penale italiano. Giappichelli, Torino, pp 333–372

Gleß S (2006) Beweisrechtsgrundsätze einer grenzüberschreitenden Strafverfolgung. Nomos, Baden-Baden

Jackson JD (2005) The effect of human rights on criminal evidentiary processes: towards convergence, divergence or realignment? Mod Law Rev 68:737–764

Jackson JD, Summers SJ (2012) The internationalisation of criminal evidence: beyond the common law and civil law traditions. Cambridge University Press, Cambridge

Jescheck H-H (1955) Entwicklung, Aufgaben und Methoden der Strafrechtsvergleichung. Mohr Siebeck, Tübingen

Kostoris RE (2008) Verso un processo penale non più statocentrico. In: Balsamo A, Kostoris RE (eds) Giurisprudenza europea e processo penale italiano. Giappichelli, Torino, pp 3–10

Pereira AC, Ambos K (eds) (2006) Mercosul e União Europeia. Lumen Juris, Rio de Janeiro

Ruggeri S (2008) Il procedimento per decreto penale. Dalla logica dell'accertamento sommario alla dinamica del giudizio. Giappichelli, Torino

Sieber U (2006) Strafrechtsvergleichung im Wandel – Aufgaben, Methoden und Theoriensätze der vergleichenden Strafrechtswissenschaft. In: Sieber U, Albrecht H-J (eds) Strafrecht und Kriminologie unter einem Dach. Duncker & Humblot, Berlin, pp 78 ff.

Vogel J (2010) Transkulturelles Strafrecht. Goltdammer's Archiv für Strafrecht 157:1–13

[12] On the perspective of a transcultural criminal law see Vogel (2010), p. 1ff.

Part II
Audi Alteram Partem in National Criminal Justice. The Perspective of Domestic Law

Chapter 2
Participatory Rights in Italian Criminal Justice and the Developments Towards a *contradictoire*-Based Model of Criminal Proceedings

Contents

A. Introductory Remarks. The Long Road of Italian Law Towards a New Model of Criminal Proceedings, Based on the Contribution of Private Parties to the Administration of Justice 13
B. The Development of a Constitutional Participatory Model of Fair Criminal Justice 17
I. Participatory Rights in the 1947 Constitution 17
II. The Enactment of a *contradictoire*-Based Model of Criminal Justice Under the Increasing Influence of International Human Rights Law 19
1. The Principle of *contradictoire* as the Core Guarantee of the Constitutional Model of a Fair Trial 19
2. A Systematic Understanding of the Constitutional Model of a Fair Trial and the Need for an Overall Balance Between the Right to Confrontation and Other Constitutional Interests 21
C. The Principle of *contradictoire* and Equality of Arms 24
I. Premise. The Link Between the Requirements of *contradictoire* and Equality of Arms in the Constitutional Model of a Fair Trial 24
II. Defence and Prosecutorial Inquiries 25
D. The Role of Private Parties in the Exercise of Criminal Prosecutions 28
I. The Role of the Victim in the Institution of Criminal Proceedings. The Relationship Between Private and Public Prosecution 28
II. Parties' Involvement in the Decision Not to Institute a Criminal Prosecution or to Drop Criminal Proceedings 32
1. The Defence's Involvement in the Decision Not to Institute a Criminal Prosecution 32
2. The Need to Balance Conflicting Interests in the Decision Whether to Prosecute or to Terminate Criminal Proceedings 34
E. The Principle of *contradictoire* and the Right to Be Informed in Criminal Proceedings 39
I. The Constitutional Model of Informed Participation in Criminal Proceedings 39
II. Information on the Accusation 41
1. Information on the Charge in the Pre-Trial Inquiry 41
2. Preventive Information About the Decision to Charge 44
3. Information on the Indictment 48
III. Information on Developments of the Criminal Inquiry and the Evidence Supporting the Charging Decision 49
IV. Notice of the Institution of Court Proceedings and the Right to Know the Initiation of a Criminal Prosecution 52

S. Ruggeri, Audi Alteram Partem *in Criminal Proceedings*,
DOI 10.1007/978-3-319-54573-8_2

F. Prosecutorial Needs and the Right of Participation in Criminal Proceedings 54
I. Premise 54
II. Prosecutorial Needs and the Right to Personally Participate in Court Proceedings. The Problem of *in absentia* Proceedings 55
1. The 1988 Rules on Default Proceedings and Developments Due to the Strasbourg Case-Law 55
2. The 2014 Reform: The Disappearance of Default Proceedings and the New Procedure for Absent Defendants 57
III. Participatory Rights in Alternative Proceedings 60
1. Premise 60
2. *Inaudito reo* Proceedings and the Problem of Criminal Conviction Without Previous Hearing. The Case of Penal Order Proceedings 61
3. Criminal Hearings *in camera* and the Right to Be Heard Fairly. The Complex Trade-Offs Required by Plea Bargaining and Abbreviated Proceedings 64
G. The Right to Have Oneself Fairly Heard 68
I. Premise 68
II. The Right to Be Fairly Heard in the Pre-Trial Phase 68
1. The 1988 Model and the Subsequent Developments in the Dynamics of the Prosecutorial Inquiry. The Progressive Re-Enhancement of the Power of the Investigative Bodies to Obtain Oral Evidence 68
2. The Weak Protection of Suspects and Victims 71
3. The Risks of the Witness Testimony of Co-Defendants Assisted by a Lawyer 74
III. The Right to Be Heard Fairly in Open Court 76
H. *Audi alteram partem* and the Collection of Evidence 80
I. Introductory Remarks. Principle of *contradictoire* in the Taking of Evidence 80
II. Participatory Rights in Evidence-Gathering in the Pre-Trial Inquiry 82
1. The Involvement of Private Parties in Prosecutorial and Police Inquiries 82
2. The Right to Confrontation in *incidente probatorio* 83
III. Participatory Rights in Evidence-Gathering at Trial 85
1. Principle of *contradictoire*, Oral Evidence and the Need for Constant Balance Among Conflicting Interests 85
2. Principle of *contradictoire* and the Collection of Expert Evidence 87
3. Principle of *contradictoire* and Documentary Evidence. Participatory Rights and the Admission of Evidence Gathered in Other Proceedings 89
4. Defendant's Consent and Evidentiary Agreements Among the Parties 91
I. Participatory Rights, the Use of Untested Evidence and the Defence's Contribution to Fact-Finding 93
I. Systematic Remarks. The High Relativism of Italian Evidence Law 93
II. Participatory Rights and Fact-Finding in the Trial Phase 96
1. Premise 96
2. Evidence Unavailable at Trial 97
3. Hearsay Evidence 100
4. Inconsistent Out-of-Court Evidence 102
III. Participatory Rights and Fact-Finding in Alternative Proceedings 109
1. Premise 109
2. Alternative Proceedings and the Waiver of the Right to Participation in Evidence-Gathering 109
3. The Impact of the Accused's Waiver on the Interests of Other Parties and on Fact-Finding 112
J. The Principle of *contradictoire* and Pre-Trial Restrictions on Freedom 113
I. Premise 113
II. Participatory Rights and Fact-Finding in the Decision on Coercive Measures. Another Endurance Test for the Distinction Between Strict and Free Assessment of Evidence 115

III. *Audi alteram partem* in the Procedure on Remand Detention and Further Restrictions on Liberty ... 117
1. Participatory Safeguards in the Procedure on the Application of Coercive Measures. The Inconveniences of Another Example of *inaudito reo* Proceedings ... 117
2. Participatory Rights in the Judicial Review Proceedings Against Coercive Measures ... 120
K. Provisional Conclusions ... 123
References ... 124

A. Introductory Remarks. The Long Road of Italian Law Towards a New Model of Criminal Proceedings, Based on the Contribution of Private Parties to the Administration of Justice

A close examination of the Italian criminal justice reveals that significant changes took place in the understanding of criminal proceedings over the last few decades. At the time of the enactment of the current code of criminal procedure (1988), criminal justice in Italy was still governed by the 1930 code, albeit largely amended. The so-called 'Rocco-code' maintained some of the main features of the original model, which left to private parties very limited room in criminal proceedings. In particular, the defence could give only indirect contribution to the taking of oral evidence in open court, since depending on the types of the proceedings, witnesses were examined by either the president of the trial court or by a district court judge (*pretore*).[1] Furthermore, evidence-gathering was largely frustrated by the widespread use of information collected by law enforcement authorities in the pre-trial stages. In particular, the drafters of the fascist code had construed the intermediate stage (*istruzione*) as the procedural phase primarily aimed at the collection of criminal evidence.[2] Most significantly, defendants were normally remanded into custody at the beginning of the judicial proceedings, being therefore deprived of the right to take part in criminal proceedings as free persons, with inevitable repercussions on their defence rights.[3] Under the 1930 model, the intermediate phase should have been headed either by an investigating magistrate or the public prosecutor.[4] However, the prosecutorial inquiry, though initially

[1] Art. 440of the 1930code.

[2] Siracusano (1973), p. 166 ff.

[3] The inclusion of the rules on both arrest and remand detention into the systematic structure of the 1930 code at the beginning of the Book concerned with the intermediate phase was clearly in line with the typically inquisitorial appreciation of pre-trial custody as the most appropriate means of forcefully achieving the collaboration (if not the confession) of the defendant, who was also viewed as an instrument for the success of the criminal inquiries rather than a right holder. Cf. Marzaduri (1994), p. 61.

[4] Investigative judges headed a formal inquiry (*istruzione formale*), whereas prosecutors an interim one (*istruzione sommaria*).

conceived as an exception to the ordinary judicial inquiry, soon gained ground in practice,[5] thus also frustrating the accused's right to be heard by an impartial body. This result was long tolerated on the ground that the public prosecutor, forming part of the judiciary, is under Italian law an independent body of justice (*organo di giustizia*).[6] Yet nothing could justify the result of an independent inquiry being conducted by the same authority that charged defendants with a criminal offence, remanded them into custody, and collected incriminating evidence against them.

Even though this system was already considerably softened by the 1980s, Italy lacked a clear model of criminal proceedings at the time in which the legislative process for a new codification started. Notwithstanding the clear intention of the Commission headed by *Pisapia* to depart from the old mixed procedure and to draw the new criminal procedure law towards the adversarial model of common law countries, only a single reference to the adversarial system was enacted in the Delegation Law for the new code,[7] which instead failed to enact any reference to specific models of criminal justice.

To be sure, the 1988 code contained some elements typical of the adversarial tradition. In particular, the drafters of the current codification strengthened the defence's contribution to evidence-gathering at trial by acknowledging the general principle that evidence should be taken at the initiative of the parties, which were in turn directly involved in the taking of testimonial evidence by being enabled to cross-examine witnesses, co-defendants and experts. Moreover, the weight of out-of-court evidence was considerably weakened through the introduction of an unprecedented distinction between the trial file (*fascicolo per il dibattimento*) and the prosecutorial file (*fascicolo del pubblico ministero*).[8] This distinction mainly aimed at preventing the decision-makers from basing the decision of guilt on police reports and hearsay evidence, while entailing the duty of using, as a rule, only the information gathered at trial. There were of course some exceptions, the first one concerning the pieces of evidence that could be inserted into the trial file. Moreover, the new code provided further situations in which out-of-court evidence could be admitted in court. All these cases, however, constituted an exhaustive list of grounds for admission at trial of hearsay evidence.[9]

Notwithstanding these positive changes, the new criminal justice maintained, albeit with some tiny adjustments, some old procedures that largely frustrated the

---

[5]Cordero (1966), p. 3 ff.

[6]Critical remarks on this concept were formulated by Chiavario (1971), p. 714 ff.

[7]Art. 1 Law 81/1987.

[8]See respectively Arts. 431 and 433 CCP. Despite the heading of the latter Article, the 'prosecutorial file' has never contained only the pieces of evidence gathered by the competent prosecutor but also the information collected by the police as well as the evidence taken in the intermediate phase by the competent judge. In the light of its comprehensive scope, it therefore constitutes a general file containing, as a rule, all the information taken in the pre-trial phase.

[9]Art. 514 CCP.

defendant's participation in criminal proceedings—in particular, the default proceedings (*processo in contumacia*)[10] and the penal order procedure (*procedimento per decreto penale*).[11] Moreover, the 1988 code made little effort to strike a balance between the defendant's participatory rights and the need to give voice to other individuals involved in criminal proceedings. In particular, although victims were granted unprecedented rights in the pre-trial inquiry, their role remained weak in the court proceedings unless they joined a civil action to criminal proceedings, a result maintained by the 1988 codification, despite serious criticisms raised in the past against this solution.[12] Furthermore, co-defendants were not free to appear in court and could coercively be brought to a prosecutorial or court hearing, though they had a general right to remain silent.[13] The rules on witness testimony were even more deficient, revealing scant attention towards the witness's right to be fairly heard. Even though minors should have been assisted by a guardian or a family member and an expert in child psychology,[14] this safeguard applied only to trial hearings. Furthermore, no specific rules protected other types of witnesses.

In a nutshell, the overall approach of the new Italian code remained far from a truly participatory understanding of criminal justice. The reform of the court proceedings stage did not depart from a rather formalistic view of the criminal process as *actus triarum personarum*, which did not rule out trials held *in absentia* or postponing the accused's participation to a higher stage or instance. Despite the clear influence of the common-law rule against hearsay evidence, the trial evidence-gathering was still largely frustrated by extremely long pre-trial inquiries, dominated by the old investigative powers of the law enforcement authorities, even where fundamental rights were at stake.[15] Notwithstanding its adversarial inspiration, the new code therefore remained largely based on the old mixed system of criminal justice.

It is thus no surprise that, despite the optimistic expectations of the drafters of the 1988 codification, the new criminal justice system imploded on itself. A few years after the code's enactment, both constitutional case-law and the legislature erased the main adversarial structures of the new codification, a result that cannot reductively be interpreted as a reaction to the 1992 anti-mafia legislation.[16] It is noteworthy that, while the European Court, as we will see, broadened the protective scope of fair trial rights far beyond the accused's side, the Italian criminal justice

[10] Art. 487 CCP.

[11] Arts. 459 et seq. CCP.

[12] Carnelutti (1963), p. 14.

[13] Art. 210 CCP.

[14] Art. 498(4) CCP.

[15] Since in Italy prosecutors are part of the judiciary (*magistratura*), they are still empowered to order a number of coercive measures, such as, in particular, searches and inspections, as well as wiretaps in urgent cases.

[16] Law Decree 306/1992 converted into the Law 356/1992. In the sense indicated in the text cf. also Marzaduri (2004b), p. 223 ff.

suffered from a drastic shift back to the inquisitorial tradition. The enhancement of the law enforcement powers of the investigative bodies in the pre-trial stage thus largely frustrated the right to *contradictoire* and the guarantee of judicial oversight in the evidence-gathering.

To be sure, both the legislature and the case-law aimed over the 1990s at striking new balances between prosecutorial needs and the participatory rights of individuals, other than the accused, involved in criminal proceedings. In the midst of the 1990s, for example, a general reform of sexual crimes[17] created a new case in the regulation on *incidente probatorio*—namely, a court procedure aimed at the collection of non-repeatable evidence in the pre-trial phase[18]—with a view to allowing the hearing of minors under 16 years old within proceedings for sexual offences. This reform strengthened the voice of vulnerable individuals, regardless of whether they were injured by the offence under investigation or had witnessed it.[19] Again, it is no coincidence that during these developments in Italian law, as we will see, the Strasbourg Court made important steps toward the acknowledgment of a statute of victims and vulnerable witnesses,[20] whereas Constitutional Court started enhancing the formal status of the European Convention in Italy.[21]

Notwithstanding that most developments had alternate motivations, the changes during this historical phase were not unproductive, revealing the need for a new approach to criminal justice beyond the traditional distinction between adversarial and inquisitorial systems. A fundamental step in this direction was the 1999 fair trial reform, carried out by Constitutional Amendment Law 2/1999, which enacted the principle of *contradictoire* in the Italian Constitution, while enshrining some of the main fair trial rights of the accused person acknowledged in the European Convention. This fundamental reform largely reversed the course of Italian law, paving the way for a new period in both the legislation and the case-law. The enhancement of the status of international human rights law in the Italian legal system, as we will see, made a decisive contribution to the development of a model of criminal justice increasingly oriented towards the qualitative requirements set forth by the Strasbourg Court.[22]

Against this background, this discussion focuses on the developments that occurred over last decades towards a new understanding of criminal proceedings, strongly based on the principle of *contradictoire*. To this end, particular weight shall be attached not only to Italian legislation but also to the case-law with a view to examining its contribution to implement the constitutional model of fair trial. The present chapter will also anticipate some of the main reforms that took place as

---

[17]Law 66/1996.

[18]Art. 392 et seqq. CCP.

[19]Di Chiara (2002), p. 553.

[20]Chapter 8, F.II&III.

[21]Chapter 16, B.II&III.

[22]On this development see among others Conti (2013), p. 103 ff.

a result of the rising influence of international human rights law and the EU legislation, though these will be analysed in detail in Chap. 16.

The analysis of Italian law highlights that, despite important innovations and the conferment to defence's lawyers of unprecedented investigative powers, the role of private parties remained weak especially in the pre-trial phase. Notwithstanding the shift towards a model of criminal justice oriented towards a stronger human rights protection in criminal proceedings, neither constitutional law nor international human rights law could erase the imbalance between the defendant and the public prosecutor. As anticipated, this leads to *contradictoire*-based evidence being still often overwhelmed by information gathered by technical means that can be requested, or in exceptional circumstances ordered, only by prosecutors (*e.g.*, interception of telecommunications).[23] Furthermore, the weight of the traditional understanding of criminal proceedings and the persistent absence of a comprehensive model of participation of private parties frustrate the possibility of a fair involvement of the individuals other than the defendant. As we will see at a later stage of this investigation, this approach, which is largely the result of the vertical concept of the individual rights in criminal justice,[24] can rarely be deemed consistent with the wide-ranging conception of the *audi alteram partem* by the Strasbourg case-law.

B. The Development of a Constitutional Participatory Model of Fair Criminal Justice

I. Participatory Rights in the 1947 Constitution

The correct understanding of the developments that have recently taken place in Italy requires us to firstly look back to the evolution of a constitutional model of fair criminal trial. At the time of the enactment of the first Republican Constitution (1947), Italy did not have a well-defined system of criminal justice. In the post-war era, the repressive approach of the 1930 code was softened somewhat and some important reforms had already been carried out. For instance, Royal Legislative Decree 288/1944 made the decision on the termination of criminal proceedings subject to the oversight of an investigative magistrate. We have seen, however, that Italian criminal justice was still strongly characterised by the mixed system, which did not leave much room (if any) for the involvement of private parties in procedural activities. Criminal inquiries and evidence-gathering were dominated by the investigative magistrate or even worse, by public prosecutors. Despite the 1944 reform, the judicial assessment of the investigating judge was based on the sole

[23]Chapter 1, A.

[24]On the developments of individual rights after the fair trial constitutional reform see Marzaduri (2004a), p. 283 ff.

information attached by the competent prosecutor without any participation of the defence.[25]

Notwithstanding the intention of the drafters of the Constitution to depart from the fascist criminal justice system, there were no clear traces of a participatory model of criminal proceedings in the 1947 Charter. It is no surprise that the Constitution did not enact any reference to the *contradictoire*, which appeared neither as a principle nor as an individual right. Remarkably, the Rocco code, unlike the code of civil procedure,[26] did not have any provision regarding the principle of *contradictoire*, nor was one enacted in subsequent years.

In sum, despite the liberal inspiration of the 1947 Constitution, the heritage of the Rocco code was still alive, and it was only after the Constitutional Court became operational (1956) that the acknowledgment of some important defence rights softened the inquisitorial character of prosecutorial investigations. Doubtless, the constitutional case-law made a decisive contribution to the renovation of the fascist model of criminal justice, giving rise to a new historical phase characterised by the enhancement of defence safeguards in criminal inquiries with inquisitorial structure (the so-called "*garantismo inquisitorio*").[27] Moreover, the lack of an explicit acknowledgment of the principle of *contradictoire* by the 1947 Constitution could not be interpreted as a sign of the indifference of constitutional law towards the involvement of the parties in the administration of criminal justice.[28] Remarkably, since its first rulings the Constitutional Court considered the right to *contradictoire* to be sufficiently protected by the constitutional provision on the inviolable right to a defence.[29]

Notwithstanding its merits, the constitutional case-law developed under the 1930 code reflected a rather simplified approach to criminal justice. As noted, the enhancement of defence rights in pre-trial investigations was not accompanied by a clear definition of a new criminal justice system, nor was there any in-depth reflection on the overall balance required by criminal proceedings. On close examination, the more general acknowledgement of the state's obligation to protect the inviolable rights of the person and human dignity[30] could also be used to strengthen the role of private parties in criminal proceedings. Nevertheless, the potential of this fundamental provision was not sufficiently exploited until relatively recent times.

---

[25] Cordero (1958), p. 1025 ff.

[26] Art. 101 CPC. See Luiso (1981).

[27] Garlati (2010).

[28] Giostra (2001), p. 3; Marzaduri (2000), p. 767.

[29] Art. 24 Const. See CConst, 46/1957. In the same sense, more recently, CConst, 117/2007.

[30] Art. 2 Const.

II. The Enactment of a contradictoire*-Based Model of Criminal Justice Under the Increasing Influence of International Human Rights Law*

1. The Principle of *contradictoire* as the Core Guarantee of the Constitutional Model of a Fair Trial

Another important factor that strongly contributed to a cultural change of the understanding of criminal justice was the rising influence of international human rights law. Even though in the 1980s the findings against Italy by the Strasbourg Court were still few, there is little doubt that the European Convention already held a relevance that went far beyond the formal status of the 1955 Ratification Law. In the 1960s, moreover, criminal law scholarship had already criticised the practice of ratifying international human rights instruments through ordinary laws, and thus called for the constitutionalisation at least of the 'substantial' guarantees of the Rome Convention.[31] The awareness of the importance of the Strasbourg case-law was widespread as the discussion started on a new code of criminal procedure. Remarkably, the 1987 Delegation Law required the Government, charged with the task of enacting the new codification, to comply with the obligations deriving from international human rights law.

Despite strengthening the link of the new criminal justice system with the European Convention, the Delegation Law neither constitutionalised this Charter nor provided it with a super-legislative status. It took more than 10 years before the European Convention gained constitutional relevance. The opportunity for the enactment into the Constitution of a set of fair trial rights acknowledged by the Convention was provided at the end of the 1990s by a controversial ruling of the Constitutional Court concerning the admissibility of untested evidence given by co-defendants out of court.[32] The constitutional judges, adopting a highly formalistic approach to the principle of *contradictoire*, largely frustrated the right to confrontation by granting the accused persons the possibility of coercively obtaining the presence at trial of their accuser, who was still allowed, however, to remain silent on any given question. This solution was clearly unsatisfactory and provoked an immediate reaction by the Parliament,[33] which enshrined at the constitutional level the requirement that criminal evidence must be taken pursuant to the principle of *contradictoire*.[34] The Italian legislature also took advantage of this opportunity to confer constitutional status to some guarantees of the European Convention.

---

[31]Chiavario (1969), p.49 ff.

[32]CConst, 361/1998.

[33]Constitution Amendment Law 2/1999. On this constitutional reform see Grevi (2000), p. 237 ff.; Marzaduri (2000), p. 762 ff.

[34]Art. 111(4) Const.

The overall result was, however, modest compared to the goals pursued. The 1999 constitutional reform not only focused solely on the guarantees of Article 6 ECHR but also acknowledged a small number of the fair trial rights of the accused.[35] Besides, these safeguards were combined with provisions of very different nature and cultural origin, which mainly aimed at satisfying the specific needs of the Italian criminal justice.[36] The constitutional fair trial reform somewhat departed from the European Convention, ranging between a rather structuralist approach and a human rights perspective. Both the principle of *par condicio* and the requirements of the neutrality and impartiality of the judiciary not only recognised individual safeguards but furthermore had to be interpreted as constituent elements of the constitutional model of a fair trial.[37] Most significantly, these requirements—as well as the principle of *contradictoire*—were not constitutionalised with exclusive reference to criminal justice.[38]

This does not mean, however, that the 1999 constitutional reform overlooked the subjective relevance of the right to be involved in judicial proceedings, a right of utmost importance especially in criminal matters, because of the serious repercussions of the criminal inquiry in the sphere of human rights. This called for a systematic interpretation of the principle of *contradictoire*, which cannot be deemed unconnected from the other requirements of Article 111(2) Const. It is hard to understand how the parties could be fairly heard in criminal proceedings without an independent and impartial judicial oversight that ensured full equality of arms. The need for systematic interpretation also deemphasized the need for a structuralist approach to the principle of *contradictoire*.[39] There is a strict link between the general provision on the principle of *contradictoire* and the other constitutional rules regarding the fair trial rights of the accused.[40] The effective exercise of the right to participate in criminal proceedings requires defendants to be

[35] Art. 111(3) Const.

[36] For instance, the constitutionalisation of the defendant's consent to the use of untested evidence, as one of the exceptions to the principle of *contradictoire* in the evidence-gathering, was mainly aimed at giving a constitutional justification for alternative proceedings structured on a consensual basis. See Art. 111(5) Const.

[37] Art. 111(2) Const. Remarkably, a lively debate also divided the Italian criminal law scholarship in the interpretation of the principle of reasonable length of criminal proceedings, raising the question of whether it should be viewed as an individual right or an objective guarantee of a fair process. See Grevi (2000), p. 326 ff.

[38] Art. 111(2) Const.

[39] Marzaduri (2000), p. 767.

[40] The term 'accused' (*accusato*) is traditionally extraneous to Italian criminal procedural law, which usually relates to the person formally charged with a criminal offence as 'defendant' (*imputato*). Over recent years, however, the rising influence of international human rights law and EU law has led to the gradual spread of this new concept in Italian law. This poses delicate problems of compatibility with the national terminology, which in turn entails substantial implications on the scope of application of fundamental guarantees.

given proper information on the charges filed against them and to have enough time to prepare their defence.[41] Moreover, the accused's right to be confronted with incriminating witnesses[42] lies at the core of the requirement of the parties' involvement in evidence-gathering, to the point that defendants cannot be convicted on the basis of evidence given by individuals who voluntarily avoided any confrontation with the accused.[43]

This confirms that the constitutional model of a fair trial makes *contradictoire* not only the best method of ascertainment of the facts, but also a fundamental requirement for a human rights-oriented exercise of criminal jurisdiction. Legal scholarship often distinguishes between a subjective and an objective appearance of the principle of *contradictoire*.[44] On close examination, this distinction oversimplifies the complex, tangled web of constitutional guarantees, each of which can only be ensured through the others.

2. A Systematic Understanding of the Constitutional Model of a Fair Trial and the Need for an Overall Balance Between the Right to Confrontation and Other Constitutional Interests

These developments had two main implications, namely (a) that the principle of *contradictoire* cannot simply be seen as another expression of the right to a defence and (b) that the participatory rights of the accused cannot be enhanced without the overall consideration of the conflicting interests existing in each concrete case.

Surprisingly, the need for such balance is generally overlooked in the field of the evidence-gathering. Moreover, the manner in which the right to confrontation was set forth in the constitutional model of a fair trial also gave rise to rather absolutist interpretations. In particular, legal scholarship held a radical ban on use of untested evidence, except for three derogations laid down by the Constitution, namely the defendant's waiver of participation in evidence-gathering, the objective impossibility of involvement of the parties and proven unlawful conduct.[45] We will see that the European Convention specified neither the mode nor the context in which defendants must be granted the right to examine or have their accusers examined.[46] By contrast, the Italian Constitution requires confrontation to take place 'before the judge'. Of course this expression cannot be interpreted in such rigid terms that confrontation could only take place before the trial judge, since this would inevitably entail the unlawfulness of any decision based on evidence gathered out of

[41] Art. 111(3) Const.

[42] *Ibid.*

[43] Art. 111(4) Const.

[44] Conti (2000), p. 198 ff.

[45] Art. 111(5) Const. On these constitutional derogations from the principle of *contradictoire* cf. Di Chiara (2009).

[46] Chapter 8, F.II.

court. However, unlike the European Convention, the Italian Constitution does not deem any confrontation sufficient to fulfil the defendants' right to *contradictoire*, instead requiring confrontation to take place, as a rule, in a court hearing with the direct involvement of the defence. Although this does not mean that an 'eye-to-eye confrontation' with the accuser is the only solution in line with the Constitution, it is clear that the constitutional arrangements exclude, as a matter of principle, out-of-court confrontation, as well as the examination of incriminating witnesses by a judicial authority.[47]

Doubtless, the 1999 constitutional reform not only strengthened the role of the defence in the taking of incriminating evidence but furthermore enhanced the link between the principle of *contradictoire* and the guarantee of judicial oversight also in the field of evidence-gathering.[48] This link was further confirmed, as noted, by the general ban on use for the purposes of rendering judgement of evidence rendered by any person who freely waived confrontation with the accused. This is surely a guarantee of utmost importance, which cannot be limited by elusive interpretations aimed at restricting the scope of the prohibition to the use of incriminating evidence as the sole basis of the accused's conviction.[49] From this it does not follow, however, that out-of-court incriminating evidence taken without the accused's contribution can never be used to prove the defendant's guilt. On close examination, even the peremptory provision that the *contradictoire* must govern the taking of criminal evidence does not support this radical conclusion. Nor does the exhaustive nature of the exceptions in paragraph 5 lead to the result that, outside these cases, the use of untested evidence is radically unconstitutional.[50] This conclusion reveals an approach that, focusing exclusively on the defendants' right to participate in the taking of evidence, overlooks the complexity of the conflicting interests inherent in criminal proceedings.

It has been noted that the 1999 reform emphasised the accused's side to such point that it locked the principle of *contradictoire* in a cage which only admits the three ways out provided for by Article 111(5) of the Constitution. All these situations, despite not requiring the legislature to enact them or to give full probative value to untested evidence,[51] confirm the somewhat unilateral approach of the fair trial reform. This approach can entail serious repercussions on the human rights of other individuals involved in criminal proceedings. Therefore, there is a need for an interpretation of the fair trial guarantees aimed at avoiding the sacrifice

---

[47]It is apparent that the Constitution, as a rule, does not allow entrusting the examination to an investigative magistrate in favour of the defence, since judges cannot clearly hear people before themselves.

[48]Marzaduri (2000), p. 783.

[49]Ferrua (2013), p. 46 f.

[50]Marzaduri (2000), p. 785.

[51]On close examination, the Constitution enabled, rather than required, the legislature to enact these derogations. In this sense cf. Giostra (2001), p. 9. Of a different opinion see Ferrua (2009), p. 20 ff.

of other constitutional interests in the name of a rigid understanding of the defendant's right to be involved in the collection of evidence.

Remarkably, legal scholarship pointed out the need for a restrictive interpretation of the constitutional derogations to the principle of *contradictoire* in evidence-gathering. In particular, it has been stressed that the Constitution cannot allow defendants to waive their right to be involved in the taking of incriminating evidence without in-depth consideration of all the interests at stake and of the overall implications on both the ascertainment of the facts and the fundamental rights of other individuals involved in criminal proceedings.[52] On the other hand, the objective impossibility for the accused to take part in the collection of evidence is by definition a neutral event that does not suffice to undermine the right to be adjudicated on the basis of evidence collected with the defence's contribution.[53]

In a nutshell, the complexity of criminal justice makes it necessary to overcome an accused-centred approach to constitutional reform, which in turn reflects the traditional bilateral understanding of criminal proceedings as the space of confrontation between (public) accuser and accused. This does not entail watering down the principle of *contradictoire* by broadening the scope of its exceptions to the extent that further derogations, which are not foreseen by the Constitution, would surreptitiously be introduced. As *Marzaduri* put it, it is noteworthy that the Constitution requires the legislature to regulate, rather than to simply provide for, exceptions from the principle of *contradictoire*.[54] This requirement lies at the core of the constitutional fair trial reform even beyond the area of criminal evidence. Remarkably, the first provision of Article 111 of the Constitution also requires the law to 'regulate' the right to fair trial according to constitutional principles. This entails a very difficult task for the legislature, which is called upon to strike delicate balances between the accused's participatory safeguards and other public and individual interests acknowledged by the Constitution. For instance, the acknowledgment of the accused's right to have any exculpatory evidence obtained cannot certainly be interpreted in the sense that the accused holds an unconditional right to evidence, which would jeopardise the need for efficient prosecution and the principle of a reasonable duration for court proceedings.[55]

These conclusions suggest in-depth consideration of the general opinion that the legislature could not depart from the principle of *contradictoire* in cases other than those provided for by the Constitution. Since statutory law must regulate both the right to *contradictoire* and its exceptions, Italian legislature is in any case called upon to balance all the constitutional interests involved in criminal proceedings. Furthermore, the drafters of the 1999 constitutional reform were certainly aware of the need to provide the highest protection to the right to effective participation in criminal proceedings. Again, the right to confrontation provides a clear example.

---

[52]Marzaduri (2000), p. 800.

[53]See, albeit from different viewpoints, Giostra (2002), p. 3291 f. and Ubertis (2002), p. 1184.

[54]Marzaduri (2000), p. 800 fn. 252.

[55]*Ibid.*, 783 f.

As noted, reproducing the formulation of Article 6 ECHR, the 1999 constitutional reform granted defendants the right to examine their accusers, or have them examined. From this it does not follow that the Constitution enabled the accused to cross-examine prosecutorial witnesses.[56] This does not mean, however, that legal assistance always suffices to ensure effective confrontation, nor that the Constitution prevents defendants from being present at the gathering of incriminating evidence if they have requested it. As we will see, Italian courts unfortunately still allow this result in the field of international cooperation.

C. The Principle of *contradictoire* and Equality of Arms

I. Premise. The Link Between the Requirements of contradictoire *and Equality of Arms in the Constitutional Model of a Fair Trial*

It has been observed that the 1999 constitutional reform laid down a strict link between the principle of *contradictoire* and the other fair trial requirements set forth by Article 111 of the Constitution. Against this framework, the connection between the right to *contradictoire* and the principle of equality of arms is of utmost importance, helping shed light on the exact terms of the parties' involvement in criminal justice.

Certainly, the complex structure of criminal proceedings makes it by definition impossible for the public prosecutor and the private parties to be placed on an equal footing. Great differences exist between the public prosecutor and the defence, differences that are mainly due to their different roles and the aims pursued. Even though prosecutors hold a number of powers in the manner of private parties, they can never have a private interest in fact-finding. In Italy, moreover, prosecutors are called upon to carry out complete and objective investigations, collecting evidence both against and in favour of the suspect.[57]

It was surely not the intention of the drafters of the 1999 constitutional reform to disrupt this set-up by imposing a perfect equality of arms. Yet the enactment of the *par condicio* principle and the right to *contradictoire* in the same general provision on the essential requirements of a fair trial calls for a stronger relationship between these two fundamental guarantees than in the past. The achievement of a real equality of arms enables effective *contradictoire* among the parties and *vice versa*, and both safeguards are further enhanced by the guarantee of impartiality and independence of the judiciary.[58] Of course, this does not mean that the

[56]*Ibid.*, 784 ff.

[57]Arts. 326 and 358 CCP.

[58]Marzaduri (2000), p. 768 f.

Constitution limited the scope of the *par condicio* principle and the right to *contradictoire* solely to court proceedings, since this would leave the defence unprotected in the pre-trial inquiry, in which the imbalance between the law enforcement authorities and private parties reaches its highest tension. One might argue that the principle of equality of arms should be recognized in an indirect manner in the preliminary phase, in that denial of defence rights would negatively affect the effective exercise of the right to *contradictoire* on an equal position at a later stage of the proceedings.[59] Yet this explication would be misleading: especially where coercive means are needed, the principle of equality of arms must play a direct role in ensuring for the defence fair participation in decisions regarding interference with fundamental rights, as well as in challenging intrusive investigative methods enforced without judicial order.

A close examination of the developments that occurred over almost 20 years demonstrates the difficulties that the Italian criminal justice had to face to fulfil the constitutional requirements of *contradictoire* and equality of arms. The following analysis will highlight the pendulum-like evolution of Italian law, which reveals the inability of the Italian legislature and the case-law to depart from an understanding of the defence rights of the accused strongly inspired by a logic of contrast with law enforcement authorities and the public prosecutor. This approach overlooks the relationship between the accused and other private parties and, more generally, the requirement for an overall balance between state-related needs and the individual interests inherent in a fair criminal law action.

II. Defence and Prosecutorial Inquiries

As noted, the enactment of the *par condicio* principle into the constitutional model of a fair trial did not aim at erasing the differences in the investigative powers of private parties and law enforcement authorities. Yet difference in the distribution of powers can give rise to an unfair balance among the parties by frustrating the aim of a proper fact-finding and by preventing the defence from being effectively involved in decisions that can lead to restrictions on fundamental rights. By implementing the 1999 constitutional reform, however, the legislature did not consistently follow this approach. The implementation of the new constitutional fair trial safeguards was carried out by two important reforms, namely Law 397/2000 and Law 63/2001.[60] The former introduced an unprecedented regulation on the defence's investigations with a view to implementing the *par condicio* principle,[61] whereas the latter focused

[59]In this sense see Marzaduri (2000), p. 769.

[60]Nobili (2001), p. 5 ff. Notwithstanding that the heading of Law 63/2001 explicitly related to the implementation of the 1999 constitutional reform, this result was therefore due to both these legislative instruments.

[61]On this topic cf. Siracusano (2008), p. 500 ff.

on the right to confrontation and re-established fair conditions on the use of untested evidence. On close examination, both these reforms formed part of an overall legislative programme, which confirmed the strict link between the fundamental requirements of *contradictoire* and equality of arms.

Notwithstanding these good intentions, the results were less positive than expected. The 2000 reform adopted a rather formalistic approach to the principle of equality of arms. This was apparent from the way the new rules were structured. Even though new investigative powers were granted to the defence lawyer (not only of the accused but of all private parties), the legislature limited itself to amending a number of provisions on investigative acts of the police and prosecutorial authorities, provisions thus tailored to the functions of the investigative bodies. Among the main innovations, moreover, the 2000 Law introduced a new statute on testimonial interviews conducted by the defence lawyer; interviews that, despite giving formal status to informal hearings which were already common practice, lacked any coercive power.[62] In particular, lawyers had no power to compel the physical appearance of a witness or co-accused at their law office, and in case of refusal to appear or refusal to answer questions, they could only request the intervention of the competent prosecutor or a judge.[63] The 2001 reform in turn strengthened the constitutional requirement of *contradictoire* from a somewhat one-sided approach, which, while enhancing the accused's participation in the taking of testimonial evidence and drastically reducing the use of untested evidence, left little room for the interests of other private parties.

Therefore, Italian legislature largely lost an important opportunity for rebalancing the structure of criminal proceedings. On close examination, these legislative reforms, far from compensating for the inevitable imbalance between the prosecutor and the defence, gave rise to new unbalanced situations.

At the pre-trial stage, the difference in the available resources in most cases put the defence on a footing of unavoidable disparity.[64] Furthermore, the 2001 reform, despite considerably restricting the conditions of use at trial of the police and prosecutorial information, left some important rules unchanged, which govern the coercive powers of the investigative bodies during the preliminary inquiry. Alongside exceptional situations that enable prosecutors to order intrusive measures in urgent cases (*e.g.*, interceptions of telecommunications),[65] we have noted that the public prosecutor, as a judicial authority (*autorità giudiziaria*), can still order some intrusive investigations, such as searches and inspections, during the pre-trial inquiry. Private parties in contrast hold no law enforcement powers. Moreover, the lack of in-depth reflection on the link among the equality of arms, the principle of *contradictoire* and the guarantee of judicial oversight led the Italian legislature to ignore the alternative of strengthening the *jus postulandi* of private parties. Except

[62] Art. 391-*bis* CCP.

[63] Art. 391-*bis*(10) CCP.

[64] Marzaduri (2000), p. 768.

[65] Art. 267(3).

in the case of access to private places or areas not open to the public that can be requested by a lawyer,[66] Law 397/2000 failed to amend the rules on other intrusive investigative measures, such as wiretaps, which can still be ordered solely upon request of the competent prosecutor. The main concern that prevented the legislature from reforming this set-up was the fear that the granting of *jus postulandi* to private parties could re-introduce the old prosecutorial inquiry in a new version, transferred to the defence and also prone to misuse.[67] On close examination, this concern was certainly excessive, taking into account that under the current code, the judicial authority is always required to give reasons when interferences with fundamental rights are needed.

Further imbalances concerned the admission and use at trial of out-of-court evidence. To be sure, the legislature established common conditions of admission at trial of untested evidence gathered by the defence and law enforcement authorities, conditions largely inspired by the requirement of *contradictoire* laid down by the 1999 constitutional reform.[68] Nevertheless, the risk of a formal equality of arms was still unavoidable. It cannot be denied that, despite the generally reduced probative value of out-of-court evidence, the information gathered by the investigative bodies is often deemed much more reliable than that gathered by the defence. This practical result was not reduced by the formal requirements set forth especially for interviews of witnesses and co-defendants by the lawyer. Thus, neither the complex set of information duties imposed on the lawyer before receiving oral statements by witnesses[69] nor the obligation, lying with counsel that chooses to take written statements, to draw up official records[70] enhanced the reliability of the oral evidence taken by the defence.

On the other hand, the granting of unprecedented powers to the defence can lead to unjustified imbalances in favour of private parties. In particular, Law 397/2000 allowed for the defence to have an official file set up at the office of the competent judge for the pre-trial inquiry (*giudice per le indagini preliminari*).[71] This innovation enabled private parties to put exculpatory evidence at the disposal of the

[66] Art. 391-*septies* CCP.

[67] Marzaduri (2000), p. 770.

[68] Art. 391-*decies* CCP, enacted by the 2000 reform, submitted the use of defensive evidence to the ordinary rules regarding out-of-court untested evidence, rules that Law 63/2001 drastically amended pursuant to the requirements set by the 1999 constitutional reform. See Arts. 500 et seqq. CCP.

[69] Art. 391-*bis*(3) CCP.

[70] Art. 391-*ter* CCP. This is a very delicate issue with a view to a correct understanding of the institutional position and the responsibility of defence lawyers. The Joint Sections of the Supreme Court acknowledged that lawyers, despite being free to receive informal statements, must draw up complete documentation if they choose to minute up the statements obtained by informants, with the result that uncompleted documentation makes them liable for falsification in an official act. From this it follows that the responsibility of lawyers as public officials is dependent on their choice to draw up official records of the statements collected. Cf. CCass, *S.L.*

[71] Art. 391-*octies* CCP.

judicial authority without the need to give it to the competent prosecutor or to request the law enforcement bodies to carry out investigations in their favour. However, unlike prosecutors, lawyers are not required to insert all the information available in the official file. This result can give rise to a considerable imbalance in the distribution of powers among the parties, making it impossible for both the decision-makers and the prosecutor to verify the information available to the defence at a certain stage of the proceedings. As we will see, this issue is of utmost importance for the purposes of the admission of out-of-court evidence that become unavailable at trial because of unpredictable circumstances.[72]

D. The Role of Private Parties in the Exercise of Criminal Prosecutions

I. The Role of the Victim in the Institution of Criminal Proceedings. The Relationship Between Private and Public Prosecution

One delicate issue concerns the involvement of private parties in the institution of a criminal prosecution.[73] Historically, private parties have not always played the same role in the conduct of criminal prosecutions in Italy. In the nineteenth century, *Carrara* had already pointed out that private prosecutions, be they initiated either by the victim or any other citizen, reflected the degree of a liberal criminal justice.[74] Surprisingly, the 1930 code, despite its authoritarian approach, also did not drop the existing forms of criminal prosecution initiated by individuals and bodies other than the public prosecutor.[75] Yet these prosecutions had a limited scope of application, which confirmed the strong orientation of the 1930 codification towards a model of criminal prosecution mainly entrusted to the public prosecutors. This result could easily be explained in the light of the hierarchical subordination of public prosecutors to the Executive under the fascist regime. Moreover, the 1930 code also enhanced the public character of criminal prosecutions in another way, that is, enabling district court judges (*pretori*) to institute proceedings in the cases falling within their jurisdiction.[76]

---

[72] *Below*, I.II.2.

[73] On this topic see Caianiello (2003). For an in-depth reconstruction of the role of the victim in the institution of criminal prosecutions see Parlato (2012), p. 113 ff.

[74] Carrara (1875), p. 4 ff.

[75] For instance, the Royal Decree 368/1904 enabled the Prefect to institute criminal proceedings in case of infringement of the rules governing the draining of the marshes. For an overview of the cases of criminal prosecution by bodies other than the public prosecutor under the 1930 code see Marzaduri (1996), p. 4.

[76] Marzaduri (1996), p. 3.

To a great extent, the public character of criminal prosecutions was historically linked with the principle of legality. Yet the 1930 code originally provided for the prosecutor's autonomous power to terminate the proceedings,[77] a decision that only entailed the duty to inform, depending on the type of procedure, the General Prosecutor or the Crown Prosecutor. As a matter of principle, this solution did not entail discretionary management of prosecution, which could only be dropped in cases of manifestly insufficient charges. However, the practical implementation of these rules gave certain leeway to use the power of termination.[78] This led the legislature to introduce judicial oversight of the termination of criminal proceedings, which aimed at eliminating the prosecutorial practice of archiving of procedural records and substituting it with a judicial decision.[79] This reform also enabled investigative judges, to which prosecutors had to lodge their request for termination of the proceedings, to institute a criminal inquiry at their own initiative whenever they considered a criminal law action necessary in a concrete case.[80] This result gave rise to a clear form of public prosecution *ex officio*.

The enactment of the principle of legality by the 1947 Constitution should be interpreted in the light of these developments. It is not surprising that this solution, quite unique in the European context, was initially seen as entailing both a strict mandatory prosecution and a monopoly on public prosecutions. On close examination, it is debatable whether the Constitution aimed at achieving these results.[81] At any rate, it took several years before Italy could depart from a state-centred approach to criminal prosecution. In the midst of the 1950s, the legislature enabled any voter to institute criminal proceedings in cases of infringement against the rules governing the composition and election of electoral bodies.[82] However, it was questionable if this reform introduced a popular criminal prosecution (*azione penale popolare*) in a strict sense rather than empowering voters to simply lodge a complaint.[83] It was only at the end of the 1960s that the Constitutional Court acknowledged the constitutionality of criminal prosecutions by individuals or bodies other than the public prosecutor,[84] a solution strongly supported by legal scholarship[85] and confirmed by subsequent rulings of the Constitutional Court.[86] This approach, however, did not exclude the public prosecutor's initiative, only legitimising the (possible) concurrence of private and public prosecution, and therefore the (possible) concurrence between discretionary and mandatory prosecution.

---

[77] Art. 74(3) of the 1930 CCP (1930 version).

[78] Carnelutti (1947), p. 48.

[79] Royal Legislative Decree 288/1944.

[80] Art. 74(3) of the 1930 CCP.

[81] On this discussion see Ruggeri (2015a), p. 63 f.

[82] Presidential Decree 570/1956.

[83] Marzaduri (1996), p. 3.

[84] CConst. 61/1967.

[85] Chiavario (1975), p. 897 f.

[86] CConst. 84/1979 and 474/1993.

The 1988 codification did not explicitly deal with the problem of private prosecutions, while enacting an exhaustive list of forms of criminal prosecution by the public prosecutor.[87] One year later, Legislative Decree 271/1989, enacting the implementation of the rules of the new code, made a clear step forward towards a public approach to criminal prosecution by repealing any previous legislation enabling bodies other than the public prosecutor to institute criminal proceedings.[88] This provision should not be interpreted in a strict sense, that is, as relating only to forms of criminal prosecution by institutions or bodies provided for by special regulations. The survival of forms of private criminal prosecution was in any case excluded by Article 207 of the 1989 Implementing Rules, which extended the application of the new code to the proceedings regulated by special legislation, except for explicit derogations.[89] The only exception to this approach was laid down in Article 577 CCP, which, in line with a tradition interrupted by the fascist code, enabled the victim who joined a civil law action to criminal proceedings for either insult or defamation to challenge the criminal judgment before a criminal court. Doubtless, this provision strengthened the role of the injured party in these delicate proceedings. However, it was debatable whether this provision, which was later repealed by the Law 46/2006, enabled the injured party to initiate a criminal prosecution at second instance.[90]

Another important innovation was brought about by Legislative Decree 274/2000, which introduced an unprecedented form of criminal jurisdiction of justices of the peace (*giudici di pace*), based on the conciliation procedure for minor crimes. This legislative reform strengthened the role of the aggrieved parties to such point that it enabled them to bring a legal action directly before the competent judge (*ricorso immediato al giudice*) instead of lodging a complaint (*querela*) before investigative bodies.[91] Although this legal action certainly allowed the injured party to have access to criminal jurisdiction, it can be doubted whether the 2000 reform enacted a form of private criminal prosecution.[92] On a formal level, the victim's legal action is a request for criminal proceedings against the defendant.[93] Moreover, Italian legislature imposed precise obligations on the victims who choose this option, requiring them to define the alleged offence in clear and exact terms. Furthermore, victims must include the information supporting their request, while specifying in advance the circumstances in which witnesses and technical advisors would give oral evidence.[94] Remarkably, *ricorso* must be signed

[87] Art. 60(1) CCP.

[88] Art. 231 RICCP.

[89] Marzaduri (1996), p. 4.

[90] *Ibid.*, 5 f. Of a different opinion see Cordero (2012), p. 1098.

[91] Art. 21 et seqq. Legislative Decree 274/2000.

[92] Ruggeri (2002), p. 655 ff.; Marzaduri (2016), p. 1121 ff.

[93] Art. 21(2)(i) Legislative Decree 274/2000.

[94] Art. 21(2)(f-h) Legislative Decree 274/2000.

by both the victim and his lawyer,[95] a requirement of utmost importance, which can impinge on the admissibility of this legal action.[96]

On close examination, the drafters of the 2000 reform did not enable the victim to institute a criminal prosecution excluding any initiative of the public prosecutor. Significantly, *ricorso* must be communicated to the competent prosecutor who is called upon to assess whether the conditions exist to bring the alleged offender to court or whether the victim's legal action should be withheld.[97] At first glance, this regulation renders the public prosecutor's initiative a necessary step for the institution of criminal proceedings, to the point that defendants could be summoned to court only after the prosecutor had indicted them. However, the prosecutor's role in this procedure is very weak. In particular, prosecutors cannot carry out any investigations to verify the merits of the victim's legal action,[98] a solution largely justified by the fact that, unlike in ordinary cases, the victim's initiative can be withheld only if manifestly unfounded. Furthermore, it may happen that the prosecutor neither prefers formal charges against the offender nor expresses a contrary opinion to the victim's *ricorso*. In the absence of any initiative, the proceedings will not stall, since the 2000 reform enabled the judge to carry out the same assessments entrusted to the prosecutor.[99] Unless the victim's legal action must be withheld, the justice of the peace will summon the parties to court and the court summons must contain the charge against the defendant.

This result gives rise to several systematic concerns. Certainly, the legal solution cannot lead to the conclusion that the victim's initiative takes on the form of a criminal prosecution *secundum eventum*, that is, depending on whether or not the prosecutor prefers a formal charge confirming or amending the indications contained in the victim's *ricorso*.[100] The Constitutional Court classified the victim's legal action as a proposal of prosecution, which remains in the exclusive hands of the public prosecutor.[101] The constitutional case-law therefore ruled out an interpretation of these rules in terms of a criminal prosecution *ex officio* by the justices of the peace. From this approach it follows that, unless *ricorso* must be withheld, the justice of the peace is not necessarily required to bring the defendant to court, but should return the case to the competent prosecutor, who must issue the indictment pursuant to Article 409(5) CCP.[102] The reference to this provision, enacted by the

---

[95] Art. 21(3) Legislative Decree 274/2000.

[96] Art. 24 Legislative Decree 274/2000.

[97] Art. 25 Legislative Decree 274/2000.

[98] Of a different opinion CConst, 381/2005. In this ruling, the Constitutional Court pointed out that the detailed contents of the *ricorso* enable the prosecutor to assess the merits of the private initiative. This conclusion cannot be sustained, since prosecutors have a very short period of time to assess the victim's legal action.

[99] Art. 26 Legislative Decree 274/2000.

[100] Of course, the prosecutorial power of amending the facts stated in the victim's *ricorso* has its limits and cannot lead to a distortion of the essential features of the offence indicated by the injured party. See Marzaduri (2016), p. 1124.

[101] CConst, 321/2008.

[102] CConst, 361/2005.

1988 code to avoid the old form of judicial prosecution,[103] might be seen as a formalistic attempt to save the public prosecutor's monopoly on the institution of criminal proceedings. However, a judicial criminal prosecution would largely frustrate the role of the parties and the possibility of effective defence. In particular, if the same judge who preventively assessed the victim's *ricorso* could later decide on the merits on the case, the impartiality of the judicial authority would inevitably be undermined.[104] On close examination, the constitutional case-law should be interpreted in the light of the aim of ensuring effective judicial oversight of the criminal prosecution without jeopardising the rights of private parties.[105]

II. Parties' Involvement in the Decision Not to Institute a Criminal Prosecution or to Drop Criminal Proceedings

1. The Defence's Involvement in the Decision Not to Institute a Criminal Prosecution

Somewhat different problems concern the role of private parties in the procedure for the termination of criminal proceedings. It has been observed that under the 1930 code, public prosecutors not only could institute court proceedings but also had full power to autonomously discontinue the pre-trial inquiry, with only the duty to inform the General Prosecutor or the Crown Prosecutor about their decision. Although the 1944 reform placed the termination of criminal proceedings under judicial control, the legislature failed to involve private parties in the decision on whether to terminate proceedings. This solution, which revealed the scant importance attached at that time to the defence's contribution to judicial decisions, lasted 44 years.

It was only in 1988 that the new code for the first time involved private parties in the decision on discontinuance of the proceedings. To be sure, the 1988 code did not end the possibility of a criminal inquiry to be terminated through a decision *inaudito reo*.[106] However, the 1988 codification clearly favoured a system that involved the defence in the decision to discontinue of the proceedings. Remarkably, the code allowed not only the suspect but also the victim to play active role in this procedure. In particular, the victim was empowered to lodge an objection against the prosecutorial request to discontinue the procedure by indicating the need for further investigations and evidence that still need to be gathered.[107] In the case of admissible objection, the victim's initiative prevents the judge from dropping the case without hearing the victim.[108] Moreover, the code has structured this

[103]For a critical approach to the legal solution of Article 409(5) CCP cf. Giostra (1994), p. 80.

[104]Marzaduri (2016), p. 1126.

[105]CConst, 361/2005.

[106]Art. 409(1) CCP.

[107]Art. 410(1) CCP.

[108]Art. 409(2) CCP.

interlocutory procedure in a manner that makes any decision[109] conditional on both private parties and the competent prosecutor[110] being given the opportunity to be heard.[111]

While the code considerably strengthened the role of the suspect in the decision on the discontinuance of criminal proceedings, it can be doubted whether this set-up provided the victims with an effective opportunity to make their voice heard. Unlike the suspect's counsel, who must always be summoned to the hearing,[112] it is questionable whether the victim's lawyer must also be summoned.[113] Moreover, since the code requires judges to hear suspects or victims only if present, Italian courts make the hearing of the victim dependent on his explicit request.[114] Doubtless, these results hamper the effective participation of the aggrieved parties in a procedure that can negatively affect their claim for justice.

The weak role of the victim in the decision to charge is further confirmed by the rules on legal remedies against the decision to terminate the proceedings. The 1988 code enabled the injured party to lodge an appeal on points of law before the Supreme Court to challenge the judicial order discontinuing inquiry. However, this appeal was allowed only in cases of violation of *contradictoire*,[115] thus protecting the victim who was not summoned, or was summoned with delay, to the court hearing. By contrast, no protection was provided in more serious violations of the right to *contradictoire*, *e.g.* where the victims, despite their request, were not informed of the application for discontinuance of the proceedings[116]; where the

---

[109]As possible alternatives, the competent judge can either order the termination of the proceedings or require the competent prosecutor to carry out further investigations or to bring the defendant to court. See Art. 409(4–5) CCP.

[110]Moreover, the court summons must be communicated to the General Prosecutor before the Court of Appeal. Cf. Art. 409(3) CCP.

[111]CCass, *Mariottini.*

[112]CConst, 418/1993.

[113]Legal scholarship advocates the need to summon also the victim's counsel pursuant to the general rules of *in camera* hearings. See Caprioli (1994), p. 418 fn. 64. The case law does not share this opinion, however. Cf. CCass, *Barlettelli.* Of course, the question is relevant in the cases in which the victims have not yet appointed a counsel, since otherwise the summons will be notified at their legal domicile pursuant to Article 33 of the code's implementing rules. See Campo (1993), p. 1497.

[114]CCass, *P.o. in proc. Mercuri.*

[115]Art. 409(6) CCP.

[116]Art. 408(2) CCP. More recently, the legislature, following the indications of the 2011 Council of Europe Convention of Istanbul on preventing and combating violence against women and domestic violence, launched a reform—namely, Law 119/2013—aimed at enhancing the criminal law protection of women also by means of procedural tools. In this light, the 2013 reform on gender-based violence strengthened the information rights of the victims who must be notified of the prosecutorial application for discontinuance of the proceedings regardless of whether they requested to be informed. This innovation only applies, however, to the cases of gender-based violence. Outside these cases, the notice of the prosecutorial application for discontinuance of the proceedings is still dependent on the request of the injured parties who may however have not been informed in the course of the pre-trial inquiry about the consequences of their inaction.

judge terminated the case before the 10-day deadline provided for the victim to lodge his challenge[117]; where the judge terminated the proceedings without considering the victim's challenge duly lodged[118]; and so on. To tackle these problems, both the criminal law scholarship and the case-law suggested extending the scope of the appeal before the Supreme Court.[119] Although both the Constitutional Court and the Joint Sections of the Supreme Court shared this approach,[120] it is questionable whether this legal remedy can be extended to violations other than those provided for by the code,[121] since this solution would infringe on the principle of legality governing procedural invalidity.[122]

These shortcomings confirm the scant involvement of the victim in criminal proceedings with regard to the decision to charge.[123] This was also a result of a formalistic approach to the role of the injured party in criminal justice. It is noteworthy that, whereas the violation of the rules on the victim's summons gives rise to an absolute form of invalidity,[124] the infringement of the rules governing his intervention in criminal proceedings leads to a relative nullity, which can only be judicially declared on the initiative of the injured party.[125]

2. The Need to Balance Conflicting Interests in the Decision Whether to Prosecute or to Terminate Criminal Proceedings

Alongside these developments, the legislature made further steps forward by requiring new compromises between prosecutorial needs and individual interests in the decision on whether to prosecute. The first remarkable intervention in this direction was contemporaneous with the new code. Presidential Decree 448/1988, introducing a comprehensive set of rules in the field of juvenile criminal justice, extended the power to drop prosecution for reasons unconnected with the merits of the charge and concerned with the features of the offence. This legislation allowed for discontinuance of prosecution when the alleged offence was criminally irrelevant (*irrilevanza del fatto*)[126] due to the low severity and occasional nature of the

---

[117] Art. 408(3) CCP.

[118] Art. 410 CCP.

[119] See, among others, Giostra (1994), p. 60; CCass, *Noschese*.

[120] See respectively CConst, 353/1991, and CCass, *Testa* (in relation to the case of unlawful declaration of inadmissibility of the victim's objection) as well as CCass, *Lo Mauro* (in relation to the case of lack of assessment of the admissibility of the objection).

[121] In this sense *Caprioli*, who shared moreover the proposed extension to the case in which the judge failed to assess the victim's objection. See Caprioli (1994), p. 430 f.

[122] Art. 177 CCP.

[123] In a different sense see Iasevoli (2007), p. 3.

[124] Art. 178(c) CCP. On the grounds for this approach see Tranchina (1989), p. 4 f.

[125] Art. 181 CCP.

[126] On this topic see Quattrocolo (2004), Cesari (2006).

conduct, and where further prosecution could affect the minor's educational needs.[127] This tool constituted the first experiment in the Italian criminal justice with enacting a model of diversion from judicial proceedings.[128]

On close examination, the new mechanism was still imperfect for several reasons. First of all, it is questionable whether the low severity and occasional nature of the conduct, alongside the minor's educational needs, truly demonstrates the irrelevance of the criminal offence. This legislative solution gives rise, moreover, to serious human rights concerns. The proceedings could be terminated either too early or too late. On one hand, the 1988 reform on juvenile criminal justice introduced a decision barring the opening of the trial phase (*sentenza di non luogo a procedere*) even during the preliminary investigations, that is, in a phase in which it is still uncertain whether and with what accusation the suspect will be brought to court. On the other, the criminal proceedings could also be terminated after the defendant being brought to court with a formal accusation, a solution that may be detrimental for the minor defendant, who would be exposed to the prejudicial effects of a criminal prosecution.

From the perspective of the present discussion, it is worth noting that the 1988 reform on juvenile criminal justice granted the parties a rather weak role in this delicate decision. To be sure, the judge, before ordering termination of the proceedings, had to hear not only the minor defendant and the holder of parental responsibility but also the victim. However, judicial authority was not bound by the information obtained by private parties, and the decision could only be challenged by the defendant and the General Prosecutor before the Court of Appeal, whereas the victims had no tool to make their voice heard.

The practical experience of this mechanism over the first decade encouraged the Italian legislature to extend to adult offenders, albeit to a limited extent, the clauses aimed at dropping prosecution in cases of minor offences. An important reform was carried out by Legislative Decree 274/2000, which enhanced, within the jurisdiction of justices of the peace, the judicial discretion in the termination of a criminal prosecution for grounds unconnected not only with the merits of the charge but also with the characteristics of the offence itself. By this means, a new form of termination of the proceedings was introduced in the case of crimes characterised by particularly low severity (*particolare tenuità del fatto*).[129]

This mechanism constituted a remarkable step forward. From the viewpoint of substantive criminal law, the low severity of the conduct does not touch upon its criminal relevance. From a procedural perspective, termination of the proceedings at the end of the investigative stage protects the suspect from the negative repercussions of a criminal charge. Moreover, a wide range of diversion criteria guides the judicial decision on the initiation of the prosecution, some of which are clearly

[127] Art. 27 Presidential Decree 448/1988.

[128] Di Chiara (2003), p. 258 ff.

[129] Art. 34 Legislative Decree 274/2000.

oriented to a stronger protection of some fundamental rights of the defendant.[130] It is noteworthy that the 2000 reform considerably strengthened the protection of the private parties and especially of the victim. In the pre-trial phase, the proceedings cannot be discontinued if the injured party has a specific interest in the initiation of a criminal prosecution.[131] Moreover, criminal proceedings can also be terminated because of the low severity of the deed after the initiation of court proceedings. In this case, however, a judgment is required, and the proceedings can only be discontinued on the condition that neither the defendant nor the victim, after being heard,[132] are opposed to this conclusion. Finally, it is worth observing that, although the low severity of the deed entails an assessment of the merits of the case, the drafters of the 2000 reform opted for a procedural solution, justified specifically on the ground of the importance attached to the victim's interest in the institution of a criminal proceeding.[133]

Furthermore, Legislative Decree 274/2000 introduced another tool aimed at an alternative conclusion to criminal proceedings, that is, the extinguishing of the offence in the case of rectifying measures.[134] Unlike the termination of the proceedings for low severity of the deed, this is a clear example of restorative justice. The importance attached by the 2000 reform to this mechanism led to the diminishing of the role of private parties other than the defendant. Although the offence can only be declared extinguished after the parties have been heard, the victim has no right to challenge.[135] On the other hand, the defendant's responsibility to find proper rectifying measures was enhanced. To avoid the risk of a sort of 'monetarisation' of criminal justice, the justices of the peace must assess the ability of the rectifying measures adopted to meet the goals of remuneration and prevention pursued by the criminal law provision, taking into account the seriousness of the concrete offence committed.[136]

More recently, Law 67/2014, while introducing a new procedure for absent defendants, enacted an unprecedented regulation on the suspension of criminal

---

[130]The low severity of the deed must be assessed not only in light of the interests protected by statutory criminal law, the damages or dangers derived from the offence, the degree of guilt and the occasional character of the criminal action but also taking into consideration the potential damage that the institution of a criminal process would cause to personal interests such as work, family, health and so on.

[131]In this sense cf. Marzaduri (2016), p. 1137 f., who pointed out that, notwithstanding clear legal indications, the prosecutor who decides to apply for a termination of the proceedings for the low severity of the deed should previously hear the victim and verify his interest in the institution of a criminal process.

[132]Marzaduri (2016), p. 1137 f.

[133]*Ibid.*, 1138.

[134]Art. 34 Legislative Decree 274/2000. In particular, judges can declare the offence extinguished if the defendants demonstrate that after the first appearance hearing, they took concrete measures to repair the damages caused by the offence committed, by means of restitution or compensation, and to eliminate the harmful or dangerous consequences of their act.

[135]Marzaduri (2016), p. 1138 f.

[136]*Ibid.*

proceedings for the purposes of probation.[137] Although a similar mechanism has been in force since the 1988 reform on juvenile justice,[138] it was only in 2014 that a probation procedure was extended to adult offenders who committed a crime punishable either with a financial penalty or with a period of detention up to a maximum of 4 years. Like in the aforementioned case falling within the jurisdiction of justices of the peace, criminal proceedings can be suspended when the defendant requests to be given a probation period to repair the harmful or dangerous consequences of the offence committed and possibly to compensate the injured party for the damages caused.[139] This mechanism, which entails also the suspension of the passage of time for the prosecution of the offence,[140] is also dependent on the performance of social community work during the probation period under the supervision of the Social Service.

Concerning the procedural arrangements, probation must be requested, as a rule, before the conclusion of the intermediate phase or the first appearance hearing at trial.[141] However, this mechanism neither presupposes the institution of a criminal prosecution nor necessarily leads to the suspension only of the court proceedings. If defendants make their request during the pre-trial phase,[142] suspension will also apply to the preliminary inquiry. In this case, prosecutorial consent is required. Otherwise, after the initiation of court proceedings, the competent judge, unless the conditions for acquittal exist, must first hear the parties, including the victim, and should eventually order an *in camera* hearing. Furthermore, defendants can be summoned to appear personally in court so that the judicial authority can verify the voluntariness of their request.[143] Like in case of the rectifying measures falling within the jurisdiction of the justices of the peace, the parties' opinion on the probation proposal is not binding. Nevertheless, the judicial authority must ascertain whether the accused proposed a proper treatment programme and whether there is sufficient evidence that he will refrain from committing further offences, taking into specific account the need to protect the injured party and to facilitate a mediation between the parties.[144]

Certainly, Law 67/2014 enhanced the protection of the victim in comparison to the similar probation tool in the field of juvenile justice, where the judge needs to hear the injured party neither before ordering the probation period nor before

---

[137] Arts. 168-*bis* et seqq. PC. The procedural arrangements are governed by Articles 464-*bis* et seqq. CCP. The procedural rules on the suspension of the proceedings for the purposes of a probation period were enacted into a new Title V-*bis* of the 6th Book of the code on alternative proceedings. Notwithstanding this systematic approach, it can be doubted whether this can be considered an 'alternative proceeding' in the sense attached to this notion by the 1988 code.

[138] Art. 28 Presidential Decree 488/1988.

[139] Art. 168-*bis* PC.

[140] Art. 168-*ter* PC.

[141] Art. 464-*bis*(2) CCP.

[142] Art. 464-*ter* CCP.

[143] Art. 464-*quarter*(1–2) CCP.

[144] Art. 464-*quarter*(3) CCP.

declaring the offence extinguished.[145] Furthermore, the 2014 reform strengthened the parties' right to challenge the decision on probation, enabling both the defendant and the public prosecutor to lodge an appeal on point of law before the Supreme Court. The aggrieved parties were in turn enabled to request a prosecutorial appeal and to challenge the judicial order either because they were not summoned or because they, despite having appeared in court, were not examined.[146] Yet the voice of the injured party is still weak, since the judge must hear the victim only in case of rescheduling of the sums due as a compensation for damages, whereas to modify the original arrangements it is sufficient that only the defendant and the public prosecutor have been previously heard.[147] Furthermore, the legislature left the participatory role of the victim rather undefined at the end of the probation period. Although the parties and the victim must be summoned to the hearing in which the defendant's conduct during the probation period is to be assessed,[148] it is unclear whether they need to be heard or whether the judicial authority can autonomously decide on the extinguishing of the offence.

Ultimately, the 2014 reform charged the Government with the task of elaborating a new general ground for exclusion of criminal liability for the low severity of the deed. By further developing the solutions existing in the field of juvenile justice and the proceedings before the justice of peace, Law 28/2015 provided a general legal basis for termination of the proceedings for low severity of the deed in cases of offences punishable with a fine or a detention of a maximum of no more than 5 years.[149] From a procedural viewpoint, it is worth observing that this mechanism has strengthened the participatory rights of the aggrieved parties even if it places them under a considerable burden. Unlike in the other cases of termination of the proceedings, the victim has the right to be informed of the application for discontinuance of the proceedings irrespective of a specific request,[150] a right aimed at a preventive challenge of the prosecutor's initiative.[151] Yet the victim's challenge must give reasons from the outset, unlike in the field of the proceedings before the justice of the peace. If the injured parties decide to challenge the prosecutorial request for discontinuance of the proceedings for the low severity of the deed, however, they must also give reasons on pain of inadmissibility.[152] Moreover, the 2015 reform also enhanced the role of the defendants by enabling them to lodge a challenge as well, a solution that is justified by the need to protect their interest in obtaining a more favourable form of discontinuance of the proceedings.[153]

---

[145] See Arts. 28–29 Presidential Decree 488/1988.

[146] Art. 464-*quarter*(7) CCP.

[147] Art. 464-*quinquies* CCP.

[148] Art. 464-*septies* CCP.

[149] Art. 411 CCP, in relation to Art. 131-*bis* PC. See among others Caprioli (2015), p. 82 ff.

[150] Caprioli (2015), p. 99.

[151] Art. 411(1-*bis*) CCP.

[152] *Ibid.*

[153] Giuliani (2016), p. 560.

It must be acknowledged, however, that the obligation for the prosecutor to involve the parties in this case of discontinuance of the proceedings has an expected price.[154] Thus the right of the suspect and the victim to be informed in any case does not entail that prosecutors must interrupt the investigations once they consider the deed to be of a low severity. On the contrary, the investigative bodies should further investigate to rule out the possibility of requesting termination of the proceedings on other grounds more favourable for the suspect, who might otherwise challenge the hurried initiative of the prosecutor. Yet the need to activate a necessary *contradictoire* with the parties may lead prosecutors not to consider the case under investigation as a priority or, even worse, to include it into the so-called 'model 45', i.e. a special register for facts that are not deemed to entail sufficient suspicion of guilt as *notitiae criminis*.[155]

E. The Principle of *contradictoire* and the Right to Be Informed in Criminal Proceedings

I. The Constitutional Model of Informed Participation in Criminal Proceedings

The first condition for the effective involvement of private parties in criminal proceedings is the possibility of receiving proper information on the ongoing investigation or prosecution. Without this fundamental requirement, any form of defensive participation turns out to be purely formal. Effective participation in the proceedings must thus be seen as informed participation.

In this regard, Italian law still reveals great deficiencies that neither the fair trial constitutional reform nor the developments that have recently occurred in the Strasbourg case-law and in EU law could erase. We have seen that the first guarantee that the 1999 constitutional reform enacted with specific regard to criminal justice is about information on the accusation. The introduction of the new concept of 'accusation', however, has given rise to heated debates on the scope of the constitutional provision. On close examination, the drafters of the 1999 constitutional reform did not reproduce exactly the formulation of the European Convention. Thus, according to Article 111 of the Constitution, defendants must be granted information on the nature and the grounds of the charge in a confidential way. Doubtless, the requirement of confidentiality does not fit the indictment best for two main reasons. First, the secrecy of the investigation and the prohibition of publicity end with the initiation of the court proceedings.[156] Second, except in the

---

[154] Caprioli (2015), p. 100 f.

[155] *Ibid.*, 101.

[156] Marzaduri (2000), p. 777.

case of penal order proceedings, defendants are always granted information on the indictment. A literal interpretation of the constitutional provision would therefore lead to the paradoxical result of recognising a guarantee that to a great extent already exists in Italian criminal justice.

This conclusion led criminal law scholarship to examine the constitutional guarantee of information in the light of the European Convention. In particular, a confrontation with European case-law, which traditionally identified the charge with any official notification of the charge,[157] paved the way for the extension of the scope of the constitutional provision to the pre-trial inquiry. Furthermore, the flexible case-law of the European Court on the decision to charge, which the Strasbourg judges considered to be entailed by very different investigative acts even within the same criminal justice system,[158] suggested shifting the approach from the formal perspective of the phases of criminal proceedings to the potential of the investigations to affect the rights of the accused.[159]

The approach followed by the Strasbourg Court should have guided the interpreter in the ascertainment of the investigative acts that, impinging on the suspect's fundamental rights, can be deemed as entailing the decision to charge.[160] Yet the Italian legislature neither walked this road nor amended the rules on the information of the preliminary charge filed in the pre-trial phase.[161] On close examination, the Constitution does not require the accused to be informed immediately and unconditionally of the charge filed against them. Remarkably, the 1999 constitutional reform departed from the requirement of 'promptness' of the English version of Article 6(3)(a) ECHR, enacting a more flexible formulation (closer to the French text), which grants the accused the right to receive information 'as soon as possible'. This expression, far from requiring the competent authorities to immediately inform the suspects on the charge filed against them, calls for a balance among conflicting interests,[162] banning, however, delays that cannot be justified on the basis of other constitutional interests.

At first glance, no constitutional provision specifically deals with the right to information on the developments of the prosecutorial and police investigations. This does not, however, mean that this fundamental guarantee has no relevance to the constitutional model of a fair trial. Alongside the general acknowledgment of the inviolability of the right to a defence under Article 24 of the Constitution, Italian constitutional law provides for a strict link between the right to information on the accusation and right to have facilities for the preparation of one's own defence, another fundamental guarantee enacted in compliance with the European

[157] *Ibid.*, 776.

[158] For an overview of the multiple applications of the notion of 'charge' to Italian procedural law see Ubertis (2009), p. 28 f.

[159] ECtHR, *Foti et al. v. Italy*, § 52. On this point see more extensively Chap. 8, D.II.2.

[160] Marzaduri (2000), p. 777.

[161] *Below*, E.II.1.

[162] Marzaduri (2000), p. 778.

Convention.[163] Certainly, the knowledge solely of the charge is insufficient for the accused to set up a proper defensive strategy and to effectively take part in criminal proceedings. Especially at the pre-trial stage, the ignorance of the strategy of the investigative bodies and the evidence collected can impinge on the defence of the suspects, frustrating the possibility of countering investigative means that can severely affect their fundamental rights.[164] It is noteworthy that under the European Convention, the guarantee of Article 6(3)(b) applies to any person 'charged' with a criminal offence, the suspect being included in this broad notion.[165]

This conclusion, while confirming the need to avoid a restrictive interpretation of the constitutional guarantee of information on the accusation, refutes the assumption that Italian constitutional law does not acknowledge the right to be duly informed of the evidence gathered by the investigative authorities. Of course, this right cannot be granted in absolute terms and similar balances to those required for the information on the accusation are also needed here.[166]

II. Information on the Accusation

1. Information on the Charge in the Pre-Trial Inquiry

It has been noted that, despite the differences *vis-à-vis* the European Convention, the constitutional fair trial reform called for in-depth reflection on the trade-offs concerning the right to information on the charging decisions, starting from the pre-trial inquiry. The examination of the development of Italian law at the time of the 1999 reform, however, highlights a considerable cultural backwardness of the Italian criminal justice and the failure by the legislature to take into consideration the severe repercussions of the lack of information for private parties involved in criminal proceedings. Of course, as noted, the institution of a criminal inquiry cannot entail the duty of the competent authorities to immediately inform the individuals that might be involved in the criminal law action. In this light, the rules of Article 335 CCP, which do not require prosecutors starting a criminal investigation to provide information at their own initiative, are exempt from criticism. The need for information arises, however, when enough evidence is collected against one or more individuals who must thus be charged with a criminal offence[167] and who take on the formal status of 'suspects'.[168]

[163] *Ibid.*, 780 f.

[164] *Ibid.*, 781 f.

[165] Chapter 8, D.III.

[166] Marzaduri (2000), p. 782.

[167] *Ibid.*, 782.

[168] Art. 335(2) CCP.

In this regard, the 1988 code provided for a radical solution, excluding any information until the defendant was brought to court.[169] This harsh solution certainly could not be deemed in line with the constitutional requirement of effective defence. It took several years before Law 332/1995 acknowledged the right of both suspects and victims to receive information on the prosecutorial charge and its eventual modifications. This reform, strengthening the right to information, revealed a clear attempt to overcome a strictly dualistic view of criminal proceedings. Nevertheless, the 1995 reform made the duty of information dependent on the request of the interested party,[170] which clearly presupposes that the individuals concerned already know the prosecutor's office that opened a criminal inquiry against them.

The main shortcomings of Law 332/1995, moreover, concerned the rules that allow for restriction or exclusion of information, rules that highlighted a considerable distance from the balance required by the Constitution. The 1995 legislation enabled prosecutors to withhold the sought information on the ground of vague investigative needs for a period no longer than 3 months.[171] Even worse, the legislature permitted the exclusion of information in cases of certain serious offences listed in Article 407(2)(a) CCP (kidnapping with the purpose of extortion, mafia-typed organised crime, terrorism, etc.).[172] This was a very questionable solution, which reflected the persistent prejudice that the abstract seriousness of the offence always entailed risks for the ongoing investigation.[173] Furthermore, it is clear that these restrictions on the right to information cannot be justified in relation to the victim and the suspect in the same terms. Doubtless, the risks for the ongoing investigation—no matter whether legally presumed or assessed in the concrete case—have a different weight with regard to the victim and the suspect. Therefore, the lack of information cannot have the same impact on the right of the suspect and the victim to be involved in criminal proceedings.

The failure to strike a proper balance between investigative needs and the right to informed on the initial charge could not be compensated for at a later stage of the proceedings. To be sure, the 1988 codification introduced a tool—namely, notice of investigation (*informazione di garanzia*)—aimed at ensuring to both suspects and victims information on the ongoing investigation.[174] The origin of this instrument can be traced back to the judicial communication (*comunicazione giudiziaria*), enacted into the 1930 code by Law 932/1969.[175] However, unlike this old tool, the new notice of investigation aimed at enabling its addressees to exercise their defence rights rather than at informing them of the charge and the developments of

[169] Art. 335(3) CCP (1988 version).

[170] Art. 335(3) CCP.

[171] Art. 335(3-*bis*) CCP.

[172] Art. 335(3) CCP.

[173] Marzaduri (2000), p. 779 fn. 110.

[174] Art. 369 CCP.

[175] Art. 304 of the 1930 CCP.

the prosecutorial inquiry.[176] The rules on the notice of investigation, as amended by the 1995 reform, weakened even more the position of both suspects and victims by restricting the duty of information of the competent authority to the case of investigations at which the lawyer could be present.

Another shortcoming of Italian law at the time of the 1999 constitutional reform concerned the contents of the information, which far from satisfied the requirement of preciseness laid down by both the European Convention and the Italian Constitution. Even though the notice of the investigation was often given at a stage in which the initial suspicion was further corroborated by additional evidence, Article 369 CCP allowed for suspects and victims to know solely the relevant criminal law provision as well as the place and time of the alleged offence. This was very scant information, which gave the interested parties little chance to set up an effective defence strategy. Moreover, Italian law did not have clear rules on the necessary linguistic assistance to ensure that the suspect and the victim were able to fully understand the contents of the information. In a historical ruling, the Constitutional Court had already stressed that in the light of the European Convention, defendants have an enforceable right to be promptly informed of the charge in a language they can understand.[177] Nevertheless, the domestic rules on information remained untouched, whereas the 1999 constitutional reform, despite acknowledging the defendant's right to follow the hearing in a language they understood, omitted any reference to the right to understand the information on the accusation.[178]

In sum, there were sufficient grounds for in-depth reform of Italian law at the time of the constitutional fair trial reform. Nevertheless, very little has been done until now and most of the deficiencies of the Italian criminal justice still affect the right to information of both suspects and victims in the pre-trial inquiry. Surprisingly, neither the 2000 Law on defensive investigations nor the 2001 Law implementing the constitutional fair trial reform brought about any innovation in the right to information in the pre-trial phase. Shortly before the enactment of Law 63/2001, another legislative instrument[179] introduced a new tool of information, namely a notice on the right to a defence.[180] This tool was, however, reserved solely to suspects and did not substantially change the function of the notice of the investigation under Article 369 CCP.

Remarkably, the 1999 constitutional reform also could not change the minimalist approach of Italian courts. According to the Supreme Court, even though the lawyer's presence at investigative measures generally reveals the potential of investigations to interfere with fundamental rights, neither the concrete features of the alleged offence nor the contents of the ongoing investigation need to be communicated to the suspect and the victim.[181] Until recent times, suspects and

---

[176]Marzaduri (2000), p. 778.

[177]CConst, 10/1993. On the systematic importance of this decision see Chap. 16, B.I.2.

[178]Marzaduri (2000), p. 780.

[179]Law 60/2001.

[180]Art. 369-*bis* CCP.

[181]CCass, *Mariano*.

victims were not even informed of subsequent changes to the information contained in the notice of the investigation—a solution that reflected the questionable argument that the private parties, after being informed of the ongoing inquiry, must take the necessary initiatives to get informed.[182]

On the other hand, it must be acknowledged that, even though investigative acts which allow for the lawyer's presence are needed, the granting of information on the charge can also jeopardise the aims of the ongoing investigation. The problem arises especially in relation to unannounced investigative means, such as searches or inspections. This delicate issue raised a lively debate in Italian case-law after the 1999 constitutional reform. This led the Joint Sections of the Supreme Court to adopt the Solomon-like solution that, although the lawyer can be present at a search or a seizure, the competent authority does not need to inform the individuals concerned beforehand.[183] According to this jurisprudence, the failure to send the notice of investigation before the performance of an unannounced investigation will not therefore affect its validity. The only obligation of the competent authority is to send the notice of investigation after the use of such investigative means—not always, however, but only if the suspect was present.[184] This questionable conclusion, which made the right to information subject to accidental circumstance, was unfortunately confirmed by subsequent case-law.[185]

2. Preventive Information About the Decision to Charge

The 1988 code also provided individuals with scant information at the end of the pre-trial inquiry. Concerning the case of termination of the proceedings, we saw that the current code made some important steps forward in comparison to the 1944 legislation, ensuring for both the victim and the suspect a hearing *in camera* aimed at the judicial oversight of the prosecutorial request for discontinuance of the proceedings. Although this procedure was of particular importance for the victim who lodged an objection to the prosecutorial request,[186] criminal proceedings could still be terminated on the basis of the sole prosecutorial request and without any hearing.[187] In this case, the drafters of the 1988 codification did not require that suspects should be informed not only on the prosecutorial request but also on the judicial order of termination of the proceedings, with the result that the individuals concerned could remain unaware of the conclusion of a criminal inquiry carried out against them.

---

[182] CCass, *Iuzzolini*.

[183] Art. 365(1) CCP.

[184] CCass, *Mariano*.

[185] CCass, *Zaccaria*.

[186] Art. 409(2) CCP.

[187] Art. 409(1) CCP.

Furthermore, private parties were not at all involved in the charging decision, which was exclusively in the hands of the competent prosecutor. As noted, the current codification strengthened the public nature of criminal prosecution, ruling out any involvement of the injured party in the decision on whether and with what forms to institute a criminal law action against the alleged offender. Unless the prosecutor decided to apply for discontinuance of the proceedings, suspects were also denied any mechanism aimed at avoiding the institution of the court proceedings, a result that exposed them to grave repercussions on their public image and family life. In sum, no preventive information was due to the individuals concerned where prosecutors decided to institute court proceedings, and all private parties were made aware of the prosecution only by means of the judicial summons and after charges had already been preferred.

At first glance, this approach was in line with the principle of legality, enshrined in the Constitution in the light of a clear *favor actionis*. On close examination, this conclusion revealed a formalistic understanding of the principle of mandatory prosecution, which cannot be read as requiring unjustified prosecutions. There is little doubt that the principle of legality must be interpreted in the light of the overall system of interests acknowledged by the Constitution, which does not tolerate the initiation of a criminal prosecution in the case of unfounded charges. It is noteworthy that the current code, departing from the approach of the 1930 legislation, strengthened the responsibility of public prosecutors for the decision to charge in that it required defendants to be brought to court with a founded accusation (albeit not necessarily exempt from contradictions and lacunas).[188] Moreover, the 1988 solution highlighted an arguably restricted interpretation of the principle of *contradictoire* as relating to the sole court proceedings. Yet it cannot be doubted that the defendant can play a proactive role in avoiding unjustified prosecutions that in turn jeopardise the efficiency of the whole criminal justice system.

It took, however, several years for legislative reform. The first one came in 1997, as the Italian legislature required prosecutors to invite the suspects to be heard before bringing them to court on pain of the annulment of the indictment.[189] Two years later, Law 479/1999 introduced an unprecedented tool—i.e., a notice on the completion of the pre-trial inquiry (*avviso di conclusione delle indagini*)—due in all cases other than those requiring the discontinuance of the proceedings.[190] The new instrument pursued two main goals, that is, informing suspects of the future indictment and giving them the opportunity to be heard before their being brought to court. The guarantees of information and *contradictoire* were here strictly linked with each other, to the point that the notice must also inform the suspect on the possibility of taking further defensive initiatives, such as submitting statements, attaching the results of defensive investigations, and requesting specific

[188] On this discussion see Ruggeri (2015a), p. 65 ff.

[189] Art. 416 CCP, as reformed by the Law 234/1997. On this reform see Marzaduri (1997), p. 759.

[190] Art. 415-*bis* CCP.

prosecutorial investigations. Although a formal accusation need not yet be filed, the charge must anticipate its exact contents, with the result that prosecutors are not allowed to subsequently change the indictment without sending another notice.

The ultimate goal of this instrument was thus to allow for the defendant to preventively challenge the decision to charge, avoiding the negative repercussions of court proceedings. This should also have required a methodological change in the understanding of the charging decision, requiring prosecutors to assess the merits of the case on the basis not only of the police investigations but also of the defence's contribution. It must however be acknowledged that, despite the merits of this preventive notice, none of the aims pursued were properly achieved. It can firstly be doubted that the information is always able to reach the suspect. Thus the 1999 reform failed to carry out an in-depth reform of the rules on judicial service, which rules still allow only formalistic information of the proceedings.[191] This clearly jeopardises the possibility for the suspect to set up a proper defensive strategy and to take the initiatives allowed by Article 415-*bis* CCP, starting with the right to give oral statements or to be heard by the prosecutor.

A delicate question is whether or not this procedural tool enables defendants to oppose the decision to charge by presenting exculpatory arguments.[192] The 1999 reform restricted the invalidity of the prosecution to two cases, i.e. (a) if the prosecutor failed to send the notice of Article 415-*bis* CCP or (b) the suspect, despite having requested to be heard, was not summoned to a hearing at the prosecutor's office.[193] On close examination, these situations are quite different from each other. At first glance, in both cases the invalidity of the proceedings depends on the conduct of the competent prosecutor. Yet in the former case the prosecution is void due to the failure of the prosecutor to send the notice on the completion of the pre-trial inquiry, whereas in the latter the validity of the court proceedings is affected if the prosecutor did not summon the suspect, provided, however, that he explicitly requested to be heard. Again, this presupposes that the suspect was personally made aware of the prosecutorial decision to bring him to court. Outside these two cases, prosecution is not void on grounds concerned with the notice under examination, with the result that prosecutors are not bound by the representations made by the suspect in the form of written statements, and can also reject any eventual request for further investigation on behalf of the suspect. This solution, despite being formally in line with the prosecutor's full responsibility for

[191]If suspects were not informed of the proceedings during the pre-trial inquiry, they need be notified pursuant to Article 157(1) CCP. However, this provision, despite starting with notification in person, provides for different forms of notification of defendants, which cannot ensure their knowledge of the proceedings. The lack of attention to the need to ensure effective information is even more evident in the provision requiring that the notification be renewed only where it is proved or probable that the defendant had no effective knowledge of the act of notification. Cf. Art. 157(5) CCP.

[192]Caprioli (2000), p. 276.

[193]Art. 416(1) CCP. A similar rule applies to the proceedings before single judges (*tribunale in composizione monocratica*). Cf. Art. 552(2) CCP.

the pre-trial inquiry, cannot, however, be deemed compatible with the obligation to carry out complete investigations on behalf of the suspects.[194] Of course, the risk that the defence may hamper the prosecution through unjustified requests must be avoided. This does not mean, however, that prosecutors can simply overlook any defensive allegation or request.

Another important deficiency of this mechanism, as it was structured by the 1999 legislation, was the exclusive focus on the accused's side. Despite the positive effects of the preventively informing the suspect, Italian legislature failed to involve other individuals in the charging decision that might be interested in the institution of court proceedings, especially the victim and the damaged party. Recently, the 2014 reform on gender-based violence amended Article 415-*bis* CCP requiring that, in cases of mistreatment within the family and stalking, notice be sent also to the victim's lawyer or, if no lawyer has yet been appointed, to the victim. The merits of this legislative reform are evident. For the first time, victims have been involved in the prosecutorial assessment of the need to initiate the court proceedings. This goal can, however, be frustrated by several factors. In particular, there are still grave deficiencies in the rules on victim's notification. Although the code requires that, in the absence of their lawyer, victims must be notified of the completion of the pre-trial inquiry, there is nothing to ensure that they will also be informed personally. Thus notice can also be served to the municipality in which the place of residence is located, or, where this is unknown, to the registry of the court.[195]

Moreover, there is no legal tool allowing for the victim to exercise similar rights to those laid down by Article 415-*bis* CCP. As a result, even though the aggrieved parties are informed about the future charge and the investigations made, they are not entitled to present written statements to the prosecutor[196] or to request that specific investigations be carried out.

The fragmentary nature of the 2014 reform of the rules on the notice of the completion of the pore-trial inquiry, therefore, demonstrates how far Italian law still is from achieving an effectively participatory understanding of the charging decision. Outside the limits laid down by the 2014 legislation, neither the victim nor the damaged party must be preventively informed about the prosecutorial decision to prefer formal charges against the defendant, a decision that can be retracted on the basis of the information produced solely by the accused. One might argue that it would be superfluous to involve the victim in a decision—namely, the decision on the institution of a criminal prosecution—that by definition aims at satisfying his claim for justice and reparation.[197] This argument would be misleading, however. A

---

[194] Art. 358 CCP.

[195] Art. 155 CCP.

[196] To be sure, Article 121 CCP enables all the parties to present statements at any stage of the proceedings. Yet this provision cannot be used for the purposes of assessment of the accusation, since it only regards statements presented to the judge.

[197] Bene (2004), p. 194.

number of different offences, other than those provided for by Article 415-*bis* (1) CCP, would equally justify the involvement of the victims in the charging decision. There is little doubt that the injured party can make a decisive contribution not only to avoid termination of the proceedings but also to orient the future prosecution towards the most appropriate type of criminal proceedings depending on the peculiarities of the case at hand. If defendants are allowed to initiate a bargaining procedure aimed at satisfying their own interests, why should victims be denied the possibility of avoiding criminal proceedings, if they will be instituted with a form that frustrates their claim for justice?

These arguments counteract the general assumption that the notice of the completion of the pre-trial investigations is not required where the prosecutor decides to institute alternative proceedings. Italian courts have long followed this approach, which was shared by Constitutional law especially in relation to the immediate proceedings,[198] on the assumption that this procedure has special pre-requisites that largely fulfil the aims of the tool of Article 415-*bis* CCP. This conclusion cannot be sustained and reveals a clear underestimation of the role of private parties in the decision regarding the most appropriate form of prosecution in a concrete case.

3. Information on the Indictment

Concerning the information on the indictment, the 1988 codification, departing from the approach of the 1930 code,[199] ruled out any possibility of an accusation without accused, that is, the possibility of criminal proceedings being initiating against unknown persons. As a result, criminal charges could only be preferred against one or more individuals who were brought to court with the formal status of 'defendants'. The indictment must in turn be filed in clear and precise terms[200] and must be attached to the judicial summons sent both to defendants and victims.[201]

Despite its linearity, this approach proved unsatisfactory during the first decade after the code's enactment. A minimalist interpretation of the requirement of precise and clear charges found wide acceptance in the case-law, which, relying on the fact that the indictment can be amended during the court proceedings,[202] excluded the invalidity of undefined indictments. Furthermore, Italian courts

---

[198]CConst, 203/2002. In the same sense CCass, *Bardi*, as well as Caprioli (2000), p. 274.

[199]Under the Rocco code, however, this approach, despite being widely shared by the case-law, had raised several criticisms by the criminal law scholarship. See Carnelutti (1949), p. 257; Cordero (1987), p. 80 ff.

[200]Art. 417(b) CCP.

[201]Art. 419 CCP.

[202]Art. 423 CCP. Precisely the legal basis of this jurisprudence has, however, given rise to several concerns among scholars, who have pointed out that the tools allowing for the prosecutor to amend the charge presuppose that the original indictment fulfilled all its requirements. In this sense see Lorusso (2008), p. 68.

considered that the judicial order returning the case to the prosecutor was void. Surprisingly, the Supreme Court confirmed this jurisprudence even after the 1999 reform,[203] thus underestimating the need to provide precise information so as to enable private parties to set up an effective defence.

III. Information on Developments of the Criminal Inquiry and the Evidence Supporting the Charging Decision

The possibility of effective defence in criminal proceedings is also largely dependent on the degree of knowledge of the developments of the prosecutorial investigations and the evidence supporting the charging decision. Doubtless, it is in the pre-trial inquiry where the tension between investigative needs and information rights reaches its highest point. Of course, private parties cannot claim their right to information to the extent that full disclosure would jeopardise the investigations carried out by the law enforcement agencies. Yet the lack of information can be particularly detrimental for the individuals concerned in that it not only hampers the possibility of defensive investigations but furthermore frustrates their participatory rights in interim decisions on the application of investigative means that interfere with fundamental rights.

It is precisely where coercive measures are at stake that the solutions provided by Italian law are largely unsatisfactory. The most problematic area concerns pre-trial detention and other forms of restriction on freedom, as we will see at a later stage of this study.[204] The 1988 code allowed for prosecutors only to disclose the pieces of evidence supporting their request for pre-trial measures. To strengthen the protection of the individuals concerned, Law 332/1995 imposed on prosecutors the duty to attach to their request all the information collected in favour of the suspect and eventual defensive statements already lodged.[205]

Notwithstanding the good intentions of the legislature, the results achieved were less significant than the expectations. Thus the notion of evidence 'in favour of the defendant' is by definition referential, which leaves to the prosecutorial authority much room for discretion in deciding what pieces of evidence will be attached to the request for a coercive measure.[206] Depending on the decision made by the competent prosecutor, a considerable part of the prosecutorial and police investigations can therefore be kept secret from the defence, which clearly frustrates the opportunity to challenge the merits of the measure applied. Furthermore, the solution adopted enables prosecutors to deny disclosure not only to the accused but also to the competent judge who is thus not in a position to assess whether the

[203] CCass, *Battistella*.
[204] *Below*, J.III.1.
[205] Art. 291(1) CCP.
[206] CCass, *Capri*. See Marzaduri (1998), p. 179.

prosecutorial decision to withhold information was justified by the need to avoid risks the ongoing inquiry and what implications it could have on the right to defence. Therefore, there is no independent oversight of the prosecutorial strategy and the protection of the right to information is entirely left to the unchallengeable decision of the competent prosecutor.

The negative repercussions of this set-up are further enhanced by the fact that Italian judges are generally called upon to rule on the prosecutorial request for a coercive measure without previously hearing the suspect, who can only challenge the judicial order after the enforcement of the proposed measure. As a result, there is a high risk that the ascertainment of the justification of the sought measure reflects the one-sided perspective of the prosecutorial authority. The Supreme Court also extended this approach to the judicial review of pre-trial measures (*riesame*), ruling that the competent court could not annul the judicial order on the basis of evidence other than that attached by the prosecutor to the initial request or the information produced in the judicial review proceedings.[207] On a deeper level still, the limitation of exculpatory evidence reflects an incorrect understanding of the right to a defence, whose full exercise often requires the knowledge of, and the possibility of contesting, incriminating evidence.

Grave concerns also arise in relation to investigative means interfering with the fundamental rights of third parties. A problematic area concerns the interception of telecommunications, a highly intrusive measure that under Italian law can only be ordered as a last resort and under similar conditions to those required in the field of restrictions on liberty. In particular, there must be strong evidence for the alleged offence (*gravi indizi di reato*).[208] Even though this demanding condition requires complex assessments, there are no statutory indications of the information that prosecutors must disclose. As opposed to the regulation on restrictions on freedom, the Italian legislature has never required that at least exculpatory evidence be attached to the prosecutorial request for interception of telecommunications. Therefore, although a judge is usually competent to order wiretaps, the judicial assessment is limited to the information that prosecutors decide to attach to their requests.[209] This can entail a doubly detrimental result, jeopardising the possibility of challenging the measure applied[210] and frustrating the tasks of the judiciary[211] in the ascertainment of the need for a hidden interference with the constitutional right to free and secret communication.[212]

---

[207] CCass, *Sanna*.

[208] The difference from the formulation used in the field of restrictions on freedom—namely, strong suspicion of guilt (*gravi indizi di colpevolezza*)—lies in the fact that the remand detention and the alternatives to custody presuppose that the criminal inquiry has already been directed against one or more individuals. Instead, there is no need that a suspect has been detected for the purposes of wiretapping, which can also be ordered against third parties. See CCass, *Zita*.

[209] Marzaduri (2008), p. 4848.

[210] Art. 268(5) CCP.

[211] Marzaduri (2008), p. 4848 f.

[212] Art. 15 Const.

It is only at the end of the pre-trial inquiry that prosecutors must provide full information on the results of their investigations. As noted, the 1988 code required full disclosure of the results of the pre-trial investigations only after the institution of judicial proceedings. It was only in 1999 that Italian legislature, introducing the notice of Article 415-*bis* CCP, anticipated disclosure at the end of the pre-trial phase. From this it follows that after the completion of the pre-trial investigations, prosecutors can no longer withdraw information from the defence but must attach the file containing all the pieces of evidence gathered by the investigative bodies as well as the judicial orders and the decisions issued during the preliminary investigations,[213] so as to enable the accused persons to set up their defensive strategy on an complete basis.

By preferring formal charges against the accused, the prosecutor must still attach the entire file. This requirement might appear to be superfluous in the light of the complete disclosure under Article 415-*bis* CCP but is not. Prosecutors may be required to carry out further investigations in response to the request of individual suspects made after the notice of the completion of the pre-trial inquiry. Furthermore, the obligation to attach the entire prosecutorial file to the request for court proceedings allows for the victims—beyond the few cases in which they must be given preventive information—to know the results of the police and prosecutorial investigations.

It may happen, moreover, that prosecutors need to take further evidence after prosecution has been instituted but before the first court hearing. If this happened before the institution of the intermediate phase, the 1988 code required the prosecutor to produce the other piece of evidence before the hearing.[214] More detailed rules governed a similar situation in the timeframe from the court decision ordering the opening of the trial phase to the first trial hearing.[215] In particular, prosecutors had limited investigative powers, being able to conduct any type of investigation except those involving either the accused persons or their lawyer, on the assumption that none of them should be 'distracted' from the preparation of a defence strategy for purposes of the trial hearing. Moreover, the evidence gathered had a particular allocation, an *ad hoc* file being set up at the prosecutor's office, with, however, the possibility for private parties to view and take copies. In order to establish equality of arms, the 2000 reform on defensive investigations amended these rules by imposing similar obligations on the lawyers of private parties. Therefore, a duty of disclosure also lies with the defence lawyers who are in turn called upon to produce at the prosecutor's office the evidence collected after the court decision ordering the opening of the trial phase.

---

[213] Caprioli (2000), p. 276.

[214] Art. 419(3) CCP.

[215] Art. 430 CCP.

IV. Notice of the Institution of Court Proceedings and the Right to Know the Initiation of a Criminal Prosecution

The shortcomings of the 1988 regulation, moreover, were not limited solely to the contents of the information but furthermore concerned the inability of the rules on judicial service to ensure the effective knowledge of the prosecution instituted. The 1988 code had serious deficiencies, which, as noted, unfortunately have yet not been solved. Pursuant to the 1988 rules, after the prosecutor preferred formal charges, the competent judge should summon both the defendants and the victim to court, while warning the former that, not appearing in court, they would be tried *in absentia*. However, both the assessment of whether the accused persons had been made aware of the proceedings and the examination of the grounds for their absence in court were reserved to the trial court, with the result that default proceedings could only be instituted in trial phase. The drafters of the 1988 code instead considered the accused's presence superfluous in the intermediate phase and that if the accused failed to appear, the competent judge should merely summon him again.[216] Moreover, a new summons could only be issued if it was proved or probable that the accused ignored the initiation of the proceedings,[217] whereas the hearing should be postponed where it was proved that the failure to appear in court was due—or probably due—to accident or *force majeure*.[218] As a result, if defendants did not appear at the intermediate hearing without justification, the proceedings continued on its course and, if no lawyer had yet been appointed, the accused was provided with a court-appointed lawyer.

This set-up became increasingly unsatisfactory in the first decade after the enactment of the new code. It took, however, more than 10 years for a new legislative intervention. Although Law 479/1999 largely reformed the intermediate phase, it did not substantially change the way the accused could participate in criminal proceedings. The main shortcoming of this legislation is that it was not preceded by an in-depth reflection on the delicate trade-offs between prosecutorial needs and the individual right to be involved in a fair manner in criminal proceedings. Therefore, it limited itself to transposing to the intermediate phase the rules on the renewal of the summons and the postponement of the hearing, maintaining, however, the general features of the 1988 solutions. Yet we have seen that these arrangements only aimed at remedying proved or probable ignorance of the proceedings[219] as well as the failure to appear in court due, or probably due, to accident or *force majeure*.[220] Moreover, the assessment of these situations

[216] Art. 420(2) CCP (1988 version).

[217] Art. 485(1) CCP (1988 version).

[218] Art. 420(4) CCP (1988 version).

[219] Art. 420-*bis*(1) CCP.

[220] Art. 420-*ter*(1–2) CCP.

left wide discretion to the judiciary and the judicial decision on whether to issue a new summons or postpone the hearing could not be challenged before a higher court.[221]

The extension of these rules to the intermediate phase, far from enhancing the protection of the accused, increased the risks for his participatory rights. In particular, default proceedings could already be instituted in the intermediate phase,[222] no matter whether there was concrete evidence about whether they had been informed of the institution of a criminal law action and, even worse, irrespective of the severity of the alleged offence or the existence of a public interest justifying the initiation of criminal proceedings *in absentia* already. The negative impact of the lack of coherent rules on the right to information was further aggravated by the weak acknowledgment of legal assistance. Even after the 1999 reform, the hearing could be postponed and a new summons should be issued—alongside the aforementioned situations concerned with the accused—if the lawyer did not appear at court because of a legitimate impediment. The consequence of this approach was that, whenever the accused did not appear in court without justification and no lawyer was present, the competent judge must declare the initiation of default proceedings and appoint *ex officio* a lawyer without any consideration of whether this arrangement could truly compensate him for the lack of *contradictoire*.

Since 1999, many things have changed and among other innovations we should mention the abolition of default proceedings.[223] Notwithstanding these positive results, the Italian criminal justice still suffers from grave methodological deficiencies, which highlight the cultural difficulty in departing from the traditional approach to the information rights of the accused in criminal proceedings. On close examination, the failure to carry out an in-depth reform of the rules on judicial service and the maintenance of the traditional arrangements on the assistance of a court-appointed lawyer reflect the clear attempt to preserve the formal understanding of criminal proceedings as *processus triarum personarum* rather than to ensure effective defence to the accused.

Furthermore, the scant attention to the need for proper notice also concerns—and to a greater extent than for the accused—other individuals involved in criminal proceedings. It has been noted that the role of the victim, despite having unprecedented rights in the pre-trial inquiry, loses most of its effectiveness at the end of the pre-trial inquiry, to the point that the prosecutor does not still generally need to send to the victim the notice of Article 415-*bis* CCP. After prosecution has been initiated, the competent judge must summon both the defendant and the victim to court. Yet it can happen that the injured party remains unaware of the initiation of a criminal law action. Again, this is mostly due to the shortcomings of the rules on judicial service, which shortcomings not only concern the accused but also the victim. In particular, the code provides that, if the identity and the residence of the victim are not known,

---

[221]See respectively Arts. 420-*bis*(2) and Art. 420-*ter*(2) CCP.

[222]Art. 420-*quater* CCP.

[223]*Below*, F.II.2.

the court summons can be lodged at the court registry[224] and by means of public announcements.[225] On close examination, these forms of judicial service are not always justified by the impossibility of personally notifying the victim.[226] Another important difference from the notification of the accused is that the validity of criminal proceedings is not affected by the lack of effective information of the victim.

The information of the damaged party is even more scant and contradictory. Under Italian law, the victim is not always entitled to a claim for damages and therefore may not be able to lodge a civil law action before a criminal court as a 'damaged party'.[227] The code's arrangements give rise to serious concerns especially where the victim is not a damaged party.[228] Unlike the victim, the damaged party can actively be involved in criminal proceedings. Surprisingly, however, the individuals entitled to claim for damages do not need to be summoned to court, with the result that they can be fully ignorant of the institution of a criminal law action, which prevents them from joining a civil law action to the criminal proceedings.[229]

F. Prosecutorial Needs and the Right of Participation in Criminal Proceedings

I. Premise

These shortcomings inevitably affect the right to take part effectively in criminal proceedings. Moreover, the way private parties can be involved in criminal hearings varies considerably according to various factors, such as the different phases or instances of the proceedings, as well as their different structures, that is, depending on whether a public hearing or a hearing *in camera*[230] is at stake. Within this quite enormous area, I shall focus on two main topics, namely (a) the right to personally participate in court proceedings, with specific regard to *in absentia* trials, and (b) the participatory rights in the field of alternative proceedings.

---

[224]Art. 154(1) CCP.

[225]Art. 155(1) CCP.

[226]Furthermore, notification at the court registry can also be ordered when a victim resident abroad failed to elect a legal domicile in Italy. Cf. Art. 154(1) CCP. As to the judicial service by means of public announcements, this solution can be the result of the number of the victims and the difficulty of reaching them by ordinary means. See Art. 155(1) CCP.

[227]The difference between victim and damaged party is particularly evident in the field of offences against the administration of justice, where the state is the victim, even though individuals suffered from damages from a criminal action. See Tranchina (1989), p. 1.

[228]Zumpano (2000), p. 347.

[229]See critically Scalfati (1999), p. 37.

[230]On the principle of *contradictoire* in the field of *in camera* proceedings see Di Chiara (1994).

II. Prosecutorial Needs and the Right to Personally Participate in Court Proceedings. The Problem of in absentia *Proceedings*

1. The 1988 Rules on Default Proceedings and Developments Due to the Strasbourg Case-Law

The first problematic area concerns proceedings held without the involvement of the accused. This result can in turn be due to two different situations, i.e. (a) a criminal law action that, despite every attempt to involve the accused, is initiated in the form of default proceedings and (b) criminal proceedings normally held in a form that always rules out the accused's participation prior to the rendering of a verdict, while allowing for the convicted person to lodge an objection, with a view to participating in a future trial. Notwithstanding the similar features of these two situations, the present discussion shall focus only on default proceedings, whereas I shall examine the problem of *inaudito reo* proceedings by respectively dealing with the participatory rights in penal order procedures[231] and in the decisions on the application of coercive measures.[232]

Concerning *in absentia* trials, it has been noted that default proceedings constituted one of the most typical expressions of the mixed model of criminal justice.[233] Despite several changes in the 1930 code over its last years of life, Italian legislature did not intervene to amend the rules on these proceedings, although in the mid-1980s, the Strasbourg Court convicted Italy for infringing the defendant's right to a fair hearing in relation to *in absentia* proceedings.[234] Underestimating the relevance of this case-law, the drafters of the 1988 code reproduced, with a few tiny adjustments, the old system of default proceedings. It has been noted, moreover, that under the 1988 regulation this procedure was only applicable to the trial hearing, the accused's absence in the intermediate phase being considered tolerable. Although the intermediate hearing had to be held with the participation of the public accuser, the accused and the judge, this requirement aimed at ensuring the validity of criminal proceedings,[235] reflecting a strong structuralist approach rather than an interest in the accused's personal involvement in criminal proceedings. This is also apparent from the wide decision-making powers of the Italian judges, who were enabled to freely assess the grounds for the defendant's absence and the requirement of proved or probable ignorance of the proceedings, assessment that, as noted, could not be challenged before a higher court.

[231] *Below*, F.III.2.

[232] *Below*, J.III.1.

[233] See recently the detailed analysis of Mangiaracina (2010), Negri (2014).

[234] ECtHR, *Colozza v. Italy*. See extensively Chap. 8, C.II.

[235] Article 179(1) CCP provides for the absolute nullity of criminal proceedings conducted without the participation of the defendants' lawyers, where the law requires their involvement in procedural activities.

Where the conditions did not exist for renewal of the court summons or the postponement of the hearing, the competent court had to declare the institution of 'contumacy' proceedings, a term that still revealed a clear reproach of a person who decided to avoid criminal justice. In this case, a lawyer was to represent the accused in court. Yet legal assistance was a weak substitute for personal participation and did not suffice to ensure that the defence strategy was in line with the accused's intentions. Thus counsel was a court-appointed lawyer, who probably did not even know the accused.

Eleven years after the code's enactment, Law 479/1999, as noted, limited itself to anticipating to the intermediate phase the examination of the reasons for the defendant's absence or ignorance of the proceedings, without reforming the conditions under which defendants could be personally involved in a court hearing, and particularly without substantially changing the rules on judicial summons and the structure of default proceedings. At the time of the 1999 reform, this set-up gave rise to two main problems. Firstly, it hindered efficient international cooperation with other European countries (especially EU Member States) which did not provide for, or which restricted to a minimum extent, the scope of *in absentia* proceedings. Secondly, it exposed Italy to the risk of being again ruled against by the Strasbourg Court on the ground of the Convention's right to personal participation in criminal proceedings. For the sake of clarity, I shall deal with the former problem while examining the Italian law on transnational surrender.[236]

The distance of Italian law from the European Convention brought about a strong confrontation with the Strasbourg Court, which culminated in two judgments against Italy in the cases *Somogyi v. Italy* and *Sejdovic v. Italy*, decided in the middle of the last decade.[237] It is worth observing that, unlike in the past, the European Court stressed that the main deficiencies of these cases should not be attributed to the way criminal proceedings had been carried out but should largely be traced back to statutory law. In particular, the Strasbourg judges stressed that Italian law not only did not ensure to defendants the right to be present at trial but furthermore made it extremely difficult to challenge a conviction issued *in absentia* after the expiration of the time allotted to do so. Even after the 1999 reform, defendants were still burdened with proving that no fault or negligence could be imputed to their ignorance of the proceedings—truly a *probatio diabolica*!

Starting from these premises, the European Court called upon the Italian legislature to conduct an in-depth reform of default proceedings. The referral of the *Sejdovic* case to the Grand Chamber made legislative reform extremely urgent and the need to avoid a new verdict against Italy by the Strasbourg Court led the Government to issue a Law Decree aimed at reforming the rules on relief from the effects of the expiration of the deadline to challenge *in absentia* convictions.[238] For the sake of clarity, I shall critically analyse in Chap. 16 the consistency of this

[236] Chapter 4, D.I.

[237] See respectively ECtHR, *Somogyi v. Italy* and ECtHR, *Sejdovic v. Italy*.

[238] Law Decree 17/2005, subsequently converted in Law 60/2005.

reform in the light of European case-law on *in absentia* proceedings as well as the subsequent responses of the Grand Chamber in the *Sejdovic* case.[239] For the purposes of the present discussion, it should be noted for now that the hurried legislation of 2005 provided inadequate solutions to the problem of default proceedings, which were maintained without any amendment. The urgency of the case and the failure to carry out a systematic examination of the relevance of the accused's personal role (and the limits of the accused's absence) in criminal justice did not allow for a consistent reform of default proceedings. The 2005 reform limited itself to facilitating access to the second instance by enabling individuals convicted *in absentia* to request relief from the effects of the deadline expiring to challenge their conviction,[240] unless the competent authority demonstrated that they were aware of the proceedings and freely waived participation. In light of these shortcomings, it might be surprising that a new legislative intervention only arrived in 2014. On close examination, this was the result of the compromise solutions adopted by the Grand Chamber, which gave the default proceedings a further 10 years of life.

2. The 2014 Reform: The Disappearance of Default Proceedings and the New Procedure for Absent Defendants

It has been noted that in 2014 the Italian legislature decided to carry out a comprehensive reform of this problematic area. Launched with the proclaimed aim of solving the problem of judgments rendered *in absentia*, Law 67/2014 not only dropped default proceedings but also introduced a new procedure for absent defendants. To be sure, a strict *in absentia* procedure already existed in the 1988 code, which allowed for a trial hearing to be held without the accused, if he either had decided not to be personally present or had behaved in such a manner as to be expelled from the courtroom.[241]

The new *in absentia* procedure has nothing to do with these proceedings, being generally unconnected from both any defensive strategy and the defendant's behaviour. On close examination, this reform was also unable to achieve a proper balance between prosecutorial needs and the individual right to participation in criminal proceedings. Despite the comprehensive goals pursued, Law 67/2014, like the 2005 reform, was not the result of in-depth consideration of the role of the accused's involvement in criminal proceedings nor did the Italian legislature aim at a systematic solution of the multiple problems connected with *in absentia* trials. Against the background of the long tradition of *in absentia* criminal proceedings, the abandonment of default proceedings did not entail a re-expansion of the right to

---

[239] Chapter 16, D.II.1.a.

[240] Negri (2005), p. 260 ff.

[241] Art. 488 CCP (1988 version).

participation but led—in inverse proportion—to the establishment of a new procedure in which the defendant was absent.

Although this reform aimed at aligning Italian law with Strasbourg's requirements,[242] the new procedure for absent defendants reflects very different situations, which in turn give rise to quite opposing consequences, that is, the institution or the suspension of criminal proceedings.[243] Concerning the cases that allow for the initiation of a procedure *in absentia*, the first situation occurs when the accused, duly informed of the initiation of a criminal law action, expressly waives his right to be present at trial. A second, and rather different, situation occurs when the accused, after being personally summoned, does not appear in court.[244] Furthermore, the new regulation reveals the dangerous shift from situations characterised by the sure knowledge of criminal proceedings to cases that only highlight a presumed knowledge, and even to situations in which the knowledge of criminal proceedings is a pure accident. Therefore, the 2014 reform allows for the institution of the new proceeding *in absentia*, even though the accused persons neither was summoned to court personally nor waived their right to participation. By equating rather different situations—namely, the knowledge of a prosecutorial criminal inquiry and information about the court proceedings—the legislature also allowed the accused to be brought to court[245] on the assumption, albeit differently qualified,[246] that the defendant, despite being aware of the preliminary investigations, voluntarily avoided being informed of the proceedings.

Alongside the risks of the presumption of knowledge of criminal proceedings, this result is inconsistent from a chronological viewpoint. Even if it is proven that the suspect was aware of the proceedings at the time of the pre-trial inquiry or even avoided information on the institution of a criminal investigation, how can this demonstrate that the defendant, after a considerable lapse of time, was also aware of the initiation of court proceedings and unequivocally chose not to participate? What can the knowledge of a pre-trial inquiry say about whether the court proceeding will ever be initiated and about the charge with which the defendant will be brought to court?

These arrangements can have very serious repercussions on the defendant's right to take part personally in criminal proceedings. Since the drafters of Law 67/2014 deemed it sufficient that suspects were in any case informed of a pre-inquiry against them, it may happen that the court proceedings are instituted even though it is certain or highly probable that the accused was not aware of the court summons.

---

[242]Quattrocolo (2014), p. 2 ff. The question will be discussed in detail in Chap. 16, D.II.1.a.

[243]See respectively Arts. 420-*bis* and 420-*quinquies* CCP.

[244]Art. 420-*bis*(2) CCP.

[245]Art. 420-*bis*(2) CCP.

[246]Here also, the code put together heterogeneous situations, i.e., (a) the fact that suspects chose their domicile in the pre-trial investigations; (b) their arrest or the adoption of pre-trial measures; (c) the decision to appoint a lawyer of their own choosing; and in general terms, (d) the circumstance that suspects were aware of the beginning of criminal inquiries against them or voluntarily avoided the information on the proceedings.

This marks a clear step backward in relation to the previous regulation under which this was a rather exceptional circumstance.[247] As a result, absent defendants—whatever the reasons for their absence—will be represented in court by their own counsel, if already appointed, or by a court-appointed lawyer[248] who will often face enormous difficulty in finding the accused. This risk is particularly high where criminal proceedings are initiated with considerable delay from the time when the first summons was handed down.

To be sure, the 2014 reform ensured subsequent remedies for absent defendants. If the accused appears in court, the judicial order that allowed the continuation of the proceedings must be revoked (even *ex officio*) and defendants can either apply for new evidence to be taken or request alternative proceedings. These defensive opportunities are subject to very demanding conditions, however. The judicial order allowing the procedure *in absentia* is revoked only if the accused appears in court prior to the verdict. Furthermore, the hearing can be postponed for the purpose of collection of new evidence only if the defendant can demonstrate either that their absence was not due to a negligent ignorance of the proceedings or that it was impossible for them to appear in court because of accident, *force majeure,* or other legal impediment, which must also be proven without delay and any fault.[249] The same burden of proof is required to apply for alternative proceedings.[250]

Moreover, the 2014 reform introduced an unprecedented remedy to allow for the accused to obtain a retrial, that is, a new form of revocation of final judgments (*rescissione del giudicato*).[251] This new remedy is, however, limited to cases of conviction, with the result that the accused tried *in absentia* cannot challenge the negative consequences deriving from an acquittal. Again, moreover, defendants can access this remedy only if they succeed in proving that the unawareness of the proceedings was not due to their negligence. This mechanism, therefore, turns out to charge individuals with the demonstration of negative circumstances rather than offloading onto the competent authority the burden of proof that the continuation of the criminal process is really needed and is based on the defendant's waiver of participation. This negative result cannot be softened by the fact that defendants can access this remedy even if they had been informed of the preliminary inquiry initiated against them.[252]

The difficulty of Italian law in achieving a proper balance between prosecutorial needs and individual rights also has bearing on cases in which the conditions for the institution of a procedure *in absentia* do not exist. In these cases, the 2014 reform requires the competent authority to declare the defendants untraceable (*irreperibile*) and to suspend the proceedings initiated against them. This result is

[247] Caprioli (2014), p. 664.
[248] Art. 420-*bis*(3) CCP.
[249] Art. 420-*bis*(4) CCP.
[250] Art. 489(2) CCP.
[251] Art. 625-*ter* CCP.
[252] Caprioli (2014), p. 667 f.

certainly excessive and does not take into due account the differences between the circumstances of absence. The absence of the defendant is in itself a neutral event, which cannot be deemed the result of negligent behaviour of the defendant, even though he was aware of the ongoing investigation. From the same viewpoint, the ignorance of preliminary investigations does not in itself demonstrate that the accused, though not appearing in court, was not aware of the court summons. Yet the indiscriminate suspension of the proceedings in any case of non-traceability of the defendant grants a protective shield to those who, despite being aware of the proceedings, are able to avoid official information. This result, while hindering the ascertainment of the facts, can ensure unjustified protection to individuals who can abscond for long periods, allowing for acquittal because prosecution of the offence is time-limited.[253] Thus the 2014 reform coupled the suspension of the proceedings with the suspension of the limitation period for the prosecution of the offence, which, however, cannot exceed the maximum time limits laid down in Article 161 (2) CC.[254]

III. Participatory Rights in Alternative Proceedings

1. Premise

Alternative proceedings constitute another relevant testing ground for the attention reserved by Italian law to the right of private parties to be involved fairly in criminal proceedings. This problematic area poses difficult trade-offs between the need for efficient prosecution, the accused's right to obtain special benefits, and the interest of other parties in defending their role in criminal proceedings and in obtaining justice and reparation for the damages suffered from the criminal offence. For the sake of clarity, I shall here focus on two main issues, i.e. (a) the problem of criminal conviction without any previous hearing and (b) the problem of criminal judgments obtained by means of a hearing *in camera*. In the latter, the tension between state-related interests, the accused's right to a rapid conclusion of the case through a reduced sentence and the participatory rights of the damaged party perhaps reaches its highest point. At a later stage of this investigation, I will re-examine alternative proceedings from the specific viewpoint of the use of untested evidence and the parties' contribution to the fact-finding.[255]

---

[253]Quattrocolo (2014), p. 10 f.

[254]See Article 159(3) CC, as amended by Article 12 of Law 67/2014.

[255]*Below*, I.III.

2. *Inaudito reo* Proceedings and the Problem of Criminal Conviction Without Previous Hearing. The Case of Penal Order Proceedings

It has been noted that, alongside the possibility of default proceedings, Italian law has another traditional procedure that excludes any participation of the accused prior to the rendering of a verdict, that is, penal order proceedings. Following the requirements of the civil justice doctrine of *inaudita altera parte* decisions, penal order proceedings lead to a criminal conviction through an *inaudito reo* procedure. Despite some similarities with *in absentia* trials, *inaudito reo* proceedings constitute the most essential form of criminal procedure, characterised by a conviction issued without any previous intervention of the defence. The inquisitorial inspiration of the Rocco code led to penal orders being issued by single district court judges who were competent to convict individuals for crimes whose sentence was a financial penalty without any prosecutorial request and any formal accusation.[256]

Notwithstanding the severe criticisms raised against the approach followed by the 1930 code,[257] the 1988 codification, as noted, reproduced this old procedure. This result was mainly due to constitutional case-law, which had since its earlier rulings defended the constitutionality of these proceedings pursuant to the doctrine of *inaudito reo* judgments.[258] According to this approach, the failure to involve the accused prior to the decision-making is justified by the fact that the conviction can be challenged in order to ensure a trial hearing. Yet it is debatable that a theoretical justification—elaborated, moreover, in the field of civil justice in relation to civil order of payment (*decreto ingiuntivo*)[259]—can fulfil the accused's right to give his contribution to the decision-making and that the postponement of *contradictoire* can compensate the defendant for the defensive opportunities lost.

To be sure, the 1988 code brought about some important innovations. In particular, penal orders could be issued in response to a prosecutorial request made after a period of investigation[260] and containing a formal charge against the accused. Even so, penal order proceedings still had a minimalist structure and constituted the only procedure in which a conviction could be issued against individuals who, though formally charged with a criminal offence, should be kept in ignorance of a criminal law action instituted against them. This is the reason why

[256]See among others Bellavista (1952).

[257]Tranchina (1961), p. 516 ff.

[258]CConst, 46/1957.

[259]On close examination, the approach followed by the Constitutional Court mixes the justification elaborated by two outstanding scholars of civil procedural law during last century, namely *Piero Calamandrei* and *Francesco Carnelutti*. The former advocated the idea of subsequent involvement of the other parties, while the latter focused on the eventual nature of their participation. See respectively Calamandrei (1926), and Carnelutti (1924), p. 270 ff. The scholar who first imported Carnelutti's doctrine to penal order procedures was *Girolamo Bellavista*. Cf. Bellavista (1952), p. 47.

[260]In 1988, the period was shorter than in normal cases (4 months) but further legislation enabled prosecutors to investigate up to 6 months.

conviction still holds here the form of an order (*decreto*) rather than of a judgment (*sentenza*). It must be acknowledged that to a certain extent penal order proceedings protect the participatory rights of the accused more than ordinary criminal proceedings.[261] Thus, request for penal order is inadmissible as long as the accused cannot be traced or it would be impossible to serve the order at the chosen domicile.[262] This does not, however, mean that, when the defendant is formally traceable, the penal order procedure will be conducted against a person whom the competent authority is always able to summon to court and to personally involve in the ongoing proceeding. In order to balance the accused's right to a defence with the doctrine of *inaudito reo* trials, Law 60/2001 required the penal order to be also served to the defendant's lawyer or, where no lawyer was appointed by the accused, to a court-appointed lawyer.[263] Doubtless, this reform made another important step forward in comparison to the 1988 regulation, which, following the approach of the Rocco code, did not provide legal assistance to the person convicted through a penal order.

Notwithstanding this positive result, the 2001 legislation failed to tackle the problem of whether the lawyer could effectively reach the accused, a task that can be particularly difficult for court-appoint lawyers.[264] The persistent disinterest of Italian law in the personal information of the accused persons makes it extremely difficult for them to decide whether to challenge the penal order issued against them. To be sure, the 1988 code also brought about two important innovations in relation to the objection against penal orders. First, the convicted person was granted a wider range of tools to react against a penal order, in that objection enabled the accused to request—as an alternative to a retrial—an abbreviated proceeding or a plea agreement with the prosecutor as well as to opt for payment of a fine. Second, departing from the approach of the former code, the drafters of the 1988 codification entitled the defendant's lawyer to file the challenge without special powers.

The combination of these innovations entailed further problems in the light of constitutional law, which, as noted, enshrines the right to *contradictoire* as an essential feature of a fair trial, while recognising the accused's right to consent to the use of untested evidence. It is apparent that, if the defence lawyer can lodge an objection against a penal order, this decision may not reflect the accused's informed decision to challenge the conviction. In this case, *inaudito reo* proceedings therefore steer away from their traditional justification, based on the postponement of *contradictoire* at request of the interested party. The case-law further aggravated this result by acknowledging the lawfulness of a challenge filed by a court-appointed lawyer.[265] In sum, the lawyer's initiative, no matter whether to challenge

---

[261] Caprioli (2004), p. 586 ff.

[262] Art. 460(4) CCP.

[263] Art. 460(3) CCP.

[264] Ruggeri (2008), pp. 104 and 159 f.

[265] CConst, 504/2000. In the same sense see CCass, *Kusi Kwaben*. Of a different opinion CCass, *Gradi*.

or not the penal order, may depart from the accused's intentions and can entail the permanent loss of some important opportunities. For instance, if a challenge is lodged, the penal order must in any case be revoked, which may frustrate the accused's interest in a reduced penalty. Moreover, the lawyer's initiative has its limitations, since lawyers cannot reach a plea agreement or request abbreviated proceedings without special powers. Therefore, the lawyer's challenge can only lead to a trial hearing, which may contrast with the accused's interest in a reduced sentence through alternative proceedings. Of course, the decision not to oppose to the penal order may also not be in line with the defendant's will to challenge the conviction.

Notwithstanding the several attempts to justify the constitutionality of penal order proceedings,[266] there is no way to defend the lawfulness of a procedure in which the lawyer, no matter whether appointed by the accused or by the state,[267] can alone decide whether to challenge the sentence imposed to untraceable individuals.[268] Nor can these negative consequences be remedied by the possibility of defendants being relieved from the effects of the expiration of the deadline to challenge a penal order that has become final. As noted, the 2005 reform enabled defendants to apply for relief from the effects of the deadline for the appeal elapsing, dropping the strict conditions laid down in 1988 for the person tried *in absentia*. Yet this remedy still presupposed that the convicted person was personally informed about the conviction issued *inaudito reo*.

Further human rights concerns arise when the lawyer succeeds in contacting the accused after filing the objection. In 2008, the Joint Sections of the Supreme Court ruled that the appeal lodged by the lawyer does not allow for the accused to separately request relief from the effects of the expiration of the deadline to challenge the decision.[269] Subsequently, the Constitutional Court reversed this doctrine by acknowledging the right of defendants unaware of the conviction or the proceedings to be relieved from the effects of the expiry of the deadline to challenge the decision, regardless of the appeal lodged by the lawyer.[270] As a consequence, Article 175(2) CCP was declared unconstitutional. Since this result was concerned solely with default proceedings, the question arises as to whether the lawyer's challenge to a penal order should prevent the defendant from applying for relief from the effects of the expiration of the deadline for filing a parallel challenge with a view to obtaining special benefits (*e.g.*, a reduced sentence through a plea bargaining). This question is still unsolved. It is also surprising that Law 67/2014—notwithstanding that the heading of its III Chapter aims to regulate the suspension of the proceedings in all cases of non-traceable defendants—fully ignored the

[266]Marzaduri (2000), p. 767 f.; Scalfati (2000), p. 530 f.

[267]Art. 460(3) CCP.

[268]Ruggeri (2008), p. 156 ff.

[269]CCass, *Huzuneanu*.

[270]CConst, 317/2009.

problem of *inaudito reo* proceedings, leaving the rules on penal order proceedings untouched.

3. Criminal Hearings *in camera* and the Right to Be Heard Fairly. The Complex Trade-Offs Required by Plea Bargaining and Abbreviated Proceedings

Different problems arise in cases of alternative proceedings that aim at a decision on guilt through a procedure *in camera*. The main examples in Italian criminal justice are plea bargaining and abbreviated proceedings.[271] It has been noted that these proceedings can be requested through the challenge to a penal order, that is, in response to a procedure initiated at the request of the sole prosecutor. Furthermore, the defence can make a plea bargain or request the abbreviated proceedings after prosecution has been instituted through the ordinary channels, and a plea bargain can be requested even during the pre-trial inquiry.[272]

Both these procedures are highly relevant from the perspective of the present discussion on at least two grounds. On the first level, both proceedings are strongly based on the accused's initiative or, in the case of a plea agreement, on the accused's consent with the prosecutorial initiative. This condition has a clear justification in view of the constitutional requirement for the defendants' waiver of their right to be involved in the taking of evidence, which entails the need for the accused's consent to the use of untested evidence. Thus there is a clear interest in the personal involvement of defendants in both plea bargaining and the abbreviated proceedings in order to verify the voluntariness of their consent or request. Furthermore, both these proceedings entail the waiver, allowed also by the European Convention, of the right to a public hearing, and in the case of a plea agreement, even though it does not entail a guilty plea under Italian law, we have seen that the accused must specifically request, or consent to, a guilty verdict.

In this regard, it is worth observing that the 1988 code provided that in case of a plea agreement, the competent judge can at any time summon the defendant, if it is necessary to verify the voluntariness of his consent.[273] More serious problems arise in relation to cases in which the defence's lawyer, despite not having special

---

[271]Under the 1988 regulation, these two proceedings shared several common features. On close examination, the drafters of the 1988 code aimed at introducing two negotiated proceedings, i.e. (a) an agreement on a financial penalty or a detention up to 2 years (*patteggiamento*) and (b) a procedural agreement (*giudizio abbreviato*). In both cases, the agreement only involved the accused and the prosecutor, and above all, the accused could benefit from a reduced sentence. There was however a big difference between the two procedures, in that the former necessarily led to a conviction, whereas the latter only aimed at a hearing *in camera*, which could lead either to the conviction or the acquittal of the accused. As will be explained in the text, the 1999 reform deeply alter the dynamics of the abbreviated proceedings, which are no longer a negotiated procedure.

[272]Art. 447 CCP.

[273]Art. 446(5) CCP.

powers, requests the abbreviated proceedings in the presence of the accused who does not contest this initiative. By relying on a formalistic interpretation of the code, in the past the Supreme Court shared the opinion that the lawyer's request should be rejected without the accused being given the possibility of being heard.[274] This doctrine, contested by subsequent case-law of single chambers, was recently abandoned by the Joint Sections, which confirmed the admissibility of abbreviated proceedings requested by the lawyer in the presence of the accused.[275]

On a second level, both a plea bargain and abbreviated proceedings, despite entailing positive advantages in terms of the decongestion of criminal justice, can also have negative repercussion on the participatory rights on individuals other than the accused, especially the victim and the damaged party. It has been observed that under the 1988 regulation, both these proceedings were based on an agreement between the prosecutor and the accused. This structure has remained unchanged in the case of plea agreements, which can negatively affect the interest of the damaged party in joining a civil law complaint to the criminal proceedings. To be sure, as noted, a plea agreement can also be reached during the pre-trial inquiry, that is, in a phase in which the damage party cannot still lodge a civil-law complaint. Yet the code also allows for the accused and the prosecutor to propose a plea bargain during the court proceedings and even after the damaged party has already joined a civil law action to the criminal proceedings. The 1988 code adopted a practical and simple solution to this case: the competent judge should not rule on the request for compensation, while the civil proceedings, suspended once the civil law complaint was filed during criminal proceedings, could resume its course. In 1990, the Constitutional Court, relying on the separation between civil and criminal law actions promoted by the 1988 code, ruled this solution consistent with the Constitution, which left to the damaged parties only one way to claim for damages before a civil court.[276] On close examination, this was a rather unfortunate argument. The general preference for separation between civil and criminal proceedings cannot allow for civil-law complaints, which have already been lodged before a criminal court, to remain undecided, nor can the damaged party be excluded from criminal proceedings beyond the cases of expulsion set forth by Article 81 CCP.[277]

Even though this ruling called for in-depth examination of the role of the damaged party in criminal proceedings, Law 479/1999 also intervened in a somehow practical way, allowing for the defendant to pay the legal costs of the damaged party, a payment moreover subject to total or partial compensation.[278] This was clearly a weak solution, which only provided a small compensation to the individuals who suffered damage from a criminal offence, instead of attempting to safeguard their right to participate in criminal proceedings. It is noteworthy that

---

[274] CCass, *Di Costanzo*.

[275] CCass, *Morini*.

[276] CConst, 443/1990.

[277] Arts. 80 et seqq. CCP.

[278] Art. 444(2) CCP.

the competent judge—though called upon to verify, if necessary, the voluntariness of the accused's plea—did not need not hear the injured party. Nor could the prosecutor reject the accused's proposal on the ground that the plea bargain would jeopardise the damaged party's right to take part actively in criminal proceedings.[279] In 2003, Italian legislature carried out a comprehensive reform of negotiated proceedings, which broadened the scope of plea agreements to a custodial sentence by allowing for the parties to agree to a detention for up to 5 years. It is surprising, however, that this reform not only was not preceded by an in-depth examination of the need for a proper fact-finding[280] (generally excluded in the original plea bargaining)[281] but furthermore did not include a redefinition of the legislative arrangements concerned with the weak participatory role of the damaged party.

At first glance, the abbreviated proceedings seem to better protect the individuals who suffered damage as a result of the criminal offence. In particular, Italian law allows for the damaged party who has already lodged a civil-law complaint not to consent to abbreviated proceedings. The decision not to consent to abbreviated proceeding has two main consequences. First, civil proceedings instituted for compensation of damages will not be suspended,[282] as generally provided for when civil proceedings are initiated after a civil-law complaint has been lodged before a criminal court.[283] Second, the damaged party does not risk any binding effects of the criminal judgment on the civil proceedings initiated by them or in their interest.

A few observations are necessary in this regard, however. In general terms, the code protects the individuals who suffered damage against the risk that the defendant's acquittal, if issued on certain grounds, can negatively affect any non-criminal proceedings instituted for the compensation of damages by them or in their interest. Thus civil or administrative courts must abide by the criminal judgment, on the condition that the damaged party either lodged a civil-law complaint before the criminal court or was in a position to do so.[284] This is not always the case, however. It has been noted that the damaged party as such does not need to be summoned to court and that the victim is not always entitled to a claim for damages. In these cases, neither the damaged party nor the victims are by definition placed in a position to take part actively in criminal proceedings.

[279] CCass, *Bosio*.

[280] Marzaduri (2004c), p. 245.

[281] Since the enactment of the code, the problem of fact-finding in plea bargaining has given rise to lively debates both in the case-law and the criminal law scholarship. For an in-depth analysis of this problem area see Gialuz (2008), p. 17 ff.

[282] Art. 441(4) CCP.

[283] Art. 75(3) CCP.

[284] See Art. 652(1) CCP, which moreover provides for the exception that either the civil law action was not transferred to the criminal proceedings or the damaged party initiated the civil proceedings where the possibility of lodging a civil-law complaint before a criminal court was no longer allowed, pursuant to Article 75(2) CCP.

It must be acknowledged that the code laid down more restrictive conditions for criminal judgments issued through abbreviated proceedings to be able to bind non-criminal courts than those applicable to ordinary criminal proceedings. Regardless of whether the accused was acquitted or convicted, civil and administrative courts must abide by the criminal judgment only if the damaged party consented to the abbreviated proceedings. Of course, this logically presupposes the effective participation of the damaged party, the abstract possibility of taking part in criminal proceedings not being sufficient for these purposes.[285] Notwithstanding this positive result, the protection provided by the code arrives late and cannot compensate for the impossibility of participation due to the persistent failure to grant the damaged party information about the institution of criminal proceedings and the charge preferred against the defendant.[286]

Ultimately, one can observe further important implications on the accused's request for abbreviated proceedings. By thoroughly reforming this procedure, Law 479/1999 dropped the prosecutorial power to request abbreviated proceedings, or to consent to the initiative of the defendants. As a result, the accused can only be tried *in camera* at his own request and on the basis only of the information gathered by investigative bodies during the pre-trial phase. Furthermore, the accused can also make his request conditional on the collection of additional evidence without the prosecutor having any possibility of requesting integrative information, except for evidence in rebuttal. Of course, it cannot certainly be affirmed that a prosecutorial right to a fair hearing was infringed. We have seen that under Italian law, prosecutors, as representatives of the judiciary, cannot have any interest in a criminal case other than that of ensuring the proper administration of justice. It is precisely in this sense, however, that the abolition of the prosecutorial power to oppose to the defendant's request for abbreviated proceedings, though justified to a certain extent,[287] can also lead to unreasonable restrictions on the defence rights of the damaged party. Moreover, this approach entails the risk of negative consequences

---

[285]See respectively Arts. 651(2) and 652(2) CCP. There are, however, some differences between the cases of conviction and acquittal. Alongside the consent of the damaged party, civil or administrative courts must abide by the defendant's conviction under the additional condition that the damaged party did not oppose the binding effects. This condition needs systematic interpretation, since the lack of opposition clearly presupposes that the damaged party was able to participate in the criminal proceedings. In this regard, see Scalfati (1999), p. 37. The fact that the requirement of consent presupposes the effective participation of the damaged party in the abbreviated proceedings leads to the result that any form of binding effects should also be ruled out if the damaged party was excluded from the criminal proceedings, pursuant to Article 80 CCP.

[286]See critically Scalfati (1999), p. 37.

[287]On close examination, the 1988 code neither specified the grounds for the prosecutorial dissent nor allowed for a judicial review in the subsequent trial phase. The Constitutional Court, sharing most of these arguments, declared the 1988 rules unconstitutional, while enabling the trial court to evaluate the reasons for the prosecutorial dissent and, if it was not justified, to apply the reduced sentence proposed by the accused. Cf. CConst, 81/1991. Furthermore, the code enabled prosecutors also to block the defendants' request—frustrating their expectation to obtain a reduced sentence or anyway a judgment *in camera*—in case of investigations negligently performed or uncompleted results achieved during the pre-trial inquiry.

for the proper ascertainment of the facts, which is certainly in the interest not only of society but also of the victim. Furthermore, the imbalance in favour of the accused can also have another negative consequence, that is, charging the competent judge of the pre-trial inquiry with the task of compensating eventual evidentiary lacunas by gathering further information *ex officio*.[288]

G. The Right to Have Oneself Fairly Heard

I. Premise

The right to have oneself fairly heard lies at the heart of the *audi alteram partem* rule in criminal proceedings. In this regard, however, different challenges arise in the court proceedings and in the pre-trial inquiry, and beyond the differences between the phases of the proceedings, a further distinction must be made depending on the diverse role and the interests brought forward by private parties in criminal proceedings. In particular, whereas defendants can only be examined at their request in the court proceedings, suspects can be compelled to undergo questioning during the prosecutorial inquiry. A similar distinction exists in relation to other parties. For the sake of clarity, I will analyse different types of hearings separately in relation to the pre-trial inquiry and the court proceedings.

II. The Right to Be Fairly Heard in the Pre-Trial Phase

1. The 1988 Model and the Subsequent Developments in the Dynamics of the Prosecutorial Inquiry. The Progressive Re-Enhancement of the Power of the Investigative Bodies to Obtain Oral Evidence

Concerning the pre-trial phase, the 1988 code enacted a simple distinction between two groups of individuals, that is, suspects and non-suspects, depending on whether suspicion of guilt had already arisen against the person to be examined. On close examination, the distinction was based on a formal issue and different rules thus governed police questioning and prosecutorial interrogation, depending on whether or not the person being questioned had been charged with a criminal offence.[289] In the latter case, the drafters of the 1988 code introduced the broad notion of ‘informants’ (*persona informata sui fatti*) to define any non-suspect. The main difference concerned legal assistance, which was mandatory in case of suspects no matter whether they were being questioned by the prosecutor or the police, whereas informants had no right (and no need) to be assisted by a lawyer.

[288] Art. 441(5) CCP.

[289] See respectively Arts. 350 and 351, and Arts. 362 and 375 CCP.

There were only a few significant exceptions. The first concerned the prosecutorial examination of co-defendants, which had to follow the rules governing the co-accused's hearing in open court, which rules required, *inter alia*, the assistance of a lawyer.[290] The second regarded the police questioning of suspects immediately after the commission of the deed. Here, legal assistance was not needed, and as compensation, the police did not have to draw up official records of the statements collected and the evidence given by the suspect could in no way be used at trial.[291] Furthermore, the code did not ignore the need to avoid a formalistic distinction between suspects and non-suspects, which could give rise to abuses and lower the protection of the individuals against whom suspicion of guilt had already been raised. An important provision required the competent authority—no matter whether the police, the prosecutor, or a judge—to stop the questioning of any person other than the suspect or the defendant, if the evidence given could lead to the institution of criminal proceedings against them.[292] Moreover, the individuals examined had to be informed of the right to be assisted by a lawyer and none of the statements previously made could be used against them.[293] The code further protected individuals, in relation to whom suspicion of guilt had already arisen from other investigations, against dilatory tactics by the investigative authorities aimed at eluding the rules on mandatory legal defence. Furthermore, if suspicion of guilt had already arisen against the person examined, who was nevertheless heard pursuant to the rules concerned with non-suspects (and therefore without legal assistance), the evidence gathered could be admitted as incriminating evidence neither against him nor against the individuals under investigation.[294]

It should taken into consideration, however, that under the 1988 rules, the police were only competent to question both suspects and non-suspects during their initial investigations. After prosecutors took over the leadership of the case, the police could investigate further only by delegation.[295] However, there were some particular investigative acts that could not be delegated to the police authority. Among them, prosecutors should personally interrogate the suspects or conduct any confrontation between them and other people.[296] From this it followed that suspects, after the institution of the prosecutorial inquiry, could no longer be questioned by law enforcement authorities and had the right to be interrogated by a representative of the judiciary. At any time, the suspect could also give spontaneous statements to the prosecutor.[297] These rules did not apply to the questioning of

---

[290] Art. 363 CCP.

[291] Art. 350(5–6) CCP.

[292] Art. 63(1) CCP.

[293] *Ibid.*

[294] Art. 63(2) CCP.

[295] Art. 348(1) CCP (1988 version).

[296] Art. 370(1) CCP (1988 version).

[297] Art. 374 CCP. Although suspects could also give spontaneous statements to the police, the evidence gathered could only be used at trial to assess the reliability of the information obtained in open court. Cf. Art. 350(7) CCP.

co-defendants, which could be delegated to the police regardless of the issues concerned. It was not a consistent approach, since the assistance of a lawyer was precisely aimed at protecting the co-accused persons against the risk of jeopardising their position.

Although some of these rules are still in force, the overall structure of the prosecutorial inquiry suffered from radical changes a few years after the code's enactment. In particular, two important innovations are noteworthy for the purposes of the present discussion. The first one was the abolition of the prosecutor's leadership of the preliminary inquiry. This radical change was firstly due to the 1992 anti-mafia legislation, which enabled the police to continue their investigations even after the prosecutor took over the case.[298] As a consequence, the police were entitled to carry out parallel inquiries to those headed by the competent prosecutor. In 2000, the reform on justices of the peace further strengthened the police inquiry by charging law enforcement authorities with ordinary investigative powers, while involving the prosecutor only in a subsequent phase.[299] The second, and no less important, innovation was the strong enhancement of police investigative powers. Here also, a radical change was made by the 1992 anti-mafia legislation, which allowed prosecutors to delegate the investigative acts initially excluded, i.e., confrontation and the suspect's interrogation.[300]

As a consequence of these two reforms, the police could both autonomously question the suspects after the institution of the prosecutorial inquiry and interrogate them with all the powers initially reserved to the prosecutor. Most significantly, the 1992 legislation also empowered the police to question co-defendants at their own initiative, co-defendants who, unlike other informants, had to be assisted by a lawyer.[301] It was an investigative power of no little importance, taking into account the relevance, especially for the purposes of proceedings regarding mafia-type crimes, of the information given by persons available for collaboration with the authorities. Almost 10 years later, Law 63/2001 introduced an unprecedented form of witness testimony for co-defendants assisted by a lawyer (*testimonianza assistita*), reserved to the individuals prosecuted in same or in other proceedings who are available to give evidence against other persons.[302] This testimony was not limited to the trial inquiry. Remarkably, the same legislation enabled both the police and prosecutors to question co-defendants pursuant to the new rules.[303]

[298] Art. 348(1) CCP.

[299] Arts. 11 et seqq. Legislative Decree 275/2000.

[300] Art. 370 CCP.

[301] Art. 351(1-*bis*) CCP.

[302] Art. 197-*bis* CCP. On this topic see Conti (2003).

[303] See respectively Arts. 351(1) and 362(1) CCP.

2. The Weak Protection of Suspects and Victims

These developments raise grave human rights concerns especially in relation to the hearing of the accused and the victim. On the accused's side, it is worth observing that Italian law provides no statutory indications about the stage of the pre-trial inquiry at which the accused should be interrogated. We have noted that under the 1988 model police questioning was limited to the initial stage and that suspects could at any time give written statements to the competent prosecutor. Yet the 1988 code did not require prosecutors to interrogate the suspect at a certain stage of the investigations and under the original rules, as noted, criminal prosecution could even be instituted without the suspect being given the opportunity to be heard. The situation changed after Law 234/1997 required prosecutors, before bringing suspects to court, to summon them to be heard, on pain of the annulment of the indictment, at the latest at the end of the pre-trial inquiry. The 1999 reform, introducing the notice of the completion of the pre-trial inquiry, provided for the invalidity of prosecution only where the prosecutor did not interrogate suspects, despite their explicit request.

We have seen, however, that this positive result still today presupposes that the suspect was personally served the information of Article 415-*bis* CCP, which the rules on judicial service do not ensure. Furthermore, the aforementioned extension of the power of the police to interrogate suspects by delegation has led to the result that during the pre-trial inquiry, the investigative bodies still retain a great margin of discretion in deciding both the form of examination and the time at which they will hear the suspect, depending on the investigative strategy. Moreover, under the current rules, the law enforcement authorities are not required to hear the suspect, who requests to be questioned.[304] In sum, suspects have no right to be heard, though the investigative bodies can coercively obtain their presence, if needed.

On the other hand, it can be doubted whether the guarantee of legal assistance suffices to give the suspect a fair hearing, if questioned by the police or interrogated by the prosecutor. By questioning suspects at their own initiative, the police are not required to provide them with any information. This approach was logical under the 1988 rules, which enabled the police to carry out autonomous investigations before the prosecutor takes over the leadership of the pre-trial inquiry. This result, however, is no longer sustainable, taking into account the fact that the police can also question the suspect after the prosecutor has preferred a charge against one or more individuals. Remarkably, both the prosecutor and the police, when acting by delegation, must inform the suspects of the charge against them prior to the interrogation. However, even then there is no requirement to give information on the investigations being conducted,[305] nor must the investigative bodies disclose even the information collected in favour of the person examined.

---

[304] CCass, *Papia et al.*

[305] Art. 375(3) CCP. The only exception relates to the immediate proceedings. Here also, however, there is no mandatory provision requiring prosecutors to disclose all the investigations conducted.

Furthermore, legal assistance can result in a purely formal guarantee if the lawyer is not sufficiently prepared for the case. This risk exists especially when neither the suspect's counsel nor the court-appointed lawyer can be present at the prosecutorial interrogation or the police questioning, so that the competent authority must appoint a lawyer who is immediately available. Moreover, the effectiveness of legal assistance largely depends on whether and to what extent lawyers can actively participate in the hearing, *e.g.* by raising objections on specific issues. In the case of police questionings, the lawyer can only be present.[306] In the prosecutorial interrogation, the defence lawyer can instead make specific requests and observations to the competent authority.[307] However, the assistance of a lawyer can rebound like a boomerang, since the statements given by suspects in a prosecutorial interrogation, if inconsistent with the evidence rendered in open court, can be read out at trial and used as incriminating evidence against them.[308]

Another weak point concerns the lack of clear rules governing access to the judicial authority. In the pre-trial inquiry, though suspects, as noted, can at any time give spontaneous statements to the investigative authorities, they have no right to be heard by a judge. Judicial hearings only take place for specific purposes, mainly if a coercive measure was enforced against the suspect. Furthermore, since the police are enabled to interrogate suspects by delegation, they cannot request to be interrogated personally by the prosecutor. In sum, a close examination of the pre-trial inquiry supports the worrisome conclusion that under the current rules, the suspect has no right to be heard by an independent body and not even by a representative of the judiciary.

The protection of the victim is even weaker. Like the suspect, the victim has no right to be heard either by the investigative authorities or by the competent judge during the pre-trial inquiry. Nor can *incidente probatorio* be requested for this purpose, unless urgent evidence is at stake. The main problem is still the lack of special rules for hearing the victim. It is surprising that the 1988 code, despite considerably enhancing the role of the victim in the pre-trial phase, did not provide for specific guarantees concerned with the examination of the aggrieved parties, who had to be questioned as any other informant by the law enforcement authorities whenever necessary for the ongoing investigations. Unfortunately, subsequent legislation maintained this approach.

Nevertheless, it must be acknowledged that over the last few decades some important innovations were brought about in relation to special types of vulnerable individuals. In 1996, as noted, Italian legislature allowed for the taking of testimonial evidence of minors by means of *incidente probatorio* beyond the cases of urgency in proceedings for sexual crimes. Remarkably, Law 66/1996 enabled the competent judge for the preliminary inquiry to take particular measures to gather the testimony of minors, requiring them to be heard outside the courtroom (*e.g.* in

[306] Art. 350(3) CCP.

[307] Art. 364(7) CCP.

[308] Art. 503(5) CCP.

their place of living). Subsequent legislation progressively extended the scope of this provision, and the Constitutional Court also contributed to this result, declaring the regulation on *incidente probatorio* unconstitutional in that it did not account for cases involving vulnerable individuals, such as the victims of corruption[309] and the mentally ill.[310] More recently, the scope of this procedure was further broadened by the 2013 reform on gender-based violence and later by Law 24/2014, which, implementing the EU Directive on preventing and combating trafficking in human beings and protecting its victims,[311] extended the rules on pre-trial hearings to the judicial hearing of various vulnerable adults.[312] Some important reforms were also made in the field of prosecutorial and police hearings. In 2012, a legislative reform, implementing the Lanzarote Convention on Protection of Children against Sexual Exploitation and Sexual Abuse, required prosecutors, while questioning minors (regardless of whether witnesses or victims) in case of particular serious crimes, to provide the assistance of an expert of child psychology or psychiatry.[313] The 2013 reform on gender-based violence later extended this requirement to the police questioning of minors.[314]

Notwithstanding these positive results, the voice of private parties is still weak at the end of the pre-trial inquiry, even though some steps forward were made through the introduction of the notice of Article 415-*bis* CCP. This instrument has clear limitations, still providing, as noted, scant protection to the victim in a number of proceedings in which the aggrieved parties would certainly have interest in knowing in advance the contents of the future charge and the form of the future prosecution. Furthermore, even in proceedings in which notice of the completion of the pre-trial inquiry is also owed to the aggrieved parties, they have no right to be examined by the prosecutor and the rejection of informal requests cannot affect the validity of the future prosecution.

Moreover, we saw that the notice of Article 415-*bis* CCP is only required where the competent prosecutor has decided to bring the suspects to court. No preventive notice of the charging decision is due when the prosecutor applies for discontinuance of the proceedings. Despite the clear attempt of the drafters of the 1988 code to enhance the role of the victim and to give voice to interested parties, discontinuance of the proceedings can be ordered without the victim or the suspect being heard. Of course, the competent judge is not bound by the prosecutorial request for termination of the proceedings and, if needed, can require the prosecutor to file a formal accusation against the suspect. In this regard, it is worth noting that both the Supreme Court and the Constitutional Court ruled out the need to notify the suspects of the completion of the pre-trial inquiry and of the decision to institute

[309] CConst, 262/1998.

[310] CConst, 63/2005.

[311] Directive 2011/36/EU.

[312] Art. 398(5-*ter*) CCP.

[313] Art. 362(1-*bis*) CCP, introduced by the Law 172/2012.

[314] Art. 351(1-*ter*) CCP.

court proceedings against them.[315] At first glance, this should not deprive the interested parties of the opportunity to be judicially examined, since the competent judge can only require the prosecutor to prefer charges after the oral hearing to which suspects and victims must be summoned.[316] However, this hearing is governed by the general rules on *in camera* proceedings,[317] with the result that both suspects and victims can request to be heard only if they appear in court,[318] which presupposes that they were personally informed of the procedure on termination of the proceedings.

In a nutshell, there is nothing to ensure that private parties obtain a fair opportunity to be heard, even though decisions are at stake which can seriously affect their rights and interest in the ongoing proceedings. The same approach was adopted in relation to the length of the prosecutorial inquiry. Thus, if prosecutors request to be authorised to carry out further investigations, the competent judge must first notify both the suspect and any victim who asked to be informed.[319] However, judges can rule on the prosecutorial request without hearing either the prosecutor or the lawyers,[320] being required to arrange an oral hearing only when it would be impossible to decide on the basis of the information available.[321] This condition clearly entails a highly discretionary assessment. Furthermore, the general rules on *in camera* hearings also apply to the decision on the extension of the period of investigation, so that private parties will also here be heard only if they appear in court.

3. The Risks of the Witness Testimony of Co-Defendants Assisted by a Lawyer

Another worrisome situation concerns the police and prosecutorial power to question co-defendants as witnesses assisted by a lawyer in the pre-trial phase. As noted, the main condition of this form of witness testimony is that the co-accused is available to give evidence on the criminal liability of other persons. Apparently, this regulation reveals a neutral approach to the co-accused's testimony, while providing the person examined with strong safeguards: in particular, co-defendants must be assisted by a lawyer and their statements will not negatively affect their position. On close examination, this is a problematic regulation, which motivates co-defendants to give evidence against other persons, while exposing them to several risks especially if questioned in the pre-trial phase.

---

[315] CCass, Barillà; CConst, 460/2002.

[316] Caprioli (2000), p. 275.

[317] Art. 127 CCP.

[318] Art. 127(3) CCP.

[319] Art. 406(3) CCP.

[320] Art. 406(4) CCP.

[321] Art. 406(5) CCP.

Like in a role-playing game, co-defendants take on a different status depending on the issues on which they are questioned. Under the 1988 rules, co-defendants had an absolute right to silence regardless of the circumstances in which they were examined.[322] This was one of the main reasons that led the Italian legislature to introduce in 2001 a new form of testimony for the co-accused, assisted by a lawyer. Thus, despite not dropping the old examination of co-defendants, this reform aimed at drastically reducing the scope of the right to silence. Pursuant to the 2001 legislation, co-defendants hold the right—in line with the general privilege against self-incrimination acknowledged to witnesses[323]—not to answer only the questions relating to their own liability as well as those concerned with issues that only partially involve other individuals.[324] Beyond these cases, however, the co-accused looses his general right to silence and must therefore exhaustively answer any question.

It might be argued that this is a free choice since the code makes the application of the rules on witness testimony dependent on the fact that the co-accused was informed on their new status prior to the examination.[325] Remarkably, as noted, this information is not only due to individuals prosecuted in other proceedings[326] but also to the defendants prosecuted jointly.[327] On close examination, this conclusion would oversimplify the problem. To start with, the information due to the accused follows a standard formulation and the competent authority does not need to provide the individuals examined with clear indications on the concrete consequences of their new status. Besides, the reference to the issues concerned with other people is extremely broad and does not presuppose that a criminal prosecution has already been initiated against the person against whom the co-accused is called upon to give evidence. The most critical point is that the new status—and the implications on the right to silence—is often far from being the result of an informed decision of the individuals examined, who must only be made aware that, while giving statements on other persons, they could be heard pursuant to

[322] Art. 210(4) CCP.

[323] Art. 198(2) CCP.

[324] Conti (2001b), p. 644.

[325] Art. 64 CCP.

[326] As a rule, pursuant to Article 197-*bis*(1) CCP, co-defendants can be summoned as witnesses only after their trial has finally been disposed of. This is the case for offences committed by several individuals either jointly or through independent actions [Art. 12(a) CCP], as well as for crimes committed to hide or execute other offences [Art. 12(c) CCP], and offences committed while other crimes were being perpetrated, or to ensure to the perpetrator the product, profit or price of another crime, or crimes several individuals perpetrated against each other, or when the proof of one crime depends upon the proof of another [Art. 371(2)(b) CCP]. Furthermore, in the two latter situations [Arts. 12(c) and 371(2)(b) CCP], co-defendants can also be summoned to be examined as special witnesses whille their proceedings are still ongoing, if they are available to give evidence in issues related to other individuals. It is worth observing, moreover, that the Constitutional Court declared Article 197-bis CCP unconstitutional it that it required legal assistance even when the co-accused was acquitted because the prosecuted offence did not exist or he did not commit it. See CConst, 381/2006 and 21/2017.

[327] Conti (2003), p. 234.

Article 197-*bis* CCP. The examination of the co-accused also does not necessarily include questions directly concerned with other individuals. Therefore, the change in testimonial status may often be the result of the future assessment by the competent authority of the incriminating testimony given by the co-defendants rather than being the consequence of their free decision.

The extension of this logic to police questioning and prosecutorial interrogation can entail grave human rights repercussions. The law enforcement authorities can, first of all, question a co-accused on apparently neutral matters and later assess whether the statements gathered can be of some interest for the definition of the position of other individuals under investigation. This gives the competent authorities an enormous margin of discretion in evaluating *ex post* whether and to what extent the evidence collected can be useful for the further investigation of other individuals,[328] and in the affirmative case, the co-accused can be forced to submit to further questioning in which he looses most of his right to silence.

These discretionary powers can be, as a result, extremely dangerous in the hands of the investigative authorities during the pre-trial inquiry,[329] in which private parties are normally kept in dark about ongoing investigations. Though assisted by a lawyer, co-defendants are informed about the possible change of their status before the questioning has started[330] and before knowing the questions on which they will be examined. Under these conditions, co-defendants must decide—in front of a police officer or the prosecutor, and with only the assistance of a lawyer whom they may have never seen before in their life—whether and to what extent to answer questions that will possibly be deemed to be concerned with other people, which will in turn expose them to the risk of further questioning pursuant to Article 197-*bis* CCP. It should also be taken into consideration that the co-accused can be prosecuted for false or incomplete statements to the prosecutor.[331] In the light of the general pressure of a police or a prosecutorial questioning, it may thus happen that co-defendants lose a clear understanding of whether and to what extent they can invoke their right to silence and as a result simply collaborate with the investigative authorities.[332]

III. The Right to Be Heard Fairly in Open Court

The hearings of private parties hold different features after the institution of court proceedings, and here also, various distinctions can be made according to the type

[328] *Ibid.*, 229 ff.

[329] Gaeta (2001), p. 442.

[330] Nobili (2001), p. 6.

[331] Art. 371-*bis* CC. More recently, Law 277/2012 extended this criminal law provision to false information given or to information withheld to the Prosecutor before the International Criminal Court.

[332] Amodio (2001), p. 3596.

of the proceedings, the stage or instance, and so on.[333] In the present discussion, I will focus on the right to be fairly heard in open court and the exceptions concerned with hearings *in camera*.

Apparently, the 1988 code provided private parties with stronger protection in the trial phase than during the prosecutorial inquiry. Not only the accused but all private parties, including a damaged party that had lodged a civil-law complaint, could only be heard at their own request. Therefore, the hearing of private parties should always be the result of a free decision. On the accused's side, the Constitutional Court deemed the requirement of consent to be constitutional on the assumption that defendants cannot be compelled to give testimony against themselves[334] nor can they be coercively brought to court for the purposes of their examination.[335] On close examination, this justification is not entirely consistent and the same grounds should also be extended to the pre-trial hearings in which suspects also cannot be compelled to give evidence against themselves. It is also worth observing that, unlike under the 1930 code, the hearing of the defendant does not take place at the beginning of the trial inquiry, but usually follows the evidence-gathering, with the result that the accused can properly assess whether to give oral evidence.

Notwithstanding these positive results, it can be doubted whether Italian law ensures full respect for the voluntariness of the decision of private parties to be examined. There is no obligation for the trial court to provide the individuals concerned with clear information about the decision to request to be examined. It should also be taken into consideration that, if defendants do not appear in court or refuse to be examined, the evidence eventually given in the pre-trial inquiry either to the prosecutor or the police, if delegated by the prosecutor, as well as the statements made in the intermediate phase can be read out at the request of any other party.[336] Under the 1988 rules, the defendant's out-of-court statements could be used unconditionally and against anybody. We will see that subsequent legislation and the Constitutional Court introduced some important conditions on the use

[333] A delicate question concerns the hearing of the accused in the intermediate phase. It has been noted that defendants, after being brought to court, can be examined only at their own request. Moreover, the drafters of the 1988 code structured the intermediate phase in such manner that further information could only be gathered in exceptional circumstances and oral evidence was taken only by the competent judge. Yet the 1999 reform entitled any party to request the cross-examination of the accused. From this it followed that, though defendants could still be heard only at their request, the initiative of any other party could expose them to the cross-examination by the prosecutor and the lawyers in a non-public hearing. See Arts. 421(2) and 422(4) CCP. For critical remarks cf. Scalfati (1999), p. 68, who considered it possible, however, to ensure the defendants' right to request to be questioned by the competent judge. It should also be taken into account that as a consequence of this reform, the evidence that the accused will give in response to the cross-examination can be read out at trial and can be used as inculpatory evidence both against the person examined and other parties (in the latter case, however, provided only that the lawyers of the individuals concerned were present in the intermediate phase).

[334] CConst, 221/1991.

[335] Art. 490 CCP.

[336] Art. 513 CCP.

of pre-trial evidence against other parties. Yet the information given by the defendants in the pre-trial phases can still be used against them, a result that is also extended to cases in which the accused, despite consenting to the trial hearing, refuses to answer specific questions.[337] Moreover, it may happen that the accused consents to be cross-examined but gives evidence different from that rendered in the pre-trial phases. In this case, the current regulation allows for out-of-court statements of the accused to be read out on request of another party. It is true that this evidence will normally be used only to scrutinise the reliability of the accused.[338] However, the statements rendered at the pre-trial stage either to the prosecutor or to the police, if acting by delegation, or to the competent judge for the pre-trial phase—if inconsistent with the evidence given in open court—can be used against the accused.[339] In these cases, therefore, the decision-makers can discretionarily decide to use the evidence given to the police or prosecutorial authority, or the information obtained in open court.

This result gives rise to serious human rights concerns. It makes little sense to grant defendants the right to silence and even to refuse to give evidence on specific issues if their previous statements can be read out and admitted at trial as incriminating evidence. The rationale of this legal set-up is that pre-trial evidence given by the accused can only be used as evidence on the stated matters if it was gathered by the judicial authority (judges or prosecutors) or by the police by delegation of a representative of the judiciary (prosecutor), which should sufficiently guarantee the suspect's right to a defence. Yet this justification does not take into account the differences between pre-trial hearings. As noted, suspects summoned to a police questioning or to a prosecutorial interrogation are provided with weak safeguards. Though assisted by a lawyer, suspects are not free to not appear at the prosecutorial questioning and can be coercively brought to the prosecutor's office or the police station. To a great extent, the possibility of the police questioning suspects at their own initiative after the institution of the prosecutorial inquiry has even more serious implications for the persons concerned, who, as noted, are provided with no information on the charge, whereas the lawyer can only be present at the questioning. Different rules govern the hearings conducted by the competent judge for the pre-trial inquiry and especially in the intermediate phase, in which defendants not only have the right to be heard at their own request but their lawyer has full access to the prosecutorial file.

It is even more questionable that the out-court-statements of defendants can be admitted at trial if they either do not consent to the trial examination or are not present in court.[340] Here also, there are considerable differences between these two

---

[337] Conti (2001a), p. 603.

[338] Art. 503(4) CCP.

[339] Before the 2001 reform, the case-law had adopted a rather broad interpretation of this provision, allowing that all the recorded evidence taken in the pre-trial phase—that is, not only the parts containing the statements contrasting with the evidence given in open court—be read out at trial. This interpretation could not be deemed in line with the constitutional acknowledgment of the principle of *contradictoire*. In the same sense see Conti (2001a), p. 603.

[340] Art. 513(1) CCP.

situations. Whereas the former reflects a clear defensive choice, the latter is a neutral situation, which neither expresses the accused's decision not to take part in criminal proceedings nor can *per se* make the out-of-court statements more reliable. The 2014 reform on default proceedings, allowing for the institution of proceedings *in absentia* under new conditions, also could not change this result.

Further human rights problems concern the trial hearing of co-defendants called upon to give evidence in relation to the statements made either in other proceedings or during the preliminary inquiry. As observed, serious concerns regarding the co-accused's testimony arise in the pre-trial inquiry. Furthermore, the current rules also allow for co-defendants to be summoned to appear in court as witnesses with legal assistance, provided that before the pre-trial questioning they were informed that they might take on this new status and if the trial court considers that the evidence give out of court can be of some interest in defining the position of other individuals under examination. Clearly, the code protects co-defendants against the risk of negative effects in relation to the offence for which they are currently being prosecuted, no matter whether in the same or in other proceedings. However, there is nothing to ensure that co-defendants will not be held liable for what they will say at trial as well as for the failure to answer the questions exhaustively. These risks, alongside the loss of the general right to silence, put the co-accused in a clearly vulnerable position, which does not fit the requirements of a fair hearing.

Over recent years, however, Italian law has made some important steps forward in relation to the trial hearing in particular cases of vulnerable individuals involved in criminal proceedings. The 1988 code had already provided for an express derogation from cross-examination in cases of minors, who should normally be questioned, taking into account further questions and objections raised by other parties, by the president of the trial court assisted by a family member and an expert in child psychology.[341] In 1997, the Constitutional Court declared the rules on cross-examination unconstitutional for not allowing the president of the trial court also to question mentally ill adults summoned as witnesses on the assumption that cross-examination could negatively affect these vulnerable persons.[342] This ruling did not, however, equate the position of minors and mentally ill adults, since in the latter the president of the trial court must discretionarily assess the need for derogation from cross-examination.[343] In the following year, Italian legislature further enhanced the rules on the hearing of minors, allowing for the extension to the trial examination of the special rules on *incidente probatorio*, with the result that in cases of serious crimes, minors can also be heard in a context other than the courtroom.[344] The same legislative reform allowed for the victims, no matter whether minors or mentally ill adults, to be heard, at their own request, through a glass mirror with an intercom system. More recently, the 2013 reform on gender-

[341] Art. 498(4) CCP.

[342] CConst, 283/1997.

[343] Di Chiara (1997), p. 2575.

[344] Art. 498(4-*bis*) CCP, introduced by the Law 268/1998.

based violence broadened this provision,[345] while requiring the trial judges to ensure the adoption of protection measures if the victim is an adult in a vulnerable position.[346]

H. *Audi alteram partem* and the Collection of Evidence

I. Introductory Remarks. Principle of contradictoire *in the Taking of Evidence*

It has been observed that one of main challenges of the 1988 code was to enhance the role of all the parties in the taking of evidence. To this end, the drafters of the current codification enacted a set of general rules on the evidence-gathering procedure.[347] As a matter of principle, evidence can be collected in open court at the request of the parties,[348] even though the judicial authority can in exceptional circumstances gather information at its own initiative.[349] At trial, moreover, the collection of evidence at the initiative of the competent court is subject to strict conditions and plays a subsidiary role to the taking of evidence requested by the parties. It is also worth observing that, after a request for evidence-gathering has been admitted, the judicial order can only be revoked after the parties have been heard.[350] This highlights the importance of evidence-gathering not only in the interests of the party that requested the collection of certain information but also for the purposes of the fact-finding.

Against this background, the 1988 code attached a central importance to the parties' contribution to the taking of oral evidence, frustrated in the 1930 code by the broad use of the information gathered in the prosecutorial inquiry or the inquiry conducted by the investigating judge. As noted, the drafters of the 1988 code

---

[345] Art. 498(4-*ter*) CCP.

[346] Art. 498(4-*quater*) CCP.

[347] 3rd Book of the code.

[348] Art. 190(1) CCP. Under the 1988 code, this also applied to the exceptional evidence-gathering intermediate phase. Since the 1999 reform, the competent judges for the pre-trial inquiry can also gather information at their own initiative in the intermediate phase. Cf. 422 CCP. It is worth observing, moreover, that in this phase the competent judge can also take evidence requested by the parties. Neither the prosecutor nor private parties, however, are entitle to cross-examine the person being heard, who is questioned by the judge on the basis of eventual observations or requests of the parties. It is not an unremarkable difference, since the fact the parties have no direct access to the source of evidence can give rise to the risk that the defence's contribution will be trivialised or even misunderstood. Relying on this difference in the method of evidence-gathering, as noted, the code still requires the evidence taken in the intermediate phase to be included in the prosecutorial file rather than in the trial file Cf. Art. 433 CCP.

[349] Art. 190(2) CCP.

[350] 190(3) CCP.

strengthened the principle of *contradictoire* by making cross-examination (except in case of the hearing of minors) the main method of obtaining evidence in open court[351] and therefore the main method of examining not only witnesses and experts[352] but also private parties[353] and co-defendants.[354] Furthermore, the parties' involvement in evidence-gathering should not be viewed in terms of a formal participation. Doubtless, the 1988 code set forth some important innovations to give effectiveness to the parties' involvement in the collection of oral evidence. It is noteworthy that any party interested in the gathering of oral evidence is required to inform, before the opening of the trial hearing, the other parties (including the prosecutor) about the persons to be examined and the circumstances on which they will be heard.[355] This is a guarantee of utmost importance, which makes cross-examination as a form of informed participation in the evidence-gathering.

Another important factor that enhanced the parties' involvement in the collection of oral evidence at trial was the introduction of the aforementioned distinction between the trial file and the prosecutorial file. This distinction, coupled with the establishment of an exhaustive list of grounds for admission of out-of-court evidence, entails that the trial court, as a matter of principle, does not know and therefore cannot admit at its own initiative the information gathered in the police and prosecutorial inquiry. Remarkably, the parties' initiative is also required in the exceptional cases in which out-of-court evidence can be read out in court. For instance, the trial judges can autonomously neither admit information that has become unavailable at trial[356] nor read out inconsistent statements of witnesses, co-defendants and any party examined at trial.[357] As a consequence, admission of out-court-evidence is in the hands of the parties, which can request it depending on the defence strategy.

The system is not airtight, however. Among the parties, public prosecutors can also request the admission of out-of-court evidence. Under the 1988 rules, the right to *contradictoire* at trial could largely be frustrated by the admission of the testimonial statements given immediately after the event, a result justified on the assumption that this information was spontaneous and intrinsically reliable. Despite the strong adversarial inspiration of the 1999 constitutional reform and the 2001 fair trial implementation, we have noted that there is still enough room for the admission—mainly at the request of the prosecutor—either of evidence given by

[351] A significant exception concerned the proceedings before district judges who, upon agreement between the parties, could examine witnesses and private parties at trial, taking into account eventual questions and objections raised by the defence and the prosecutor. The 1999 reform, dropping district judges, maintained this solution for the new proceedings before single judges (*tribunale monocratico*). Cf. Art. 559(3) CCP.

[352] Art. 501 CCP.

[353] Art. 503(3) CCP.

[354] Art. 210(5) CCP.

[355] Art. 468 CCP.

[356] Art. 512 CCP.

[357] See Arts. 500 and 503 CCP.

co-defendants or the accused during the prosecutorial inquiry or of information gathered by the police by delegation, notwithstanding the scant safeguards that still characterise the evidence-gathering at the pre-trial stage.

For the sake of clarity, I shall here focus on two main topics, namely (a) the parties' involvement in the evidence-gathering in the pre-trial inquiry and (b) the involvement of private parties in the collection of evidence at trial.

II. Participatory Rights in Evidence-Gathering in the Pre-Trial Inquiry

1. The Involvement of Private Parties in Prosecutorial and Police Inquiries

We have already examined some of the main developments concerned with the prosecutorial and the police inquiry. It has been observed that, despite its strong adversarial approach, the 1988 code enhanced the pre-trial inquiry in comparison to the fascist codification, while maintaining some important decision-making powers on the part of prosecutors as representatives of the judiciary. The years following the code's enactment led to a further enhancement of the police investigative powers during the prosecutorial inquiry. It is also noteworthy that the developments that occurred in subsequent years in the Italian criminal justice both at the statutory and case law level did not largely concern evidence-gathering in open court but the conditions on which out-of-court evidence can be admitted at trial.

Against this background, a close examination of the pre-trial phase highlights various forms of involvement of the parties in the collection of evidence by the investigative authorities. Legal scholarship often uses the definition of 'imperfect *contradictoire*',[358] which can in turn have different features depending on the degree of involvement of private parties in the investigations carried out by the police and the prosecutor. Despite the clear attempt to enhance participatory rights in the pre-trial inquiry, it can be doubted whether the individuals concerned can have a fair opportunity to be involved in the police and prosecutorial investigations. Clearly, the absence of an impartial body and the dominant role of the investigative authorities cannot satisfy the constitutional requirements of fair evidence-gathering, based the principle of equality of arms. As long as prosecutors lead their investigations, the involvement of the defence will inevitably be secondary. It has been noted that the police questioning of suspects only allows for the passive presence of a lawyer. Although the defence lawyer has a more active role in the prosecutorial interrogation, being able to make specific requests and observations to the competent authority, there is no formal means to avoid inadequate questioning for the suspect.

[358] Cordero (2012), p. 891.

As noted, some legislative reforms strengthened the defence rights of particular informants examined in the pre-trial inquiry, such as co-defendants and, more recently, minors, either as victims or witnesses of certain serious crimes. Yet these reforms, despite enhancing the participatory rights of the person examined, ignored the problem of guaranteeing the right to confrontation of the addressee of the evidence that informants give to the police or the prosecutor. A particularly delicate case concerns the co-defendants summoned to be examined as witnesses pursuant to Article 197-*bis* CCP. Even though a lawyer must assist them in this crucial decision, neither the police nor the prosecutor need summon the addressees of the co-accused's statements or their counsel.[359]

The most complete form of involvement of private parties in prosecutorial inquiries in the pre-trial phase concerns the surveys conducted by technical advisors appointed by the prosecutor. In urgent cases, prosecutors must follow the procedure laid down by Article 360 CCP, which allows for the suspect and victim not only to involve their lawyers but also to appoint technical advisors of their own choosing. Even though technical and legal assistance allows for the individuals concerned to actively participate in the appointment of the technical investigation, the conducting of this survey still remains in the hands of the prosecutor. As noted, the (potential) involvement of private parties can also backfire. The fulfilment of the statutory conditions allows for the inclusion of this information into the trial file as non-repeatable evidence, regardless of whether private parties had a fair opportunity to contribute to the prosecutorial investigation.[360]

2. The Right to Confrontation in *incidente probatorio*

It has been noted that the 1988 code, while dropping both the prosecutorial evidence-gathering and the inquiry of an investigating judge, introduced a court procedure aimed at the collection of evidence in the pre-trial phase: *incidente probatorio*. This procedure was mainly concerned with urgent evidence, that is, evidence that could not possibly be collected in open court.[361] At first glance, the parties play a dominant role in this court procedure on several grounds. The need to obtain urgent evidence must assessed in advance and the individuals concerned can make reservations, objections, and so on. Furthermore, the code required the application in *incidente probatorio* of the same rules governing the trial evidence-gathering.[362] As a rule, the taking of evidence cannot be extended to issues concerned with individuals whose lawyers were not present[363] and at trial, the

[359]Tonini (2001), p. 272.

[360]See Article 360(5) in conjunction with Article 431 CCP.

[361]To be sure, the 1988 rules already provided for an important case of evidence-gathering unconnected from urgent reasons. Pursuant to Article 392(2) CCP, complex expert evidence should, as a rule, be taken in the pre-trial stage to avoid excessive congestion of the trial phase.

[362]Art. 401(5) CCP.

[363]Art. 401(6) CCP.

information obtained cannot, as a rule, be used against persons not represented in court.[364]

Despite these positive results, it is questionable whether this procedure allows for private parties to have a fair opportunity to be involved in gathering of evidence, which will later be inserted into the trial file.[365] Even though the code proclaimes that *incidente probatorio* is governed by the same rules applicable to the trial evidence-gathering, there are still considerable differences from the collection of evidence in open court. The main point of difference concerns the lack of information on the results of the prosecutorial and police investigations. It has been noted that at trial, the parties are granted previous information on the oral evidence to be gathered. In the prosecutorial inquiry, on the contrary, the defence is normally kept in dark of the information obtained by the investigative bodies. The 1988 code did nothing to ensure information to the persons involved in *incidente probatorio*. The problem arose a few years later, as the Constitutional Court pointed out the need for the public prosecutor to disclose previous statements given by the persons to be examined either at either the police or the prosecutor's office no later than the day of the court hearing.[366] It was clearly a compromise solution, which left almost no time to prepare effective defence. Italian legislature intervened only in 1996,[367] requiring disclosure from the prosecutors at the latest 2 days before the oral hearing.[368] Although this solution marked an important step forward, its scope of application was restricted solely to the case in which oral evidence was to be taken and even in this case, the defence could only have access to the previous statements of the person to be examined, which was a rather accidental situation.

It should also be taken into consideration that these developments occurred in the period of return to inquisitorial practices following the 1992 legislation, which dropped some of the main innovations brought about by the 1988 code to avoid the unconditional use of out-of-court evidence. To compensate for the strengthening of hearsay evidence, both the constitutional case-law and the legislature introduced some important innovations, which contributed to the enhancement of *incidente probatorio*. In 1994, the Constitutional Court extended the scope of *incidente probatorio* to the intermediate phase,[369] which in turn altered the general dynamics of this procedure: as noted, in the intermediate phase, unlike in the pre-trial inquiry, the accused has full access to the prosecutorial file.

Three years later, Italian legislature uncoupled two important cases of *incidente probatorio* from reasons of urgency,[370] namely the hearing of co-defendants, no matter whether prosecuted in the same or other proceedings, provided, however,

---

[364] Art. 403 CCP.

[365] Art. 431(1)(e) CCP.

[366] CConst, 74/1991.

[367] Law 267/1997.

[368] Art. 398(3) CCP.

[369] CConst, 77/1994.

[370] Art. 392(1)(c-d) CCP, as reformed by the Law 267/1997.

that they were to be questioned on issues concerned with other persons. This reform clearly attempted to contrast the increasing use of prosecutorial evidence at trial by strengthening the taking of information by means of a court procedure *in camera* during the pre-trial inquiry. This result was of utmost importance in the field of serious organised crimes, in which co-defendants can make a highly useful contribution to the ongoing investigation. Yet these developments confirmed the traditional tendency of Italian criminal justice to anticipate the taking of evidence—and by this means, also the fact-finding—to the pre-trial stages. Since the 1997 reform, the examination of co-defendants can ordinarily take place out of court, at request of prosecutors, regardless of whether concrete grounds exist that justify the anticipation of evidence-gathering and the derogation from the requirement of publicity.

Remarkably, *incidente probatorio* was further strengthened after the fair trial constitutional reform was issued and after the legislature re-oriented most of the original rules on the admission of out-of-court evidence to the principle of *contradictoire*. Unfortunately, these developments were not accompanied by the enhancement of the information rights in the pre-trial stage. On the other hand, it must be acknowledged that some human rights problems can also arise from indiscriminate disclosure. It has been observed that Law 66/1996 enacted a new ground for *incidente probatorio* for the purposes of the examination of minors under 16 years old in proceedings for sexual offences. This reform also required prosecutors to disclose all the investigations conducted in cases of sexual crimes. It is questionable whether this obligation also applied to the case in which evidence is collected at the accused's request.[371] At any rate, this legislation required the competent prosecutor to allow for defendants to access the entire file of the pre-trial inquiry and therefore also the evidence gathered in relation to other individuals. This result is certainly excessive and can severely jeopardise the effective conduct of the pre-trial inquiry.

III. Participatory Rights in Evidence-Gathering at Trial

1. Principle of *contradictoire*, Oral Evidence and the Need for Constant Balance Among Conflicting Interests

Concerning the evidence-gathering at trial, we have observed that the 1988 code strongly aimed at strengthening the role of the parties in the taking of oral evidence in open court. Even though cross-examination still lies at the core of the Italian law of evidence and the principle of *contradictoire* governs the taking of information in criminal proceedings, Italian legislature not only has enhanced the admissibility of hearsay evidence at trial but has also progressively enacted some important innovations with a view to balancing the accused's right to confrontation with the need

---

[371] Bargis (1996), p. 504.

to protect particular types of witnesses. In particular, Law 119/2013 strengthened the possibility of special forms of confrontation (*e.g.*, shields testimony with intercom system) to protect minors or adults in cases of some serious crimes (sexual crimes, stalking, trafficking of human beings, and so on).[372] We will also see at a later stage of this study that, as a result of the implementation of EU law, Italian legislature has recently provided for the general use of protective means of examination in cases of victims in a particularly vulnerable condition.[373] These innovations are of utmost systematic importance, notwithstanding their limited scope of application, which only relates to the hearing of the aggrieved parties.

Further derogations from the rules on cross-examination in open court are aimed to protect the right to life and physical integrity of the person being examined in specific circumstances. In particular, Italian law allows for certain precautions to be ordered either *ex officio* or at request of the parties in cases of individuals admitted to a witness protection programme.[374] Special arrangements are also provided for in the case of the hearing of undercover officers, including foreign police officers, who conducted their investigations pursuant to Law 146/2006, which ratified the UN Convention on transnational organised crime, arrangements that are aimed at protecting the person being examined through shielding their face.[375] In cases of mafia-typed crimes and other serious crimes as well as in the case of undercover officers in the situations falling within the scope of Law 146/2006, the trial examination has to take place by videoconference. The need to avoid negative repercussions on the persons being examined and their next of kin, moreover, justifies the provision that relieves undercover officers, including foreign police officers, members information and security services, as well as auxiliary and third parties involved in the undercover investigations under Law 146/2006, from the general duty to give their personal information.[376] It is a typical case of (almost) absolute anonymous witness testimony, in that the real identity of the person examined is hidden not only to the defence but also to the competent court (only the prosecutor can request to be informed about the real identity of the individuals involved in undercover investigations).

These provisions confirm the complexity of the current legal set-up, which does not allow us to give cross-examination an absolute value. In the delicate field of oral evidence, the principle of *contradictoire* is therefore to be constantly re-defined in relation to the interests at stake. This calls for proper trade-off between the need for efficient prosecution, the participatory rights of the accused and the protection of the fundamental rights of the individuals being examined.

---

[372] Art. 498(4-*ter*) CCP.

[373] Art. 498(4-*quater*) CCP, as amended by Legislative Decree 212/2015. See Chap. 16, D.V.1.a.

[374] Art. 147-*bis* RICCP.

[375] Art. 147-*bis*(1-*bis*) RICCP, introduced by Law 136/2010, enacting an extraordinary anti-mafia programme.

[376] Art. 497(2-*bis*) CCP, introduced by Law 136/2010 and further enhanced by the anti-terrorism reform of Law 43/2015.

2. Principle of *contradictoire* and the Collection of Expert Evidence

Another complex issue concerns the parties' contribution to the taking of expert evidence. It is noteworthy that expert evidence is one of the few exceptional cases in which evidence can be gathered at the initiative of the trial court[377] beyond the conditions that normally allow for the collection of evidence *ex officio*.[378] The fact that both the prosecutor and private parties have usually no specific knowledge in technical matters, however, should not diminish the importance of their contribution in the gathering of technical evidence. Significantly, Italian law acknowledges the defendants' right to be present, at their own request, at the hearing of witnesses, experts and technical advisors of the parties, examined in their domicile in exceptional cases.[379]

To compensate for the lack of technical knowledge, the 1988 code enhanced the participatory rights of the defence and the public prosecutor, allowing them to appoint technical advisors after the judge orders the taking of expert evidence.[380] Technical advisors are allowed to take part in the phase in which the tasks of the court-appointed expert are defined. Moreover, experts must in turn take into account specific requests and observations of the parties' technical advisors while carrying out their work,[381] and requests and observations must be inserted into the expert's final report. Doubtless, the possibility of technical advisors being fairly involved in a court-ordered technical survey is of utmost importance to ensure the effective contribution of the parties in the collection of expert evidence. Remarkably, the 1988 code granted private parties the right to be assisted by court-appointed technical advisors under the same conditions provided for legal aid.[382] A delicate issue is whether technical advisors can cross-examine court-appointed experts at trial. A part of the criminal law scholarship shared this opinion,[383] which is, however, rejected by the prevailing case-law. on the assumption that the provision on the expert's examination is governed by the rules on the witness's hearing.[384] This is a rather formalistic argument, which does not take into account the difference between the examination on factual and on technical issues.

The 2000 reform on defensive investigations, moreover, ensured to lawyers a proactive role, enacting a mechanism similar to the procedure laid down for the urgent prosecutorial technical surveys. Thus Law 397/2000 enabled the defence to

---

[377] Art. 508 CCP.

[378] Pursuant to Article 507 CCP, additional evidence can be gathered at the initiative of the trial judges only if necessary for the rendering of a verdict and after all the information requested by the parties has been collected.

[379] Art. 502 CCP.

[380] Art. 225(1) CCP.

[381] Art. 230 CCP.

[382] Art. 225(2) CCP.

[383] Kostoris (1993), p. 337.

[384] CCass, *Ferrara*.

carry out their own technical surveys, to which special rules, however, apply in case of non-repeatable evidence. The defence must inform the public prosecutor who could appoint a prosecutorial technical or request *incidente probatorio* to have the expert evidence obtained by means of a court procedure.[385] Another peculiarity of the prosecutorial involvement is that the defence is not free here to choose whether attach the information to its official file. Thus the results of the defence's technical survey in which the prosecutor took part must be inserted into the lawyer's file, or, if the survey can no longer be repeated, directly into the trial file.[386]

It should be noted, however, that in Italy, complex expert surveys usually take place prior to the trial phase. We saw that, derogating from the general approach to *incidente probatorio*, the 1988 code allowed for the collection of expert evidence in the pre-trial phase regardless of the existence of risks for the sought information. Alongside urgent cases concerned with risks for the source of evidence,[387] technical surveys can also be ordered at the pre-trial stage in complex cases in which, if technical investigations were carried out during the trial-phase, they would lead to the suspension of the trial hearing for more than 60 days. More recently, Law 85/2009, aimed at accession to the 2005 Prum Treaty and while introducing a DNA database, amended the rules on *incidente probatorio* by allowing for the use of this *in camera* procedure to obtain samples of biological materials from a living person out of trial.[388] The common goal of these cases is to ensure the greatest possible focus and speediness in the trial phase.

This set-up raises several human rights concerns. The main problem probably lies in the characteristics of *incidente probatorio*, which procedure can only be activated at the request of either the prosecutor or the accused. This requirement has remained unchanged over almost three decades, notwithstanding the considerable developments that have occurred in the Italian criminal justice involving this court procedure. Yet there is no doubt that expert evidence is of utmost importance for reliable fact-finding. This explains why expert investigations can be ordered *ex officio* by the trial court, an approach confirmed by the new rules on technical inquiries aimed at DNA tests.[389] In the light of this, there is no valid reason for which the performance of technical surveys of particularly complex nature or interfering with personal freedom should be subject to the request of the parties. Furthermore, it can be doubted that only the public prosecutor and the suspect can be interested in technical inquiries. Although during the pre-trial inquiry the victims may also have interest in the taking of technical information, their voice is still limited to an indirect request through the prosecutor. Surprisingly, these rules were not properly adapted to the extension of *incidente probatorio* to the intermediate phase, in which the injured person may have already lodged a civil-law complaint.

---

[385] Art. 391-*decies*(3) CCP.

[386] Art. 391-*decies*(4) CCP.

[387] Art. 392(1)(f) CCP.

[388] Art. 392(2) CCP.

[389] Art. 224-*bis* CCP.

Another weak point concerns the possibility of private parties actively contributing to the taking of expert evidence in *incidente probatorio*. Again, the main shortcomings often arise in the pre-trial inquiry. It has been observed that in urgent cases prosecutors will normally find no advantage in requesting this court procedure, since they can appoint their own technical advisors to carry out a survey under Article 360 CCP, whose results will be inserted into the trial file as unrepeatable evidence. Where no urgency reasons exist, *incidente probatorio* is often preceded by a prosecutorial technical survey that allows neither the lawyer's participation nor the appointment of a technical advisor. This situation can in turn negatively affect the effectiveness of the contribution of private parties in *incidente probatorio*. As noted, if the procedure aims at the gathering of oral evidence, prosecutors must disclose the results of any previous hearing of the person to be examined. Nevertheless, Italian law does not still grant private parties the right to have access to the record of the prosecutorial technical survey, nor can the parties' technical advisors control the survey conducted by the court-appointed expert.

3. Principle of *contradictoire* and Documentary Evidence. Participatory Rights and the Admission of Evidence Gathered in Other Proceedings

At first glance, the constitutional acknowledgment of the principle of *contradictoire* in the taking of evidence may seem to be concerned solely with oral or in any case dynamic evidence.[390] This conclusion is misleading, however. For instance, the parties can make their contribution by submitting arguments on the admissibility and assessment of documentary evidence.[391] Besides, the role of private parties in the taking of documentary evidence is already apparent at the time in which the admissibility of the sought information is at stake. Thus the trial court can only obtain documentary evidence after the parties have had the opportunity to consult the sought documents beforehand.[392] Although this requirement is certainly of high importance, some problems can arise in case of complex documents, since Italian law does not require the requesting party to disclose the documents to other parties beforehand, as in case of testimonial evidence.

A particularly complex issue concerns the evidence taken in other proceedings. The 1988 code introduced special rules in this regard, rules that were, surprisingly, enacted into the regulation on documentary evidence.[393] As a result, the information gathered in other proceedings, no matter whether documentary or oral evidence, constitutes documentary evidence from the viewpoint of the criminal proceedings in which it is to be admitted. Under the 1988 code, two main provisions governed this matter. First, as a rule, external evidence gathered either at trial or in

[390] Marzaduri (2000), p. 790 f.

[391] Orlandi (2010), p. 52 f.

[392] Art. 495(3) CCP.

[393] Art. 238 CCP (1988 version).

incidente probatorio could be taken unconditionally, as could be non-repeatable evidence. Second, evidence gathered neither at trial nor through *incidente probatorio* could only be used to assess the reliability of the oral evidence given in open court.

Doubtless, this solution revealed a formalistic understanding of the principle of *contradictoire* and turned out to be inadequate just a few years after the code's enactment. On close examination, the fact that external evidence was taken at trial in proceeding A, in which the lawyers of the individuals B and C were present, does not at all entail that the right to *contradictoire* was also satisfied for party D, against whom the statement obtained should be used in proceeding E. The 1992 anti-mafia reform, while dropping a number of the original restrictions on the use of pre-trial evidence, thoroughly reformed the rules on the gathering of external evidence. On one hand, this legislation strengthened the contribution of the accused against whom external evidence was to used. In particular, consent of the individual defendants was required to enable the use of external information obtained, if it was gathered neither at trial nor in *incidente probatorio* in other proceedings.[394] On the other hand, external evidence could be used under the same limitations applying to pre-trial evidence, limitations enormously softened, however, in 1992. Subsequent legislation strengthened the right to *contradictoire* by introducing a new provision specifically concerned with testimonial evidence taken in other proceedings, evidence that could only be used against the defendants whose lawyers took part in the hearing in other proceedings.[395] Notwithstanding its merits, this solution also reflected a formal approach to the parties' involvement in the evidence-gathering, since no attention was attached to the conditions under which the lawyer took part in the testimonial examination in other proceedings. Yet the defence strategy largely depends on the offence under prosecution,[396] so that even the same lawyer can play a different role according to the diverse interests of his client in criminal proceedings.

The constitutional enshrinement of the principle of *contradictoire* by the 1999 reform called for in-depth reflection on the conditions of use of oral evidence obtained in other proceedings. However, the legislative implementation of the constitutional fair trial reform limited itself to adjusting the existing provisions. In particular, the subjective limitations on the use of testimonial evidence gathered in other proceedings remained unchanged, with the result that the formal condition that the lawyers were present at the testimonial hearing in other proceedings can alone justify the use of this information, without any consideration of qualitative requirements of legal assistance.

A highly worrisome issue concerns the admissibility of final criminal judgments, issued in other proceedings, as evidence of the facts decided. The 1992 anti-mafia

---

[394] Art. 238(4) (1992 version).

[395] Art. 238(2-*bis*) CCP.

[396] In this sense Marzaduri (2002b), p. 167, who shared a criticism raised by Lozzi (1997), p. 687.

reform introduced a specific provision for this purpose, allowing for lax conditions of use of judicial decisions as documentary evidence.[397] This can in turn frustrate the goals pursued by the rules on the admission of information obtained in other proceedings,[398] in that the limits laid down by Article 238 CCP for the admission and use of external evidence may be eluded by obtaining the decision that ruled on the same information. It is surprising that over more than two decades—and despite the 1999 fair trial reform—this dangerous provision has remained unchanged.

4. Defendant's Consent and Evidentiary Agreements Among the Parties

For the last decades, Italian has increasingly enhanced the possibility of evidentiary agreements among the parties. To a great extent, this tendency was a further development of the relevance attached to the accused's consent to the use of untested evidence and the general role of the parties in evidence-gathering. It has been observed that the growing focus on this problem led the Italian legislature to enact into the Constitution the accused's consent as an exception from the general principle of *contradictoire* in the taking of criminal evidence. The professed aim of this choice was to give constitutional justification to the alternative proceedings that aim, upon the defendant's consent, at a out-of-court decision on the merits of the case mainly on the basis of the evidence obtained during the police and prosecutorial inquiry.[399] At the time of the constitutional reform, however, there had already been in-depth discussion on the limits within which defendants can waive their right to *contradictoire* in the taking of criminal evidence in open court.[400]

Doubtless, the new constitutional framework provided the basis for a further enhancement of the defence's role in the evidence-gathering.[401] Nevertheless, the 2001 implementation led to somewhat unsatisfactory results. For instance, it is debatable that Italian law allows for defendants to consent to the use of evidence taken in other proceedings[402] without any consideration of the repercussions on the interests of other individuals involved in criminal proceedings.[403] Another delicate question is whether defendants must personally waive their right to participation in the gathering of evidence and what role their lawyers can play in this decision.[404] This issue has become of utmost importance since Law 479/1999 introduced a

[397] The case must be finally disposed of and the decision can only admitted if relevant for the fact-finding in the proceedings of destination. Moreover, it can be assessed as evidence of the matters under prosecution, provided that corroborating evidence exists.

[398] Art. 238-*bis* CCP.

[399] Marzaduri (2009), p. 189 ff.

[400] *Ibid.*, 197.

[401] Di Bitonto (2004).

[402] Art. 238(4) CCP.

[403] Marzaduri (2009), p. 208.

[404] By contrast, no problem arises in relation to other private parties who are always represented in court by their lawyers. Cf. Art. 100(1) CCP.

flexible mechanism allowing for the parties (including the public prosecutor) to agree that specific pieces of evidence gathered by either the police or the prosecutor or the defence are inserted into the trial file. Agreements can be reached either at the end of the pre-trial phase(s), i.e. at the time in which the two files are set up, or at a later stage of the proceedings.[405] Under the current rules, there are no limitations on the accused's side, so that lawyers can reach an agreement with the prosecutor and the other parties no matter whether their clients provided them with the special power to do so and even regardless of whether the defendants were in any case informed on this important decision.

This approach raises several concerns in the light of an overall consideration of the *audi alteram partem* rule. Since evidentiary agreements alter the overall information usable for the decision-making and can therefore heavily impinge on the fact-finding, defendants should be duly conscious of the consequences of this decision, which can lead to the use of incriminating evidence.[406] This solution is even more inadequate in cases of *in absentia* trials, in which the impossibility of contacting the accused charges the lawyer with the burden of facing such a difficult decision alone. It is debatable whether better results can be expected from the new proceedings for absent defendants, which, as noted, do not ensure that individuals can always be made aware of the institution of criminal proceedings against them. These arguments also raise serious concerns on the constitutionality of this set-up. On one hand, the Constitution certainly requires that the waiver of *contradictoire* reflect a decision personally made by the defendant. On the other, the constitutional fair trial reform, while enabling the legislature to enact rules allowing for the use of untested evidence upon the accused's consent, called for an overall balance among conflicting interests. The Italian Constitutional Court, however, has followed a more formalistic approach on the assumption that lawyers, thanks to their knowledge in legal matters, can make the most proper decision in the interest of their clients.[407]

Against this background, it should be examined whether Italian law provides for tools aimed at compensating for the expansionary force of evidentiary agreements. To be sure, the code does not clarify whether the judicial authority should assess the contents of the agreement reached by the parties. Clearly, a negative solution can have serious repercussions on fact-finding, enabling the parties to obtain information that may be irrelevant, if not also misleading, for the rendering of a verdict.[408]

---

[405] See Arts. 431(2), Art. 493(3) and 500(7) CCP.

[406] In the same sense cf. Marzaduri (2009), p. 215 f., who moreover considered an intervention of the Constitutional Court unnecessary to enable the defendant to personally consent to the use of untested evidence.

[407] CConst, 182/2001.

[408] For in-depth analysis of this issue see Marzaduri (2009), p. 217 ff. Besides, the role of the judiciary is quite different depending on whether the evidentiary agreement is reached at the end of the pre-trial inquiry or of the intermediate phase, or during the trial inquiry. The main difference is that, whereas in the intermediate phase the competent judge has full access to all the evidence gathered by the investigative bodies, the knowledge of the trial court is limited to the contents of the trial file.

In should also be noted that the 1999 reform, while strengthening judicial initiative in evidence-gathering in the intermediate proceedings and in the abbreviated proceedings, enabled the trial court to collect at its own initiative evidence inserted into the trial file upon agreement of the parties.[409] This solution reveals the awareness by the Italian legislature of the different reliability of the evidence taken at trial and the information gathered by individual parties out of court, although included into the trial file upon the parties' agreement. This approach also holds great practical importance, since judicial initiative helps fill eventual knowledge gaps in the evidentiary agreement, which can seriously affect the decision-making. Unfortunately, Italian legislature failed to lay down clear rules on the use of this judicial power, which enhances the discretion of trial judges in compensating for the lack of *contradictoire*.

I. Participatory Rights, the Use of Untested Evidence and the Defence's Contribution to Fact-Finding

1. Systematic Remarks. The High Relativism of Italian Evidence Law

The rules on the participatory rights in evidence-gathering largely affect the contribution that private parties can make to fact-finding. As a matter of principle, the lack of a fair opportunity for the defence to participate in the taking of evidence also impinges on the reliability of decision-making. Doubtless, there is a strict link between evidence and the proof of the facts, accentuated in Romance languages by the common linguistic roots of the two notions (*prova*, *prueba*, *preuve*, etc.), which encompass a very complex phenomenon that goes from the gathering of certain information to its assessment to prove certain facts.[410] Furthermore, both evidence and fact-finding are legal concepts—and by definition referential notions—which do not only relate to the proof of guilt and the decision on the merits. Since fact-finding largely depends on the matter at stake, the probative relevance of the evidence gathered also varies according to the decision at hand.

In the Italian criminal justice, this result may seem to be confirmed by the distinction between the trial and the prosecutorial file. As noted, this distinction was introduced to mark a clear dividing line between the information that can be used for the trial decision and the information that cannot be used for these purposes. On close examination, the drafters of the 1988 code aimed at importing in structural terms the rules, long developed in common law countries, on the limited use of hearsay evidence. In the light of the important implications of this

[409] Art. 507(1-*bis*) CCP.

[410] See among others Cordero (1963), Ubertis (1995), p. 296 ff.; Ferrua (2013), p. 1 ff.

distinction, it is surprising that the 1988 code enabled the administrative staff of the competent judge for the pre-trial inquiry to set up the two files. To be sure, the distribution of the evidence between the two files was unrelated to the use of the information gathered. Under the current rules also, the evidence contained in the trial file cannot be used for the decision-making without being first read out at trial.[411] Moreover, it cannot be ruled out that the evidence initially included in the trial phase will later be declared inadmissible.[412] On the other hand, it should be reminded that the distinction between the two files artificially prevents the fact-finders from having access to information that may be both valid and reliable, thus entailing drastic consequences on the outcome of criminal proceedings. In 1988, however, this was deemed to be the necessary price to eradicate inquisitorial practices still strongly based on the widespread use of police reports and out-of-court evidence gathered by the investigative bodies without the contribution of the defence.

Yet we saw that this system did not exclude any probative relevance of the police and prosecutorial evidence, which could still be used for the purposes of interlocutory decisions as well as in the alternative proceedings that lead to a decision on the merits out of court. Remarkably, the first commentators of the current code already pointed out the high relativism of the new Italian evidence law, highlighted by an unprecedented form of invalidity, that is, the non-usability of evidence (*inutilizzabilità*).[413] On close examination, this invalidity should not only concern evidence unlawfully gathered but furthermore reflected a more ordinary phenomenon. In a *contradictoire*-based model, it is no surprise that certain pieces of evidence—namely, the information gathered by the investigative bodies—can still be used for specific decisions within criminal proceedings, despite being unusable for the purposes of the trial decision on the merits.[414]

At first glance, the distinction between the two files reflects the principle of separation between the trial phase and the pre-trial stages, which includes the following two concepts:

- All the decisions to be issued in open court should be based on evidence gathered at trial as well as on out-of-court evidence, provided that it was lawfully admitted at trial
- All the decisions to be issued in the pre-trial phases—i.e., intermediate and interlocutory decisions, as well as the decision on guilt by means of alternative proceedings *in camera*—can indistinctly be based on the police and prosecutorial evidence, on the information taken through defence investigations as well as

---

[411]Art. 511 CCP.

[412]Grifantini (2007), p. 179 ff.

[413]The first scholar who clearly analysed this phenomenon after the enactment of the 1988 code was *Massimo Nobili*. Cf. Nobili (1998), p. 10 ff.

[414]In 2000, the Join Sections of the Supreme Court shared the distinction between 'pathological' and 'physiological' non-usability of evidence. See CCass, *Tammaro*.

on the evidence taken by the competent judge for the pre-trial inquiry with the defence's contribution.

On close examination, this distinction reflects too simplified an understanding of fact-finding, which does not take into account that very different decisions can be issued within the same phase of criminal proceedings. The trial court is often called upon to ascertain issues unrelated to the defendant's guilt,[415] *e.g.* ruling on jurisdictional issues or deciding on questions only indirectly concerned with the merits (for instance, the existence of unlawful conduct against the witness). A distinction between the phases of the proceedings is even more questionable in relation to the pre-trial stage, in which various decisions can be issued which, although not aimed at the defendant's conviction, deal with issues strictly linked with the charge. The main case is the decision on the suspicion of guilt as a necessary prerequisite for the adoption of coercive measures.[416] A clear example is the decision to remand the defendant into custody as well as the decision on the use of interception of telecommunications. In both cases, the assessment of *fumus delicti* entails a provisional ascertainment of the defendant's guilt,[417] which, albeit based on the information available at a certain stage of the pre-trial inquiry, cannot, however, make unconditional use of untested evidence. From a human rights perspective, the distinction between the two files also cannot lead to the result that coercive measures adopted during the trial phase cannot be revoked on the information contained in the prosecutorial file but must be maintained until evidence is gathered in open court.[418]

Against this background, criminal law scholarship has progressively become aware that the distribution of information between the trial and the prosecutorial file cannot entail a rigid distinction based on the dividing line between the trial and the pre-trial phase.[419] Starting with the distinction between *Strengbeweis* and *Freibeweis*, developed in German literature,[420] *Negri* in particular pointed out the strict link between methods of evidence-gathering, the rules on fact-finding and the different types of criminal decisions. This approach led him to re-define the terms of the relativism of the Italian evidence law, while proposing a new distinction between decisions on substantive and decisions on procedural issues.[421] The 1988

---

[415]See Negri (2004), p. 136 fn. 6, starting with the studies of Többens (1979), p. 7 ff.

[416]This requirement was enacted into the new Swiss code of criminal procedure. Cf. Art. 197(1) (b) CCP-Switzerland. See Pieth (2012), p. 118.

[417]In this context see the detailed analysis of Negri (2004), p. 52 ff., who used the German doctrine of *Sachgestaltungsvoraussetzungen*, which highlights the procedural projection of the criminal offence for purposes other than those of the decision on the merits. In the German literature see Volk (1978), p. 147 f.

[418]Negri (2004), p. 166.

[419]*Ibid.*, 133 ff.

[420]For an in-depth reflection in Italy on the co-existence of different evidentiary methods in criminal proceedings see already Orlandi (1992), pp. 50 and 221.

[421]Negri (2004), p. 133 ff.

code appears to support this approach, distinguishing between the proof of facts concerned with the charge, the defendant's punishment and the determination of sentences and security measures, and the proof of procedural issues.[422] According to this approach, the distinction between issues concerned with the defendant's guilt and procedural facts conditions the materials that can be used for the ascertainment of the facts. As a matter of principle, the former should—rigorously—be proved only on the basis of evidence taken with the parties' contribution, except specific cases allowing for the use of untested evidence. By contrast, the latter could—freely—be proved on the basis of any information lawfully obtained, no matter whether the defence could participate in the evidence-gathering.[423]

Doubtless, this approach marked great cultural progress in the understanding of criminal decision-making, strengthening the accused's contribution to the fact-finding. However, a close examination of the complex trade-offs among the conflicting interests in criminal justice can shed new light on this problematic area and can help overcome the barriers posed by rigid distinctions between methods of fact-finding. In the present discussion, I shall focus on participatory rights concerned with the decision on the merits of the case by separately analysing the decision-making at trial and in alternative proceedings. For the sake of clarity, I shall examine participatory rights concerned with decision-making in the field of the remand decision and the decision on other restrictions on freedom at a later stage of the investigation.[424]

II. Participatory Rights and Fact-Finding in the Trial Phase

1. Premise

It has been observed that the choice to insert prosecutorial and police evidence into a separate file was mainly aimed at preventing the trial court from ruling on the defendant's guilt on the basis of evidence gathered through secret investigations without the defence's contribution. Despite this strongly adversarial approach, the

---

[422] Art. 187 CCP.

[423] On the assessment of procedural issues see Catalano (2002), p. 521 ff. Italian courts may seem to support this distinction, *e.g.* by ruling out that the unpredictability of the event which rendered certain information unavailable at trial can only be proved on the basis of the evidence gathered in open court or anyway contained in the trial file. See CCass, *XY*. Pursuant to this approach, the procedural nature of an assessment should justify the use of all the information available, no matter who gathered it and with which methods it was gathered. However, one should not overlook the implications that this approach can have on the defendant's fundamental rights, *e.g.* negatively affecting the right to confrontation. Further consequences can be observed in relation to other individuals (for instance, the right of the accused's next of kin, who claim their right not to testify at trial).

[424] *Below*, J.I.

1988 code did not rule out the use of untested evidence, which could be admitted at trial in at least three main situations:

- Testimonial statements rendered either to the police or the prosecutor could be admitted if the evidence could no longer be taken at trial on unpredictable grounds[425];
- Testimonial evidence given orally to the court about facts the witness heard from someone else was generally allowed and the testimony given by indirect witnesses could be used without the direct witness being heard under certain conditions[426];
- Testimonial evidence rendered either to the police or the prosecutor could be admitted at trial in the case of inconsistent testimonial evidence given in open court.[427]

All three situations of these, which largely correspond to some of the traditional common-law exceptions from the rule against hearsay evidence,[428] have suffered from radical changes over the last three decades. More recently, new developments have occurred as a consequence of the growing impact of Strasbourg case-law. For the sake of clarity, I shall focus separately on the problem of information unavailable at trial, the use of hearsay evidence and the use of inconsistent out-of-court evidence. All these issues pose very difficult challenges from a human rights perspective, calling for an approach aimed at striking a balance not only between prosecutorial needs and the accused's right to confrontation but furthermore among the conflicting interests of different individuals involved in criminal proceedings.

2. Evidence Unavailable at Trial

As noted, Italian law uses the term 'non-repeatability' rather than 'unavailability', a linguistic preference that reveals the persistent tendency to anticipate the collection of information. In this study, however, I prefer to adopt the more neutral notion of 'unavailability', which will hopefully facilitate a comparison with the European Convention. Evidence can be unavailable at trial for various grounds. In some cases, it can already be foreseen in the preliminary inquiry that certain information will probably not be able to be taken in open court. In these cases, specific safeguards are required. We have seen that the code laid down specific requirements for prosecutors to order urgent technical investigations. Moreover, *incidente probatorio* provides a general means of taking evidence through a court procedure

[425] Art. 512 CCP.

[426] Art. 195 CCP.

[427] Art. 500 CC8pP.

[428] Spencer (2014), p. 5 f.

in camera, which requires the application of the same rules on trial evidence-gathering.

On close examination, none of these tools can ensure the effective involvement of the defence in the collection of evidence. Concerning *incidente probatorio*, we have already examined the difficulties in ensuring to the suspect the full exercise of defence rights. It must be acknowledged, however, that Italian law enacted some rules aimed at avoiding the use of evidence gathered by means of this procedure against individuals not represented in the hearing *in camera*. As noted, evidence-gathering cannot be extended to issues concerned with defendants whose lawyers had not been summoned. If needed, the hearing must be postponed to summon the other interested parties, unless it would jeopardise the collection of the requested information.[429] These rules are still further reinforced by the provision that, as noted, forbids the use of information gathered through *incidente probatorio* against defendants whose lawyers could not participate in the taking of evidence.[430] Yet this result only applies to the trial decision, so that remand decisions and a guilty verdict in alternative proceedings held *in camera* can still be based on untested evidence,[431] without any consideration of the reasons that made the accused's involvement impossible.

Further problems arise where the evidence gathered through an investigation not initially urgent has become unavailable at trial. This situation mainly concerns testimonial evidence and thus coincides to a great extent with the topic of absent witnesses, according to the terminology used by Strasbourg case-law. As noted, the 1988 code provided for specific rules on the use of evidence gathered by the prosecutor, making the admissibility of untested evidence that became unavailable at trial conditional on the existence of unpredictable circumstances that arose after the preliminary inquiry.[432] This condition required the trial court to ascertain whether the event that rendered the evidence non-repeatable at trial could have been foreseen in the pre-trial inquiry on the basis of the information available. This assessment aimed at preventing prosecutors, well aware of the risks regarding the sought information, from carrying out autonomous investigations instead of activating the judicial procedure of *incidente probatorio*.

Subsequent legislation, though maintaining this requirement, progressively broadened the scope of this regulation by enabling the parties also to request the admission of unavailable evidence gathered by the police at their own initiative and, more recently, even by the lawyers of private parties. Doubtless, this extension strengthened the rights of the defence, while giving voice to individuals heard by the defence lawyer. Yet the broadening of the scope of the original provision

429 Art. 402 CCP.

430 The only exception concerns the case of suspicion of guilt arisen only after the end of the pre-trial procedure, if the evidence collected has already become unavailable. Cf. Art. 403(1-*bis*) CCP. On the problems concerned with this case see Cordero (2012), p. 877.

431 Galantini (1992), p. 68 f.

432 Art. 512 CCP (1988 version).

radically changed the mechanism of admission of unavailable evidence, requiring a condition that is somewhat unreasonable in several cases. To be sure, the 1988 code had already required the same condition for the admission of non-repeatable evidence collected by the competent judge in the intermediate phase, notwithstanding that judges cannot activate *incidente probatorio* at their own initiative, and that this procedure was initially circumscribed to the sole pre-trial inquiry. Yet the requirement of unpredictable circumstances has become even more questionable in relation to the police and the lawyers of private parties other than the defendant, since none of them is entitled to request *incidente probatorio*. Specific problems arise in relation to unavailable evidence gathered through defensive investigations, mainly because of the structure of the lawyer's official file. As noted, the lawyer does not need to insert all the information collected but can only include the pieces of evidence they wish to be taken into consideration by the judicial authority. This situation makes it by definition impossible for both the trial court to scrutinise the information available to the lawyers during their investigations and therefore to ascertain whether they were already aware of the circumstances that later made the evidence unavailable at trial.

Without any consideration of these shortcomings, the 2001 fair trial legislation further enhanced the admissibility of untested evidence that has become unavailable at trial, extending the condition of unpredictable circumstances to information obtained in other proceedings.[433] This provision gives rise to further unreasonable results. There is nothing to ensure that party A, who in proceedings B took a certain piece of evidence which party C requests to be admitted in proceedings D, could apply for *incidente probatorio* in proceedings E.

A delicate question, which allows us to observe a significant change in the understanding of unavailable evidence, is whether non-repeatability of evidence must also be unrelated to a subjective decision of the person summoned to give oral evidence at trial. The question arose in the midst of the 1990s, as the Constitutional Court deemed it lawful that statements rendered in the pre-trial inquiry by the accused's next of kin, who claim their right not to testify at trial,[434] were read out in open court. Yet this situation, despite being the result of a subjective strategy, cannot often be predicted in advance. The question gained new relevance after the 1999 fair trial reform, which enabled the legislature to depart from the principle of *contradictoire* by allowing for the use of untested evidence if the involvement of the parties in the evidence-gathering is absolutely impossible on objective grounds. This led the Constitutional Court to overrule its previous jurisprudence in relation to the evidence given by the accused's next of kin to the police or the prosecutor during the pre-trial inquiry.[435]

---

[433] Art. 238(3) CPP.

[434] CConst, 179/1994.

[435] CConst, 440/2000.

3. Hearsay Evidence

At first glance, hearsay evidence may appear to be another form of unavailable evidence. Here, however, the problem does not coincide with that of unavailable evidence, which relates to the information gathered out of court that cannot be repeated at trial. In cases of hearsay evidence, instead, witness testimony is often rendered in open court, albeit not by the direct source of evidence. In light of this, we can therefore say that here the unavailability concerns the direct testimony, not the information in itself. The 1988 code acknowledged the general admissibility of hearsay evidence, although under some conditions. On the one hand, it enabled judges to collect first-hand evidence at their own initiative.[436] On the other, it ruled out the use of hearsay evidence, if one party requests the hearing of the direct witness who does not, however, appear in court, except only in case of death, illness and non-traceability.[437]

This approach, which has largely remained unchanged until today, is not entirely consistent with a participatory understanding of criminal justice. Clearly, the general admissibility of hearsay evidence was intended to give voice not only to normal witnesses but also to individuals affected by the criminal offence, such as the victim. However, the choice of excluding any use of the hearsay evidence on grounds possibly unrelated to the indirect witness is questionable, revealing scant consideration of the intrinsic reliability that the second-hand testimony may have in a concrete case. Furthermore, the exceptions of death, illness and non-traceability can unjustifiably restrict the possibility of using hearsay evidence. The main problems relate to the case of illness, a notion that, despite not exclusively relating to physical illness, requires a situation that can be classified as a sickness (physical or mental illness). This should not, therefore, allow for the use of indirect witness in cases of vulnerable individuals that would certainly suffer from a particular stress if confronted with the defendant. It is worth observing, however, that the Supreme Court has progressively extended the exception of illness to cases in which the court hearing of minors, especially victims of sexual crimes, would cause a serious disturbance of their mental and emotional equilibrium.[438] The fact that a part of the case-law rigorously requires the presence of minors,[439] despite their fragile psychological equilibrium, demonstrates a rigid understanding of the principle of *contradictoire*, which does not take into account the complex human rights challenges posed by the *audi alteram partem* rule.

Another delicate problem concerns the admissibility of indirect testimony given by law enforcement authorities on facts they learned during their investigations. The 1988 code prohibited the taking of hearsay evidence by police officers and agents in open court. The main ground for this radical approach was to avoid

---

[436] Art. 195(2) CCP.

[437] Art. 195(3) CCP.

[438] CCass, *Scardaccione.*

[439] CCass, *Muscas.*

eluding the exclusionary rules on untested and inconsistent evidence. Furthermore, the police cannot be treated as normal witnesses, performing specific duties while gathering oral evidence during their investigations. Over the last few decades, however, this regulation has undergone several changes and to a great extent, it may be said that the new Italian law of evidence started sagging as this prohibition was dropped. This occurred in 1992, as the Constitutional Court declared the ban of police hearsay evidence unconstitutional, thus paving the way for the erosion of the original rule against narrative.[440] Certainly, the original restrictions on the use of out-of-court inconsistent statements given to the investigative bodies could no longer be maintained if the same information could in any case be obtained at trial through the indirect testimony of the police officer or agent.

Notwithstanding that several criticisms were raised against this constitutional ruling, it took several years for a further statutory intervention. Only in 2001 did the legislative implementation of the fair trial constitutional reform restore both the rule against narrative and the ban on police hearsay evidence, albeit in a rather different form from the original regulation. The ban on collection of hearsay evidence by the police was circumscribed to the cases of information recorded by the investigative authority[441] and consequently to statements gathered by the police while performing their duties.[442] The goal of the new regulation was not only to protect the defendant's right to participation in the gathering of incriminating evidence but also to preserve the police's obligation to record the evidence collected during official investigations.[443] In this light, however, the wording of the new provision was unjustifiably limited. This led the Supreme Court to re-interpret the legal prohibition as relating not only to the statements recorded but also to the cases in which the police must draw up official records of the statements collected.[444] The Constitutional Court shared this interpretation by declaring the rules on the police hearsay evidence unconstitutional.[445] Yet police hearsay evidence is still not banned in the remaining cases, being subject to normal conditions where testimonial evidence was gathered in exceptional or urgent circumstances as well as in cases in which the police should report statements given by third parties without a specific hearing.[446]

Notwithstanding considerable steps forward, the current rules on police hearsay evidence give rise to human rights concerns. Of course, there are no risks to the right to *contradictoire* in relation to the defendant's statements, which can never be admitted at trial through indirect testimony.[447] Yet the case-law still allows for the

[440] CConst, 24/1992.

[441] Arts. 351 and 357(2)(a-b) CCP.

[442] Art. 195(4) CCP, as amended by Law 63/2001.

[443] Caprioli (2002), p. 83.

[444] CCass, *Torcasio*.

[445] CConst, 305/2008.

[446] CCass, *Torcasio*.

[447] Art. 62 CCP.

wide use of police hearsay evidence in undefined exceptional cases. This lack of definition can lead to abuses and does not seem to be in line with the general approach of the code, which provides for the entering into the record of witness statements at a later stage of the proceedings only in exceptional circumstances.[448] On the other hand, the general ban on police hearsay evidence in relation to recorded statements appears excessively rigid insofar as it excludes the use of police testimony on victims' statements that in particular situations could only with great difficulties be repeated at trial. As noted, this especially applies to the evidence rendered to the police by minors in case of serious offences, which requires the adoption of special precautions, such as the presence of an expert of psychology or child psychiatry appointed by the prosecutor.

4. Inconsistent Out-of-Court Evidence

The distinction between the trial and the prosecutorial file poses the problem of how inconsistencies between the information gathered in open court and the evidence taken out of court should be handled. In 1988, the main problem was whether and to what extent inconsistent statements rendered to the investigative bodies in the pre-trial inquiry could be used at trial. Doubtless, allowing for full probative use to out-of-court testimonial evidence, as in the past, would have negatively affect the accused's right to participate in the gathering of incriminating evidence. Of course, this reasoning could not apply to inconsistent evidence given by the same accused to the investigative bodies, it being instead necessary to protect the defendant's right to silence. The problem of inconsistent evidence took on further significance as Law 397/2000 enacted rules on the use of inconsistent testimony given by informants to the lawyers of private parties. All these cases, however, have a common feature. Unlike in case of unavailable and hearsay evidence, the direct source evidence is here available at trial. The individual examined gives oral evidence in open court, evidence that is, however, contradicted by statements rendered by the same person out of court. Comparing this case to that of absent witnesses, it might say that here the problem concerns inconsistent witnesses or parties.

The most difficult challenges from a participatory understanding of criminal justice arise in relation to inconsistent testimony. On one hand, pursuant to a rigorous understanding of the principle of *contradictoire*, defendants could only be convicted on the basis of evidence given in open court. On the other hand, pre-trial evidence may be of particular relevance in a concrete case and cannot therefore be simply forgotten or considered as never having existed—especially in an extremely slow criminal justice system, like in Italy, where pre-trial inquiries can last years. The 1988 codification, departing from the Rocco code, attempted to balance these two needs by means of a unprecedented exclusionary rule, based on

[448]Criticisms were also raised by Balsamo and Lo Piparo (2004), p. 226.

the double assumption that untested evidence, as a matter of principle, can never be used to prove the facts and can only be used to assess the reliability of the person examined (and consequently the reliability of the evidence given in open court).[449]

Doubtless, this solution strengthened the participatory role not only of the accused by furthermore of private parties in various fashions. Unlike the 1930 codification, which allowed for the police file to be put at the disposal of the decision-makers, the 1988 code kept the trial court in ignorance of the information collected in the pre-trial inquiry. This enabled the parties, who had access to the prosecutorial file, to check the consistency of the trial testimony and to request that eventual inconsistent statements rendered out of court be read out at trial. In this way, the accused's right to contribute to the taking of oral evidence was preserved, whereas the reading out of pre-trial statements only aimed at testing the reliability of the trial evidence, any further use for the proof of the facts stated being excluded.

To be sure, the drafters of the 1988 code did not invent this solution, which had already emerged in the 1960s in a period of critical reflection on prosecutorial inquiry and the problem of use of out-of-court evidence under the Rocco code.[450] This discussion was strongly oriented towards the adversarial tradition of common-law countries which had long elaborated a rule against narrative.[451] This approach was, however, imported to Italy in terms of a rigid exclusionary rule, flanked by only one exception concerning the case of testimonial statements rendered either during a search or immediately after the fact, on the assumption, as already mentioned, that this evidence was presumably reliable. It is also important to note that the restriction on the use of inconsistent evidence to checking of the reliability of the person examined (like the rule against hearsay evidence) was elaborated in common-law countries in which criminal justice was mainly characterised by guilty verdicts not accompanied by a reasoned justification and issued by (often) non-literate people.[452] These exclusionary rules, instead, took on new significance in Italian criminal justice, which requires the decision-makers to give reasons for the use of the evidence obtained.

It has been observed that this strong barrier became unreasonable after the Constitutional Court declared the prohibition of police hearsay evidence unconstitutional. A few months later, the Constitutional Court also declared the provision containing a ban on the use of inconsistent statements to prove the facts

---

[449]Art. 500(3) CCP (1988 version).

[450]See Cordero (1966), p. 189 ff. Moreover, an important reform draft of a new code of criminal procedure, elaborated by *Carnelutti* in the 1960s (known as 'Carnelutti draft'), had already provided for the possibility of pre-trial statements being produced at trial to assess the reliability of witnesses or defendants. This proposal was, however, dropped in the amended reform draft. Cf. Carnelutti (1963), respectively 76 and 155.

[451]In England and Wales, the 1865 Criminal Procedure Act already allowed the use of out-of-court inconsistent testimonial statements to undermine the witnesses' reliability.

[452]Vogler (2014), p. 186. Legal scholarship, however, contrasted this argument on the grounds that jury service was originally reserved to middle class. Cf. Spencer (2014), p. 2.

unconstitutional.[453] In the same year, the anti-mafia legislation followed the way paved by the constitutional case-law by means of a radical reform on the rules governing the use of out-of-court statements, inspired by a more flexible approach. To be sure, the rule limiting the use of inconsistent testimony to evaluate the reliability of the person examined remained untouched. Since the exclusionary rule was dropped, however, this provision only held a rhetorical meaning, which could no longer impede the use of inconsistent evidence for fact-finding, provided that further elements confirmed its reliability.[454] Another significant innovation was the possibility of using inconsistent information where the witness refused to testify on the specific circumstances referred to in the pre-trial hearing.[455] This innovation was of utmost systematic importance, blurring the distinction between unavailable and inconsistent evidence, which by definition presupposes at least two versions of the same facts. On the other hand, the original exception was dropped and replaced by two new cases allowing for the use of inconsistent statements as evidence of the matters stated, i.e. (a) if evidence was given in the intermediate phase[456] or (b) the person examined was likely to have been blackmailed or threatened or in any way subject to psychological pressure in order to cause them to change their original testimony or not to testify at all.[457]

On close examination, some flaws vitiated the 1988 regulation, which presupposed conditions that could rarely be fulfilled in the Italian criminal justice on organizational grounds. First of all, the resistance of the rule against narrative required the possibility of rapid and focused proceedings,[458] aimed at allowing oral evidence to be taken in open court with the shortest distance from the fact. Certainly, the 1992 legislation originated from the need to bolster the fight against mafia at the beginning of the 1990s. Yet this tendency was in line with a progressive relaxation of the rule against narrative, which was already underway in several common-law countries. In England and Wales, this weakening culminated in the 2003 Criminal Justice Act, which converted the original exclusionary rule in a rule of assessment of hearsay evidence for the purposes of the fact-finding.[459] The exception of the admission of inconsistent evidence because of fear was also a typical common-law exception to the rule against hearsay evidence, an exception significantly maintained by the 2003 UK legislation.[460] In Italy, however, the failure to define the elements that should corroborate the reliability of out-of-court statements inevitably gave rise to abuses.[461] It is therefore not surprising

[453]CConst, 255/1992. This ruling was strongly criticised by many scholars. See Ferrua (1992), p. 1455 ff.

[454]Art. 500(4) CCP (1992 version).

[455]Art. 500(2-*bis*) CCP (1992 version).

[456]Art. 500(6) CCP (1992 version).

[457]Art. 500(5) CCP (1992 version).

[458]Rivello (1993), p. 100.

[459]S. 119 CJA 2003. See Spencer (2014), p. 221 ff.

[460]S. 116(2) CJA 2003.

[461]This risk had been foreseen by Cordero (1992), p. 236.

that 8 years later, the Constitutional Court extended the 1992 solution to the case of inconsistent testimonial statements rendered in other proceedings as well as to inconsistent evidence given by co-defendants who, after being coercively brought to court, claimed their right to silence.[462]

It has been noted that the legislature reacted to this constitutional ruling with the 1999 constitutional fair trial reform, which not only enshrined the principle of *contradictoire* at constitutional level but also enacted a general prohibition of use of untested evidence for the purposes of the defendant's conviction. To fulfil these requirements, Law 63/2001 moved back towards the 1988 solutions, bringing about, however, some important innovations. On close examination, the 2001 reform did not reproduce the original ban on use inconsistent testimony as evidence of the matters stated. Nevertheless, the dropping of the provision allowing for the use of out-of-court statements in case of corroborating evidence led to the result that the rule on the scrutinization of reliability of the person examined recovered its original features as a typical exclusionary rule. Besides, as noted, Italian law provides for an exhaustive list of the cases in which out-of-court evidence can be used for the decision on the merits. Thirteen years after the entry into force of the code, moreover, the legislature provided the rule against narrative with a wider range of exceptions. To be sure, this result should not necessarily be viewed as a further relaxation of the rule against narrative. For instance, the legislature strengthened the conditions under which out-of-court inconsistent statements can be admitted as evidence of the matters stated, if the individuals examined changed their opinion or refused to testify because of fear or another psychological pressure.[463] Under the current rules, these situations can no longer be presumed but must be proved on the basis of concrete circumstances or pieces of evidence.[464]

Although the Constitutional Court has on several occasions deemed this set-up in line with fair trial principles,[465] it can be doubted that the 2001 reform provided the only solutions compatible with the constitutional requirement of *contradictoire* in evidence-gathering. At a deeper level still, it is debatable whether the legal solutions can properly fulfil the overall requirements of the constitutional model of a fair trial,[466] which requires a balance of all the conflicting interests involved in criminal proceedings. Certainly, the strict link between the principle of *contradictoire* and the ban on use of the out-of-court statements of those who have always freely avoided any confrontation with the accused leaves no room for interpretations aimed at unconditionally allowing the use of the statements of the individuals who instead accepted confrontation.[467] As noted, this situation by definition occurs if the person examined at trial does not refuse to answer the

[462]CConst, 361/1998.

[463]Art. 500(4) CCP.

[464]Art. 500(5) CCP. On this topic see Busetto (2009).

[465]CConst, 32/2002 and 36/2002.

[466]In this sense see instead Ferrua (2012), p. 135 ff.

[467]*Ibid.*, 136 f. Of a different opinion Grevi (2000), p. XVIII.

questions, despite giving different evidence. Thus subsequent confrontation with the defendant does not change the nature of the inconsistent out-of-court statements, which remain information collected without the defence's contribution. This does not mean, however, that the principle of *contradictoire* always allows for the use of the evidence given in open court, notwithstanding that its reliability was undermined by the pre-trial statements of the person examined. On close examination, the Constitution also does not require pre-trial evidence to remain useless for the purposes of the fact-finding.

Of course, the fact that out-of-court evidence undermined the reliability of the information given at trial does not necessarily mean that it provides truthful evidence. This does not mean, however, that inconsistent statements never provide reliable information and therefore never deserve to be assessed by the decision-makers for the purposes of the decision on the merits. Such conclusions would tighten the right to confrontation even more than in some common-law countries with a strong adversarial tradition and in which the right to confrontation also holds constitutional relevance. In the US, for instance, since the 2004 landmark decision *Crawford v. Washington*[468] the Supreme Court has progressively enhanced the right to confrontation as a 'dignitarian right',[469] drastically reducing the room for admission of untested evidence. However, it is noteworthy that this case-law was mostly developed in relation to the cases of witnesses who either are unavailable or in any case refuse to testify at trial, that is, cases in which no problem of consistency with out-of-court statements by definition arises. Moreover, the US Supreme Court circumscribed this strong approach to the sole case of testimonial evidence collected, albeit out of court, for the purposes of criminal proceedings.[470]

Different problems arise when the individuals examined at trial do not refuse to answer the questions but give oral evidence contrasting with their previous statements. On close examination, producing out-of-court statements does not only serve the purpose of a better confrontation with the accused but also gives the individuals examined the opportunity to be confronted with themselves and with their past. Witnesses and co-defendants can therefore profit from this opportunity to explain the ground for contradiction and to eventually rectify the statements rendered at trial. If this happens, the contradiction disappears. The problem is when contradiction remains after confrontation has taken place. In the light of the opportunity offered to the person examined, however, it does not seem that the rigid ban on use of out-of-court statements to prove the matters stated reveals a reasonable solution in every case.

From the perspective of constitutional law, we saw that the Italian Constitution generally requires judges to give reasons for their rulings.[471] From this it follows

[468] 541 U.S. 36 (2004).

[469] Ashworth and Redmayne (2010), p. 365.

[470] Thus, in *Davis v. Washington* the US Supreme Court considered emergency calls made to the police office admissible at trial. Cf. 547 U.S. 813 (2006).

[471] Art. 111(6) Const.

that the defendant's conviction is invalid if the trial court cannot explain why it relied on the oral evidence given at trial, even though it was undermined by the out-of-court statements. Surprisingly, judges are instead not required to give reasons why they relied on inconsistent pre-trial statements, while admitting them as evidence of the matters stated in one of the statutory exceptions (*e.g.*, in case of proved unlawful conduct against the person examined). Even more worryingly, judges do not need to give reasons why they give no credit to out-of-court evidence if it does not fit the exceptions laid down by the law, even though it may be both intrinsically coherent and consistent with the overall information available.

This *contradictoire*-based system is not airtight, however. In particular, Italian law, while generally excluding the use of inconsistent statements, does not rule out the possibility of recovering the information contained in these statements, if obtained by other means. For instance, if the person examined told his original version to a third person and the police but later gives different evidence at trial, the code, while prohibiting the hearsay evidence of the police, allows for the examination of the indirect witness. By means of the hearsay evidence of a third person, therefore, the inconsistent testimonial information can be fully used at trial regardless of the existence of the exceptions laid down by Article 500 CCP. Further concerns arise where the original communications were wiretapped. By this means, the inconsistent out-of-court evidence, provided that it was lawfully collected, can also be read out at trial and can be used to prove the facts under prosecution.

These situations lead to the paradoxical conclusion that out-of-court testimonial statements cannot directly be used at trial if inconsistent with the oral evidence given by the same person in open court, even though the information may be in line with the overall evidence available, whereas its contents can easily be obtained by other means. When the out-of-court statements were gathered through wiretaps, this result is even more paradoxical from a human rights perspective, since evidence is obtained not only without the defence's contribution but also through a means interfering with the private sphere of a third party in a hidden way.

A highly problematic case concerns the admission of evidence if it is proven that an unlawful conduct was carried out against the person examined. It has been observed that Italian legislature tightened the conditions for the admission of inconsistent evidence in case of fear, threats and other forms of unlawful conduct against the person examined. Despite the acknowledgment of this exception in the Constitution, it can be doubted that the use of inconsistent evidence can here properly compensate for the lack of *contradictorie*. On close examination, this case does not exclusively concern inconsistent evidence but also untested evidence. Thus fear may also have prevented the person examined from giving evidence at trial, which leads to the result that the question at stake is whether to admit information not obtained at trial.

Notwithstanding the 2001 reform, the constitutional requirement of 'proved' unlawful conduct is still often blurred especially in cases of criminal proceedings for mafia-type crimes.[472] Besides, the way this exception was laid down can have drastic consequences on the defendant's right to contribute to the taking of incriminating evidence, since Italian law requires the trial court neither to assess whether the accused contributed to the alleged unlawful conduct nor to evaluate the impact of inconsistent (or untested) evidence on the decision-making. In other words, if the unlawful conduct needs to be demonstrated in an objective way and if sufficient proof is achieved, the decision-makers need not ascertain any fault on the part of the defendants. Clearly, the legal solution aims at avoiding the rule against narrative being eluded by means of unlawful actions indirectly carried out by the accused. Yet it is unreasonable that the code does not require the trial court to scrutinise whether the unlawful conduct was carried out by the accused's next of kin or by persons in any way linked with him. It is also unreasonable that Italian law does not require assessing whether all the defendants played an active role in the unlawful conduct against the person examined.

This situation can lead to at least two negative results. On one hand, out-of-court statements, once admitted at trial, can be used against all the accused persons regardless of whether the individual defendants had any contact with the person examined and did anything to undermine *contradictoire*.[473] On the other, this undifferentiated use of inconsistent (or untested) evidence can be detrimental for the fairness and reliability of fact-finding. As noted, once out-of-court evidence has been lawfully admitted at trial, the trial court has the ordinary duty to give reasons for its use. Yet it is clear that the proof of unlawful conduct against the individuals examined does not make the previous statements more reliable in itself.

Even more worryingly, the 2001 reform, despite enacting a wider range of exceptions, followed a rigid approach, which reveals an understanding of the principle of *contradictoire* unconnected with other relevant interests. This problem, however, requires us to broaden the area of investigation by analysing whether and to what extent the current rules on inconsistent evidence fit the requirements of the constitutional model of a fair trial and are also in line with the European case-law, which looks at the whole set-up of conflicting interests rather than on individual fundamental rights, such as the right to *contradictoire*. It should also be examined whether the Italian rules on inconsistent evidence properly fulfil the specific needs of international cooperation, especially in the EU area. For the sake of clarity, I shall examine this problem in Chap. 16.

---

[472]See Morosini (2009), p. 402 ff.; Maggio (2010), p. 499 ff.

[473]Carcano and Manzione (2001), p. 57. The Supreme Court has largely shared this approach. Cf. CCass, *Capozza*. Of a different opinion Ubertis (2013), p. 159, who considered the use of pre-trial testimonial statements against all the defendants unlawful if only one of them or even a third person unlawfully led the witnesses to change their version or not to testify.

III. Participatory Rights and Fact-Finding in Alternative Proceedings

1. Premise

It has been observed that the distinction between the trial file and the prosecutorial file does not render the evidence included into the latter useless for the purposes of any decision. The main field in which this information can be used is again that of the alternative proceedings aimed at an out-of-court decision on the merits—namely, plea bargaining, the abbreviated proceedings and the penal order procedure. Furthermore, as noted, the main purpose of the enactment into the Constitution of the exception of the accused's consent to the use of untested evidence was to provide justification to the proceedings characterised by a decision on guilt issued on the basis of the information gathered by the investigative bodies.[474] Thus, it is precisely the accused's consent that legitimises the use of untested evidence for the purposes of the decision on the merits, which should therefore compensate for the lack of involvement in the evidence-gathering. On close examination, it is debatable whether all the aforementioned alternative proceedings can be based on this justification. Furthermore, like in the field of evidentiary agreements, it should be examined whether only the accused is entitled to consent to the use of untested evidence and above all, what impact the accused's initiative can have on the interests of other individuals involved in criminal proceedings and fact-finding.

2. Alternative Proceedings and the Waiver of the Right to Participation in Evidence-Gathering

Concerning the first question, serious problems especially arise in the field of penal order proceedings. We have noted that after the 1999 fair trial reform, criminal law scholarship justified this procedure on the basis of the doctrine of subsequent *contradictoire*, developed by the Constitutional Court since the 1950s to save the lawfulness of penal order procedures. Pursuant to this doctrine, the defendant's initiative, unlike in any other proceedings, follows the decision-making in the sense that, by not challenging the penal order, the accused consents to the conviction

[474]Exceptionally, this result can also be achieved at trial. The 1988 code provided for one single exception, that is, when the defendant—after being brought to court through the so-called 'direct proceedings' (*procedimento direttissimo*)—requests to be tried by means of the abbreviated proceedings. In this case, the direct proceedings are converted into abbreviate proceedings, with the result that the trial court must abide by rules governing the abbreviate proceedings, rules that allow, *inter alia*, the use of the evidence gathered through police and prosecutorial investigations for the purposes of the decision-making. Cf. Art. 452(2) CCP. The Constitutional Court introduced a similar result by means of the ruling 333/2009, which enabled defendants to re-present at trial the request for the abbreviate proceedings rejected in the intermediate phase, if the indictment was exceptionally amended.

based on prosecutorial and police evidence, whereas objection entails a disagreement with the use of untested evidence.

On close examination, this conclusion oversimplifies the dynamics of penal order procedures, mainly because the alternatives 'challenge or not challenge' cannot always reflect the defendant's will.[475] As noted, the 1988 code, departing from the approach of the previous codification, enabled the lawyer to lodge an objection without special powers. This approach surely cannot be deemed in line with the Constitution, which requires a strict link between the waiver of *contradictoire* and the defendant's will;[476] and the distance from the constitutional requirements of a fair trial further increases where objection is lodged by a court-appointed lawyer who could not reach the convicted person. From this it follows that penal orders against which objection was lodged do not necessarily justify the use of untested evidence on the ground of the constitutional exception of the accused's consent. Moreover, objection against a penal order does not necessarily express the accused's disagreement with the use of prosecutorial and police evidence. On close examination, penal order proceedings need to be justified in the light of the general requirement of participation in criminal proceedings. It is noteworthy that the doctrine of subsequent *contradictoire* degraded penal orders to provisional rulings (*decisioni preliminari*), as pointed out on several occasions by the Constitutional Court.[477] This approach provides a rather artificial justification of penal order procedures, which reveals a clear underestimation of the importance of the parties' involvement for the purposes of the decision-making. It cannot seriously be affirmed that the parties' contribution to the fact-finding still holds its utility after the decision has been issued.

It is worth observing that the Constitutional Court, after having long defended the lawfulness of *inaudito reo* decisions,[478] has recently become more aware of the problems concerned with the participatory rights of the accused in this alternative proceeding. Significantly, the constitutional judges no longer maintained the traditional conception of penal orders as provisional rulings,[479] shifting towards a new understanding of these proceedings.[480] Regrettably, this new case-law draws little attention to the need for a wide-ranging view of penal order proceedings in the light of all the interests at stake. This is apparent from a recent ruling in which the Constitutional Court examined the complainant's right to a preventive challenge to a penal order in case of criminal proceedings for offences that can only be prosecuted after a lawsuit by the victim.[481] This case highlights a further deficiency

[475] On this topic see Ruggeri (2009), p. 133 ff.

[476] *Ibid.*, 150 ff.

[477] Cf., among others, CConst, 8/2003.

[478] CConst, 8/2003.

[479] CConst, 323/2007.

[480] CConst, 317/2009.

[481] CConst, 23/2015. For some criticisms see Ruggeri (2015b).

of penal order proceedings, which also frustrate the victim's right to participation in criminal proceedings. Unlike the 1930 code,[482] the 1988 regulation did not allow for the damaged party to join a civil law action to criminal proceedings when the prosecutor requested a penal order. In 1999, Italian legislature softened this approach by enabling the complainant to lodge a preventative objection to a penal order proceeding.[483] In 2015, however, the Constitutional Court declared this provision unconstitutional. Alongside some inconsistencies, this decision reveals a further development in the constitutional case-law, which highlights a dangerous understanding of criminal proceedings. By emphasising the constitutional need for a speedy and efficient prosecution, the Court leaves little room for the interest of private parties other than the accused to be fairly involved in criminal justice.

Further problems arise in relation to the abbreviated proceedings. As noted, these proceedings are characterised by the fact that the competent judge is called upon to rule on the merits, at the defendant's request, on the basis of the police and prosecutorial evidence as well as of the information gathered by the defence and the evidence eventually taken through *incidente probatorio*.[484] Here also, moreover, the defendant's initiative only conditions the rules on fact-finding at a secondary level, since it firstly modifies the ordinary structure of criminal proceedings. The first difference from the ordinary proceedings, therefore, concerns the first structure of this procedure, which aims at a decision *in camera*. Despite the abbreviated proceedings also being governed by the same rules on the trial decision-making,[485] the structure of this *in camera* procedure affects the way not only the accused but also other parties can contribute to fact-finding.

As in the case of penal order, can we affirm that the defence's initiative reflects the defendant's waiver of the right to participate in evidence-gathering? The examination of statutory law should lead to the affirmative answer, since abbreviated proceedings can be requested either by the accused or by his lawyer with a special power. However, we have noted that the Supreme Court deemed the special power given to the lawyer equivalent to the silence of the defendant present in the hearing, if the accused does not contradict the lawyer's request. This conclusion, based on the assumption that the competent judge can at any time verify the accused's free will, cannot be sustained unconditionally. It is precisely the presence of the accused that should require the judicial authority not only to hear him but also to inform him of the implications of the abbreviated proceedings.

---

[482]Under the 1930 code, the decision to join a civil law action to the criminal proceedings precluded the recourse to the penal order procedure. See Cordero (1987), p. 757.

[483]Art. 459(1) CCP, as amended by the Law 479/1999. The 1988 code did not allow for the recourse to the penal order procedure in relation to such offences.

[484]Art. 442(1-*bis*) CCP.

[485]Art. 442(1) CCP.

3. The Impact of the Accused's Waiver on the Interests of Other Parties and on Fact-Finding

The second problem concerns the implications of the accused's decision to renounce a public trial on the interests of other parties involved in criminal proceedings and on the decision-making. This complex question concerns all the proceedings aimed at avoiding the trial judgement at request or with the consent of the defendant. Moreover, a distinction should be made depending on whether the guilt is proven solely on the basis of information available (plea bargaining and penal order proceedings) or whether further evidence can be taken in a hearing *in camera* (abbreviated proceedings). Another distinguishing feature of plea bargaining and penal order proceedings, in comparison to the abbreviated proceedings, is that the initiative of the parties or the prosecutorial request does not generically aim at a decision on the merits but at the immediate conviction of the accused. This aim, while allowing for the exceptional use of untested evidence, requires the competent judge to assess this information not just in terms of provisional evidence, which will probably be replaced by the evidence taken at trial, but as the only information on which the conviction will be based.[486]

This situation can lead to serious practical problems in cases of plea-bargaining. The information available may be incomplete or even contradictory. Yet the structure of the plea bargain proceedings allows neither the parties nor the competent judge to undertake further initiatives aimed at gathering supplementary evidence. In these situations, both case-law[487] and criminal law scholarship[488] rule out the application of the ordinary rules governing trial decision-making, with the result that judges should paradoxically convict the defendant who requested it, even in case of incomplete or contradictory evidence. Furthermore, we have noted that the initiative of the prosecutor and the accused leaves no room for further participation of the aggrieved parties, even if they have already lodged a civil-law complaint. Serious problems also arise in case of penal order proceedings, which lead to a radical change of the normal rules on sentencing as a consequence of the initiative of the sole prosecutor.[489]

486 Marzaduri (1990), p. 730.

487 Cass, *Cardoni*.

488 For an overlook of this problem see Gialuz (2008), p. 13 ff. It is noteworthy, moreover, that even *Marzaduri*, who pointed out the need that the bargaining decision be supported by enough inculpatory evidence, excluded the application of the trial rules on the decision-making, which require defendants to be acquitted not only in cases of lack of evidence against them but also in cases of incomplete or contradictory evidence. Cf. Marzaduri (1990), p. 730.

489 For some criticisms see Ruggeri (2008), p. 236 f. On the relationship between judicial conviction (*richterliche Überzeugung*) and the assessment of strong suspicion of guilt (*Tatverdachtsgewinnung*) from the viewpoint of German penal order procedures see Ebert (2000), p. 193 ff.

Different human rights concerns relate to the abbreviated proceedings from the perspective of the present discussion, since here further evidence can be taken in the hearing *in camera*. As anticipated, the defendant's request for abbreviated proceedings can frustrate the right to evidence of other parties and can also negatively affect the quality of the fact-finding. Whereas defendants can make their request conditional on the taking of further information, the public prosecutor is only entitled to produce evidence in rebuttal.[490] More worryingly, the injured party, though enabled to decide whether to accept this procedure, cannot request any further evidence. Further risks to a proper decision-making arise from the fact that the competent judges for the abbreviated proceedings, as noted, can gather at their own initiative integrative evidence in order to fill any knowledge gap. This task, which was certainly extraneous to the original functions of the competent judge for the pre-trial inquiry,[491] can give rise to a dangerous return to the old investigating magistrate.[492]

J. The Principle of *contradictoire* and Pre-Trial Restrictions on Freedom

I. Premise

Complex problems from the perspective of the participatory safeguards of the individuals concerned arise in the field of coercive measures. A highly problematic

[490] Under the current rules, prosecutors can request evidence in rebuttal if the accused requested supplementary information. Furthermore, the Constitutional Court extended this power to cases in which the defence, despite not requesting further evidence, produces the results of investigations previously carried out. See CConst, 184/2009.

[491] As noted, moreover, the 1999 reform enhanced the power of the competent judges for the pre-trial phases by enabling them also to take information at the intermediate stage at their own initiative. This power can only be exercised, however, in case of exculpatory evidence manifestly aimed at the termination of the proceedings in the intermediate phase.

[492] To be sure, the code's provision is quite ambiguous and has led to the case-law following different interpretations. Unlike the old investigating magistrates, the competent judge for the abbreviated proceedings must abide by the charges preferred by the prosecutor and can neither amend the prosecutorial charge nor elaborate different investigative strategies to prove the offence under prosecution. In this sense see Illuminati (2003), p. 82. Nevertheless, as noted, these judges can gather evidence at their own initiative when they consider that the state of the proceedings is not fit for judgment. This gives them unprecedented powers in the collection of evidence, which certainly go beyond their ordinary functions both in the pre-trial inquiry and in the intermediate phase. On close examination, the fact that the state of the proceedings is not fit for judgment is by definition a referential parameter that can be understood in very different fashions. If any judicial intervention is excluded in cases of complete information (in this sense see Fiorio 2008, p. 90), the need for integrative evidence can emerge either from the arguments brought about in the hearing *in camera* or from the evidence requested by the defence together with the request for abbreviate proceedings.

area concerns the procedure on the application of remand detention and further restrictions on freedom.[493] The decision on remand—based on the assessment of the two requirements of *fumus delicti* and *pericula libertatis*, of clear civil-law inspiration—may seem to provide a clear example of the aforementioned distinction between strict and free evaluation of evidence. On close examination, the complex human rights challenges of the decision on coercive measures do not entirely correspond to this formal distinction. On one hand, despite the valuable attempt to orient *fumus delicti* towards the requirement of *contradictoire*, the assessment of the suspicion of guilt is still largely based on untested evidence. On the other, the competent judge, while scrutinising the risks to the ongoing criminal inquiry, often needs to assess issues linked with the merits of the case and to make forecasts on substantial questions (*e.g.*, the severity of the sentence[494]).

Furthermore, the 1988 code, while largely relying on the last amendments of the previous codification,[495] dropped the possibility of coercive measures being adopted (like in the past) by the investigative prosecutor or the investigating magistrate, thus setting up a clear division of roles between the prosecutorial request and the decision-making. As a result, prosecutors could no longer apply coercive measures, which could only be enforced on the basis of a judicial order of the competent judge for the pre-trial inquiry who in turn needed a prosecutorial request. Despite these important structural innovations, as noted, the code did not give voice to the accused prior to the decision on the application coercive measures, which were therefore ordered solely on the basis of prosecutorial evidence. The result was, with a few minor exceptions, another example of decision *inaudito reo*, with the possibility of the individuals concerned being be heard after the judicial order has been issued and enforced.

In the light of this complex problematic area, the present discussion focuses on two main questions, i.e. (a) the participatory rights concerned with fact-finding in

---

[493]It should be taken into account that under Italian law, control measures (*e.g.*, suspension of the exercise of parental authority, the exercise of a public office or service or a certain business or occupation) are subject to the same general conditions laid down for remand detention and the alternatives to pre-trial custody.

[494]In some cases, the assessment of sentence thresholds is limited to statutory provisions. For instance, if remand detention is needed because of the risk of the suspect committing other offences of the same type as that under investigation, the competent judge must verify whether the other crimes are punishable with imprisonment of a maximum of at least 5 years. In this sense cf. Article 274(c) CCP, as amended by a recent reform on pre-trial measures—namely Law 47/2015—which raised the amount of sentence required to remand suspects in custody. In other cases, instead, the assessment of sentence thresholds entails concrete forecasts. For instance, under Article 274(b) CCP, the risk of absconding can only hold relevance for the purposes of the application of both control and coercive measures if a sentence is likely to be imposed of at least 2 years of imprisonment. This imposes on the competent judge the difficult task of determining, on the basis of the information available, the severity of the sentence pursuant to the general requirements set forth by Article 133 et seqq. CC.

[495]At the beginning of the 1980s, two important reforms largely amended the rules on remand detention. See Law 532/1982 and Law 398/1984. Shortly before the enactment of the new code, Law 330/1988 brought about further important innovations.

the decision on the application of coercive measures and (b) the participatory guarantees of the individuals concerned in the procedure on remand detention and further restrictions on liberty.

II. Participatory Rights and Fact-Finding in the Decision on Coercive Measures. Another Endurance Test for the Distinction Between Strict and Free Assessment of Evidence

Concerning the first problem area, we have noted that the fact that the application of coercive measures requires the assessment of the two requirements of *fumus delicti* and *pericula libertatis* apparently fit the distinction between the decision on substantial issues and the evaluation of procedural issues. Doubtless, suspicion of guilt is strictly linked with the merits of the case, whereas the risks of absconding or tampering with evidence may seem to concern questions unrelated with the alleged offence. From this it also follows that fact-finding should be based on different methods and types of evidence in the two cases. On close examination, this result, which highlights a rather formalistic understanding of this complex problem area, does not fit best the approach of the 1988 code. Thus the failure to enact clear rules on the assessment of evidence in the field of pre-trial measures[496] has allowed for wide use also of untested evidence for the purposes of the assessment of both *fumus delicti* and *pericula libertatis*.

Furthermore, the dynamics of the remand decision, initially based solely on the prosecutorial request, normally lead to the use of the information obtained by the investigative authorities. Of course, this does not apply to further decisions within the remand proceedings (*e.g.*, the decision on the continuation of imprisonment or its replacement with another measure of coercion), decisions which usually presuppose the contribution of the defence. For these grounds, however, one cannot expect that the decision on remand only relies on evidence collected in court, which would lead to the result that the information gathered by the defence lawyer should not be used. From a human rights perspective, this would entail grave repercussions on the right to freedom where coercive measures are underway during the trial inquiry. As noted, a rigid approach to fact-finding would lead to the result that even a request for release, justified on the subsequent loss of *fumus delicti*, could not be based on the information available, but that defendants should await the gathering of *contradictoire*-based evidence in their favour. Furthermore, if prosecutors had to await the collection of incriminating evidence at trial, it would give rise to dangerous forms of immunity for the accused.[497]

In sum, the assessment of suspicion of guilt, notwithstanding its strict link with the charge and the merits of the case, cannot ban the use of untested evidence and

[496] Negri (2004), p. 27 ff.

[497] Marzaduri (1996), p. 65 f.; Negri (2004), p. 166.

cannot entirely follow the methods of fact-finding governing the trial decision on guilt.[498] This does not mean, however, that the judicial authority can ignore the most basic requirements of the trial decision-making, *e.g*. by not requiring corroborating evidence in case of evidence given by a co-accused to the law enforcement authorities.[499] Over the 1990s, legal scholarship became increasingly aware of this problem and it is therefore to be welcomed that Law 63/2001 required the fulfilment of some important conditions of the trial fact-finding.[500]

Even so, the fragmentary nature of this legislation still left several questions open.[501] In particular, there are no clear statutory indications on the rules governing the decision on remand during the trial phase. On one hand, we have noted that the distinction between the trial file and the prosecutorial file cannot entail that any decision issued during the trial file can only be based on the evidence contained in the former. On the other, the widespread relevance of the information gathered by individual parties does not mean that untested evidence can unconditionally be used even though the information contracts with that collected in open court. The principle of proportionality especially requires the competent judge—and therefore also the trial court—to decide on the application or the maintenance of coercive measures as well as to make reliable forecasts regarding the accused's guilt and the sentence that will probably be imposed.[502] The weakening of the requirements of fact-finding can have serious implications in proceedings against serious offences and especially against mafia-type crimes. Here, Italian law, departing from the general understanding of pre-trial detention as *extrema ratio*, allows defendants to be remanded in custody solely on the basis of suspicion of guilt.[503]

---

[498]German scholars traditionally distinguish the proof of *Tatbestand* from that of *Tatverdacht*. The latter takes on particular characters in the field of interim decisions (*Tatverdachtsurteile*) not only due to the incompleteness of the information available but also because of the prognostic features of the fact-finding. On the *Tatverdachtsurteile* see Paeffgen (1986), p. 192. For an in-depth reflection on this topic see Negri (2004), p. 70 ff.

[499]In the light of the aforementioned criticisms on the gathering of evidence by co-defendants in the pre-trial inquiry, it is clear that not requiring corroborating evidence entails a further departure from the rules on the trial fact-finding, since suspects have no right to be present at the questioning of the co-accused.

[500]Art. 273(1-*bis*) CCP.

[501]Marzaduri (2002a), p. 266; Negri (2004), p. 143 f.

[502]For an in-depth analysis of this problem area in the light of principle of proportionality see Negri (2004), p. 150 ff. and 236 ff.

[503]The 1992 legislation provided for a very controversial regulation with regard to mafia-related crimes (mafia-type association, crimes committed using the typical conditions of mafia-type association and crimes of mafia abetting). Over more than two decades, this regulation has been largely amended. Recently, the legislature extended the scope of Article 275(3) CCP to the area of sexual offences and other serious crimes. This reform was largely countered by the Constitutional Court, which further narrowed the application of this exceptional mechanism. Cf. Di Chiara (2002), p. 133. Following the approach of the constitutional case-law, Law 47/2015 distinguished the special rules on remand detention according to two groups of serious crimes. In the case of the offences under Articles 270, 270-*bis* and 416-*bis* CC (subversive association, criminal association aimed at national and international terrorism and at subverting democratic order, and mafia-related

These observations also partially apply to the assessment of *pericula libertatis*, which, despite largely concerning issues unrelated to the alleged offence, cannot be based on any piece of evidence, including untested evidence. Furthermore, we have noted that this complex ascertainment does not exclusively concern procedural facts and that some risks of the ongoing proceedings are strictly connected with the merits of the case. The prognostic assessment of the probable punishment would inevitably provide unreliable results if it were based on information that the trial court could not use in determining the sentence to be imposed. Moreover, the evaluation of risks unconnected with the merits (*e.g.*, the risk of tampering with evidence) can also entail severe implications with regard to the right to liberty, determining the type of coercive measure and the degree of intrusiveness.

III. Audi alteram partem *in the Procedure on Remand Detention and Further Restrictions on Liberty*

1. Participatory Safeguards in the Procedure on the Application of Coercive Measures. The Inconveniences of Another Example of *inaudito reo* Proceedings

It has been observed that the 1988 code construed the new procedure on the application of pre-trial measures, with certain exceptions,[504] pursuant to the traditional doctrine of *inaudito reo* decisions. As a result, individuals restricted in their most precious rights for the purposes of an ongoing criminal inquiry (right to liberty, right to free movement, etc.) can only be heard after the judicial order and, even worse, after

criminal association), remand detention is applied if suspicion of guilt arises, unless it was proven that no risk exists to the ongoing inquiry. In the case of other serious crimes (murder, sexual crimes, etc.), the same mechanism applies, with the difference, however, that alternatives to custody can also be applied in cases of attenuated risks to the proceedings.

At first glance, it appears that Italian law provides for proper balance among conflicting interests, allowing for the application of remand detention on the basis of a rebuttable presumption of dangerousness of defendants charged with these crimes. However, the code exonerates the judicial authority from assessing the real existence of any concrete risk to the ongoing inquiry. Thus evidence in rebuttal must, as a rule, be produced by the defendant. Furthermore, the possibility of overturning the presumption of dangerousness depends on very exigent proof on the part of the defence. From the perspective of the present discussion, the fact that the assessment of suspicion of guilt provides the sole justification of remand detention appears to be highly problematic especially in the cases of mafia-related criminal association and of sexual crimes, in which one can observe the widespread tendency of proving *fumus delicti* on the basis of dangerous inferences and presumptions. On the fact-finding in the field of mafia-typed crimes see the comprehensive analysis of Maggio (2010), p. 491 ff.

[504]In particular, the accused must be previously examined when a coercive measure is to be applied in the hearing aimed at validating arrest and when a new period of detention is needed after a previous pre-trial detention has expired because of the failure to bring the accused to the judicial authority. Cf. respectively Arts. 294(1) and 302 CCP.

the measure has been enforced. Here also, like in the field of penal order procedures, the main question is whether this abstract mechanism can ensure for the accused a fair opportunity to be heard and to contribute to the decision-making. Furthermore, it must be examined whether a subsequent hearing allows for a fair re-assessment of the lawfulness and justification of restriction on fundamental freedoms.

Unlike other European Constitutions,[505] the Italian Constitution did not require the judicial authority to hear the individuals subject to long-term restrictions on freedom—not only prior to the judicial order but also afterwards. Doubtless, this significant lacuna impinged on the further developments that occurred in Italian criminal justice. It is therefore not surprising that the 1988 code not only did not acknowledge the accused's right to be heard prior to the decision-making but also construed the subsequent hearing in a highly questionable way. Apparently, the code strengthened the participatory rights of the individuals concerned by requiring a short-distance judicial hearing of the accused on pain of loss of validity of the ongoing measure.[506] Yet, as noted, this solution had considerable shortcomings, which severely affected the right of the person concerned to be fairly heard and to effectively participate in the procedure. Notwithstanding the guarantee of a judicial hearing, prosecutors could originally question the defendant before the judicial authority and the lawyer's presence at the hearing was not mandatory, with the result that defendants had to face alone the same authority who requested the coercive measure.

This approach became be inadequate already in the first years after the enactment of the new code. However, it took several years before the legislature brought about some changes. The first important reform was carried out by Law 332/1995, which banned prosecutorial questioning before the individuals concerned had been heard by the judicial authority.[507] Yet prosecutorial questionings were still allowed after provisional arrest and even in the hearing after the enforcement of remand detention,[508] the accused was not always assisted by a lawyer. It was only the 2001 fair trial legislation that enhanced the right to a defence by requiring the assistance of a lawyer in the remand hearing,[509] thus making the questioning conducted without a counsel void. We will also see that a recent reform, implementing EU law, enacted into the code new rules requiring defendants to be informed in an

[505]For instance, German Basic Law grants the individuals concerned the right to be informed of the grounds for arrest, a fundamental right that, moreover, entails the duty of the competent authority to hear them and allow them to raise objections and complaints against the arrest order. Cf. Art. 104(3) Basic Law. Remarkably, these guarantees also apply when the judicial authority orders pre-trial detention. This highlights that Germany enshrined at the constitutional level the right of detained individuals to obtain an independent assessment of the lawfulness of detention on the basis of their allegations and claims. Cf. Gusy (2010), p. 1091; Müller-Franken (2010), p. 103.

[506]Art. 294(4) CCP.

[507]Art. 294(6) CCP.

[508]CConst, 384/1996.

[509]Art. 294(4) CCP.

understandable language, *inter alia*, of their right to know the charge filed against them and the evidence supporting the coercive measure adopted.[510]

Notwithstanding these developments, it can be doubted that Italian law can still ensure full compensation for the failure to involve the defence prior to the application of pre-trial measures. To start with, it is clear that the effectiveness of legal assistance in remand hearings largely depends on the possibility of defendants communicating with their lawyer. During the pre-trial inquiry, however, prosecutors can request the competent judge to postpone the interview between the detained suspects and their lawyer.[511] It is true that the prosecutorial request must be justified by specific and exceptional grounds but these rather vague statutory indications can give rise to abuses. From this it follows that defendants may happen to meet with (or even be introduced to) their lawyer only at the judicial hearing, which makes legal assistance, despite its mandatory nature, a purely formal guarantee.[512]

This situation is highly detrimental especially for defendants remanded into custody, who can remain up to 5 days without communication with their lawyer. Since this is the same time limit for the judicial authority to examine them,[513] defendants will inevitably loose any possibility of setting up a defensive strategy before the judicial hearing.[514] The conditions for effective defence are further reduced when taking into account the fact that prosecutors can also request the moving forward of the remand hearing to within 48 h from the enforcement of the coercive measure.[515] If this result offers the advantage of moving forward the judicial guarantee, the postponement of the communications between the accused and his lawyer can have serious repercussions on the participatory rights and the right to freedom.

Doubtless, this set-up reveals the scant attention paid by Italian law to the defence's contribution to the assessment of the lawfulness of coercive measures. A fair lawfulness test should require the fulfilment of specific qualitative conditions to enable the defence to produce exculpatory evidence and to contest the prosecutorial information that supported the judicial order. Yet Italian law still has considerable backwardness in this regard, notwithstanding some recent steps forward resulted from the implementation of EU law.[516] To a great extent, the fairness of the judicial hearing also depends on the impartiality of the competent authority. Nevertheless, Italian law does not provide for any mechanism to prevent the accused from being heard by the same judge who remanded him into custody or

[510] Legislative Decree 101/2014. See Chap. 16, D.VI.1.b.

[511] Art. 104(3) CCP.

[512] In these cases, the hearing is void only if the postponement of the interview with the lawyer was unlawfully ordered. Cf. Montagna (2010), p. 3156.

[513] Art. 294(1) CCP.

[514] The negative effects of the postponement are reduced in case of house arrest, further coercive means and control measures, since the hearing must here take place within 10 days.

[515] Art. 294(1-*ter*) CCP.

[516] Legislative Decree 101/2014. See Chap. 16, D.VI.3.

ordered another restriction on freedom against him on the basis of prosecutorial and police evidence. This makes it extremely difficult for the defence to obtain an impartial re-examination of the justification of the measure applied.[517]

2. Participatory Rights in the Judicial Review Proceedings Against Coercive Measures

Another problematic issue is whether defendants who have been submitted to a coercive measure can undertake a legal action and which participatory rights Italian law ensures to them in these proceedings. The approach followed by the Rocco code, which excluded any initiative on the part of the accused, became inadequate after the 1947 Constitution that enabled the individuals concerned to lodge an appeal before the Supreme Court against any judicial order entailing restriction on liberty.[518] Even though it certainly constituted an important step forward, the appeal before the Supreme Court did not raise the danger of the unjustified prolongation of remand detention.[519] The shortcoming was clearly due to the minimalist solution, which guaranteed to the individuals concerned a slow judicial control, limited, moreover, to the sole points of law.

This approach became unsatisfactory after the ratification in Italy of the European Convention and the International Covenant, which granted any person deprived of liberty the right to undertake proceedings with a view to obtaining rapid judicial oversight on the lawfulness of detention. It took, however, several years for a legislative intervention, a result probably due not only to the self-restraint of the European Court, which considered the guarantee of *habeas corpus* 'absorbed' in the case of detention ordered by the judicial authority,[520] but also to the former European Commission[521] that deemed the appeal before the Supreme Court a proper solution.[522] It was only Law 532/1982 that introduced a specific remedy aimed at ensuring to the accused, at his own request, a review by a special court (*tribunale della libertà*) of the lawfulness of coercive measures, a judicial review that, unlike the judicial examination by the Supreme Court, also allowed a full oversight of the merits of the coercive measure.[523] This tool, redefined by the 1984

---

[517] Italian courts rule out, however, that the hearing conducted by a different judge is void. Cf. CCass, *Caruso*.

[518] Originally, this provision was enacted into the paragraph 2 of Article 111 of the Constitution. By means of the 1999 constitutional fair trial reform, this provision was shifted to paragraph 7 of the same Article.

[519] Marzaduri (1986), p. 773.

[520] Chapter 8, G.III.

[521] EComHR, *Bonazzi v. Italy*.

[522] Chiavario (1984), p. 356 ff.; Marzaduri (1986), p. 773.

[523] Art. 263-*bis* of the 1930 CCP.

reform on pre-trial measures, was reproduced by the 1988 code in the context of a general reform of the remedies against coercive measures.

The arrangements of the current codification allow for wide judicial oversight of the lawfulness of coercive measures. Defendants who are subject to restrictions on liberty or free movement[524] can either lodge an appeal on points of law before the Court of Cassation[525] or request a court review by *tribunale della libertà*.[526] The review proceedings can be activated by both the accused and his lawyer who do not need to challenge the judicial decision ordering a coercive measure by including specific complaints into their request for review.[527] Therefore, the competent court is not called upon to scrutinise specific issues of the judicial order but must re-assess the overall lawfulness and justification of the coercive measure applied. Unlike in the judicial hearing under Article 294 CCP, coercive measures are here assessed by a court other than the judge who ordered them. Further shortcomings of that hearing do not arise in the field of review proceedings. In particular, Law 332/1995 strengthened the right to effective defence by excluding from the calculation of the deadlines for requesting the judicial review the days in which the interview with the lawyer was postponed.[528] More recently, Law 47/2015 enhanced the participatory rights in the review hearing by acknowledging the accused's right to appear in court personally,[529] right that was previously subject to the ordinary rules on hearings *in camera*. It is important to note that the rules on the review proceedings lay down a powerful means of ensuring a rapid decision, providing for that the judicial order ceases to have effect if the competent judge who ordered the coercive measure does not submit within 5 days all the necessary documents to *tribunale della libertà*, which must in turn decide within the short term of 10 days.[530]

Notwithstanding these merits, the judicial review also presents certain drawbacks, and further problems have recently arisen from the changes made by the 2015 reform on pre-trial measures. The period available for requesting the judicial review is still relatively short (10 days) and if the defendant requests it personally within 2 days after being served of the judicial order, Law 47/2015 allowed for the competent court to postpone the hearing.[531] Of course, this innovation aims at enabling the accused to consult his lawyer and to prepare a better defence strategy. However, this arrangement also entails the postponement of the deadline for

[524]Control measures fall outside the scope of this judicial review.

[525]Art. 311(2) CCP.

[526]Art. 309 CCP.

[527]Art. 309(6) CCP. The 2015 reform enabled the defendant who requested judicial review to state new reasons before the hearing.

[528]Art. 309(3-*bis*) CCP.

[529]Art. 309(8-*bis*) CCP. The 2015 reform also enabled the public prosecutor who requested the coercive measure to appear in court instead of the prosecutor before *tribunale della libertà*.

[530]Art. 309(10) CCP.

[531]Art. 309(3-*bis*) CCP.

decision, which impinges on the maintenance of the effects of the judicial order. It should also be noted that the 2015 reform softened the previous radical solution, which provided for the expiration of the measure enforced, by allowing for the possibility of a new coercive means being applied in exceptional cases.[532]

A highly problematic issue concerns the information on which decision will be based. In this regard, the 2015 reform missed an important opportunity for an in-depth reflection on the solution of Article 291 CCP, which, as noted, allows for prosecutors to withhold relevant information from both the defence and the competent court to review coercive measures. Consequently, Law 47/2015 did not bring about any innovation on this important point, with the result that the competent judge must only submit to *tribunale della libertà* the documents already attached by the prosecutor to the request for a coercive measure as well as the all the elements in favour of the individuals concerned, which emerged afterwards.[533] This will probably lead Italian courts to maintain their previous approach, which, relying on the distinction between 'documents' and 'elements', allows for prosecutors even to submit extracts from the deeds and documents available.[534] There is little doubt that this approach can negatively affect the participatory rights of the individuals concerned, jeopardising their right to contrast the incriminating evidence gathered by the investigative bodies. Apparently, the 2015 reform strengthened the relevance of the proactive role of the defence by requiring *tribunale della libertà* to annul the judicial order if it did not give any reasons not only on the justification of the measure applied but also if it did not assess the information produced by the defence.[535] Yet the innovative force of this provision is reduced, taking into account that coercive measures are usually ordered *inaudito reo* and that several hurdles can impede the effective exercise of the defence rights in the hearing under 294 CCP.

Ultimately, it should be noted that the judicial review has a limited scope of application, being only allowed against the judicial decision that ordered a coercive measure. Any further decision within the remand proceedings and, more generally, any further decision during the enforcement of the measure applied (*e.g.*, the decision on the extension of the length of the measure applied) can be challenged through a special appeal.[536] This is however governed by the general rules on hearings *in camera*, with the result that defendants must only be heard if they appear in court.[537] As an alternative, the accused can at any time request a review of the justification of the measure applied by the competent judge for the stage of the proceedings in which the measure is underway, and the judicial authority can

[532]Art. 309(10) CCP. Even though the competent court must give reasons of these 'exceptional grounds', the vague formulation enacted leaves a great margin of discretion.

[533]Art. 309(5) CCP.

[534]CCass, *Plaku*.

[535]Art. 309(10) CCP.

[536]Art. 310 CCP.

[537]Art. 310(2) CCP.

revoke or replace the measure within another.[538] However, the general rules on hearings *in camera* also apply to this review and Italian law does not require the competent judge to hear the accused prior to the decision-making, except if new elements have arisen.[539] Furthermore, this tool has evident limitations. It may happen that the same judge who ordered the coercive measure will rule on the defence's request for revocation or substitution with a less intrusive measure. Moreover, the Supreme Court has widely developed a form of *ne bis in idem* with a view to avoiding that the defence requests the competent judge to review the lawfulness of pre-trial measures in relation to issues already assessed by a higher court *tribunale della libertà* through a final decision.[540] Most worryingly, there is no obligation for the competent judge to review the lawfulness of a long-term measure at certain intervals of time. As we will see, this issue is very problematic in the light of the findings of the European case-law.[541]

K. Provisional Conclusions

The analysis of Italian law reveals a highly complex scenario, which still has several deficiencies and contradictions. The 1988 code marked a fundamental step for the abandonment of certain old practices of the mixed system and the enhancement of the role of private parties in criminal proceedings. However, this was a long road and several developments have occurred over almost 30 years after the code's entry into force. It took more than 10 years before a constitutional model of a fair criminal trial was enacted and since then, neither statutory law nor Italian courts have followed coherent lines.

It must be acknowledged that several steps forward were made to satisfy the new constitutional requirements, especially under the growing influence of the Strasbourg case-law and, more recently, of EU law, as we will see at a later stage of this study. Among the most significant developments, we can observe the rising tendency to abandon a dual understanding of criminal justice and to draw the focus towards individuals involved in criminal proceedings, other than the accused. A close examination of Italian law provides, however, a fragmentary picture and the lack of a uniform approach to criminal justice. The contradictions of some important recent reforms (in particular, the legislation on default proceedings and pre-trial measures) highlight the difficulties in shifting from the old culture of criminal justice to a model truly inspired by the idea that the balanced involvement of private parties in criminal proceedings is an essential condition of a reliable fact-finding.

---

[538] Art. 299 CCP.

[539] Art. 299(3-*ter*) CCP.

[540] For criticisms against the so-called '*ne bis in idem* cautelare' see Ruggeri (2010).

[541] Chapter 8, G.II.

References

Amodio E (2001) Giusto processo, diritto al silenzio e obblighi di verità dell'imputato sul fatto altrui. Cassazione penale, pp 3592 ff

Ashworth A, Redmayne M (2010) The criminal process, 4th edn. Oxford University Press, Oxford

Balsamo A, Lo Piparo A (2004) La prova "per sentito dire". La testimonianza indiretta tra teoria e prassi applicativa. Giuffrè, Milano

Bargis M (1996) Commento all'art. 13 legge 66/1996. La Legislazione penale, pp 498ff

Bellavista G (1952) Il processo penale monitorio, 2nd edn. Giuffrè, Milano

Bene T (2004) L'avviso di conclusione delle indagini. ESI, Napoli

Busetto ML (2009) Il contraddittorio inquinato. Cedam, Padova

Caianiello M (2003) Poteri dei privati nell'esercizio dell'azione penale. Giappichelli, Torino

Calamandrei P (1926) Il procedimento monitorio nella legislazione italiana. Unitas, Milano

Campo A (1993) Sulla legittimazione della persona offesa a ricorrere per cassazione ex art. 409 comma 6 c.p.p. avverso il provvedimento di archiviazione emesso in violazione del contraddittorio. Cassazione penale, pp 1496–1500

Caprioli F (1994) L'archiviazione. Jovene, Napoli

Caprioli F (2000) Nuovi epiloghi della fase investigativa: procedimenti contro ignoti e avviso di conclusione delle indagini preliminari. In: Peroni F (ed) Il processo penale dopo la riforma del giudice unico. Cedam, Padova, pp 245–285

Caprioli F (2002) Palingenesi di un divieto probatorio. La testimonianza del funzionario di polizia nel rinnovato assetto processuale. In: Kostoris RE (ed) Il giusto processo tra contraddittorio e diritto al silenzio. Giappichelli, Torino, pp 59–91

Caprioli F (2004) "Giusto processo" e rito degli irreperibili. In: La Legislazione penale, pp 586 ff

Caprioli F (2014) Indagini preliminari e udienza preliminare. In: Conso G, Grevi V, Bargis M (eds) Compendio di procedura penale, 7th edn. Wolters Kluwer Italia/Cedam, Padova, pp 512–686

Caprioli F (2015) Prime considerazioni sul proscioglimento per particolare tenuità del fatto. Diritto penale contemporaneo (rivista trimestrale 2/2015), pp 82–105

Carcano D, Manzione D (2001) Il giusto processo. Commento alla legge 1 marzo 2001, n. 63. Giuffrè, Milano

Carnelutti F (1924) Nota intorno alla natura del processo monitorio. Rivista di diritto processuale civile, pp 270 ff

Carnelutti F (1947) Lezioni sul processo penale. II vol. Ed. dell'Ateneo, Roma

Carnelutti F (1949) Processo contro ignoti. Rivista italiana di diritto processuale, II, pp 257 ff

Carnelutti F (1963) Verso la riforma del processo penale. Morano, Napoli

Carrara F (1875) Azione penale. Rivista penale, pp 4 ff

Catalano EM (2002) L'accertamento dei fatti processuali. Indice penale, pp 521–570

Cesari C (2006) Le clausole di irrilevanza del fatto nel sistema processuale penale. Giappichelli, Torino

Chiavario M (1969) La Convenzione europea dei diritti dell'uomo nel sistema delle fonti normative in materia penale. Giuffrè, Milano

Chiavario M (1971) Il pubblico ministero organo di giustizia? Rivista italiana di diritto e procedura penale, pp 714–743

Chiavario M (1975) Appunti sulla problematica dell'"azione" nel processo penale italiano: incertezze, prospettive e limiti. Rivista trimestrale di diritto e procedura civile, pp 864 ff

Chiavario M (1984) Processo penale e garanzie della persona, II, Le garanzie fondamentali, 3rd edn. Giuffrè, Milano

Conti C (2000) Le due anime del contraddittorio. Diritto penale e processo, pp 197–202

Conti C (2001a) Principio del contraddittorio e utilizzabilità delle precedenti dichiarazioni. Diritto penale e processo, pp 592–607

Conti C (2001b) Giusto processo (diritto processuale penale). In: Enciclopedia del diritto, vol V Agg. Giuffrè, Milano, pp 627–649

Conti C (2003) L'imputato nel procedimento connesso. Diritto al silenzio e obbligo di verità. Cedam, Padova
Conti C (2013) Contraddittorio. In: Digesto delle discipline penalistiche, vol VII Agg. Utet, Torino, pp 103–122
Cordero F (1958) Archiviazione. In Enciclopedia del diritto, vol II. Giuffrè, Milano, pp 1025–1035
Cordero F (1963) Tre studi sulle prove penali. Giuffrè, Milano
Cordero F (1966) Ideologie del processo penale. Giuffrè, Milano
Cordero F (1987) Procedura penale, 9th edn. Giuffrè, Milano
Cordero F (1992) Codice commentato, 2nd edn. Utet, Torino
Cordero F (2012) Procedura penale, 9th edn. Giuffrè, Milano
Di Bitonto ML (2004) Profili dispositivi dell'accertamento penale. Giappichelli, Torino
Di Chiara G (1994) Il contraddittorio nei riti camerali. Giuffrè, Milano
Di Chiara G (1997) Testimonianza dei "soggetti deboli" e limiti all'esame incrociato. Giurisprudenza costituzionale pp 2564 ff
Di Chiara G (2002) Incidente probatorio. In: Enciclopedia del diritto, VI Agg. Giuffrè, Milano, pp 546–565
Di Chiara G (2003) Diritto processuale penale. In: Fiandaca G, Di Chiara G (eds) Una introduzione al sistema penale. Per una lettura costituzionalmente orientata. Jovene, Napoli, pp 189–365
Di Chiara G (ed) (2009) Eccezioni al contraddittorio e giusto processo. Un itinerario attraverso la giurisprudenza. Giappichelli, Torino
Ebert A (2000) Der Tatverdacht im Strafverfahren unter spezieller Berücksichtigung des Tatnachweises im Strafbefehlsverfahren. Peter Lang, Frankfurt am Main
Ferrua P (1992) La sentenza costituzionale n. 255 del 1992: declino del processo accusatorio. Rivista italiana di diritto e procedura penale, pp 1455ff
Ferrua P (2009) La dialettica regola-eccezioni nell'impianto dell'art. 111 Cost.: il quadro sistematico. In: Di Chiara G (ed) Eccezioni al contraddittorio e giusto processo. Un itinerario attraverso la giurisprudenza. Giappichelli, Torino, pp 3–40
Ferrua P (2012) Il 'giusto processo', 3rd edn. Zanichelli, Bologna
Ferrua P (2013) La prova nel processo penale: profili generali. In: Ferrua P, Marzaduri E, Spangher G (eds) La prova penale. Giappichelli, Torino, pp 1–56
Fiorio C (2008) La nuova prova nel processo penale. Giappichelli, Torino
Gaeta P (2001) Le modifiche alla disciplina delle informazioni assunte dal pubblico ministero e dalla polizia giudiziaria. In: Tonini P (ed) Giusto processo. Nuove norme sulla formazione e valutazione della prova. Cedam, Padova, pp 431–443
Galantini N (1992) L'inutilizzabilità della prova nel processo penale. Cedam, Padova
Garlati L (ed) (2010) L'inconscio inquisitorio. L'eredità del Codice Rocco nella cultura processualpenalistica italiana. Giuffrè, Milano
Gialuz M (2008) Applicazione della pena su richiesta delle parti. In: Enciclopedia del diritto, Annali II-1. Giuffrè, Milano, pp 13–47
Giostra G (1994) L'archiviazione. Lineamenti sistematici e questioni interpretative, 2nd edn. Giappichelli, Torino
Giostra G (2001) Contraddittorio (principio del): II) Diritto processuale penale. In: Enciclopedia giuridica Treccani, vol VIII. Treccani, Roma, pp 1–13
Giostra G (2002) Prova e contraddittorio. Note a margine di una garbata polemica. Cassazione penale, pp 3288–3292
Giuliani L (2016) Indagini preliminari e udienza preliminare. In: Conso G, Grevi V, Bargis M (eds) Compendio di procedura penale, 8th edn. Wolters Kluwer/Cedam, Padova, pp 457–591
Grevi V (2000) Alla ricerca di un processo penale giusto. Giuffrè, Milano
Grifantini FM (2007) Utilizzabilità in dibattimento degli atti provenienti dale fasi anteriori. In: Ferrua P, Grifantini FM, Illuminati G, Orlandi R (eds) La prova nel dibattimento penale, 3rd edn. Giappichelli, Torino, pp 167–313
Gusy C (2010). Article 104. In: von Mangoldt H, Klein F, Starck C (eds) Kommentar zum Grundgesetz, III vol. (Arts. 83–146), 6th edn. Vahlen Verlag, München, paras. 1–78

Iasevoli C (2007) Persona offesa dal reato. In: Enciclopedia giuridica Treccani, vol XXIII. Treccani, Roma, pp 1–8
Illuminati G (2003) Il giudizio senza oralità. In: Verso la scoperta di un modello processuale. Giuffrè, Milano, pp 67 ff
Kostoris RE (1993) I consulenti tecnici nel processo penale. Giuffrè, Milano
Lorusso S (2008) Una scelta di efficienza processuale che non legittima forzature o abusi. Guida al diritto 11:67ff
Lozzi G (1997) I princìpi di oralità e del contraddittorio nel processo penale. Rivista italiana di diritto e procedura penale, pp 669–693
Luiso FP (1981) Principio del contraddittorio ed efficacia della sentenza verso terzi. Giuffrè, Milano
Maggio P (2010) Prova e valutazione giudiziale dei comportamenti mafiosi: i risvolti processuali. In: Fiandaca G, Visconti C (eds) Scenari di Mafia. Orizzonti criminologici e innovazioni normative. Giappichelli, Torino, pp 491–519
Mangiaracina A (2010) Garanzie partecipative e giudizio in absentia. Giappichelli, Torino
Marzaduri E (1986) Riesame dei provevdimenti restrittivi della libertà personale. In: Novissimo digesto italiano, Appendice. Utet, Torino, pp 771–787
Marzaduri E (1990) Brevi considerazioni sui poteri del giudice nell'applicazione della pena su richiesta delle parti. Cassazione penale, pp 729–733
Marzaduri E (1994) Misure cautelari personali (princìpi generali e disciplina). In: Digesto delle discipline penalistiche, vol VIII. Utet, Torino, pp 59 ff
Marzaduri E (1996) Azione: d) diritto processuale penale. In: Enciclopedia giuridica Treccani, vol V. Treccani, Roma, pp 1–23
Marzaduri E (1997) Commento agli artt. 2-3 legge 234/1997. La Legislazione penale, pp 750–765
Marzaduri E (1998) Commento all'art. 275. In: Chiavario M (ed) Commento al nuovo codice di procedura penale, vol III Agg. Utet, Torino, pp 162–192
Marzaduri E (2000) Commento all'art. 1 legge costituzionale 2/1999. In: La Legislazione penale, pp. 762-804
Marzaduri E (2002a) Giusto processo e misure cautelari. In: Kostoris RE (ed) Il giusto processo, tra contraddittorio e diritto al silenzio. Giappichelli, Torino, pp. 261ff.
Marzaduri E (2002b) Commento all'art. 3 l. 63/2001. La Legislazione penale, pp 164–172
Marzaduri E (2004a) Note minime in tema di giusto processo penale. In: Various Authors, Nuove forme di tutela delle situazioni soggettive. Aspetti pubblicistici. Giuffrè, Milano, pp 283–298
Marzaduri E (2004b) Indagini preliminari e modello processuale: profili di incoerenza originaria del codice Vassalli. In: Verso la riscoperta di un modello processuale. Giuffrè, Milano, pp 223–226
Marzaduri E (2004c) Commento agli artt. 1-3 legge 134/2003. La Legislazione penale, pp 241–258
Marzaduri E (2008) Spunti per una riflessione sui presupposti applicativi delle intercettazioni telefoniche a fini probatori. Cassazione penale, pp 4833–4853
Marzaduri E (2009) La prova negoziata e l'art. 111 Cost.: tra deroga al contraddittorio e valorizzazione dei profili dispositivi dell'accertamento penale. In: Di Chiara G (ed) Eccezioni al contraddittorio e giusto processo. Un itinerario attraverso la giurisprudenza. Giappichelli, Torino, pp 189–224
Marzaduri E (2016) Procedimento penale davanti al giudice di pace. In: Conso G, Grevi V, Bargis M (eds) Compendio di procedura penale, 8th edn. Wolters Kluwer Italia/Cedam, Padova, pp 1099–1147
Montagna M (2010) Art. 294. In: Giarda A, Spangher G (eds), Codice di procedura penale commentato. I Tomo, 4th edn. Ipsoa, Milano
Morosini PG (2009) Provata condotta illecita e processo per fatti di criminalità organizzata. In: Di Chiara G (ed) Eccezioni al contraddittorio e giusto processo. Un itinerario attraverso la giurisprudenza. Giappichelli, Torino, pp 387–411

Müller-Franken S (2010) Art. 104. In: Stern K, Becker F (eds) Grundrechte-Kommentar, Carl Heymanns Verlag, Köln, paras. 1–129

Negri D (2004) *Fumus commissi delicti*. La prova per le fattispecie cautelari. Giappichelli, Torino

Negri D (2005) Commento all'art. 1 Decreto-legge 17/2005. La Legislazione penale, pp 260–291

Negri D (2014) L'imputato presente al processo. Una ricostruzione sistematica. Giappichelli, Torino

Nobili M (1998) Scenari e trasformazioni del processo penale. Cedam, Padova

Nobili M (2001) Giusto processo e indagini difensive: verso una nuova procedura penale? Diritto penale e processo, pp 5–14

Orlandi R (1992) Atti e informazioni dell'autorità amministrativa nel processo penale. Giuffrè, Milano

Orlandi R (2010) L'attività argomentativa delle parti nel dibattimento penale. In: Ferrua P, Grifantini FM, Illuminati G, Orlandi R (eds) La prova nel dibattimento penale, 4th edn. Giappichelli, Torino, pp 3 ff.

Paeffgen H-U (1986) Vorüberlegungen zu einer Dogmatik des Untersuchungshaftsrechts. Carl Heymann, Mainz

Parlato L (2012) Il contributo della vittima tra azione e prova. Torri del Vento, Palermo

Pieth M (2012) Schweizerisches Strafprozessrecht, 2nd edn. Helbing Lichtenhahn Verlag, Basel

Quattrocolo S (2004) Esiguità del fatto e regole per l'esercizio dell'azione penale. Jovene, Napoli

Quattrocolo S (2014) Il contumace cede la scena processuale all'assente, mentre l'irreperibile l'abbandona. Riflessioni a prima lettura sulla nuova disciplina del procedimento senza imputato. www.penalecontemporaneo.it. Accessed 30 Apr 2014

Rivello PP (1993) Commento all'art. 7 Decreto-legge 306/1992. La Legislazione penale, pp 92–103

Ruggeri S (2002) Esercizio dell'azione penale, pubblico ministero e persona offesa nella prospettiva del procedimento davanti al giudice di pace. Giurisorudenza italiana, pp 655–660

Ruggeri S (2008) Il procedimento per decreto penale. Dalla logica dell'accertamento sommario alla dinamica del giudizio. Giappichelli, Torino

Ruggeri S (2009) Il procedimento per decreto penale. In: Di Chiara G (ed) Eccezioni al contraddittorio e giusto processo. Un itinerario attraverso la giurisprudenza. Giappichelli, Torino, pp 133–188

Ruggeri A (2010) Corte costituzionale e Corti europee: il modello, le esperienze, le prospettive. Centro di documentazione europea (Università di Catania), http://www.cde.unict.it/sites/default/files/19_2010.pdf

Ruggeri A (2015a) "Dialogue" between European and national courts, in the pursuit of the strongest protection of fundamental rights (with specific regard to criminal and procedural law). In: Ruggeri S (ed) Human rights in European criminal law. New developments in european legislation and case law after the Lisbon treaty. Springer, Heidelberg, pp 9–29

Ruggeri S (2015b) Investigative and prosecutorial discretion in criminal matters: the contribution of the Italian experience. In: Caianiello M, Hodgson J (eds), Discretionary criminal justice in a comparative context. Carolina Academic Press, Durham (North Carolina), pp 59–85

Scalfati A (1999) L'udienza preliminare. Profili di una disciplina in trasformazione. Cedam, Padova

Scalfati A (2000) Le nuove prospettive del decreto penale. In: Peroni F (ed) Il processo penale dopo la riforma del giudice unico. Cedam, Padova, pp 521 ff

Siracusano D (1973) Istruzione del processo penale. In: Enciclopedia del diritto, vol XXIII. Giuffrè, Milano, pp 166–204

Siracusano F (2008) Investigazioni difensive. In: Enciclopedia del diritto, Annali II-1. Giuffrè, Milano, pp 496–518

Spencer JR (2014) Hearsay evidence in criminal proceedings, II edn. Hart Publishing, Oxford

Többens HW (1979) Der Freibeweis und die Prozessvoraussetzungen im Strafprozess. Freiburg i.Br

Tonini P (2001) Riforma del sistema probatorio: un'attuazione parziale del "giusto processo". Diritto penale e processo, pp 269–273

Tranchina G (1961) Il procedimento per decreto penale e l'art. 24 della Costituzione. Rivista di diritto processuale, pp 516 ff
Tranchina G (1989) Persona offesa dal reato. In: Enciclopedia giuridica Treccani, vol XXIII. Treccani, Roma, pp 1 ff
Ubertis G (1995) Prova (in generale). In: Digesto delle discipline penalistiche, vol X. Utet, Torino, pp 296–338
Ubertis G (2002) Prova e contraddittorio. Cassazione penale, pp 1182–1184
Ubertis G (2009) Principi di procedura penale europea, 2nd edn. Raffaello Cortina, Milano
Ubertis G (2013) Sistema di procedura penale, Principi generali, vol I, 3rd edn. Utet, Torino
Vogler R (2014) Criminal evidence and respect for fair trial guarantees in the dialogue between the European court of human rights and national courts. In: Ruggeri S (ed) Transnational evidence and multicultural inquiries in Europe. Developments in EU legislation and new challenges for human rights-oriented criminal investigations in cross-border cases. Springer, Heidelberg, pp 181–192
Volk K (1978) Prozeßvoraussetzungen im Strafrecht. Zum Verhältniss von materiellem Recht und Prozeßrecht. Ebelsbach am Main
Zumpano MA (2000) Rapporti tra processo civile e processo penale. Giappichelli, Torino

Chapter 3
Participatory Rights in Brazilian Law and the Requirements of *contradictoire* and Full Defence in Criminal Proceedings

Contents

A. Premise 130
B. Participatory Safeguards in the Constitutional Model of a Fair Trial. The Right to *contradictoire* and Full Defence 130
C. *Audi alteram partem* and Equality of Arms 132
D. The Role of Private Parties in the Decision to Charge 135
I. Participatory Rights of the Victim in the Initiation of Criminal Proceedings. The Forms of Private Criminal Prosecution 135
II. The Involvement of Private Parties in the Decision Not to Institute or to Drop a Criminal Prosecution 136
E. The Principle of *contradictoire* and Right to Information in Criminal Proceedings 138
I. The Right to Information in the Pre-Trial Stage 138
II. Charging Decision and the Need for Proper Information on the Initiation of Criminal Proceedings 140
F. Prosecutorial Needs and the Right to Take Part Personally in Criminal Proceedings. The Problem of *in absentia* Procedures in Brazilian Law 141
G. Investigative Needs and the Right to Be Fairly Heard 145
I. The Right to Be Fairly Heard in the Pre-Trial Phase 145
II. The Right to Be Fairly Heard in Court Proceedings 146
H. *Audi alteram partem* and the Collection of Evidence 149
I. The Right to *contradictoire* in Obtaining Oral Evidence 149
II. The Right to *contradictoire* in the Taking of Expert Evidence 151
III. The Right to *contradictoire* and Documentary Evidence 152
I. *Audi alteram partem* and the Proof of Guilt 153
J. *Audi alteram partem* and the Use of Measures of Coercion 155
I. Premise 155
II. The Right to *contradictoire* and Restrictions on Freedom 155
1. Participatory Safeguards in Remand Proceedings 155
2. *Audi alteram partem* and Provisional Arrest 159
3. The Right to Be fairly Heard in Cases of Temporary Detention 160
III. The Right to Be fairly Heard and Investigative Interferences with Fundamental Rights 161
IV. *Audi alteram partem* in *habeas corpus* Proceedings 162
1. *Habeas corpus* in Brazilian Law 162
2. Participatory Rights in *habeas corpus* Proceedings 163
K. Interim Conclusions 164
References 165

S. Ruggeri, Audi Alteram Partem *in Criminal Proceedings*,
DOI 10.1007/978-3-319-54573-8_3

A. Premise

In his book '*O devido processo penal*', *Giacomolli* pointed out that Brazilian courts, with rare exceptions, still largely follow practices reflecting an authoritarian understanding of criminal justice.[1] It would be misleading to say, however, that this result is still due to the original authoritarian approach of the 1941 code of criminal procedure. Although clearly inspired by the 1930 Italian code,[2] Brazilian criminal justice has undergone several developments over last decades, which have steered it away from the initial state-centred approach.

Doubtless, the 1988 constitutional reform marked a fundamental step in the enhancement of several fair trial guarantees, and although various institutions have not yet been fully adapted to constitutional requirements, there is no doubt that the constitutional model of due process provides fundamental solutions for the renovation of criminal justice. Furthermore, the most recent constitutional case-law highlights the need to re-define the constitutional model of a fair trial in the light of the rising impact of Inter-American case-law in Brazilian law. Therefore, Brazilian criminal justice should be submitted to a double check of compliance with constitutional and international human rights law.[3] I shall start the present discussion by analysing the participatory requirements arising from constitutional law. I shall instead examine the influence of international human rights law at a later stage of this research, after having analysed the solution models provided by Inter-American case-law.

B. Participatory Safeguards in the Constitutional Model of a Fair Trial. The Right to *contradictoire* and Full Defence

Despite the state-centred origin of the Brazilian criminal justice, it is noteworthy that the principle of *contradictoire* has a long tradition in Brazilian constitutional law. It was first enacted into the 1937 Constitution[4] and was later maintained in the further Constitutions of 1946[5] and 1967.[6] Before the enactment of the 1988 Federal Constitution, there had been much discussion on whether this constitutional requirement should apply to any type of court proceedings or solely to criminal proceedings.[7] The current Constitution eliminated this uncertainty by enshrining

[1]Giacomolli (2014), p. 12 ff.

[2]Casara and Melchior (2013), p. 19.

[3]Giacomolli (2014), p. 12 ff.

[4]Art. 122(11) of the 1937 Constitution.

[5]Art. 141(25) of the 1946 Constitution.

[6]Art. 140(16) of the 1967 Constitution.

[7]Scarance Fernandes (2010), p. 60.

contradictoire with a very broad scope of application, which explicitly encompasses both judicial and administrative proceedings.[8]

In the field of criminal justice, it is worth observing that the 1988 Constitution did not acknowledge *contradictoire* as a principle but in terms of a fundamental right of the individuals accused of a criminal offence, namely as the right to participate in the criminal proceedings instituted against them. This acknowledgment does not mean, however, that the Constitution only looked at the accused's side and therefore ignored the importance of the contribution of other parties to fact-finding. In Brazil, like in Italy, the strict link with the *par condicio* principle[9] suggests a broad interpretation of the fundamental requirement of *contradictoire*, which must therefore be extended to other private parties and even to the public prosecutor. Remarkably, the institution of a public prosecutor in Brazil historically aimed at protecting individuals from the risk of being adjudicated by the same body who preferred charges against them.[10] A multilateral understanding of the *audi alteram partem* rule was clearer in the 1967 Constitution, which linked the requirement of *contradictoire* with criminal proceedings without any reference to individual parties.[11] At first glance, it may appear that the formulation used by the 1988 Constitution in relation to criminal proceedings is unjustifiably more limited than that referred to other court proceedings, in which the guarantee of *contradictoire* was ensured to all the litigant parties. However, the notion of 'judicial proceedings' is sufficiently broad as to also encompass criminal proceedings, or at least the court hearings, notwithstanding that the reference to 'litigant parties' must be adapted to the peculiarities of criminal justice.

On the other hand, it is worth observing that the 1988 Constitution, returning to the approach of the 1937 Constitution, coupled the accused's right to *contradictorie* with the right to full defence (*ampla defesa*), a guarantee that must be granted 'with all means and resources inherent' to the defence rights.[12] Certainly, the strict link between the guarantees of *contradictoire* and full defence enhances the participatory role of private parties in the administration of criminal justice. Furthermore, the focus on a 'full' defence calls for an interpretation of these constitutional requirements that prevents formal arrangements both at the legislative level and in the practice.[13] From this it follows that the competent judge cannot rule on the evidence attached by individual parties without giving the others the opportunity to be properly heard and produce information supporting their allegations.[14] In the

[8]Art. 5(LV).

[9]Pellegrini Grinover (1990), p. 11. The two guarantees should instead remain separate according to Scarance Fernandes (2010), p. 61.

[10]Scarance Fernandes (2010), p. 61.

[11]Art. 153(16), following the new enumeration laid down by the 1969 constitutional amendment.

[12]On the strict link between *contradictoire* and full defence see Pellegrini Grinover et al. (2001), p. 77.

[13]Pellegrini Grinover (1990), p. 12.

[14]*Ibid.*, 6 fn. 25; Lopes Jr (2017), p. 97 f.

light of the requirement of 'fullness', moreover, the judicial authority cannot maintain a passive role but must actively engage in removing the barriers to effective participation of the parties. On close examination, this result does not affect the impartiality of the decision-makers.[15] An important consequence of the proactive role required from the competent judge by the guarantees of *contradictoire* and full defence is that the competent authorities must provide individuals with the necessary safeguards to ensure their effective involvement in criminal proceedings. Certainly, the main prerequisite is the possibility of having proper information on the proceedings and the offence being prosecuted.

As far as the scope of these requirements is concerned, the reference to 'judicial proceedings' does not mean that the 1988 Constitution, following the approach of its predecessor, restricted the guarantee of *contradictoire* solely to the criminal inquiry (*instrução criminal*). Under the 1967 Constitution, legal scholarship had already pointed out the need for a broad interpretation of this constitutional requirement, which could not be limited to evidence-gathering, encompassing all the necessary procedural activities to prepare the judge's conviction.[16] The requirements set forth by the 1988 Constitution surely entail the right to a judicial hearing,[17] even though it does not necessarily take place in the court proceedings. Even the reference to the 'accused person' cannot justify the restriction on the scope of these fundamental guarantees to judicial proceedings.[18] A restrictive interpretation would have negative repercussions, weakening the protection of the individuals involved in the investigative phase in which they are most vulnerable, being often exposed to different interferences with fundamental rights. Remarkably, the 1988 Constitution expressly acknowledged the right to *contradictoire* and full defence for all the defendants 'in general terms' (*em geral*). This expression calls for a broad understanding of the constitutional guarantee, which must be extended to suspects,[19] notwithstanding their different positions and the peculiarities of the pre-trial phase.

C. *Audi alteram partem* and Equality of Arms

It has been observed that there is a strict link between the principle of equality of arms and the guarantees of *contradictoire* and full defence. As *Lopes Jr.* put it relating to *Carnelutti*'s doctrine, the requirement of *contradictoire* can only serve

[15]Pellegrini Grinover (1990), p. 12 f.

[16]*Ibid.*, 10.

[17]Lopes Jr (2017), p. 97.

[18]Lauria Tucci (2004), p. 211. Of a different opinion Scarance Fernandes (2010), p. 62, who moreover admits the need to grant suspects the protection of their most relevant interests in the pre-trial inquiry.

[19]Lopes Jr (2017), p. 171 f., 538.

its goals if a balanced distribution of powers allows for effective contraposition of the parties in criminal proceedings.[20] Certainly, the principle of equality of arms cannot be understood in formal terms, but require the state to distribute the parties' procedural powers in a way that prevents the overall position of a single party from being unreasonably disadvantaged in comparison to other parties.[21] Criminal justice cannot level out the social and economic inequalities of the parties, especially in the complex Brazilian society. Yet precisely the existence of such inequalities requires a proactive stance by the state. To a certain extent, it can be said that *contradictoire* highlights the dynamic features of the *par condicio* principle, requiring the state to actively engage in a fair division of procedural rights and resources.[22]

We have seen that the Brazilian Constitution links the guarantee of *contradictoire* to the right to a full defence, which must significantly be assured with all the means and forms available. Moreover, the requirements of *contradictoire* and full defence must be interpreted in the general context of Article 5 of the Constitution, which aims at guaranteeing to both Brazilians and foreign citizens resident in Brazil equal treatment, as well as the right to freedom, security, and respect for property. This acknowledgment suggests a systematic interpretation, aimed at constantly linking the right to participation in criminal proceedings with the general requirement of equality of arms. This approach is certainly in line with the American Convention, which strictly links the principle of equality of arms with the due process guarantees. It is noteworthy that these guarantees, unlike the presumption of innocence, are not an exclusive prerogative of the accused but must be ensured to any person 'with full equality'.

The need to strengthen the link between the *audi alteram partem* rule and the *par condicio* principle is particularly evident in the pre-trial inquiry, in which fundamental rights are often exposed to the most serious attacks. The greatest difficulties, however, lie in the structure of the pre-trial phase, which in Brazil is still characterised by a police inquiry (*inquérito policial*). The drafters of the 1941 code maintained this model mainly due to the enormous territorial extent of Brazil,[23] thus opting for a clearly state-centred understanding of criminal inquiries. Not only can the police institute investigations, as a rule, at their own initiative but they can also autonomously decide when and whether to charge one or more individuals with a criminal offence (*indiciamiento*).[24]

Against this background, there is little doubt that the constitutional requirements of *contradictoire* and full defence can play a decisive role in compensating for the prevailing role of the police in the preliminary stage and the potentials of the right to defence must be exploited to ensure to individuals concerned the opportunity to

---

[20]Lopes Jr (2017), p. 362.

[21]Gomes and Mazzuoli (2010), p. 113.

[22]Pimenta Lopes (2013), p. 6 f.

[23]Lopes Jr (2017), p. 121.

[24]Moraes Pitombo (1983), p. 313 ff.

be fairly heard. In particular, suspects must be given the opportunity to communicate with their lawyers before being questioned.[25] Traditionally, the structure of the police inquiry allowed for limited exercise of the right to defence, which mainly held an exogenous function at the pre-trial stage, *e.g*. by means of *habeas corpus*.[26] More recently, Law 13.245/2016 amended the rules governing defence lawyers, thus strengthening the lawyer's participation also in the pre-trial investigations. Even so, there are still some methodological deficiencies in Brazilian criminal justice. For instance, it is a weak safeguard that the defence can request the police to perform specific investigations in its favour.[27] This solution still reflects a rather paternalistic view of defence rights, which in Brazil, like in Italy, is far from the conferment to the defence of a *jus postulandi* and the possibility of direct access to the competent court.

Over recent years, we have also witnessed considerable changes in the functions of the judicial authority, changes that, while enhancing the powers of the judiciary in the pre-trial inquiry, have led to a progressive shift away from the original model of a judge responsible for procedural safeguards. Among the most significant innovations, Law 11.690/2008 empowered judges to collect, at their own initiative, urgent evidence during the pre-trial inquiry. This power—albeit subject to compliance with the principles of necessity, adequacy and proportionality of the measure adopted—can, however, give rise to misuses, allowing for judges to follow their own investigative goals. This can further distort the balance between the police and the individuals charged with a criminal offence.[28] Serious human rights concerns also arise from Law 11.719/2008, which, enacting parts of the legislative project 4.207/2001, modified Article 396 CCP in a manner that enabled the institution of court proceedings without the suspect being heard. This reform, therefore, lost the opportunity to introduce an intermediate hearing in which the defence can contribute to the decision on whether to open the trial phase.[29] Even worse, under the current rules, the defendant does not have the right to be judicially heard after the initiation of the court proceedings, as had been provided for before 2008.[30] Following the example of the Law 11.689/2008, Brazilian legislature radically reformed jury trials, requiring the competent judge, after formal charges have been preferred (*denúncia* or *queixa*), to summon the defendants, who can reply in writing within 10 days.[31]

[25] Lopes Jr (2013), p. 236.

[26] *Ibid*.

[27] Art. 14 CCP.

[28] Lopes Jr (2017), p. 124.

[29] Lopes Jr (2013), p. 286.

[30] Art. 394 CCP (before 2008).

[31] Art. 396 CCP.

D. The Role of Private Parties in the Decision to Charge

I. Participatory Rights of the Victim in the Initiation of Criminal Proceedings. The Forms of Private Criminal Prosecution

In Brazilian law, private parties can also play a proactive role in the initiation of criminal proceedings. The role of the victim, in particular, depends on the different types of offence and the forms of proceedings provided for by the law.

In cases of offences for which unconditional public criminal action (*ação penal pública incondicionada*) is foreseen, the institution of criminal proceedings depends solely on the initiative of public bodies. Since the police are competent to conduct the pre-trial inquiry, the investigations are instituted at their own initiative. Once sufficient information is gathered to bring defendants to court, the public prosecutor will then proceed against them with a formal accusation (*denúncia*) regardless of both the existence of aggrieved parties and their interest in the initiation of a criminal prosecution. Also in the case of unconditional public prosecution, however, Brazilian law grants some powers to the victim, in order to compensate for the eventual inaction of the investigative bodies. In particular, alongside the general acknowledgment of the possibility for anybody to report the commission of a criminal offence, the code enables the victim to formally request the institution of a criminal inquiry in cases of police inaction. Although this request is subject to the discretion of the police authority,[32] it is noteworthy that Brazilian law requires the victim to provide the police authority with concrete elements justifying the beginning of criminal investigations.[33]

Furthermore, there are specific types of crimes, which allow for the aggrieved parties to be more actively involved in the institution of a criminal prosecution. This firstly applies to the cases in which the criminal law provision makes the public criminal law action conditional on the victim's request for proceedings (*representação*). In these cases, the code gives such relevance to the victim's will that not only the prosecutor's action but also the police initiative is barred until the injured person requests the initiation of the proceedings.[34] Although the law provides for a formal request by the injured party, the case-law has progressively smoothed this requirement, calling for a broad interpretation of the victim's will.[35] It is noteworthy, however, the prosecutor's law action following the victim's

[32]Moreover, the code entitles the victim to lodge a complaint before the Chief of Police as well as to make another to the public prosecutor who, while agreeing with the request, will require the police to begin the investigations.

[33]Art. 5 CCP.

[34]Art. 5(4) CCP.

[35]Lopes Jr (2017), p. 137 f.

request for proceedings is still a public prosecution, which remains in the hands of the competent prosecutor.

Moreover, Brazilian law further strengthened the role of the aggrieved parties by entitling them to initiate a private criminal prosecution within the limits laid down by Article 29 CCP. In particular, the victim's prosecutorial initiative is subsidiary to the public law action in the sense that it presupposes the inactivity of the competent prosecutor within the legal time-limit.[36] This exceptional type of private prosecution, which was confirmed by the 1988 Constitution,[37] is of utmost importance in Brazilian law in order to avoid negligence or omissions by the competent prosecutor. Remarkably, the code also enabled the next of kin of the victim in cases of judicially declared death or absence.[38]

Ultimately, it is worth noting that, although the Federal Constitution acknowledges the public prosecutor's responsibility to institute criminal proceedings,[39] Brazilian criminal justice has traditionally provided for minor offences that can only be prosecuted through a private criminal action.[40] Defendants can therefore be brought to court with a charge preferred through an act having a different form from the prosecutorial *denúncia*, namely through *queixa*. In these cases, the court proceedings cannot be instituted without the victim's initiative, whereas the police inquiry does not usually take place. The code, however, enabled the aggrieved parties to avail themselves of the state's authority to achieve the activation of criminal investigations, whenever the information available is still not enough to justify the initiation of criminal proceedings.[41] In these cases, the police can start a criminal inquiry at request of the victim.[42]

II. The Involvement of Private Parties in the Decision Not to Institute or to Drop a Criminal Prosecution

Compared to the role of the injured party in the institution of criminal proceedings, Brazilian law traditionally leaves almost no room for the participation of private parties in the decision not to initiate or to terminate a prosecution. By anticipating the solution enacted in Italy in 1944, which made the decision on the termination of criminal proceedings subject to the oversight of the investigative judge, the Brazilian code enacted a model of termination of the proceedings ordered by the

[36] Art. 29 CCP.

[37] Art. 5(LIX) Const.

[38] Art. 31 CCP.

[39] Art. 129(I) Const.

[40] Art. 30 CCP. According to Law 9.099/2005, as amended by Law 11.313/2006, minor offences are those punishable up to 2 years of imprisonment.

[41] Lopes Jr (2017), p. 139.

[42] Art. 5(5) CCP.

competent judge upon request of the prosecutor. Notwithstanding the dominant role of the law enforcement authority in the pre-trial inquiry, therefore, Brazilian law rules out the possibility of the proceedings being discontinued at the initiative not only of the police but also of the prosecutor. There is no room, instead, for the participation of the private parties in the decision not to institute criminal proceedings. This lacuna is even more detrimental to the defence taking into consideration that the prosecutorial authority still plays considerable role in the decision on discontinuance of the proceedings. Thus, not only is the judicial authority called upon to rule on the information provided by the competent prosecutor but furthermore the judge, not agreeing with the prosecutorial request, must forward the case to the General Prosecutor, who can either prefer charges against the suspect, forward the case to another public prosecutor, or reiterate the request for discontinuance of the proceedings. In the latter case, the competent judge must abide the prosecutorial request.[43] Brazilian law only provides for a weak form of involvement of the defence at the federal level. In the case of proceedings in which the public prosecution depends on a private *representação*, the Federal Public Prosecutor's High Council requires the competent prosecutor to forward the request for termination of the proceedings to any interested person, who can attach documents or arguments with a view to a new assessment of the case.[44] The concept of 'interested person', however, is highly undefined and the only result of the private initiative is a new assessment on the part of the competent prosecutor, the victim still lacking the power to challenge the prosecutorial request before an independent authority.

The question arises, moreover, whether Brazilian law involves the interested parties in the decision to terminate the proceedings prior to the initiation of a criminal prosecution on grounds other than the merits of the case. In the proceedings falling within the jurisdiction of the provincial states, the individuals investigated for less serious offences can be admitted to a form of pre-trial diversion, which entails the application of measures other than detention (*e.g.*, social work). Under Brazilian law, diversion is usually ordered prior to the preferment of formal charges, which prevents defendants from being exposed to the risk of a public hearing. Here also, however, the proceedings are discontinued without involving the victims, although they are often formally heard. Recently, moreover, the reform on organised crime carried out by Law 10.850/2013, enacted a new form of provisional suspension of prosecution, which by definition involves the defendant. This new mechanism, inspired by the US form of deferred prosecution, enables public prosecutors to suspend the initiation of prosecution up to maximum 6 months (which can be extended to other 6 months) as long as the requirements of collaboration are fulfilled.

---

[43] Art. 28 CCP.

[44] See Art. 14(1) Resolution 77/2004, http://csmpf.pgr.mpf.mp.br/documentos-e-publicacoes/resolucoes/resol_77_set_2004.pdf.

E. The Principle of *contradictoire* and Right to Information in Criminal Proceedings

I. The Right to Information in the Pre-Trial Stage

Different problems arise in relation to the involvement of private parties in criminal proceedings instituted mainly by means of a public prosecution. It has been observed that active participation in criminal proceedings presupposes specific qualitative requirements. Among these conditions, it is of utmost importance that the individuals concerned are ensured proper information on the charge and the results of the inquiries carried out by the investigative bodies.[45] Doubtless, information constitutes the most basic condition of the effective exercise of the right to *contradictoire*, which in these terms must already be granted in the pre-trial phase. Moreover, it has been noted that the Federal Constitution acknowledged the right to *contradictoire* for the accused in general terms, which calls for possibly the broadest protection of all the individuals charged with a criminal offence.[46] Nevertheless, criminal law scholarship has traditionally rejected that the principle of *contradictoire* should govern the police inquiry. Even after the 1988 Constitution, the pre-trial phase was still viewed as an administrative procedure, which only aimed at verifying the conditions for the institution of a criminal prosecution. In this context, the suspect is reduced to a mere object of the state's legal action and does not hold defence rights.[47]

A close examination of Brazilian legislation and especially of its practical arrangements displays a rather worrisome picture. It has been observed that Brazilian law empowers the police to charge individuals with a criminal offence in the pre-trial phase pursuant to specific forms. In practice, however, suspects are not charged with a formal act, with the result that they are not put in a position to know whether they will be questioned as suspects or witnesses. This result is certainly unconstitutional, depriving the individuals concerned of their right to silence.[48] Of course, the police charge presupposes sufficient suspicion of guilt against the suspects[49] and, in the absence of sufficient justification, Brazilian law allows for *habeas corpus* because of illegal coercion, a powerful legal action aimed at judicial oversight of the reasons for the police charge.[50] *De lege ferenda*, it should be examined whether the maintenance of the police competence to charge individuals with a criminal offence is a proper solution from a human rights perspective. At any

---

[45] Lopes Jr (2017), p. 539.

[46] In this sense see already Lauria Tucci and Cruz e Tucci (1993), p. 25 ff.

[47] For an overview of the main opinions expressed before and after the 1988 Constitution see Hassan Choukr (1995), p. 109 ff.

[48] Lopes Jr (2017), p. 102 fn. 86.

[49] *Ibid.*, 168.

[50] Lopes Jr (2013), p. 335.

rate, a list of charging acts should be laid down at the statutory level. By this means, the charging decision would be reflected in a formal act once sufficient suspicion of guilt arises against the suspect. This should in turn entail the obligation of the competent authority to hear the suspects after a formal charge has been preferred,[51] while providing them with proper information, as required by the American Convention.[52]

Of course, the duty of information must always be balanced with the need to prevent the charge from producing effects of social stigmatisation.[53] It is noteworthy that Brazilian law, although generally requiring the police to keep their inquiry confidential, entitles, as a rule, the defendant's counsel to access the information gathered. This was confirmed in 2009 by the Federal Supreme Tribunal that, in its binding precedent (*Súmula vinculante*)[54] No. 14, acknowledged the defence's right to access the results of the police investigations, albeit with two important limitations. First, since the access must be in the interest of the defendant, lawyers should only have access to information strictly concerned with their clients. Second, access should only be granted to information already gathered, with the exclusion of evidence collected through investigations that are still underway.[55] As noted, Law 13.245/2016 strengthened the lawyer's participation rights in the investigations. In particular, this legislative reform emphasised the right to *contradictoire* in the police inquiry by enhancing the possibility of the lawyer accessing the information gathered by the investigative bodies and by providing for the absolute invalidity of the suspect's investigation where the lawyer is prevented from being effectively involved in the investigations.[56]

Even so, Brazilian law does not still require the police, while starting a criminal investigation on their own initiative, to inform individuals other than the suspect. In particular, victims and their relatives, who might be unaware of the initiation of the criminal inquiry (especially if the offence under investigation is subject to public prosecution), need be given information neither on the police inquiry nor on the police charge. This solution cannot be deemed in line with the need to allow the aggrieved parties to take part actively in criminal proceedings, *e.g.* by assisting the public prosecution through a subsidiary criminal law action. Moreover, the possibility for the victims to request further investigations also presupposes that they are given proper information on the development of the police inquiry, especially if the victim's initiative led to the institution of criminal proceedings.

---

[51] Lopes Jr (2017), p. 169.

[52] Chapter 9, D.

[53] Lopes Jr (2013), p. 337 fn. 58.

[54] The constitutional amendment reform 45/2004 enacted into the Constitution a new Article 103-A, which enables the Federal Supreme Tribunal to issue, either *ex officio* or upon request, binding precedents on constitutional law issues.

[55] Lopes Jr (2017), p. 174.

[56] *Ibid.*, 173.

II. Charging Decision and the Need for Proper Information on the Initiation of Criminal Proceedings

After the court proceedings have been initiated, providing ineffective information on the proceedings impinges on the validity of the procedure.[57] Traditionally, the main goal of the court summons was to promote the active participation of defendants in the proceedings, while enabling them to make their voices heard. This also explains why the defence must be given full knowledge of the accusation contained in the *denúncia* or *queixa*.[58] Subsequent legislation considerably changed the purpose of the court summons, which no longer aims at the hearing of the defendant, who can only reply in writing. Over the last decades, the case-law has become increasingly aware of need for effective information, which has led the Federal Supreme Tribunal to declare the court summons by edict (*citação por edital*) void in cases of detained defendants.[59] On this basis, Law 10.792/2003 reformed the rules on the court summons, providing that detained defendants must be personally summoned to court.[60]

The examination of Brazilian law reveals, moreover, the recent attempt of the legislature to tilt up the balance between the individual right to information and the prosecutorial needs towards the protection of state-related interests. In particular, Law 11.719/2008 enacted an unprecedented form of court summons, typical of civil proceedings, that is, the so-called '*citação com hora certa*'.[61] By this means, judicial officers who, after attempting to find the defendants at their domicile three times, consider them to have absconded to avoid notification will inform either a family member or, in their absence, a neighbour, that the court summons will be served again at a given time.[62] Yet the basis for this form of notification—namely, the risk of absconding—leaves to judicial officers a great margin of discretion. This can give rise to abuses, increasing the risk that defendants are only granted an apparent knowledge of ongoing proceedings.[63] It is true that once the notification *com hora certa* is performed, the accused who does not appear in court will be granted a court-appointed counsel. However, Article 363(1) CCP, as amended by Law 11.719/2008, provides that criminal proceedings are valid if the defendant was in any case summoned to court. The only guarantee for the accused in the case of notification *com hora certa* is a strict judicial oversight, and unless it is proven that the failure to appear in court or to send a lawyer was really due to the defendant's free decision not to take part in the proceedings, the proceedings must

[57] *Ibid.*, 540.

[58] *Ibid.*, 543.

[59] STF, *Súmula vinculante* No. 351.

[60] Art. 360 CCP.

[61] Art. 362 CCP.

[62] Art. 227 CPC.

[63] Lopes Jr (2013), p. 547 f.

be suspended.[64] It must, however, be acknowledged that the absence of clear criteria also enhances judicial discretion, which calls into question the constitutionality of this form of notification.[65]

Furthermore, the 2008 reform also maintained the possibility of defendants being summoned by edict,[66] notwithstanding the radical criticisms expressed by legal scholarship.[67] Pursuant to this procedure, a notice is published in the official press and in a newspaper circulating nationwide, and defendants have a period of time, up to a maximum of 15 days, to appear in court either personally or through their lawyers. It is clearly a fictitious form of notification, and in this sense legal scholarship rightly stresses that all further means must be used to reach the defendant, who can only be summoned by edict in the last resort.[68]

Another delicate problem concerns the contents of the information with particular regard to the indictment preferred against the accused. It is obvious that an abstract accusation or the preferment of generic charges impede the ability to set up a proper defence, determining a cultural shift back to the time of objective liability, which is clearly inconsistent with the requirements of a fair trial.[69] Brazilian constitutional case-law adopted a strong approach on this point, stressing the need for concrete charges, which in case of more than one defendant must also specify the individual contribution of the accused persons involved.[70]

F. Prosecutorial Needs and the Right to Take Part Personally in Criminal Proceedings. The Problem of *in absentia* Procedures in Brazilian Law

These observations allows us not to analyse how Brazilian law deals with inactivity of the defence and which rules specifically govern the defendant's failure to appear in court. This issue is of utmost importance not only in the light of the constitutional requirement of *contradictoire* but also—as we will see at a later stage of this research[71]—in relation to the approach of the American Convention to the right to have personal access to court.

As a matter of principle, Brazilian law considers the accused's participation in criminal proceedings as an absolute individual right. There is no obligation to cooperate with the administration of justice, nor can defendants be compelled to

[64] *Ibid.*, 548.
[65] In this sense Marques da Silva (2008), p. 37.
[66] Art. 361 CCP.
[67] Delmanto Jr (2004), p. 152.
[68] Lopes Jr (2017), p. 546.
[69] Giacomolli (2014), p. 128.
[70] STF, *HC* 84.580-1/SP, rel. Celso de Mello.
[71] Chapter 9, C.

take part in procedural activities than can jeopardise their right not to introduce evidence against themselves.[72] This reveals the unreasonableness of the judicial power to bring the defendant to court coercively,[73] a solution that clearly highlights the persistent inquisitorial understanding of the accused as a means that can be used for the purposes of the criminal inquiry. In the light of this, two main situations should be distinguished. The first one is the case in which defendants, after being personally informed of the proceedings, neither appear in court nor send their lawyer. The second concerns the more complex situation in which defendants neither could be personally summoned to court nor in any case replied within the time limit of 15 days laid down in the summons by edict. Legal scholarship distinguishes between a real and a fictitious inactivity, restricting the possibility of defendants being declared absent to the former case. On close examination, both situations require a proper balance between the individual right to personal participation and the public interest in efficient prosecution.

Certainly, the accused's absence, insofar as it is due to his free choice, cannot affect the course of the proceedings. Moreover, since in Brazil the right to a defence is not only an individual interest but also constitutes a public requirement, the code requires that defendants also be granted a court-appointed lawyer in the case of voluntary absence and that the lawyer reply in writing to the court summons.[74] Yet this requirement, introduced by Law 11.719/2008, is somewhat unfortunate, generally referring to any case in which defendants did not reply to the court summons and therefore also to the case in which they were summoned *com hora certa*. To avoid constitutional violations, the only way, as noted, is to summon by edict defendants who have not replied to the notification *com hora certa* and to order, in case of persistent inactivity, the suspension of the proceedings. Furthermore, it can be doubted that under Brazilian law the defendant's absence expresses their free will to not take part in the proceedings. It is true that Law 9.721/1996 dropped the old default proceedings (*em revelia*), which took place in any case of defendants who, duly summoned, did not appear in court without justification.[75] However, the 1996 reform, although requiring the defendants to be summoned personally, maintained the possibility of criminal proceedings being conducted against absent defendants who either failed to appear in court without a justified reason or failed to communicate their new residence.

Concerning the second situation considered above, the defendant's absence certainly is more akin to a fictitious lack of defensive reaction, since the likelihood that defendants summoned by edict become aware of the proceedings initiated against them is surely low. In this case, the 1996 reform provided for the suspension not only of criminal proceedings but also of the time limit laid down for the prosecuted offence. The only procedural activities allowed in this lapse of time

[72] Lopes Jr (2017), p. 559. Of a partially different opinion Nucci (2014), p. 767.

[73] Art. 260 CCP. Against this solution see Lopes Jr (2017), p. 559 f.

[74] Art. 396-A(2) CCP.

[75] Art. 366 CCP (before 1996).

are the collection of urgent evidence and the possibility of the competent judge remanding defendants into custody pursuant to Article 312 CCP.[76] More precisely, the time limit is first suspended after the judicial authority receives the *denúncia*, and will be subsequently suspended if the defendant does not appear in court.

Notwithstanding its merits, this regulation has given rise to strong criticisms by criminal law scholarship and to very different interpretations by case-law. In particular, the suspension of criminal proceedings appeared to be an improper solution in Brazilian criminal justice, which departed from the traditional assumption that a criminal law action can be carried out without the accused's contribution.[77] Further human rights concerns arise in relation to the suspension of the time limit for prosecuting the alleged offence especially because the code neither lays down a maximum period for this suspension, nor restricts this result to specific types of offences. These arguments did not, however, lead the Federal Supreme Tribunal to declare the unconstitutionality of the 1996 legislation. According to the federal judges, the Constitution does not ban the suspension of the time limit, nor does this case give rise to a hidden absence of such a limit (*imprescritibilidade*), a result that the legislature could, moreover, extend to cases other than those laid down in Nos. LXII and LXIV of Article 5 of the Constitution.[78]

Legal scholarship strongly criticised these arguments. As *Lopes Jr*. points it out,[79] this approach is questionable from the viewpoint of constitutional, substantial and procedural criminal law. To start with, the lack of any legal specification on the maximum length of the suspension of the time limit, although it is not exactly equivalent to the lack of statutory limitations for the prosecuted crime, gives rise to a similar result.[80] Even admitting a substantial difference between this case and those laid down in Article 5,[81] the Constitution does not tolerate the unlimited suspension of the time limit for any offence irrespective of its seriousness.[82] Suspending indefinitely the time limit of petty crimes would clearly be a disproportionate result.[83] In general terms, moreover, the indefinite extension of the time limits for prosecuting criminal offences reveals an out-dated concept of prescription, which runs counter to the modern right to have the offence forgotten.[84]

---

[76]Art. 366 CCP.

[77]Pacelli (2012), p. 613.

[78]*RE* 460.971, rel. Sepúlveda Pertence.

[79]Lopes Jr (2017), p. 552 ff.

[80]Hassan Choukr (2011), p. 565 f. Similarly Lopes Jr (2017), p. 551, who points out that the Constitution did not empower the legislature to set forth further cases of offences that can be prosecuted without time limits.

[81]In this sense cf. Tourinho Filho (2010), I vol., 930 f.

[82]Moreover, the recent Law 12.683/2012 introduced an important derogation from the general suspension of time limits in cases of economic crimes under Law 9.613/98. For criticisms on this reform see Lopes Jr (2013), p. 762.

[83]Tourinho Filho (2010), I vol., 929 ff.

[84]*Ibid*., 929; Lopes Jr (2017), p. 553 fn. 18.

On close examination, the solution of suspending criminal proceedings without time limits and allowing for the re-opening of the process after decades can also give rise to complicated problems. In particular, prosecution will probably be directed against a completely different person,[85] which, in case of conviction, can inevitably frustrate the goal of resocialisation of the criminal being punished. Furthermore, what evidence can be obtained in non-urgent cases after decades?

The Superior Court of Justice, strongly contrasting with the approach of the Federal Supreme Tribunal, shared these arguments in a *Súmula* of 2009.[86] This ruling followed the opinion, relying on a reform project of the code of criminal procedure,[87] that had long argued for the introduction of a maximum period of suspension of the time limit for prosecuted offences. According to the Superior Court of Justice, this period should correspond to the statutory limitations laid down in Article 109 CC, calculated in relation to the maximum sentence threshold. Despite its merits, this solution also raises some concerns from a human rights perspective. Its greatest shortcoming is perhaps that it provides for general statutory limits which may not fit the needs of the prosecuted case.[88] Moreover, recourse to the time limit laid down for the maximum instead of the minimum sentence threshold appears to be arbitrary.[89] On close examination, any abstract solution can give rise to disproportionate results. A legislative reform is therefore necessary to ensure that the state's failure to inform defendants who remain unaware of proceedings through no fault of their own cannot jeopardise them.[90]

Even within these limits, the rules on suspension of the proceedings must be interpreted in a strict way, especially because of the risks arising from the procedural acts allowed during the suspension period. It has been observed that, during the period of suspension of the proceedings, the competent judge can order the collection of urgent evidence and remand defendants into custody. Both these powers can affect the fundamental rights either of the defendants or third parties. The anticipation of taking urgent evidence can frustrate the defendants' right to be confronted with their accusers. From this it follows that proper reasons must be given for the decision to obtain evidence during the suspension of the proceedings and evidence must be taken in such a way as to compensate for the lack of the defendant's contribution. In this regard, any technical means available (*e.g.* audio

---

[85]In this sense see already Lopes Jr and Badaró (2009), p. 14.

[86]*Súmula* No. 415.

[87]Code's reform project 4.207/2001.

[88]Lopes Jr (2013), p. 760 f.

[89]Hassan Choukr (2011), p. 565.

[90]In this sense see Lopes Jr (2017), p. 354 f., who moreover invoked the Spanish rules on time limits for criminal offences, which provide for the interruption of the statutory limitations where the defendant, if also summoned by edict, does not appear in court and is formally declared absent (*rebelde*) (p. 354 fn. 21). Although the Spanish *rebeldía* also leads to the suspension of criminal proceedings, the declaration of absence does not entail—unlike in Brazil—the suspension of prescription, with the result that the time limit for the offence can lapse while the prosecution still suspended.

or videotaping) should be used to guarantee the reliability of evidence-gathering.[91] The Superior Court of Justice also expressed a similar position, stressing the need for proper reasoning to avoid the simple passage of the time being used to justify the anticipation of the taking of evidence.[92] Furthermore, it is clear that the non-appearance of defendants in court cannot justify the use of restrictions on freedom beyond the normal conditions.[93] The practice of automatically remanding absent defendants into custody is therefore certainly unlawful.[94]

G. Investigative Needs and the Right to Be Fairly Heard

I. The Right to Be Fairly Heard in the Pre-Trial Phase

Personal participation in criminal proceedings remains a weak guarantee if the accused is not ensured the necessary tools to exercise effective defence. A fundamental guarantee is certainly the granting of a fair opportunity to be heard. In the pre-trial inquiry, this condition may seem to be impossible due to the dominant role of the law enforcement authority. Yet we have seen that the constitutional requirements of *contradictoire* and full defence also largely apply to the police inquiry. It is noteworthy that among other tasks, the police must question the suspect according to the guarantees laid down for the court hearings.[95] To ensure full compliance with these safeguards, the 1941 code required the notes on the questioning to be signed by two witnesses present at the reading out.[96] On close examination, this provision could scarcely protect the suspect, since the two witnesses need not be present at the moment of the police questioning. Nevertheless, the use of the term 'hearing' and the reference to the rules on the court examination reveal the clear attempt of the Brazilian legislature to make fair hearing a general guarantee, which applies throughout the criminal proceedings.

The requirement of fairness necessitates specific qualitative conditions to be met to allow the effective exercise of the right to *contradictoire*. In particular, suspects can claim their right to silence, expressly acknowledged in the Federal Constitution,[97] before the police authority. Moreover, counsel must assist the suspect in the police questioning, as required by Article 185 CCP, reformed by Law 10.792/2003. It must be acknowledged, however, that the practical application of these rules is unfortunately very different from what the law foresees. As noted, the lack of a

[91]Lopes Jr (2017), p. 558.

[92]*Súmula* No. 455.

[93]Lopes Jr (2017), p. 557.

[94]Tourinho Filho (2010), I vol., 936.

[95]Arts. 185 et seq. CCP.

[96]Art. 6(V) CCP.

[97]Lopes Jr (2017), p. 141.

clear statutory definition of the exact stage at which individuals can be charged with a criminal offence (*indiciamento*) leads to the police often taking oral evidence from the suspects without duly informing them of their formal status.[98]

It is worth observing that alongside the suspect, the police are also required to hear the victim. It has been observed that Brazilian law attaches the victim a proactive role in minor cases for the purpose of the initiation of a criminal prosecution.[99] As a matter of principle, the modes of the victim's questioning by the police should also be consistent with the rules on the court hearing of the injured party.[100] In this regard, it must be taken into account that in Brazil victims cannot be heard as witnesses,[101] and consequently they neither are required to tell the truth nor can be prosecuted for false statement.[102] On the other hand, victims can coercively be brought to the police station for the purposes of the police hearing. Unlike suspects, however, the aggrieved parties cannot claim the right to silence,[103] a solution that is mainly justified on the assumption that the police inquiry is often initiated at the victim's initiative. Despite its importance, the victim's testimony must be handled with great caution and prudently taking into account the media. This especially applies to the case of sexual crimes allegedly committed against minors. Here, the negative consequences on the defendant's life of incriminating statements, taken by the police with the assistance of specialists, can be irreparable, as highlighted by the *Escola Base* case in São Paulo.[104]

II. The Right to Be Fairly Heard in Court Proceedings

Over the last few years, the court hearings of private parties have undergone radical reforms, with a view to enhancing the defence rights of the person examined. Doubtless, some reforms were the result of the enshrinement of fair rights guarantees at the constitutional level. Until 2003, the code, starting with a distorted understanding of the right to silence,[105] required trial judges, before examining defendants, to inform them that their silence could be interpreted to the detriment of their defence.[106] This formulation turned out to be inconsistent with the right to silence acknowledged by both the Federal Constitution and the American Convention.[107] It took, however, several years before Law 10.792/2003 required judges to

[98] *Ibid.*

[99] Art. 4(IV) CCP.

[100] Art. 201 CCP.

[101] Scarance Fernandes (1995), p. 212.

[102] Lopes Jr (2017), p. 454.

[103] *Ibid.*, 454 f. In the same sense Pacelli (2012), p. 425.

[104] Lopes Jr (2017), p. 477 ff.

[105] Tourinho Filho (2010), I vol., 597.

[106] Art. 186 CCP (old version).

[107] Lopes Jr (2017), p. 446.

inform the accused, before starting the hearing, of the charges preferred and of the right to remain silent. Unlike in the past, silence can no longer be interpreted to the detriment of the accused's defence.[108]

On the other hand, the 2003 reform also strengthened the role of defence lawyers. The 1941 code had made counsel a sort of guest of stone during the examination of their clients, in which they could intervene in no way.[109] Under Brazilian law, the judicial authority still plays a dominant role in conducting the hearing of the accused, who cannot be cross-examined by the parties.[110] Since 2003, however, the code has required judges to verify, after examining the defendants, whether further facts need to be ascertained or the parties (and their lawyer) wish to pose further questions.[111]

Subsequent reforms aimed at balancing the individual right to be fairly heard with other relevant interests, either concerned with the criminal prosecution or with other private parties. In particular, Law 11.900/2009 introduced a new regulation on the hearing of detained defendants by videoconference or other technological means of transmission of sounds and images in real time. This regulation allows for recourse to these techniques in exceptional cases, not only for grounds relating to public security or *ordre public*[112] but also to satisfy individual defence needs, such as that of facilitating the defendants' participation, if illness or other circumstances can make it difficult for them to appear in court.[113] Significantly, these technical arrangements can also be justified to balance the defensive safeguards of different individuals, especially the defendants' right to be heard and the need to avoid negative influences on the victims and witnesses.[114] Of course, the existence of these needs must be properly considered, since videoconferencing deprives the accused not only of the right to be personally heard but also of the right to take part directly in the taking of evidence.[115] At any rate, it is quite obvious that defendants must be granted the possibility of following, by the same technical means, the procedural activities carried out at trial.[116] Furthermore, the code aims at ensuring to detained defendants heard by videoconference similar defence conditions to those applicable during ordinary trial hearings. In particular, defendants must always be given the right to a private interview with their counsel before the judicial hearing. Moreover, the accused must be given access to special telephone channels to communicate privately with a lawyer in prison, who will in turn be in constant, and equally private, contact with the lawyer present at trial.[117] However,

[108] Art. 186 CCP (new version).

[109] Art. 187 CCP (old version).

[110] As we will see, a different method has been introduced since 2008 for witnesses' examination.

[111] Art. 188 CCP (new version).

[112] For some criticisms on the vagueness of these legal requirements see Lopes Jr (2013), p. 650 f.

[113] Art. 185(2)(II) CCP.

[114] Art. 185(2)(III) CCP.

[115] Lopes Jr (2017), p. 450 f.

[116] Art. 185(4) CCP.

[117] Art. 185(5) CCP.

these arrangements are rather cumbersome and can jeopardise effective defence, especially if defendants appointed only one counsel. In this case, the defence lawyer must face the alternative of either being present at trial, while the accused will be assisted by a public defender in prison, or providing assistance in prison without taking part in the trial activities.[118]

On the other hand, the 2009 reform had a scope that went beyond only the defendant's hearing. Thus the main rules on the examination of defendants by videoconference apply, *mutatis mutandis*, to the hearings of detained victims and witnesses.[119] These hearings pose delicate problems, which not only concern the defence of the examined person but also the possibility of other parties present at trial being effectively involved in evidence-gathering. Moreover, the possibility of witnesses being heard by videoconference goes beyond only cases of detention. Before 2008, where judges considered that the defendant's presence at trial could humiliate or frighten a witness, or cause constraint to him, the accused could be banned from the courtroom. After Law 11.690/2008, judges are firstly required to verify whether the witness can be examined by videoconference. Only if this arrangement is not possible can the competent judge ban the accused from the courtroom and continue with the hearing, at which the lawyer must in any case be present.[120] Of course, the judicial authority can only order technical arrangements, which inevitably affect the right to *contradictoire*, in exceptional cases and must give reasons for this decision.[121]

Another indisputable merit of the 2008 reform was the enhancement of the victim's right to participate in court proceedings. The 1941 code had only enacted one very short provision on the victim's hearing, a provision that empowered the judicial authority to bring the victim to court coercively.[122] The 2008 legislation introduced a more extensive regulation, which aimed at strengthening the right to participation for victims in a vulnerable position. In particular, victims must be granted a separate space in the courtroom[123] and multidisciplinary assistance—especially psychological, medical and juridical assistance—must be put at their disposal at the expense either of the offender or the state.[124] Before the 2008, as noted, judges could ban defendants from having access to the courtroom only if their presence at trial could affect the witness. Yet restriction only on behalf of the witness was clearly unjustified since the same risks could concern the victim. It is

[118]Lopes Jr (2013), p. 651.

[119]Art. 185(8) CCP.

[120]Art. 217 CCP. It is worth noting, however, that in the practice the defendant is still often banned from the courtroom whenever the victim or the witness requests it. Hearings by videoconference are more used in other situations, *e.g.* where the examination concerns a victim or a witness residing in a place other than that in which the trial is held.

[121]Lopes Jr (2017), p. 475.

[122]Art. 201 CCP (old version).

[123]Art. 201(4) CCP.

[124]Art. 201(5) CCP.

therefore to be welcomed that the 2008 reform extended this solution in Article 217 CCP.[125]

It is also of great importance that Brazilian law empowers the competent judge to adopt all necessary measures to protect the victim's hearing from external repercussions, which can affect their right to private and family life, as well as their right to honour and image. Among these measures, the judicial authority can order the maintaining of the secrecy of the ongoing investigations with a view to avoiding the disclosure of the victim's hearings and statements to the media.[126] Yet secrecy cannot be opposed to the accused's defence, which must in any case be given access to the victim's statements.[127] These measures, if properly backed by reasons, can provide a good balance between the accused's right to a defence and the need to protect the private sphere of other individuals affected by the alleged offence.

H. *Audi alteram partem* and the Collection of Evidence

I. The Right to contradictoire *in Obtaining Oral Evidence*

The examination of the developments that have occurred in Brazilian law over the last years also reveals the enhancement of the parties' contribution in the field of evidence-gathering. In this context, the collection of oral evidence poses difficult human rights challenges that require delicate trade-offs between conflicting interests. Some of the observations made heretofore can also be used in the light of the present discussion.

As anticipated, one of the most significant reforms carried out by Law 11.690/2008 was the replacement of the old form of judicial questioning of witnesses with cross-examination conducted by the parties.[128] Doubtless, this reform strengthened the constitutional requirement of *contradictoire* and full defence. In this context, the exceptional power of the judiciary to order the examination by videoconference must be restricted to cases in which the defendant's presence can truly cause humiliation or constraint to the witnesses or victims.[129] An even more cautious approach is required to the decision to ban defendants from the courtroom, a decision that, notwithstanding the wording of Article 217 CCP, cannot automatically follow the simple impossibility of ordering videoconferencing. Notwithstanding the lawyer's presence, defendants excluded from the courtroom are clearly deprived of the possibility of properly following the taking of incriminating

---

[125]Tourinho Filho (2010), I vol., 656.

[126]Art. 201(6) CCP.

[127]See Lopes Jr (2017), p. 456.

[128]Art. 212 CCP.

[129]Lopes Jr (2017), p. 475.

evidence. At any rate, defendants maintain their right to have the last word, which clearly requires them to be given the opportunity (and the necessary time) to access the records of the witness testimony.[130]

Furthermore, the 2008 reform also enhanced the impartiality of the judicial authority, without converting it into a passive onlooker. In particular, judges are called upon to assess the relevance and properness of the questions put to witnesses as well as to stop questions aimed at inducing them to certain responses. This oversight is of utmost importance not only for the purposes of fact-finding but also in order to protect the witness's memory and his right to a fair examination, especially if the witness is a minor. Moreover, the judicial authority can integrate the cross-examination of the parties by putting further questions to the witness. However, this power only aims at clarifying issues other than those covered by the parties' questions and must therefore be exercised with great caution. It must certainly be avoided that judges, in assuming a leading role in the taking of testimonial evidence or remedying the failures of the prosecutorial authority, reverse the implementation of the new system of cross-examination.[131] There is still, however, great uncertainty in the case-law on the consequences that a dominant role by the competent judges can have on the parties' right to be directly involved in the gathering of oral evidence. The examination of the case-law of the higher courts reveals a clear tendency, albeit with some exceptions,[132] to relativize this invalidity,[133] with the result that the proceedings can only be declared void if the defence proves an injury suffered.[134]

As noted, defendants cannot be cross-examined but must still be examined by the trial court. It has been observed, moreover, that the 2003 reform, departing from the 1941 approach that excluded any intervention of the defence, required the competent judges to ascertain whether the parties wish to have further issues clarified. At any rate, the maintenance of a solution that entrusts to the judiciary the conduct of the accused's hearing can be easily explained in the light of the characteristics of this court examination. Although largely governed by the rules on criminal evidence, the accused's hearing is not a means of obtaining evidence in a strict sense but must be viewed in the light of the guarantees acknowledged to defendants by both the Constitution and the American Convention, starting with the presumption of innocence.[135]

---

[130] *Ibid.*, 476.

[131] See STJ, *REsp* 1.259.482, rel. Marco Aurélio Bellize, which declared the proceedings void because the judge replaced the absent public prosecutor by putting questions to the witness. Cf. Lopes Jr (2017), p. 460.

[132] STJ, *HC* 153.140, rel. Felix Fischer.

[133] See STJ, *HC* 151.357, rel. Og Fernandes; STF, *HC* 110.623, rel. Ricardo Lewandowski.

[134] For an overview of the case-law of the higher courts in this respect see Hassan Choukr (2011), p. 375 f.; Lopes Jr (2017), p. 458 ff.

[135] Lopes Jr (2017), p. 442 f.

II. The Right to contradictoire *in the Taking of Expert Evidence*

The involvement of private parties in the taking of expert evidence can be of utmost importance in the complex contemporary era, characterised by the growing role of scientific evidence. In this scenario, there is an increased need for specialised knowledge that makes the traditional role of the judge as a *peritus peritorum* rather out-dated. Certainly, this approach can no longer be maintained on the grounds of the official preparation of the court-appointed experts,[136] instead requiring the competent authority to establish the necessary conditions for the parties to give their contribution to the collection of this type of evidence.

The 1941 code entrusted technical inquiries to court-appointed experts and the assessment of the information gathered solely to the judge. Even after the enactment of the 1988 Constitution, it took two decades to steer Brazilian criminal justice towards a participatory model of collection of expert evidence. An in-depth reform was carried out by Law 11.690/2008, which strengthened the role of the parties in various fashions. The defence was permitted to appoint private experts,[137] and both private parties and the public prosecutor were given the right to obtain a technical assistant (*assistente técnico*) to follow the technical inquiry carried out by the court experts.[138] It is noteworthy that this right was not only granted to the accused but also to the complainant and the victim, even though in the latter case it can only be claimed after the victim has taken over the role of a prosecutorial assistant.[139] The tasks of technical assistants are of utmost importance from the very beginning of the expert inquiry, allowing parties to put special questions or formulate requests for the ascertainment of certain issues. Furthermore, technical assistants are called upon to make a critical assessment of the expert's report,[140] which is essential to put the parties in a position to properly exercise their right of criticism. The work of technical assistants can also help detect eventual deficiencies in the inquiry of the court expert and the parties can always request the expert to be examined in order to clarify specific issues.[141] It must be acknowledged, however, that Brazilian law does not go so far as to grant private parties technical assistance at the state's expenses, assistance that still remains a privilege of wealthy people.[142]

The most delicate problems concerned with the involvement of the defence in technical inquiries arise in the pre-trial phase. This is especially due to the

[136] Art. 159(1) CCP.

[137] Lopes Jr (2017), p. 428 f.

[138] Art. 159(3) CCP.

[139] Lopes Jr (2017), p. 426.

[140] Art. 159(4) CCP.

[141] Art. 159(5)(I) CCP.

[142] Tourinho Filho (2010), I vol., 558 ff.

aforementioned practice of the police postponing the preferment of the charge, notwithstanding the existence of sufficient evidence against the suspects.[143] Taking into consideration that most complex expert inquiries are carried out at the pre-trial stage, suspects should be allowed to put special questions to the police-appointed experts and especially to follow the investigation by means of their own assistants.[144] However, Brazilian law is still deficient in this regard. Technical assistants can start their activity after being admitted by the judge, a solution that seems to exclude the possibility of experts appointed by the police.[145] A better solution would probably be to enact a court procedure with a view to obtaining, *inter alia*, expert evidence in the pre-trial phase.

III. The Right to contradictoire *and Documentary Evidence*

Like in Italy, it would be misleading to say that the constitutional requirements of *contradictoire* and full defence only concern oral evidence. The strict link between these two requirements and the right to be tried in a reasonable time also entails that prosecutorial documents must be put at the disposal of the defence, which must have the necessary time to analyse them and express its opinion.[146] Law 11.689/2008 aimed at satisfying this requirement in the field of jury trials, enacting into the code the ban against reading out at trial documents that were not produced at least 3 days before the hearing.[147] In ordinary proceedings, Brazilian courts often invoke a deadline of 5 days along the same lines as the civil proceedings, notwithstanding that the code of criminal procedure does not contain specific provisions in this regard.[148]

A close examination of documentary evidence in the light of constitutional law, moreover, helps prevent infringements of the right to *contradictoire*, deriving from the use of documentary evidence as a surrogate for the information that should be gathered in open court with the parties' contribution. Certainly, out-of-court witness testimony cannot unconditionally be used at trial, since the code requires witnesses to give evidence orally, while banning written statements.[149] Particular concerns arise in relation to the prosecutors' practice of continuing their inquiry, in parallel with the court proceedings, after formal charges have been preferred—an unregulated practice that frustrates the fundamental requirement of *contradictoire*.[150] Further problems concern the admissibility of evidence gathered

[143]Lopes Jr (2017), p. 429 fn. 12.

[144]*Ibid.*, 429.

[145]Tourinho Filho (2010), I vol., 558.

[146]Lopes Jr (2017), p. 504.

[147]Art. 479 CCP.

[148]Lopes Jr (2013), p. 704.

[149]Art. 204 CCP.

[150]Lopes Jr (2017), p. 503 f.

in other proceedings. The unconditional use of this information not only entails clear risks for the right to *contraditoire* but also reveals the underestimation of the important role that both the procedural context and the factual background play in the collection of criminal evidence.[151] Similar concerns also relate to the admissibility of criminal judgments or bargaining decisions issued in other proceedings, which are mainly used to determine the defendant's dangerousness. Of course, judges must exercise the utmost caution in admitting this evidence.[152]

I. *Audi alteram partem* and the Proof of Guilt

Different problems arise in relation to decision-making. Brazilian law has progressively assimilated the need for the contribution of the parties to fact-finding. Whereas the use of evidence taken in open court is unquestionable, a lively debate has long divided legal scholarship as to the admissibility of untested evidence gathered in the police inquiry. Before the 1941 code, the codifications of some provincial states provided that the police inquiry should 'accompany' the prosecution. This entailed that the information gathered by the police during their investigations had to be attached to the trial file and could be used until the contrary was proven. The 1941 code maintained that formulation, while significantly dropping, however, any reference to the relevance of the police evidence.[153] This rules out any possibility of interpreting the new provisions in the old sense. The fact that the police inquiry accompanies the charging decision should only enable the trial judges to assess the admissibility of the prosecution initiated.[154] Nevertheless, Brazilian courts have not always followed this approach and it took two decades after the enactment of the 1988 Constitution before the legislature could properly fulfil the constitutional requirements of *contradictoire* and full defence.

An in-depth reform was carried out by Law 11.690/2008, which radically amended the general provisions on decision-making. Until then, Brazilian law was strongly based on the full freedom of criminal judges from any formality governing other judicial proceedings.[155] Except the proof of civil status, the principle of free assessment of evidence (*livre apreciação da prova*) governed fact-finding in criminal matters.[156] The 2008 reform, while maintaining the principle of free motivated belief, linked judicial freedom in the assessment of evidence with the information gathered with the parties' contribution. This in turn entailed the prohibition of ruling on the defendant's guilt on the exclusive basis of the

[151] *Ibid.*, 384.
[152] *Ibid.*, 382 f.
[153] Art. 12 CCP.
[154] Lopes Jr (2017), p. 155.
[155] Art. 155 CCP (old version).
[156] Art. 157 CCP (old version).

information collected in the pre-trial inquiry, except in the cases of precautionary evidence, non-repeatable evidence and anticipated evidence (*provas cautelares, não repetíveis e antecipadas*).[157] There is no doubt that the aim pursued by the drafters of the 2008 reform was to enhance the principle of *contradictoire*, while restricting the use of pre-trial evidence, as a rule, to the investigative stage and the charging decision.[158] Nevertheless, the added provision on the prohibition of exclusive use of the results of pre-trial investigations did not suffice to rule out any use of untested evidence for the purposes of the trial decision.[159] This requires us to analyse the extent to which this approach can be deemed to be in line with the Brazilian Constitution.

Certainly, where the information gathered during the police inquiry contradicts the evidence gathered at trial, the court cannot use it to convict the defendant.[160] Serious risks for the principle of *contradictoire* arise from the practice of basing the defendant's conviction on judicial evidence combined with the results of police investigations.[161] Article 155 CCP still allows this practice, which could be removed, according to legal scholarship,[162] by only banning the inclusion of police evidence into the trial file pursuant to the Italian model. Moreover, the accused's right to be involved in the gathering of incriminating evidence can also be infringed as a result of the exceptions foreseen in Article 155 CCP.

On close examination, these exceptions have few common elements and provide different levels of guarantees. The most protective case is that of anticipated evidence, that is, of evidence gathered by means of a court procedure before the trial inquiry, a procedure that can be activated where the real risk arises that the sought information, if not gathered soon, will be deteriorated or get lost. From this it follows that, when a piece of evidence is unlikely to be collected at trial, it should in principle be gathered at the pre-trial stage before a judicial authority and pursuant to the requirements of *contradictoire* and full defence.[163] However, the rules on this procedure are very scant and certainly need to be reformed[164] in order to avoid infringements of the right to *contradictoire*. Except a specific provision concerned with witness testimony, there are no general provisions governing the anticipated collection of evidence. A rather generic reference is laid down by Article 156(I) CCP.

---

[157] Art. 155 CCP.

[158] Lopes Jr (2001), p. 119 ff.; Polastri Lima (2002), p. 4 f.

[159] Lopes Jr (2017), p. 163 f. It is noteworthy that Brazilian legislature enacted the proposal made by the 'Grinover Commission' (a Commission appointed in 2000 by the Ministry of Justice with the aim of elaborating guidelines for the reform of criminal justice). This proposal, however, left no room for the use of pre-trial evidence, except the sole cases of pre-trial evidence taken in the context of coercive measures, non-repeatable evidence and anticipated evidence. See Hassan Choukr (2011), p. 275.

[160] Tourinho Filho (2010), I vol., 522 f.

[161] For an overview of the case-law see Hassan Choukr (2011), p. 278 f.

[162] Lopes Jr (2017), p. 165. In the same sense see already Pellegrini Grinover (1996), p. 239 f.

[163] Lopes Jr (2017), p. 161 f.

[164] *Ibid.*, 162.

It is a rather dangerous provision, which, collocated among the general rules on criminal evidence, empowers judges during the police inquiry to collect—pursuant to the requirements of necessity, adequacy and proportionality—any piece of evidence considered to be urgent and relevant for the decision-making. Moreover, this court procedure cannot always be activated in case of risks for the sought information. For instance, in cases of personal recognition or examination of the *corpus delicti*, the investigative authorities are allowed to gather non-repeatable evidence on their own initiative. This raises further delicate questions. Under which conditions can some information be deemed non-repeatable and what guarantees shall apply to these investigative activities? Furthermore, which rules shall govern the admission of evidence that became non-repeatable after its collection at the pre-trial stage? Brazilian law still provides no statutory responses to these questions.

J. *Audi alteram partem* and the Use of Measures of Coercion

I. Premise

Although the use of coercive means is unavoidable for the achievement of the aims of a criminal investigation, their adoption puts individuals in a particularly vulnerable position. This poses very difficult challenges to any criminal justice system oriented toward human rights protection. In Brazil, delicate trade-offs are required to ensure the individuals' involvement in the decision on the application of measures that interfere with fundamental rights without frustrating investigative needs. Moreover, difficult problems also arise in relation to judicial proceedings aimed at oversight of the lawfulness of coercive measures. For the sake of clarity, I shall separately analyse pre-trial restrictions on freedom and other investigative means relevant to fundamental rights. This discussion will finally deal with the right to be fairly heard in the field of *habeas corpus* proceedings.

II. The Right to contradictoire *and Restrictions on Freedom*

1. Participatory Safeguards in Remand Proceedings

Brazilian law provides for two main forms of provisional imprisonment *in itinere judicii*, that is, imprisonment *in flagrante delicto* and preventive imprisonment. These two types of imprisonment broadly correspond to the provisional arrest and the remand detention in the sense used by international human rights instruments. Another form of restriction on liberty is the temporary detention (*prisão temporária*). Among these types of detention, preventive imprisonment constitutes another important testing ground for the capacity of Brazilian law to provide vulnerable defendants with a fair opportunity to be heard. In the light of the

American Convention, to which Brazil is bound, it must be examined whether detainees have the right to a be promptly brought before a judge or another authority entitled to exercise judicial powers in order to be tried in a reasonable time or to be released. These guarantees supplement the general right of any person to be heard, with due guarantees and within a reasonable time, by an independent court. As we will note, the Inter-American case-law considers that the procedural safeguards laid down in the field of personal freedom can also be satisfied by a hearing following the deprivation of liberty.[165] Legal scholarship also called for a legislative reform in this direction of Brazilian law,[166] which did not traditionally allow for the participation of the defence in remand proceedings.[167] This approach, however, required in-depth reflection on the form in which defendants, after being restricted in their most valuable freedom, must have an effective opportunity to be heard and contrast the measure applied.

Recently, the Brazilian legislature, while reforming the code's rules on pre-trial measures, introduced an unprecedented form of *contradictoire* prior to the detention order.[168] After the 2011 reform, Brazilian judges, before ruling on a request for coercive measures, must summon the 'opposing party', except in urgent cases and unless a risk for the effectiveness of the coercive means exists.[169] The merits of this approach are unquestionable and it must be acknowledged that in most cases, the previous *contradictoire* does not entail further risks for the effectiveness of the coercive intervention.[170]

On close examination, this reform enhanced the participatory rights of individuals deprived of liberty in a rather contradictory way. Alongside the fact that the defendant can be deemed the opposing party of neither the prosecutor nor the judge, the code does not specify the aim and the consequences of this judicial summons.[171] The best solution would certainly be that defendants could be given the opportunity to be heard rather than replying in writing.[172] Yet the 2011 reform left this important issue undefined, which negatively impinges on the effectiveness of the defensive participation. Although the code requires judges to attach both the request and the necessary information to the judicial summons, it is not clear whether defendants must be given access to the overall information available.[173] Brazilian law also does not clarify whether defendants can count on enough time to prepare their defensive strategy and to search for information to rebut the justification of the restriction on liberty.[174]

---

165 Chapter 9, G.II.

166 Lopes Jr (2017), p. 586 f.

167 Hassan Choukr (2011), p. 443 f.

168 Law 12.403/2011.

169 Art. 282(II)(3) CCP.

170 Pacelli (2012), p. 521.

171 Lopes Jr (2011), p. 16.

172 Giacomolli (2014), p. 365.

173 Hassan Choukr (2011), p. 445.

174 Lopes Jr (2017), p. 587.

On the other hand, previous *contradictoire* is neither always possible nor is a reasonable solution, especially in cases in which the granting of information can frustrate the needs of criminal proceedings.[175] As noted, the code provides for derogations from the general duty of summoning the defendant, without clarifying, however, when risks for the effectiveness of the coercive means arise. On close examination, urgent cases may be due to a delay in the request due to the prosecutorial negligence. Above all, the 2011 reform has not specified which safeguards defendants must be given in these cases. Certainly, Article 282(II)(3) CCP cannot be interpreted in the sense that defendants could be restricted in their personal freedom or liberty of movement without having the opportunity to challenge the measure applied, since this would run counter to the approach of the American Convention. Even in exceptional cases in which no summons is due prior to the detention order, defendants should therefore be granted the right to be heard by a court, albeit after the detention order being enforced.[176]

Further concerns arise in relation to the way the procedure on the application of pre-trial measures can be initiated. In particular, it must be taken into consideration that, even after the Law 12.403/2011, Brazilian law allows for judges to order pre-trial detention *ex officio*.[177] There is no doubt that this power jeopardises the impartiality of the judicial authority,[178] thus affecting the possibility of the defendant subject to coercive measures being fairly heard by an independent body. Moreover, the 2011 reform maintained the code's rules, which enabled, alongside the prosecutor, both the police and the complainant (*querelante*) to request the adoption of pre-trial detention.[179] This autonomous power of the police, despite being in line with the general Brazilian approach to the pre-trial inquiry, can give rise to human rights concerns. Furthermore, it is not clear what role the victim can exactly play in the initiation of the remand proceedings. On close examination, the legal formulation is misleading in that it generally refers to the complainant. However, Article 311 CCP surely cannot be interpreted as also empowering the complaining to request pre-trial detention in cases of private criminal action, which is allowed where the minimum sentence is less than 4 years of imprisonment, i.e., the threshold laid down by Law 12.403/2011 as the minimum sentence to order remand detention.[180] The only case in which the complainant can request the defendant's remand detention is therefore that of private legal action subsidiary to the public prosecution.[181] However, the victim plays a rather ambiguous role in

[175]Giacomolli (2014), p. 364.

[176]Lopes Jr (2017), p. 587. Similarly Nucci (2014), p. 645.

[177]Art. 311 CCP.

[178]Lopes Jr (2017), p. 629 f.; Giacomolli (2014), p. 376 f.

[179]Art. 311 CCP.

[180]Lopes Jr (2017), p. 630. Of a different view Pacelli (2012), p. 519 f., who considers the lack of legitimation of the victim on the investigative stage incompatible with the Brazilian system of private legal action.

[181]Lopes Jr (2017), p. 630.

remand proceedings, since the code does not provide for any form of hearing of the victim either before or after the measure has been enforced.

Another deficiency of Brazilian law concerns the length of remand proceedings. Unlike in case of temporary detention whose duration cannot, as a rule, exceed 5 days with the possible prorogation of further 5 days,[182] the 1941 code does not traditionally provide for maximum time limits of provisional imprisonment. Nor are detained individuals granted the right to have this coercive means reviewed by an independent authority at fixed intervals, even though pre-trial measures are by definition of a temporary nature and lose their justification after fulfilling the goal for which they were applied.[183] This set-up in turn entails negative implications on the right to *contradictoire*, since the code says nothing about whether—and in the affirmative case, with which safeguards—defendants should be heard in the course of remand proceedings. This right is of utmost importance especially when the measure applied must be replaced with another or aggravated.[184]

In this regard, Law 12.403/2011 missed another important opportunity, failing to lay down a maximum length of pre-trial detention, one of the core goals pursued by the project of a code's reform No. 4.208/2001. The 2011 reform also did not enact the proposal of a new No. 7 of Article 282 CCP, a proposal that required judges to re-examine the justification of the coercive measure the latest every 60 days, or even earlier if needed.[185] Indirectly, maximum periods of detention might be deduced by the maximum time limits introduced by Law 11.719/2008 in relation to the criminal inquiry (as well as from other time-limits laid down by further legislation). Brazilian case-law has also contributed to filling this legal lacuna, starting with the leading case of the Tribunal of Justice of Minas Gerais, which for the first time fixed an "81 days-rule".[186] Nevertheless, the absence of legal indications makes it difficult to challenge the lawfulness of pre-trial detention because of its excessive duration, a result that entails a complex assessment of the characteristics of the concrete case.[187] Thus the duration of pre-trial detention inevitably depends on the balances struck in the specific case and on the subjective evaluation of the 'necessity' of the measure applied. An important factor that undoubtedly contributes to this result is also the limited use of the alternatives to custody, introduced by the 2011 reform and provided for by Article 319 CCP. Although judges increasingly use alternatives measures, it will probably take a long time to change the culture of a considerable part of the Brazilian judiciary, which largely explains the excessive use and the unnecessary length of remand detention.

Yet there is no doubt that the establishment of mechanisms to restrain the undue length of coercive means has certainly become a constitutional requirement since

---

[182]Law 7.960/1989.

[183]Giacomolli (2014), p. 366.

[184]Lopes Jr (2017), p. 588. In the same sense see already Pacelli (2012), p. 522.

[185]Lopes Jr (2017), p. 593.

[186]For in-depth analysis of the case-law cf. Jopes and Badaró (2009), p. 96 ff.

[187]Giacomolli (2014), p. 367.

the 2004 constitutional reform enshrined the right to be tried within a reasonable time.[188] By laying down that individuals cannot be deprived of their freedom and assets without a due process established by the law, furthermore, the Constitution requires the Brazilian legislature to grant the detained individuals the right to obtain a constant check of the justification of their detention.[189] This seems in turn to entail also the defendant's right to be heard during remand proceedings.

2. *Audi alteram partem* and Provisional Arrest

In the absence of a reasoned judicial order, people can only be provisionally arrested *in flagrante delicto* pursuant to the strict conditions established by the Constitution.[190] Brazilian constitutional law lays down detailed duties of information, which go beyond the requirements set forth by the American Convention. The compliance with these duties of information is a prerequisite of the lawfulness of the arrest procedure, which must otherwise lead to the immediate release of the arrested person.[191] Alongside the judicial authority, the police must inform the family of the arrested individuals, as well as any further person eventually indicated by them, of the arrest and place they are detained.[192] Furthermore, detainees must be duly informed of their rights, starting with their right to silence, and their family and lawyer must be given the possibility of assisting them.[193]

The code's rules are generally in line with these requirements. Recently, Law 12.403/2011 also introduced a duty of communication to the public prosecutor with the view to enhancing the protection of prosecutorial needs. The information of the prosecutor can thus lead to the adoption of further, more long-term measures of coercion, including pre-trial detention. The infringement of these duties of information affects the lawfulness of the procedure, requiring the judicial authority to immediately released the arrested person. Outside this case, the code empowers judges to two further decisions, that is, converting the arrest into provisional imprisonment by remanding the arrested person into custody, if other means of coercion prove inadequate to tackle the risks at stake, and ordering the provisional release, either with or without sureties.[194] On close examination, these powers must be interpreted in the light of the Constitution, which allows the imprisonment to be ordered and maintained only where bail is legally inadmissible.[195] From this it follows that defendants can be remanded into custody not only where other coercive

[188] Art. 5(LXXVIII) Const. See Giacomolli (2014), p. 366 ff.

[189] *Ibid.*, 368.

[190] Art. 5(LXI) Const.

[191] Art. 5(LXV) Const.

[192] Art. 5(LXII) Const.

[193] Art. 5(LXIII) Const.

[194] Art. 310 CCP.

[195] Art. 5(LXVI) Const.

means are inadequate—i.e., the alternative measures provided for by Article 319 CCP—but also when they cannot be granted bail. In this regard, it must be taken into account that the 2011 reform dropped the traditional concept of bail as a state's concession,[196] so that bail is now the first option that judges are called upon to assess while maintaining the provisional arrest. Unfortunately, this reform was not carried out in a consistent manner with its own aims. Remarkably, Article 321 CCP still makes the granting of provisional release conditional on the lack of the requirements of pre-trial detention.[197]

Surprisingly, Brazilian law does not require judges to hear the arrested person. The conversion of provisional arrest into pre-trial detention or another coercive measure is therefore a single-handed decision of the judicial authority, which involves neither the defence nor the prosecutor.[198] Even the Federal Constitution, while granting imprisoned people the right to know the identity of the officials responsible for the police questioning,[199] does not acknowledge the right to be heard by the judicial authority, notwithstanding the risks arising from the maintenance of the arrest. The practice is generally in line with this approach.[200] However, taking into account the intrusiveness of the coercive measures into which the provisional arrest can be converted (from conditional bail to provisional imprisonment), defendants should be granted the opportunity to be heard in order to contrast the need for remand detention.[201]

3. The Right to Be fairly Heard in Cases of Temporary Detention

It has been observed that the 1989 reform enacted another form of provisional detention, called 'temporary detention' because of its relatively short duration, compared to the undefined length of remand detention. Even though Brazilian law requires this coercive measure to be necessary to the pre-trial investigations,[202] the temporary detention mainly aims at satisfying the needs of the police inquiry. Therefore, the police can have the suspect at their disposal for a maximum period of 5 days. On close examination, this is not a short period of time, exposing suspects to the vulnerable situation of being confronted with police officers often interested in obtaining their confession or testing their availability to accuse other co-offenders.[203]

---

[196] Article 310 CCP expressed it literally before 2011. See Hassan Choukr (2011), p. 498.

[197] *Ibid.*, 499.

[198] *Ibid.*, 496.

[199] Art. 5(LXIV) Const.

[200] Giacomolli (2014), p. 364.

[201] Pacelli (2012), p. 522.

[202] Art. 1(I) Law 7.960/1989.

[203] Lopes Jr (2017), p. 142.

To avoid these risks, it is essential that the police properly fulfil their obligation to provide the detainees with full information on their rights enshrined in Article 5 of the Constitution,[204] starting with their right to silence. Moreover, the guarantee of judicial oversight should be enhanced. To be sure, temporary detention can only be enforced pursuant to a judicial order, which in turn presupposes request either of the police or the public prosecutor. In this context, however, the defence does not ned to be heard. The defence lawyer can only request that the detained individual be brought to court. Yet this request remains subject to the discretionary assessment of the competent judge, who will decide whether to hear the detainee.[205] It can be doubted that this result can be deemed consistent with the Federal Constitution.

III. The Right to Be fairly Heard and Investigative Interferences with Fundamental Rights

Investigative means can also endanger individual rights and new generations of interferences with fundamental rights do not even entail coercion in a strict sense. A particularly sensitive topic in the recent history of Brazilian law concerns the collection of genetic material for the purposes of criminal identification. The possibility of individuals being subject to criminal identification has its legal basis in the Constitution, which requires, in addition, a legislative arrangement.[206] The legislature recently intervened with Law 12.037/2009, which empowered judges to authorise—either *ex officio* or upon request of the public prosecutor or the police or the defence—coercive identifications for investigative purposes.[207] Law 12.654/2012 subsequently reformed this regulation, providing for the possibility of criminal identification by means of genetic information.[208]

Doubtless, these investigations can seriously affect fundamental rights, starting with the right to physical integrity and the right privacy. Moreover, as noted, suspects are exposed to the risk of coercively giving evidence against themselves.[209] In the light of this, the 2012 reform enhanced the guarantee of jurisdiction. Notwithstanding this guarantee, the broad way the judicial oversight was construed gives rise to several human rights concerns. It is particularly worrisome that criminal identification by means of genetic information must satisfy investigative needs, a rather generic formulation which can be interpreted in different ways according to the challenges posed by each concrete case. Moreover, the fact that the competent judge can order the coercive collection of genetic information can

[204]Art. 2(6) Law 7.960/1989.

[205]Art. 2(3) Law 7.960/1989.

[206]Art. 5(LVIII) Const.

[207]In the latter case, the identification is of course not of compulsory nature.

[208]Lopes Jr (2017), p. 143.

[209]*Ibid.*, 144 ff. and 434.

jeopardise the impartiality of judicial oversight. There is also the risk of judges following their own investigative strategy, or supporting that of the police, instead of guaranteeing the lawful use of means impinging upon fundamental rights.[210] It is therefore of utmost importance that this power is used under strict limits and only where the coercive collection of genetic material is truly essential to the ongoing criminal inquiry.[211] On the other hand, it is regrettable that Brazilian legislature failed to define the crimes in relation to which this measure is allowed.[212] The lack of statutory indications entails the risk that this serious coercion may also be used for investigating offences punishable with financial sentence.

IV. Audi alteram partem *in* habeas corpus *Proceedings*

1. *Habeas corpus* in Brazilian Law

In Brazil, people suffering from illegal detention and unlawful coercion are granted a special legal action, namely *habeas corpus*. Today, *habeas corpus* has its legal basis in the 1988 Constitution[213] and is also regulated by the current code of criminal procedure.[214] However, *habeas corpus* constitutes a procedure independent from criminal proceedings. Not only can it be initiated either before or after the institution of criminal proceedings but furthermore it can be lodged independently from other criminal law remedies.

Habeas corpus is strongly rooted in Brazilian law tradition. The origin of *habeas corpus* proceedings in Brazilian law dates back to the imperial period in the nineteenth century.[215] Relying on the English model, Brazilian legislature enacted *habeas corpus* for the first time into the 1832 code.[216] The first model of *habeas corpus* was clearly structured as a reaction to an ongoing coercion (habeas corpus *liberatório*), viewed in terms not only of illegal imprisonment but also of any further illegal interference with freedom (*prisão ou constrangimento ilegal em sua libertade*). However, Brazilian legislature soon broadened the scope of *habeas corpus* proceedings. The 1832 code was amended through an unprecedented form of preventive *habeas corpus*, aimed at countering not only illegal ongoing coercion but also the threat of imminent illegal restriction on liberty.[217] It cannot be ruled out that this reform was influenced by other legal actions, such as the Spanish *recurso*

---

[210] Lopes Jr (2013), p. 312.

[211] *Ibid.*

[212] *Ibid.*, 311 f.

[213] Art. 5(LXVIII) Const.

[214] Arts. 647 et seq. CCP.

[215] See Pontes de Miranda (1979), p. 123 ff. Cf. also Lopes Jr (2017), p. 1109 f.

[216] Arts. 340 et seq. 1932 CCP.

[217] Law 2.033/1871.

de manifestaciones de personas, which had already been in force in the Kingdom of Aragon from 1428 to 1592,[218] as well as the *firma de derecho*. Thus, these ancient instruments allowed not only the counteracting but also the prevention of illegal detentions.[219]

It is worth observing that *habeas corpus* was enshrined, with such double functions, in the first Republican Brazilian Constitution of 1891.[220] This Constitution failed however to define the type of coercion individuals must be undergoing or must be about to undergo. This legal lacuna gave rise to a stormy debate.[221] A constitutional reform, carried out in 1926, amended the rules on *habeas corpus*, whose scope of application was restricted to illegal imprisonment and illegal coercion of the liberty of movement (*liberdade de locomoção*). The 1934 Constitution amended this set-up, dropping the reference to 'movement'.[222] The 1941 code enacted the *habeas corpus* in this version, which was later enacted the 1988 Federal Constitution. Despite its very broad scope of application, *habeas corpus* can therefore only be invoked in case of illegal coercion of the *liberté d'aller et de venir*, as the Federal Supreme Tribunal pointed out in the *Súmulas* Nos. 693 and 695.[223] Moreover, it is noteworthy that Brazilian *habeas corpus* can be used in cases of coercion carried out not only by administrative authorities but also by the judicial authority. This makes it a very useful tool to counter unjustified imprisonment as well as, after the 2004 constitutional reform, the excessive length of remand detention.[224]

2. Participatory Rights in *habeas corpus* Proceedings

Habeas corpus constitutes a tool of utmost importance and is very often used in Brazil. It has a very broad scope, perhaps the broadest among the countries in which this instrument is acknowledged. Not only can it be used to challenge illegal detention but furthermore it is a powerful tool to counter illegal action or abuse of power made especially by public authorities.[225] As an instrument of 'collateral attack', *habeas corpus* can be used, for instance, to challenge a procedural invalidity as well as the termination of the proceedings without justified reasons. In general terms, *habeas corpus* provides individuals with a law action of constitutional relevance to protect their fundamental rights in criminal proceedings and

[218] Gimeno Sendra (2007), p. 537.

[219] Lopes Jr (2013), p. 1334 f.

[220] Art. 72(22) 1891 Const.

[221] Tourinho Filho (2010), II vol., 522 ff.

[222] *Ibid.*, 526 f.

[223] Lopes Jr (2013), p. 1342.

[224] *Ibid.*, 1342 ff.

[225] On the use of *habeas corpus* in cases of coercion made by private people see Lopes Jr (2017), p. 1123 f.

during the investigations, enabling them to request a judicial oversight in relation to any question that can entail the manifest invalidity of the proceedings under Article 648 CCP.

Notwithstanding the great importance of *habeas corpus*, the individuals concerned have surprisingly scant participatory rights in these proceedings. To be sure, pursuant to the origin of this legal action, the code enables the competent judicial authority to order that the complainant will be brought to court. However, the complainant must appear in court only if necessary.[226] By issuing a preliminary injunction (*liminar*), the competent judge often does not even consult the public prosecutor in order not to frustrate the goals of the procedure. The public prosecutor will usually be heard in the case of rejection of the request for preliminary ruling, a situation that, according to the Federal Supreme Tribunal's *Súmula* 691, should prevent individuals from requesting a new *habeas corpus* until the competent court rules on the merits of the case.[227] Complainants are allowed to make oral submissions very rarely and are often denied information on the court hearing, which clearly reflects negatively on their right to defence and effective participation in *habeas corpus* proceedings.

In the light of this, the Superior Court of Justice has in some rulings considered the decision on *habeas corpus* void when it was issued without counsel being informed about the court hearing, even though the complainant had expressly asked to be summoned to court in order to render oral statements.[228] In other rulings, however, the Superior Court of Justice followed the doctrine expressed by the Federal Supreme Tribunal in its *Súmula* No. 431,[229] which clearly excluded the invalidity of the *habeas corpus* decision due to the failure to summon the complainant's lawyer. There is little doubt that the Federal case-law should review its doctrine in order to enhance the protection of the right to a defence.[230]

K. Interim Conclusions

The examination of Brazilian law reveals the clear tendency to depart from its traditional inquisitorial approach to criminal proceedings. Doubtless, the 1988 Constitution provided a strong contribution to orienting criminal justice to the requirements of *contradictoire* and full defence. This brought about important innovations, such as the elimination of default proceedings, a typical example of criminal proceedings aimed solely at serving prosecutorial needs. More recently,

[226] Art. 656 CCP.

[227] Lopes Jr (2017), p. 1131 f., who points out, moreover, that the STF has recently smoothed this doctrine in cases of manifest unlawfulness of coercion.

[228] STJ, *HC* 93.557, rel. Arnaldo Esteves Lima.

[229] STJ, *HC* 19.506, rel. Felix Fischer.

[230] Lopes Jr (2017), p. 1133.

Brazilian legislature strengthened judicial guarantees in the field of coercive measures. Notwithstanding considerable steps forward, Brazil is, however, far from a participatory understanding of criminal justice and defence rights are still weak especially in the pre-trial phase, a result that is mainly due to the overwhelming role of the law enforcement authority.

References

Casara R, Melchior AP (2013) Teoría do Processo Penal Brasileiro. Vol. I, Dogmática e Crítica: Conceitos Fundamentais. Lumen Juris, Rio de Janeiro

Delmanto R Jr (2004) Inatividade no Processo Penal Brasileiro. Revista dos Tribunais, São Paulo

Giacomolli NJ (2014) O devido processo penal. Abordagem conforme a Constituição Federal e o Pacto de São José da Costa Rica. Atlas S.A., São Paulo

Gimeno Sendra V (2007) Derecho procesal penal, 2nd edn. Colex, Majadahonda

Gomes LF, Mazzuoli V d O (2010) Comentários à convenção americana sobre direitos humanos: Pacto de San José da Costa Rica, 3rd edn. Revista dos Tribunais, São Paulo

Hassan Choukr F (1995) Garantias constitucionais na investigação criminal. Revista dos Tribunais, São Paulo

Hassan Choukr F (2011) Código de Processo Penal. Comentários Consolidados e Crítica Jurisprudencial, 5th edn. Lumen Juris, Rio de Janeiro

Lauria Tucci R (2004) Direitos e garantias individuais no processo penal brasileiro. Saraiva, São Paulo

Lauria Tucci R, Cruz e Tucci JR (1993) Devido Processo Legal e Tutela Jurisdicional. Revista dos Tribunais, São Paulo

Lopes A Jr (2001) Sistemas de Investigação Preliminar no Processo Penal. Lumen Juris, Rio de Janeiro

Lopes A Jr (2011) O Novo Regime Jurídico da Prisão Processual, Liberdade Provisória e Medidas Cautelares Diversas. Lumen Juris, Rio de Janeiro

Lopes A Jr (2013) Direito Processual Penal, 10th edn. Saraiva, São Paulo

Lopes A Jr (2017) Direito Processual Penal, 14th edn. Saraiva, São Paulo

Lopes A Jr, Badaró GH (2009) Direito ao Processo Penal no Prazo Razoável, 2nd edn. Lumen Juris, Rio de Janeiro

Marques da Silva IL (2008) Reforma Processual Penal de 2008. Revista dos Tribunais, São Paulo

Moraes Pitombo SM (1983) O indiciamento como Ato de Polícia Judiciária. Revista dos Tribunais 577:313–316

Nucci G de Souza (2014) Código de Processo Penal Comentado. 13th edn. Forense, Rio de Janeiro

Pacelli E (2012) Curso de Processo Penal, 16th edn. Atlas, São Paulo

Pellegrini Grinover A (1990) As garantias constitucionais do processo. In: Pellegrini Grinover A (ed) Novas tendências do direito processual. Forense Universitária, Rio de Janeiro, pp 1–119

Pellegrini Grinover A (1996) Influência do Código-Modelo de Processo Penal para Ibero-América na legislação latino-americana. Convergências e dissonâncias comos os sistemas italiano e brasileiro. In: Pellegrini Grinover A (ed) O Processo em Evolução. Forense Universitária, Rio de Janeiro, pp 218–241

Pellegrini Grinover A, Scarance Fernandes A, Magalhães Gomes Filho A (2001) As nulidades no processo penal, 7th edn. Revista dos Tribunais, São Paulo

Pimenta Lopes MV (2013) A paridade de armas no processo penal. www.conteudojuridico.com.br

Polastri Lima M (2002) A Prova Penal. Lumen Juris, Rio de Janeiro

Pontes de Miranda FC (1979) História e Prática do Habeas Corpus, 8th edn. Saraiva, São Paulo

Scarance Fernandes A (1995) O papel da vítima no processo criminal. Malheiros, São Paulo

Scarance Fernandes A (2010) Processo penal constitucional, 6th edn. Revista dos Tribunais, São Paulo

Tourinho Filho F da Costa (2010) Código de Processo Penal Comentado vol I–II, 10th edn. Saraiva, São Paulo

Part III
Audi Alteram Partem in Transnational Criminal Justice. The Perspective of Domestic Law

Chapter 4
Participatory Rights in Transnational Criminal Justice Under Italian Law

Contents

A. General Remarks on the Rules Governing Transnational Criminal Inquiries 170
I. The Domestic Rules on Legal Assistance and the Influence of International Law Instruments 170
II. The Domestication of EU Law on Legal Assistance 171
B. Human Rights Developments in the Italian Law on Transnational Criminal Justice. Introductory Remarks 172
C. Participatory Rights in National Cases with Transnational Features 174
D. Participatory Rights, Right to Freedom and International Surrender Procedures. The Italian Law on Extradition 176
I. *In absentia* Trials and International Surrender 176
II. The Right to Be Fairly Heard and to Challenge the Lawfulness of the Surrender Procedure 179
III. Coercive Means and the Right to a Judicial Hearing 181
1. Coercive Means in Surrender Procedures 181
2. The Hearing of the Person Subject to Measures of Coercion 183
IV. The Role of the Judiciary in Extradition Procedures 185
E. Participatory Rights and Transnational Evidence 188
I. Models of Gathering Evidence Abroad 188
II. Participatory Rights in the Taking of Evidence Abroad 190
III. Defence Rights and the Use of Overseas Evidence 192
1. Premise 192
2. Movement of Evidence and Defence Rights in the Admission of Information already Gathered Abroad 192
3. Defence Rights and the Use of Evidence Taken Abroad in Response of an Italian Request for Legal Assistance 194
4. The Lax Approach of Italian Courts to the Use of Overseas Evidence 196
IV. Defence Rights in Gathering Evidence Requested by Other Countries 197
F. Provisional Conclusions 199
References 199

S. Ruggeri, Audi Alteram Partem *in Criminal Proceedings*,
DOI 10.1007/978-3-319-54573-8_4

A. General Remarks on the Rules Governing Transnational Criminal Inquiries

I. The Domestic Rules on Legal Assistance and the Influence of International Law Instruments

Different problems arise in the two countries in the field of transnational criminal justice. Italian law does not provide for comprehensive rules on transnational cases, which are governed by various legal instruments with different status and origin. The rules on international cooperation have basically two sources, namely domestic and international law. National rules are mainly concentrated within the 11th Book of the code, which governs international judicial cooperation with foreign countries. The current codification departed from the approach of the 1978 draft for a new code of criminal procedure. This draft proposal had proposed placing the rules on extradition, letters rogatory and the execution of foreign judgments after the general rules on the subjects and acts of criminal proceedings, the law on evidence, and pre-trial measures. Ten years after the failure of this project, the 1988 codification confirmed the traditional approach of the Rocco code, enacting the rules on the tools of legal assistance at the end of the code—quite an appendix to the provisions governing domestic cases.[1] By this means, the code's drafters also rejected the model, adopted a few years earlier by German-speaking countries at the beginning of the 1980s, of a separate statute on international cooperation in criminal matters.[2]

The choice to maintain the rules on legal assistance within the code of criminal procedure, however, confirmed the traditional approach, which, in line with the French model, linked international cooperation with the main principles governing domestic criminal proceedings. It is noteworthy that, although the code did not go so far as to domesticate international treaty law on legal assistance, the domestic rules on legal assistance were intended to have subsidiary application. Following the Rocco code, the 1988 codification gave prevalence to the international instruments on legal assistance in force in Italy.[3] As a result, national law can only be applied where the sought legal assistance lacks international law basis or with the view to filling lacunas existing in international law instruments. In these cases, all the code's rules—that is, not only the regulation of the 11th Book but also the ordinary provisions on domestic proceedings—must be applied to international cooperation.

This arrangement clearly aimed at preserving Italy's obligations towards the international community while ensuring coherence in the new model of criminal justice. The experience of the years ahead, however, demonstrated that the initial

[1] Chiavario (1991), p. 662.

[2] *Ibid.*, 663.

[3] Art. 696(2) CCP.

expectations were excessively optimistic. The enactment of international instruments on legal assistance into Italian law has been a long process and is still incomplete. A close examination of the international law instruments in force in Italy highlights the backwardness of Italian law.[4] At the Council of Europe level, Italy has never ratified the 2001 Second Additional Protocol to European Convention on Mutual Assistance in Criminal Matters, though it signed it more than 10 years later (January 2013). Therefore, the 1959 European Convention on mutual assistance in criminal matters, integrated by the 1990 Convention on the implementation of the Schengen agreement, was the main instrument governing the taking of evidence overseas.

Over the last decade, moreover, Italy has domesticated some important international law instruments. A clear example was provided by Law 146/2006, which ratified the UN Convention on transnational organised crime and the Protocols thereto. This led to Italian law opening up to mutual assistance that enhanced the international cooperation at the police level through new forms of transborder investigations, such as joint inquiries and undercover investigations. Despite these positive results, however, the use of the new investigative tools is limited to the scope of application of the individual international instruments, whereas the code's rules on international cooperation have still remained largely untouched.

II. The Domestication of EU Law on Legal Assistance

Further concerns arise in relation to EU law. Although Italy was actively engaged in the EU legislation under the former Third Pillar, most tools of international cooperation among member states have never been implemented into national law. For a quite long time, the EAW Framework Decision, domesticated with considerable delay,[5] remained almost the only tool of EU legal assistance in force in Italy. Until now, moreover, Italy has implemented neither the 2002 Framework Decision on joint investigation teams[6] nor the 2008 EEW Framework Decision.[7] As a result, there was until recently no legal basis for the carrying out of joint criminal inquiries with the authorities of other member states, and by cooperating with other EU countries, the Italian authorities also could not use more modern instruments of evidence-gathering than letters rogatory. This situation did not change after the entry into force of the Lisbon Treaty. We will see in Chap. 16 that, notwithstanding the rising engagement of Italy in domesticating the EU legislation issued after 2009, these developments mainly concern national proceedings, whereas among the instruments of legal assistance, only the EAW Framework was slightly amended.

---

[4]Caprioli (2013), p. 440 ff.

[5]Law 69/2005.

[6]FD 2002/465/JHA.

[7]FD 2008/978/JHA.

The consequence of the persistent closure towards EU law was in turn that the national law on international cooperation with other member states was not updated to meet the specific needs and especially the new challenges of the mutual recognition-based legal assistance. Moreover, the same legislative instrument used to domesticate the EAW Framework Decision—namely an ordinary Law or an equivalent legal instrument—was adopted to implement subsequent EU legislation on other forms of legal assistance.[8] On close examination, this result could not be deemed the necessary consequence of the approach followed by the 1988 code. The maintenance of national subsidiary rules on legal assistance, applicable to any case not covered by international treaties, does not prevent the legislature from adopting a similar approach to that of the French code, which enacted specific rules on the *entraide judiciaire internationale* between France and other EU countries.

Even more worryingly, Italy stood out until recently among the few countries that had not yet ratified either the Brussels Convention on Mutual Assistance in Criminal Matters among the EU Member States or its 2001 Additional Protocol. Therefore, the 1959 European Convention found application—and because of the failure ratify the 2001 Second Additional Protocol, in a highly out-dated way—even in the international cooperation with other EU countries. In January 2016, however, a Ministerial Committee took office for the purposes of elaborating a project of reform of 11th Book of the code of criminal procedure and updating Italian law to more modern instruments of international cooperating, starting with the Brussels Convention. As a result of this discussion, Law 149/2016 has recently ratified the Brussels Convention, while charging the Government with a double delegation in order both to enact the necessary rules of implementation of the 2000 Convention and to reform the provisions of the code's 11th Book. We can hope that the implementation of Law 149/2016, by means of an in-depth reform of the code's rules on legal assistance will also have positive effects in the near future on the international cooperation outside the EU area.

B. Human Rights Developments in the Italian Law on Transnational Criminal Justice. Introductory Remarks

The slowness of Italian law in domesticating instruments of international law on legal assistance has negatively affected not only the efficiency of international cooperation but also the protection of the fundamental rights of the individuals involved in transnational cases. From the perspective of the present discussion, it is

[8]For instance, Legislative Decree 161/2010 transposed the Framework Decision 2008/909/JHA on application of the principle of mutual recognition to judgments in criminal matters imposing custodial sentences or measures involving deprivation of liberty for the purpose of their enforcement in the European Union.

worth observing that the code still pays very scant attention to the role of private parties in transborder inquiries. This is apparent in the field of overseas evidence, which pursuant to the code's rules can only be taken by means of letters rogatory. Concerning the form and procedure of evidence-gathering, the 1988 code followed the approach adopted by various international instruments, allowing for the combination of *lex loci* with specific procedures of *lex fori* for the purposes of the collection of information sought by a foreign country.[9] By contrast, the taking of evidence abroad was originally governed solely by *lex loci*. It was only in 2001 that a legislative reform allowed for the application of Italian procedures abroad,[10] albeit only if provided for by a specific international agreement.[11] Pursuant to the current rules, however, *lex fori* can only be applied, in both cases, insofar as it was requested by the country seeking legal assistance. This demonstrates that the combined method primarily aims at safeguarding the prosecutorial needs of the state where the relevant proceedings are ongoing. The protection of the individuals involved in a transnational procedure remains instead in the background, so much so that the rules on letters rogatory do not even mention whether and to what extent the defence can participate in the taking of overseas evidence or information sought for the purposes of foreign prosecutions. Over the last decades, moreover, the failure to enact more modern tools of gathering transnational evidence has led to the case-law developing the practice of informal agreements with foreign authorities, agreements aimed at the collection of evidence for domestic purposes and its subsequent transfer to Italian proceedings. This practice raises serious concerns from a human rights perspective. The main shortcoming is that the taking of information is often hidden to the defence, which is thus deprived of any possibility of being involved in evidence-gathering.[12]

Further concerns arise in relation to extradition, notwithstanding that the 1988 code largely aimed at strengthening the protection of individual rights in the field of surrender procedures. In particular, the use of coercive measures—above all, pre-trial detention—was no longer deemed a necessary condition of surrender procedures. Moreover, the code's drafters redefined the overall relationship between governmental and the judicial authorities with a view to reducing the Minister of Justice's powers and enhancing court oversight of extradition decisions.[13] Despite these innovations, however, extradition remained largely based on the traditional dualistic approach, which left wide powers to the governmental authority. More specifically, the rules on coercive means in cases of incoming requests for extradition give the sought person no possibility of preventing restrictions on fundamental freedoms. Like in domestic cases, the individuals concerned need not be heard before decision-making. On the other hand, compared to the 1930

[9]Art. 725(2) CCP.

[10]Law 367/2001.

[11]Art. 727(5-*bis*) CCP.

[12]Caprioli (2013), p. 451 ff.

[13]Marzaduri (1983), p. 611 ff.

codification, the 1988 code provided for a more active involvement of the requesting country in the surrender decision.[14]

Surprisingly, Italian law also attaches little weight to the participatory rights of the individuals involved in transborder inquiries governed by the new tools of international cooperation within the EU area of freedom, security and justice. In particular, the Italian rules on the European arrest warrant, despite providing a general framework based on the mutual recognition principle, grant the defence few opportunities to take part actively in the surrender procedure. More recently, as noted, some adjustments were made to adapt national regulations to the recent EU legislation on some defence rights. Yet Law 69/2005 still lacks protective rules to ensure a fair hearing in the EAW procedure. In addition, Italy has never implemented the Framework Decision 2009/299/JHA, which largely reformed the 2002 legal solutions in relation to the problem of *in absentia* proceedings.[15] As a result, surrender procedures are still governed by out-dated rules on *in absentia* trials, which cannot properly fulfil the individual right to effective participation in surrender proceedings. Nor does Law 67/2014, which introduced a new procedure for absent defendants, suffice to prevent these shortcomings in a near future.

C. Participatory Rights in National Cases with Transnational Features

Against this background, I shall now analyse the developments that occurred in Italian law towards a participatory approach to transnational criminal justice by focusing on two main areas, namely criminal proceedings having transnational features and international cooperation in criminal matters. Concerning the first area, it is apparent that prosecutorial needs usually have a dominant weight where a domestic inquiry is at stake and there is a clear tendency to deal with foreign elements in such a way as to avoid hurdles for the ongoing investigation. This negatively affects the possibility of the persons involved participating in criminal proceedings. Certainly, providing proper and understandable information is the first condition for effective participation in criminal cases involving individuals who either do not live in the trial country or do not understand the language of criminal proceedings. Under the 1930 code, the failure to grant non-Italian speaking defendants the right to be informed about proceedings by means of judicial notification

[14]Chiavario (1991), p. 672.

[15]It might be argued that Italy has implicitly implemented this legislation through the 2014 reform, which abolished contumacy judgments. Yet this conclusion would be misleading. Whereas the new type of *in absentia* proceedings reproduce some of the situations covered by the old default proceedings, the rules on judicial service of the court summons, as noted, have largely remained unchanged.

(*comunicazione giudiziaria*) written in their own language had already led to the European case-law acknowledging a breach of Article 6(3)(a) ECHR.[16]

The 1988 code brought about some improvements by enacting special rules on the way defendants living abroad must be informed of the initiation of criminal proceedings, rules that, albeit with tiny reforms, have remained untouched until now. Italian law distinguishes the case in which the defendant's place of residence or stay abroad is known from that in which the competent authority, albeit knowing that the accused does not live in Italy, ignores their place of residence or stay abroad. In the former case, the judge or the prosecutor must send them, by registered post with recorded delivery, a letter providing information on the competent authority and the charge preferred. By means of the same letter, defendants are called upon to choose their legal domicile in Italy within 30 days. This requirement is of utmost importance. Where no counsel was appointed within the foreseen time limit or the indication on the address for service is incomplete or inadequate, the letter must be served on a court-appointed lawyer.[17] The result is not different when the exact place of residence or stay abroad is unknown. The only difference, however, is that the competent authority must first order further searches outside the national territory under the limits laid down by international agreements and, in the case of negative result, can institute the procedure provided for non-traceable defendants.[18]

At first glance, these rules provide defendants with stronger safeguards than in domestic proceedings. Notwithstanding some similarities with the general duty of information on the ongoing investigation under Article 369 CCP, defendants resident abroad must be granted the aforementioned special information irrespective of whether the law enforcement authorities must carry out an investigation at which their lawyer can be present. Moreover, this special information does not rule out the general notice on the proceedings, which can be useful especially to keep defendants updated about eventual changes to the charge.

Notwithstanding these merits, the code's rules far from properly protect the right to effective participation of the individuals concerned. Despite the broader scope of application of the information due to non-resident defendants than that applicable in purely national cases, the competent authority is not required to make the accused persons aware of the consequences of the failure to choose their legal domicile in Italy.[19] This lacuna is of utmost relevance especially in cases of defendants who are familiar neither with the Italian language nor with Italian law. Certainly, the 1988 codification improved the approach of the Rocco code under which, whenever the defendant failed to choose their domicile or residence in Italy, any further notification should be made at the court's registry.[20] This solution raised serious human

[16] ECtHR, *Brozicek v. Italy*.

[17] Art. 169(1) CCP.

[18] Art. 169(4) CCP.

[19] Grilli (1990), p. 308.

[20] Art. 177-*bis* 1930 CCP. It is noteworthy that the Constitutional Court deemed these rules constitutional. See CConst, 184/1980.

rights concerns, since the reasons the defendant failed to choose a legal domicile in Italy could depend on several grounds. However, the current arrangements, allowing the continuation of criminal proceedings by sending all further notification to a court-appointed lawyer, cannot be deemed satisfactory, entailing the risk of decoupling the defence strategy from the defendant's will. This risk is particularly high where the competent authority only knows that the defendant has a provisional residence abroad, an element often subject to change.

The shortcomings of the current regulation are enhanced where the defendant's stay abroad is known, since the need for further searches pursuant to international agreements is only an intermediate step towards the procedure established for untraceable defendants, a procedure aimed mainly at justifying prosecutorial needs. Worryingly, as we will see, the 2014 legislative reforms, while enacting new procedural safeguards by implementing the EU legislation on some defence rights in criminal proceedings, left this regulation in the same substantial terms drafted almost 30 years ago. There is no doubt that the right to prepare an effective defence strategy can be largely frustrated if criminal proceedings can be instituted on the sole condition that a lawyer possibly unaware of the defendant's needs was appointed.

D. Participatory Rights, Right to Freedom and International Surrender Procedures. The Italian Law on Extradition

I. In absentia *Trials and International Surrender*

More complex problems concern the participatory rights of the individuals involved in international cooperation. In the present discussion, I shall examine the developments that occurred in the field of extradition procedures. For the sake of clarity, I will analyse in Chap. 16 whether and to what extent Italian law properly enacted the procedural safeguards introduced by the EU legislation on the European arrest warrant and is consistent with the supranational reforms issued on defence rights in criminal proceedings and surrender procedures after the entry into force of the Lisbon Treaty.

As far as extradition is concerned, the first problem relates to the consequences on the surrender procedure of the absence of the accused in the relevant proceedings. The 1988 code did not enact any specific rules into the 11th Book. This result is to a certain extent understandable: it would have been rather contradictory to require foreign countries to fulfil conditions that domestic law could not satisfy.[21] It cannot be overlooked, however, that some years before the code's enactment Italy had ratified the Second Additional Protocol to the 1957 Extradition Convention.[22] This led to the introduction of some important solutions which, despite not banning

[21]Chiavario (2013), p. 64.

[22]Law 755/1984.

in absentia procedures, aimed at submitting the risks for personal freedom to stricter conditions than in the past. On close examination, the arrangements of the 1978 Protocol were clearly a compromise. On one hand, the requested party was allowed to deny extradition for the purposes of carrying out a sentence or detention order imposed by a decision rendered against *in absentia*, if it considered the proceedings conducted abroad as not satisfying the minimum defence rights granted to everyone charged with criminal offence. On the other, extradition should in any case be granted if the requesting party gave an assurance considered sufficient to guarantee to the person claimed the right to a retrial that safeguarded the rights of defence.[23]

Notwithstanding these steps forward in Italian law, the 1988 code, as noted, ignored the problem of the defendant's absence for the purposes of extradition with non-European countries. In the following years, however, Italian legislature showed a rising awareness of the specific problems arising from *in absentia* trials in the field of international cooperation. Bilateral agreements with both European and non-European countries introduced similar solutions to those provided for in the 1978 Protocol, while progressively reducing the margins of appreciation given to the requested country. For instance, the 2003 Addition Protocol to the 1987 Extradition Convention between Italy and Argentina enabled the contracting parties to refuse extradition in cases of *in absentia* proceedings that did not guarantee the minimum defence rights. At the same time, this international instrument required the requested state to surrender the sought person if the requesting country demonstrated that its law granted the person convicted *in absentia* the right to apply for a retrial.[24]

Italian legislature, however, is still far from a coherent approach to this very delicate issue, a result certainly due to the lack of satisfactory solutions at the national level. In particular, the bilateral agreements in force with non-European countries provide for very different arrangements. Some extradition treaties rule out refusal of extradition in case of criminal proceedings rendered *in absentia* abroad[25] or, in light of the formal regularity of the information given to defendants, consider *in absentia* trials equivalent to the proceedings effectively involving the accused.[26] The case-law has in turn deemed some domestic remedies to be proper assurances for the purposes of the surrender to a foreign country of individuals prosecuted in Italy *in absentia*. In particular, the Supreme Court

[23] Art. 3(1) SAP ECE.

[24] Art. 1(1–2). It is noteworthy, moreover, that the same Protocol requires only Italy to fulfil certain conditions aimed at demonstrating the regularity of the court summons and the adequacy of the information given to defendants. See Chiavario (2013), p. 65.

[25] This is the case of Article 5(a) of the extradition treaty between Italy and Brazil. As we will see, this agreement, although acknowledging the refusal of surrender of the persons who were not granted the minimum defence rights, expressly excludes that extradition can be denied on the sole ground that default proceedings were carried out in the trial country. Cf. Chapter 5, D.I.

[26] See, for instance, Article 16(b) of the 1970 Convention on Mutual Legal Assistance between Italy and Lebanon.

considered defendants to be sufficiently protected if they can apply for a judicial oversight of the conviction in the executive phase (*incidente esecutivo*).[27] The same conclusion applies if the accused can be relieved from the effects of the expiration of time to the appeal against the final judgment rendered *in absentia*,[28] or can have the conviction reviewed through an extraordinary appeal (*revisione*).[29]

On close examination, all these solutions can adequately satisfy neither the right to freedom nor the right to effective participation of the individuals involved in cross-border criminal cases. This result is largely due to the limitations of these domestic remedies. In particular, it is apparent that enabling application for judicial oversight only in the executive phase deprives the accused of the possibility of contributing to the decision-making, especially because *incidente esecutivo* mainly deals with the enforceability of the conviction rather than with the merits of the case. Another unsatisfactory solution is removing the effects deriving from the expiration of the time limits laid down for lodging an appeal against the conviction rendered *in absentia*, as this remedy, albeit facilitating the access to a second instance, cannot compensate defendants for the loss of the defensive opportunities provided for in the first instance. The extraordinary appeal of *revisione* may seem to be a more appropriate remedy, especially after a constitutional ruling that extended its scope of application to all cases in which a final conviction entailed the infringement of one of the fair trial guarantees of Article 6 ECHR.[30] One should not undervalue, however, the limitations of this particular appeal, which is a typical second instance hearing that does not allow for the full exercise of the defence rights.

All this calls for legislative reform of the national rules on extradition with a view to protecting the right to freedom and to ensuring the accused's active involvement in criminal proceedings. Law 67/2014 enhanced the need for legislative intervention. As noted, this reform, while enacting a new procedure for absent defendants, introduced an unprecedented, civil justice-oriented form of revocation of final judgments. Although this tool enables the individuals convicted *in absentia* to obtain participation in the proceedings at first instance, this mechanism also has evident limitations. In particular, we have observed that defendants can have the conviction revoked only if they succeed in proving that they remained unaware of the proceedings for reasons other than their negligence. Notwithstanding these limits, the need to avoid unjustified distinctions with domestic cases should lead to the Supreme Court reviewing its previous jurisprudence.

---

[27]CCass, *Fà*.

[28]CCass, *Perri*.

[29]CCass, *Greco*.

[30]CConst, 113/2011. On this judgment see the contributions to the roundtable published in *La Legislazione penale* (2/2011).

II. The Right to Be Fairly Heard and to Challenge the Lawfulness of the Surrender Procedure

Rather different problems arise in relation to the right of the sought individuals to take part in the surrender procedure. In this regard, we must examine whether and to what extent Italian law grants the requested person a fair opportunity to be heard and to challenge the lawfulness of the ongoing procedure. It has been observed that the 1988 code followed the dualistic approach of the 1930 code,[31] making the governmental decision on extradition conditional on the favourable decision of the court of appeal. Yet extradition does not necessarily presuppose judicial oversight, which the sought individuals can waive in giving their consent to the surrender to a foreign country. Moreover, extradition proceedings do not immediately involve the judicial authority since the Ministry of Justice must first forward the request to the Attorney-General before the competent court of appeal, whose tasks are mainly to identify the sought individuals and receive their eventual consent. As a result, the individual right to be heard must firstly be satisfied before the prosecutorial authority. In this regard, the 1988 code, closing a gap in the former codification, required the Attorney-General not only to inform the sought persons of their right to legal assistance but also to appoint a lawyer for defendants not represented by their own counsel, while informing the lawyer at least 24 h before the hearing.[32]

The appropriateness of these legal arrangements, moreover, should be assessed in the light of the complexity of the prosecutorial tasks, which are not limited to formal oversight, but include the questioning of the sought person on substantial issues.[33] The main goal of this examination is to prepare a report that must be presented to the court of appeal at the end of the preliminary inquiry carried out by the Attorney-General, a report aimed at enabling the judicial authority to assess at best the conditions for extradition. Moreover, the prosecutorial hearing gives to the sought individuals an important opportunity to challenge the lawfulness of the extradition procedure. This hearing also provides the Italian authorities with information of utmost importance to ascertain both the fairness of the proceedings conducted overseas and the compliance of the punishment imposed or expected abroad with the fundamental principles of Italian law. Yet the 1988 code failed to establish clear qualitative requirements of the prosecutorial hearing. In particular, it is questionable that General Prosecutors are not called upon to inform the sought individuals in clear terms of the consequences of their consent.[34] Furthermore, the code still ignores the need to appoint an interpreter to individuals who do not understand Italian, notwithstanding that the Supreme Court has long acknowledged the right to interpretation in the field of surrender procedures.[35]

---

[31] Art. 662 CCP (1930).

[32] Art. 703(2) CCP.

[33] Marchetti (1990), 40.

[34] *Ibid.*, 39.

[35] CCass, *Rabei Osman*.

At a deeper level still, it should be questioned why the 1988 codification, maintaining the approach of the Rocco code, entrusted these delicate tasks to the prosecutorial rather than to the judicial authority. Under the 1930 code, the immediate involvement of General Prosecutors was due to the fact that the extradition procedure usually started with the arrest of the sought person. The requested individuals were normally arrested upon order of either the Attorney-General, or the local prosecutor upon request of the Ministry of Justice,[36] and, after being arrested, they were put at the disposal of the local prosecutor or the *pretore*, who were entitled to hear them first. Significantly, this arrest was completely unconnected with the existence of risks either for the extradition procedure or the foreign prosecution[37] and was only intended to allow the requested state to properly fulfil its international obligations.[38] Besides, this set-up was in line with the general approach of the former code that, as noted, provided prosecutors with coercive powers in the investigative phase, enabling them to remand the defendant into custody at the very beginning of the criminal inquiry. The 1988 code dropped most coercive powers of prosecutors in the field of personal freedom, while making radical changes in extradition procedure. In particular, it enabled the police to arrest the sought person for urgent grounds only in case of risk of flight,[39] and after the Ministry of Justice has been informed of the arrest, the arrested person must be put at the disposal of the court of appeal.[40] Nevertheless, the code maintained the main role of General-Attorney who, despite not having prosecutorial tasks in the extradition procedure, leads the first hearing of the requested individuals, who are often called upon to make difficult decisions in a vulnerable situation in a foreign country (*e.g.*, by giving their consent to extradition).

Furthermore, Italian law acknowledges the right to a fair hearing in a rather formalistic way even in the court procedure activated in the requested country. The courts of appeal are called upon to check the lawfulness of the request for extradition after carrying out the necessary inquiries. To this end, both the Attorney-General and the defence lawyer must be heard, whereas the sought individuals and the representative of the requesting state must be examined only if they appear.[41] From this it follows that the judicial authority could only hear the Attorney-General and a court-appointed lawyer, even if scarcely familiar with the specific problems of the requested person and the problems of the foreign prosecution. Italian courts also contributed to watering down the right to *contradictoire*. According to the

[36] Art. 663(1) CCP (1930). See Cordero (1987), p. 839.

[37] Moreover, the police could arrest the sought person without a prosecutorial order, if they learned of a foreign arrest warrant or a similar act and provided that a risk of flight existed. Cf Art. 663 (2) of the 1930 CCP. In contrast, the risk of absconding was not required for the purposes of the arrest by the Attorney-General.

[38] Gaito (1987), p. 1680.

[39] Art. 716(1) CCP.

[40] Art. 716(2) CCP.

[41] Art. 704(2) CCP.

Supreme Court, the failure to inform the lawyer appointed by the requested person is an intermediate form of invalidity (*nullità a regime intermedio*),[42] which the competent judge can only declare prior to the formal standing hearing for the parties (*regolare costituzione delle parti*).[43] According to the case-law, the right to be personally heard by the court is also subject to the same regime.

III. Coercive Means and the Right to a Judicial Hearing

1. Coercive Means in Surrender Procedures

Specific problems arise when measures of coercion must be applied in the field of surrender procedures. Again, the solutions adopted by Italian law diverge considerably depending on whether an international agreement governs the surrender in a concrete case or the rules of the code apply to it. Traditionally, the 1957 European Convention on Extradition was the main multilateral instrument used in Italy with other European countries (and still used with non-EU countries). As noted, this Convention provided for the 'provisional arrest' of the sought individuals upon request of the requesting state.[44] This rather unfortunate definition may seem to encompass both the arrest and the provisional imprisonment, as clearly emerges from the maximum time-limits of detention, which do not certainly fit the usual short length of arrest.[45] This procedure can however only be activated in urgent cases and with a view to anticipating the extradition request in order to avoid the risk of the surrender proceedings being frustrated by the escape of the requested person. Significantly, although the requested country can always order the provisional release, it must anyway take all necessary means 'to prevent the escape of the person sought'.[46] This provision is of utmost systematic importance, demonstrating that the 1957 Convention did not rule out the possibility of further 'measures' being adopted,[47] measures aimed, however, at preventing the main risk that led to the provisional arrest being ordered.

A general overview of the bilateral instruments signed by Italy with individual countries, both inside and outside Europe, reveals a varied picture,[48] which highlights solutions that differ considerably from those of the Council of Europe's

---

[42]Chiavario (2013), p. 110.

[43]CCass, *Venezia*.

[44]Art. 16 ECE.

[45]According to Article 16(4) ECE, the provisional arrest can be terminated if the requested party has not received the request for extradition and the documents mentioned in Article 12 within a period of 18 days after arrest. In any event, the detainee must be released after 40 days from the date of arrest.

[46]Art. 16(4) ECE.

[47]Chiavario (2013), p. 148.

[48]*Ibid.*, 144 ff.

Convention on Extradition. Some agreements foresee various coercive means whose application is not always confined to a stage prior to the forwarding of the request for extradition. Among these bilateral agreements, the 1973 Extradition Treaty between Italy and UK significantly linked the arrest of fugitives to an ongoing extradition procedure.[49]

The 1988 code, following the approach adopted for the application of pre-trial measures in domestic proceedings, introduced detailed rules on provisional coercions in the field of passive extradition. The link between these provisions and the ordinary rules on pre-trial measures is so close that the code requires, as a rule, the application of the overall regulation of the 1st Title of the 4th Book. There are however some important exceptions, which give rise to some human rights concerns. In particular, the exclusion of any assessment of the strong suspicion of guilt, revealing the persistent underestimation of the human rights implications of the extradition procedure, cannot be deemed in line with the constitutional requirements on the right to freedom.[50] On close examination, the general reference to the ordinary rules on pre-trial measures also cannot be justified *in toto*. Thus, coercive measures adopted during surrender procedures have very different goals and needs from those of the pre-trial measures that can be adopted in a national criminal inquiry. This is mainly due to the fact that the risks concerned with extradition procedures cannot be compared with those that pre-trial measures aim to prevent in criminal proceedings. Therefore, the application of the rules on the general aims of pre-trial measures should be by definition precluded. Remarkably, the code justifies the adoption of coercive measures in the light of the need to prevent the sought person from avoiding surrender.[51]

This acknowledgment highlights further deficiencies in the approach followed by the Italian criminal justice, with particular regard to respect for the principle of proportionality. At first glance, Italian law properly protects the right to freedom by providing for the application of a wide range of coercive measures other than the provisional detention.[52] Yet some of the ordinary pre-trial measures, restricting the freedom of movement to a low extent, do not fit the main goal pursued, being unable to properly prevent the risk of flight of the sought individuals. This delicate issue, moreover, leads to questioning the adequacy of the distribution of competences laid down for the adoption of pre-trial measures. Unlike in domestic cases, coercive measures cannot be ordered upon request of the competent prosecutor but must be requested by the Ministry of Justice.[53] This confirms the traditional admixture between political and legal assessments within a procedure that can lead to serious restrictions on individual rights. The right to liberty also cannot be

[49] Art. 10.

[50] Marzaduri (1993), p. 234 f.

[51] Art. 714(2) CCP.

[52] Art. 714(1) CCP.

[53] The case-law has pointed out the essential character of the Ministry's initiative. See CCass, *Askin*.

deemed as properly guaranteed by the requirement that the extradition procedure must already have been instituted. This solution can be detrimental for the sought individuals, taking into account the long period of duration of the coercive means. Significantly, this period not only goes far beyond the expiration periods laid down in the 1957 European Convention on Extradition but furthermore is often not proportional to the different degrees of intrusiveness of the measures adopted.[54]

Under the rules of the code, moreover, coercive measures can also be applied before a request for extradition has been lodged. Along with the case of arrest, enacted in line with the 1957 Convention, the code provided for another situation, characterised by the 'provisional application' of coercive measures at the request of both the foreign country and the Italian Ministry of Justice.[55] This form of coercion turns out to affect the overall set-up on pre-trial means in the field of passive extradition. On one hand, the existence of a provisional application of coercive means confirms the (potentially) long-term character of the restrictions on freedom ordered under Article 714 CCP. On the other, the requirement of the request of the foreign country and the Italian Ministry of Justice raises doubts as to whether the ordinary application of pre-trial measures is linked with real risks concerned with the foreign prosecution, as here coercive means are adopted regardless of any initiative of the foreign State. By contrast, the case of provisional application of coercive means seems to fit the requirements of the 1957 Convention. This case primarily aims at avoiding that the future request for extradition is frustrated by the escape of the sought person, which, as noted, is the only justification for coercion in the field of surrender procedures.[56] Furthermore, the maximum duration of the coercive means cannot here exceed 40 days without a request for extradition and the necessary documents arriving either at the Ministry of Foreign Affairs or at the Ministry of Justice.[57]

2. The Hearing of the Person Subject to Measures of Coercion

Against this background, we should now examine whether and in which terms the individuals subject to coercive means must be granted a fair opportunity to be heard. In case of police arrest within an extradition procedure, the code requires the police to inform the Ministry of Justice instead of the competent prosecutor, as usually provided for in domestic cases. This does not, however, make the procedure unconstitutional, since the police must bring the arrested person, within 48 h, before the president of the court of appeal, who is the competent authority to validate the arrest. Some concerns arise, instead, from a constitutional law perspective in relation to the validation procedure and the decisions following the validation of

[54]Marchetti (1993), p. 461.

[55]Art. 715 CCP.

[56]Art. 715(2)(c) CCP.

[57]Art. 715(6) CCP.

the arrest. Since the code says nothing about the characteristics of the validation procedure, the case-law has generally ruled out that the arrested person should be heard by the president of the court of appeal, who must carry out a rather formal review on the basis of the information available.[58] The sought person will be heard only 5 days after the arrest has been maintained.[59] Unlike in domestic proceedings, moreover, the code requires that coercive means be ordered in case of validation of the arrest.[60] This solution, if interpreted as giving no discretion to the judicial authority in choosing whether to order another measure of coercion, would certainly be unconstitutional since it could lead to the adoption of a long-term restriction on fundamental freedoms even without real justification—a conclusion the case-law has rightly rejected.[61]

Doubtless, the 1988 code put a greater focus on the hearing of the person subject to pre-trial detention and other restrictions on freedom, requiring, unlike in domestic cases, the detained person be heard in any case within 5 days from the execution of the measure adopted.[62] On close examination, the right to be fairly heard was here guaranteed in a rather weak manner. Whereas the case-law deems this deadline non-peremptory,[63] the code says nothing about the consequences of the failure to hear the sought person within 5 days. This gap can give rise to clear discrimination *vis-à-vis* defendants against whom a national investigation is ongoing, defendants who could profit from the expiration of the measure applied. Moreover, the code may seem to attach a rather formal aim to this hearing, that is, the identification of the sought person and the eventual consent to surrender. The accused was not enabled to challenge substantial issues,[64] as confirmed by the radical choice of excluding, as noted, any assessment by the requested country of the justification of the foreign detention order that activated the extradition procedure. The guarantee of legal assistance is also weaker than in national cases. Although detained individuals must be granted a court-appointed lawyer, if they are not represented by their own counsel, lawyers must be informed only 24 h before the hearing and their participation is not mandatory.[65]

---

[58] CCass, *Gorduna*.

[59] Marzaduri (1993), p. 249.

[60] Art. 716(3) CCP.

[61] Chiavario (2013), p. 156.

[62] Art. 717(1) CCP.

[63] CCass, *Sava*.

[64] Chiavario (2013), p. 157.

[65] Art. 717(2) CCP.

IV. The Role of the Judiciary in Extradition Procedures

To a great extent, the effectiveness of the right to a fair participation in international surrender proceedings also depends on the role of the judiciary in the requested country. The 1988 code strengthened judicial powers in line with the general enhancement of the role of the judiciary in criminal proceedings. The area in which most significant changes were made in this direction is that of coercive means, which under the 1930 code largely fell within the competence of prosecutors. Pursuant to this approach, the Rocco code enabled the Attorney-General to order, pending an extradition procedure, the provisional detention of the sought individuals.[66] Doubtless, this result hardly guaranteed their right to freedom, taking also into account that the Attorney-General must in turn follow a request of the Ministry of Justice. Even more questionably, the detainee's provisional release was also in the hands of the Attorney-General, who was called upon to assess the lawfulness of detention and to decide whether to maintain it.[67] It is noteworthy that, although several legislative reforms strengthened judicial oversight in the field of personal freedom over the 1980s,[68] the case-law maintained this approach until the last years of the 1930 code, ruling out, albeit with a few exceptions, the application of the ordinary guarantees on the restriction on personal freedom.[69]

Despite the lack of specific indications in the 1989 Delegation Law on international cooperation,[70] the 1988 code dropped the prosecutorial power to order provisional coercions pending the extradition procedure, entrusting this delicate power to the judiciary. This change was a part of a broader reform that charged the court of appeal with the task of assessing the lawfulness of requests for extradition, a task from which this court can only be released in case of consent of the sought person.[71] From this approach it followed that the sought individuals could no longer be extradited without the favourable decision of the court of appeal.[72]

These developments were not accompanied, however, by a systematic reflection on surrender procedures and, in more general terms, on international cooperation in criminal matters. As a result, the case-law interpreted the enhancement of the judiciary in light of old categories that, just a few years before the code's enactment, had led to denying the character of extradition procedures as judicial proceedings.[73] Legal scholarship also adopted a similar approach, classifying surrender procedures as a form of non-contentious jurisdiction (*giurisdizione*

[66]Art. 663 of the 1930 CCP. See Marchetti (1990), p. 33 ff.

[67]Art. 663(2) of the 1930 CCP.

[68]From Law 532/1982 to Law 330/1988.

[69]CCass, *Torresan*.

[70]On these developments see Marzaduri (1993), p. 1 f. and 155 f.

[71]Art. 701(2) CCP.

[72]Art. 701(1) CCP.

[73]CCass, *Carboni*.

volontaria)[74]—a rather ambiguous classification of half-jurisdictional and half-administrative proceedings, derived from civil procedural law and applied to extradition procedures until now.[75] In other words, the code's drafters followed the traditional understanding of extradition as a procedure both structurally and functionally different from the proceedings carried out against a person charged with a criminal offence.[76]

This heritage led the underestimation of the new functions of the judiciary, which were interpreted in the light of general features of traditional concept of extradition.[77] Still today, we can observe the dominant position of the Ministry of Justice, whose action can inhibit the effectiveness of transnational prosecution, *e.g.* by not allowing extradition despite the positive response of the court of appeal. Indeed, neither the favourable decision of the judicial authority nor the person's consent obliges the Ministry to authorise the sought extradition.[78] This demonstrates that extradition still holds a political character that can thus contaminate the national criminal law action, carried out for the purposes of a foreign prosecution, with assessments of political expediency. For instance, although the Attorney-General has no jurisdiction to restrict individual freedoms, the Ministry can, at any stage of the extradition procedure, apply for provisional limitations of personal liberty of the sought people and request the seizure of their assets.[79]

This approach can not only frustrate the goals of the criminal prosecution carried out by the trial country but can also affect the ordinary conduct of the criminal law action carried out by the requested country, a legal action that can have negative repercussions—on national territory—on fundamental rights. There is no doubt that the adoption of a human rights perspective would lead to a correct understanding of the function of the judiciary in surrender procedures and the criminal law character of extradition procedure. This calls for in-depth reflection not only on the repercussions of the foreign proceedings on the sphere of individual rights[80] but also on the implications of the decision on surrender from a constitutional law perspective.[81] In the light of this, the task of the judicial authority certainly cannot be restricted to the assessment of the formal requirements of the requests for extradition but should also encompass the lawfulness of the surrender procedure. This oversight should be conducted with specific regard both to the risks to fundamental

---

[74]In this sense see Cordero (1991), p. 1031, who thus reproduced the opinion expressed under the 1930 code. Cf. Cordero (1987), p. 839.

[75]Cordero (2012), p. 1251.

[76]Marzaduri (1993), p. 171 ff.

[77]Cordero (2012), p. 1251.

[78]Art. 701(3) CCP.

[79]Art. 714(1) CCP.

[80]Under the Rocco code, the Constitutional Court had already dealt with this issue by declaring the unconstitutionality of Royal Decree 5276/1870, which had ratified the Convention between Italy and France that allowed the extradition for crimes punishable with death penalty. Cf. CConst, 54/1979. On this judgment see Marzaduri (1993), p. 178 f.

[81]*Ibid.*, 176 ff.

rights arising from the foreign prosecution and to the requirements set forth by the constitutional law of the requested country.[82]

Italian constitutional law would certainly favour such a reconstruction, pursuing, as noted, among its core goals the protection of inviolable human rights,[83] while posing the right to liberty at the top of the inviolable freedoms of the person.[84] From this it follows that criminal jurisdiction, albeit carried out for the purposes of international cooperation, must be exercised in full compliance with the overall implications of surrender procedures.[85] This should also entail the possibility of the national authorities scrutinising the merits of the case prosecuted abroad, a review that cannot be restricted to the ascertainment of the dual criminality requirement or the abstract punishability of the prosecuted act in both countries.[86] However, the code provides for scant solutions in this regard and the need not to frustrate the international cooperation with foreign countries still prevails. In cases of extradition to a foreign country, the Italian judicial authority can only scrutinise the existence of a strong suspicion of guilt in the absence of an international instrument in force in Italy or if international agreements do not provide otherwise.[87] Over the last years, furthermore, the Supreme Court has gradually broadened the scope of this oversight, requiring national authorities to also test the merits of foreign prosecutions where an international agreement, although being in force, provides nothing in this regard.[88] From this it follows that the competent authority must assess the merits of the foreign prosecution unless an international agreement provides for an explicit derogation.[89] Legal scholarship had already advocated this conclusion at the beginning of the 1990s.[90] This approach is to be welcomed, since the direct implications of the extradition procedure on the right to freedom of the sought person surely require national authorities to assess the justification required for restricting personal freedom in similar terms to those provided for in domestic cases.[91]

---

[82]Article 705(2) CCP requires the judicial authority to issue an unfavourable decision, among others, when the person to be extradited has been subject, or risks subjection to. a process that does not respect fundamental rights, as well as if the foreign judgment infringes the basic principles of Italian law.

[83]Art. 2 Const.

[84]Art. 13(1) Const.

[85]For a similar approach see already Marzaduri (1993), p. 190 f.

[86]*Ibid.*, 191 f.

[87]Art. 705(1) CCP.

[88]CCass, *Maksymenko*. For a different approach to the treaty on extradition between Italy and the USA, notwithstanding that it requires the requesting state to provide the cooperating country with information able to allow assessing the existence of probable cause concerned with the prosecuted offence, see Chiavario (2013), p. 114 f. Especially in the past, moreover, the Supreme Court had on several occasions pointed out that, in cases of international agreements in force in Italy, the national authority was limited to a formal review of the merits of the request for extradition. Cf., among others, CCass, *Odigie Obeide*.

[89]CCass, *Von Pinoci*. In the same sense cf. Marchetti (1990), p. 64 ff.

[90]Marchetti (1990), p. 64 ff.

[91]Marzaduri (1993), p. 195.

E. Participatory Rights and Transnational Evidence

I. Models of Gathering Evidence Abroad

Further delicate problems arise in the field of transnational evidence. In this regard, the 1988 code also faithfully followed the traditional approach, according to which letters rogatory are the only means of gathering evidence abroad.[92] Various international instruments signed by Italy, especially with non-European countries, adopt the same approach. At the EU level, we have noted that the 1959 Convention on Mutual Assistance long constituted the main instrument used by Italy to collect overseas evidence, since Italy had until recently neither ratified the Brussels Convention on Mutual Assistance nor implemented mutual recognition-based instruments aimed at the collection of evidence in other EU countries. Moreover, Italy failed to enact further instruments of legal assistance, such as the Second Additional Protocol to the Council of Europe's European Convention on Mutual Assistance and the 2001 Additional Protocol to the EU Convention.

All this leads to the result that Italian cooperation with foreign countries—at least if based on international agreements—still largely follows traditional modes of legal assistance, which requires, as a rule, the application solely of the *lex loci*. In the absence of an international law basis, we have noted that the 1988 code, while allowing for partial application of *lex fori* in case of letters rogatory requested by foreign country, followed a similar approach in cases of evidence taken abroad upon Italian request. Thus the drafters of the code did not provide for any possibility of national authorities requesting the application of domestic procedures with a view to the collection of evidence abroad. It took several years before Law 367/2001 enabled the Italian authorities to request the fulfilment of formalities of Italian law by requesting foreign states to obtain evidence for the purpose of a national prosecution. This possibility, however, still has a limited scope of application, being conditional on the existence of a specific international agreement.[93] However, the new Article 727(5-*bis*) CCP, enacted in 2001, did not introduce a new power for Italian authorities, which can forward their request to foreign countries only as long as it is foreseen in international law agreements. The real innovation is instead a limitation for the Italian authorities, which can only request the application of the domestic rules affecting the admissibility at trial of the evidence taken.

Nonetheless, Italian legal assistance in the field of evidence is still characterised by the strong governmental character of letters rogatory and it is early to foresee how the implementation of the Brussels Convention will reform the international cooperation between Italy and other member states. The shortcomings of the traditional forms of legal assistance—in particular, the slowness of the procedure and the great uncertainty about the admissibility at trial of the evidence gathered by

---

[92] See among others Marchetti (2008), p. 1035 ff.

[93] Law 367/2001.

this means[94]—have therefore led the case-law to develop more flexible forms of international cooperation. The main one is perhaps the informal exchange of evidence already gathered by foreign authorities.[95] In Europe, several international instruments provide for this form of legal assistance, strongly based on the principle of availability of information.[96] Among the bilateral agreements signed by Italy, the 1988 Agreement on Judicial Cooperation between Italy and Switzerland includes the exchange of information pertaining to criminal offences in the area of judicial cooperation, an exchange aimed at assisting the requesting state in initiating or carrying out investigations or proceedings.

International law acknowledges such exchanges solely in relation to evidence already gathered and some legal instruments even emphasise the 'spontaneous' nature of these exchanges.[97] Nevertheless, Italian authorities have increasingly used this mode of legal assistance over recent years in a quite different fashion. The main concern arises from the fact that informal procedures are often used to bypass the difficulties of legal assistance. In order to avoid the inadmissibility of evidence laid down in the field of letters rogatory,[98] Italian authorities often lodge informal requests with foreign countries, aimed at initiating a proceeding abroad with the aim of collecting specific pieces of evidence for the purposes of a national prosecution in Italy. There is little doubt that this form of cooperation cannot be deemed spontaneous.[99] One of the most worrisome points is that evidence from abroad can be used to institute a national investigation. Although some international instruments allow for this possibility,[100] it is rather unclear on what basis and within which limits any investigations took place abroad. On close examination, there is a high risk that the availability principle turns out to legitimise suspicionless procedures addressed to the collection of evidence abroad for the purposes of a national investigation.[101] Even more worryingly, these procedures often lead to the adoption of measures that can seriously impinge on the sphere of individual rights.[102]

In Italy, these practices have also gained ground because of the lack of general rules on joint cross-border inquiries.[103] Despite some legislative proposals, there was until the 2016 reform no comprehensive legal basis for criminal investigations

---

[94]Art. 729(1-*bis*) CCP. This provision, which was also enacted by the 2001 reform, forbids the use at trial of evidence gathered abroad by means of letters rogatory according to procedures other than those requested by Italian authorities pursuant to Article 727(5-*bis*) CCP. For the need to give a restrictive interpretation of this provision see Caprioli (2013), p. 450.

[95]See among others Marchetti (2008), p. 1071 ff.; Caprioli (2013), p. 451 ff.

[96]Böse (2007).

[97]In this sense see Article 7 of the Brussels Convention.

[98]Caprioli (2013), p. 452.

[99]*Ibid.*

[100]See Article 11(1) of the Second Additional Protocol to the 1959 Council of Europe's Convention.

[101]Melillo (2009), p. 103; Caprioli (2013), p. 453.

[102]Ruggeri (2013), p. 561.

[103]Caprioli (2013), p. 453.

being carried out in joint venture with foreign authorities,[104] except in specific criminal law areas[105] and in relationship to some countries.[106] Yet joint investigations have increasingly gained relevance in police practice, and notwithstanding the lack of general rules, common task forces were set up with foreign authorities over last years, as in the *Duisburg* case.[107] Joint investigations differ from another form of intervention of national authorities in the collection of overseas evidence, through the so-called 'joint letters rogatory'. In Italy, this form of legal assistance mainly takes place on the basis of the 1959 Council of Europe's Convention.[108] However, the possibility of joint letters rogatory is conditional on the consent of the foreign country and only allows for mere presence at the evidence-gathering without any possibility of investigations conducted by the Italian authorities and without any law enforcement powers on foreign territory.[109]

II. Participatory Rights in the Taking of Evidence Abroad

Against this background, the effective exercise of participatory rights in transborder inquiries depends on the mode of legal assistance used in a concrete case. The traditional system of letters rogatory makes the involvement of the defence in the taking of evidence abroad conditional on the provisions of the law of the requested country. Moreover, the 1959 Council of Europe's Convention had already provided for a limited form of intervention not only of national authorities but also of private parties in the execution of letters rogatory. Since the entry into force in Italy of the 1959 Convention (1962), this mode has therefore enabled defence lawyers to be involved in the gathering of overseas evidence. Italian legal scholarship usually adopts the definition of 'participatory' or 'joint letters rogatory" (*rogatorie partecipate* or *concelebrate*) to indicate the direct involvement in the taking of overseas evidence.[110] This does not reflect, however, the terms of the participation of both the defence and the Italian authorities, which, as noted, does not go beyond the mere presence at foreign investigations that under this international instrument, furthermore, can be carried out on the basis solely of *lex loci*.

A more enhanced form of participation of the defence can take place where Italian authorities are allowed to request the application of specific forms of *lex fori*

[104]Marchetti (2008), p. 1065.

[105]See Law 146/2006, which ratified the UN Convention on transnational organised crime.

[106]Cf. the 1998 Swiss-Italian Agreement.

[107]Scella (2011), p. 222.

[108]Art. 4 of the 1959 Convention.

[109]Exceptions require the explicit consent of the foreign competent authority, as happened in the 1990s in the *Big John* case. See Di Chiara (1994), p. 1 ff.

[110]See, albeit with some differences, Pisani (2001), p. 557; Marchetti (2008), p. 1057; Caprioli (2013), p. 450 f.

abroad. It has been observed, however, that under the code's rules this possibility depends on the existence of a specific provision in an international agreement in force in Italy. On close examination, this form of limited application of Italian law may not suffice to ensure the participation in evidence-gathering of the interested parties, which depends on various factors, such as the way national authorities formulated the request for letters rogatory or the exact terms of the international agreement applicable to a concrete case.

Further concerns arise in the relation to the other aforementioned forms of legal assistance. Concerning joint inquiries, the few international instruments providing for this form of investigation leave to the competent authorities a great margin of discretion in defining, *inter alia*, the law applicable to the investigations necessary in a concrete case.[111] This inevitably impinges on the possibility of private parties being involved in evidence-gathering. Moreover, in complex transnational cases, in which the team needs to carry out investigations in the territory of several countries, evidence-gathering will be governed by different *leges loci*. This gives rise to great uncertainty as to the limits of the powers of the law enforcement authorities, limits that are often unpredictable *ex ante*.

The most serious problems, moreover, arise from the practice of informal evidentiary exchanges. The main concerns do not relate here to forms of evidence-gathering—forms that, due to the national nature of the investigations, will follow *lex loci*—but to the involvement of the defence. It is precisely the informal nature of information exchanges that deprives the individuals concerned of any possibility of not only taking part at the collection of evidence but also challenging the lawfulness of the procedures followed abroad. It is clear that, especially when the exchange of information is preceded by informal requests aimed at the collection of evidence useful to a national prosecution, legal assistance is 'played on a field that is [...] hidden *a posteriori* from the eyes of the defence'.[112]

A final question to be addressed is whether the defence can have a proactive role in the collection of overseas evidence. In this respect also, Italian law reveals an out-dated approach, ruling out any initiative by defence lawyers, who are not entitled to request letters rogatory, being required to submit their request to the judicial authority that will assess the need for this procedure. Nor can counsel carry out investigations abroad, as allowed, in contrast, in national cases. The Supreme Court excluded this possibility, envisaged by legal scholarship,[113] on the assumption that Article 391-*bis* et seqq. CCP lay down an exhaustive list of investigative tools acknowledged to the defence, a list that does not allow for direct investigations overseas.[114] This conclusion gives rise to discriminatory results, taking into account that public prosecutors—as representatives of the judiciary—can activate the procedure of letters rogatory. Moreover, we have seen that the Supreme Court

[111]Marchetti (2008), p. 1065.

[112]Caprioli (2013), p. 454.

[113]Curtotti Nappi (2007), p. 14.

[114]CCass, *Kaneva*.

allows the admission of evidence gathered by foreign authorities upon informal request of the Italian judicial authority, including the public prosecutor.

III. Defence Rights and the Use of Overseas Evidence

1. Premise

Against this background, the question arises as to whether and to what extent information gathered abroad can be used in national criminal proceedings. In general terms, both legal scholarship and Italian courts consider the admissibility of overseas evidence a question of a purely domestic relevance, being therefore subject solely to national law. Moreover, the possibility of obtaining overseas evidence largely depends on the way the information was gathered and on the mode of legal assistance used in a concrete case. The code distinguishes two main situations, depending on whether the sought evidence was already taken abroad or whether Italy must engage in international cooperation to obtain information overseas.

2. Movement of Evidence and Defence Rights in the Admission of Information already Gathered Abroad

The first situation occurs where the sought evidence was already gathered abroad independently from a request for legal assistance. Unlike letters rogatory, this case does not pose problems of evidence-gathering but of movement of evidence. The 1988 code did not explicitly deal with this problem. Furthermore, the code's rules of implementation submitted the admission of evidence already collected by foreign authorities to almost the same conditions established for the use of information taken in other domestic proceedings, as laid down in Article 238 CCP.[115] From this it follows that Italian courts can only admit, as a rule, evidence obtained abroad either at trial or in any case through a procedure aimed at guaranteeing the defence's participation. Moreover, statements taken abroad, after being admitted at trial, can only be used against those defendants whose lawyers could take part in the examination abroad. Defendants who were not represented at the time of evidence-gathering abroad must consent to the use of the information obtained against them, otherwise it will be used within the general limits laid down by the code. The only exception concerns the case of non-repeatable evidence taken by the police in foreign proceedings, evidence that can be used at trial either upon common agreement between the parties, or after the person whose statements were obtained has been examined by means of letters rogatory.[116]

[115] Art. 78(1) RICCP.

[116] Art. 78(2) RICCP.

At first glance, this set-up fulfils the constitutional requirements of defence and *contradictoire*. However, the technique used—namely, the quite automatic reference to the general rules governing the transfer of evidence from other national proceedings—does not fit best the specific needs of transnational cases, while ensuring a rather formal degree of participation in the evidence-gathering. In some cases, the legal arrangements pose rather unrealistic conditions, as in the case of incriminating evidence given by witnesses or co-defendants abroad. It is extremely improbable, for example, that the lawyer of the defendant A, against whom the national proceeding A1 was initiated, had the opportunity to be involved in the taking of evidence in the foreign trial B1 instituted against the accused C and D, a trial possibly unconnected with A1. In other cases, the application of the ordinary rules is by definition excluded, depending on conditions strictly linked with national legal instruments. For instance, several countries do not provide for a pre-trial evidentiary procedure similar to the Italian *incidente probatorio*,[117] which makes the requirement of unpredictable non-repeatability of evidence by definition impracticable.[118] Further concerns arise in relation to consent to the use of untested evidence. On close examination, the requirements of the accused's consent to the admission of incriminating evidence and the agreement between the parties with the use of non-repeatable evidence taken by the police do not necessarily reflect the defendant's decision to allow for the admission of such information. Especially where the accused cannot be traced, the defence lawyer on his own initiative and even a court-appointed lawyer can agree with the use of untested evidence—a risk particularly high in transnational cases. Of course, the accused can apply for the renewal of evidence-gathering and above all, can request a new examination of his accuser in Italy. Like in domestic case, however, the fulfilment of the right to confrontation is subject to the limits laid down for serious crimes by Article 190-*bis* CCP, which still leaves a great margin of discretion to the competent authorities.

On the other hand, it cannot be overlooked that the application of the ordinary rules to the admission of evidence gathered abroad can jeopardise the interests of other individuals involved in a criminal law action. Where the aforementioned conditions cannot be met, the testimonial evidence obtained abroad will normally be used only to assess the reliability of witnesses or co-defendants, provided they appear in court and give evidence in the Italy. Yet this approach, despite not excluding the use of inconsistent statements to prove the facts in exceptional circumstances,[119] is also modelled on the requirements of national proceedings. This poses obstacles to the use of information that not only may be consistent with the overall information gathered but furthermore may be intrinsically reliable

---

[117]Under the 1930 code, moreover, the Supreme Court pointed out that the fulfilment of the exact conditions laid down by national law could not be required and that the performance of a procedure aimed at taking evidence before an impartial authority with the parties' contribution sufficed to justify the admission of overseas evidence at trial. See CCass, *Ballinari et al.*

[118]Some scholars point out, moreover, the need for coordination with the general provision of Article 526(1-*bis*) CCP. Cf. Scella (2002), p. 104.

[119]In this sense see instead Galantini (1992), p. 416.

(or may have been taken through a procedure aimed at ensuring its reliability). Doubtless, the aprioristic underuse of untested evidence can affect the right especially of non-resident victims to make their voice heard in national criminal proceedings.

3. Defence Rights and the Use of Evidence Taken Abroad in Response of an Italian Request for Legal Assistance

Different problems arise where the sought information was not taken abroad and legal assistance is needed to collect it. Under the code rules, the use of evidence taken abroad by means of letters rogatory is subject to strict conditions, modelled on two main situations. Both non-repeatable and documentary evidence (*e.g.*, the results of DNA analysis) taken by means of letters rogatory can be admitted into the trial file without further conditions.[120] By contrast, repeatable oral evidence gathered through letters rogatory (*e.g.*, witness statements) can be admitted at trial under the condition that the lawyers could be present at the evidence-gathering and could exercise the same powers acknowledged by Italian law.[121] A particular situation concerns the case of statements given in the pre-trial stage by a person living abroad by means of letters rogatory, statements that, despite being originally repeatable, have become non-repeatable for subsequent circumstances. The code allows for this evidence to be read out only if the person examined, although summoned, did not appear in court, and examination at trial is absolutely impossible.[122]

Notwithstanding the clear attempt of the code's drafters to make the use of evidence gathered through letters rogatory consistent with the approach of the 1988 criminal justice system, these situations cannot achieve a proper balance between prosecutorial needs and the participatory rights of the defence. It is questionable that Italian law treats in the same manner the cases of documentary and non-repeatable evidence, allowing for the quite automatic admission of both types of evidence taken through letters rogatory. This solution, which is quite obvious in case of documentary evidence, is debatable in case of urgent evidence. Precisely the existence of risks to evidence-gathering in open court should have justified, as a rule, the involvement (even through technical means) of the defence in the collection of evidence abroad. Moreover, admitting non-repeatable information without any consideration of whether the defence's participation at the evidence-gathering abroad was objectively impossible cannot deemed in line with the Constitution. Italian case-law raises further concerns. Starting with a literal interpretation of Article 431(1)(f) CCP, Italian courts allow for the use of testimonial evidence on the sole condition that the defence lawyer could take part in the execution of letters rogatory, even though the accused expressly requested personal

[120] Art. 431(1)(d) CCP.

[121] Art. 431(1)(f) CCP.

[122] Art. 512-*bis* CCP.

participation.[123] There is no doubt that this interpretation frustrates the *audi alteram partem* rule, giving a rather formalistic sense to the right to be fairly involved in the collection of oral evidence.

Concerning the use of evidence given by non-resident witnesses, Article 512-*bis* CCP, as it was introduced by the 1992 anti-mafia reform, only required that the person either be not summoned or, being summoned, did not appear at trial. The current version of this provision, reformed by Law 479/1999, makes the admission of testimonial evidence conditional on the absolute impossibility of a trial examination in Italy. Italian courts have interpreted this condition in a strict sense, providing for the fact that evidence could not be obtained through letters rogatory with the defence's participation, for grounds unconnected from the accused's intent. However, the requirement of the impossibility of the witness examination in open court should be viewed in objective terms. As a consequence, the Italian authorities should not engage in assessing whether the non-resident witness ever accepted confrontation with the accused. The Supreme Court took the same view by allowing evidence to be read out if the foreign state did not consent to the hearing by means of letters rogatory.[124] Doubtless, this situation cannot be deemed in line with the constitutional requirement of objective impossibility of the accused's participation,[125] which calls upon the Italian authorities to ascertain the grounds on which no confrontation could take place with the accuser. It is therefore debatable that the lack of consent of the foreign country can allow for the use of the statements, at least when it is proven that the witness refused confrontation with the defendant. This calls for a systematic interpretation of this provision in the light of the general rule of Article 526(1-*bis*) CCP, which forbids the accused's guilt to be based on untested evidence if the accuser voluntarily refused confrontation with the defendant.[126] It can be doubted, however, that this case-law will be maintained in a near future in the EU judicial area. As we will note, the EIO Directive introduced comprehensive rules on hearings by videoconference, rules that considerably circumscribe the possibility of the authorities of other member states refusing the witness's examination.[127]

On the other hand, Italian law allows for the reading out of statements given by non-resident persons in such terms that the Italian authorities are called upon to make an overall assessment on the case. On a first level, the requirement that 'other circumstances' must also be taken into account clearly gives a great margin of

---

[123]CCass, *De Falco*.

[124]CCass, *Remling*.

[125]Of a different view Caprioli (2013), p. 443.

[126]In this sense see CCass, *Iamundo*. According to criminal law scholarship, the party requesting the admission of the overseas statements must prove that the witness did not refuse confrontation with the defendant. In this sense see Grifantini (2007), p. 258. Yet this further condition, which is not foreseen by the provision under discussion, cannot be required in absolute terms. In particular, it would be excessive to require defendants to prove of the lack of the witness's voluntary refusal of confrontation by requesting the admission of exculpatory evidence.

[127]Chapter 13, C.II.2.b.

discretion to the competent authority. This can also lead to the refusal of admission of exculpatory evidence that has become non-repeatable for objective reasons. This result clearly infringes the accused's right to support his version of the facts—and to defend his status as an innocent person—through exculpatory evidence.[128]

As noted, moreover, the Italian authorities have increasingly used informal channels of legal assistance to avoid the shortcomings of letters rogatory. From the viewpoint of the present discussion, this raises the problem of the admissibility of the information gathered by these means and the implications on the defence rights of the individuals concerned. On close examination, this particular situation can be traced back to none of the two cases examined. On a formal level, since the information transferred to Italy was already taken abroad, the problem should only concern the movement of evidence. Yet we have seen that information exchanges are often preceded by informal requests for evidence-gathering by national authorities. To be sure, resorting to this practice does not ensure unconditional admissibility of evidence. By gathering the sought information, the foreign authorities only followed their own law, which can be different and even incompatible with the requirements set for the use of evidence by Italian criminal procedure law. Remarkably, Italian case-law requires that the evidence obtained abroad through this practice must also pass the check of admissibility pursuant to Article 78 of the code's implantation rules.[129] At any rate, it should be taken into consideration that, whatever the results of the overseas investigations are, the foreign authorities have full discretion in selecting the elements that can be forwarded to the requesting authority.[130]

4. The Lax Approach of Italian Courts to the Use of Overseas Evidence

Alongside the way evidence was collected abroad, Italian courts tend to adopt a rather lax approach to the use of overseas evidence. In the case of information obtained through letters rogatory, this result is largely justified by the demanding character of this procedure. Here, however, two main situations should be distinguished, depending on whether overseas evidence should be used for the purposes of the decision on the merits of the case or with a view to interim decisions. Concerning the former situation, the case-law makes the use of overseas evidence conditional on the general assessment of compliance with the main principles of Italian law.[131] Remarkably, this condition applies to any case of evidence taken abroad, no matter whether it was gathered at request of the Italian authorities or had already been collected by the foreign authorities. Italian courts adopt a very different approach to the latter case, allowing for full use of evidence taken abroad

[128] Cesari (2001), p. 79.

[129] CCass, *Pozzi*. See Caprioli (2013), p. 452.

[130] Melillo (2009), p. 103 f.

[131] CConst, 379/1995. See also CCass, *Pozzi*.

for the purposes of intermediate decisions and the application of coercive means, irrespective of whether the main guarantees of Italian law were infringed upon abroad and whether defendant consented to the use of the sought evidence.[132]

Both solutions give rise to serious concerns from a human rights perspective. To be sure, the test of consistency with the fundamental principles of domestic law aims at providing a further barrier to the massive use of evidence gathered through means other than those allowed under Italian law. However, the result of this assessment has usually been the opposite one, legitimising the use of evidence obtained by other means and with very different guarantees from those allowed by Italian law under the sole condition that the basic principles of domestic law were not jeopardised. As a result, the requirement of compatibility only with the main principles of Italian law has led to the inevitable lowering of fundamental rights protections in the field of evidence-gathering in Italy.[133] A particular worrisome situation concerns the defendant's right to be involved in the taking of criminal evidence. For instance, the Supreme Court deemed statements given abroad admissible at trial, even though the witness was examined only by the judicial authority without any *contradictoire*, if it is allowed by *lex loci*.[134] This conclusion, which cannot be shared in purely domestic cases, gives therefore rise to clear distinctions among defendants, distinctions that, depending on accidental factors (*e.g.*, the location of the source of evidence), cannot be justified from a human rights perspective. The approach to the use of overseas evidence for the purposes of interim decisions—and especially of decisions on coercive means—is even more questionable. This conclusion can produce a double negative result, not only frustrating the accused's right to take part in evidence-gathering but also overlooking the interference with individual rights deriving from decisions based on untested evidence.

IV. Defence Rights in Gathering Evidence Requested by Other Countries

At first glance, minor problems may seem to arise in relation to the collection of evidence requested by other countries. In this regard, Italian law does not provide for specific rules governing the participatory role of the defence. It has been observed, however, that the code—despite acknowledging the application, as a rule, of Italian law—allows for foreign countries to request that the execution of letters rogatory follow specific procedures of *lex fori*. Significantly, the drafters of the code had already enacted this possibility in 1988 with a view to facilitating the use of the information taken for the purposes of foreign prosecutions. Furthermore,

132 CCass, *Pizzata*.

133 Caprioli (2013), p. 445 ff.

134 CCass, *Russo*.

the fact that combination with *lex fori* does not depend on the existence of *ad hoc* provision in an international agreement leads to the result that foreign procedures can be requested to allow for the participation of private parties even in investigative acts that do not involve the defence under Italian law. Here also, moreover, the application of *lex fori* depends on the explicit request of foreign authorities. This requirement does not ensure the participation of the defence, while leaving great uncertainty as to the overall procedure that will be applied in a concrete case.

Furthermore, the code also provides for scant guarantees as to the participation of the defence in the previous phase of *exequatur* by the competent court of appeal. In particular, Article 724 CCP not only does not require the intervention of the competent prosecutor—who, while appearing in court, must in any case be heard—but also does not expressly acknowledge the participation of the individuals concerned and their lawyers. Legal scholarship has raised doubts on the constitutionality of the code rules under Article 24(2) of the Constitution.[135] However, the lack of specific references does not exclude the defence's involvement, taking into account that the *exequatur* procedure must follow the general rules on hearings *in camera*, which allow for the participation of the defence.[136] In some cases, moreover, the sought person must be personally heard in court, *e.g.* if free consent is a prerequisite for the *exequatur*.[137] In other cases, the involvement of the defence in the *exequatur* phase can jeopardise the effective execution of letters rogatory, especially when hidden investigations are at stake. In these cases, a proper solution is to postpone the intervention of the defence.[138]

Ultimately, it must be taken into account that Law 367/2001 dealt with the case in which an international law agreement enables a foreign administrative authority to request legal assistance to Italy in a proceeding for a criminal offence.[139] Despite providing for the jurisdiction of the competent judge for the pre-trial inquiry, the code requires the Italian authorities to apply under ordinary conditions the procedure requested by the administrative authority. This provision reveals scant attention to the forms of evidence-gathering, taking into consideration that administrative authorities are not always bound by the same obligations as the judicial authority. It is not clear pursuant to what criteria and within which limits the requesting authority can ensure respect for the guarantees of *lex fori* and to what extent the defence has therefore the right to be involved in the sought investigation.

---

[135]Cordero (2012), p. 1261.

[136]Marchetti (2016), p. 1031.

[137]*Ibid.* Indeed, Article 724(5) CCP provides for two situations in which the consent of the requested person is needed, i.e. (a) when the fact does not constitute a criminal offence under Italian law and (b) when specific requirements relating to race, religion, nationality, and so on, can affect the execution or the results of letters rogatory.

[138]Marchetti (2005), p. 94.

[139]Art. 726-*ter* CCP.

F. Provisional Conclusions

The examination of Italian law highlights a largely out-dated approach to transnational criminal justice, especially where Italy is engaged in international cooperation in criminal matters. However, slow steps forward could be observed in the field of legal assistance over the last years, especially in the international cooperation with other EU countries. The constitutional fair trial reform has surely contributed to the enhancement of the defence rights of private parties in transborder inquiries, *e.g.* reinforcing the barriers against the use of untested evidence. Notwithstanding these developments, the participatory safeguards of the defence are far from the standards of national criminal justice and the voice especially of vulnerable individuals involved in cross-border cases is still weak. Furthermore, despite the recent ratification of the Brussels Convention, the implementation of the EU legal instruments launched after the entry into force of the Lisbon Treaty, due to their limited scope of application, will probably have scant effects on forms of legal assistance other than the EAW proceedings.

References

Böse M (2007) Der Grundsatz der Verfügbarkeit von Informationen in der strafrechtlichen Zusammenarbeit der Europäischen Union. Bonn University Press, V&R Unipress

Caprioli F (2013) Report on Italy. In: Ruggeri S (ed) Transnational inquiries and the protection of fundamental rights in criminal proceedings. A study in memory of Vittorio Grevi and Giovanni Tranchina. Springer, Heidelberg, pp 439–455

Cesari C (2001) "Giusto processo", contraddittorio ed irripetibilità degli atti di indagine. Rivista italiana di diritto e procedura penale, pp 56–87

Chiavario M (1991) Cooperazione internazionale ed obiettivi di garanzia e di efficienza nella nuova disciplina dei rapporti con autorità giudiziarie straniere. In: Chiavario M (ed) Commento al nuovo codice di procedura penale, vol VI. Utet, Torino, pp 661–678

Chiavario M (2013) Manuale dell'estradizione e del mandato d'arresto europeo. Utet, Torino

Cordero F (1987) Procedura penale, 9th edn. Giuffrè, Milano

Cordero F (1991) Procedura penale, 1st edn. Giuffrè, Milano

Cordero F (2012) Procedura penale, 9th edn. Giuffrè, Milano

Curtotti Nappi D (2007) I nuovi orizzonti investigativi del difensore: le informazioni assunte all'estero. Osservatorio del processo penale 2:14 ff

Di Chiara G (1994) Cooperazione tra Stati ed assunzione della rpova in territorio straniero. Trasferte giudiziarie e recenti esperienze: il processo c.d. *Big John*. In: Di Federico G, Di Chiara G (eds) Cooperazione tra Stati ed assunzione della rpova in territorio straniero. Lo Scarabeo, Bologna, pp 1ff

Gaito A (1987) Commento all'art. 663. In: Conso G, Grevi V (eds) Commentario breve al codice di procedura penale. Cedam, Padova

Galantini N (1992) L'inutilizzabilità della prova nel processo penale. Cedam, Padova

Grifantini FM (2007) Utilizzabilità in dibattimento degli atti provenienti dale fasi anteriori. In: Ferrua P, Grifantini FM, Illuminati G, Orlandi R (eds) La prova nel dibattimento penale, 4th edn. Giappichelli, Torino, pp 167–313

Grilli L (1990) Le notificazioni penali. Giuffrè, Milano
Marchetti MR (1990) L'estradizione: profili processuali e principio di specialità. Cedam, Padova
Marchetti MR (1993) Commento all'art. 714. In: Chiavario M (ed) Commento al nuovo codice di procedura penale. 1st Agg. Utet, Torino, pp 456ff
Marchetti MR (2005) L'assistenza giudiziaria internazionale. Giuffrè, Milano
Marchetti MR (2008) Rogatoria (dir. proc. pen.) In: Enciclopedia del diritto, Annali II-1. Giuffrè, Milano, pp 1035–1074
Marchetti MR (2016) Rapporti giurisdizionali con autorità straniere. In: Conso G, Grevi V, Bargis M (eds) Compendio di procedura penale, 8th edn. Wolters Kluwer Italia/Cedam, Padova, pp 989–1072
Marzaduri E (1983) Autorità giudiziaria ed autorità amministrativa nel procedimento di estradizione passiva. Rivista italiana di diritto e procedura penale, pp 611–644
Marzaduri E (1993) Libertà personale e garanzie giurisdizionali nel procedimento di estradizione passiva. Giuffrè, Milano
Melillo G (2009) Tecniche investigative speciali e squadre investigative comuni. In: Illuminati G (ed) Prova penale e Unione Europea. Bononia University Press, Bologna, pp 93–111
Pisani M (2001) In tema di assunzione all'estero delle prove da oarte dell'autorità giudiziaria italiana. Rivista italiana di diritto e procedura penale, pp 557–573
Ruggeri S (2013) Transnational inquiries and the protection of fundamental rights in comparative law. Models of gathering overseas evidence in criminal matters. In: Ruggeri S (ed) Transnational inquiries and the protection of fundamental rights in criminal proceedings, A study in memory of Vittorio Grevi and Giovanni Tranchina. Springer, Heidelberg, pp 533–573
Scella A (2002) Tutela del contraddittorio e utilizzazione di prove formate in altri procedimenti. In: Kostoris RE (ed) Il giusto processo tra contraddittorio e diritto al silenzio. Giappichelli, Torino, pp 92 ff
Scella A (2011) Verso le squadre investigative comuni: lo scenario italiano. In: Rafaraci T (ed) La cooperazione di polizia e giudiziaria in materia penale nell'Unione europea dopo il Trattato di Lisbona. Giuffrè, Milano, pp 215–229

Chapter 5
Participatory Safeguards in Transnational Criminal Justice Under Brazilian Law

Contents

A. General Remarks on the Brazilian Rules Governing Transnational Criminal Justice 201
B. Human Rights in Brazilian Transnational Inquiries 203
C. Participatory Rights in Domestic Criminal Proceedings with Transnational Features 205
D. *Audi alteram partem* and the Protection of Personal Freedom in Extradition Procedures 206
I. The Problem of *in absentia* Trials 206
II. The Right to a Fair Hearing and the Role of the Judiciary in Extradition Procedures 207
E. Participatory Rights and the Taking of Evidence in Transnational Cases 210
I. Modes of Gathering Overseas Evidence 210
II. The Right to a Defence and Equality of Arms in the Taking of Overseas Evidence 211
III. Participatory Rights in the Collection of Evidence Requested by Foreign Countries 213
F. Provisional Conclusions 215
References 215

A. General Remarks on the Brazilian Rules Governing Transnational Criminal Justice

Like Italy, Brazil also does not have comprehensive rules on transnational criminal justice. Although the drafters of the 1941 code enacted a few rules on international cooperation with foreign authorities, these rules only concerned two legal assistance instruments, that is, letters rogatory and the homologation of foreign judgments. By contrast, no provision governed extradition, even though it is certainly the oldest form of judicial assistance in Brazil. Significantly, the Constitution in force at the time of the code's enactment—namely, the 1934 Constitution—had already conferred to the Federal Supreme Tribunal jurisdiction in extradition procedures. This situation has remained largely unchanged since then and there are still no codified rules on extradition. The enactment in 1980 of a comprehensive Law on

S. Ruggeri, Audi Alteram Partem *in Criminal Proceedings*,
DOI 10.1007/978-3-319-54573-8_5

the legal status of aliens (*Estatuto do Estrangeiro*) certainly contributed to this result, introducing specific provisions on extradition procedures.[1]

In 1941, however, a number of international agreements were already in force. Since then, new legal instruments have been enacted and have governed international cooperation with other countries inside and outside South America. This has led to the result that the rules on international cooperation in force in Brazil are today largely spread among legal sources of different origin and nature. Furthermore, international instruments follow very different approaches with a view to fulfilling specific needs of cooperation with the relevant countries. Certainly, the lack of a general statute on judicial assistance in criminal matters has negatively affected the consistency of Brazilian law on transnational criminal cases. The failure by the drafters of the 1988 Constitution to lay down clear requirements of international cooperation has accentuated this result.

It must be acknowledged, however, that the enactment of the 1988 Constitution raised attention towards international cooperation in criminal matters. This is apparent from the introductory provisions, which acknowledge Brazil's obligation to cooperate with other countries for the swift progress of mankind,[2] while requiring Brazil to engage in economic, politic, social and cultural integration with other countries from Latin-America, with a view to the creation of a Latin-American community.[3] More specifically, the Federal Constitution laid down important human rights clauses in the field of extradition, which is not allowed in cases of foreign citizens prosecuted for offences of opinion and political crimes.[4] Extradition is also excluded in case of Brazilian citizens, except naturalised citizens who have committed a criminal offence before the naturalisation, or in the case of their involvement in drug trafficking under the legal conditions.[5] Concerning the extradition procedure, furthermore, the Federal Constitution confirmed the Federal Supreme Tribunal's jurisdiction in the field of extradition procedures.[6] Pursuant to the 1988 constitutional set-up, the Federal Supreme Tribunal was also competent for the homologation of foreign judgments and the *exequatur* of letters rogatory. The 2004 constitutional reform, however, transferred the latter two competences to the Superior Court of Justice.[7] It is also noteworthy that the Constitution provided for a general jurisdiction of federal courts in all cases based on international agreements with foreign countries.[8]

The process of re-democratisation of the country following the 1988 constitutional reform led to Brazil ratifying new important international instruments to

---

[1]Law 6.815/1980.

[2]Art. 4(IX) Const.

[3]Art. 4 Const.

[4]Art. 5(LII) Const.

[5]Art. 5(LI) Const.

[6]Art. 102(I)(g) Const.

[7]Art. 105(I)(i) Const.

[8]Art. 109(III) Const.

govern the judicial assistance in criminal matters, both with other states in Latin America and with European countries.[9] Moreover, other factors have also contributed to this process, such as the need to provide a legal basis for enhanced forms of international cooperation aimed at countering the exponential growth of serious types of organised crimes that have a transnational dimension.[10] In this context, Brazil also adhered to some important multilateral agreements at the regional level, such as the 1996 Mercosur Protocol on Mutual Legal Assistance in Criminal Matters[11] and the 1992 Inter-American Convention on Mutual Assistance in Criminal Matters and its 1993 facultative Protocol.[12] These developments in turn accentuate the need for a general statute with a view to establishing a common approach that eliminates the legal fragmentation of the current law on international cooperation in criminal matters. This statute would also serve as a model for future international agreements.[13] Even though various initiatives have been presented since the last decade in this direction, none of them have yet been implemented.

Ultimately, it must be taken into consideration that legal assistance is not the only area that deserves legal intervention in the field of transnational criminal justice. Domestic proceedings can also have transnational elements. In this respect, it is worth observing that over the last decades Brazilian law has enhanced the use of the tools of international cooperation in case of criminal proceedings characterised by some transnational features. A clear example is the general application of letters rogatory to summon defendants resident outside Brazil, as reformed by the Law 9.271/1996. This legislation dropped the original provision that limited this possibility to cases of crimes not subject to bail (*delitos inafiançáveis*), whereas in other cases defendants must be summoned by edict.

B. Human Rights in Brazilian Transnational Inquiries

Apart from the aforementioned provisions on extradition, the Federal Constitution does not explicitly provide for further specific human rights clauses concerned with other tools of international cooperation in criminal matters. This does not mean, however, that under constitutional law transnational cases are neutral to fundamental rights or, even worse, only aim at fulfilling state-related interests. It has been noted that the Constitution requires Brazil to engage in promoting relationships

[9]For an overview of the international both bilateral and multilateral instruments signed by Brazil Abade (2013), p. 227ff.

[10]Abade (2013), p. 233.

[11]The Protocol was promulgated by the Decree 3.468/2000.

[12]Both the Convention and its Protocol were promulgated by the Decree 6.340/2008.

[13]*Ibid.*, 233f.

with other countries with a view to the swift progress of mankind, a general expression that certainly encompasses the search for higher levels of protection of the fundamental rights of the people involved in transnational procedures. Moreover, Brazilian higher courts have increasingly become aware that some of the fundamental rights acknowledged by the Constitution apply to transnational cases and are exposed to particularly high risks in the field of international cooperation.

International legal assistance instruments also do not ignore the need to protect the individuals rights of the persons involved in cross-border procedures. Originally, human rights provisions were particularly enacted in international agreements on extradition, which is not generally allowed in cases of military and political crimes, in cases of discriminatory prosecutions, for the purposes of the execution of the death penalty, torture or other inhumane treatment, and so on.[14] Over the last decades, moreover, it was possible to see the rising attention towards individual rights in transnational inquiries through international instruments adopted after the 1988 Constitution. This was already evident in the 1989 extradition treaty between Brazil and Italy, which encompassed not only a general fundamental rights clause[15] but also a more specific provision concerned with the right to a defence.[16] In this agreement, therefore, defence rights played a double role in transborder cases, i.e. (*a*) as a condition preventing the requested party from extraditing the sought person and (*b*) as requirements of a fair surrender procedure in the requested State. However, the Italian-Brazilian extradition treaty required respect for the right to a defence to a minimum extent, since extradition could only be refused in the case of infringement of the minimum defence rights. Moreover, the sought individuals must be granted legal assistance and, if needed, the assistance of an interpreter only if provided for by, and only pursuant to the requirements of, the law of the requested party, no matter whether eventual deficiencies of *lex loci* have negative repercussions on the effective exercise of the defence rights.

Some of these shortcomings were amended by subsequent bilateral agreements. For instance, the 1996 extradition treaty between Brazil and France required both the contracting parties to refuse extradition, *inter alia*, when the sought persons had been tried before a court unable to properly protect their fundamental and defence rights.[17] Significantly, no further specification was here made to the minimum content of these rights. On the other hand, this treaty also provides for almost nothing in the way of the right to defence in relation to surrender procedures. Defence rights remain therefore governed by the domestic criminal law of the requested country, which might be entirely unknown to the individuals involved.

---

[14]For an overlook of these clauses see Abade (2013), p. 236f.

[15]Art. 5 ExT Brazil-Italy.

[16]Art. 8 ExT Brazil-Italy.

[17]Art. 4(c) ExT Brazil-France.

C. Participatory Rights in Domestic Criminal Proceedings with Transnational Features

It has been noted that domestic criminal proceedings can also have transnational features, posing difficult human rights challenges. The main problem is to ensure proper information where defendants do not live in Brazil and possibly do not speak Portuguese. Until 1996, as noted, the code provided for different rules on the court summons of defendants resident abroad, depending on whether the prosecuted offence was subject to bail or not. In the former case, the court summons followed the procedure by edict with a deadline of at least 30 days, within which they should appear in court, whereas in the latter defendants were summoned by means of letters rogatory.[18] The use of letters rogatory did not pose particular problems, provided the defendant's place of residence was known. Serious human rights concerns arose instead from the fact that the code allowed for defendants to be summoned by edict—a type of court summons that, as noted, relies on a legal fiction of notice of the proceedings—irrespective of whether their place of resident was known. In these cases, the failure to appear in court led inevitably to the result that criminal proceedings were conducted *in absentia* without the accused being given a fair opportunity for participation.

The 1996 reform, while dropping the old procedures *em revelia*, changed the rules on court summons of defendants whose place of residence outside Brazil is known, with the result that they must always be informed by means of letters rogatory, regardless of whether bail can be granted or not.[19] Of course, this solution also cannot ensure that the accused will be made aware of the proceedings. If the defendant cannot be found, however, criminal proceedings will no longer be continued *in absentia*. Moreover, proceedings will only be suspended after the notification by edict.[20] It is noteworthy that, unlike in domestic cases, the running period of prescription is suspended not only after the suspension of the proceedings but also during the performance of letters rogatory.[21] This result is questionable from a human rights perspective, giving rise to discriminatory situations, since suspension is ordered on the sole grounds that the defendants are not resident in Brazil and without any proof of their having voluntarily absconded.

[18] Art. 367 CCP (original version).

[19] Art. 368 CCP.

[20] Lopes Jr (2017), p. 543.

[21] Art. 368 CCP.

D. *Audi alteram partem* and the Protection of Personal Freedom in Extradition Procedures

I. The Problem of in absentia *Trials*

The tension between the public interest in efficient transnational prosecution and the right to participation in criminal proceedings reaches its highest point in the field of extradition, in which the sought individuals can experience direct consequences on their personal freedom. Here, the first delicate problem is whether and to what extent the absence of the sought person in the relevant proceedings impinges on the surrender procedure.

The way Brazilian law deals with this issue gives rise to some human rights concerns. Law 6.815/1980 provided nothing on the effects of *in absentia* proceedings on extradition and an overview of the international agreements in force shows that Brazil generally adopts a rather minimalist approach.[22] Whereas most international instruments contain no specific clause concerned with *in absentia* procedures, the extradition treaty between Brazil and Spain allows the requested party to refuse extradition only if it considers that the proceedings conducted *in absentia* in the requesting state violated the minimum defence rights.[23] The extradition treaty between Brazil and France provides even less protection, foreseeing that the simple fact that the sought individuals were prosecuted *em revelia* does not constitute a ground to refuse their surrender, unless their absence in the relevant proceedings can be considered a presumed confession.[24] The extradition treaty between Brazil and Italy does not even leave room for exceptions. As noted, this treaty, while confirming the approach of the extradition treaty with Spain with regard to the relevance of the minimum defence rights, rules out that the sole fact that the proceedings were conducted *em revelia* can lead to refusal of extradition.[25] Instead, the extradition treaty between Brazil and Portugal highlights greater attention towards the defendant's absence in the relevant proceedings. This treaty, however, remains bound by the traditional legal assistance approach according to which surrender cannot be refused if the law of the requesting state ensures that the sought person can challenge the decision issued *in absentia* or has a right to a retrial after extradition.[26]

At any rate, it is worth observing that all these extradition treaties were signed at a time in which criminal proceedings could still be conducted *em revelia* in Brazil. Doubtless, the qualitative requirements of *contradictoire* and full defence, alongside the 1996 abolition of *revelia*, should lead to a review of these agreements in

[22] Abade (2013), p. 237f.

[23] Art. 7 ExT Brazil-Spain.

[24] Art. 4(c) ExT Brazil-France.

[25] Art. 5(c) ExT Brazil-Italy.

[26] Art. 5 ExT Brazil-Portugal.

order to avoid a deficit in human rights protections as compared with domestic cases. This reform certainly cannot be deemed detrimental to an efficient international cooperation with foreign countries. Fair transnational cooperation can no longer be based on the disregard—justified by the respect for foreign sovereignty—of how foreign countries deal with the relevant human rights issues. Furthermore, the maintenance of the current legal set-up does not only entail risks for the defendants' participatory rights in the relevant criminal proceedings but can have further negative consequences as a result of the surrender procedure, especially in terms of restrictions on personal freedom, assets, and so on.

II. The Right to a Fair Hearing and the Role of the Judiciary in Extradition Procedures

A different question is whether and in which terms the sought individuals must be granted a fair opportunity to participate in the surrender procedure initiated against them. In this regard, Brazilian law also reveals a certain backwardness from a human rights perspective. *Estatuto do Estrangeiro* contains scant provisions on this point, notwithstanding that a recent reform amended some important rules on pre-trial measures in the field of extradition procedures.[27] In urgent cases, the trial country can request the pre-trial detention of the sought person.[28] This form of detention can be maintained, without any possibility of alternative measures, as long as the Federal Supreme Tribunal has not ruled on the request for extradition,[29] which must be transmitted within 90 days after the foreign country has been informed of the provisional imprisonment.[30] Nevertheless, there is no specific provision requiring the requested person to be heard on the lawfulness of the provisional detention, which may not be justified on the basis of real risks for the surrender procedure. The sought person will only be heard after the foreign state has sent its request for extradition. In this regard, moreover, Law 6.815/1980 follows a minimalist approach. It is true that a lawyer must be appointed if the requested individuals are not represented by their own council and the hearing can take place the earliest 10 days after that moment.[31] However, nothing is specified as to further issues of utmost importance to ensure the effectiveness of this hearing, such as whether the detained persons can communicate with their lawyers, whether an interpreter must also be appointed if they do not understand Portuguese, and so on. Most extradition agreements have attached even less attention to these issues. For instance, both the treaties with France and Italy have failed to require the sought

[27] Law 12.878/2013.

[28] Art. 82 Law 6.815/1980.

[29] Art. 84 Law 6.815/1980.

[30] Art. 82(3) Law 6.815/1980.

[31] Art. 85 Law 6.815/1980.

individuals to be heard even when they were deprived of their liberty in the requested state.

The traditional understanding by the higher courts of extradition in terms of *ad hoc* non-contentious procedure has also here probably contributed to this result, attenuating the need to ensure to both the requested individual and the requesting country the full exercise of the right to defence and *contradictoire*.[32] It is noteworthy, moreover, that the requesting country has progressively gained a more active role in extradition procedures, a role that today encompasses the possibility of submitting written observations and even oral statements, thus giving rise to a direct participation known as '*Amicus curiae*'.[33] By contrast, the voice of the sought individuals has still little weight.

Another factor that impinges on the effective exercise of the right to a defence, which is far from the constitutional requirement of 'fullness',[34] is the rather formal role that the judiciary still plays in extradition procedures. According to federal case-law, the consent to extradition, while making the hearing of the requested person superfluous, does not release the judicial authority from its obligation to assess the overall lawfulness of the surrender procedure.[35] Yet this assessment is usually limited to a general check (*delibação*) of the formal conditions of the surrender.[36] A clear example of this approach emerges from *Estatuto do Estrangeiro*, which limits both the tasks of the judiciary to the assessment of the identity of the sought person, the examination of formal errors of the submitted documents and the unlawfulness of extradition.[37] By contrast, the oversight of the lawfulness of extradition leaves no room for challenging issues concerned with the relevant proceedings in the requesting state.[38] To be sure, the 1928 Inter-American Convention of Private International Law, known as '*Código Bustamante*', had already enhanced the assessment of the merits of the case, by requiring the requesting country to submit the necessary documents aimed at demonstrating, by means of reasonable information, the liability of the sought person.[39] Yet the federal case-law deemed this requirement to have been dropped by subsequent extradition agreements.[40] In the *Donnini* case, dealt with after the 1988 Constitution, the Federal Supreme Tribunal rejected any objection concerned with the lack of full defence and *contradictoire* in extradition procedures.[41] According to the

[32] Abade (2013), p. 253f.

[33] *Ibid.*, 254.

[34] Fraga (1985), p. 341f.

[35] STF, *Ext.* 1.098, rel. Cezar Peluso.

[36] According to Abade (2013), p. 256f., this confirms the indirect relevance of fundamental rights in the extradition procedure.

[37] Art. 85(1) Law 6.815/1980.

[38] Abade (2013), p. 257.

[39] Art. 265 *Código Bustamante*.

[40] Abade (2013), p. 258.

[41] STF, *Ext.* 541.

federal case-law, as noted, the only derogation allowed (albeit partially) by the Constitution concerns the case of naturalised Brazilians who can be extradited if their involvement in drug trafficking was demonstrated.[42] The Federal Supreme Tribunal confirmed this approach in the 1996 *DEBSS* case, rejecting the exception of unconstitutionality of the model adopted by *Estatuto do Estrangeiro*.[43]

In sum, the scant defensive opportunities of the sought individuals are consistent with the system of limited judicial oversight for the Brazilian judiciary, a system that during the military regime was based on the logic of non-inquiry and aimed at not jeopardising the need for enhanced international cooperation. Remarkably, the first time under the former Constitution that the problem of the direct application of the Brazilian constitutional system of fundamental rights protection was dealt with, the question was whether extradition could be allowed in the case of life sentences. The question gave rise to a strong critical reaction by most constitutional judges,[44] which led to the Federal Supreme Tribunal adopting a doctrine, known as the *Rezek* doctrine, aimed at limiting the scope of application of constitutional requirements solely to the range of Brazilian jurisdiction.[45]

However, things had to change under the new constitutional framework, which revealed the need to bring international cooperation in line with constitutional requirements. In an important ruling issued after the 1988 Constitution, Min. *Celso de Mello* pointed out Brazil's obligation to engage in the assessment of the respect for due process requirements both during and following the person's surrender.[46] The arguments used were such as to destroy the *Rezek* doctrine. In particular, the sole fact that foreigners are subject to extradition does not deprive them of their dignity as human beings, which entails the need for full protection of their fundamental rights, starting with due process guarantees. This required Brazilian authorities to avoid the risk that the fundamental rights of the sought individuals could be violated after their surrender to a foreign country.[47] Another important implication of this approach was the enhancement of the role of the defence in challenging before Brazilian courts errors of the relevant proceedings entailing negative consequences for the fundamental rights of the individuals concerned.

A close examination of the developments that have taken place in the federal case-law, moreover, paints a rather confused picture, which does not make it clear to what extent Brazil must assure direct compliance with its own constitutional requirements in surrender procedures.[48] In general terms, the voice of private parties has remained weak and it is unclear whether and within which limits the

---

[42] Abade (2013), p. 262.

[43] STF, *Ext*. 669.

[44] Abade (2013), p. 289ff.

[45] Opinion rendered by Min. Francisco Rezek in STF, *Ext*. 426.

[46] STF, *Ext*. 663.

[47] Abade (2013), p. 299ff.

[48] *Ibid*., 306.

sought person can claim before the Supreme Federal Tribunal violations concerned with the foreign criminal proceedings.

E. Participatory Rights and the Taking of Evidence in Transnational Cases

I. Modes of Gathering Overseas Evidence

Further problems arise in the field of transnational evidence-gathering. In Brazilian law, evidence can traditionally be taken overseas by means of letters rogatory (*cartas rogatórias*). Although this tool was already used during the imperial period in the midst of the nineteenth century, it was only through Law 221/1984 that specific rules on letters rogatory in criminal matters were introduced.[49] The enormous territorial extension of the country led the Brazilian legislator to opt for a centralised *exequatur* procedure, in order to avoid inequalities in the treatment of foreign requests for legal assistance. Notwithstanding rising computerisation and the need to speed up international cooperation, the Constitutional Amendment Law 45/2004 confirmed this approach, shifting the competence for *exequatur*, as noted, from the Federal Supreme Tribunal to the Superior Court of Justice. As a result, the few attempts to enact a model of mutual recognition with countries belonging to the Mercosur area by means of direct contacts with foreign judicial authorities encountered immediate reaction by the Federal Supreme Tribunal, which required respect for the new powers of Superior Court of Justice.[50]

Despite the need to preserve the jurisdiction of Superior Court of Justice in the field of letters rogatory, moreover, the higher courts have over the last decades increasingly developed a new form of direct assistance (*auxílio direto*). This form of international cooperation—acknowledged by several international instruments since the 1990s—consists of a request for assistance presented by a foreign country to the Central Brazilian Authority, which directly refers the case to the national body competent for the sought measure without seeking a preliminary ruling by the Superior Court of Justice. Although the procedure is activated at the initiative a foreign country, the request is only a prerequisite of the sought investigation that, unlike in case of letters rogatory, is deemed to be of a domestic nature and, as such, is subject to national law. An important implication is that Brazilian authorities are here allowed to assess the merits of the case prosecuted abroad, whereas in the field of letters rogatory the merits can only be dealt with in exceptional circumstances, when problems of sovereignty and public order arise.[51] Therefore, the fact that the Superior Court of Justice is not involved in direct assistance procedures can be

[49] *Ibid.*, 310f.

[50] *Ibid.*, 323.

[51] In this sense see Article 6 Resolution 9/2005 of the Superior Court of Justice.

somewhat compensated for by the broader oversight carried out by national authorities.[52]

The Federal Supreme Tribunal had already deemed *auxílio direto* constitutional before the 2004 constitutional reform.[53] Yet this approach changed rapidly and a few years later the constitutional judges engaged in defending the new jurisdiction of the Superior Court of Justice, pointing out that investigations can only be carried out in Brazil upon request of foreign States by means of letters rogatory.[54] The Superior Court of Justice shared this doctrine initially.[55] However, this approach did not last long, since the Superior Court of Justice's Special Court recently rescued direct assistance from the risk of unconstitutionality.[56]

II. The Right to a Defence and Equality of Arms in the Taking of Overseas Evidence

It has been observed that the 1941 code had enacted a few provisions relating to letters rogatory. These provisions, however, concerned only the procedure on incoming requests for legal assistance. Still today, there is no provision relating to outgoing requests for letters rogatory. Nor does the code lay down specific restrictions on the use of overseas evidence in Brazilian criminal proceedings, evidence that can therefore be admitted pursuant to the same rules applicable to the information obtained in other national proceedings. The lack of specific rules governing outgoing requests for letters rogatory does not mean that the code ignores the problem of the modes in which other countries should provide legal assistance. Two provisions are relevant in this regard. The first one, as noted, concerns the court summons of defendants whose place of residence abroad is known. The second, relating to witness testimony, was introduced by the Law 11.900/2009 with a view to deterring dilatory behaviour of the defence in requesting the collection of evidence abroad. Pursuant to the new Article 222-A CCP, the sought evidence must be not just useful and relevant for the ongoing criminal inquiry but the requesting party must demonstrate the absolute need (*imprescindibilidade*) for letters rogatory and must cover the costs concerned with this procedure.

It has been noted that the use of letters rogatory to summon non-resident defendants can give rise to discriminatory situations. The same risk arises in relation to letters rogatory used for the purposes of the collection of witness testimony.[57] Thus defendants seeking to support their version of the facts by

---

[52]Similarly Abade (2013), p. 319.

[53]STF, *Carta Rog*. 10920.

[54]STF, *HC* 83.588.

[55]STJ Special Court, *AgRg* 2484.

[56]Abade (2013), p. 320f.

[57]*Ibid*., 328ff.

means of overseas evidence are unjustifiably subject to worse treatment than the Public Prosecutor, whose requests are supported by the state. Disadvantaged defendants can be frustrated in their attempt to prove their innocence by bearing the costs of legal assistance, which possibly go beyond their financial capabilities. It is true that, if the competent judge deems the sought evidence to be particularly relevant for fact-finding, the accused can be granted a free-of-charge legal assistance. Yet this is an exceptional measure, while defendants must normally bear the costs of legal assistance, even if they succeed in proving the real need to take the information at stake.

This result not only undermines the accused's right to evidence but furthermore reveals a mistaken understanding of evidence-gathering. Even though evidence is normally taken at the initiative of the parties, evidence-gathering does not aim at fulfilling the interests of individual parties. It is in the interests of all the individuals involved in a criminal inquiry and, on a deeper level, in the interest of the best ascertainment of the facts that relevant information is collected. The Federal Supreme Tribunal dealt with this issue in the *Mensalão* case, a complex case involving the alleged corruption of congressmen. However, the approach adopted remained uncritically faithful to the new legal provision.[58]

It is noteworthy, moreover, that the national provisions on letters rogatory have not yet been updated to new forms of evidence-gathering, which vary the terms of the defence's participation in particular cases. Surprisingly, the 2009 reform did not extend to letters rogatory the rules on the taking of witness evidence by videoconferencing or through other technological means,[59] rules that expressly provide for the participation of the defence.[60] *De lege ferenda*, a proper solution could be to set up a similar tool for the collection of overseas evidence, eventually subjected to a financial agreement on the technical arrangements with the foreign state. This solution would release the defence from undue and unjustified costs.

It should be considered, however, that some international instruments of legal assistance in force in Brazil provide for the application of specific forms of *lex fori*, provided it does not jeopardise the essential principles of the requested country.[61] Within the scope of the application of these agreements, application of *lex fori* can allow for the involvement of the defence, similarly to what happens in national cases. Yet, there is no certainty that this will happen in a concrete case. Here also, the most serious shortcoming of this solution is that the application of *lex fori* is conditional on the explicit request of the 'requesting party'. This expression makes, therefore, the defence's participation dependent not only on the judicial discretion but furthermore on the political evaluation of the Government of the requesting state. Other bilateral agreements give rise to a further imbalance between the

[58] *Ibid.*, 329f.

[59] Thus, Article 222-A CCP only relates to the paragraphs nos. 1 and 2 of the previous Article 222 CCP.

[60] Art. 222(3) CCP.

[61] In this sense see Article 8(1) TLA Brazil-Italy.

defence and competent authorities of the requesting country. For instance, the 1997 Agreement on Mutual assistance between Brazil and Colombia makes it clear that neither authorities nor private parties of the requesting country can exercise in the territory of the requested country the same powers acknowledged by *lex fori*.[62] At the same time, this instrument provides for a significant exception, which enables only the authorities of the trial State, upon consent of the requested country, not only to be present but also to play active role in the execution of letters rogatory.[63]

III. Participatory Rights in the Collection of Evidence Requested by Foreign Countries

Brazilian courts tend to follow a similar approach to incoming requests for legal assistance as that used for the admission of overseas evidence. Just as evidence obtained from abroad can be used in domestic criminal proceedings pursuant to the rules of national law, information can be taken in Brazil for the purposes of foreign inquiries within the limits laid down by *lex loci*.

The Federal Supreme Tribunal has recently dealt with the question of whether and to what extent the constitutional requirements of *contradictoire* and full defence must be complied with in the execution of letters rogatory in Brazil.[64] By ruling on a case in which the validity was contested of the procedure before the Superior Court of Justice, which granted *exequatur* to the requested country without the interested party being given access to the case file, the Federal Supreme Tribunal acknowledged the need to ensure full respect for the right to *contradictoire*. However, this conclusion was considerably weakened by the fact that, according to the constitutional judges, the interested party should specifically prove the damage suffered in a concrete case.[65] Concerning the forms of participation of the defence, a delicate problem is whether the individuals concerned must be heard before the carrying out of the sought measure.[66] In its Resolution 5/2005, the Superior Court of Justice adopted a rather vague approach, allowing the requested investigation to be carried out without previous hearing of the interested party if the involvement of the defence could undermine the efficiency of international cooperation.[67] However, the individuals concerned should be involved after the sought investigation has been completed, within the limits laid down in domestic cases.[68]

---

[62] Art. 1(3) ALA Brazil-Colombia.

[63] Art. 13(3) ALA Brazil-Colombia.

[64] Abade (2013), p. 341ff.

[65] STF, *RE* 554.410-ED.

[66] Abade (2013), p. 342f.

[67] Art. 8 Resolution 9/2005.

[68] Abade (2013), p. 343.

This approach cannot be followed in absolute terms. Of course, the principle of *contradictoire* cannot be complied with in such a rigid way that it would frustrate Brazil's obligation to cooperate with foreign countries with a view to an efficient investigation of crimes, especially with a transborder dimension. This does not mean, however, that the interested parties can unconditionally be denied the right to be involved in the collection of evidence. Where the sought cooperation concerns measures without confidentiality constraints, the failure to involve the individuals concerned means depriving them of their right not only to challenge eventual errors of the procedure but also to avoid undue—and often irreparable—restrictions on their fundamental rights.[69] In this regard, the Federal Supreme Tribunal adopted a more protective approach than that followed by the Superior Court of Justice, allowing the execution of letters rogatory without the prior involvement of private parties only when this could jeopardise the specific aim of the requested investigation.[70]

Doubtless, the need to hear the individuals concerned is of utmost importance when fundamental rights are at stake. A delicate issue dealt with by federal case-law on several occasions is whether letters rogatory can be executed in Brazil for the purposes of blood collection, without the consent of the individuals concerned.[71] It is noteworthy that Brazilian law does not allow such investigations to be carried out coercively, since it would undermine, albeit indirectly, the privilege against self-incrimination. Since the end of the 1990s, moreover, the Federal Supreme Tribunal has extended this approach to transborder cases, acknowledging that collecting blood against the will of the individual concerned would certainly run counter to the Brazilian *public ordre*.[72] Furthermore, coercion can also be produced in an even more indirect manner, *e.g.* when the persons concerned are heard without being free to choose whether and to what extent they can give oral evidence. In this regard, the question has recently arisen as to whether Brazil can provide legal assistance to a foreign country by examining co-defendants as witnesses. This result not only considerably reduces the scope of the right to silence but also entails the risk of co-defendants being exposed to criminal liability for false or reticent statements if they do not tell the whole truth about the facts they know.[73] Since Brazilian law does not allow co-defendants to be examined as witnesses, the request for assistance was rejected on the ground that the application of the rules of witness testimony would jeopardise the co-defendant's right to be fairly heard.[74] This approach demonstrates that Brazilian courts are well aware of the human rights implications of criminal investigations carried out for the purposes of foreign prosecutions.

---

[69] Cervini (2000), p. 76f.

[70] STF, *HC* 90.485/SP. See Abade (2013), p. 344.

[71] Abade (2013), p. 343ff.

[72] STF, *Carta Rog.* 8.443.

[73] Abade (2013), p. 345.

[74] STF, *HC* 87.759/DF.

F. Provisional Conclusions

The analysis of Brazilian law highlights the increasing attention towards human rights in transnational criminal justice. To a great extent, the process of strengthening defence rights in transnational inquiries was also the result of the 1988 Constitution, which engaged both the Brazilian legislature and the higher courts in the enhancement of fair trial guarantees, especially in the field of international cooperation. In this context, some important multilateral agreements of legal assistance were enacted into national law. Yet Brazil still lacks comprehensive statutory rules on transnational criminal justice and the 1941 code, despite some recent reforms, still contains isolated provisions on legal assistance that charge the individuals concerned with burdens inexistent in domestic cases. Some important achievements are also due to the case-law. Altogether, the examination of the two problem areas of extradition procedures and the transnational evidence reveals that Brazilian law is still far from the standards of protection of the constitutional requirements of *contradictoire* and full defence laid down in the field of domestic criminal justice.

References

Abade D (2013) Direitos fundamentais na cooperação juridical internacional. Saraiva, São Paulo

Cervini R (2000) Princípios de cooperação judicial penal internacional consagrados no Projeto de Protocolo de Assistência Jurídica Mútua em assuntos penais do Mercosul. In: Cervini R, Tavares J (eds) Princípios de Cooperação Judicial Penal Internacional no Protocolo do Mercosul. Revista dos Tribunais, São Paulo, pp 25–162

Fraga M (1985) O Novo Estatuto do Estrangeiro Comentado. Forense, Rio de Janeiro

Lopes A Jr (2017) Direito Processual Penal, 14th edn. Saraiva, São Paulo

Part IV
Convergences and Divergences in the National Understanding of Participatory Rights in Domestic and Transnational Criminal Justice

Chapter 6
Common Developments and Deficiencies of the Domestic Approach to Participatory Safeguards in Criminal Proceedings

Contents

A. Premise 220
B. The Constitutionalisation of the Principle of *contradictoire* and Its Contribution of to a Human Rights-Oriented Understanding of Criminal Justice 222
C. *Audi alteram partem* and the Principle of Equality of Arms. The Weak Role of the Judiciary and Persistent Imbalances in the Pre-trial Inquiry 225
D. Criminal Prosecution and the Role of Private Parties 227
I. The Proactive Role of the Injured Party in the Institution of Criminal Proceedings. The Problem of Private Prosecutions 227
II. The Involvement of Private Parties in the Decision Not to Institute or to Drop a Criminal Prosecution 230
E. Principle of *contradictoire* and Information in Criminal Proceedings 234
I. The Right to Information on the Charge, Right to Know Relevant Evidence and the Difficult Trade-Offs Required in the Investigative Phase 234
II. Information on the Initiation of a Criminal Law Action and Recent Legal Arrangements to Involve the Accused Personally in the Proceedings 237
F. The Right to Personal Participation in Criminal Proceedings and the Problem of *in absentia* Proceedings 239
G. Investigative Needs and the Right to Be Fairly Heard in Criminal Proceedings 241
I. The Right to a Fair Hearing, Legal Assistance and the Role of the Judiciary in the Pre-trial Examination of the Accused 241
II. The Right to a Fair Hearing of Individuals Other Than the Accused and the Lack of Comprehensive Rules on Different Informants 245
III. The Right to Silence, Defensive Choices and the Right to Be Fairly Heard in Judicial Proceedings 246
IV. Methods of Examination and the Guarantees of a Fair Hearing 248
H. *Audi alteram partem* and the Collection of Criminal Evidence 250
I. Participatory Rights in the Taking of Oral Evidence and the Role of the Judiciary 250
II. The Right to Confrontation, Documentary Evidence and the Use of Information Gathered in Other Proceedings 253
III. The Right to *contradictoire*, Technical Investigations and Expert Evidence 255
I. The Parties' Contribution to the Decision-Making and the Requirements of *contradictoire*-Based Fact-Finding 257
I. Relativism of Criminal Evidence and the Different Probative Value Depending on the Decision at Stake 257
II. Principle of *contradictoire*, the Proof of Guilt and the Principle of Free Assessment of Evidence 259

S. Ruggeri, Audi Alteram Partem *in Criminal Proceedings*,
DOI 10.1007/978-3-319-54573-8_6

J. *Audi alteram partem* and Pre-trial Restrictions on Freedom ... 261
I. Premise ... 261
II. The Right to *contradictoire* and Short-Term Restrictions on Liberty ... 262
III. Pre-trial Measures and the Guarantee of a Fair Hearing of the Accused and the Victim in Remand Proceedings ... 265
IV. Participatory Rights in the Proceedings Activated by the Defence on Judicial Oversight of Restrictions on Freedom ... 267
K. Provisional Conclusions ... 268
References ... 269

A. Premise

The comparative-law examination of the developments that have occurred in Italy and Brazil in order to enhance participatory safeguards for private parties in criminal proceedings highlights various common lines. As noted, the Brazilian 1941 code was largely inspired by the Italian codification of 1930. The subsequent history of both criminal justice systems was the constant (albeit not always linear) attempt to depart from this starting point and therefore from the strong inquisitorial tradition that had long characterised the Italian and Brazilian criminal procedural law. Yet Brazil is still governed by the old 1941 codification, whereas in 1988 Italy enacted a new code of criminal procedure, after the failed attempt to launch a new codification in the 1970s.

Despite the ideological influence of the Rocco code on Brazilian law, the two criminal justice systems have undergone somewhat different developments. Doubtless, constitutional law has had enormous relevance to these developments. In Italy, the 1947 Constitution paved the way for a new approach to criminal justice. This was, however, a slow process, and it was mainly thanks to the Constitutional Court that some important defensive safeguards were enacted in the pre-trial inquiry. The 1988 codification walked a slightly different road by strengthening the role of the defence, especially in the evidence-gathering in the trial phase. However, various innovations brought about by the 1988 code were rooted in the centuries-long common law tradition and could not survive against the different cultural background of the Italian criminal justice. Moreover, the Italian code also reproduced a number of procedures, such the default proceedings and the penal order procedures, which were based on abstract doctrines rather than on the effectiveness of the defence rights.[1] Even the new system of pre-trial measures, despite some important innovations, postponed the defence's intervention until after the decision of the court.[2] Brazilian criminal justice also saw important developments as a consequence of the 1988 Federal Constitution, significantly enacted in the same year as

[1]Cf. Chapter 2, respectively, F.II.1. and F.III.2.

[2]Chapter 2, J.III.1.

the Italian new code of criminal procedure entered into force. Doubtless, the enshrinement of the right to *contradictoire* and full defence at the constitutional level played an important role in the recent evolution of Brazilian procedural law.[3] The renovation of Brazilian criminal justice, however, was also a long process, notwithstanding that some important reforms were already carried out in the 1990s, such as eliminating default proceedings.

Furthermore, other important factors have also contributed to these developments in both countries. In particular, we will note that over the last decades, international human rights law has had an increasing influence on both Italian and Brazil criminal justice. More recently, important changes have also occurred in Italy as a result of the general obligation to implement EU law in criminal matters.[4]

Notwithstanding several steps forward, both criminal justice systems are still far from a truly participatory understanding of criminal justice. The main methodological deficiency is probably the failure to provide a comprehensive balancing of the complex interests that characterise most criminal proceedings in the current era. A modern picture of criminal justice cannot be reduced to the traditional dualistic conflict between the accuser and the accused, as it reveals a number of overlapping interests that require the involvement of various bodies and individuals, albeit in different fashions and with different roles. The Italian code, while maintaining the possibility of the damaged party taking part in criminal proceedings, has progressively strengthened the role of the victim under the strong influence of the Strasbourg case-law. Yet Italian law still lacks comprehensive rules in this respect and the voice of private parties other than the accused has remained weak[5] in important areas, especially in the field of alternative proceedings, pre-trial measures, and evidence-gathering. Brazilian law shows a quite different picture. The reforms aimed at the implementation of the constitutional requirements of *contradictoire* and full defence have contributed to strengthening the defendant's participatory rights in various ways. As far as the aggrieved parties are concerned, even though they can in certain cases play a proactive role in the initiation of criminal proceedings, the role of the victims in judicial hearings is still largely undefined. On close examination, victims are not even consistently involved in criminal decisions on questions that can affect their interests, such as in the decision on discontinuance of the proceedings (*arquivamento*).[6]

[3]Chapter 3, B.

[4]On both issues see extensively Chapter 16.

[5]Chapter 2, G.II.2.

[6]Chapter 3, D.II.

B. The Constitutionalisation of the Principle of *contradictoire* and Its Contribution of to a Human Rights-Oriented Understanding of Criminal Justice

In general terms, we have seen that in both countries constitutional law has had enormous relevance in the process of 'humanisation' of criminal proceedings.[7] In this context, the acknowledgment of the guarantee of *contradictoire* at the constitutional level was of utmost importance for establishing a model of fair criminal justice in both countries.

In Brazil, the principle of *contradictoire* had already been enshrined in the 1937 Constitution and was later maintained in the subsequent Constitutions of 1946 and 1967. At that time, however, this fundamental guarantee had a more limited scope of application than in the 1988 Constitution, which for the first time acknowledged the requirement of *contradictoire* with a formulation encompassing both the judicial and administrative proceedings.[8] In Italy, the 1999 constitutional fair trial reform enacted the principle of *contradictoire* into the Constitution with a view to defining the essential characteristics of a constitutional model of fair trial. Significantly, this model was intended to apply to any type of proceedings, that is, both to judicial and administrative proceedings. It would be a mistake, however, to assume that Italian constitutional law did not ensure the guarantee of *contradictoire* before 1999. The failure to enact an explicit reference into the 1947 Italian Constitution can largely be explained taking into account the characteristics of the 1930 code. In the post-war era, as noted, Italian law was still inspired by a strongly inquisitorial approach to criminal proceedings. Depending on the type of the proceedings, a prosecutorial judge (the investigating magistrate) or a prosecutor charged with judicial powers (the public prosecutor) headed the pre-trial investigations, remanding defendants into custody and obtaining evidence in secret and without almost any intervention of the defence.[9] In court proceedings, the accused did not have a fair opportunity to participate in criminal hearings in the case of default proceedings, and the defence's contribution to the evidence-gathering was substantially inhibited by the widespread use of police and prosecutorial evidence.

Despite the heritage of the Rocco code, the 1947 Italian Constitution did not ignore the defence's role in criminal proceedings, enshrining the inviolable right to a defence at every stage of the proceedings.[10] Since its first rulings, the Constitutional Court invoked precisely this fundamental provision to demonstrate the constitutional relevance of the principle of *contradictoire*. By relying on the inviolable right to a defence, the constitutional case-law, as noted, played a decisive role in renovating the old approach to criminal justice, acknowledging

[7]Giacomolli (2014), p. 12ff. As to Italian criminal justice, see the fundamental contribution of Conso (1969).

[8]Chapter 3, B.

[9]Chapter 2, A.

[10]Chapter 2, B.I.

unprecedented defensive safeguards in the pre-trial inquiry. The 1988 code further enhanced the guarantee of *contradictoire* by limiting the use of out-of-court evidence and by laying down the cross-examination as the main method of gathering oral evidence at trial. By reacting to the tort reforms of the 1990s, Constitutional Amendment Law 2/1999 aimed at explicitly acknowledging the principle of *contradictoire* at the constitutional level, while giving it independent relevance beyond the right to a defence. Yet the structuralist approach of the 1999 constitutional reform raised new doubts as to whether the guarantee of *contradictoire* should be viewed as an individual guarantee or as laying down the objective features of a new constitutional model of criminal proceedings.[11] The heated debate on the scope of the principle of *contradictoire*, therefore, did not lead to an in-depth reflection of the role of the parties in criminal justice.

The relationship between the principle of *contradictoire* and the right to full defence followed a different road in Brazilian constitutional law. The link between the two guarantees, introduced by the 1937 Constitution, re-appeared in the 1988 Constitution, which acknowledged them 'with all means and resources' that are inherent to the right to a defence. This important specification helps avoid formalistic interpretations of the constitutional requirements, calling for effective protection of the participatory rights of the individuals involved in criminal proceedings.[12] This specification can explain how the general acknowledgment of the principle of *contradictoire* led in a few years to important reforms, such as eliminating default proceedings.

Concerning the scope of the guarantee of *contradictoire*, both the Italian Constitution and the Brazilian Constitution may seem to exclusively focus on the parties' involvement in the court proceedings. This is clear in the Brazilian Constitution, which ensures to 'defendants' the right to *contradictoire*,[13] whereas the Italian Constitution, transposing the approach of the European Convention, introduced the unprecedented concept of 'accused person' (*accusato*).[14] These differences do not entail, however, that the two Constitutions only protect the participatory rights of the individuals involved in criminal proceedings in the judicial hearings. This restrictive interpretation would oversimplify the structure of criminal proceedings, which are always characterised by a number of delicate intermediate decisions. Especially at the pre-trial stage, the defence can play an essential role in decisions on the adoption of measures severely restricting individual rights, and even in cases of hidden interference with fundamental rights, the possibility of oversight of the competent prosecutor and law enforcement authorities ought to be ensured, as well as the ability to challenge the application of such measures. In this light, the intervention of the public prosecutor can also play an important role from a human rights perspective. In Italy, in particular, the

[11]Chapter 2, B.II.2.

[12]Chapter 3, B.

[13]*Ibid.*

[14]Chapter 2, B.II.1.

introduction of the prosecutorial request for pre-trial measures did away with the old tradition of coercive measures being applied by the same body in charge with the investigations.

On close examination, both the Brazilian and the Italian Constitution acknowledge a broad concept of '*contradictoire*'. In Brazil, the reference to the accused 'in general terms' should be interpreted as also encompassing the suspects' right to participate in decisions that can affect their status.[15] In Italy, the state's involvement in protecting the inviolable right to defence and ensuring a fair distribution of procedural powers calls for extension of the principle of *contradictoire* to the entire scope of criminal proceedings, albeit with necessary differences in each phase. Furthermore, the way some of the fair trial guarantees (*e.g.*, the right to information on the charge) were constitutionalised in Italy requires a re-interpretation of constitutional provisions to also ensure protection to the suspect during the preliminary inquiry.[16]

Another delicate issue concerns the holders of the guarantee of *contradictoire*. Doubtless, both the Italian and the Brazilian Constitution exalt the participatory right as an individual guarantee of the defendant. In very clear terms, as noted, the Brazilian Constitution ensures to defendants in general the right to *contradictoire* and full defence. In Brazil, however, the strict link with the *par condicio* principle suggests a broad interpretation of the requirement of *contradictoire*, which, unlike the right to a defence, must also be ensured to the public prosecutor.[17] In the Italian Constitution also, the link with the principle of equality of arms enriches the axiological scope of the principle of *contradictoire*.[18] Furthermore, the fact that the guarantee of *contradictoire* also constitutes an essential condition of fair fact-finding should rule out restrictive interpretations.

Nevertheless, the risk of a fragmentary approach to criminal justice—characterised by conflict between state and individual parties—is still apparent from the constitutional law of both countries, especially in the field of evidence-gathering. To be sure, the 1988 Brazilian Constitution opted for a broad acknowledgment of the right to *contradictoire*, departing from the 1967 Constitution, which ensured it solely in the criminal inquiry.[19] In Italy, the 1999 constitutional reform enabled defendants to agree to the use of information taken without their participation, while banning the use of untested evidence for the purposes of the accused's conviction. Most significantly, the Italian Constitution, in addition to the guarantees laid down in the European Convention, enacted a provision that seems to grant defendants an unconditional right to have exculpatory evidence obtained. Unfortunately, the implementation of these requirements, while strengthening the accused's safeguards in evidence-gathering, largely enhanced a two-sided understanding of

[15]Chapter 3, B.

[16]Chapter 2, E.I.

[17]Chapter 3, C.

[18]Chapter 2, C.I.

[19]Chapter 3, B.

the right to *contradictoire* without a proper consideration of the overall balances required by criminal proceedings. This calls for systematic interpretation of the constitutional model of a fair trial.[20]

C. *Audi alteram partem* and the Principle of Equality of Arms. The Weak Role of the Judiciary and Persistent Imbalances in the Pre-trial Inquiry

Against this background, there can be little doubt that both in Brazil and in Italy, the strict link between the guarantee of *contradictoire* and the principle of equality of arms helps avoid reductive interpretations of the role of the parties in criminal proceedings. In Brazil, the right to *contradictoire* and full defence must be seen in the general context of Article 5 of the Constitution, aimed at granting both Brazilian and foreign citizens resident in Brazil equal treatment, as well as the right to freedom, security and respect for property.[21] In Italy, we have seen that the guarantee of *contradictoire* laid down by 1999 constitutional fair trial reform should not only be linked with the general principle of equal treatment in Article 3 of the Constitution but furthermore—and more specifically—with the explicit acknowledgment of the principle of equality of arms in judicial proceedings.[22] There is a two-sided link between these two fundamental guarantees. On the one hand, effective *contradictoire* cannot take place without a balanced distribution of safeguards and procedural powers. On the other, a constitutional model of fair trial cannot ignore the social and economic inequalities of the parties. In criminal proceedings, great imbalances always exist between the prosecutorial authority and the defence especially during the pre-trial inquiry, differences that by definition do not put the parties on an equal footing.[23]

This situation enhances the need for the state's active engagement in a fair distribution of rights, powers and resources in order to ensure effective participation in criminal proceedings. In Italy, the constitutional acknowledgement of *par condicio* strengthens the role of the judiciary. Remarkably, the principles of *contradictoire* and equality of arms are strictly coupled with the guarantee of an independent oversight of the proceedings. Again, this systematic link cannot lead to the conclusion that under Italian constitutional law, the requirements of

[20]Chapter 2, B.II.2.

[21]Chapter 3, B.

[22]Chapter 2, C.I.

[23]Chapter 2, C.II.

contradictoire and *par condicio* acknowledge the right of the parties to be involved solely in judicial hearings. Particularly where decisions can affect the individuals concerned, national law must also strengthen the judicial oversight at the pre-trial stage.[24] The need for a fair distribution of powers and rights among the parties in the pre-trial phase is also apparent in Brazil, where the structure of the police inquiry still reveals a state-centred understanding of criminal investigations. A broad interpretation of the constitutional acknowledgment of full defence to the accused 'in general terms', therefore, calls for the enhancement of the participatory safeguards in decisions on measures relevant to fundamental rights.[25]

The legislative implementation of the constitutional requirements of *contradictoire* and equality of arms, however, has not always followed consistent lines in the two countries. This is apparent in the field of evidence-gathering. In Brazil, Law 11.690/2008 enhanced the powers of the judiciary during the pre-trial inquiry, enabling judges to order at their own initiative the collection of urgent evidence. Although this new judicial power must be exercised pursuant the principles of necessity, adequacy and proportionality of the measure adopted, it can lead judges to follow their own investigative strategy, which can in turn further alter the imbalance between the police and the individuals concerned.[26] In Italy also, both the Constitutional Court and the legislature have progressively strengthened the judicial collection of pre-trial evidence by broadening the scope of *incidente probatorio* beyond the case of urgency. In the 1990s, the extension of this court procedure was mainly due to the need to counterbalance the enhancement of the use of prosecutorial and police evidence at trial.[27] Unlike in Brazil, however, the taking of evidence in a judicial hearing in the pre-trial phase has always remained dependent on the initiative of either the prosecutor or the defendant. Furthermore, Law 397/2000 aimed at strengthening the constitutional requirement of *par condicio* by giving a formal status to the investigations of the lawyers of private parties. By this means, Italian legislature attempted to compensate for the imbalance between the defence and the law enforcement authorities. The result, however, largely frustrated the principle of *contradictoire* by enhancing the possibility for both the prosecutor and private parties to gather evidence prior to the trial autonomously.[28]

On close examination of both countries highlights an understanding of equality of arms that, far from reflecting a reasonable distribution of powers and rights among the parties, can give rise to further imbalances both against and in favour of the defence. On the one hand, Italian law, submitting the use of the information gathered by the defence to almost the same conditions laid down for the prosecutorial evidence, does not take into account the different degree to which the

[24]Chapter 2, C.I.

[25]Chapter 3, B.

[26]Chapter 3, C.

[27]Chapter 2, H.II.2.

[28]Chapter 2, C.II.

information collected by the defence and by the investigative bodies is held to be reliable for the decision-makers. On the other, providing the private parties with an official file in a similar form to that of the prosecutorial file, without the obligation for the lawyer to insert all the information gathered, gives to the defence unquestionable advantages, while jeopardising the tasks of the competent authority.[29] In Brazil, the empowerment in the police inquiry of the competent judges to gather evidence at their own initiative confers them a proactive investigative role similar to that of the investigative magistrates, which can affect their impartiality.[30]

Ultimately, both Italy and Brazil not only still allow for intrusive investigations to be ordered out during the pre-trial inquiry by the prosecutor as a representative of the judiciary but furthermore give weak relevance to the *jus postulandi* of private parties. In Italy, even forms of interference with fundamental rights, which require a previous judicial order (*e.g.*, wiretaps), can be ordered by the prosecutor in urgent cases.[31] In general terms, most coercive measures falling with the competence of the judiciary can only be ordered at request of the competent prosecutor, while the defence is not entitled to request for them. The *jus postulandi* of private parties is also weak in relation to the prosecutor, who is generally not required to perform the investigations requested by the defence. In Brazil, the defence also has limited ability to request that the police perform certain investigations.[32]

D. Criminal Prosecution and the Role of Private Parties

I. The Proactive Role of the Injured Party in the Institution of Criminal Proceedings. The Problem of Private Prosecutions

Private parties can play different roles in the initiation of a criminal prosecution depending on the constitutional model of criminal proceedings. In several countries, the public-law understanding of criminal justice traditionally led to the charging decision being the exclusive prerogative of public prosecutors. An anticipated expression of this approach was the dominant role of law enforcement authorities in the pre-trial phase.

Historically, Italy had a strong public-law tradition of criminal prosecutions, although limited forms of private criminal law action existed in the past, even under the 1930 regime. It is therefore no surprise that the enactment of the principle of legality into the 1947 Constitution was initially interpreted as the acknowledgment of the monopoly of public prosecutors on the institution of criminal proceedings.[33] In the years ahead, further types of private criminal prosecution, such a popular

[29] *Ibid.*

[30] Chapter 3, C.

[31] Chapter 2, C.II.

[32] Chapter 3, C.

[33] Chapter 2, D.I.

criminal prosecution, were introduced. In the 1960s, the Constitutional Court advocated a flexible interpretation of the constitutional requirement, recognising the lawfulness of criminal proceedings instituted by individuals or bodies other than the public prosecutor. The 1988 codification, while enacting an exhaustive list of prosecutorial forms, abolished any form of criminal prosecution by bodies other than the public prosecutor, who was given exclusive competence to institute first a criminal pre-trial inquiry and then a criminal process.[34]

Brazilian law had a quite different historical development. Like the Italian Constitution, Brazilian constitutional law charges public prosecutors with the responsibility to institute criminal proceedings. Nevertheless, this responsibility cannot be seen in terms of a monopolistic power of public prosecutors in initiating criminal proceedings.[35] The 1941 code granted the victim several powers to remedy the inaction of either the police or the prosecutor.[36] In cases of offences for which unconditional public criminal action is required, victims can formally request the police to initiate a criminal inquiry, although the injured party is required to attach concrete information to justify this result. Nevertheless, in these cases, the opening of criminal investigations falls entirely within the purview of the police, who have wide discretion in assessing the victim's justification.

Furthermore, Brazilian law also ensured a more active role to the injured party, although the forms of private prosecution depend on the types of criminal offence. By departing from the Rocco code, the 1941 Brazilian code enabled the victim to initiate a criminal prosecution through an act having a different form from the prosecutorial *denúncia* (*queixa*). Since the victim can undertake this initiative in cases of offences for which a public-law action is provided, the victim's prosecution remains of a subsidiary nature and the public prosecutor can amend or integrate it. Private prosecutions have historically been of utmost importance in Brazilian law, so much so that the 1988 Constitution acknowledged a subsidiary private prosecution in the case of inactivity of a public Prosecution.[37] Doubtless, this solution enhanced the victim's role compared to the coeval 1988 Italian code, which provided private parties with no tool to remedy prosecutorial inaction, enabling, however, the General prosecutors to remove the case from the jurisdiction of the competent prosecutor and deal with the case themselves.[38] In addition to these powers, Brazilian law further strengthened the victim's role, providing for minor offences that can only be prosecuted through a private criminal action.[39] Despite their limited scope of application, these cases have a great systematic importance and provide a more straightforward solution than the victim's *ricorso* before the justices of the peace under Italian law.

---

[34] *Ibid.*

[35] Of a different opinion Tourinho Filho (2010), I vol., p. 163.

[36] Chapter 3, D.I.

[37] Chapter 3, D.I.

[38] Art. 412 CCP-Italy.

[39] Chapter 3, D.I.

Moreover, the victim also plays an important role in cases of offences in which public criminal law action is conditional on their request. The importance attached in Brazil to the initiative of the aggrieved parties in these cases is consistent with the general openness of Brazilian law towards private prosecution. Although the lack of private initiative not only hinders the prosecutor's action but also the police investigations, Brazilian courts tend to soften this strong approach, calling for a broad interpretation of the victim's will.[40] In Italy, in contrast, the prosecutorial registration of the case as an offence requiring a victim's lawsuit (*querela*) does not impede police and prosecutorial investigations as long as the injured party has not lodged his complaint. Under Italian law, when the pre-trial inquiry confirms the legal classification, the proceedings will be discontinued in the absence of the victim's lawsuit.[41] However, if the prosecutor does not request the termination of the proceedings, but prefers formal charges against the defendant, the criminal proceedings are not void nor is the prosecutorial action barred, the judge being required only not to open the trial, because of the lack of the victim's lawsuit. This demonstrates that the private legal action, far from being a condition of the public-law prosecution, affects the decision-making, preventing the competent court from ruling on the merits of the case, no matter whether the defendant must be acquitted or convicted.

The increasing role played by the injured party in the institution of criminal proceedings poses the further problem of ensuring independent oversight of the private legal action, in order to avoid both overloading the criminal justice system and exposing defendants to the possible burden of undue criminal prosecution. In Italy, the concerns arising from the victim's legal action traditionally led to the constitutional case-law not going beyond the compromise solution of a parallel public prosecution.[42] More recently, similar concerns led Legislative Decree 274/2000 to introduce a weak form of private prosecution, while involving the public prosecutor in the procedure instituted by the victim's *ricorso* before the justice of the peace. In Brazil, there was until recently no legislative tool to reject the victim's prosecution, so that defendants had no possibility of challenging the decision receiving the victims' *queixa* and the only legal action at their disposal was *habeas corpus*, albeit within the limitations of this mechanism.[43] Moreover, Law 11.719/2008 enacted an important innovation into both ordinary proceedings and jury trials, introducing an unprecedented form of rejection *in limine litis* of the prosecutorial initiative.[44] In particular, the competent judge can reject the prosecution initiated for alternative or generic charges, which imposes upon the victim the duty of providing precise and complete charges.[45]

---

[40] Chapter 3, D.I.

[41] Art. 411 CCP-Italy.

[42] Chapter 2, D.I.

[43] Lopes Jr (2017), p. 726.

[44] Art. 396 CCP-Brazil.

[45] Lopes Jr (2017), p. 727f.

Furthermore, the negative consequences of generic accusations on the right to a defence are not only an issue in private legal actions but also in public prosecutions. In Italy, in the absence of clear statutory rules, the Joint Sections of the Supreme Court, putting an end to a disagreement among individual Sections, ruled out that judges could declare the criminal proceedings void due to a generic indictment, returning the case to the prosecutor who can prefer new charges against the defendant.[46] According to the Supreme Court, in line with a previous ruling of the Constitutional Court,[47] the judicial authority should require the competent prosecutor to amend or integrate the charge within the same hearing pursuant to Article 423 CCP-Italy. Only in the absence of prosecutorial initiative would judges be allowed to return the case to the competent prosecutor, notwithstanding that the prosecutorial legal action was not invalid.

Despite the clear attempt to strike a compromise aimed at reducing negative consequences on the proceedings, this solution is questionable on various grounds. From a procedural viewpoint, the prosecutorial power to amend the indictment during the court proceedings presupposes a valid charge. Yet this is not the case in the situation at hand, since here return of the case to the competent prosecutor entails a clear regression of the proceedings to the pre-trial stage, which in turn requires the annulment of the prosecutorial request for court proceedings and therefore the invalidity of the indictment preferred. It is also questionable that some judges, if prosecutor does not take any initiative, adopt the practical arrangement of specifying the charge rather than declaring the proceedings void. On close examination, Italian law provides for the invalidity of the indictment in this case, classifying the procedural errors concerned with the institution of a criminal prosecution among the general forms of invalidity of criminal proceedings.[48] The adoption of a human rights perspective further supports this conclusion. Doubtless, there is a need to provide the defence with proper information on the charge in order to set up a proper defence strategy.

II. The Involvement of Private Parties in the Decision Not to Institute or to Drop a Criminal Prosecution

The possibility of private parties giving their own contribution to the termination of criminal proceedings has been the result of long developments in both countries. In Italy, the 1930 code strengthened the role of prosecutors, who, as representatives of the Executive, could autonomously drop the pre-trial inquiry without any judicial oversight and with the only obligation to inform the General Prosecutor or the

[46]Chapter 2, E.II.3.

[47]CConst, 131/1995.

[48]Arts. 178(b) and 179 CCP-Italy.

Crown Prosecutor of their decision, depending on the type of proceedings.[49] Italian case-law also allowed for abandoning criminal proceedings instituted against unknown defendants. These solutions lasted until Royal Legislative Decree 288/1944 abolished the prosecutorial power to terminate criminal inquiries, while enabling the investigative judge to scrutinise the prosecutorial request for discontinuance of criminal proceedings. Notwithstanding the merit of creating independent oversight, this procedure left no room for the participation of private parties in the judicial decision.[50] Certainly, the intervention of the interested parties would have been justified, taking into account that the investigative judge, when disagreeing with the prosecutorial request, could autonomously institute criminal proceedings. It took almost 50 years for an in-depth reform of this situation. The 1988 code involved both the victim and the suspect, albeit not in a consistent way, in the judicial procedure on discontinuance of the pre-trial inquiry, while ruling out the possibility of criminal proceedings being instituted against unknown defendants.[51]

Despite the clear influence of the Rocco code, the 1941 Brazilian codification somewhat departed from the Italian approach. Despite being charged with the responsibility of the pre-trial inquiry, the police could not autonomously terminate the proceedings[52] but had to forward a report to the competent prosecutor, who could either bring the defendant to court through *denúncia* or request the termination of the proceedings.[53] Unlike in the Italian 1930 code, the responsibility for the latter decision lay in the hands of the judicial authority.[54] When disagreeing with the prosecutorial request, the judge should forward the case to the General Prosecutor (*procurador-geral*) who could either prefer charges against the suspect, forward the case to another public prosecutor, or reiterate the request for discontinuance of the proceedings, by which request the competent judge should now abide.[55] This solution, which is still in force, can give rise to a sort of subordination of the judicial authority to the General Prosecutor's assessment of the case. By contrast, Italian law enables judges, when rejecting the request for termination of the pre-trial inquiry, to require the competent prosecutor to institute criminal proceedings.[56] From the viewpoint of the present discussion, the main problem in the Brazilian solution is that there is no room for both the suspect and the victim to be involved in the judicial procedure on dropping criminal proceedings, nor do they have any ability to challenge the judicial decision. Yet, despite enhancing the role

---

[49]Chapter 2, D.II.1.

[50]*Ibid.*

[51]*Ibid.*

[52]Art. 17 CCP-Brazil.

[53]Chapter 3, D.II.

[54]*Ibid.*

[55]Art. 28 CCP-Brazil.

[56]Chapter 2, D.II.1.

of the victims, Italian law left them limited room for challenging the judicial order of discontinuance of the proceedings.

Further human rights concerns arise in relation to the defence's contribution to the termination of a criminal prosecution after the institution of the court proceedings. In Brazil, Law 11.719/2008, while enabling judges to reject *in limine litis* the prosecution instituted through *denúncia* or *queixa*, introduced a particular form of provisional acquittal (*absolvição sumária*).[57] The grounds for this provisional termination of the judicial proceedings are mostly concerned with the merits of the case. In this instance, however, the Brazilian solution can give rise to dangerous results from a human rights perspective. In most cases, there is little room for a preliminary rejection of the prosecution, taking into account that the competent judge only knows the information attached by the (public or private) prosecutor, information from which exculpatory evidence rarely emerges. The reasons for a provisional acquittal will normally arise from the response that the defence must provide in any case that does not lead to a preliminary rejection of the prosecution under Article 396 CCP-Brazil.[58] In this regard, however, it must be born in mind that the 2008 reform dropped the original solution according to which defendants must be summoned to be heard in court. As a result, defendants must provide a written response within 10 days, a response that is usually provided by the lawyer. Both the accused and the suspect will be examined at the hearing set by the judge after receiving *denúncia* or *queixa*,[59] which entails that criminal proceedings can be ended with a provisional acquittal without private parties having given their personal contribution to the decision-making.

By means of this form of provisional acquittal, Brazilian law enacted a solution similar to that existent under the 1930 Italian code, which had enhanced the central role of *istruzione* to the extent that it allowed for the accused to be acquitted in the intermediate phase. Although the Rocco code provided for two forms of acquittal (at the end of the trial and in the intermediate phase respectively), the latter was not however a provisional termination of criminal proceedings, since the pre-trial inquiry aimed at gathering the necessary information for the decision on the merits of the case. As noted, the 1988 code departed from this approach by abolishing both the investigative judges and the possibility of collecting evidence at the pre-trial stage with a view to fact-finding, except in specific circumstances. As a result, criminal proceedings can be terminated at the intermediate stage through a ruling that, despite maintaining the old form of a judgment (*sentenza*), does not acquit the defendant but only reveals the lack of the necessary evidence to justify the opening of the public hearing (*non luogo a procedere*).[60] This does not mean that termination of the court proceedings entails a purely procedural decision. Even before Law

[57] Art. 397 CCP-Brazil.

[58] Lopes Jr (2017), p. 733f.

[59] Art. 400 CCP-Brazil.

[60] Art. 425 CCP-Italy.

479/1999 strengthened the intermediate phase, the decision of the intermediate phase largely dealt with the merits of the case, albeit only on the basis of the available information.

Against this background, the 1988 code enhanced the role of the defence for the purposes of termination of the judicial proceedings in the intermediate phase. The 1987 Delegation Law left the door open for a model of the intermediate phase characterised by an examination of the criminal prosecution solely on the basis of the information already gathered by the investigative bodies during the pre-trial inquiry. The drafters of the 1988 code, despite structuring the intermediate phase mostly with a view of the assessment of the records of prosecutorial and police evidence, enabled defendants to be examined at their own request. Moreover, if the competent judge considered the information available insufficient for the decision-making, both the public prosecutor and the private parties could request the collection of integrative evidence, which, despite not being normally admissible at trial, should be a basis for the decision on whether to open the trial phase.[61] The collection of such evidence, however, was confined to exceptional cases, so that the practical incidence of the parties' initiative on the decision-making was minimal. The 1999 reform, in the light of an in-depth reform of the intermediate phase, abandoned the possibility of taking inculpatory evidence, which frustrated the right to evidence of both the prosecutor and the damaged party who had already joined a legal action to the criminal proceedings.[62] The possibility of gathering integrative information *in camera* was circumscribed to cases of exculpatory evidence, significantly either at request of the defence or upon the judicial initiative. Although evidence-gathering in the intermediate phase remained limited to exceptional cases, the accused had much more room to demonstrate the superfluity of the trial phase, which would no longer be opened only in cases of manifest proof of innocence.

This set-up has largely remained unchanged until now in Italy. Despite the enhanced right to evidence for the accused, however, it must be taken into account that the 1999 reform also enabled all the other parties—including the public prosecutor—to request the accused's cross-examination at the intermediate stage.[63] This result weakens the right of defendants to make their voice heard by a judge and to avoid the opening of the public trial. The utility for the defence to request a court examination is reduced, if the initiative of other parties can expose defendants to the cross-examination, with the further risk of their statements being admitted at trial.

[61] Art. 422 CCP-Italy.

[62] For some criticism on this mechanism see Cordero (2012), p. 914f.

[63] Arts. 421(2) and 422(4) CCP-Italy.

E. Principle of *contradictoire* and Information in Criminal Proceedings

I. The Right to Information on the Charge, Right to Know Relevant Evidence and the Difficult Trade-Offs Required in the Investigative Phase

The involvement of private parties in criminal proceedings remains a formalistic requirement without providing them with proper information. Information must be given both on the initiation of a criminal law action and on substantial issues. In the former sense, we will see that notice of the proceedings is an essential condition to decide whether and how to participate in criminal hearings. In the latter, information must be provided on the charge and the developments of the proceedings. Yet substantial information does not exclusively relate to the judicial proceedings. There can be no doubt that the contrast between the individual right to information and the need to preserve the effectiveness of the ongoing investigations is enhanced in the pre-trial inquiry in both countries under examination.

Both the Italian and the Brazilian Constitution acknowledge the right to information as a necessary prerequisite for the effective exercise of the guarantee of *contradictoire* in criminal proceedings. In Brazil, the extension of the right to *contradictoire* and full defence to the police inquiry calls for the enhancement of the defendants' right to be informed on the investigation initiated against them.[64] In Italy, the 1999 fair trial reform, following the approach of the European Convention, constitutionalised the right of the defendants to be confidentially informed as soon as possible of the charge preferred against them. As noted, this guarantee cannot be restricted to information on the indictment, of which defendants must be notified almost in any case.

On the other hand, it is essential that information on criminal proceedings does not exceed strict limits to avoid the negative effects of social stigmatisation of the alleged perpetrator.[65] The reference to the requirement of confidentiality by the Italian Constitution[66] should also be read in the light of this, especially in relation to the pre-trial inquiry, in which the indiscriminate disclosure of still provisional data can have a negative impact on the suspects and their reputation. Moreover, this risk not only concerns information on the charge but also access to the results of the ongoing investigation. It is noteworthy that, in order to balance the right to information with respect for the reputation of other individuals and their relatives, the Brazilian Federal Supreme Tribunal has acknowledged the defence's right to information on the results of the police inquiry, while limiting the lawyers' access solely to information strictly concerned with their clients.[67]

---

[64]Chapter 3, E.I.

[65]*Ibid.*

[66]Chapter 2, E.I.

[67]Chapter 3, E.I.

The extension of the right to information to the pre-trial phase, moreover, poses difficult challenges because of the need to avoid negative implications for the efficiency of the ongoing inquiry. Remarkably, the Italian Constitution, departing from the English text of the ECHR provision on the right to information on the accusation, requires defendants to be informed 'as soon as possible'. In the light of this formulation, Italian Constitution does not grant the suspect the right to be informed immediately and without conditions but calls for a balance among conflicting interests, requiring delays in the information to be justified on the basis of other constitutional values.[68] The same applies to information on the results of the police and prosecutorial investigations, information that the Italian Constitution, albeit not explicitly, acknowledges through the general reference to the defendants' right to have facilities for the preparation of their own defence. Despite its absolute terms, this reference cannot be interpreted as the unconditional acknowledgment of the suspect's right to information on the ongoing inquiry.[69]

In this respect, the comparative analysis of Brazil and Italy reveals that the procedural law of both countries is still far from achieving a proper balance among conflicting interests. In Brazil, the police are still competent to charge individuals with a criminal offence in the pre-trial phase. In the practice, however, we have seen that suspects are often not formally charged, with the result that the police do not enable them to know whether they will be questioned as suspects or witnesses.[70] This situation, which deprives individuals of their right to silence, cannot be deemed in line with the Constitution. In Italy, the 1988 code concentrated the power to make the charging decision in the hands of public prosecutors, who must immediately register any *notitia criminis*. Nevertheless, Italian law does not contain clear time limits[71] and prosecutors still hold great discretion in choosing the legal classification of the alleged offence. Even more worryingly, there is still no room for judicial oversight of the prosecutorial charge, although the choice of *nomen juris* can have severe implications on the suspect's rights, affecting the overall length of the preliminary inquiry, allowing for the use of coercive means beyond the ordinary conditions, and so on.

Under Italian law, the initiation of criminal investigations does not necessarily entail a duty of information. Especially where a criminal inquiry is instituted against unknown persons or investigations not having implications on individual's rights are conducted, information is not due. However, once enough evidence is gathered to charge one or more individuals with a criminal offence and criminal investigations can affect their position, information should be required in principle. By departing from the 1988 regulation, which postponed the notification to the initiation of court proceedings, Law 332/1995 allowed for both victims and suspects to access to the registration of the charge upon their request. Since then, the

[68]Chapter 2, E.I.

[69]Chapter 2, E.III.

[70]Chapter 3, E.I.

[71]Art. 335 CCP-Italy.

granting of information has been dependent on private initiative rather than being an obligation of the competent authority.[72] Moreover, Italian law does not provide stronger guarantees at a later stage of the prosecutorial inquiry, since notice of the investigation under Article 369 CCP-Italy is only due in cases of investigations at which the lawyer can be present.[73]

In Italy, neither the implementation of the constitutional fair trial reform nor. as we will note,[74] the obligation to comply with the requirements laid down by EU law have brought about substantial changes to this set-up. The granting of information on the ongoing inquiry still presupposes the defence's initiative and is largely dependent on the strategy of the investigative authorities. Furthermore, information, whenever provided, is scant and may not suffice to guarantee effective defence. The individuals concerned will normally have their right to information satisfied only at the end of the investigation. Yet also this does not always happen. In cases of termination of the proceedings, information is only due to suspects who were deprived of their personal freedom during the pre-trial inquiry. Information is always due where the competent prosecutor decides to institute court proceedings through the notice on the completion of the pre-trial inquiry. However, notice under Article 415-*bis* CCP-Italy—a tool unknown in Brazilian law—provides information on the charge at a very late stage of the proceedings and the eventual contribution of the defence can rarely contend with the prosecutorial initiative.[75]

Further problems concern the scope of the guarantee of information. To a great extent, the Italian legislature has, questionably, adopted the same approach to the right of information for both defendants and victims, despite their very different interests in criminal proceedings. This undifferentiated approach was extended to the rules on restriction or exclusion of information. These rules reveal the inability of Italian law to strike a proper balance between investigative needs and the individual right to information, allowing for information to be denied or postponed because of either the abstract seriousness of the investigated offence or vague investigative needs.[76] In Brazil, the police, when starting a criminal investigation on their own initiative, need not inform individuals other than the suspects on the charge filed and the ongoing inquiry. As a result, where the aggrieved parties did not request the initiation of the police inquiry, they will remain unaware both of the criminal charge and the police investigations,[77] unless they are questioned by the investigative authority.

Even more worryingly, little weight is generally given to the information rights of individuals restricted in their fundamental rights. In Italy, during the pre-trial inquiry, suspects and victims must only be informed within the strict limits laid down for the notice of the investigation and even in case of coercive means, except

[72]Chapter 2, E.II.1.

[73]*Ibid.*

[74]Chapter 16, D.III.1.a.bb.

[75]Chapter 2, E.II.2.

[76]Chapter 2, E.II.1.

[77]Chapter 3, E.I.

the cases of pre-trial detention and further restrictions on freedom, information does not generally exceed the formal requirements set forth by Article 369 CCP. Further shortcomings concern the disclosure of the results of the prosecutorial and police investigations. Prosecutors still have great discretion in selecting the pieces of evidence can be attached to their requests for wiretaps or pre-trial detention, except, in the latter case, the information gathered in favour of the defendant. This result inhibits both the possibility of effective defence and the judicial oversight prescribed by the law.

II. Information on the Initiation of a Criminal Law Action and Recent Legal Arrangements to Involve the Accused Personally in the Proceedings

It has been observed that, along with information on substantial issues, the individuals concerned need proper information about the initiation of a criminal law action in order to be able to decide whether and how to participate in criminal proceedings. Over the last decades, considerable developments have occurred both in Italy and in Brazil in the attempt to strike new balances between the individual right to information and the need for effective prosecution.

To start with, new developments have taken place as to the goal of the information provided. In Brazil, as noted, the traditional purpose of the court summons was to promote the active participation of the defendants in criminal trials, allowing them an opportunity to be heard. This set-up was, however, recently reformed and defendants summoned to court are nowadays called upon to reply in writing.[78] This innovation has considerably reduced the personal contribution of the accused, since the lawyer usually provides the written response. In Italy, we saw that notice on the completion of the pre-trial inquiry under Article 415-*bis* CCP-Italy anticipates the information about the proceedings before formal charges have been preferred. This notice, moreover, allows for the defence to know in advance the future indictment and the evidence collected by the investigative bodies during the pre-trial inquiry, while enabling the accused to undertake active initiatives, such as producing written statements and requesting an oral hearing before the initiation of the court proceedings. Yet the wide range of defensive opportunities is more apparent than real. Prosecutors can ignore the arguments expressed by the defence in written statements, whereas the defendants' hearing, although affecting the validity of the procedure, provides a mostly theoretical opportunity to avoid the prosecutorial initiative, since the accused does not know exactly the form of the proceedings that the competent prosecutor will institute.[79]

[78] Chapter 3, C.

[79] Chapter 2, E.II.2.

A second development that can be observed in both countries concerns the possibility of the defendants being personally served with the proceedings instituted against them. In Brazil, Law 11.719/2008 extended to criminal justice the *citação com hora certa*, a form of court summons typical of civil proceedings.[80] Doubtless, this type of judicial service gives to judicial offices great powers in assessing the defendant's desire to abscond and cannot guarantee notification of the accused in person. The only way to reduce the danger of abuses is to strengthen judicial oversight. One should not overlook, however, the risks that arise from the judicial assessment of the justification of this court summons. In Italy, for instance, the problems deriving from uncontrolled judicial discretion were enhanced by Law 479/1999, which transposed to the intermediate phase the rules on the renewal of the summons and the postponement of the hearing.[81] As a consequence of this legislation, the competent judges for the pre-trial inquiry also had great leeway particularly since their assessment could not be challenged before a higher court. This reform, therefore, did not strengthen the defendants' right to be made aware of the proceedings initiated against them. Nor was this set-up improved by the hurried 2005 reform, which, in order to avoid further convictions by the Strasbourg case-law, acknowledged the right of defendants unaware of the conviction or the proceedings to be relieved from the effects of the expiration of the time to challenge the decision.[82]

It was only after almost 10 years that the Italian legislature intervened again in this delicate field, abolishing default proceedings.[83] This radical reform, however, was accompanied by the introduction of a new *in absentia* procedure, which to a great extent still relies on dangerous assumptions of the defendant's knowledge of the proceedings. Doubtless, these arrangements were largely due to the failure of Italian law to carry out an in-depth reform of the rules on judicial service. The risks of similar assumptions, moreover, are also apparent in Brazilian law, which almost 20 years after the abolition of default proceedings maintained the possibility of defendants being summoned by edict, a procedure that clearly assumes a fictitious knowledge of criminal proceedings.[84] It is therefore to be welcomed that the Brazilian legislature, on the basis of federal case-law, reformed the rules on the court summons, providing that detained defendants must be personally summoned to court.[85] At any rate, the possibility of defendants being summoned by edict should remain a last resort.

[80]Chapter 3, E.I.

[81]Chapter 2, E.II.3.

[82]Chapter 2, F.II.1.

[83]Chapter 2, F.II.2.

[84]Chapter 3, E.II.

[85]*Ibid.*

F. The Right to Personal Participation in Criminal Proceedings and the Problem of *in absentia* Proceedings

In both countries, therefore, the performance of personal notice enables defendants to decide whether and to what extent they can make their own contribution to the criminal inquiry. There can be little doubt that even in criminal justice systems with high-developed forms of legal assistance, the possibility of being personally involved in criminal hearings is of utmost importance with a view to fair criminal proceeding. In Italy, the right to personal participation is reserved to the defendant, since other private parties are represented in court by their lawyers. This does not negate, however, the importance of the personal contribution of private parties other than the accused in some judicial hearings (*e.g.*, in *incidente probatorio*).

Unlike other civil-law countries, both Brazil and Italy consider the defendants' participation in the proceedings as an individual right rather than a duty of collaborating with the criminal inquiry. As a result, defendants should not be compelled to intervene in investigative activities that can jeopardise their right not to adduce evidence against themselves. Neither of the two criminal justice systems is consistent with this approach, however. In Brazil, where defendants, after being duly summoned, do not appear in court, the judicial authority can bring them to court coercively for the purposes of questioning, a confrontation with other people, and so on.[86] In Italy, the situation varies depending on the phase. During the pre-trial inquiry, suspects can be compelled to cooperate with questioning by the prosecutor or the police. The situation changes after the opening of court proceedings. In the intermediate proceedings, defendants can be examined only upon their request and at trial also, judges cannot compel defendants to appear in court for the purposes of their examination. Aside from these limits, the 1988 code allowed for absent defendants or defendants tried through default proceedings to be coercively brought to court, a provision that the 2014 reform restricted to the case of absent defendants.[87]

Neither Italy nor Brazil has traditionally had clear legal arrangements to distinguish the defendants' voluntary absence from the amorphous situation in which defendants simply do not appear in court. Notwithstanding the need to balance efficient prosecution and the defendant's right to be present at trial, the default proceedings were long maintained in both countries. As noted, both Italy and Brazil needed to walk a long road to get rid of this inquisitorial procedure, which allowed for *in absentia* proceedings by replacing the defendant's personal participation with the representation of a court-appointed lawyer. Brazil needed almost half a century to abandon *em revelia* proceedings, which were abolished shortly after the enactment of the 1988 Constitution. In Italy, we saw that default proceedings were

[86] Art. 260 CCP-Brazil.

[87] Art. 490 CCP-Italy.

dropped more than 25 years after the 1988 codification and almost 70 years after the Republican Constitution.

The way both countries departed from this understanding of criminal justice was somewhat tortuous and the need to maintain some forms of proceedings *in absentia* led to gradual changes. In the 1988 Italian code, absence and contumacy could in principle be distinguished, albeit not in very clear terms.[88] Absence was always a free choice of the defendants who requested the proceedings to be continued without them or refused to appear in court. By contrasts, contumacy was the conclusion of a complex procedure that aimed at remedying only the cases in which the defendants' failure to appear in court was due to their ignorance or probable ignorance of the proceedings, situations that, as noted, the competent judge could assess freely and without any oversight by a higher court. Far from granting effective knowledge of the proceedings, therefore, the 1988 code provided the judiciary with wide discretion in assessing cases of ignorance or probable ignorance of the court summons. The same standards applied to the assessment of the grounds for non-appearance in court, that is, accident and *force majeure*. In any other case, neither a new summons nor a postponement of the hearing was needed, and the defendant, when not appearing in court, was to be provided with a court-appointed lawyer and the proceedings held in contumacy. This situation applied both to defendants who either were possibly unaware of the proceedings or chose not to participate in the proceedings. As we will note, this intrinsic ambivalence led the Strasbourg Court to rule not always in a consistent way in relation to Italian default proceedings.[89]

The traditional approach of Brazilian law to default proceedings was even more drastic.[90] Defendants who, duly summoned, did not appear in court were automatically declared absent and the proceedings continued *em revelia*. The abolition of contumacy, however, did not entail the abandonment of the practice of criminal proceedings being held in the absence of the defendant who after being summoned personally failed either to appear in court without justification or to communicate their new residence. This result can be deemed in line neither with the Constitution nor with the American Convention. The fact that the defendants were personally summoned to appear in court does not entail in itself that their non-intervention reflects their choice not to take part in the proceedings. On close examination, similar criticisms arise in relation to the presumption of knowledge of the proceedings that allow for the institution of criminal proceedings pursuant to the 2014 Italian reform. Even more worryingly, Italian law extended these assumptions from the cases in which defendants are personally summoned to court to situations in which the suspects were only made aware of the initiation of criminal investigations against them.[91]

---

[88] Chapter 2, F.II.1.

[89] Chapter 16, D.II.1.a.

[90] Chapter 3, F.

[91] Chapter 2, F.II.2.

In Brazil, we have noted that, 12 years after the 1996 reform, Law 11.719/2008 introduced the controversial form of summons *com hora certa*. Notwithstanding its limits and the maintenance of *citação por edital*, Law 9.271/1996 had the merit of introducing unprecedented mechanisms to deal with the defendant's absence at trial. As noted, both the proceedings and the time limit for the prosecution of the offence are to be suspended, with the judge having solely the power to order the collection of urgent evidence and pre-trial detention.[92] Neither solution is exempt from human rights concerns, and the unlimited suspension of the time limit for the prosecution of the offence poses especially delicate problems of constitutional, criminal and criminal procedural law.[93] Furthermore, there is no doubt that allowing for criminal proceedings to be re-opened after several years, regardless of the seriousness of the offence, is an unreasonable solution that can seriously jeopardise the right of all individuals to have their acts forgotten after a certain period of time.

Over recent years, Brazilian federal case-law has attempted to mitigate the negative consequences of the vague legislative solution, acknowledging the defendants' right for there to be a time limit on the prosecution of their offence, a period corresponding to the statutory limitations laid down in Article 109 CC, calculated in relation to the maximum sentence threshold.[94] Concurrently, the Italian legislature introduced a similar solution to compensate for the shortcomings of the 2005 reform. Italian Law 67/2014 also provided for the suspension both of the proceedings and of the time limit for the prosecution of the offence, a period that cannot exceed the maximum time limits laid down in Article 161(2) of the criminal code.[95] Beyond the similarities with the Brazilian solution, however, the scope of the suspension of criminal proceedings in Italy can be narrower as a result of the broad range of situations in which the presumption of knowledge of the proceedings allows for a prosecution to be carried out against absent defendants.

G. Investigative Needs and the Right to Be Fairly Heard in Criminal Proceedings

I. The Right to a Fair Hearing, Legal Assistance and the Role of the Judiciary in the Pre-trial Examination of the Accused

Providing the individuals involved in criminal proceedings with a fair opportunity to be heard stands out among the most difficult challenges of any criminal justice

[92] Chapter 3, F.

[93] *Ibid.*

[94] *Ibid.*

[95] Chapter 2, F.II.2.

system, requiring delicate balances between state-related needs and individual interests. The way this aim was pursued in the two countries, however, differs considerably according to the different phases of the proceedings.

In Italy, the legal set-up rapidly changed in the early years after the code's enactment. We saw that the 1988 code aimed at a centralised model of prosecutorial leadership of the preliminary investigations, which ruled out the suspect's examination by the police, even upon delegation of prosecutorial authority.[96] The solution of the drafters of the 1988 codification, which required the prosecutor as a part of the judiciary to question suspects personally, was aimed at protecting them against the risk of abuses. This did not exclude the possibility of the police questioning the suspect immediately after the fact and even without their counsel being present.[97] However, the results of this questioning should neither be recorded nor could in any way be admitted at trial. Furthermore, the police could question informants and co-defendants. The autonomous investigations of the police, however, were chronologically limited to the phase before the opening of the pre-trial inquiry. After the prosecutor took over the leadership of the case, the police could only carry out further investigations if delegated to do so by the prosecutorial authority. This set-up only lasted a few of years, however. By overriding the original relationship between police and prosecutorial inquiries, the 1992 anti-mafia legislation empowered the law enforcement authorities to continue their investigations even after the prosecutor took over the case, while allowing prosecutors to also delegate the defendant's hearing to the police.[98] This reform was of utmost systematic importance, bringing about an in-depth change to the overall structure of the pre-trial inquiry. From the perspective of the present discussion, it is noteworthy that throughout the pre-trial inquiry, the suspect's examination can today be delegated to the police pursuant to the rules governing the prosecutorial hearing and the police can also question the suspect at their own initiative.

In Brazil, police leadership of the pre-trial inquiry calls for a balance between the need for efficient investigation and the individual right to a fair opportunity to be heard.[99] The use of the same terminology for the preliminary and trial hearings highlights the requirement that the police must grant the suspects, as a rule, the same safeguards laid down for the court examination, starting with the right to silence. In this regard, Italian law instead distinguishes, even from a terminological viewpoint, the defendant's trial examination (*esame*) from the prosecutorial questioning of the suspect (*interrogatorio*), no matter whether carried out by the police or by the prosecutor. Moreover, different legal rules apply under Italian law to the two types of hearing. Even though both suspects and defendants have the right to silence, we have noted that in the court proceedings, defendants can only be examined at their own request, whereas in the pre-trial inquiry suspects can be

---

[96] Chapter 2, G.II.1.

[97] *Ibid.*

[98] *Ibid.*

[99] Chapter 3, G.I.

compelled to be questioned by the investigative authorities.[100] In the light of the mixed structure of the intermediate phase as a pre-trial judicial hearing *in camera*, the drafters of the 1988 code introduced special rules on the defendant's examination in this phase, rules that excluded any form of coercion aimed at obtaining the defendant's presence in court.

A necessary condition of a fair hearing is legal assistance. In Brazil, it was only in 2003 that the legislature acknowledged the suspect's right to be assisted by counsel during the police examination.[101] Under Italian law, except in the case of police questioning immediately after the commission of the offence, both suspects and defendants must be granted the assistance of a lawyer during their examination. Italian law also ensured the same guarantee to co-defendants whom prosecutors must question pursuant to similar rules to those governing their hearing in the court proceedings.[102] Since 2001, legal assistance has also been ensured to the co-accused summoned to be examined on issues concerned with other individuals (*testimonianza assistita*).

Although legal assistance must therefore be provided to any person charged with a criminal offence in both countries, some differences can be observed. In Italy, the mandatory nature of this guarantee impinges on the validity of the overall proceedings. In Brazil, the practical application of the 2003 reform still gives rise to serious human rights concerns because of the lack of a clear statutory definition of the exact moment in which—and the procedural act through which—individuals must be charged with a criminal offence (*indiciamento*). By departing from the approach of the Rocco code, Italian law links the status of 'suspect' with the formal registration of individual data in the prosecutorial register, while providing an exhaustive list of the procedural acts through which the accused can be brought to court with a formal indictment.[103] To compensate for this formal approach, the 1988 code requires the competent authority—no matter whether the police, the prosecutor or a judge—to stop the questioning of any person other than the suspect or the defendant, who gives statements that can lead to the initiation of a criminal law action.[104] In this case, the person examined will be granted the right to be assisted by a lawyer and the statements previously made will not be used against them. These fundamental requirements highlight a substantial approach, which is further enhanced by the provision that the statements of the individuals already suspected of having committed an offence, against whom, however, no criminal investigation has yet been initiated, can be admitted as inculpatory evidence neither against them nor against the individuals currently being investigated if the competent authority has examined them without the guarantees acknowledged to the suspect or the defendant.[105] This important provision aims at protecting individuals,

[100]Chapter 2, G.I.
[101]Chapter 3, G.I.
[102]Chapter 2, G.II.1.
[103]Art. 60(1) CCP-Italy.
[104]Chapter 2, G.II.1.
[105]*Ibid.*

against whom suspicion of guilt has already arisen from other investigations, against dilatory tactics of the investigative authorities.

Furthermore, the comparative analysis of the two countries highlights the limits of legal assistance in pre-trial hearings. In Italy, the scant information that is generally provided to the defence jeopardises the right to be fairly heard at the pre-trial stage.[106] By questioning suspects at their own initiative, the police are not required to provide them with any information. This situation, which was initially based on the choice of the drafters of the 1988 code to limit autonomous police inquiries before the competent prosecutor took on leadership of the investigations, seems to be no longer justified today. Thus prosecutors must inform suspects on the provisional charge, as it stands at present. However, no information is due, as a rule, on the investigations conducted, nor is there a general obligation to disclose the evidence collected in favour of the accused. A somewhat different situation can be observed in Brazil. Even though suspects must be given the opportunity of a private interview with their lawyers before the hearing, Brazilian law had not until recently specified what information was to be granted both to the lawyers and their clients, nor what rights counsel has during the examination. However, we saw that Law 13.245/2016 brought about significant changes to the rules governing defence lawyers (Law 8.906/94), strengthening not only the right of suspects to be assisted by lawyers during the police inquiry and especially in the police questioning but also the possibility of counsel accessing the information collected by the investigative bodies.[107] Consequently, the competent authority will only be entitled to delimit access to relevant information where a concrete risk arises to the efficiency of the ongoing investigation or to its goals.[108]

Another factor that negatively affects the possibility of a fair hearing in the pre-trial phase is the weak role of the judiciary in both countries. Certainly, the enhancement of judicial hearings would constitute a proper alternative to the questionings by the investigative bodies, which remain unable to provide individuals with the opportunity to have themselves heard in the delicate phase of the pre-trial inquiry. Italian law acknowledges the right to be heard by a judge in specific situations, especially in cases of remand detention and alternatives to custody. However, there is no general possibility for the suspect to be heard by a judge, as spontaneous statements can only be given to the competent prosecutor. The court procedure of *incidente probatorio* also cannot ensure this result, since defendants, although being entitled to request it, can only be examined on issues concerned with other individuals.

---

[106] Chapter 2, G.II.2.

[107] Art. 7(XXI) Law 8.906/94.

[108] Art. 7(11) Law 8.906/94.

II. The Right to a Fair Hearing of Individuals Other Than the Accused and the Lack of Comprehensive Rules on Different Informants

Another common deficiency of both countries is the failure to provide comprehensive rules on the hearing of individuals other than the accused. In Italy, the 1988 code introduced the broad notion of 'informants' with a view to marking a basic distinction between the person charged with a criminal offence and other private subjects. Consequently, different rules govern both the police and the prosecutorial questionings depending on whether the person to be examined had been charged with a crime or not. The rather vague notion of 'informants' therefore had a residual character. The only type of questioning governed by special rules concerned the co-accused, who must be heard pursuant to a procedure intermediate between witness testimony and a suspect's examination.[109] Thus, although co-defendants could be coercively brought to the prosecutor's office, they were to be granted the assistance of a lawyer and could claim their right to silence. As noted, the pre-trial hearings of co-defendants have undergone various legislative changes over subsequent years. In 1992, the legislature enabled the police to question co-defendants at their own initiative pursuant to the rules governing the prosecutorial hearing. In 1997, the Italian legislature uncoupled the hearing of co-defendants through *incidente probatorio* from the original cases of urgency. Five years later, the 2001 fair trial reform, while introducing the aforementioned testimony of the co-accused assisted by a lawyer (*testimonianza assistita*), empowered both the police and prosecutors to question co-defendants pursuant to the new rules.

In both countries, furthermore, there have never been comprehensive rules on the pre-trial hearing of the aggrieved parties, notwithstanding their different position in criminal proceedings from that of potential witnesses and other informants. The 1988 Italian code did not provide for specific provisions on the examination of vulnerable individuals at the pre-trial stage and it was only in 1996 that the rules of *incidente probatorio* were for the first time extended to the pre-trial hearing of minors in cases of sexual crimes. Subsequent legislation progressively broadened the scope of this mechanism.[110] In recent years, the need to fulfil the requirements set by the EU Directive on preventing and combating human trafficking and protecting its victims has brought about the extension of these rules to the case of judicial hearings of some vulnerable adults.[111] Further international developments led the Italian legislature to introduce *ad hoc* rules on the prosecutorial and police questioning of minors who, no matter whether witnesses or victims, in cases of particular serious crimes must be heard with the assistance of an expert in child

[109] Chapter 2, G.II.1.

[110] Chapter 2, G.II.2.

[111] *Ibid.*

psychology or psychiatry. We will see that in 2015 the legislature, implementing the 2012 Directive on victims' rights, provided highly vulnerable victims with special support if questioned by the police or by the prosecutor, while enhancing the possibility for them to be ordinarily heard through *incidente probatorio*.[112]

In Brazil, one of the main tasks of the police during the pre-trial inquiry is to question the aggrieved parties, questioning that must in principle follow the rules governing the victim's examination in open court. Unlike in Italy, however, victims are not examined pursuant to the rules governing witness testimony.[113] Consequently, although victims can be coercively brought to the police station, they cannot be compelled to tell the truth nor can they be prosecuted for false statements. From this it also follows that the injured party cannot claim the right to silence, a solution that can be reasonably accepted taking into account that the police inquiry is often initiated on the victim's initiative. Like Italy, Brazil has also recently paid rising attention to the testimony of victims especially in cases of sexual crimes, a testimony that must be handled with great caution to avoid negative irreparable repercussions on the defendant's life.[114]

III. The Right to Silence, Defensive Choices and the Right to Be Fairly Heard in Judicial Proceedings

A delicate issue in both countries concerns protection against the risk of being compelled to give evidence against oneself. In Brazil, the 1941 code for more than 60 years required judges to inform defendants, prior to their examination, that silence could be interpreted to the detriment of their defence. Surprisingly, even though the 1988 Constitution enshrined the general right of defendants to be presumed innocent and the right of any detained person to remain silent, it took 15 years before the Brazilian legislature amended this provision, which distorted the right to silence and seriously jeopardised the possibility of a hair hearing.[115] Moreover, the 2003 reform did not change the possibility of judges forming their opinion on the basis of the defendant's silence, which, notwithstanding that it cannot be interpreted as a confession, can affect the decision-making.

Italian law, as noted, expressly rules out that defendants can coercively be brought to court for the purposes of their examination. Like other private parties, defendants can only be questioned with their consent and can always claim their right to silence on any matter stated. Yet coercion can be used by indirect means, *e.g.* if silence or refusal to be examined can negatively affect the defendant's position. It is noteworthy that the 1992 reform enacted into the rules on witness

[112]Chapter 16, D.IV.1.

[113]Chapter 3, G.I.

[114]*Ibid.*

[115]Chapter 3, G.II.

testimony a provision that allowed for out-of-court statements to be read out not only in cases of inconsistency with the evidence rendered at trial but also if the person examined refused to answer the questions.[116] This provision, which clearly blurred the distinction between the reading out of inconsistent and unavailable pre-trial evidence, survived for almost 10 years and its scope of application was broadened to the extent that it deeply influenced the overall treatment of hearsay evidence in Italy. The extension of this rule to the hearing of private parties enhanced the human rights risks to the individuals examined at trial. As far as the accused is concerned, the 1988 code had already enabled the parties, when the defendant did not appear in court or refused to the examined, to request the admission of his statements given to either the prosecutor or if delegated by the prosecutor, the police, as well as to the judge in the pre-trial inquiry or the intermediate phase.[117] Surprisingly, the 2001 fair trial reform of the rules on witness testimony, while abolishing the old Article 500(2-*bis*) CCP-Italy, did not amend the provision of Article 513 CCP and therefore out-of-court evidence given by the defendant can also be read out at trial if the accused, despite consenting to the court hearing, refuses to answer specific questions.

This result is questionable from a human rights perspective. It is debatable that typical defensive options, such as the choice not to appear in court or the refusal to be examined, should allow the use of incriminating evidence on the assumption that it was obtained with the lawyer's presence. It has been observed that very different guarantees apply to the prosecutorial hearing and the examination conducted by the competent judge for the pre-trial inquiry. Furthermore, it appears to be contradictory that, while defendants possess the right to silence, their refusal of examination or of individual questions allows for other parties to request the admission of information that can severely jeopardise them. This result raises even more serious concerns if the accused simply does not appear in court, an event that does not necessarily reflect a free defensive choice.

From the viewpoint of the right to silence of the accused, further complex problems concern the conditions of use of incriminating statements rendered out of court by co-defendants. Italian law, in particular, gives rise to several human rights concerns. The 1988 code provided nothing in this regard. The attempt of the Italian legislature in 1997 to hinder the unconditional use of this information by requiring the consent of the addressee of the pre-trial statements or agreement among the parties[118] was erased by the Constitutional Court through judgment 361/1998. This ruling achieved two main results, i.e. (*a*) it compelled—even coercively—the co-defendants who gave incriminating evidence to appear in court and (*b*) it allowed for the admission of their out-of-court statements (no matter whether gathered in the pre-trial inquiry or in other proceedings) not only to solve inconsistencies with the evidence given at trial but also in cases of

[116] Chapter 2, I.II.4.

[117] Art. 513 CCP-Italy (1988 version).

[118] Art. 513(1-2) CCP-Italy (1997 version).

refusal of examination or refusal to answer specific questions. In both cases, information could be used against other co-defendants, provided that other pieces of evidence supported its reliability. This judgment overruled the protective scope of the principle of *contradictoire* by severely restricting the participatory rights both of the person examined and of the addressee of the incriminating evidence. On the one hand, co-defendants, even prosecuted in the same proceedings, could be brought to court *manu militari*, loosing their right to choose whether to be examined and thus being exposed to a forced confrontation with the addressee of their previous statements. On the other hand, the addressee of the incriminating evidence, despite being allowed silence on any matter stated, was exposed to the wide use of hearsay evidence gathered without any defensive participation.

Since Law 67/2001, this result has no longer been in force, so that today out-of-court statements of co-defendants cannot be used against other people without their consent. However, witness testimony of co-defendants assisted by a lawyer raises several concerns as to the consequences of the refusal of examination or individual questions.[119] In particular, it must be ascertained whether and to what extent in these cases the person examined can suffer from indirect pressure that restricts their right to silence and to a fair hearing. The 2001 fair trial reform provided co-defendants who choose to give evidence as witnesses with a broad protective umbrella against the risk of worsening their own position both in the same and other proceedings. Nonetheless, we have seen that Italian law acknowledges to the competent authority wide discretion in assessing whether the statements given concern other people. Provided that the co-defendants were informed prior to the questioning, prosecutors can request their being summoned at trial as witnesses with legal assistance, if their pre-trial statements can be used for the decision on other individuals. By this means, the individuals examined lose their unconditional right to silence, and whereas their previous statements cannot negatively affect their position, they are exposed to criminal responsibility not only for what they will say at trial but also for their refusal to answer the new questions exhaustively. This result gives a great power to the competent authority, while putting co-defendants in a vulnerable position that does not allow them to make their defensive options freely.

IV. Methods of Examination and the Guarantees of a Fair Hearing

Ultimately, the comparative analysis has highlighted another problematic issue concerned with the guarantee of a fair questioning, namely the method of examination of the individuals involved in criminal proceedings. This issue distinguishes Brazilian and Italian law considerably. As noted, the 1941 Brazilian code did not

[119]Chapter 2, G.II.3.

differentiate between witnesses and defendants, who were questioned by the trial judge in open court.[120] Although judicial questioning certainly protected defendants from the risks of cross-examination, the impossibility for the counsel to intervene during the hearing made lawyers a sort of guest of stone, leaving the person examined alone. Recent reforms have distinguished the examination of witnesses and defendants. Whereas Law 11.690/2008 enabled the parties to cross-examine witnesses under judicial supervision, the 2003 legislature maintained the judicial examination of the accused, while strengthening the role of defence lawyers, who can today suggest further facts and indicate issues to be clarified after the completion of the judicial questioning.[121]

In Italy, it has been observed that different methods govern the taking of oral evidence in the intermediate phase and at trial. In the former case, although defendants must consent to their examination, Law 479/1999 has entitled any party to request the defendant to be cross-examined, which exposes the accused who asks to be heard *in camera* to the risks of direct confrontation. Concerning the trial hearings, the 1988 code made the cross-examination the main method of questioning of any person at trial with the sole exception of the proceedings before *pretore*. As a result, not only witnesses and experts but also the parties, who accepted or requested to be heard, had to be cross-examined by other parties, including the prosecutor. This situation has remained substantially unchanged. Unlike in Brazil, the party that requests the hearing has always had an active role by starting the examination and having the right to ask new questions.[122]

Notwithstanding the constitutional requirement of *contradictoire*, moreover, Italian law derogates from the method of direct confrontation to protect individuals other the parties from the risks of cross-examination.[123] The 1988 code had already allowed for minors to be questioned as witnesses by the president of the trial court who, taking into account further questions and objections raised by other parties, should be associated by a family member or guardian and an expert in child psychology. Of course, this was not the only case of vulnerable witnesses and therefore in 1997, the Constitutional Court enabled the trial court's president to question also vulnerable adults who could be jeopardised by the parties' examination. In 1998, the Italian legislature extended these rules to the hearing of minors through *incidente probatorio* at the pre-trial stages. For the first time, moreover, Italian law addressed the problem of the hearing of victims by allowing the use of a glass mirror with an intercom during their examination, a solution recently broadened by the 2013 reform on gender-based violence.

Brazilian legislature has also recently focused on the use of modern technical means to tackle problems concerned with specific types of examination.[124] The hearing of detained defendants by videoconference, introduced in 2009, can be

---

[120] Chapter 3, G.II.

[121] *Ibid.*

[122] Art. 503(2) CCP-Italy.

[123] Chapter 2, G.III.

[124] Chapter 3, G.II.

ordered not only to safeguard the public security or *ordre public* but also to enable the participation, albeit by different means, of the person examined in the proceedings, whenever the defendant's illness or other circumstances can make his appearance at trial difficult. Of course, the participatory rights of the accused are not absolute and therefore these technical arrangements can also be justified to balance the defence needs of different individuals, that is, the defendants' right to be heard with the need to prevent them from having a negative influence on the victims and witnesses. The use of technical means has led to the legislature also protecting individuals other than the accused, while relaxing rigid solutions that drastically deprived defendants of their right to participation in the taking of evidence. Traditionally, when judges considered that the defendants' presence at trial could humiliate, frighten, or cause constraint to the witnesses, defendants were to be banned from the courtroom. This situation changed in 2008, as a legislative reform required the judicial authority firstly to verify whether the witness can be examined by videoconference, and, only if this arrangement is not possible, permitted the defendant to be banned from the courtroom, where the defendant's lawyer will in any case be present.

H. *Audi alteram partem* and the Collection of Criminal Evidence

I. Participatory Rights in the Taking of Oral Evidence and the Role of the Judiciary

Both countries have progressively enhanced the role of the parties in the taking of criminal evidence. This is especially apparent in the field of oral evidence. Italian law of evidence is strongly based on the rule that criminal evidence should in principle be gathered in open court at the request of the parties and by means of the method of cross-examination.[125] In Brazil, the fact that the 2008 reform submitted the taking of testimonial evidence to cross-examination by the parties not only enhanced the participatory rights of the defence but also strengthened the impartiality of the judiciary, which can put supplementary questions.[126] Yet Brazilian law still requires defendants to be examined by the trial judges, a solution justified on the assumption that the accused cannot be seen as a means of evidence. Both countries, however, provide for various exceptions from the rule of trial evidence-gathering and especially from the rule of cross-examination in open court to protect the interests of specific individuals, such as victims or particular types of witnesses. In Italy, these solutions not only aim at protecting vulnerable

[125] Chapter 2, H.I.

[126] Chapter 3, H.I.

witnesses (*e.g.*, minor witnesses) but also the family members of particular informants (*e.g.*, undercover agents).[127] In Brazil, we have noted that recent legislation has also enhanced recourse to technical arrangements—especially hearing by videoconference or other technological means of transmission of sounds and images in real time—not only to allow for remote hearing of defendants but also to balance the right to confrontation with the need to avoid negative influences on the victims and witnesses.

Moreover, the proactive role of the parties in the taking of oral evidence does not only relate to the cross-examination but also to further initiatives, which can be exercised during the hearing of witnesses or co-defendants. In particular, it is noteworthy that under Italian law, inconsistent out-of-court statements can only be read out at trial at the request of the parties.[128] This result is the inevitable consequence of the distinction between prosecutorial and trial file, which entails that unlike in the past, the trial judges have no access to the evidence obtained out of court. That the reading out of out-of-court evidence lies in the hands of the parties, however, also gives great power to the public prosecutor. On close examination, the main problem lies in the changing role of prosecutors, who are required to carry out impartial investigations during the preliminary inquiry, investigations that can often entail serious restrictions on individual rights. The role of public prosecutors changes after the initiation of the court proceedings, since the prosecutor takes on the role of a public accuser and can exercise almost all the procedural rights of private parties. Yet the effects of the pre-trial investigations do not remain restricted to the preliminary phase. Even in cases in which hearsay evidence is only used to prove the credibility of the person examined, we have seen that prosecutors, reading out statements rendered in the preliminary inquiry, can impeach private parties, informants and co-defendants during trial examination.

This result alters the balance between the rights of the parties in the taking of oral evidence, nor can it be compensated for by the possibility of the private parties reading out at trial out-of-court statements obtained through defence's investigations. Thus public prosecutors, flanked by law enforcement bodies, are often equipped with more powerful tools to obtain evidence at the pre-trial stage and the information collected by the investigative bodies will often inevitably have a greater weight for the decision-makers.

The enhanced role of the parties in the taking of evidence should also be assessed in the light of the competences of the judiciary. At first glance, the method of gathering oral evidence and the role reserved to the judicial authority are not necessarily issues related to each other. That the judge admits some pieces of evidence, which were not requested by the parties, says nothing about the forms according to which they must be gathered. As noted, however, the entitlement of the parties to cross-examine informants enhances the impartiality of the competent judge. Inquisitorial models not only largely entrust the gathering of evidence to investigative magistrates but also provide for a wide range of possibilities for

---

[127] Chapter 2, H.III.1.

[128] Art. 500(1) CCP-Italy.

information to be gathered *ex officio* at trial. In adversarial models, the testimonial hearing ordered *ex officio* must also be governed by the cross-examination. Both countries have increasingly reduced judicial initiative in evidence-gathering, while leaving less room for the direct intervention of the competent judge in testimonial hearings. Italian law provides clear provisions, which submit to strict conditions the gathering of integrative evidence taken by trial judges at their own initiative[129] and judicial intervention in the witness examination conducted by the parties.[130]

Certainly, a proper balancing of the relationship between the parties' initiative and judicial intervention aims to avoid the risk of the judiciary re-assuming a leading role in the taking of testimonial evidence, especially supporting the tasks or remedying the failures of the public prosecution. Under Italian law, the gathering of integrative evidence at the initiative of the trial court must follow the collection of the information requested by the parties. In the early 1990s, the Supreme Court re-interpreted this power by allowing the trial judges to obtain evidence *ex officio* also where the competent prosecutor failed to present a testimonial list on time and even if the parties requested no pieces of evidence.[131] The Constitutional Court ruled that admitting evidence *ex officio* was constitutional in the absence of any request of the parties.[132] More recently, the Supreme Court confirmed the lawfulness of evidence-gathering at the initiative of the trial court in cases of inactivity of the parties.[133] This case-law, however, gives rise to human rights concerns and various practical difficulties in Italian criminal justice, characterised by the distribution of the available information between the two files. Thus the limited information available in the trial file trial can often make it extremely difficult for the trial judges to ascertain whether further evidence is strictly necessary for the decision-making.

Brazilian legislation also limits judicial intervention in the witnesses' examination, although the case-law tends to make the invalidity of the proceedings conditional on the proof of a concrete damage suffered by the defence.[134] Certainly, the excessive use of judicial power to gather new pieces of evidence or supplement the collection of evidence requested by the parties can alter the equilibrium among the parties. Especially where the trial judges aim at saving incriminating evidence, the defence, suffering from a clear disadvantage from the judicial initiative, must be granted a tool of reaction in order to compensate for the lack of previous disclosure of the sought evidence. The Italian Constitutional Court has recently shared this approach,[135] thus satisfying the requirements set by Strasbourg case-law, which

---

[129] Art. 507 CCP-Italy.

[130] Art. 506 CCP-Italy.

[131] CCass, *Martin*.

[132] CConst, 111/1993.

[133] CCass, Joint Sections, *Greco*.

[134] Chapter 3, H.I.

[135] CConst, 73/2010.

calls upon national judges to collect evidence to compensate for the imbalance in the burden of proof.[136]

II. The Right to Confrontation, Documentary Evidence and the Use of Information Gathered in Other Proceedings

In both countries, despite the lack of specific indications in the respective Constitutions, the principle of *contradictoire* cannot be interpreted as concerning the collection solely of oral evidence. In Italy, the general acknowledgment by the Constitution of the involvement of the parties in evidence-gathering should be read as encompassing the overall procedure of evidence-gathering rather than the strict phase of taking evidence. In this context, there is little doubt that the collection of documentary evidence also requires the contribution of the parties. Furthermore, it is of utmost importance that documentary evidence will not be used as a surrogate for oral evidence.[137]

In particular, the defence can make a relevant contribution in the admission of documentary evidence. A delicate issue concerns the possibility for the defence to have a fair opportunity to examine the sought documents prior to their admission. Doubtless, this opportunity affects the effectiveness of the right to a full defence and, as far as the defendants are concerned, their right to have the time and the facilities for the preparation of their defence. In both Brazil and Italy, this issue holds specific relevance under both international human rights law and constitutional law. Nevertheless, Italian legislation follows a worrisome approach, since the 1988 code, while acknowledging the parties' right to examine documents after their admission at trial,[138] does not require them to communicate their request to the other parties beforehand, as in case of oral evidence. Brazilian law also lacks clear statutory indications in this respect and except in cases of jury trials, in which documents must be produced at trial at least 3 days prior to the trial hearing, there is no provision concerned with ordinary proceedings—a lacuna that the case-law usually fills by invoking the rules governing civil proceedings.[139]

A particularly delicate problem in both countries is obtaining pieces of evidence gathered in other proceedings. Doubtless, criminal proceedings cannot be seen as islands and often need information collected in other contexts. On the other hand, criminal justice systems based on the principle of *contradictoire* cannot tolerate that the collection of external evidence frustrates the parties' contribution to the gathering especially of oral evidence. Certainly, the parties can critically assess external evidence and especially written statements. Admitting information collected in other proceedings, however, deprives the parties of the possibility of taking part

[136] See Chiavario (2015), p. 531.

[137] Chapter 2, H.III.3.

[138] *Ibid.*

[139] Chapter 3, H.III.

actively in evidence-gathering. Moreover, the massive use of external information as a substitute for oral evidence that should instead be gathered in the same proceeding does not only entail risks for the right to *contradictoire* but can also jeopardise the decision-making. Both in Italy and Brazil, legal scholarship points out that the procedural context plays an essential role in the collection of criminal evidence.

To tackle these problems, the 1988 Italian codification, departing from the approach followed by the Rocco code, specific detailed rules governing the admission and use of external evidence.[140] The main principle was that external evidence should have been gathered either at trial or in a court procedure in the pre-trial phase. Despite its merits, this solution reflected a rather formalistic approach to right to *contradictoire*, which as an individual guarantee, has by definition a relative value. The fact that a witness gave certain statements at trial in the presence of the lawyers for the parties B and C does not at all mean that the parties D and E were involved in the gathering of evidence. From the viewpoint of the latter parties, no confrontation therefore took place.

The Italian law on the use of evidence taken in other proceedings walked the same tortuous road that led to the several amendments of the rules governing the use of pre-trial and hearsay evidence.[141] As noted, the first reform was carried out by the 1992 anti-mafia legislation, which, despite its shortcomings, undoubtedly strengthened the participatory role of the addressee of the external evidence. On one hand, the single defendants were permitted to consent to the use of the information obtained, if it was not gathered at trial or *incidente probatorio*. On the other, a new limitation on the use of testimonial evidence taken in other proceedings was introduced, in that the witness statements could only be used against the accused whose counsel had been in a position to take part in the other hearing. On close examination, this result also reveals a formalistic understanding of the right to *contradictoire*, since in Italy, as in Brazil, the lawyer's contribution always depends on the subject matter of the proceeding in which the evidence is taken. Moreover, the lack of the defendant's consent did not ban at all the use of external evidence, which was allowed under the soft limitations introduced by the 1992 reform. Although the 2001 reform tightened these limits, it must be acknowledged that the legislative implementation of the constitutional fair trial reform missed the opportunity for an in-depth reflection on this delicate field, while limiting itself to a mere readjustment of the existing rules.

The comparative examination of the two countries has highlighted further human rights risks, which arise from the obtaining of external rulings for evidentiary purposes. Although Brazil does not have special rules on this problem, legal scholarship is well aware that decisions issued in other proceedings, especially decisions in proceedings intended to scrutinise the accused's dangerousness, should be admitted at trial with great caution.[142] In Italy, the 1992 anti-mafia reform

---

[140] Art. 238 CCP-Italy.

[141] Chapter 2, H.III.3.

[142] Chapter 3, H.III.

introduced a new provision—namely Article 238-*bis* CCP-Italy—which allows for the use of external rulings as documentary evidence to prove the facts under prosecution.[143] Although the lack of almost any limit to the use of external decisions clearly frustrates the strict conditions laid down in relation to the collection of external evidence, there has still been no legislative intervention to align this problematic provision to the fair trial requirements.

III. The Right to contradictoire, *Technical Investigations and Expert Evidence*

Expert evidence has increasingly gained importance in criminal proceedings worldwide. Doubtless, the traditional state-centred approach, based upon the exclusive role of court appointed experts and the wide discretion of the judge as a *peritus peritorum*, can no longer fulfil the challenges of modern criminal justice and the developments that increasingly occur in science and technology. Nevertheless, there are still visible traces of this old approach both in Brazil and in Italy, as shown by the dominant role of court-appointed experts in a number of criminal proceedings. In Italy, expert evidence holds special importance in the court procedure of *incidente probatorio,* and in the trial phase expert evidence is one of the few cases in which information can be taken at the initiative of the competent court.[144] In Brazil, the 1941 code entrusted technical inquiries to court-appointed experts, while submitting the assessment of expert evidence to judicial discretion.[145]

Against this background, there is no doubt that a participatory model of criminal proceedings necessitates the involvement of the parties in the taking of expert evidence as a necessary condition for reliable decision-making. In most cases, however, neither the prosecutors nor the lawyers have enough preparation to follow technical inquiries. Therefore, modern criminal justice systems have progressively enhanced the role of technical advisers, appointed by the parties. The ways technical advisors can carry out their tasks, however, are different in the two countries. The comparative analysis of Brazil and Italy highlights two main developments, that is, the involvement of the parties' appointed technical advisors in the court-appointed expert's investigation, and the conduct of autonomous technical inquiries. Brazilian law only recently allowed for the participation of the parties' technical advisors in the court-appointed expert's investigation, despite the clear implications on the constitutional requirements of *contradictoire* and full defence.[146] There is still no possibility for autonomous investigations by the parties' technical advisors, whose role is limited to following the technical inquiry

[143]Chapter 2, H.III.3.

[144]Chapter 2, H.III.2.

[145]Chapter 3, H.II.

[146]*Ibid.*

carried out by the court-appointed experts. At any rate, their tasks are of utmost importance, especially to allow the effective participation of private parties in the taking of expert evidence. This not only applies to the accused but also to the victims, provided they have already taken over the role of prosecutorial assistants. Moreover, technical assistants can give a very useful contribution to the decision-making by providing a critical assessment of the court expert's report. In the light of this, it is regrettable that Brazilian law does not grant the defence a technical advisor at the state's expense, which makes technical assistance a privilege of wealthy people.[147]

The 1988 Italian code strengthened the role of the parties' technical advisors in the overall procedure for obtaining expert evidence.[148] Technical advisors can first make their contribution in the phase in which the court appoints its expert by making requests and observations, which will in turn appear in the final report of the court expert. There is, however, some uncertainty as to whether technical advisors can also cross-examine the court-appointed expert at trial. In the light of the importance of the tasks of technical advisors and the effective exercise of the right to *contradictoire*, Italian law grants the private parties the assistance of court-appointed technical advisors under the same conditions provided for legal aid. It is also noteworthy that Law 397/2000 enabled the defence to conduct autonomous technical inquiries.[149] Only in the case of non-repeatable technical investigations must the defence inform public prosecutor who can exercise the rights, if compatible, acknowledged to the defence by Article 360 CCP-Italy. Despite the evident similarities with non-repeatable technical surveys ordered by the prosecutor, it cannot be denied that the prosecutorial inquiry often has greater influence on the decision-makers than that conducted by the technical advisors of private parties.

A delicate issue in both countries is whether and to what extent the parties can be involved in the taking of expert evidence in the pre-trial phase. This issue is of utmost importance, also taking into account that most technical surveys must be conducted on perishable sources of evidence that need to be collected as soon as possible. In Brazil, the practice of postponing the preferment of charges against the suspect makes it often difficult for the defence to be involved in the police's technical investigations. Moreover, the 2008 reform did not provide clear indications as to whether private parties can appoint technical assistants during the police inquiry.[150]

In Italy, the 1988 code provided different safeguards depending on whether or not the technical prosecutorial inquiry concerns non-repeatable or repeatable evidence.[151] As noted, specific information duties are required in the former case. No information is, however, due where prosecutors consider that the technical

---

[147] *Ibid.*

[148] Chapter 2, H.III.2.

[149] *Ibid.*

[150] Chapter 3, H.II.

[151] Chapter 2, H.III.2.

investigation can be repeated at trial, with the result that both the victim and the suspect are deprived of the possibility of participating in the prosecutorial inquiry by means of either their lawyer or a technical advisor of their own choice. Further problems arise where another technical investigation through *incidente probatorio* follows the inquiry carried out by the technical advisor appointed by the competent prosecutor. Although evidence must be obtained pursuant to the rules governing trial evidence-gathering, the defence has no access to the records of the prosecutorial investigation nor can private parties' technical advisors oversee the inquiry conducted by the court-appointed expert. Irrespective of whether a previous technical prosecutorial survey was conducted, the structure of *incidente probatorio* does not appear to be adequate to tackle the modern challenges posed by complex technical inquiries and to grant the defence a fair opportunity for participation.[152] The fact that *incidente probatorio* can only be activated at the request of the parties does not seem to be consistent with the goals of expert evidence, which aims at ensuring the reliability of evidence-gathering and fact-finding. In this context, it is also debatable that victims still have a weak proactive role, not being entitled to request to the competent judge the collection of expert evidence.

I. The Parties' Contribution to the Decision-Making and the Requirements of *contradictoire*-Based Fact-Finding

I. Relativism of Criminal Evidence and the Different Probative Value Depending on the Decision at Stake

In inquisitorial systems of criminal justice, information is gathered, as a rule, in secrecy and out of court, while maintaining probative value throughout the proceedings irrespective of the forms and the context of its collection. The main consequence is that the pieces of evidence collected by the investigative bodies during their preliminary inquiries can also be used to obtain the guilty verdict. The same does not apply, however, to private parties. Information gathered by the defence was traditionally viewed with suspicion and was not deemed reliable enough to guide the decision-making.

Criminal justice both in Brazil and in Italy was long based on this tradition. In Brazil, the codes of some provincial states required the police inquiry to 'accompany' the prosecution, which also entailed that police information would be attached to the trial file and would have full probative value unless contrary information was obtained.[153] In Italy, as noted, the structure of criminal

[152] *Ibid.*

[153] Chapter 3, I.

proceedings under the 1930 code was characterised by an emphasis on the pre-trial inquiry, in which the investigative magistrate or the prosecutor gathered evidence for the purposes of deciding guilt. As a consequence of this approach, the information collected before the trial could be used as proof of the defendant's guilt, as much as the evidence taken in open court. The emphasis placed on evidence collected in the pre-trial phase was crucial in understanding criminal trials, which were conducted in the shadow of the police report, whose file contained all the information taken by the police during their pre-trial investigation (*preistruzione*).[154]

The shift away from this tradition was not rapid as one might imagine. The 1941 Brazilian code retained the ambiguous expression requiring the police inquiry to 'accompany' the prosecution, however without any further reference to the probative value of the police investigations.[155] Although this change should have been interpreted as banning any form of probative incidence of the police evidence on the trial decisions, Brazilian courts long maintained the old practice, which lasted more than 60 years and that not even the 1988 Constitution could quickly eradicate. In Italy, legal scholarship had long called for an in-depth reform of the rules governing the trial decision-making especially with a view to the enhancement of the participatory rights of the individuals against whom incriminating evidence should be used. The 1988 code partially drew on these suggestions. Among the main innovations, the distinction between the prosecutorial and the trial file did away with the undifferentiated probative value of criminal evidence throughout the proceedings. The first commentators welcomed this reform by highlighting the unprecedented relativism of criminal evidence.[156]

The examination of Brazilian criminal justice reveals similar developments. Law 11.690/2008, issued 20 years after the enactment of the Constitution, also drastically reduced the use of out-of-court evidence.[157] As a result, the decision-makers can only use evidence taken in open court pursuant to the principle of *contradictoire*. This does not entail, however, that pre-trial evidence is deprived of any probative value. On the contrary, the information gathered during the police inquiry will be used at the investigative stage and for the purposes of the charging decision, which confirms the intrinsic relativism of Brazilian evidence law as well.

It must be acknowledged, furthermore, that an approach based on the division between pre-trial and trial decisions oversimplifies the problem at hand. It is noteworthy that in Italy the implementation of the constitutional fair trial reform did not only entail a restoration of the central role of the trial phase but also led to an in-depth reflection on the complexity of criminal evidence, which can hold different probative value even within the same phase, depending on the decision at stake. Before the 1992 reform, legal scholarship had already pointed out the potentials of

---

[154]Siracusano (1973), p. 167ff.

[155]*Ibid.*

[156]Chapter 2, I.I.

[157]Chapter 3, I.

the new principle of non-usability of evidence, which can make a certain piece of evidence usable against some defendants and unusable against others.[158] After the 2001 implementation of the constitutional reform, Italian scholars acknowledged that the relative value of criminal evidence is due to the functional and structural differences among the decisions rather than to the phases of criminal proceedings.[159] On one hand, the rulings on procedural issues (*e.g.*, on the establishment of jurisdiction), which can also be issued during the trial phase, should follow the rules governing the pre-trial decisions. On the other, it is questionable whether out-of-court evidence can unconditionally be used for the purposes of all decisions in the pre-trial stage. Where the adoption of measures interfering with fundamental rights is at stake (*e.g.*, remand detention), the decision entails a provisional assessment of the merits of the case, in terms of suspicion of guilt, proportionality of the sought measure with the expected sentence, and so on. For the purposes of such assessments, out-of-court evidence cannot be equated with the eventual information gathered with the parties' contribution. On the contrary, the decision-makers are called upon to check the probative value of the available evidence in the light of the forms pursuant to which information was taken and of the intrusiveness of the measure applied.

II. Principle of **contradictoire**, *the Proof of Guilt and the Principle of Free Assessment of Evidence*

Against this background, there can be no doubt that the decision on guilt poses the most difficult challenges in both countries in light of the *contradictoire*-based understanding of evidence-gathering and the need to set specific conditions to the use of information gathered without the involvement of the defence. In Brazil, the 2008 reform, while maintaining the principle of free conviction of judges, based this freedom solely on information obtained pursuant to the requirement of *contradictoire*. This rule, however, was considerably smoothed by the provision that banned the 'exclusive' use of pre-trial evidence, except in cases of precautionary evidence, non-repeatable information and evidence collected prior to the trial by means of *ad hoc* procedure.[160] This rather vague formulation leaves, therefore, a great margin of judicial discretion in the assessment of information taken without the parties' contribution. This risk also exists in Italian law, which in 2001 enacted into the code the constitutional exclusionary rule prohibiting the accused's liability to be proven 'on the basis' of the statements of a person who freely refused any confrontation with the accused.[161] This formulation, if interpreted as banning only

[158] Chapter 2, I.I.

[159] *Ibid.*

[160] Chapter 3, I.

[161] Art. 526(1-*bis*) CCP-Italy.

the exclusive use of untested evidence, could undermine the general provision of Article 526(1) CCP-Italy, which enables the decision-makers to use only evidence lawfully obtained at trial. Despite strong criticism on the part of legal scholarship, we will see that the Italian Supreme Court shared this lax interpretation in the light of the Strasbourg doctrine on the sole and decisive evidence.[162]

In sum, the practice of basing the defendant's conviction on evidence gathered in open court combined with the results of the pre-trial investigations is still alive in both countries. Different results, however, have arisen in cases of repeatable evidence, especially where contradictions emerge between the information that prosecutorial witnesses give in open court and the statements taken in pre-trial questionings. This case highlights a very different interpretation of the constitutional requirement of *contradictoire* in the two countries examined. In Brazil, in the absence of explicit statutory rules, legal scholarship rules out any probative value of pre-trial evidence contradicted at trial.[163] In Italy, the 1988 code introduced specific provisions to govern these cases, provisions revolving around what was called the 'golden rule' of the new criminal justice system,[164] namely the rule limiting the probative value of out-of-court inconsistent statements to assessing the reliability of the witness, rather than the merits of the case. Both the Constitutional Court and the legislature brought about considerable changes in 1992, and it took almost 10 years before the original golden rule was restored, albeit flanked by a broader range of exceptions that still allow the admission and wide-ranging use of untested evidence if read out in open court. It is worth observing, furthermore, that a great part of Italian legal scholarship did not deem this set-up a necessary solution in the light of the constitutional principle of *contradictoire* in the evidence-gathering.[165] According to this approach, the fact that witnesses appear in court and assent to answer the questions suffices to satisfy the constitutional requirements of *contradictoire* and confrontation, even if contradictions emerged between out-of-court statements and the results of the trial examination. The main argument is based, again, on a flexible understanding of fact-finding, pursuant to which the accused's guilt can be proved through a combination of out-of-court evidence and trial evidence. Despite the rigorous requirements set forth by the Italian Constitution, this reasoning reveals a more flexible approach to the principle of *contradictoire* than that adopted by Brazilian legal scholarship.

Further problems concern the decision on the merits in the case of alternative proceedings. As far as Italian law is concerned, the 1988 code did not provide general indications as to the rules that should govern the fact-finding in the case of alternative proceedings. In the following years, the Italian legislature specified this rather undefined approach, allowing the use of the information contained in the prosecutorial file with a view to the proof of guilt in the abbreviate proceedings,

---

[162]Chapter 16, D.V.2.a.

[163]Chapter 3, I.

[164]Ferrua (2012), p. 142ff.

[165]See among others Conti (2001), p. 637.

while requiring the application of the same rules governing the decision-making at trial.[166] Even more worryingly, Law 479/1999 altered the balance between the need for timely criminal justice and respect for the participatory rights of the individuals tried in alternative proceedings. In particular, Italian law emphasized the defendant's waiver of the right to *contradictoire*, acknowledged by the constitutional fair trial reform shortly before, to the point that it not only abolished the prosecutorial consent to the request for abbreviated proceedings but also the prosecutorial power to challenge the judgment issued through this procedure.[167] This approach highlights a one-sided understanding of the principle of *contradictoire*, which largely overlooks the strict link between the defence's right to be involved in the evidence gathering and the need for reliable fact-finding. Remarkably, the 1999 reform also eliminated the judicial power to reject requests for abbreviated proceedings, which did not fit the requirements of this procedure and entailed risks for the decision-making. Over the last decade, the Constitutional Court dealt with the problem of whether the defence can attach exculpatory evidence to the request for abbreviated proceedings. The constitutional case-law, while recognising the lawfulness of this practice, acknowledged the lower trustworthiness of the decision on the merits than that of trial judgements issued in a public hearing and pursuant to the principle of *contradictoire*.[168] Surprisingly, similar concerns have not yet been raised in relation to the guilty verdicts that are issued by means of plea-bargaining or in penal order proceedings, notwithstanding the shortcomings of the unconditional use of untested evidence in alternative proceedings activated respectively by the agreement between the defence and the prosecutor, and solely by the initiative of the prosecutor.

J. *Audi alteram partem* and Pre-trial Restrictions on Freedom

I. Premise

The wide use of coercive measures has always characterised the history of criminal proceedings in continental countries. Moreover, the developments that have occurred in science and technology over the last decades have led to increasing use of hidden forms of interference with fundamental rights and of measures that go far beyond the traditional restrictions on individual freedoms.[169] The use of measures of coercion also poses new challenges from the viewpoint of the present discussion, raising the question of whether and to what extent private parties can be involved in the decision on the adoption or the oversight of measures relevant to

[166] See particularly Article 442(1-*bis*) CCP-Italy, which was introduced by Law 479/1999.
[167] Chapter 2, I.III.3.
[168] CConst, 184/2007.
[169] For a comparative analysis of hidden criminal investigations see Hauck (2014).

fundamental rights. Of course, participation in the proceedings on coercive measures takes on different features depending on the type of the measure used and the interests at stake.

In the light of the comparative examination carried out in this study, I will here focus on restrictions on liberty. Here, the main difficulty lies in guaranteeing the right to a fair hearing in a way that allows the defence to dispute the justification of the coercion beforehand. For the sake of clarity, I will separately analyse this problem in relation to three main areas, namely *a)* short-term restrictions on freedom, *b)* long-term restrictions on freedom and *c)* the proceedings on judicial review of the lawfulness of arrest and detention with specific regard to *habeas corpus*.

II. The Right to **contradictoire** *and Short-Term Restrictions on Liberty*

The first problematic area concerns the involvement of the defence in the proceedings on the application or oversight of short-term restrictions on liberty. In both countries, in the absence of a judicial warrant, the police can provisionally arrest the suspect under certain strict conditions. Both the Italian and the Brazilian Constitution lay down detailed rules to govern short-term restrictions on freedom, rules that primarily aim at taking individuals from the police's control and putting them at the disposal of the judicial authority as soon as possible. Notwithstanding these requirements, none of the two Constitutions clarify whether and with which guarantees suspects have the right to be heard by an independent authority. This lacuna has evident implications on the human rights sphere, especially taking into account the risks connected with the validation of provisional arrest and the coercive measures that the judicial authority can adopt afterwards.

In Italy, the 1988 code strengthened the procedural safeguards in the procedure on the validation of the police arrest, providing for the necessary participation at the hearing of both the prosecutor and the defendant's lawyer.[170] Moreover, the competent judge must hear the arrested individuals and their lawyer, or at least the latter, if the arrested person could not be or refused to be examined.[171] Although the police were not entitled to question the arrested person,[172] the right to be heard by a judge could be largely undermined by the provision that enabled the prosecutor, as a part of the judiciary, to question the arrested person.[173] This power was of utmost importance for prosecutors, who were called upon to decide whether to release the arrested person or request the judicial validation of the arrest procedure.

[170] Art. 391(1) CCP-Italy (1988 version).

[171] Art. 391(3) CCP-Italy (1988 version).

[172] The police could not exercise their general power to question the suspect, laid down in Article 350 CCP-Italy, where the person was arrested.

[173] Art. 388 CCP-Italy.

A few years after the enactment of the new code, Italian legislature reduced the role of the prosecutor, who still today does not need to be present at the validation hearing.[174] Yet prosecutors have remained empowered to question arrested individuals before they are brought before the competent judge.

More recently, Italian legislature, under the influence of EU law, reformed the provision on the information duties of the police after the suspect's arrest. By transposing the EU Directive 2012/13, Legislative Decree 101/2014 required the police to inform the arrested individuals in an understandable language, *inter alia*, about their right to know the charge filed against them, their right to silence and their right to be promptly brought before the competent judge.[175] However, the information that the prosecutor must provide to the arrested individuals while questioning them is still limited to the charge under investigation. Moreover, unlike in cases of coercive measures, information must only be provided on the evidence that supported the arrest procedure,[176] with the result that prosecutors do not need to disclose any eventual information collected in the defendant's favour. Despite the acknowledgment of the right to silence, the vulnerable position of the arrested person makes the prosecutorial questioning an extremely dangerous confrontation with the judicial authority, and the criminal law consequences arising from their refusal to provide complete and truthful information considerably reduce the suspect's freedom to remain silent.

This situation can in turn affect the results of the validation procedure, which can lead to the adoption of a coercive measure of a longer duration (including the pre-trial detention) on the basis of the information collected and the statements given at the court hearing by the defence's lawyer and eventually the arrested person.[177] It is noteworthy that, where the suspect was arrested under Article 381 (2) CCP-Italy or the provisional arrest is allowed after the commission of the offence, coercive measures can be adopted also beyond the ordinary statutory limits.[178] Of course, the adoption of coercive measures is far from being an automatic result of the validation procedure. However, the fact that the competent judge can release the arrested person in the absence of the necessary requirements for the application of pre-trial measures[179] reveals that freedom is still largely conceived as an alternative to provisional coercion.

Similar problems can be observed in Brazilian law. To be sure, the Federal Constitution, while enabling the police to provisionally arrest people, provides for strict conditions and information duties on the part of the law enforcement authorities.[180] In particular, the police must not only inform the arrested individuals about

---

[174]See Art. 391 CCP-Italy, as amended by the Legislative Decree 12/1991.

[175]Art. 386 CCP-Italy.

[176]Art. 388(2) CCP-Italy.

[177]Art. 391(5)(first period) CCP-Italy.

[178]Art. 391(5)(second period) CCP-Italy.

[179]Art. 391(6) CCP-Italy.

[180]Chapter 3, J.II.2.

their rights, including the right to silence, but also their next of kin. Arrest must in any case remain a very provisional coercion and the judicial authority before which the arrested person must be brought is competent to assess the lawfulness of the arrest procedure. The 2011 reform introduced an unprecedented duty of communication to the public prosecutor, who can request further coercive means after the arrest has been validated. In this regard, the Brazilian Constitution expressly prohibits individuals to be imprisoned or kept in custody where the law allows their provisional release, either with or without sureties. However, the code still reveals an inverse relationship between bail and pre-trial detention, which leads to the case-law granting to suspects provisional release only where the conditions for being remanded into custody do not exist in a concrete case.[181] This result is further aggravated by the fact that Brazilian law does not require the competent judge, who is called upon to rule on the conversion of provisional arrest into pre-trial detention or another coercive measure, to examine the arrested person.[182] As a result, the adoption of a long-term restriction on liberty constitutes a unilateral decision of the judicial authority. This result cannot be deemed to be unconstitutional, since, as noted, the Brazilian Constitution does not acknowledge the right of the arrested person to be heard by the judicial authority.

Further concerns arise from other forms of provisional restrictions on freedom. In Italy, prosecutors can order the provisional detention of the suspect in cases of risk of absconding (*fermo d'indiziato*),[183] a detention that, albeit subject to strict limits, gives rise to almost the same human rights problems relating to the provisional arrest. In 1989, Brazilian legislature brought about another form of provisional detention, that is, temporary detention.[184] This short-term imprisonment, aimed at fulfilling the needs of ongoing investigation, allows the police to have the suspect at their disposal for a maximum of 5 days. During this period, suspects are often in the vulnerable situation of being confronted with police officers interested in obtaining their confession or testing their availability to accuse other co-offenders. The weak voice of the defence is also extended to the initiation of this procedure, since temporary detention, even though it can be enforced only pursuant to a judicial order, can only be requested by the police and the public prosecutor. The individuals concerned are not entitled to be heard and, although the defence lawyer can request the detained person be brought to court, this request is subjected to the discretionary assessment of the competent judge, who will decide whether or not to hear the detainee.

---

[181] *Ibid.*

[182] *Ibid.*

[183] Art. 384 CCP-Italy.

[184] Chapter 3, J.II.3.

III. Pre-trial Measures and the Guarantee of a Fair Hearing of the Accused and the Victim in Remand Proceedings

Different problems arise in relation to the proceedings on the application of long-term restrictions on freedom and particularly remand proceedings. In this regard, the main problem is that neither Italian nor Brazilian law has traditionally provided tools to ensure a preventive hearing of the individuals against whom restrictions on liberty should be applied. The 1988 Italian code confirmed this approach. By enacting comprehensive rules on pre-trial measures (*misure cautelari*), the drafters of the current code did not require judges to hear the defence prior to ordering remand detention or alternatives to custody, nor in cases of control measures. As a sort of compensation, the 1988 code introduced a mandatory hearing of the suspect after the adoption of pre-trial measures.[185] Surprisingly, this radical approach was not justified by the existence of concrete reasons that require the postponement of the right to *contradictoire*, that is, concrete risks for the ongoing investigations or the aims of the criminal prosecution. On close examination, Italian law reveals a similar understanding of the right to *contradictoire* to that of penal order procedures; and here also, it can be doubted that a subsequent hearing, especially if the individuals concerned could not consult a lawyer beforehand, can compensate them for lost opportunities.[186] The guarantee of judicial oversight, in particular, does not provide adequate safeguards if the same judge who ordered the coercive measure is the one who examines the suspect. Despite heated debates in the criminal law scholarship, the 2015 reform on pre-trial measures missed an important opportunity to enhance the preventive role of the defence.

Brazilian law has recently adopted a different approach, requiring judges, before ruling on a request for coercive measures, to summon the 'opposing party', except in urgent cases and unless a risk for the efficiency of the coercive measure exists.[187] Notwithstanding the merits of the 2011 reform on pre-trial measures and bail, which has for the first time enacted a form of preventive *contradictoire* into the Brazilian rules on provisional imprisonment, the legal solution provides extremely scant information on both the aim of this judicial summons and the practical implications of this procedure.[188] It is not clear whether suspects, after being summoned, can be judicially examined or must reply in writing. In both cases, Brazilian law specifies neither the information to which the defence can have access nor how much time the individuals concerned have at their disposal to prepare their defence strategy. Further human rights concerns arise from the statutory exceptions, since the 2011 reform did not clarify which reasons of urgency and which risks for the efficiency of the sought coercion release judges form their obligation to

[185] Chapter 2, J.III.1.

[186] *Ibid.*

[187] Chapter 3, J.II.1.

[188] *Ibid.*

summon the suspects, and, particularly, which guarantees must be granted to them in these cases. It appears to be reasonable that the suspect will be judicially heard at least after the provisional imprisonment has been enforced.

The lack of clear statutory indications on the defendant's right to be fairly heard also has negative implications on the subsequent stages of the remand proceedings. In Italy, although the 1988 code enacted detailed maximum time limits for remand detention and its alternatives, there are no legal minimum time limits, which entails the practical consequence that the normal duration of pre-trial detention often tends to be the maximum one. Even more worryingly, the overall system of pre-trial measures is designed to work without requiring judges to scrutinise the justification of the coercion applied at regular intervals. This situation has not yet changed despite the openness shown by the Italian Supreme Court towards the need for periodical scrutiny of coercive measures in the field of EU international cooperation.[189] In this light, the mandatory subsequent hearing of the accused can backfire, since defendants, after the first examination, will no longer be heard by the judge, unless either the defence requests it or the prosecutor asks for a more intrusive measure. Brazil still lacks legal rules on the maximum length of provisional imprisonment.[190] Despite attempts by the case-law to fill this lacuna, the 2011 reform also missed an important opportunity to regulate this problem. However, there is a need for urgent legislative intervention in the light of the constitutional requirements of *contradictoire* and full defence, in order to restrain the undue duration of pre-trial detention. Furthermore, Brazilian law says nothing about whether, and about the guarantees with which, defendants should be examined in the course of remand proceedings, and there are still no rules on the suspect's hearing even when the measure applied is to be intensified.[191]

Another important issue concerns the entitlement to activate the proceedings on pre-trial measures. In Brazil, unlike in Italy, both the victim and the police play an important role in the remand proceedings.[192] The 2011 reform maintained the traditional approach, which enabled not only the prosecutor but also the police and the complainant (*querelante*) to request the defendant's pre-trial detention. Certainly, the fact that the police are entitled to request coercive measures can give rise to human rights concerns. Brazilian law, however, does not make it clear what role the victim exactly can play in the institution of remand proceedings. The only case in which the complainant can request the defendant being remanded in custody is that of private legal action subsidiary to the public prosecution.[193]

---

[189]Chapter 16, E.II.4.

[190]Chapter 3, J.II.1.

[191]*Ibid.*

[192]*Ibid.*

[193]*Ibid.*

A different question is whether and to what extent individuals other than the accused—particularly the victim—can be involved in decision on remand proceedings. In this regard, Brazilian code does not provide for any form of hearing of the victim, either before or after the measure has been enforced.[194] In Italy, over the last few years, the legislature has increasingly oriented the use of pre-trial measures towards the protection not only of public security but also of the rights of the victim. In 2001, the legislature had already introduced an unprecedented form of restriction on the defendant's right to free movement, namely coercive removal from the family home,[195] whose scope of application was recently broadened beyond the statutory sentence limits laid down for remand detention in case of sexual crimes.[196] Eight years later, Italian legislature enacted a general provision governing bans on approaching areas usually frequented by the victim.[197] Notwithstanding these new tools, the victim does not still play any proactive role in the procedure on the application of pre-trial measures, which can only be requested by the competent prosecutor. Furthermore, the voice of the victim is still weak and the fact that the aggrieved parties need to be heard neither before nor after the coercive measure being enforced reveals a rather paternalistic view of pre-trial measures in Italian law.

IV. Participatory Rights in the Proceedings Activated by the Defence on Judicial Oversight of Restrictions on Freedom

Finally, I will examine whether and with what safeguards the selected countries involve the individuals concerned in the proceedings activated by the defence on judicial oversight of restrictions on freedom. In this regard, the comparative examination of Brazilian and Italian law highlights a systematic difference. In Brazil, the individuals suffering from illegal detention and unlawful coercion can lodge a special legal action to obtain judicial oversight, namely *habeas corpus*. This tool, which is strongly rooted in Brazilian law and has its legal basis in the Brazilian Constitution, constitutes a procedure independent from criminal proceedings.[198] In Italy, the special proceeding of *riesame*, introduced in the 1980s under the influence of the European Convention to provide an alternative to the oversight by the Supreme Court, ensure to the individuals subject to restrictions on liberty a judicial

---

194 *Ibid.*

195 Art. 282-*bis* CCP-Italy, introduced by Law 154/2001. More than 10 years later, Law-Decree 93/2013, converted into Law 119/2013, enabled the police to remove the suspects from their family home in urgent cases. See Article 384-*bis* CCP-Italy.

196 Art. 282-*bis*(6) CCP-Italy, as amended by Law 172/2012 and later by Law-Decree 93/2013, converted into Law 119/2013.

197 Art. 282-*ter* CCP-Italy, introduced by Law-Decree 11/2009, converted into Law 38/2009.

198 Chapter 3, J.IV.1.

review of the lawfulness of measures ordered by the competent judicial authority.[199] This review, however, is designed to work within criminal proceedings.

Despite the long tradition of *habeas corpus* in Brazilian law, the participatory safeguards of the individuals concerned are still weak. Complainants are summoned to appear in court and can make oral submissions only if necessary, while Brazilian case-law has not reached common positions about the validity of *habeas corpus* where the decision is issued without even the lawyer being informed of the court hearing.[200] The 1988 Italian code had followed a similar approach. By submitting the judicial review of *riesame* to the ordinary rules on hearings *in camera*, the drafters of the code made the examination of the individuals subject to coercive measures conditional on the fact that they appeared in court.[201] In 2015, Italian legislature enhanced the participatory rights in the review hearing by ensuring the right to appear in court personally to the accused who expressly requested it.[202]

A delicate problem in both countries is the scant information guaranteed to the individuals concerned in the judicial review activated by them. In Brazil, the defence is often denied information on the court hearing, which does not allow the complainant to set up a proper defence strategy in *habeas corpus* proceedings.[203] Italian law has since Law 332/1995 applied in the field of *riesame* a similar compromise solution to that adopted in relation to the information rights in the decision on the application of coercive measures, a solution that restricts the information due to the defence to that attached by the competent prosecutor to the request for the measure at hand as well as the to the elements in favour of the individuals concerned, which emerged afterwards.[204] Unfortunately, the 2015 reform did not bring about any innovation to this legislative set-up, which considerably limits the ability to mount a proper and effective defence.

K. Provisional Conclusions

The comparative-law analysis of the two selected countries highlights the rising attention towards the role of private parties in criminal proceedings. To a great, this result was due to the worldwide influence of adversarial models. However, further factors have also contributed to this development, which largely reflects the strong impact of international human rights case-law—and as far as Italy is concerned, the increasing influence of EU law—on the evolution of criminal justice. The renovation of domestic case-law is also a long process, characterised by progressive

[199] Chapter 2, J.III.2.

[200] Chapter 3, J.IV.1.

[201] Chapter 2, J.III.2.

[202] *Ibid.*

[203] Chapter 3, J.IV.1.

[204] Chapter 2, J.III.2.

adjustments of new approaches to criminal proceedings to the mixed system of inquisitorial origin, which still largely inspires the criminal justice of both countries.

In general terms, considerable steps forward have led to the enhancement of participatory and information safeguards for the accused in several problem areas, such as the gathering of evidence, the application of coercive measures, and so on. However, other private parties still have a weak role and their involvement in criminal proceedings does not yet follow consistent lines. In particular, both countries still lack a comprehensive statute on the role of the victim, notwithstanding that some important reforms have recently strengthened the guarantees of vulnerable individuals in specific situations and in relation to particular (organised) crimes. The need for coherent rules is enhanced by the recent developments that in recent years have increasingly oriented the criminal justice policies towards unprecedented aims, such as protecting new forms of public security. This poses in both countries the difficult challenge of balancing the need to ensure the effective participation of the individuals involved in a criminal law action and the pursuit of security aims.

References

Chiavario M (2015) Diritto processuale penale, 6th edn. Utet, Torino
Conso G (1969) Costituzione e processo penale. Giuffrè, Milano
Conti C (2001) Giusto processo (diritto processuale penale). In: Enciclopedia del diritto, vol V Agg. Giuffrè, Milano, pp 627–649
Cordero F (2012) Procedura penale, 9th edn. Giuffrè, Milano
Ferrua P (2012) Il 'giusto processo', 3rd edn. Zanichelli, Bologna
Giacomolli NJ (2014) O devido processo penal. Abordagem conforme a Constituição Federal e o Pacto de São José da Costa Rica. Atlas S.A., São Paulo
Hauck P (2014) Heimliche Strafverfolgung und Schutz der Privatheit. Mohr Siebeck, Tübingen
Lopes A Jr (2017) Direito Processual Penal, 14th edn. Saraiva, São Paulo
Siracusano D (1973) Istruzione del processo penale. In: Enciclopedia del diritto, vol XXIII. Giuffrè, Milano, pp 166–204
Tourinho Filho F da Costa (2010) Código de Processo Penal Comentado, vol I–II, 10th edn. Saraiva, São Paulo

Chapter 7
Similarities and Shortcomings of the National Understanding of Participatory Rights in the Field of Transnational Criminal Justice

Contents

A. Constitutional Law Safeguards and the Slow Enhancement of Participatory Rights in Transnational Criminal Cases 272
B. Information Rights and the Conduct of a Criminal Law Action with Transnational Elements 274
C. *Audi alteram partem* and International Surrender Procedures 276
I. Premise 276
II. Participatory Rights in the Trial Country and Surrender Procedures. The Rising Influence of International and Constitutional Law, and the Enhancement of the Procedural Safeguards in the Field of *in absentia* Proceedings 276
III. Participatory Rights in the Surrender Procedure 278
1. Giving a Voice to the Sought Person 278
a) Procedural Safeguards in the Prosecutorial Hearing and the Right to be Fairly Heard by a Judge 278
b) Surrender Procedures, Coercive Means and the Right to a Fair Hearing 281
2. The Role of the Judiciary in the Surrender Procedures and the Right to Challenge the Lawfulness of the Proceeding 282
D. Participatory Rights and Transnational Evidence 284
I. Models of Gathering Transnational Evidence. The Traditional Approach of the Brazilian and Italian Law and the Rising Development of Informal Modes of International Cooperation 284
II. Participatory Safeguards in the Collection of Evidence Abroad 285
1. Defence Rights in the Evidence-Gathering and the Right to Obtain Exculpatory Evidence 285
2. Participatory Safeguards and the Admissibility of Overseas Evidence 287
III. Participatory Rights in the Collection of Evidence Requested by Foreign Countries 289
E. Interim Findings 290
References 290

S. Ruggeri, Audi Alteram Partem *in Criminal Proceedings*,
DOI 10.1007/978-3-319-54573-8_7

A. Constitutional Law Safeguards and the Slow Enhancement of Participatory Rights in Transnational Criminal Cases

A rather different scenario emerges from the comparative-law analysis of the selected countries in the field of transnational criminal justice. As far as international cooperation in criminal matters is concerned, Brazil and Italy at first glance provide different legal frameworks. Whereas the Italian 1988 code enacted a set of domestic rules inspired by the main principles governing domestic criminal proceedings,[1] the Brazilian code of criminal procedure has only a few rules that are concerned with tools of international legal assistance, and in this area Brazilian law is still overwhelmingly governed by instruments of international law.[2] In Brazil, the main instrument of international cooperation is extradition, which is mainly regulated by the Law on the Legal Status of Aliens (*Estatuto do Estrangeiro*).[3] In Italy, the rules concerned with domestic proceedings with transnational features are few and rather uncoordinated with each other, whereas the Italian code also provides a subsidiary regulation on international cooperation in criminal matters in instruments of international law.[4] Most significantly, notwithstanding the recent ratification of the Brussels Convention, Italian law has still largely not updated to the new forms of international cooperation in the EU area.[5]

Notwithstanding this legal fragmentation, the constitutional law of the two countries provides important safeguards in the field under examination. Although both the Italian Constitution and the Brazilian Constitution explicitly focus on extradition, banning especially international surrender for political offences, it cannot be affirmed that the constitutional law of the two countries adopts a neutral position in relation to other tools of international cooperation or ignores the complex human rights challenges of transnational criminal cases. It is worth observing that the 1948 Italian Constitution agreed, albeit on conditions of equality with other States, to the 'limitations of sovereignty necessary for an order that ensures peace and justice among Nations', while promoting and encouraging 'international organizations having such ends in view'.[6] More recently, a constitutional reform[7] amended the rules governing the distribution of legislative powers between state and regional government authorities (regions, provinces, municipalities) by requiring any legislation to be issued 'in compliance with the Constitution and with the constraints deriving from EU-legislation and international

[1] Chapter 4, A.I.
[2] Chapter 5, A.
[3] Law 6.815/1980.
[4] Chapter 4, A.I.
[5] Chapter 4, A.II.
[6] Art. 11 Const.-Italy.
[7] Constitution Amendment Law 3/2001.

obligations'.[8] In Brazil, the 1988 Constitution gave even more explicit attention to international cooperation, including in criminal matters, requiring Brazil's engagement in a cooperation with other countries for the swift progress of mankind and, more specifically, in the economic, politic, social and cultural integration with other countries from Latin America with a view to the creation of a Latin American community. It is also noteworthy that the Federal Constitution lays down the exclusive jurisdiction of the higher courts—namely, the Federal Supreme Tribunal and Superior Court of Justice—in the field of two of the main tools of international cooperation, that is, extradition and letters rogatory.[9] Even though the Constitution provides for a general jurisdiction of federal courts in all cases based on international agreements with foreign countries, this centralised approach was justified by the need to ensure consistency in the case-law on extradition and legal assistance, given the huge territorial dimension of the country.

Furthermore, these references are certainly not the only constitutional provisions applicable to transnational cases. The main principles governing criminal justice must also be applied to criminal proceedings with transborder dimensions. In particular, we should mention fundamental safeguards, such as the presumption of innocence and certain fair trial guarantees, as well as the main guarantees protecting the right to freedom. There can be little doubt that the right to full defence and the right to *contradictoire*, as well as the principle of *par condicio*, hold even more relevance in the delicate field of transborder proceedings, which often place the individuals concerned in a condition of high vulnerability.

Nonetheless, the potential of constitutional law has not yet been fully utilised. To be sure, the enshrinement of the principle of *contradictoire* by Brazil at the constitutional level led to legislative reform of the rules on the service of court summonses in the case of a defendant resident abroad. This reform dropped the old practice of summoning defendants subject to bail by edict. In order to ensure effective information about the proceedings, the guarantee of notification by means of letters rogatory was extended to all defendants, no matter whether subject to bail or not. In Italy, the individuals involved in transnational proceedings still have scant participatory safeguards. The code's rules on letters rogatory and extradition attach very little importance to the involvement of the defence, and the same still applies to legal instruments implementing EU legislation. Italian case-law has also shown scant interest in this issue. The Supreme Court often refuses to demand full respect for domestic rules on evidence-gathering in order not to jeopardise cooperation with foreign countries. This case-law reveals a rather minimalist approach, which does not require detailed fulfilment of Italian law but only of the fundamental principles of domestic law.[10] In some cases, the Supreme Court has gone so far as to justify the use of untested evidence collected abroad in the light of one of the constitutional exceptions from the principle of *contradictoire*,

[8]Art. 117 Const.-Italy.

[9]Chapter 5, A.

[10]Chapter 4, E.III.4.

that is, the objective impossibility of obtaining evidence with the involvement of the parties. Yet this argument is certainly out of place.[11]

Another important implication of the constitutional focus on transnational criminal justice was the enactment of a new generation of international agreements, which reveal a rising focus on individual rights in transnational inquiries. A clear example involving the two countries under examination is the 1989 extradition treaty between Brazil and Italy, an agreement that, significantly, was signed shortly after Italy enacted the current code of criminal procedure and the 1988 Brazilian Constitution started a process of re-democratization of the country. This agreement acknowledged participatory rights in the extradition proceedings between Italy and Brazil in a double fashion, i.e. (*a*) as a condition preventing the requested party from extraditing the sought person where the right to a defence was not fulfilled in the requesting country and (*b*) as a requirement of a fair surrender procedure in the requested State. In both regards, however, the right to a defence still plays a rather minimal role in the extradition treaty between Brazil and Italy. Extradition can only be refused in the case of infringement of the minimum defence rights. Moreover, as far the defence rights in the requested country are concerned, this international instrument only acknowledged the need for respect of the guarantees laid down by *lex loci*.

B. Information Rights and the Conduct of a Criminal Law Action with Transnational Elements

A domestic criminal law action can also have elements of transnationality. This can be due to various grounds, such as the different nationality of the accused or of other individuals involved in criminal investigations, defendants that do not reside in the country where the proceedings were instituted, and so on. The comparative examination of the two countries highlights considerable developments that have recently occurred particularly to improve the notice on the proceedings due to the accused who does not reside in the trial country and often does not even understand the language of the proceedings. There is little doubt that the performance of proper notice constitutes the first condition for a fair trial where such transnational cases are at stake. Brazil and Italy, however, found rather different legal arrangements in this regard.

For some time, Brazilian law followed similar lines to those of the Rocco code, which provided that, where defendants resident abroad failed to choose their domicile or residence in Italy, any further notification should be at the court's registry.[12] In Brazil, different rules on the court summons of defendants resident abroad applied depending on whether the prosecuted offence was not subject to bail

[11] Chapter 4, E.III.3.

[12] Article 177-*bis* of the 1930 CCP-Italy.

or bail could be granted.[13] The bailee must be summoned by edict and had a deadline of at least 30 days to appear in court. Clearly, both arrangements were widely unsatisfactory from a human rights viewpoint, relying on mechanisms of fictitious knowledge of the proceedings. Even more worryingly, the Brazilian solution relied on the summons by edict irrespective of whether or not the accused's place of resident was known. This led to the result that the defendants who did not appear in court should in any case be tried *in absentia*.

The 1988 Italian code aimed to avoid these shortcomings by distinguishing the cases where the defendant's place of residence abroad is known from those in which the competent authority, despite knowing that the accused does not live in Italy, ignores their place of residence abroad. Even though procedure differed somewhat in the two situations, criminal proceedings should in any case be continued pursuant to the rules on non-traceable defendants, which entailed that a court-appointed lawyer must represent the absent accused. This set-up has remained untouched until now and it is surprising that neither Law 67/2014, which did away with default proceedings, nor Legislative Decree 101/2014 implementing the EU legislation on the right to information in criminal proceedings brought about any change of this regulation. Despite some steps forward, the Italian rules on judicial service also give rise to serious concerns even in the case of defendants whose place of residence abroad in known. The failure to amend the rules on notification and the procedure for non-traceable defendants cannot ensure that the accused is personally informed of the initiation of criminal proceedings in Italy. On close examination, even the choice of not appointing a national lawyer does not demonstrate waiver of personal participation. Further risks arise from the simplified procedure applicable to foreign defendants, taking into account that the rules of Article 169(1) CCP must also be followed where the competent authority only knows that the defendant is abroad, a situation that is by definition provisional and often subject to several changes.

As noted, Brazil adopted quite different arrangements to tackle the problem of non-resident defendants being tried without any notice of the proceedings.[14] On one hand, as noted, the 1996 reform changed the rules on court summons of defendants whose place of residence outside Brazil is known, requiring the accused to be always informed by means of letters rogatory irrespective of whether bail should be granted or not. On the other, the same legislation abolished the old procedures *em revelia* in such absolute terms that the abolition also applied to transnational cases. Even though default proceedings can no longer be held, these solutions do not eliminate the risk that the accused does not receive personal notice about the proceedings. Unlike in Italy, however, a criminal law action cannot be conducted against unaware defendants in Brazil, since the proceedings must here be suspended after the notification by edict. This solution is certainly preferable, notwithstanding some discriminatory results. In particular, it is questionable that the time limit for

[13]Chapter 5, C.

[14]*Ibid.*

the prosecution of the alleged offence is not only suspended after the suspension of the proceedings but also during the performance of letters rogatory.

C. *Audi alteram partem* and International Surrender Procedures

I. Premise

Even more complex problems arise in the field of international cooperation, in which the tension between conflicting interests is enhanced by the need to balance the state-related interests of more than one country and to ensure high standards of protection to the individuals concerned, who must often face enormous difficulties due to linguistic barriers, the limited familiarity with the cultural and legal framework of one of the states involved, and so on. These difficult challenges strengthen the need to improve the participatory safeguards of the people involved in the procedures of international cooperation.

Against this background, international surrender procedures pose further problems, calling for a proper balancing of prosecutorial needs, defence guarantees and the right to freedom. In this respect, the comparative analysis of the relevant countries reveals two main problematic areas. The first one relates to the relevance in the requested country of the participatory rights of the sought persons in the trial country. The second concerns the requirements of a fair involvement of the requested person in the surrender procedure. Among these requirements, I shall focus on the right to be heard by an independent authority and the right to challenge the lawfulness of the cross-border procedure, including the merits of the case investigated abroad. The latter issue will allow us to draw some comparative conclusions on the role of the judiciary in the field of surrender procedures.

II. Participatory Rights in the Trial Country and Surrender Procedures. The Rising Influence of International and Constitutional Law, and the Enhancement of the Procedural Safeguards in the Field of in absentia *Proceedings*

Concerning the first problematic area, a particularly delicate issue concerns the implications for the surrender procedure of the defendant's absence in the relevant proceedings. In this regard, both Italy and Brazil paint a quite worrisome picture. A close examination of the domestic rules reveals the lack of any specific provisions concerned with this problem. Both the Italian 1988 code and the Brazilian *Estatuto do Estrangeiro* ignored the problem of the defendant's absence for the purposes of extradition. From a historical viewpoint, this result could be easily justified. Since at the time of these legislative reforms both countries allowed wide use of domestic criminal proceedings held *in absentia*, requiring foreign countries to fulfil conditions that domestic law could not satisfy would have been highly contradictory. Yet this conclusion only partially applies to Italian law. Thus, some years before the entry into force of the new code, Italy had already ratified the Second Additional Protocol to the 1957 Extradition Convention, thus enacting certain solutions that, despite not banning *in absentia* procedures, submitted surrender to stricter conditions than in the past.[15] Notwithstanding the specific focus on *in absentia* trials, this international instrument only struck a clear compromise among conflicting interests, requiring the requested country to surrender the sought person, provided, however, that the trial country gave proper assurances that he could obtain a retrial.

In both countries, moreover, the enshrinement at the constitutional level of the requirements of *contradictoire* and full defence not only gave rise to in-depth reforms of domestic criminal justice but also led to a new generation of international agreements, with a more specific focus on the problem under examination. After the 1988 Constitution, Brazil signed a number of extradition agreements with European countries, agreements that explicitly dealt with the issue of *in absentia* trials.[16] In Italy, the 1999 constitutional fair trial reform also led to the signing of new extradition agreements with non-European countries, which followed a similar approach to that of the Second Additional Protocol to the 1957 Extradition Convention.

A close examination of these extradition instruments, however, reveals a rather minimalist approach to the repercussions on the surrender procedure of the accused's absence in the relevant proceedings. Even though Italy has long abandoned the approach of the old agreements that considered *in absentia* trials as equivalent to the proceedings held in the presence of the accused (*e.g.*, the 1970 extradition treaty with Lebanon), some of the bilateral instruments adopted after the 1999 constitutional reform still displayed a weak understanding of the participatory safeguards in the field transnational criminal justice. For instance, the 2003 extradition treaty between Italy and Argentina only allows refusal of extradition in case of *in absentia* proceedings that did not guarantee the minimum defence rights. Brazil also adopted a similar approach after the 1988 Constitution: *e.g.*, the limit of compliance with minimum defence rights was enacted into the 1990 extradition agreement with Spain. Extradition treaties with other European countries highlight an even laxer approach. A clear example is the 1996 extradition treaty with France, which, despite being signed in the same year in which default proceedings were abolished in Brazil, ruled out that the simple fact that the sought individuals were prosecuted *em revelia* could be a ground to refuse their surrender, unless their absence in the relevant proceedings could be considered a presumed confession.

[15] Chapter 4, D.I.

[16] Chapter 5, D.I.

The 1989 extradition with Italy was even more inflexible, leaving room for no exception.

On close examination, that the sole fact that the sought person was prosecuted *em revelia* in the requesting state cannot in itself allow refusal of surrender does not mean that the defendant's absence has no relevance for the purposes of the extradition procedure. It is precisely this formulation that should require the requested state to assess the overall circumstances of the concrete case and especially the grounds that led to the prosecution *in absentia*.[17] In most extradition agreements signed both by Brazil with various European states and by Italy with non-EU countries, however, this assessment does not go beyond ensuring respect for minimum defence rights.

Other bilateral instruments may seem to attach greater weight to *in absentia* proceedings, providing for flexible mechanisms with a view to allowing the surrender of the sought person, provided that he can apply for a retrial at which he can take part personally. In this regard, however, there is a delicate problem concerning the nature of the assurances that the requesting country should provide to obtain the extradition of the individuals concerned. The concept of 'proper assurances' is by definition relative, which leaves a great margin of discretion to the national authorities, while ensuring to the sought individuals little certainty as to whether they will be surrendered to the trial country. The analysis of Italian case-law gives a clear example of the concreteness of these risks, since Italian courts considered very different remedies to be adequate to protect the individuals sought for a domestic prosecution.[18] Alongside the heterogeneity of these tools and their intrinsic limitations, the solutions adopted by the Italian Supreme Court fall short of the new standards laid down for national proceedings by Law 67/2014. Likewise in Brazil, an in-depth reflection on the constitutional requirements of *contradictoire* and full defence should lead to a reform of the international instruments in force, which satisfy themselves with conditions that since 1996 have been done away with in national criminal proceedings.

III. Participatory Rights in the Surrender Procedure

1. Giving a Voice to the Sought Person

a) Procedural Safeguards in the Prosecutorial Hearing and the Right to be Fairly Heard by a Judge

The second problem concerns the participatory safeguards that the requested person holds in the surrender procedure. In particular, we should examine whether and to

[17] Galgani (2013), p. 175.

[18] Chapter 5, D.I.

what extent the sought individuals can obtain a fair opportunity to be heard by an independent body in the requested country.

The comparative examination of the two countries reveals a worrisome approach to this problem. In Italy, since the sought person must first be questioned by the Attorney-General, the requirements of a fair hearing must initially apply to a prosecutorial examination.[19] Historically, this was the task of the General Prosecutors, justified on the grounds that the extradition proceedings usually started with the arrest of the sought person, which was ordered either by the Attorney-General or by the local prosecutor upon request of the Ministry of Justice. As noted, these prosecutorial powers were in line with the dominant role of prosecutors in the criminal justice system of the 1930s. Despite dropping most of the coercive powers of prosecutors in national criminal proceedings and strengthening the tasks of the judiciary in the field of international cooperation, the drafters of the 1988 code maintained the old approach that empowered General Prosecutors to conduct the first hearing of the sought person. This hearing not only aims at formal assessments but also concerns substantial issues that must be clarified in the report that the Attorney-General must forward to the competent court of appeal. The most delicate question that will be addressed during the prosecutorial hearing is whether the sought individuals wishes to give their consent to extradition.

In the light of the delicate character of this questioning, the Attorney-General must appoint a lawyer to individuals who are not represented by their own counsel. Legal assistance may however be insufficient to protect the sought person, who is often unfamiliar with the host country and must face the difficult decision on whether to waive the judicial hearing. Notwithstanding, Italian law requires the Attorney-General neither to appoint an interpreter to foreign individuals nor to inform them of the consequences of their consent. Certainly, the particular vulnerability of the individuals sought for the purposes of extradition should require a higher level of protection, *e.g.* providing them with the necessary information in order to make it sure that they will be fully aware of the consequences of any decision they will make. *De lege ferenda*, a good solution could be to entrust the first hearing on substantial issues to the competent court or a delegated judge. Anticipating judicial oversight is certainly the best opportunity for an overall assessment of the conflicting interests at stake, including those concerned with the prosecution carried out in the requesting state.[20] Significantly, where an extension of extradition is requested to further acts committed prior to the surrender, the Italian code requires the judicial authority to hear the extradited person and the evidence gathered will be attached to the request for extension.[21]

Moreover, weak safeguards also apply to the court procedure. In Italy, after the Attorney-General forwards his report to the competent court of appeal, the court will carry out specific inquiries to assess the lawfulness of the request for

[19]Chapter 4, D.II.

[20]Chiavario (2013), p. 108.

[21]Art. 710 CCP.

extradition. However, whereas the Attorney-General and the defence lawyer must always be heard, the sought individuals and the representative of the requesting state must be examined only if they appear in court. As a result, the hearing of the requested person is only accidental. Italian courts pay even scanter attention to the requirement of effective participation of the sought persons. For instance, the Supreme Court considers that the failure to appear in court, even though the requested individuals waived judicial oversight without understanding the consequences of their decision, gives rise to a form of invalidity of the proceedings that is remedied if a lawyer (even a court-appointed lawyer) is present at the hearing and does not contest the validity of the procedure.[22]

Surprisingly, Italian law has not made many steps forward while implementing the EU legislation on EAW procedures, although this instrument was not only intended to improve international cooperation with other member states but also to enhance the fundamental rights protection of the individuals concerned in line both with the Italian Constitution and with the European Convention. As we will see, Law 69/2005 largely reproduced the solutions adopted in the field of extradition, requiring the court of appeal, before ruling on the arrest warrant, to hear only the Attorney-General and the defence lawyer, whereas the sought person and the representative of the foreign country must be examined only if present in court.[23] To be sure, the case-law has somewhat enhanced the participatory rights of the sought person, requiring the court hearing to be postponed in case of legal impediment. Since the rules on judicial service were not changed, however, the requested individuals may unintentionally ignore the existence of an extradition procedure instituted against them.

Brazil also provides the person requested for the purposes of extradition with scant guarantees as to the right to be fairly heard by a court.[24] Notwithstanding the recent reform of pre-trial measures, *Estatuto do Estrangeiro* requires the sought individuals to be heard only after the trial country has forwarded its request for extradition. Unlike Italy, therefore, the competent court must always hear the individuals concerned, and Brazilian law does not provide for exceptions from this rule. The due process guarantees relevant to this hearing are still weak, however. Although legal assistance is ensured to individuals not represented by their own council and lawyers have a period of at least 10 days to prepare their defence strategy, Law 6.815/1980 failed to lay down further qualitative requirements of a fair hearing. In particular, it is not clear whether the sought individuals can communicate with their lawyer prior to their court examination and, importantly, whether interpretation must be granted if they do not speak or understand Portuguese.

---

[22] CCass, *Poporogu.*

[23] Chapter 16, E.II.2.

[24] Chapter 5, D.II.

b) Surrender Procedures, Coercive Means and the Right to a Fair Hearing

Further concerns arise when measures of coercion are applied in the requested country during the surrender procedure. In Brazil, despite the 2013 legislative reform, *Estatuto do Estrangeiro* still provides that extradition procedures can be initiated through a request of pre-trial detention of the sought person, lodged by the trial country before the request of extradition to secure the aims of the ongoing procedure in urgent cases. Remarkably, there are no alternatives to this form of detention, which, unlike provisional arrest, has a quite long duration. Extradition imprisonment lasts until the Federal Supreme Tribunal ruling on the request for extradition, which must be transmitted up to 90 days after the foreign country has been informed of the provisional imprisonment. Despite the consistent restriction on the right to freedom, Brazilian law does not grant the detainee a court hearing before the request for extradition has been forwarded. From this it follows that the individuals concerned have no means to challenge the lawfulness of the imprisonment ordered.

In Italy, we have noted that the Rocco code made the arrest of the sought person the first step in extradition proceedings. It is worth observing that this coercive measure was not justified by concrete risks either for the extradition procedure or the foreign prosecution, aiming only to allow the requested country to properly fulfil its international obligations. The 1988 code made in-depth changes, linking the provisional arrest with a concrete risk to the ongoing procedure (risk of absconding), while requiring the arrested person to be put at the disposal of the court of appeal rather than the prosecutorial authority. The validation of the provisional arrest can lead the competent authority to order the provisional detention of the sought person. Unlike in Brazil, moreover, detention is not the sole coercion applicable, since a wide range of alternative means can be adopted. The surrender procedure governed by the European Convention on Extradition also allows alternatives to detention, while requiring any coercion to be justified on the ground of the risk of absconding. As we will see, the same approach applies to coercive means adopted in the context of EAW procedures.[25]

Notwithstanding these positive developments, the individuals concerned have rather scant opportunities to be fairly heard by a court. In cases of police arrest, the Italian code failed to specify whether the arrestee should be heard at all. The case-law tends to exclude this conclusion on the ground that the president of the court of appeal is called upon to carry out only a formal review on the basis of the information available, so that the sought person will be heard only 5 days after the arrest has been maintained. The procedural safeguards in case of detention ordered after the validation of the provisional arrest are also weak, compared to national cases. Despite requiring the competent court to hear the detainee within 5 days from the execution of the measure, the Italian code does not clarify the

[25] Chapter 16, E.II.3.

consequences of the non-fulfilment of this time-limit, which the case-law also considered non-peremptory. Moreover, even though the detained individuals must be granted a court-appointed lawyer if they are not represented by their own counsel, defence lawyers—unlike in domestic cases—must only be informed twenty-four hours prior to the hearing and their participation is not mandatory.

In Brazil, the weak role of the defence has become even more questionable, taking into account the fact that Brazilian law has increasingly ensured to the requesting country a more active role in extradition procedures, allowing for a form of direct participation known as '*Amicus curiae*'. In Italy, one would have expected rather different results from the introduction of EAW proceedings, which the EU institutions construed in terms of court procedures, relegating the governmental authority to administrative functions. As we will note, however, changes have not been as significant as those announced.[26]

2. The Role of the Judiciary in the Surrender Procedures and the Right to Challenge the Lawfulness of the Proceeding

In both countries, the increasing role of the judiciary has had a strong impact on the effective exercise of the right to participation in surrender procedures. Certainly, the ambiguous understanding of the extradition proceedings has long justified the maintenance of a model characterised not only by the dominant role of the governmental authorities but also by the law enforcement powers of the police and the competent prosecutors. These two factors, however, were not unconnected form each other.

In Italy, we have seen that the Rocco code had provided general prosecutors with consistent decision-making and coercive powers, which were not limited to the issuing of detention orders during an extradition procedure but furthermore affected the length of remand detention, since provisional release was also in the hands of the prosecutor. In the light of the hierarchical subordination of public prosecutors to the Executive, the fascist code submitted the legal action of the Attorney-General to the instructions provided by the Ministry of Justice, who therefore also played an enhanced role in the surrender proceedings. Although this set-up, after being confirmed by the 1941 Courts Act,[27] was dropped after the fall of the fascist regime[28] and the Republican Constitution was enacted the following year, the case-law maintained for more than 40 years the traditional approach to extradition proceedings by denying application of the ordinary safeguards laid down in the field of restrictions on freedom in domestic proceedings.

Surprisingly, even the 1989 Delegation Law for the new code contained no specific rules on international cooperation, thus maintaining the traditional

[26] *Ibid.*

[27] Art. 69 of Royal Decree 12/1941.

[28] Royal Legislative Decree 511/1946.

ambiguity of extradition proceedings. On close examination, the silence of the Delegation Law should not be viewed as a sign of indifference towards the right to defence and personal freedom in international cooperation and it is thus to be welcomed that the 1988 code abolished the prosecutorial power to order provisional coercions, pending the extradition procedure. As noted, this reform was in line with the overall approach of the new Italian criminal justice, which considerably strengthened the decision-making powers of the judiciary. In particular, the court of appeal must review the lawfulness of requests for extradition and its favourable decision is a prerequisite for surrender to another country. Yet these innovations were not preceded by in-depth reflection on surrender procedures, which, despite being widely regulated by the code of criminal procedure, continued to be viewed in terms of non-contentious proceedings rather than of proceedings aimed at the ascertainment of the accused's guilt. Consequently, the prevailing case-law continued to conceive of the role of the judiciary as entailing the obligation to review only the formal requirements of the request for surrender rather than the overall lawfulness of the ongoing procedure.

Brazil has long followed a similar approach. Here also, the weak guarantees provided to the person sought for the purposes of international surrender were mainly due to the ambiguous understanding of extradition. Still today, the higher courts tend to view the extradition proceeding in terms of a non-contentious procedure. This understanding of the surrender procedure has historically produced two negative results, that is, it softened the fair trial requirements and reduced the role of the judiciary to the minimum extent. Although the case-law has long acknowledged the need for judicial examination of the lawfulness of the surrender procedure even in case of consent by the sought person, the tasks of the judiciary were traditionally limited to reviewing rather formal requirements. The need not to jeopardise international cooperation and to avoid undue interference with foreign prosecutions has led to the Federal Supreme Tribunal denying (surprisingly, even after the 1988 Constitution) that *Estatuto do Estrangeiro*, which does not allow challenging the merits of the case in the requested country, infringes on the constitutional requirements of *contradictoire* and full defence. This model of limited cognition by the Brazilian case-law of violations of fair trial requirements in foreign proceedings has long been justified on the basis of the so-called 'Rezek doctrine' according to which respect for constitutional requirements should be ensured only within Brazilian jurisdiction.

Over the two last decades, however, significant developments have occurred in both countries. In Brazil, the federal case-law has largely departed from the 'Rezek doctrine' since an important ruling in 1996, on the ground that the 1988 Constitution lays out Brazil's obligation to engage in the assessment of the respect for due process requirements both during and following the surrender procedure. Since the 1990s, awareness has also grown in Italy that the adoption of a constitutional law perspective provides a better understanding of extradition proceedings that takes into account the repercussions of the foreign proceedings not only on the fundamental rights of the extradited person but also on the constitutional requirements of the requested country. In the light of the criminal law character of the extradition proceedings, legal scholarship acknowledged that the role of the judiciary cannot be restricted to the assessment of the formal requirements of the request for surrender but must also encompass the overall lawfulness of the procedure.

D. Participatory Rights and Transnational Evidence

I. Models of Gathering Transnational Evidence. The Traditional Approach of the Brazilian and Italian Law and the Rising Development of Informal Modes of International Cooperation

Both in Brazil and in Italy, the collection of transnational evidence follows a traditional approach, which is still strongly based on old tools of legal assistance. In both countries, letters rogatory still constitute the main means of taking either evidence requested by foreign countries or information abroad and in most cases information is taken pursuant to the traditional model of legal assistance. The main consequence is that governmental authorities still plays a considerable role in international evidence-gathering, notwithstanding that in both countries the execution of letters rogatory presupposes the *exequatur* decision by the judicial authority. Unlike in Italy, where *exequatur* lies in the hands of the competent courts of appeal, the 1988 Brazilian Constitution confirmed the centralised model chosen by Law 221/1984, entrusting to the Federal Supreme Tribunal, alongside the decision on the extradition requested by a foreign country, the *exequatur* decision on letters rogatory,[29] a solution certainly justified by the constitutional relevance of the interests at stake. The fact that the 2004 constitutional reform shifted this competence to the Superior Court of Justice confirmed the traditional centralised model, justified, as noted, by the enormous territorial extent of the country. In Italy, the recent ratification of the Brussels Convention will hopefully allow the use of more modern tools of legal assistance with other EU countries, which intervention are no longer based on governmental logics but on the direct contacts between national authorities.

Because of the lack of a general modernisation of transnational evidence-gathering, the case-law of both countries has over the last decades increasingly developed new flexible forms of international cooperation, aimed at overcoming the shortcomings of the traditional model of rogatory letters. The circumstances that have led to the enactment of these new modes of international cooperation are not identical in the two countries examined. Whereas in Italy the main aim was to overcome the rigid rules on inadmissibility of evidence obtained through letters rogatory, the Brazilian case-law has indirectly sought alternatives to the *exequatur*

[29] Art. 102(I)(h) Const.-Brazil.

procedure without dropping it. At any rate, a common tendency can be observed in both countries, a tendency clearly aimed at deformalizing the procedure of transnational evidence-gathering. In Italy, the competent authorities have increasingly engaged in informal exchanges of evidence gathered abroad without having recourse to letters rogatory. In Brazil, a similar form of international cooperation is *auxílio direto*, notwithstanding that this mode of mutual assistance is less 'direct' than what its description would suggest, since foreign requests for assistance must in any case be presented to the Central Brazilian Authority. Following this procedure, however, foreign requests do not need to pass the check of the Superior Court of Justice.

II. Participatory Safeguards in the Collection of Evidence Abroad

1. Defence Rights in the Evidence-Gathering and the Right to Obtain Exculpatory Evidence

From the viewpoint of the present discussion, the collection of overseas evidence poses two main problems, namely (*a*) whether and to what extent private parties can be involved in the evidence-gathering abroad and (*b*) how defence rights should be respected in admitting the information obtained abroad. Concerning the former question, the degree to which the individuals concerned can participate in the taking of information abroad largely depends on the type of legal assistance used.

As far as the traditional modes of legal assistance are concerned, the 1959 Convention on Legal Assistance enables both Italian authorities and private parties to be present at the execution of letters rogatory. Although legal scholarship deems it a form of 'joint' or 'participatory' letters rogatory,[30] this form of participation of national authorities in evidence-gathering is rather different from that of joint investigations. In particular, the intervention both of Italian authorities and of private parties presupposes the consent of the foreign country and usually consists of a passive assistance at the evidence-gathering. Italian authorities also do not have any law enforcement powers on foreign territory since foreign authorities are competent to collect evidence on the basis of their own law. The recent ratification of the Brussels Convention will now probably enable the participation of the defence pursuant either to the requirements of *lex loci* or to the formalities of *lex fori*, provided, however, that the authorities of the trial country requested them. From this it follows that the private parties involved in Italian criminal proceedings can take part in the gathering of overseas evidence as long as the competent authorities request it and this does not infringe on the general principles of *lex loci*. Even greater uncertainty exists in transborder investigations in a strict sense.

[30] See among others Caprioli (2013), p. 450f.

The legal instruments in force in Italy, which provide for the setting up of joint inquiries, leave to the competent authorities a great margin of discretion in establishing both the forms of obtaining evidence and the involvement of private parties, thus giving rise to an evident imbalance that undermines the effective exercise of defence rights.

Serious concerns also arise from new informal procedures. As far as Italy is concerned, the practice of informal requests for evidence-gathering abroad for the purposes of Italian investigations does not allow for any participation by the defence. Notwithstanding the advantages of informal exchanges of evidence, one should not overlook the risks to the participatory rights of the individuals concerned. In particular, bypassing the *exequatur* procedure deprives the interested parties of any possibility of challenging the lawfulness of the requested investigations prior to their enforcement, investigations that can severely impinge on fundamental rights. In case of information exchange, moreover, the sought evidence is taken pursuant to the national law of the requested country, which makes the participation of the defence at the investigations conditional on the provisions of the sole *lex loci,* with which the accused could be wholly unfamiliar. Furthermore, evidentiary exchanges are often preceded by informal requests addressed to foreign authorities and aimed at the gathering of evidence useful to an Italian prosecution, which renders the defence's participation by definition impossible.

Brazilian law also grants the defence rather scant forms of participation in new evidence-gathering procedures. In cases of *auxílio direto*, the national relevance of this mode of legal assistance leads to the result that the forms and limits of the defence's involvement are entirely dependent on *lex loci*. Moreover, Brazil enacted various bilateral agreements that enable the trial country to request the fulfilment of specific procedures of its own law in the execution of letters rogatory. This limited application of *lex fori*, despite depending on the solutions adopted by the requesting country in each concrete case, allows for the involvement of private parties within the limits laid down by Brazilian law, thus compensating for the lack of specific rules on the participation of the defence in hearings by videoconference in transborder cases. Yet there still exists a considerable imbalance between national authorities and the defence in various bilateral agreements, which, in certain exceptional circumstances, allow for the participation only of the authorities specified in the request for legal assistance at the execution of letters rogatory.

Despite these negative repercussions on individual rights, the higher courts of both countries tend to advocate the lawfulness of these procedures. Except the Federal Supreme Tribunal, which, after a previous favourable ruling, defended the *exequatur* jurisdiction of the Superior Court of Justice in Brazil, practical considerations clearly influenced by state-related interests have strongly affected the jurisprudence of the higher courts in both countries.

Another delicate problem is the weak and rather contradictory acknowledgment in both countries of the accused's right to obtain exculpatory evidence in transborder cases. In Italy, a great imbalance can be observed between prosecutors and the defence. Unlike public prosecutors, defence lawyers cannot directly apply for letters rogatory but must submit their request to the judicial authority (including the competent prosecutor), which will assess the need for this procedure. Nor can counsel carry out investigations abroad, the information gathered being inadmissible at trial. Apparently, Brazil follows an undifferentiated approach, which potentially allows for all the parties of the proceedings to request letters rogatory, while submitting the gathering of overseas evidence to more strict conditions than in national cases. On close examination, the defence must not only prove the absolute need for letters rogatory but also bear the costs concerned with this procedure, whereas the costs of prosecutorial requests are covered by the state. This result is highly debatable, enhancing social inequality in Brazil.

2. Participatory Safeguards and the Admissibility of Overseas Evidence

The second problem is under which conditions the information gathered abroad can be admitted in the relevant proceedings and which participatory safeguards are due to the individuals concerned, and especially to the addressee of incriminating evidence. At first glance, the comparative analysis reveals a rather different approach in the two countries to this complex issue. Since Brazil has no specific rules in this regard, overseas evidence can be admitted at trial under the same conditions applicable to evidence obtained in other national proceedings.[31] By contrast, the Italian code has a few rules on the conditions under which information gathered through letters rogatory can be included into the trial file and non-repeatable evidence collected overseas can be used at trial, while the code's implementing rules specifically govern the use of evidence taken abroad.[32]

On close examination, the distances between the two countries are smaller than what one would imagine. Since the use of evidence in criminal proceedings is generally deemed to be a question of a national relevance, domestic law is also in Italy competent to lay down the relevant rules. In this regard, we saw that Italian law distinguishes between two situations, namely the use of evidence gathered abroad independently from any legal assistance procedure activated by Italy and the admission of evidence collected in response to a request for legal assistance.[33] Concerning the former situation, Italian law adopts an approach that does not considerably differ from that of the Brazilian law. The implementing rules of the Italian code largely refer to the general rules on the admissibility of evidence gathered in other domestic proceedings (no matter whether criminal or civil proceedings), except the sole case of non-repeatable evidence gathered by the police abroad. This common approach is highly debatable, revealing the clear underestimation of the specific challenges concerned with transborder cases. A quick overview of Italian law highlights that some conditions can rarely be fulfilled in transnational cases (*e.g.*, the presence of the defence lawyer at the hearing of

[31]Chapter 5, E.II.

[32]Chapter 4, E.III.3.

[33]See Chapter 4, respectively, E.III.2 and E.III.3.

incriminating witnesses or co-defendants abroad), while others are strictly linked to purely domestic legal tools (*e.g.*, a court procedure aimed at the collection of evidence in the pre-trial phases). Concerning the second situation, the Italian code had instead introduced specific rules on the use of evidence gathered abroad in response of a request for legal assistance, that is, different rules according to whether Italian courts aim at admitting at trial non-repeatable and documental evidence or oral repeatable evidence. In the latter case, Italian law requires the defence lawyers to be present at the evidence-gathering and to exercise the same powers acknowledged by Italian law. This solution, however, gives rise to various concerns as to the effectiveness of the accused's participatory rights and the case-law has in turn contributed to weak interpretations of these provisions.

Even though the division line between these two main regulations is clearly established at the statutory law level, Italian courts widely allow for the admission of evidence gathered by foreign authorities in response to informal requests made by Italian authorities to bypass the rules on letters rogatory. This does not mean, however, that the information obtained by these means can be used at trial without conditions. Notwithstanding that this case cannot be deemed equivalent to the transfer of evidence already gathered in foreign proceedings, the Supreme Court submits the admission of evidence obtained through informal exchanges to the rules of Article 78 RICCP.

Ultimately, two further aspects can be observed in the countries under examination. On a first level, whereas Brazil requires the application of the ordinary rules on the admission of external evidence, the Italian case-law, as noted, has until now adopted a rather lax approach to the admission of overseas evidence.[34] In order not to undermine international cooperation with foreign countries and to overcome the difficulties concerned especially with letters rogatory, information gathered abroad can be used unless its admission infringes on fundamental principles of Italian law, a limit that clearly lowers the standards of individual protection in comparison to national cases. The second issue concerns the forms of evidence-gathering abroad. It has been observed that the application of the procedures of *lex fori* in the execution of letters rogatory largely aims at facilitating the admission of evidence that, if obtained solely pursuant to *lex loci*, could otherwise remain useless in the requested country. Whereas Brazil has increasingly enacted this system in several bilateral agreements, the Italian code has until recently submitted the possibility of requesting the application of Italian law to the existence of a specific provision in an international agreement. As noted, it can be reasonably expected that the recent ratification of the Brussels Convention will strengthen the application of combined methods of evidence-gathering in Italy. This will in turn require the Italian authorities to request in advance the respect for the rules on evidence-gathering, if necessary to ensure the protection of the individuals concerned and the admissibility of the sought information. In the case of the request for specific procedures of *lex fori*, respect solely for the general principles of the Italian law does not suffice and

[34] Chapter 4, E.III.4.

the evidence obtained can only be admitted if it fulfils the ordinary rules on evidence-gathering.

III. Participatory Rights in the Collection of Evidence Requested by Foreign Countries

Different problems concern the participatory safeguards regarding the collection of evidence requested by other countries. The comparative analysis of the selected countries highlights two main problem areas, which are respectively concerned with the *exequatur* procedure and evidence-gathering for the purposes of a foreign criminal law action. As to the first problem, neither Brazil nor Italy expressly provide for the involvement of the defence in the *exequatur* procedure. Nevertheless, the case-law has significantly acknowledged this possibility through various means. In Italy, alongside the cases in which defendants must personally appear in court and give their consent to the procedure, the referral to the general rules on hearings *in camera* allows for the participation of the defence, unless the foreign request concerns a measure that must be carried out in a hidden manner.[35] The case-law follows a more restrained approach in Brazil. Despite acknowledging that the requirements of *contradictoire* and full defence apply also to the *exequatur* procedure, with the result that the defence should be given access to the case file, the Federal Supreme Tribunal offloads onto the interested party the burden of proving the damages suffered in a concrete case.[36]

Also in relation to the taking of evidence, Italy reveals more openness towards the participation of the defence, which is allowed even in cases for which Italian procedure law does not provide for it, if the trial country expressly requested it pursuant to its own law.[37] In Brazil, the Superior Court of Justice tends to consider the subsequent participation of the defence a preferable solution where the involvement of interested parties in the execution of letters rogatory can jeopardise the efficiency of legal assistance.[38] Although the need for efficient international cooperation is also in Brazil an interest of constitutional relevance, this requirement cannot be used in vague terms to deny participation of the individuals concerned. In this light, the Federal Supreme Tribunal adopted a more convincing approach, acknowledging the lawfulness of letters rogatory enforced without the involvement of the defence only when that involvement could undermine the specific goal of the sought investigation.[39]

---

35 Chapter 4, E.IV.

36 Chapter 5, E.III.

37 Chapter 4, E.IV.

38 Chapter 5, E.III.

39 *Ibid.*

E. Interim Findings

Even more than in the field of national criminal justice, transnational cases need the involvement of the individuals concerned. The comparative-law examination of the selected countries highlights the rising attention to the participatory safeguards in proceedings having transnational features as well as in the two problem areas of international surrender and evidence-gathering procedures. The still largely traditional approach of both Italy and Brazil to transnational criminal justice, however, can explain the existence of considerable shortcomings, which give rise to several human rights concerns. In particular, the weak assistance provided to the person involved in transborder inquiries still makes judicial oversight a mainly formal guarantee, notwithstanding its enhancement by the Italian and Brazilian law. The spread of informal procedures also increases risks for private parties, while ensuring scant certainties as to the applicable law and the possibility of effective participation of the defence.

References

Caprioli F (2013) Report on Italy. In: Ruggeri S (ed) Transnational inquiries and the protection of fundamental rights in criminal proceedings. A study in memory of Vittorio Grevi and Giovanni Tranchina. Springer, Heidelberg, pp 439–455

Chiavario M (2013) Manuale dell'estradizione e del mandato d'arresto europeo. Utet, Torino

Galgani B (2013) Extradition, political offence and the discrimination clause. In: Ruggeri S (ed) Transnational inquiries and the protection of fundamental rights in criminal proceedings. A study in memory of Vittorio Grevi and Giovanni Tranchina. Springer, Heidelberg, pp 167–191

Part V
Evolution of a Wideranging Participatory Approach to Criminal Justice in International Human Rights Law and EU Law

Chapter 8
Audi alteram partem in Criminal Proceedings Under the European Convention on Human Rights

Contents

A. Introductory Issues. The Right to a Fair Hearing and the Need for Overall Balance of Conflicting Interests ... 294
B. *Audi alteram partem* and the Principle of Equality of Arms ... 296
C. Prosecutorial Needs and the Right to Be personally Involved in Criminal Proceedings. The Flexible Approach of the Strasbourg Case-Law ... 297
I. The Right to Be Present in Criminal Proceedings and Individual Duties of Diligence ... 297
1. The Right to Be Present at Trial ... 297
2. The Right to Be Present Before a Higher Instance ... 299
II. The Problem of *in absentia* Procedures ... 300
III. *Inaudito reo* Proceedings and the Right of the Injured Party to Participate in Criminal Hearings ... 302
D. Information Rights and Requirements of Effective Participation in Criminal Proceedings ... 304
I. Premise ... 304
II. The Right to Know and Understand the Accusation ... 305
1. Information on the Charge ... 305
2. Decision to Charge and Information Rights in the Pre-Trial Inquiry ... 308
III. Information on the Evidence Gathered and the Right to Access to the Prosecutorial File ... 310
E. The Guarantee of a Fair Hearing and the Privilege Against Self-Incrimination ... 313
I. The Accused's Right to Be fairly Heard by an Independent Body and Qualitative Requirements of Pre-Trial Questionings ... 313
II. Prosecutorial Needs and the Right of Individuals Other than the Accused to Make Their Voice Heard in Criminal Proceedings ... 314
III. The Right Not to Be Heard in Criminal Justice. Developments in the Principle of *nemo tenetur se detegere* ... 315
F. Defence's Contribution to the Evidence-Gathering and the Requirements of a Fair Decision-Making ... 319
I. Premise ... 319
II. Participation Rights in the Collection of Criminal Evidence ... 321
1. The Right to Confrontation and the Need for an Overall Balance of Conflicting Interests in Criminal Proceedings ... 321
2. Methods of Confrontation ... 321
a) Direct and Indirect Examination ... 321
b) Anonymous Witnesses and the Use of Alternative Means of Confrontation 323

S. Ruggeri, Audi Alteram Partem *in Criminal Proceedings*,
DOI 10.1007/978-3-319-54573-8_8

3. The Right to Confrontation and Inconsistent Testimony 326
III. The Right to Confrontation and the Proof of Guilt 327
1. Premise 327
2. Out-of-Court Confrontations and the Use of Evidence Obtained Without the Defence's Participation in the Case of Subsequent Confrontation 327
3. Absent Witnesses and the Use of Untested Evidence 329
a) The Traditional Approach of the Strasbourg Case-Law: The Sole and Decisive Evidence Doctrine 329
b) The Developments in the European Case-Law After the *Al-Khawaja and Tahery* Judgment: The Progressive Softening of the Sole and Decisive Evidence Test 330
IV. The Contribution of Private Parties to the Decision-Making. *Audi alteram partem* Rule and Argumentation in Criminal Proceedings 331
G. *Audi alteram partem* and Measures of Coercion in Criminal Proceedings 335
I. Deprivation of Freedom and the Right to Information. The Soft Approach of the European Case-Law 335
II. The Right to a Fair Hearing and the Guarantee of Prompt Judicial Review of Arrest or Detention 337
III. Participatory Rights in *habeas corpus* Proceedings 340
H. Provisional Conclusions 343
References 343

A. Introductory Issues. The Right to a Fair Hearing and the Need for Overall Balance of Conflicting Interests

The examination of the developments that have occurred in the domestic law of the selected countries and the persistent deficiencies in both the areas of domestic and transnational criminal justice provide the basis for the subsequent discussion. At this point, the present study should now focus on the models for solutions provided by international human rights law and EU law to solve the deficiencies existing in Brazilian and Italian criminal justice in relation to the issues under examination.

It is widely recognised that, along with constitutional law, international human rights case-law has also made a decisive contribution to the process of humanisation of criminal proceedings.[1] The European Court on Human Rights, in particular, has promoted a convergence towards a new understanding of criminal justice strongly based on the involvement of the parties in the conduct of criminal proceedings,[2] providing solutions that have gone far beyond the scope of the contracting parties. One of the most significant benefits of Strasbourg case-law is that, even though the Rome Convention mainly focuses on the fair trial rights of the person charged with an offence, it has progressively re-defined the meaning of several procedural safeguards in the light of an overall view of the right to a fair hearing. Far from creating an opposition between the accused's rights and prosecutorial needs, the European jurisprudence reflects a much more complex concept of criminal proceedings as a listening space where conflicting interests must be balanced with each

[1]On this issue also see from the viewpoint of Brazilian law Giacomolli (2014), p. 12 ff.
[2]Jackson (2005), p. 737 f.; Balsamo and Lo Piparo (2008), p. 334 f.

other. The right to confrontation provides a clear example. The Strasbourg case-law reconstructed this guarantee in a manner that does not only look at the defendants' side, calling for delicate balances with the need to protect the interests of other people, especially those of the victim and of vulnerable witnesses.[3]

This does not entail, however, that the European Convention promotes an objective conception of the right to a fair hearing. Significantly, the Rome Convention, like other international human rights instruments, does not acknowledge the *audi alteram partem* rule as such, nor is there any reference to the principle of *contradictoire* in the terms that various countries, especially those of continental Europe, acknowledge it. As *Ubertis* put it, the reference to a 'fair hearing' requires that the individuals charged with a criminal offence be put in a fair condition to be heard, to expose their arguments and to challenge the arguments put forward by other parties.[4] Yet, as noted, these requirements can certainly not be considered an exclusive prerogative of defendants. On close examination, the European Convention does not simply grant defendants the right to be fairly heard; it recognises their right to be tried in a proceeding that provides a fair hearing of all the involved parties.[5] In other words, the Rome Convention ensures to defendants the right not only to have access to criminal justice but also to be fairly involved in a proceeding in which all the interests at stake must be balanced with each other and all the parties must also be given the opportunity of making their voice heard prior to the decision-making.

This participatory approach lies at the core of Strasbourg case-law. It is noteworthy that the European Court has increasingly broadened the scope of the right to a fair hearing in various fashions. Like the International Covenant,[6] the European Convention, despite not linking the general fair trial rights solely with a criminal law action, ensures more specific safeguards to the addressee of a 'criminal charge'.[7] This expression has led the Strasbourg case-law to develop a wide jurisprudence, which extends the scope of this fundamental guarantee not only beyond the sphere of the judicial criminal proceedings but even outside the field of criminal justice, as structured at the national level. Since *Imbrioscia v. Switzerland*,[8] the Strasbourg Court has strongly elaborated an autonomous notion of 'criminal charge',[9] extended to the pre-trial phases of criminal proceedings and

---

[3] *Below*, F.II–III.

[4] Ubertis (2009), p. 49.

[5] It is noteworthy that the English version of Article 6(1) ECHR acknowledges the right to 'a fair hearing', whereas the French text may seem to adopt a more subjective perspective by granting the accused the right that '*sa cause soit entendue équitablement*'. Most translations into Romance languages have followed the same perspective.

[6] Art. 14(1) ICCPR provides for that "In the determination of any criminal charge against him, or of his rights and obligations in a suit at law, everyone shall be entitled to a fair and public hearing by a competent, independent and impartial tribunal established by law".

[7] Art. 6(1) ECHR.

[8] ECtHR, *Imbrioscia v. Switzerland.*

[9] For an overview of Strasbourg case-law on the notion of 'charge' from the perspective of the right to a trial in a reasonable time cfr. Ubertis (2009), p. 26 ff.

even to *ad hoc* procedures, such as *habeas corpus* proceedings. As far as criminal proceedings are specifically concerned, the Rome Convention thus requires the contracting states to adapt the features of the safeguards concerned with the *audi alteram partem* rule to the different structure of the proceedings. The need for a constant balance among conflicting interests entails that the right to a fair hearing cannot be unconditionally restricted due to the structure of higher instances or their concrete management. This approach is clearly expressed in *Quadrelli v. Italy*, in which the European Court found an infringement of Article 6 ECHR, in that the Italian Supreme Court had failed to consider a memorandum of the defence.[10] Similar problems have subsequently arisen in the Strasbourg case-law regarding other states.[11]

B. *Audi alteram partem* and the Principle of Equality of Arms

Against this background, one can affirm that under the European Convention the *audi alteram partem* rule constitutes a sort of meta-value, which cuts across the whole set of the fair trial rights. This result is enhanced by the strict link between the right to a fair hearing and the principle of equality of arms, which provides a constant means of compensation for any tendency to strengthen the rights of the accused disproportionately. As noted, one of the main achievements of the Strasbourg system of human rights protection was not the enhancement of individual rights but a complex, flexible reconstruction of the right to a fair hearing. In particular, the case-law developed by the Strasbourg Court over the last two decades highlights the constant attempt to overcome the traditional accused-centred view of criminal justice[12] by extending the focus to all the individuals who either directly or indirectly are affected by criminal inquiries, without this result leading to a new partiality in favour of other parties, such as the victim.[13]

Since its earlier jurisprudence, the European Court has attached such importance to the relationship between the *audi alteram partem* rule and the principle of equality of arms[14] that one might affirm that under the European Convention the former safeguard cannot exist without the other. This approach confirms the Strasbourg Court's broad vision of the right to a fair hearing, which has led to an interesting re-definition of the accused's safeguards in the light of the state-related interest in a proper investigation and prosecution of the alleged facts. As acknowledged by the European Court on various occasions (and in relation to countries with different legal cultures),

---

[10]ECtHR, *Quadrelli v. Italy*.

[11]For further references see Trechsel (2005), p. 91 f.

[12]See Chiavario (2008), p. 21, who calls for the introduction of international general statute of victim's rights.

[13]Findlay (2011), p. 112.

[14]ECtHR, *Neumeister v. Austria*.

> the right to an adversarial process, as required by Article 6 of the Convention, means that both the prosecution and to the defense must be given the opportunity to have knowledge of and comment on the observations filed and the evidence adduced by the other party.[15]

At first glance, this approach may appear to contradict the spirit of the Convention, which does not enable prosecutors to claim state-related interests before the Strasbourg institutions.[16] On close examination, this important acknowledgment confirms that prosecutorial needs must also be taken into consideration in the complex balances entailed by the right to a fair hearing. This does not mean that prosecutors can unconditionally prevent both the defence and the judicial authority from examining relevant pieces of evidence. The European Court has negatively assessed this conduct, which not only jeopardises the exercise of an effective defence but also the possibility for the judicial authority to exercise its tasks fairly—a detrimental result that cannot be compensated for by providing the defence with proper information in a higher instance.[17] In the Strasbourg case-law, therefore, the defendant's contribution to the decision-making takes on a significance that goes beyond the right to a defence by itself, involving the public interest in a qualitative ascertainment of the facts according to the requirements of fairness and the rule of law.[18] This also explains why the right to a fair hearing cannot be unconditionally dispensed with at the defendant's initiative without the overall consideration of the negative repercussions on both the fundamental rights of other parties and the goals of criminal proceedings.

C. Prosecutorial Needs and the Right to Be personally Involved in Criminal Proceedings. The Flexible Approach of the Strasbourg Case-Law

I. The Right to Be Present in Criminal Proceedings and Individual Duties of Diligence

1. The Right to Be Present at Trial

Doubtless, the guarantee of personal participation in criminal proceedings stands among the most remarkable expressions of the right to a fair hearing under the European Convention. Personal involvement can in turn have various features according to national criminal justice. Several European countries do not allow for self-defence in the criminal process, requiring the competent authorities to

[15]ECtHR, *Fodale v. Italy*, § 42. In this sense see already ECtHR, *Laukkanen and Manninen v. Finland*, § 34.

[16]In this sense cf. Trechsel (2005), p. 90.

[17]ECtHR, *Rowe and Davis v. United Kingdom.*

[18]Trechsel (2005), p. 89.

appoint a lawyer where the accused persons have not chosen their own counsel. Moreover, the decision to appoint a lawyer of one's own choosing is also a form of direct participation in criminal proceedings, which can significantly affect the defence strategy. On close examination, legal assistance and self-defence are not necessarily alternative forms of the right to a defence, since the defendants must have the opportunity of giving their own contribution even where a lawyer represents them in court. Remarkably, all criminal justice systems provide for specific decisions that personally lie in the interested party.

Against this framework, a particularly delicate issue dealt with by the Strasbourg case-law is the right to be present at trial. To be sure, like other international human rights instruments, the European Convention does not expressly provide for the right to personally participate in criminal trials. Thus this right appears neither among the general features of the right to a fair hearing nor among the minimum guarantees acknowledged to the person charged with a criminal offence. Notwithstanding the lack of statutory indications, however, the European Court, relying on the non-exhaustive nature of the fair trial guarantees listed in Article 6(3) ECHR, has long recognised, since the leading case *Colozza v. Italy*,[19] the right of defendants to be tried in their own presence. There is little doubt that the right to take part personally in criminal proceedings is strictly linked with, and somehow presupposed by, other fair trial guarantees, starting with the right to have the time and facilities to defend oneself. This confirms that, despite the English wording of Article 6(3)(c) ECHR,[20] the guarantee of personal participation in criminal hearings cannot be viewed as an alternative to the right to be represented by a lawyer. On the one hand, the competent authority may have appointed the defence lawyer without the defendant having had the possibility of choosing his own counsel.[21] On the other, as noted, the decision to appoint a lawyer of one's own choosing is by definition a form of personal involvement in the defence strategy.

On close examination, most procedural safeguards enshrined in Article 6 (3) ECHR are expressed in such a manner that they are at least compatible with the right to be personally involved in criminal proceedings. In particular, the very first guarantee acknowledged to the individuals charged with a criminal offence—namely the right to detailed information on the charge in a language they can understand—clearly aims at their direct involvement in criminal proceedings.[22] Moreover, defendants must personally appear in court to be heard by the competent authority and their personal participation is the prerequisite for them to give their own contribution to the evidence-gathering, *e.g*. by adducing exculpatory evidence and especially by cross-examining prosecutorial witnesses.[23] Finally, the right to

[19]ECtHR, *Colozza v. Italy*.

[20]'[Everyone charged with a criminal offence has the following minimum rights:] (c) to defend himself in person *or* through legal assistance of his own choosing [...]'.

[21]Trechsel (2005), p. 244.

[22]*Below*, D.II.

[23]*Below*, F.II.

take part personally in the proceedings takes on more specific meanings where coercive measures are ordered against the accused person[24] who, in cases of arrest or detention under Article 5(1)(c) ECHR, must be brought to the judicial authority and 'release may be conditioned by guarantees to appear for trial'.[25]

2. The Right to Be Present Before a Higher Instance

Under the European Convention, the right to personal participation is not confined solely to the trial phase. A delicate issue is whether and under which conditions the accused can be personally involved in the procedure before a higher instance. In the Strasbourg case-law, the question holds relevance from the viewpoint of the right to effective defence in the appeal proceedings. The European Court has in principle acknowledged the guarantee of personal participation before a higher instance by stressing that the human rights protections provided by the Convention must potentially be extended to legal remedies. Of course, this right has different features depending on the characteristics of the procedure before higher instances, as structured at the national law level. In general terms, the Court acknowledges that, where an appeal aims at both a factual and a legal review of the decision, the proceedings must, as a rule, be held in oral and public form,[26] especially if defendants have material arguments against the judgment issued at first instance, or are interested in requesting the collection of further evidence. The same arguments, however, led the Court to acknowledge the fairness of proceedings conducted in written form and without the defendants' participation, if the appeal proceedings only aim at a legal revision of the decision without engaging the higher court in further factual inquiries.[27]

These findings are clearly inspired by those European countries in which the appeal on a point of law is structured in such a manner as to require the defendants to appoint a lawyer (who must often be specifically entitled to appear before a higher court) to represent them.[28] Nevertheless, the Court's approach gives rise to human rights concerns, depriving defendants of the possibility of giving their contribution to the decision-making in a higher instance. In particular, the arguments used do not appear to be consistent with the European case-law, which has on several occasions expressed preference for the personal participation of defendants equipped with legal knowledge.[29] Moreover, the appeal proceedings can also entail negative consequences for the defendants, since Protocol No. 7 to the European

---

[24]*Below*, G.

[25]Art. 5(3) ECHR.

[26]ECtHR, *Constantinescu v. Romania*.

[27]ECtHR, *Döry v. Sweden*.

[28]See, *e.g.*, Art. 613(1) CCP-Italy.

[29]*Below*, F.IV.

Convention does not protect them from the risk of *reformatio in pejus*.[30] Even the appeals on a point of law can worsen the appellant's position, so that the simple fact that the competent authority is called upon to examine the legal foundation of the case is not a sufficient ground for excluding the accused's participation. It is noteworthy, moreover, that that the European Court, while allowing for appeal proceedings to be held without involving the defendants, does not engage in assessing whether their defence rights were properly protected, while this assessment is required in the case of derogation from the right to a public hearing at first instance.[31]

II. The Problem of in absentia *Procedures*

Despite the acknowledgment of the right to be present at trial, the European Court has never gone so far as to consider proceedings held *in absentia* incompatible with the Convention. This result is certainly due to the tradition of some contracting states, especially of continental Europe, which generally allow for criminal proceedings to be held in the accused's absence. To be sure, there are no unequivocal provisions in the European Convention, which forbid these procedures. The Court, however, requires that *in absentia* procedures fulfil strict conditions and that specific safeguards be met to ensure the overall fairness of the proceedings.

In general terms, the Strasbourg case-law attaches great weight to the grounds for non-appearance in court, distinguishing the cases in which it stems from the free decision not to take part at trial from those in which there are no clear indications on the accused's intentions. Certainly, the addressees of a criminal enquiry cannot be charged with the burden of proving the reasons for their lack of awareness of the proceedings, nor especially with the burden of proving that non-appearance in court was due to *force majeure* or other unforeseeable circumstances.[32] Since the *Colozza* case, moreover, the Court has made it clear that the national authority are responsible for informing the accused persons about the charge filed against them, which also entails the obligation to demonstrate that the accused was made personally aware of the initiation of a criminal law action. Significantly, the competent authorities cannot be released from responsibility even in the case of conduct of the accused that could be relevant in the field of administrative law, such as the failure to communicate a change of residence.[33]

Notwithstanding these findings, the European Court has always been quite flexible while assessing whether there was a breach of the obligation to inform the accused of the accusation. Thus the failure to duly inform the accused does not necessarily affect the lawfulness of the procedure conducted *in absentia*, provided,

[30] Trechsel (2005), p. 362.

[31] ECtHR, *Liebreich v. Germany*.

[32] ECtHR, *Colozza v. Italy*, § 30.

[33] ECtHR, *F.C.B. v. Italy*.

however, that one of the following two circumstances occurs: (a) the defendants knowingly waived their right to participate in the proceedings,[34] or (b) they were granted a proper opportunity to have access to a retrial or a remedy aimed at allowing a new decision on the merits of the case. The Court laid down specific requirements for both these situations.

Concerning the former case, the Strasbourg case-law has clarified, since the *Neumeister* case, that the waiver decision must be provided with specific guarantees.[35] Moreover, the Court requires defendants to waive their right to be present at trial, if not explicitly, in an unequivocal manner, after being made aware of the consequences of their decision. It is worth observing, however, that the European Court has never given entirely favourable consideration to the waiver of personal participation in criminal proceedings, which still remains, as noted, the preferred solution in particular situations, *e.g.* where the defendant has a personal expertise in legal issues.[36] The disfavour of the Strasbourg case-law towards the decision not to personally participate in the proceedings goes so far as to acknowledge the lawfulness of some sort of sanction by the competent authorities[37] in order to 'discourage unjustified absences'.[38] Nevertheless, the Court has not yet given very clear indications in this respect.[39] As a matter of principle, the Court rules out that national law can adopt drastic measures to obtain the defendant's presence by coercive means, *e.g.* by requiring that defendants should undergo pre-trial imprisonment to challenge a conviction issued against them.[40] National authorities also cannot sanction defendants who choose not to take part personally in the proceedings by depriving them of the right to appoint a lawyer of their own choosing—a decision that, according to the Court, must remain unimpeded.[41] This approach, while highlighting the importance of legal assistance, reveals the existence of a core content of the right to personal involvement in criminal proceedings which cannot be restricted.

Further requirements apply to the case in which the accused is ensured the possibility of accessing a retrial or a remedy aimed at a new ruling on the case. The Court held that the right to be present at trial can be structured in different ways, provided that defendants are granted the opportunity to participate in a fair hearing, no matter whether this follows or precedes the decision on their guilt. Since the *Colozza* case, the Court has stressed that, even if national law does not provide

[34]To be sure, in *Colozza v. Italy*, the Court left open the question of whether the right to personal participation could be waived. Cf. Trechsel (2005), p. 255 f.

[35]ECtHR, *Neumeister v. Austria*.

[36]In *Franquesa Freixas v. Spain*, the Court regarded with disfavour the defendant's choice not to defend himself precisely because he was a lawyer.

[37]Trechsel (2005), p. 256.

[38]ECtHR, *Poitrimol v. France*, § 35.

[39]Negri (2014), p. 149 ff.

[40]ECtHR, *Poitrimol v. France*, § 38.

[41]See, among others, ECtHR, *Lala v. The Netherlands*.

for mechanisms capable of granting defendants knowledge of the proceedings, the overall fairness of the procedure is not undermined if defendants are given, either upon request or by the court, 'a fresh determination of the merits of the charge [...]'.[42] It is worth noting that in the *Colozza* judgment, the Strasbourg judges had already pointed out that the new examination of the case must be made 'from a court which has heard' the accused.[43]

This approach constitutes a clear compromise solution aimed at saving the lawfulness of some national arrangements that provide for subsequent mechanisms in order to grant the individuals convicted *in absentia* the opportunity of a judicial review by a higher court. Notwithstanding the benefits of the requirements set forth by the Strasbourg case-law, comparison with EU law will highlight that the condition of a 'fresh determination of the merits of the case' in a retrial or in a higher instance may not be sufficient to erase the shortcomings of a procedure held *in absentia*, which can severely weaken the humanitarian function of the right to personal participation in criminal proceedings.[44]

III. **Inaudito reo** *Proceedings and the Right of the Injured Party to Participate in Criminal Hearings*

Rather different problems arise in relation to *inaudito reo* proceedings, which exclude the defendants' involvement prior to the decision-making on the assumption that a subsequent challenge will ensure a trial hearing compensating them for the previous loss of defence opportunities. Although this procedure may seem to follow the same scheme adopted by the Court in the field of the default proceedings, the mechanism is quite different, since *inaudito reo* proceedings are usually carried out not only without the accused's participation but also without the trial and any court hearing.

The Strasbourg Court has not had many opportunities to examine the lawfulness issue of subsequent remedies in relation to *inaudito reo* proceedings. The recent case *Gray v. Germany*, however, gives us a rather clear picture of the Court's understanding of this procedure, while highlighting some new problematic aspects.[45] In the case at hand, the applicants complained under Article 2, read in conjunction with Article 1 ECHR, that shortcomings in the British health system in connection with the recruitment of *locum* doctors and supervision of out-of-hours *locum* services had led to their father's death as a consequence of medical malpractice by a German *locum* doctor.[46] Although the case did not mainly concern the

---

[42]*Colozza v. Italy*, § 29.

[43]*Ibid.*

[44]Chapter 14, D.II.

[45]ECtHR, *Gray v. Germany*.

[46]*Ibid.*, § 3.

right to a fair hearing, the complaint focused on two important aspects of penal order proceedings. In particular, the applicants stressed that the summary proceedings instituted in Germany had not 'involved a proper investigation or scrutiny of the facts of the case or the related evidence' and, more specifically, that 'the German authorities had failed to inform them of the proceedings and had thus deprived the deceased's next of kin of any possibility to get involved and participate in the latter'.[47] These complaints highlighted the problematic nature of the penal order procedure from a rather different perspective, which concerns its justification in terms of the need for proper investigation and the possibility for the aggrieved parties to be involved in a criminal law action. Of course, the latter problem did not relate to the stage prior to decision-making but to the trial phase, in which, pursuant to German law, the applicants could have joined the prosecution as plaintiffs. This result did not materialise, however, since the penal order was not challenged and the applicants only learned of the procedure after the conviction had already become final.

This new focus, therefore, shifted the problem of participation in criminal proceedings to individuals other than the accused. By rejecting the complaint relating to Article 2 ECHR, the Strasbourg judges incidentally provided some indications on penal order proceedings. Concerning the lack of involvement of the applicants, the Court, relying quite uncritically on the Government's arguments, recognised that German law neither requires the aggrieved parties to be informed of a penal order procedure nor enables them to challenge the conviction with a view to joining the prosecution as plaintiffs.[48] The Court further excluded that the obligation to involve them can derive from Article 2 ECHR, as conversely acknowledged in relation to situations in which the responsibility of state agents in connection with a victim's death had been at stake.[49]

The reasoning used to support this conclusion is rather unconvincing. Like in *Hugh Jordan v. United Kingdom*, the Strasbourg judges did not rule out that, as regards medical negligence, 'the next of kin of the victim must be involved in the procedure to the extent necessary to safeguard his or her legitimate interests',[50] provided, however, that the 'circumstances surrounding the death were suspicious or unclear'.[51] Also in this regard, the Court limited itself to concurring with the Government's argument that 'the circumstances of the case had been sufficiently established in the course of the investigative proceedings', with the result that 'a participation of the applicants in a potential main hearing, even if it might have a cathartic effect for the victim's next of kin, could not have further contributed to the trial court's assessment of the case'.[52] This argument is rather difficult to understand

[47] *Ibid.*, § 61.

[48] *Ibid.*, § 87.

[49] *Ibid.*

[50] ECtHR, *Hugh Jordan v. United Kingdom*, § 109.

[51] ECtHR, *Gray v. Germany*, § 87.

[52] *Ibid.*, § 91.

without an overall consideration of the Court's reasoning, which comes to the conclusion that 'the applicants have not specified which aspect' of the offender's 'responsibility for medical negligence causing the applicants' father's death has not been sufficiently clarified'.[53]

This functional approach leads to somehow paradoxical results. Pursuant to the Strasbourg case-law, the European Convention only protects the right of the aggrieved parties to be involved in a criminal inquiry as long as they can demonstrate the usefulness of their potential contribution in a public hearing. This argument is as surprising as maintaining that, under the European Convention, defendants should be granted the right to be informed about the accusation only if it is proven that insufficient information would jeopardise the effective exercise of the defence in a specific case.[54] It is not easy to understand that the injured party holds the right to participation in criminal proceedings but cannot claim it. By stating that 'in the sphere of medical negligence the procedural obligation imposed by Article 2 does not necessarily require the provision of a criminal-law remedy',[55] the Court makes it clear that the European Convention cannot grant the injured party a subsequent remedy if not provided for by national law. Nevertheless, the main question raised by the aggrieved parties—namely, whether 'in an unusual and sensitive case like the present one the prosecution authorities' decision to apply for a conviction'[56] through a proceeding that excludes their involvement was justified, notwithstanding sufficient evidence gathered against the accused – remained unanswered.

D. Information Rights and Requirements of Effective Participation in Criminal Proceedings

I. Premise

The physical presence of defendants does not suffice to ensure their effective participation in criminal hearings without further conditions. As noted, the European Convention formulated most of the fair trial rights of the accused persons in a manner that their involvement in criminal justice does not remain at a merely formal level. In general terms, the Court has on several occasions stressed the requirement of effective participation, specifying that the overall set-up of Article 6 ECHR aims at guaranteeing not only the right of the accused 'to be present, but also to hear and follow the proceedings'.[57]

---

[53] *Ibid.*

[54] *Below*, D.II.1.

[55] ECtHR, *Gray v. Germany*, § 91.

[56] *Ibid.*, § 91.

[57] ECtHR, *Stanford v. United Kingdom*, § 26. See Trechsel (2005), p. 253.

The right to effective participation in criminal hearings has various expressions, and the forms largely depend on whether national law allows for defendants to defend themselves or through a lawyer. It has been observed that the right to personal participation in criminal proceedings should not be viewed as an alternative to the guarantee of legal assistance. The Strasbourg Court, however, has never gone so far as to find an infringement of the European Convention as a consequence of the approach followed by those states which impose a court-appointed counsel on absent defendants who are not represented by their own lawyer. Moreover, the European case-law has not always provided clear indications on the safeguards due to the accused if legal assistance is ensured. As a matter of principle, if national law allows for defendants to defend themselves, they must be provided with the necessary tools to prepare their defence strategy, starting with personal access to the prosecutorial file.[58] However, the Court does not make the right to prepare one's own defence inflexible to the point that it would be incompatible with the Convention to allow only the lawyer to access the file.

This result cannot be sustained in general terms. Irrespective of whether defendants can choose their own counsel or are represented by a court-appointed lawyer, they must be put in a position to make their own contribution to the ongoing inquiry. The Court dealt with this delicate issue in *Stanford v. United Kingdom*, where it rejected the application of a defendant who complained that he had not had the opportunity to participate effectively in the proceedings since he had been placed in a glass-fronted dock.[59] In this ruling, the Court, despite acknowledging that the applicant had 'difficulties in hearing some of the evidence given during the trial', stressed that he had sufficiently represented by his counsel. This was surely a rather unfortunate argument, which revealed the Court's underestimation of the importance of the possibility of the defendant following the proceedings personally within the limits of their capacities.[60]

II. The Right to Know and Understand the Accusation

1. Information on the Charge

Certainly, under the European Convention also, the granting of proper information is the first condition of effective participation in criminal hearings. In this respect, two main guarantees must be ensured, namely the information on the charge and the information on the evidence available. It is quite obvious that any defence strategy is always set in relation to a specific charge. There is no doubt that denying the possibility of knowing the meaning of the act with which the accused was charged

[58]ECtHR, *Foucher v. France*.

[59]ECtHR, *Stanford v. United Kingdom*.

[60]In the same sense Trechsel (2005), p. 253 fn. 41.

gives rise to a 'Kafkaesque situation'.[61] There is a strict link between this right and other fair trial guarantees enshrined in the Convention. Without knowing the charge, defendants cannot make themselves heard. Moreover, informing the defendants of the charges preferred against them enables them to appoint a lawyer of their own choosing with specific competence in a specific criminal law area, as well as to decide whether and to what extent they can take part in the proceedings personally within the limits laid down by national law. Furthermore, the defence's contribution to the evidence-gathering is also oriented towards a specific charge. This not only applies to the collection of exculpatory evidence but also to the taking of incriminating evidence. Doubtless, the lack of information negatively affects the right to be confronted with prosecutorial witnesses, a result that is magnified by the fact that pursuant to the Strasbourg case-law, confrontation can also be ensured out of court.

Despite this systematic approach to the guarantee of information, the Strasbourg Court has on several occasions emphasised the functional relationship between the right to be informed about the accusation and the right to a defence, to such a point, however, that it often engages in scrutinising whether insufficient information jeopardised the effective exercise of the defence in the case at stake.[62] This approach not only weakens the right to information about the accusation[63] but also charges the European Court with the difficult task of evaluating a hypothetical situation, that is, whether the defence's opportunities would have been different by providing the accused with proper information. On close examination, the Court is neither 'equipped to do this' nor does the Convention require proof that the lack of information or misleading information undermined the exercise of the defence rights, and consequently whether better information would have enhanced the defendant's strategy.[64]

Furthermore, the focus on the repercussions of the lack of information on the right to a defence has led to the Court considerably departing from the doctrine expressed in the *Rowe et al.* case, in which it stressed that the negative consequences for the defence rights can be compensated for in a further instance.[65] This approach reveals a rather reductive understanding of the guarantee of information about the charge, as if the defendants only deserved to be protected to the extent that they were concretely jeopardised in the preparation of their defence. This perspective has made the Court lose sight of the importance for the accused to be properly informed in the light of an overall consideration of the right to a fair hearing. There is little doubt that depriving the defendant of the necessary information to set up a successful defence strategy not only affects the right to an effective defence but furthermore can negatively impinge upon a fair fact-finding. However, the failure to

[61] *Ibid.*, 193.

[62] ECtHR, *Mattoccia v. Italy*.

[63] In this sense see also Kühne (2009), Rn. 494.

[64] Trechsel (2005), p. 194 f.

[65] ECtHR, *Sipavicius v. Lithuania*.

adopt a more rigid approach—as that shared, for instance, in relation to further fair trial requirements such as the impartiality of the judge,[66] which cannot be compensated for or integrated in further instances—has not enabled the Strasbourg Court to exploit the potentials of the right to the information on the accusation.[67]

This conclusion is further corroborated by the way the European Court classifies the right to information, which is not usually viewed as entailing the obligation of national authorities to make defendants aware of the charges preferred against them,[68] provided that they can in any case obtain proper information. From this it follows that information on the charge is usually seen as a weak guarantee for the individuals concerned rather than as the obligation for the competent authorities to inform them (and keep them informed) on the accusation.[69]

On the other hand, it must be acknowledged that the adoption of a functional perspective has led the Strasbourg Court to establish some qualitative requirements that must be satisfied to avoid negative repercussions on the defence rights. The European case-law does not merely require defendants to be provided with any information on the charge but also stresses the need for detailed information on the nature and type of the accusation in a language the accused can understand. There is little doubt that the requirements of detailed and understandable information set the core conditions for the accused's effective participation in criminal proceedings. Moreover, the European Convention stands out among other international human rights instruments in that it attaches specific attention to the linguistic understanding of the charge. Significantly, the Court examined this delicate question for the first time in a transnational case, namely *Brozicek v. Italy*, where it adopted an integrated approach to the guarantee of information of the charge.[70] In this ruling, the point at stake was not just the lack of information but the lack of information that the defendant could understand, which jeopardised his right to take part effectively in criminal proceedings. Thus the failure to provide the applicant with understandable information prevented him from being present at trial and led to his conviction *in absentia*. The link between the right to information and the right to exercise an effective defence was further developed in *Mattocia v. Italy*, where the Court pointed out the repercussions of insufficient information on the guarantees listed in lit. (*b*) and especially (*d*) of Article 6(3) ECHR.[71]

---

[66]ECtHR, *De Cubber v. Belgium*.

[67]See already Trechsel (2005), p. 194.

[68]This is not always the case. In *Mattoccia v. Italy*, the Court clearly stresses that information 'rests entirely on the prosecuting authority's shoulders'.

[69]Trechsel (2005), p. 204.

[70]Chapter 11, C.

[71]Trechsel (2005), p. 201.

2. Decision to Charge and Information Rights in the Pre-Trial Inquiry

These developments lead us to analyse two further issues, namely the time at which defendants must be granted information and the degree of information required. The two questions are strictly linked with each other under the European Convention, which stands out among other human rights charters in that it links the right to information with the preferment of an 'accusation'. This reference may seem to provide this guarantee with a more restrictive scope than that of the other fair trial guarantees laid down in Article 6(3) ECHR, which, as noted, were recognised for any person 'charged' with an offence. Significantly, some commentators interpreted the right to information as relating to the act through which the court proceedings are instituted.[72] This conclusion appears to be further corroborated by a comparison with the provision on the right to information under Article 5 (2) ECHR, which expressly relates to the 'charge'. Moreover, the requirement of detail provided for by Article 6(3)(a) ECHR does not appear to fit best the investigative phase, whose goal is to gather all the information required to decide whether the defendant must be brought to court.[73]

This approach cannot be sustained for several reasons. On a first level, focusing on specific procedural acts aimed at charging the defendant with an offence not only restricts the scope of the guarantee but also deprives it of much of its dynamic force. From a human rights perspective, linking the right to information to the beginning of the court proceedings would mean accepting that the Convention left individuals largely unprotected in the pre-trial inquiry, notwithstanding that most intrusive measures are usually carried out in this phase. Moreover, this negative result would not remain limited to the right to information. As noted, the fair trial rights are strictly connected with each other: without information on the charge, suspects would not be able to properly prepare their defence, make themselves heard, and so on.

At any rate, the European Court has never followed a restrictive interpretation. Traditionally, the Strasbourg case-law has adopted a flexible approach that largely departs from the understanding of 'charge' acknowledged by national laws, highlighting an autonomous concept of the right to information on the accusation. This independent approach, oriented towards the overall purposes of protection of the right to a fair hearing under the Convention, looks at the impact of a criminal inquiry on the fundamental rights of the individuals concerned.[74] It is noteworthy that the Strasbourg case-law, dealing with the reasonable length of the proceedings, required national authorities to provide suspects with information on the charges that 'substantially affects' their position.[75] This reference highlights a clear human rights-oriented approach, which cannot remain confined to the assessment of the reasonable duration of criminal proceedings, imposing on the competent authority

[72] *Ibid.*, 198 f.

[73] *Ibid.*, 199 f.

[74] ECtHR, *Brozicek v. Italy*.

[75] Cf. ECtHR, *Deweer v. Belgium*; ECtHR, *Eckle v. Germany*; ECtHR, *Corigliano v. Italy*.

precise obligations aimed at enabling the effective exercise of fair trial rights. These obligations also entail that national authorities must promptly inform defendants of any change of the accusation that can impinge on their position and defence rights.[76]

The approach followed by the Strasbourg case-law raises the question of which criteria should determine the substantial repercussions of a criminal inquiry on the suspect's fundamental rights. Article 5(2) ECHR gives an important indication in this regard, requiring the arrested or detained individuals not only to be granted information on the grounds for the deprivation of their freedom but also on the charge filed in a language they can understand.[77] One might argue that the reference to 'any charge' would be meaningless if suspects were always to be informed of the accusation preferred against them. On close examination, this is not the correct sense of this guarantee, whose scope potentially fits all the cases listed in paragraph 1.[78] Of course, the need for information on the charge does not exclusively concern cases of provisional arrest or detention, since criminal investigations expose suspects to the risk of several measures impinging on other fundamental rights acknowledged by the European Convention. Moreover, although investigative measures can interfere with individual rights in very different ways, the application of coercive measures must always be justified by a suspicion of guilt,[79] which usually requires the competent authority to formally charge the suspect with a criminal offence.

Of course, this does not entail an absolute duty of information on the side of the competent authority. At its earlier stage, criminal inquiries generally need to be maintained secret, and in a later phase, criminal investigations often require the adoption of investigative means (online search, wiretaps, etc.) that, as noted, can strongly affect fundamental rights even in a hidden way. Nevertheless, the need for effective investigation cannot certainly be held to endure longer than the time required to complete the necessary investigative activities. Beyond these limits, there is no need to deprive the individuals concerned of the necessary information on the charge. In the light of these limits, Article 6(3)(a) ECHR can be interpreted in the sense that suspects, whenever affected or limited in their fundamental rights, must be granted information on both the charge and on any subsequent change, unless a concrete risk for the ongoing investigation arises and the authority in charge of prosecution proves it. This calls for an approach that looks at the right to information on the accusation as a dynamic guarantee rather than as a static right related to specific procedural stages.[80] From this it also follows that the degree of detail of information cannot be defined in abstract terms[81] but should be

[76]ECtHR, *Drassich v. Italy*.

[77]Trechsel (2005), p. 458 f.

[78]*Ibid.*, 458.

[79]*Ibid.*, 154.

[80]Vogler (1986), Rn. 477; Kühne (2009), Rn. 496.

[81]Trechsel (2005), p. 458.

adapted to different stages of the proceedings, varying also in relation to the eventual changes to the accusation, depending on the course of the investigation.

III. Information on the Evidence Gathered and the Right to Access to the Prosecutorial File

Under the European Convention also, information on the charge does not suffice to ensure effective participation in criminal proceedings. It has been noted that there is a strict link between the guarantees acknowledged by lists. (a) and (b) of Article 6 (3) ECHR.[82] Yet, in the *Haxhia* case, the European Court ruled out that the notification of the accusation should necessarily entail the disclosure of supporting evidence to enable the accused to prepare for trial.[83] This result can be satisfied on the basis of Article 6(3)(b) ECHR, however.[84] There is no doubt, moreover, that not only defendants but also suspects must be granted the necessary 'facilities' for the preparation of their defence, facilities that surely entail the right to have access to the file containing the results of the investigations carried out by the investigative bodies in the pre-trial phase.[85] To be sure, the early case-law of the European Commission was 'rather prudent in this respect – the right of access was considered to arise, at the very latest, from the moment that the indictment was presented'.[86] Subsequent case-law, however, acknowledged in much clearer terms that the right to information on prosecutorial evidence applies to all the phases of criminal proceedings, including the police inquiry, if national law enables the police authority to investigate autonomously.

To be sure, this case-law was elaborated mainly in relation to cases in which the applicants had been deprived of their right to freedom. One might argue, however, that a similar approach should apply whenever during the pre-trial inquiry a charging decision is made against one of more individuals, especially because these decisions, as noted, are often coupled with interferences with fundamental rights.[87] At any rate, an important aspect distinguishes the guarantees of information on the charge and the access to prosecutorial evidence. Investigative needs can justify the postponement and even the denial of information on the charge, which, however, cannot be deprived of its necessary contents depending on the stage of the proceedings.[88] By contrast, access to relevant evidence and the investigative file

[82] *Ibid.*, 222.

[83] ECtHR, *Haxhia v. Albania*.

[84] Trechsel (2005), p. 200 f.

[85] *Ibid.*, 200.

[86] *Ibid.*, 232.

[87] *Ibid.*, 234.

[88] According to *Kühne*, the risk of tampering with evidence should instead be taken into account also in relation to the prosecutorial interest not to communicate details that might undermine the investigation. See Kühne (2009), Rn. 494.

can not only be denied but also be limited to specific pieces of evidence to avoid risks to the ongoing investigation.

Certainly, suspects cannot claim their right to access relevant evidence in absolute terms. In most continental countries, the risk of tampering with evidence is a typical justification for pre-trial detention. It is reasonable, therefore, that defendants, despite being granted proper information on the reasons of their detention and the charge filed, are denied access to the file, if a concrete risk is expected to jeopardise the investigation and the collection of evidence. Even in this case, information can, however, be denied at the latest until the evidence at risk has been gathered.[89] Moreover, national law can provide for further limitations, *e.g.* restricting the access to the file solely to the lawyer. Although the European Court has acknowledged the lawfulness of this limitation on various occasions,[90] this solution can be justified in the case of risks to the ongoing inquiry, particularly in the field of organised crime.

A delicate issue is whether the European Convention allows for the prosecutor to decide what information the suspect should be permitted to access. A number of countries empower the prosecutorial authority to withhold from the defence the information gathered during the pre-trial investigations, which power can be justified not only on ground of procedural economy (*e.g.*, if certain information turned out to be of no relevance for the proceedings) but also for human rights purposes, such as the need to respect the private life of individuals not involved in the ongoing inquiry.[91] Notwithstanding the indisputable relevance of such interests, the main question is who should decide whether and to what extent relevant pieces of information can be withheld from the accused.[92] It is clear that leaving this decision in the hands of the prosecutorial authority entails great risks for the defence. Knowing the incriminating evidence may also be of utmost importance to enable the defendants to challenge the relevance of the information taken by the investigative bodies.

To avoid the dangers of arbitrary selection, prosecutors should 'disclose to the defence all material evidence for or against the accused'.[93] The Strasbourg Court adopted this approach in *Edwards v. United Kingdom*, notwithstanding that it found no infringement of the Convention by considering that the lack of information had been remedied in the second instance. Although this radical solution can be in principle justified where coercive means are adopted against the suspect, such a solution can jeopardise the right to privacy of third parties and the goals of the ongoing investigation. At the early stages of the pre-trial inquiry, a selection of the information gathered is unavoidable in order not to frustrate the goals of the investigation. This does not entail, however, that the prosecutor has an unlimited

---

[89]Weigend (2000), p. 385.

[90]ECtHR, *Kremzow v. Austria*.

[91]Trechsel (2005), p. 225.

[92]*Ibid.*, 225 f.

[93]ECtHR, *Edwards v. United Kingdom*, § 36.

power of selection and, even more, that the prosecutorial authority is the most appropriate body to strike the delicate balances concerned with the disclosure of investigative materials. An alternative could be to restrict the disclosure solely to the information favourable to the defence. This solution, despite being proposed by some commentators on the Convention,[94] raises the problem of what information should be deemed 'favourable' to the defence and who should decide it. For instance, the accused may have interest in knowing incriminating evidence given by an unreliable witness.[95]

Notwithstanding the findings of the *Edwards* judgment, it does not appear that the European Convention rules out limited forms of information on the available evidence. This approach was confirmed in the *Jasper* case, in which the Court pointed out that the limitations on the right to know prosecutorial evidence must be restricted to a minimal extent and that the competent authority must adopt proper means to compensate for them.[96] In the light of this, one can affirm that the European Convention requires that clear criteria be established to determine the extent to which limitations can be tolerated and that an independent body be charged with the task of balancing the interests concerned with the selection of the information that can be disclosed to the defence.[97] On the other hand, it has been noted that the Strasbourg case-law requires the contracting states to put in place the necessary tools to allow a proactive participation not only of the accused but also of the prosecutor. In particular, the fact that both of them must be given the opportunity to know and comment on the observations filed and the evidence adduced by other parties confirms the existence of a strict link between the right to active participation in criminal proceedings and the principle of equality of arms. The particular focus on the *par condicio* principle, furthermore, has often led to the Court calling for a balance between the right to active participation and other interests acknowledged by the Convention. In this way, the Court avoids focusing exclusively on the accused's participation, while assessing the adequacy of the balance achieved in the light of the overall fairness of criminal proceedings.[98]

---

[94] Stavros (1993), p. 181 ff.

[95] Trechsel (2005), p. 229.

[96] ECtHR, *Jasper v. United Kingdom*.

[97] Trechsel (2005), p. 227.

[98] *Ibid.*, 93, who moreover considers the Court's self-restraint as realistic and unavoidable.

E. The Guarantee of a Fair Hearing and the Privilege Against Self-Incrimination

I. The Accused's Right to Be fairly Heard by an Independent Body and Qualitative Requirements of Pre-Trial Questionings

It may appear to be surprising that the European Convention does not expressly grant defendants a right to be fairly examined and that there es no a specific provision enabling them to make their voice heard in criminal proceedings. There is no doubt, however, that this guarantee lies at the heart of the Convention's understanding of a fair trial. It has observed that the very notion of a 'fair hearing', far from relating solely to the court proceedings, makes the criminal proceedings a listening space. It is noteworthy that not only does the accused have the right to be adjudicated by an independent and impartial body but furthermore that the judgment must be rendered in public. This safeguard is of utmost importance, highlighting both the need to allow for society to know the way criminal justice is administrated and the right of defendants to make their version of the facts publicly heard.

Doubtless, there is a strict link under the Convention between the right to be fairly heard and other fair trial rights. In particular, the right to be personally involved in a criminal trial not only enables the defendants to follow the court proceeding for themselves but also entails the competent authority granting them a fair opportunity to be heard. It has been observed that in the *Colozza* case, the Court, while dealing with the problem of *in absentia* procedures, had already stressed that the accused must at least be granted a fresh determination of the merits of the case 'from a court which has heard' him. Although this decision made it clear that giving the accused the opportunity to give evidence in his favour is a basic condition of a fair decision-making, the European case-law has not always been consistent with this approach. Again, the usual understanding of criminal proceedings as a whole has led the Strasbourg judges to allow for compensating means to be adopted in a higher instance.

We will note that the guarantee of a fair hearing becomes of utmost importance where restrictions on freedom are ongoing, which requires the arrested or detained person to be immediately brought before the judicial authority or another body enabled by national law to exercise judicial powers.[99] In this context, the European Court attaches particular weight to the need that the arrestee and detainee appear in person before the judicial authority, so that the court can be put in a position to hear their objections to the coercion measures adopted.[100]

On the other hand, the Convention lacks explicit indications of the requirements that should govern out-of-court hearings of the accused. However, in the first case in which the right to an impartial and independent tribunal was dealt with, the

---

[99] Art. 5(3) ECHR.

[100] Trechsel (2005), p. 514.

Strasbourg Court examined the lawfulness of a trial before a court presided over by a judge who had previously acted as a prosecutor in the same case.[101] It might be argued that the conviction of Belgium due to the infringement of Article 6 ECHR revealed a considerable mistrust not only towards the lawfulness of a court hearing conducted by a former prosecutor but also towards the ability of the authority in charge of the pre-trial investigations to ensure a fair hearing to the suspect. Yet police and prosecutorial questionings are often a necessary step of criminal inquiries and it is debatable whether a prosecution can be instituted without the suspect having been given the opportunity of giving evidence in his favour. In the light of this, there is also a need for the main fair trial guarantees to be extended to pre-trial hearings. Remarkably, in the *John Murray* case, the European Court pointed out that Article 6 ECHR also allows for the accused to benefit from the assistance of a lawyer at the initial stage of police interrogation, although this can be restricted for good cause in a specific case.[102] This conclusion, which was further developed in subsequent cases,[103] led to the acknowledgment of the suspect's right to communicate with the counsel prior to the investigative hearing.

II. Prosecutorial Needs and the Right of Individuals Other than the Accused to Make Their Voice Heard in Criminal Proceedings

The wide-ranging conception of the right to a fair hearing by the Strasbourg case-law raises the further question of whether the guarantee of a fair examination should be to the accused. At first glance, there are no provisions in the Convention concerned with the right to a fair examination of other individuals involved in a criminal inquiry. We will note, however, that the Strasbourg case-law increasingly calls for delicate balances among conflicting interests in the field of the right to confrontation.[104] For the purposes of the present discussion, it can be anticipated that the Strasbourg Court has always avoided a formalistic approach to evidence law, allowing for untested evidence or incriminating evidence obtained through anonymous testimony to be used at trial, albeit only under certain conditions. The extent to which this information can be admitted in court has considerably increased in the recent European case-law since the *Al-Khawaja and Tahery* judgment, which has enhanced the weight of evidence given by absent witnesses.[105]

Of course, it is not easy to determine the extent to which the right to confrontation should be balanced with the need to avoid the waste of relevant information. However, it is also apparent that the increasing importance attached to untested

[101]ECtHR, *Piersack v. Belgium*. See Trechsel (2005), p. 66 f.

[102]ECtHR, *John Murray v. United Kingdom.*

[103]See, among others, ECtHR, *Magee v. United Kingdom.*

[104]*Below*, F.II.1.

[105]*Below*, F.III.3.b.

evidence and to the information taken through alternative means of confrontation highlights the Court's interest in preserving the voice of other individuals who can no longer appear in court. This does not mean legitimising the unconditional use of untested evidence regardless of the grounds for the unavailability of the witness or the victim. Even in its former case-law, the Court had been particularly keen to scrutinise the reasons for the impossibility of confrontation with the accused. As we will note, the protection of the interest in ensuring a fair hearing to specific types of witnesses can also require technical arrangements to avoid a face-to-face confrontation with the alleged offender (*e.g.* by hiding the witness's identity). An enlightening example is *Doorson v. The Netherlands*, in which the Court stressed the need to balance the accused's right to confrontation not only with the need to save useful information for the fact-finding but also with the protection of the human rights of other individuals involved in a criminal trial during their examination.[106] The need for such solutions increases in cases of vulnerable witnesses and especially in cases of victims of sexual offences. The European case-law has always shown a protective approach to vulnerable individuals by calling for forms of out-of-court examination with a view to granting them a fair opportunity to be heard.[107]

III. The Right Not to Be Heard in Criminal Justice. Developments in the Principle of **nemo tenetur se detegere**

The right to be fairly heard, moreover, has another important aspect in criminal proceedings, that is, the right to decide to what extent one should give evidence when examined. In particular, the question arises whether and under which conditions the individuals involved in criminal proceedings hold the right not to give evidence against themselves. In this respect, the *audi alteram partem* rule highlights another important feature, namely the right not to be compelled to incriminate oneself. Certainly, a human rights-oriented model of criminal justice cannot tolerate that individuals will be used for investigative purposes to the point that they would be forced to give evidence against themselves.

Unlike the International Covenant,[108] the European Convention does not provide explicit provisions in this regard. Yet the principle *nemo tenetur se detegere* holds great relevance in the Strasbourg case-law, which has long filled the legal lacuna by developing a comprehensive jurisprudence on the conditions under which individuals can claim their right not to be compelled to incriminate themselves. The first judgment in which the European Court acknowledged the privilege against self-incrimination was *Funke v. France*.[109] According to the Strasbourg judges, this

[106] ECtHR, *Doorson v. The Netherlands*.

[107] ECtHR, *S.N. v. Sweden*.

[108] Art. 14(3)(g) ICCPR.

[109] ECtHR, *Funke v. France*.

principle lies at the heart of the right to a fair hearing, providing a general guarantee against the use of abusive coercion by the competent authority.[110] As the Grand Chamber put it in *Saunders v. United Kingdom*, the *nemo tenetur* principle is also an expression of the presumption of innocence.[111] Since these judgments, the European Court has further developed the *nemo tenetur* principle in a considerable number of cases, while progressively broadening its scope of protection. As a result, not only can defendants claim their right not to be compelled to make a confession against themselves on facts already under prosecution[112] but under certain circumstances they can also refuse to answer any question and even to go to the witness box.[113] Significantly, this broad understanding of the privilege against self-incrimination has led the Court to extend the right to silence to individuals not charged with a suspicion of guilt. This especially applies to the witness who refuses to give evidence on facts that, despite not being under investigation, could lead to their conviction in a future criminal proceeding.[114]

A delicate question is whether the privilege against self-incrimination can be invoked where coercion is needed to protect other human rights acknowledged by the Convention. In *Gäfgen v. Germany*, the Grand Chamber was called upon to examine whether the threat of intolerable pain by a police officer could be accepted to save a child's life. Despite acknowledging the justification of the officer's conduct, the Court pointed out that

> the prohibition on ill-treatment of a person applies irrespective of the conduct of the victim or the motivation of the authorities. Torture, inhuman or degrading treatment cannot be inflicted even in circumstances where the life of an individual is at risk. No derogation is allowed even in the event of a public emergency threatening the life of the nation.[115]

This case-law makes it clear that, far from restricting the scope of the *nemo tenetur* principle, unlawful coercion, even if needed to save another human being, results in another breach of the Convention, namely in the prohibition of inhuman treatment. It is noteworthy that, according to the Court, the fact that 'the threats of deliberate and imminent ill-treatment were made in the context of the applicant being in the custody of law-enforcement officials, apparently handcuffed', put the suspect 'in a state of vulnerability'.[116]

Notwithstanding its great importance, however, the *nemo tenetur* principle does not ensure unconditional protection to the individuals involved in a criminal law

---

[110] Zacchè (2008), p. 181.

[111] ECtHR, Grand Chamber, *Saunders v. United Kingdom*. See Trechsel (2005), p. 348.

[112] ECtHR, *Lückhof and Spanner v. Austria*.

[113] Zacchè (2008), p. 180.

[114] The question was dealt with in *Serves v. Italy*, in which the Court did not engage, however, in assessing whether the investigating judge's decision to summon the applicant to appear as a witness rather than charging him, due to the existence of substantial evidence against him, gave rise to a coercion incompatible with the privilege against self-incrimination.

[115] ECtHR, Grand Chamber, *Gäfgen v. Germany*, § 107.

[116] *Ibid.*, § 106.

action. Although the privilege against self-incrimination does not entirely coincide with the right to silence,[117] the European Court traditionally confined its protective scope, as a rule, to situations in which individuals could claim their right to silence.[118] As a result, the Strasbourg case-law excluded from the area of the *nemo tenetur* principle the use of information gathered independently from the accused's will,[119] such as a blood sample for the purposes of a DNA analysis[120] or a vocal sample with a view to a confrontation.[121]

This does not mean, however, that the protection of the privilege against self-incrimination provided by the Convention should remain circumscribed to the area of oral evidence.[122] In the *Funke* case, the European Court had already found that the attempt of the competent authority to compel the applicant to hand over documents that could incriminate him infringed the Convention.[123] More recently, the *Jalloh* judgment led to a further development of European case-law, which stressed that the use of evidence obtained through interference with the physical integrity of the person gives rise to a double breach of the Convention.[124] In this case, the question at stake was whether national courts could administrate emetics in order to force the applicant to regurgitate the drugs he had swallowed and whether the evidence obtained by this means could be used to convict him. Although the Court acknowledged that the administration of emetics was lawful under domestic law, it did not hesitate to consider this measure an inhuman treatment, convicting Germany for the violation of both Article 3 and Article 6 ECHR because of the use of the information gathered. This judgment is of utmost importance not only because of its conclusions but also because it opened up unprecedented perspectives for a more modern understanding of the relationship between the *nemo tenetur* principle and the taking of biological materials by coercive means.[125]

Even if the scope of application of the *nemo tenetur* principle overlaps with the right to silence, moreover, the Court makes the infringement of the privilege against self-incrimination conditional on the nature and degree of the compulsion as well as on the existence of any relevant safeguards in national proceedings.[126] An interesting question concerns the relevance of the accused's silence for the purposes of the decision-making. The Court dealt with this issue for the first time in the *John Murray* case. In this important ruling, the European judges, while stressing that the

---

[117] Trechsel (2005), p. 342.
[118] Zacchè (2008), p. 183.
[119] ECtHR, Grand Chamber, *Jalloh v. Germany*, § 102.
[120] ECtHR, Grand Chamber, *O'Halloran and Francis v. United Kingdom.*
[121] ECtHR, *P.G. and J.H. v. United Kingdom.*
[122] Trechsel (2005), p. 342.
[123] ECtHR, *Funke v. France.*
[124] ECtHR, Grand Chamber, *Jalloh v. Germany*, § 102.
[125] Zacchè (2008), p. 190 f.
[126] ECtHR, Grand Chamber, *Jalloh v. Germany*, § 102.

right to silence is not an absolute guarantee,[127] examined whether English law, which allowed for the decision-makers to draw inferences from the failure to appear in court and to give evidence, was compatible with the right of a fair hearing. In this regard, the Court pointed out that two main interests should be taken into consideration. First, the *nemo tenetur* principle cannot prevent the accused's silence from being 'taken into account in assessing the persuasiveness of the evidence adduced by the prosecution'.[128] Second, the privilege against self-incrimination prevents the decision-makers from basing the conviction 'solely or mainly on the accused's silence or on a refusal to answer questions or to give evidence himself'.[129] According to the Court, a proper balance between these two interests should avoid a violation of Article 6 ECHR.

Although the *John Murray* doctrine was confirmed in subsequent judgments,[130] it gives rise to serious human rights concerns. Of course, national law can provide for various means to require witnesses or co-defendants to give evidence on the matters on which they are questioned, and their silence or incomplete statements can lead to the institution of criminal proceedings against them. However, as noted in relation to Italian law, it appears to be rather contradictory that, on the one hand, individuals can claim their right to silence on issues that may lead to their criminal liability being declared in another proceeding and, on the other, their silence can be adversely evaluated against them.

The main concern, moreover, regards the application of the sole and decisive evidence doctrine in the field of the right to silence, which leaves the door open for serious consequences, provided that further evidence supports the inferences drawn from the conduct of the person examined. On close examination, this application of the sole or decisive evidence doctrine further blurs the Court's approach to the law of evidence. We will see that the decisiveness test governed the traditional approach of the Strasbourg case-law to the guarantee of confrontation in the case of absent and anonymous witnesses, with a view to protecting the accused against the use of untested evidence or evidence taken in any case by means of alternative forms of confrontation.[131] The extension of this approach to the area of the privilege against self-incrimination considerably lowered the human rights protection of the individuals concerned, in that the fairness of the proceedings is only undermined in the case of main or exclusive use not just of evidence but of the arguments deduced by the silence of the person examined. Yet silence is by definition a neutral event that cannot be interpreted in any direction, so that it is rarely conceivable that there can be evidence supporting it.

It is noteworthy that the Court partially departed from this approach while dealing with the relevance in criminal proceedings of statements obtained during an administrative investigation. In this regard, the Strasbourg judges acknowledged

---

[127]ECtHR, *John Murray v. United Kingdom*, § 47.

[128]*Ibid.*

[129]*Ibid.*

[130]See, *inter alia*, ECtHR, *Condron v. United Kingdom*.

[131]*Below*, F.III.3.a.

that administrative or inspective authorities are not called upon to comply with the same guarantees of criminal proceedings during their investigations, as it would hamper the effective regulation in the public interest of complex financial and commercial activities.[132] Nevertheless, the use of evidence obtained under compulsion by an administrative authority with coercive powers, which do not leave the individuals examined free to decide whether and to what extent they can answer the questions, cannot be deemed to be compatible with the right to a fair hearing.[133] In *Saunders v. United Kingdom*, the Grand Chamber, starting with the differences between administrative and criminal inquiries, further broadened the scope of protection of the *nemo tenetur* principle beyond the sphere of incriminating evidence, stressing that

> the right not to incriminate oneself cannot reasonably be confined to statements of admission of wrongdoing or to remarks which are directly incriminating. Testimony obtained under compulsion which appears on its face to be of a non-incriminating nature – such as exculpatory remarks or mere information on questions of fact – may later be deployed in criminal proceedings in support of the prosecution case, for example to contradict or cast doubt upon other statements of the accused or evidence given by him during the trial or to otherwise undermine his credibility. Where the credibility of an accused must be assessed by a jury the use of such testimony may be especially harmful. It follows that what is of the essence in this context is the use to which evidence obtained under compulsion is put in the course of the criminal trial.[134]

This acknowledgment contrasts with the Court's common assumption that the privilege against self-incrimination is not an absolute right.[135] On close examination, the *Saunders* judgment makes it clear that a violation of the Convention can arise even if the information gathered was not used in criminal proceedings to incriminate the defendants or did not provide a decisive contribution to convict them. This conclusion counteracts the idea that defendants must only be protected against the sole and decisive use of incriminating evidence obtained against their will.

F. Defence's Contribution to the Evidence-Gathering and the Requirements of a Fair Decision-Making

I. Premise

It is widely recognised that the European Convention neither contains specific rules on the collection of criminal evidence nor consequently ensures to the individuals

---

[132]ECtHR, Grand Chamber, *Saunders v. United Kingdom*, § 67.

[133]ECtHR, *Shannon v. United Kingdom*.

[134]ECtHR, Grand Chamber, *Saunders v. United Kingdom*, § 67.

[135]Trechsel (2005), p. 344.

involved in criminal proceedings the right to contribute to the criminal inquiry and the decision-making. Moreover, the European Court has on several occasions pointed out that the admission of evidence is in principle a matter of national law.[136] However, some of the fair trial rights of the individuals charged with a criminal offence clearly reveal their right to be involved in the taking of evidence. As noted, both the information on the charge and the access to the prosecutorial file also hold specific relevance from this viewpoint, as does the right to be assisted by an interpreter in order to follow the court hearings. Furthermore, whereas the Convention grants the accused the right to obtain the examination of exculpatory witnesses,[137] the Strasbourg case-law, as noted, has long acknowledged the privilege against self-incrimination, a guarantee of such importance that it goes far beyond the sphere of a criminal law action. Even more significantly, the Convention recognises the defendants' right to be confronted with their accuser,[138] which not only constitutes an individual safeguard but also the core method of evidence-gathering in modern criminal justice.[139]

In the light of this, it would probably more exact to say that the Convention's approach to the law of evidence should be interpreted within its general understanding of the right to a fair hearing. This approach can also explain the longstanding tendency of European case-law to deal with the right to confrontation from the viewpoint of the proof of guilt rather than from that of the taking of evidence. This does not mean that the Strasbourg case-law exclusively focuses on the probative value of criminal evidence, while overlooking the complex challenges concerned especially with new forms of evidence-gathering. As anticipated, the Court has increasingly provided indications on alternative means of confrontation in a clear attempt to strike a balance with the need to protect the person examined. Ultimately, it has been noted that the Strasbourg case-law has also attached great weight to the argumentative contribution of the defence to the decision-making.

For the sake of clarity, I shall focus on three main areas, namely (a) the defence's involvement in the taking of evidence, (b) the use of untested evidence for the purposes of the proof of guilt and (c) the argumentative contribution of private parties to the decision-making.

---

[136] ECtHR, *Doorson v. The Netherlands.*

[137] Art. 6(3)(d) ECHR.

[138] *Ibid.*

[139] According to *Trechsel* the right to confrontation is the only guarantee specifically concerned with criminal evidence. Cf. Trechsel (2005), p. 293.

II. Participation Rights in the Collection of Criminal Evidence

1. The Right to Confrontation and the Need for an Overall Balance of Conflicting Interests in Criminal Proceedings

The right to be confronted with the accuser is of such high importance that it is enshrined not only in various Constitutions[140] but also in most international human rights charters, albeit with some different features.[141] The right to confrontation also has a strict link with other fair trial guarantees. In particular, the right to be present at trial enables the defendants to give their own contribution to the examining of prosecutorial witnesses, either by putting questions themselves, if allowed by national law, or by suggesting new issues to be examined by their counsel. This explains why the Court emphasises the requirement that confrontation normally take place in the presence of the accused.[142] Moreover, the knowledge of the accusation and possibility of setting up a proper defence strategy are necessary conditions of effective confrontation, which in turn requires that the accused be given adequate legal assistance.

At a deeper level still, we have seen that the right to confrontation is at the centre of a complex web of conflicting interests, which goes far beyond the fair trial rights of just the defendant. On the one hand, the possibility of the defendant being confronted with their accuser not only strengthens their right to an effective defence but is also the necessary condition for a reliable fact-finding and a fair decision-making.[143] On the other, the accused's right to confrontation must be balanced with the protection of the fundamental rights of other individuals and even of the accuser, especially if the latter is in a vulnerable position.

2. Methods of Confrontation

a) Direct and Indirect Examination

It has been observed that the link between the guarantee of confrontation and the right to personally participate in criminal proceedings is not only justified by the need to ensure the physical presence of the accused at the examination of prosecutorial witnesses but also by the fact that the accused holds the right to contribute to

[140] As noted, the Italian fair trial reform of 1999 enacted the right to confrontation into Article 111 of the Constitution. Outside Europe, the US Constitution still contains one of the most significant expressions of the right to confrontation. Over the last decade, the Sixth Amendment to the US Constitution has been re-interpreted by the US Supreme Court from the aforementioned landmark decision *Crawford v. Washington* onwards.

[141] For a comparative overview cf. Trechsel (2005), p. 291.

[142] ECtHR, *Asch v. Austria*.

[143] Trechsel (2005), p. 292 f.

the taking of incriminating evidence. Moreover, like the International Covenant,[144] the European Convention ensures to the accused the right either to examine or to 'have examined the witnesses against him'. At first glance, this solution reflects the alternative between self-defence and legal assistance, allowing for the examination of incriminating witnesses by the defence lawyer in the countries that do not enable defendants to cross-examine prosecutorial witnesses. On close examination, the drafters of the European Convention aimed at striking a compromise between two main forms of confrontation existent in the European countries, which broadly correspond to cross-examination, typical of common-law countries, conducted by the parties and the continental tradition of witness's examination conducted by a third body (presiding judge of the tribunal, investigating magistrate, etc.).[145] In this light, the Convention ensures a broad protective umbrella, allowing for both direct and indirect examination of incriminating witnesses, provided that the defence rights are properly satisfied and effective confrontation in the accused's interests is ensured.

The Court has further broadened the guarantee of Article 6(3)(d) ECHR, to an extent, however, which is questionable from a human rights perspective. In *Isgrò v. Italy*, the Strasbourg case-law ruled out a violation of the Convention even in the case of direct confrontation between the witness and the accused, although the latter was not assisted by counsel.[146] Doubtless, this solution largely frustrates the humanitarian goal of the right to confrontation, while underestimating the importance of the lawyer's presence with a view to the effectiveness of the right to a defence.[147] Even more delicate problems arise in case of indirect examination. It is debatable whether the examination conducted by an independent authority can satisfy the requirements of effective confrontation, even though the parties are allowed to be present at the court hearing and can forward eventual questions to the witness through the judge. This is especially true if the defence lawyer's is only allowed to put a few additional questions, after the witness has been long examined by the judicial authority.[148] To be sure, we will note that judicial hearing often provides the best solution so as not to jeopardise fundamental rights of other individuals. Yet there is little doubt that judicial examination cannot grant the defence the same opportunities as direct confrontation.

Furthermore, indirect confrontation poses serious problems even when incriminating witnesses are cross-examined by the lawyer. In particular, doubt arises as to whether court-appointed lawyers, who have never had the opportunity to contact their clients, can properly represent them in the examination of the accusers. Of course, there cannot be abstract answers to this delicate question, which highlights, however, a tension in which the failure to provide the accused with the opportunity

---

[144]Art. 14(3)(e) ICCPR.

[145]Trechsel (2005), p. 311. Similarly cf. Maffei (2012), p. 17; Spencer (2014), p. 48.

[146]ECtHR, *Isgrò v. Italy*, § 36.

[147]Trechsel (2005), p. 310.

[148]Jackson and Summers (2012), p. 349.

to be present at trial inevitably affects the effective exercise of the right to confrontation. Further human rights concerns arise in the area of the recent developments occurred in the European case-law in relation to terrorism-related procedures.[149] By extending for the first time the findings of the Grand Chamber's judgment *A. et al. v. United Kingdom*[150] to criminal justice, the European Court has recently stressed that the *habeas corpus* safeguards must be adapted to the specific challenges relating to terrorist crimes, as the ordinary requirements set by Article 5 (1)(c) ECHR

> should not be applied in such a manner as to put disproportionate difficulties in the way of the police authorities in taking effective measures to counter organised terrorism in discharge of their duty under the Convention to protect the right to life and the right to bodily security of members of the public.[151]

From this it follows that Article 5(4) ECHR still requires national authorities to disclose adequate information to enable the detained individuals to know the nature of the allegations against them and have the opportunity to produce exculpatory evidence. Moreover, the detainee and his lawyer should be put in a position to effectively participate in the court proceedings concerning continued detention. In the *Sher et al.* Case, however, the Court made it clear that the Convention 'cannot require disclosure of such material or preclude the holding of a closed hearing to allow a court to consider confidential material'.[152] This conclusion, while extending the scope of *in camera* hearings to substantial issues,[153] confirms the lawfulness—even in the field of criminal justice—of national arrangements aimed at disclosing confidential evidence solely to a 'special advocate'. From this result the way is short to a decision on guilt based, albeit partially, on confidential evidence examined by informants through a special advocate procedure, and it is debatable whether this solution can truly fulfil the requirements of the right to confrontation.

b) Anonymous Witnesses and the Use of Alternative Means of Confrontation

Traditionally, the Strasbourg Court acknowledged that, as a matter of principle, all evidence should be produced not only in the presence of the accused but 'at a public hearing with a view to adversarial argument'.[154] Depending on the circumstances of the case, however, these ideal conditions may not be technically feasible, especially in the case of witnesses resident abroad. Most significantly, the court examination does not always positively contribute to a reliable fact-finding, the public hearing enhancing the pressure at least of particular types of witnesses. At the national

---

[149]For in-depth analysis see Vogel (2017), p. 28 f.

[150]ECtHR, Grand Chamber, *A. et al. v. United Kingdom.*

[151]ECtHR, *Sher et al. v. United Kingdom*, § 149.

[152]*Ibid.*

[153]For further criticisms cf. Vogel (2017), p 29 ff.

[154]ECtHR, *Asch v. Austria.*

level, we have noted that different arrangements are increasingly adopted either to obtain evidence at risk or to avoid the negative repercussions of a trial confrontation on the person examined.

Delicate problems arise in cases in which there is a concrete risk that prosecutorial witnesses were scared of either the defendants or people from their environment, as well as in the case of witnesses for whom a particular need of protection of their identity and physical integrity arises (*e.g.*, undercover agents). Since in these situations a face-to-face confrontation with the alleged offender would certainly expose the person examined to great risks, we have seen that national law generally provides for alternative forms of questioning prosecutorial witnesses—especially anonymous testimony, often coupled with special programmes of witness protection.

This problematic area allows us to observe one of the more interesting developments in the European case-law that, as anticipated, has led the Court to include the right to confrontation in the overall set of human rights enshrined in the Convention. Since the landmark decision *Doorson v. The Netherlands*, the Court has required enhanced protection of the witness and the victim, while stressing the need to ascertain the impact of a direct confrontation on the fundamental human rights of individuals other than the defendant.[155] This approach calls for a balance between the right to confrontation and other essential interests acknowledged by the Convention, especially the right to life and physical integrity, which cannot certainly deemed to be a prerogative of the accused. Where the arrangements adopted at the national level aim at preserving the witness's anonymity, the Court not only rules out that the evidence obtained by this means can solely or decisively be used for the conviction but also stresses that the difficulties caused to the defence must be properly counterbalanced.[156]

In this light, the Court has always attached particular importance to the assessment of the justification of anonymity and the measures applied to compensate for the lack of direct confrontation. In the *Doorson* judgment, the Strasbourg judges justified the witness's anonymity on the grounds of the risks of threat and violence arising from drug dealers and the experience previously suffered by one of the witnesses. Although this did not automatically lead to the acknowledgement of the lawfulness of the anonymous testimony, the Court deemed the domestic solution a proper arrangement, since an investigative judge who knew the identity of the anonymous witnesses examined them in the presence of the defendant's lawyer who, despite not being able to verify their identity, was allowed to submit questions.[157]

Notwithstanding the focus on the need for rigorous justification of the reasons for anonymity, the flexible logic of the Strasbourg case-law has led to different

[155]ECtHR, *Doorson v. The Netherlands*. On the importance of this judgment see among others Chiavario (2008), p. 21. More recently cf. ECtHR, *Bocos-Cuesta v. The Netherlands*.

[156]ECtHR, *van Mechelen v. The Netherlands*, §§ 54 et seq.

[157]ECtHR, *Doorson v. The Netherlands*, § 60.

results depending on the weight attached to the interests at stake. Where the primary grounds for anonymity are the need to preserve the identity of undercover informants, anonymity should have extensive justification. Here, a direct confrontation in a public hearing would jeopardise the ongoing undercover inquiry, while exposing the agents examined and their relatives to great risks. The question was dealt with in *van Mechelen v. The Netherlands*, in which, however, the European judges considered the domestic arrangements to be inadequate, although both the defendant und his counsel had been placed in an adjacent room and could follow the witness' examination and ask questions.[158] This result was probably influenced by the fact that the witnesses were police officers. It was a rather unfortunate conclusion, taking into consideration that the Convention's protection of the right to life, physical integrity and security must certainly be ensured to all the persons involved in a criminal law action. It is noteworthy that the Strasbourg Court has broadened the trade-offs concerned with the right to confrontation even beyond the sphere of the parties of the proceedings in a strict sense, taking on the protection of the families of prosecutorial witnesses and their next of kin.[159]

The direct form of confrontation in a public hearing, furthermore, can be inadequate in the case of minor witnesses. Here also, anonymity can be an effective means of avoiding undue risks for the person to be examined. The question was dealt with in *S.N. v. Sweden*, where the Court accepted the national arrangements, since the alleged victim of sexual acts—namely, a boy of 11 years old who was afraid of being faced with his accuser in a trial hearing—was first interviewed by the police who videotaped the questioning. The defence had the opportunity to watch the tape and pose questions with a view to a second examination, which took place at the boy's home. This interview was recorded only on audiotape and took place in the presence the victim's parents, while the applicant's lawyer was allowed neither to be present nor to follow it in an adjacent room. The Court, however, found no violation of the right to confrontation, since the defendant's lawyer failed to request the videotaping of the interview and had in any case the opportunity to hear the audiotape and check the transcripts.[160]

This judgment is of utmost importance from a methodological viewpoint, confirming the Court's engagement in the protection of vulnerable witnesses, notwithstanding the differences existing between various situations. It must be acknowledged, however, that the arrangement found by the Swedish authorities was not the best that one could imagine. Certainly, a connection in real time would have enabled the defence to follow the witnesses' examination and to immediately react to their answers.[161] It is to be welcomed, therefore, that in more recent cases

[158]ECtHR, *van Mechelen v. The Netherlands.*

[159]Trechsel (2005), p. 319 f.

[160]ECtHR, *S.N. v. Sweden*, § 49.

[161]Trechsel (2005), p. 322.

the Strasbourg judges allowed for defendants or their lawyers, properly informed, to follow the hearing by means of a video-recording and with the further possibility of contextual or subsequent questions.[162]

3. The Right to Confrontation and Inconsistent Testimony

Different problems arise when prosecutorial witnesses are cross-examined by the defence in court but give evidence inconsistent with their previous statements gathered out of court (i.e., in the pre-trial phases of the same proceedings or in other proceedings). Despite the lack of explicit rules in the European Convention, the European Court had a few opportunities to examine this issue, providing some important methodological indications.[163]

The first case in which the Court dealt with the problem was again *Doorson v. The Netherlands*, where it ruled out that it can be decided in abstract terms whether

> evidence given by a witness in open court and on oath should always be relied on in preference to other statements made by the same witness in the course of criminal proceedings, not even when the two are in conflict.[164]

Almost 4 years later, the European case-law confirmed this approach in another decision, in which it added an important clarification. In *Camilleri v. Malta*, the Court stressed that the opportunity for the applicant to cross-examine prosecutorial witnesses before the Magistrates' Court had allowed him to request clarifications on the reasons the witnesses' testimony had changed. According to the Strasbourg judges, this enabled him to 'undermine the probative value' of the previous incriminating statement, thus widely compensating 'any alleged disadvantage which may have resulted from the fact that the statement was made in circumstances in which he was unable to challenge its veracity'.[165]

One might argue that these conclusions, which led the Court to exclude a violation of the Convention in both cases, were the result of the flexible approach of the European case-law that, as noted, has never required confrontation always to take place at the time the incriminating evidence was given, although the defence could not be present. Yet this argument would be misleading. On close examination, European case-law may seem to avoid a formalistic understanding of the problem of inconsistent testimony, shifting again the focus from the formal value of out-of-court inconsistent evidence to the requirements of effective confrontation.

[162]ECtHR, *A.S. v. Finland*.

[163]On the importance of European case-law in this problematic area see Balsamo and Lo Piparo (2008), p. 362 f.; Spencer (2014), p. 53 ff.

[164]ECtHR, *Doorson v. The Netherlands*, § 78.

[165]ECtHR, *Camilleri v. Malta*.

III. *The Right to Confrontation and the Proof of Guilt*

1. Premise

These developments allow us to understand properly the approach followed by Strasbourg case-law in relation to the defence's contribution to the decision on guilt. The aforementioned requirement that the evidence should, as a rule, be obtained 'in the presence of the accused at a public hearing with a view to adversarial argument' raises the question of the relevance that the European Convention attaches to the information collected out of court for the purposes of the fact-finding. This is a very delicate question especially in continental countries, which are still largely characterised by the dominant role of pre-trial inquiries and consequently by the widespread use of the information gathered by investigative bodies. The analysis of the Strasbourg case-law requires us to examine two main questions. The first one is whether and to what extent out-of-court evidence gathered without the accused's participation can be admitted at trial where the defendants had the opportunity to be confronted with their accuser at a later stage of the proceedings. The second question concerns the opposite situation in which confrontation has never taken place.

2. Out-of-Court Confrontations and the Use of Evidence Obtained Without the Defence's Participation in the Case of Subsequent Confrontation

The first question leads us to examine the problem of the context of confrontation. To a great extent, the trial provides the best conditions for the parties to have the opportunity to contribute to the evidence-gathering, a procedure that in several continental countries is still widely conducted by the same body called upon to decide on the merits of the case.[166] For the same reasons, the guarantee of confrontation must also be satisfied before a higher instance, especially where the competent court can re-examine the merits and even overrule the acquittal issued at the first instance by convicting the accused for the first time.[167]

It has been observed, however, that the Strasbourg Court has never emphasised this approach to the extent that it deemed the trial confrontation to be the only solution compatible with the Convention. As was stressed in *Asch v. Austria*, confrontation in open court can be an unachievable or undesirable result. Especially when oral evidence is collected at the early stage of the pre-trial inquiry, often no suspect has yet been found. In the case of serious organised crimes, the prompt (out-of-court) collection of evidence by incriminating witnesses or co-defendants is usually of utmost importance both for a clear reconstruction of complex situations

[166]Trechsel (2005), p. 305 f.

[167]*Ibid.*, 309.

and in order to avoid undue risks for the person examined. In the case of minor witnesses, furthermore, the more time passes, the greater the risk is of weakness and loss of memory, which requires the collection of testimonial evidence not to be excessively delayed from the time of the events. In more general terms, the first hearing often constitutes a rather unique occasion for a reliable fact-finding, providing essential information that will be the basis of further statements by the same person in subsequent stages of the proceedings. This enhances the need to grant defendants a fair opportunity for confrontation with their potential accusers at the pre-trial stage,[168] even if through technical means.

As noted, European countries are more and more aware of these problems, providing a number of different means to anticipate the taking of urgent evidence. In order to avoid the shortcomings of delayed collection of oral evidence, common law countries traditionally aim to ensure the most rapid institution of the court proceedings possible.[169] By contrast, we have noted that various continental countries still have long and complex pre-trial inquiries, while providing for specific tools aimed at the collection of urgent evidence, such as the Italian *incidente probatorio*. Although the Strasbourg Court has not explicitly clarified whether the Convention also acknowledges the right to confrontation in the pre-trial phase, the positive answer was implicit in the decision *Imbrioscia v. Switzerland*, in which it ruled out a violation of the right to confrontation because neither the lawyer nor the defendant had asked to be present at the police questioning of a witness.[170] This approach confirms the existence of a positive aspect of the right to confrontation, which requires (as also highlighted in *S.N. v. Sweden*) a certain degree of diligence on the part of the defendants, who should request to be involved in the taking of evidence that will potentially be used against them. On the other hand, the Court's focus on the requirement that defendants be given a proper opportunity of confrontation at a later stage of the proceedings reveals a clear underestimation of the importance of the context in which confrontation should take place.[171] On close examination, the approach is similar to that adopted in relation to the right to personal participation, which, according to the Strasbourg case-law, can take place either at the time of the first questioning of (potentially) incriminating witnesses or in a subsequent phase.

The general favour towards the use of out-of-court evidence where defendants had a later opportunity of confrontation with their accuser is not unlimited, however, in the European case-law. In particular, the Court traditionally held that—where confrontation took place through alternative means, such as anonymous

[168] *Ibid.*, 307.

[169] For instance, Scotland has a historical 110 day rule within which serious cases must be brought to court. See s. 65 of the Criminal Procedure (Scotland) Act 1995. England and Wales lack exact time-limits on the institution of the trial phase, which has given rise to many criticisms. See, among others, Jackson and Johnstone (2005), p. 3 ff.; Vogler (2012), p. 96.

[170] In the same sense Trechsel (2005), p. 309.

[171] ECtHR, *Barberá, Messegué and Jabardo v. Spain*.

testimony—the defendants suffered from difficulties that hindered the full exercise of their defence rights. As a consequence, the evidence gathered in an anonymous hearing should never be the only or primary factor in support of the accused's conviction.[172] In recent years, however, the Court has largely departed from this rigorous approach by extending the *Al-Khawaja* doctrine to anonymous testimony.[173]

3. Absent Witnesses and the Use of Untested Evidence

a) The Traditional Approach of the Strasbourg Case-Law: The Sole and Decisive Evidence Doctrine

The second question concerns the use of evidence gathered without the defence's participation where confrontation could not take place at a later stage of the proceedings. There can be various grounds for the impossibility of confrontation. The European Court has long dealt with several cases of absent witnesses, i.e., (a) dead or seriously ill individuals, (b) untraceable people, (c) witnesses heard abroad by foreign authorities and (d) individuals who can claim their right to silence or who could be endangered by the trial examination.[174] These are very different situations, which partially overlap with some cases that we have already examined above. For instance, a risk to the life or the physical integrity of the person examined can not only concern vulnerable witnesses or undercover informants but also co-defendants, especially in the field of mafia-typed organised crime, as highlighted in *Lucà v. Italy*. In other cases, moreover, a trial confrontation is not impossible in a strict sense but can take place in the abstract, even though it can entail considerable difficulties. Certainly, technical arrangements can today help overcome a number of practical difficulties, *e.g.* in the case of witnesses resident abroad. Furthermore, even a real impossibility of confrontation can depend on very different factors, which can be unrelated to the witnesses' will (*e.g.*, death) or, by contrast, can be the result of their defence strategy (*e.g.*, the choice of the accused's relatives not to give incriminating evidence against him).

Notwithstanding these differences, the European Court has traditionally adopted a rather common approach by ruling that, if defendants had no opportunity to face their accusers in any phase of the proceedings, they cannot be convicted exclusively or mainly on the basis of untested evidence. At first glance, the sole and decisive evidence doctrine reflects the attempt to strike a compromise between a rigid interpretation of the right to confrontation and the cultural traditions of individual criminal justice systems, which have long been based on the use of untested

---

[172] ECtHR, *Doorson v. The Netherlands*, § 76; ECtHR, *van Mechelen v. The Netherlands*, § 55.

[173] ECtHR, *Ellis and Simms v. United Kingdom*, §§ 74 et seqq.; ECtHR, *Pesukic v. Switzerland*, §§ 45 et seqq.

[174] Balsamo and Lo Piparo (2008), p. 346.

evidence. On close examination, the Court largely departed from the formalistic approach to evidence law, shifting again the focus from the formal use to the probative value—and therefore to the assessment—of the information gathered without the accused's participation.

Furthermore, the sole and decisive evidence test reflects the general decision-making of the European Court, which is called upon to scrutinise individual cases after all the domestic instance have been exhausted and is therefore in a position to evaluate the 'decisive' weight attached to a piece of evidence in a concrete proceeding. On the other hand, this approach to the use of untested evidence may seem to be in line with usual understanding of the European Court of the fair trial guarantees as parts of the overall right to a fair hearing. It is worth observing, however, that this case-law is not entirely consistent with the Convention's approach to the law of evidence. In particular, a different approach was applied in the *Saunders* case, in which the Strasbourg Court, while also examining the privilege against self-incrimination in the light of the overall fairness of the procedure, found an infringement of the Convention solely on the grounds that the incriminating evidence was admitted at trial, regardless of whether it played a decisive role in the decision-making.[175] Significantly, the Strasbourg Court also found a breach of Article 6 ECHR in relation to the right to confrontation, because there were no sufficient reasons for the witnesses' absence, although their statements had not played a decisive role in the decision-making.[176]

b) The Developments in the European Case-Law After the *Al-Khawaja and Tahery* Judgment: The Progressive Softening of the Sole and Decisive Evidence Test

Over recent years, as anticipated, things have considerably changed in the field of the right to confrontation. Remarkably, changes began in relation to the problem of absent witnesses. In two recent cases jointly dealt with in the landmark judgement *Al-Khawaja and Tahery v. United Kingdom*, the Grand Chamber departed from the Court's traditional approach.[177] This judgement—issued after a heated confrontation between the Court's 4th Chamber and the English judiciary—led the European Court to overcome the 'Pillars of Hercules' of its jurisprudence on the right to confrontation. By dealing with the *Al-Khawaja* case, the Grand Chamber engaged in an in-depth analysis of English evidence law and of other common law countries, reconstructing the terms within which limited hearsay evidence can be admitted at trial. The conclusion was that the decisive use of testimonial evidence for the conviction of defendants who could never exercise their right to confrontation does not necessarily lead to the infringement of Article 6 ECHR, provided,

[175] ECtHR, *Saunders v. United Kingdom*.

[176] ECtHR, *Pello v. Estonia*.

[177] ECtHR, Grand Chamber, *Al-Khawaja and Tahery v. United Kingdom*.

however, that national law allows for adequate means to compensate the accused for the lack of confrontation and these means are properly applied in the case at hand.

This judgement is noteworthy from several viewpoints. Certainly, the *Al-Khawaja* doctrine has allowed the Court to enter the territory of admissibility of hearsay evidence, which was traditionally considered to be extraneous to the European Convention. To be sure, the Court did not formally deny the prohibition on the main or exclusive use of untested evidence. However, the centre of gravity in the Strasbourg's reasoning was shifted towards a different ascertainment, the Court scrutinising, as noted, whether national law provides for adequate mechanisms not only aimed at compensating for the lack of confrontation but also at preserving the reliability of pre-trial evidence.

To a certain extent, this unprecedented approach might be considered a further evolution of the case-law adopted in relation to anonymous witnesses. It has been observed that the European Court found no infringement of the Convention, as alternative forms of confrontation were adopted at the national level to balance the right to confrontation with the need to protect the physical integrity or life of witnesses and victims. The *Al-Khawaja* doctrine on absent witnesses solidifies the need to prevent a concrete risk for the fundamental rights of individuals other than the accused. The assessment of counterbalancing factors, however, here shifts the Court's focus towards the reliability of untested evidence. This approach was further developed in subsequent cases regarding not only absent witnesses[178] but also anonymous testimony.[179]

Ultimately, it is worth observing that the *Al-Khawaja* judgment entailed a significant extension of the decision-making of the Strasbourg Court. Whereas the sole and decisive evidence doctrine was largely based on the relevance attached to untested evidence by the national decision-makers, this case-law enables the Court to scrutinise the suitability of the arrangements made by the national authorities in order to counterbalance the lack of confrontation. In this way, the European Court can today evaluate—according to its own criteria—the adequacy of the domestic solutions and consequently the reliability of untested evidence.

IV. The Contribution of Private Parties to the Decision-Making. **Audi alteram partem** *Rule and Argumentation in Criminal Proceedings*

Finally, the analysis of the Strasbourg case-law allows us to observe another form of the parties' contribution to the decision-making, namely the argumentative role

[178]ECtHR, *Schatschaschwili v. Germany*.

[179]*Above*, F.III.2.

of the parties in the fact-finding. To a great extent, this side of the *audi alteram partem* rule overlaps with other issues examined above. It has been noted that the right to know and make observations on the file and the evidence adduced by other parties lies at the heart of the right to confrontation. This can explain why the European Court has generally viewed in a negative way national authorities unconditionally depriving the defence of the possibility of examining relevant pieces of evidence. On close examination, denying defendants the access to the file and to relevant evidence not only undermines their right to take part actively in the taking of evidence but also to produce new arguments to challenge the charge filed against them.

In this context, the Strasbourg Court found a violation of the right to a fair hearing in a case in which national law did not enable defendants to reply and make observations on the prosecutorial allegations.[180] Significantly, in most legal systems defendants must generally be granted the last word.[181] The Court also focused on the argumentative contribution of the parties in the proceedings before higher courts. As noted, in *Quadrelli v. Italy*, the Strasbourg Court found an infringement of Article 6 ECHR since the Italian Supreme Court had failed to consider a defence's memorandum.[182] The increasing role of parties' argumentation in the European case-law was probably the consequence the growing importance attached to the demonstrative value of oral evidence gathered in the pre-trial phases as an alternative to the approach, widespread in various European countries, based on rigid exclusionary rules.

A delicate question is whether the Convention also protects the accused's right to argue on the legal characterisation of the alleged offence.[183] From the perspective of national criminal justice, this issue leads to the further question of whether fair criminal justice needs the argumentative contribution of private parties to the definition of legal issues. Traditionally, continental countries, relying on the *iura novit curia* principle, entrusted solely to the judiciary the definition of the correct legal characterisation of the criminal act. Consequently, the decision-makers can depart from the *nomen juris* chosen by the prosecutorial authority.

The European Convention is surely not indifferent to the opportunity for the defence to contribute to the definition of the legal characterisation of the offence at hand, an issue that considerably affects several important aspects (*e.g.*, the type and severity of the sentence to which defendants can be exposed). As noted, the European Court stressed the importance of the defendants being properly informed of the legal characterisation of the charges preferred against them by linking this guarantee with the right to effective defence.[184] This approach may be viewed as the logical consequence of the way applicants have usually complained about the

---

[180] ECtHR, *Brandstetter v. Austria*.

[181] Trechsel (2005), p. 90.

[182] *Above*, A.

[183] On this issue see Quattrocolo (2011), p. 3 ff.; Casiraghi (2012), p. 115 ff.

[184] ECtHR, *I.H. and others v. Austria*.

infringement of Article 6(3)(a) ECHR in relation to the right to be informed on the legal characterisation of criminal charges. The Strasbourg case-law, however, leads to two unsatisfactory results. On the one hand, the Court makes—consistently with its general approach to the right to information—the infringement of the Convention conditional on a concrete restriction on the right to defence, thus engaging in the difficult task of assessing what the defendant could have done more if properly informed.[185] On the other, the European judges tend to oversimplify the scope of the guarantee of information on the legal characterisation of the charge. According to the Strasbourg case-law, this guarantee not only aims at allowing effective defence for the purposes of the evidence-gathering but furthermore requires national authorities to provide defendants with the necessary information to give their personal contribution to the decision-making. As anticipated, the Court usually adopts a more rigorous approach to the right to personal participation in criminal proceedings by requiring a specific duty of diligence by defendants with legal knowledge.

Particular problems arise in the case in which the trial court amends the charge after the evidence-gathering but shortly prior to the pronouncement of the judgement, or even convicts the accused for offences not provided for in the indictment. In such cases, the Court scrutinises whether the appeal proceedings allow for an overall review of the judgment issued at first instance. According to the Strasbourg judges, it must be ascertained whether the accused was

> entitled to contest his conviction in respect of all relevant legal and factual aspects before the Court of Appeal, which heard the parties at an oral appeal hearing and reviewed the applicant's complaints about the reclassification of the charge from both the procedural and substantive point of view.[186]

This approach cannot be sustained in absolute terms, since it charges the defendant with the burden of ensuring, through his appeal, the fairness of the procedure. Again, this shortcoming may seem to be the result of the systematic approach adopted by the European case-law. Yet invoking the overall fairness of criminal proceedings cannot in itself justify compensation in higher instances where fundamental rights are at stake. The main question is whether the conviction issued at the first instance for another offence or in relation to a charge amended without informing the accused can be deemed lawful under the Convention. It is apparent from the Strasbourg case-law that this conclusion presupposes minimum qualitative requirements, particularly that the accused is given the opportunity to be heard and to give evidence on the basis of the new legal classification of the offence.

A different question is whether and within what limits the Convention allows for the legal characterisation of the charge to be changed in the proceedings before

---

[185]ECtHR, Grand Chamber, *Pélissier and Sassi v. France*, § 60. The Court overcame this approach in its subsequent case-law. See among others ECtHR, *Drassich v. Italy*. For a similar criticism to that expressed in the text see De Matteis (2008), p. 222 f.

[186]ECtHR, *Sipavičius v. Lithuania*, § 31.s.

higher courts. The European Court dealt with this issue for the first time in *Pélissier and Sassi v. France*, where it found an infringement of the Convention not just because the court of appeal had convicted the defendants for an offence different from that provided in the indictment but because the decision to amend the legal classification of the charge had not been made through adversarial argument. This conclusion highlights the importance of the decision-makers hearing the defence arguments not only on the facts but also on the legal classification of the charge. The question has more recently arisen in the case *Drassich v. Italy*, followed by the case *D.M.T. and D.K.I. v. Bulgaria*.[187] In these judgments, moreover, the Strasbourg Court departed from its traditional approach, in that it did not engage in assessing whether a concrete risk or damage resulted for the defence, basing instead its reasoning on the presumption that a prompt information on the legal re-classification of the charge would have allowed the defendant to adopt a different defence strategy. Doubtless, this new approach reveals a clearer understanding of the importance of the argumentative side of the *audi alteram partem* rule. The reasoning adopted in the cases was particularly enlightening. Notwithstanding that the decision to change the legal qualification of the charge was issued by a higher court, the competent authority must grant the accused a proper opportunity to steer the decision-making through arguments against the new legal basis of the charge.

In *D.M.T. and D.K.I. v. Bulgaria*, the Court considered the proceedings unfair because the Supreme Court should have granted the accused the

> possibilité au requérant de débattre des nouvelles charges de tentative d'escroquerie aggravée. Elle aurait pu, par exemple, ajourner l'audience pour permettre aux parties d'exposer leurs arguments ou encore leur indiquer de soumettre des mémoires écrits sur cette question.[188]

Despite its merits, this solution does not seem to be entirely satisfactory, relying on a strict distinction between factual and legal issues, a distinction which, at least in its traditional terms, has long given rise to criticisms in various countries.[189] Yet fact and law are inseparable components of any judgement and the re-classification of the legal elements of the offence cannot be conducted *in vitro*. On close examination, the solution of allowing the defence to give new arguments against the new *nomen juris* may not always be enough to save the fairness of criminal proceedings, especially where the new legal characterisation highlights the need to take new evidence. In the light of this, national law should put in place the necessary measures to enable defendants to give further evidence to counter the judgement pronounced on the basis of the new legal classification. Also, higher courts should annul the decision and remit the case to a lower instance competent to take new evidence and make a new comprehensive assessment of both fact and law.

---

[187]See respectively ECtHR, *Drassich v. Italy* and ECtHR, *D.M.T. and D.K.I. v. Bulgaria*.

[188]ECtHR, *D.M.T. and D.K.I. v. Bulgaria*, § 83.

[189]From the perspective of the countries selected in this study, see, as far as Italy is concerned, Quattrocolo (2011), p. 61 ff., and, in relation to Brazil, Lopes Jr (2017), p. 889 f.

G. *Audi alteram partem* and Measures of Coercion in Criminal Proceedings

I. Deprivation of Freedom and the Right to Information. The Soft Approach of the European Case-Law

Restrictions on the right to freedom not only cause significant suffering but also put the individuals concerned at objective disadvantage if they are subject to a criminal prosecution, hindering them from appearing in court as free persons.[190] To compensate the arrestee and detainee for their vulnerable position, the European Convention, like other international human rights instruments, provides for enhanced safeguards, which are primarily aimed at ensuring the independent assessment of the lawfulness of the measure applied.

It has been observed that the link between the information rights and the guarantee of a fair hearing takes on particular relevance where restrictions on freedom are ordered in criminal proceedings. Remarkably, the right to receive information stands out at the top of the guarantees laid down by the Convention not only to the person charged with a criminal offence but furthermore to all individuals deprived of the right to liberty.[191] Compared to the general information due in criminal proceedings, however, the information duties of the competent authorities are enhanced in the case of restrictions on freedom, since, as noted, the individuals concerned must not only be made aware of the charge but more specifically must be made aware of the grounds for arrest or detention.[192] The prudent formulation used by the Convention, which relates to 'any charge', can be explained in the light of the very broad scope of this guarantee, which applies to all the situations listed in Article 5(1) ECHR, i.e., also to forms of restrictions on freedom not linked with criminal proceedings.[193]

The European Convention does not provide for clear indications about the aims of this information. Traditionally, the Strasbourg Court links the right to information with the guarantee of Article 5(4) ECHR by stressing that the knowledge of the grounds for arrest is the necessary condition for individuals to undertake proceedings in order to obtain judicial review of the lawfulness of their arrest or detention.[194] This link was so exclusive in the earlier case-law that the Court found no ground to ascertain a violation of the Convention under paragraph 2 if paragraph 4 was infringed.[195] The Court departed from this approach in *van der Leer v. The*

[190] Vogler (2012), p. 88 f.

[191] Art. 5(2) ECHR.

[192] To be sure, national law does not always require the arrested person to be formally charged with a criminal offence. See Trechsel (2005), p. 502 f.

[193] *Ibid.*, 458.

[194] In the same sense see Peukert (2009), Rn. 91.

[195] ECtHR, *X. v. United Kingdom.*

Netherlands, which emphasised the autonomous meaning of the two guarantees.[196] Certainly, the granting of adequate information on the reasons of arrest or detention is a necessary precondition to successfully challenge of the measure applied. This point highlights a clear distinction between this right to information and the general guarantee of information on the accusation laid down by Article 6 ECHR.[197] It can be doubted, however, that this is the only justification of information. Since *Fox, Campbell and Hartley v. United Kingdom*, the Court has pointed out that 'any person arrested must be told, in simple, non-technical language that he can understand, the essential legal and factual grounds for his arrest'.[198] On close examination, the requirement of simple and understandable information not only provides the individuals concerned the ability to undertake proceedings against the measure applied but also to face the hearing before the judicial authority to which they must promptly be brought under paragraph 3.[199]

These findings, therefore, highlight the general humanitarian function of this information, which aims at the best fulfilment of both the judicial guarantees of paragraphs 3 and 4 of Article 5 ECHR. In the light of this, it is surprising that in the *Fox, Campbell and Hartley* case, the Court allowed for the applicants to be granted a 'bare indication of the legal basis for the arrest' at the time of the arrest, on the assumption that they were later informed of the reasons for their suspected of being terrorists during their police interrogation.[200] This result was debatable, providing the arrested person with no substantial information to cope with the police questioning. Although it is rather obvious that granting information only during the police questioning increases the vulnerable condition of the applicants, making them unable to improvise a defence strategy, the Court found no violation of Article 5(2) ECHR. It was even more unsatisfactory that the European Court failed to establish 'even the most rudimentary elements of formal qualities',[201] while requiring the arrested persons to understand on their own the grounds for arrest or detention.[202] Subsequent case-law further developed this approach, as is apparent from the *John Murray* case, in which the Strasbourg judges reached the conclusion that the arrestee could infer the reasons from the questioning.[203]

Despite the guarantee of simple and understandable information, the Strasbourg case-law also provides rather scant indications about the time in which information should be granted. The statutory requirement that information must be given 'promptly' is clearly too generic. If the Convention, like the International Covenant,

[196]ECtHR, *van der Leer v. The Netherlands.*

[197]Trechsel (2005), p. 458.

[198]ECtHR, *Fox, Campbell and Hartley v. United Kingdom*, § 40.

[199]Art. 5(3) ECHR.

[200]ECtHR, *Fox, Campbell and Hartley v. United Kingdom*, § 41.

[201]Trechsel (2005), p. 461.

[202]ECtHR, *Fox, Campbell and Hartley v. United Kingdom*, § 41.

[203]Trechsel (2005), p. 461.

had required information to be given 'at the time of the arrest',[204] the *Fox, Campbell and Hartley* case would have probably had a different solution. Moreover, nobody can be deprived of his liberty if justification does not already exist at the time of the arrest, so that it is hardly understandable why information should be delayed.

On close examination, the guarantee of Article 5(2) ECHR, despite providing for richer information than that required by Article 6(3)(a) ECHR, ensures limited protection to the arrested or detained person. In particular, it is not clear whether the European Convention requires the competent authority to inform the arrested individuals of their right to access relevant evidence, notwithstanding that this information is of utmost importance for the purposes of both the judicial hearings of paragraphs 3 and 4 of Article 5 ECHR. Even more worryingly, the Convention does not acknowledge the right to be informed on relevant decisions issued during the deprivation of liberty.[205] This issue holds specific relevance in the case of remand proceedings in which the competent authority is often called upon to re-assess the initial justification at a later stage. The European case-law has rarely dealt with this problem and, except for the case of rejection of a request for release, it is not clear whether the detained person should be granted information on subsequent decisions.

II. The Right to a Fair Hearing and the Guarantee of Prompt Judicial Review of Arrest or Detention

It has been observed that the aims of the information due to the individuals deprived of liberty cannot be circumscribed to the law action that the person concerned is entitled to under paragraph 4 but furthermore should be interpreted in the light of the right to be promptly brought before the judicial authority or other authority empowered to exercise judicial functions. In the latter regard, the Rome Convention stands out among other international human rights charters, in that it explicitly reserves this safeguard solely to the restrictions on liberty laid down in paragraph 1 (c) of Article 5 ECHR. This does not entail that the right to a prompt judicial review is confined solely to cases of remand detention,[206] since the Convention explicitly grants it to both the arrested and detained individuals.

This is apparent from the general goals of the guarantee under examination. Traditionally, the European judges consider that the main purpose of the right to be promptly brought before the judicial authority guarantee is to protect individuals

---

[204] *Ibid.*, 459 f.

[205] On this delicate issue see Peukert (2009), Rn. 92.

[206] Trechsel (2005), p. 502.

against arbitrary interferences by the state with their right to freedom,[207] protection ensured by means of an independent assessment of the lawfulness of the measure applied. Although it does often not constitute its official justification,[208] furthermore,

> prompt judicial intervention may lead to the detection and prevention of life-threatening measures or serious ill-treatment which violate the fundamental guarantees contained in Articles 2 and 3 of the Convention.[209]

In this light, the need for independent review is clearly stronger in the case of arrest, which usually enforced without previous judicial order. Of course, the need for independent assessment does not exclusively relate to these situations. Remarkably the Court recognised the applicability of this guarantee to a case of restriction on freedom ordered by the judicial authority and even in the presence of the defendant's lawyer.[210] This situation was clearly dealt with in *McGoff v. Sweden*, in which the Court, although focusing on the fact that the applicant had not been brought to court promptly enough, highlighted the need that the arrested person be heard in person by the judicial authority.[211]

This requirement tightens the link between the guarantee of prompt judicial review and the right of all the individuals arrested or detained in criminal proceedings to make their voice heard by an independent authority.[212] This raises a further criticism against the solution adopted in the *Fox, Campbell and Hartley* case, in which the Court found no violation of the Convention, notwithstanding, as noted, that the applicants were first examined by the police that only provided them with information during the police questioning. Of course, the right to a personal hearing holds particular importance in the case of remand detention. In this area, the delicate question arises whether detainee should be confronted alone with the competent authority or whether he has the right to legal assistance. In the latter case, the further question arises whether or not the Convention allows for the detainee to await the judicial hearing without having the possibility to communicate with his counsel.

To be sure, the Convention provides no indication as to whether the accused has the right to be assisted by a lawyer either after or during the judicial hearing. Starting with this premise, the earlier European case-law had given a negative response to this question.[213] The Strasbourg Court, however, departed form this approach in the *John Murray* case. By examining the guarantee at hand in conjunction with the general right to a fair hearing, the European judges found a breach

---

[207]See among others ECtHR, *Kurt v. Turkey*, § 123. On the protection against arbitrary detentions see Marzaduri (2012), p. 18 ff.

[208]Trechsel (2005), p. 505.

[209]ECtHR, *Kurt v. Turkey*, § 123.

[210]Trechsel (2005), p. 506.

[211]ECtHR, *McGoff v. Sweden*.

[212]Trechsel (2005), p. 514.

[213]ECtHR, *Schiesser v. Switzerland*.

of the Convention because the applicant was denied access to a lawyer during the first 48 hours of his police detention.[214] As far as the legal assistance during the questioning is concerned, it has been noted that in the same ruling, the Court acknowledged that Article 6 ECHR, as a rule, requires that 'the accused be allowed to benefit from the assistance of a lawyer already at the initial stages of police interrogation'. The Strasbourg judges, however, softened this conclusion by clarifying that this right

> may be subject to restrictions for good cause. The question, in each case, is whether the restriction, in the light of the entirety of the proceedings, has deprived the accused of a fair hearing.[215]

It took several years before the European case-law recognized, in the 2010 *Brusco* case, the right of detained defendants to be heard in presence of their lawyer. Of course, the initial hearing may not be enough, especially in the case of long-term detention. This leads to the further question of whether defendants in remand detention also have the right to be heard in subsequent stages of the remand proceedings and how they can claim this right. In particular, the point at stake is whether the Convention burdens the person concerned with the task of requesting a further hearing or requires the competent authority to carry out subsequent oversight.

In this regard, the Convention still does not provide for any clear indication. This difficult area, however, allows us to observe one of the most creative contributions by the European case-law, which has long reinterpreted the guarantee of paragraph 3 in the light of its main goals. According to the Strasbourg case-law, the purposes of the guarantee of a prompt judicial control are not limited to the assessment of the initial justification of detention but also entail a constant review of the reasonableness and the grounds for maintaining detention[216] at reasonable intervals.[217] From this approach it might be inferred that paragraph 3 requires the detainee to be regularly heard as well. On close examination, the Convention does not go so far, nor does national law always grant the detainee the right to be present at any decision in the course of the remand proceedings. As noted, the Convention does not even make it clear whether the detainee has the right to be kept informed of the results of any decision concerning detention.

---

[214]Trechsel (2005), p. 514 f.

[215]ECtHR, *John Murray v. United Kingdom*, § 63.

[216]ECtHR, *Tomasi v. France*. See extensively Trechsel (2005), p. 523 ff.

[217]Maggio (2012), p. 37.

III. Participatory Rights in habeas corpus *Proceedings*

Alongside the right to be promptly brought before the judicial authority, the European Convention grants the individuals arrested or detained a proactive guarantee, that is, the right to undertake proceedings against the measure adopted. Unlike the right to prompt judicial review, this safeguard goes beyond the sphere of criminal justice, not being reserved to the cases of arrest or detention under paragraph 3(c). The great importance of this safeguard can explain the enhanced role of the judiciary, since only a judge can scrutinise the lawfulness of detention in response to the initiative of the interested party. By means of this guarantee, the Convention acknowledged the right to *habeas corpus*, whose origins are usually traced back, in England, to the 1205 Magna Carta and, centuries later, acknowledged by the 1679 *Habeas Corpus* Act. Most interestingly, a similar procedure also existed in continental Europe—in particular, as noted, it was already operational in the Kingdom of Aragon between 1428 and 1552. In English law, *habeas corpus* has for centuries constituted a powerful device to obtain a prompt judicial control of the lawfulness of detention. By this means, individuals deprived of their liberty were granted a quick and effective remedy consisting of a summons of the custodian demanding that the person be handed over to the judicial authority for the lawfulness of detention to be examined.[218]

This precedent certainly had a strong influence on the drafters of the Convention, to the point, as noted, that they extended the guarantee to all the situations listed in paragraph 1. In the 1970 ‘Vagrancy case’, however, the Court circumscribed the scope of application of *habeas corpus*, ruling out that detainees can obtain judicial oversight of a deprivation of freedom ordered or already reviewed by a court.[219] This doctrine, which is known as the ‘doctrine of incorporation’, aimed at restricting the guarantee of judicial control to the cases of arrest or detention ordered by administrative authorities. Over the following decades, however, the Strasbourg case-law progressively softened this approach, which, viewed in strict terms, raised serious human rights concerns.[220] In particular, the focus on the existence of a previous judicial review did not take into account the dynamics of restrictions on freedom, which may become unlawful because of subsequent circumstances, thus posing the need to activate another judicial control. Doubtless, *habeas corpus* is of utmost importance in relation to pre-trial detention ordered in criminal proceedings. It has been noted that the guarantee of Article 5(4) ECHR had enormous influence on Italian law, leading to the introduction of a judicial review of coercive measures applied in criminal proceedings.[221]

A delicate question is also whether the competent court must grant the person arrested or detained a fair opportunity to be heard prior to the decision-making.

---

[218]Vogler (2012), p. 90.

[219]ECtHR, *De Wilde, Ooms and Versyp (‘Vagrancy’) v. Belgium.*

[220]For extensive criticisms see Trechsel (2005), p. 470 ff.

[221]Chapter 2, J.III.2.

Whereas there is extensive case-law on this requirement in relation to the situations of Article 5(1)(c) ECHR,[222] the Court has not given an explicit response on whether the arrested person must be personally examined in the other situations of paragraph 1, and the arguments used in *Sanchez-Reisse v. Switzerland* were rather 'cryptic'.[223] Of course, the right to be personally heard must be balanced with the requirement of speediness of the procedure. As a result, the national judges were released from responsibility in a case in which the decision was issued in the absence of the person against whom an arrest warrant was ordered, notwithstanding that it could not be executed since the person concerned was fugitive.[224] In general terms, the Court acknowledges that *habeas corpus* must satisfy the requirements of a fair trial insofar as an adversarial procedure and full respect for the *par condicio* principle are ensured.[225]

Notwithstanding these findings, the Court has always been much more cautious in the assessment of the infringement of fair trial requirements under Article 5 ECHR than in relation to criminal proceedings in general.[226] Moreover, the development of European case-law has not always followed a linear path. In the 1990 *Keus* case, the Court, relying on Dutch law, justified the failure to inform the lawyer, during the period in which the applicant was a fugitive, about the hearing and the decision to extend the applicant's confinement.[227] It took 15 years before the Court departed from the national standards of human rights protection, recognising that both the detainee and the counsel must in principle be informed of the hearing.[228] From this it does not follow, however, that the Convention requires the person concerned to be always heard. In *Varbanov v. Bulgaria*, the Court suggests that the personal participation of the detained person can be unnecessary where 'some form of representation' is guaranteed.[229] Unfortunately, subsequent case-law could not clarify what representation should exactly be necessary.

This point raises the question of whether the Convention requires the individuals concerned to be provided with legal assistance in *habeas corpus* proceedings. Despite the lack of explicit provisions, it is quite clear that the possibility of effectively challenging the lawfulness of the deprivation of freedom are very low if the person concerned is left alone.[230] This especially applies after a long period of detention, as the 1st Chamber highlighted and the Grand Chamber confirmed in the

---

[222]See among others ECtHR, *Wloch v. Poland.*

[223]In these terms cf. Trechsel (2005), p. 480 f.

[224]ECtHR, *Keus v. The Netherlands.*

[225]ECtHR, *Garcia Alva v. Germany*, § 39.

[226]For this observation see Trechsel (2005), p. 484.

[227]ECtHR, *Keus v. The Netherlands*, § 25.

[228]ECtHR, *Fodale v. Italy.*

[229]ECtHR, *Varbanov v. Bulgaria*, § 58.

[230]On this issue see Trechsel (2005), p. 486.

Öcalan case.[231] Moreover, the Court has always stressed that the guarantee of *habeas corpus* requires that individuals in a particular vulnerable situation, such as confinement in a psychiatric institution[232] or minors,[233] be represented in court. This has led to the Strasbourg judges even recognising the right of the arrestee or detainee to legal aid.[234] In *Megyeri v. Germany*, the reasoning of the Court—and in particular, the acknowledgment that legal assistance must be ensured 'unless there are special circumstances'[235]—suggests the existence of a sort of 'presumption in favour of legal aid'.[236]

Over the last decades, there have been considerable developments in the Strasbourg case-law in relation to the information that must be provided to the arrestee or detainee in *habeas corpus* procedures. In the 1989 *Lamy* case, the Court had already pointed out that the defence must be granted access to the file and the essential information on which basis the competent court should decide.[237] Subsequent case-law reiterated this solution in the light of the principle of equality of arms,[238] to the extent, moreover, that the person on remand should be entitled to access the entire investigative file.

On close examination, this 'far-reaching proposition'[239] gives rise to some problems, jeopardising the needs of the ongoing investigation. The Court dealt with the problems deriving from the solution of allowing full access to the investigative file in *Garcia Alva v. Germany*. In this case, the Strasbourg judges stressed that withholding the information available—despite being justified by the need to preserve the efficiency of the ongoing inquiry and to avoid the risk that the suspect tampers with evidence—cannot be satisfied to the extent that the arrested person suffers from 'substantial restrictions on the rights of the defence'. The conclusion was that 'information which is essential for the assessment of the lawfulness of a detention should be made available in an appropriate manner to the suspect's lawyer'.[240] To be sure, accessing the whole investigative file can also cause detriment to the interests of other parties to which some pieces of evidence may relate. The Court had the opportunity of analysing this issue in the *Garcia Alva* case. Here, however, the infringement of the Convention does not seem to have been the result of German law, which explicitly requires that,

[231] See respectively ECtHR, 1st Chamber, *Öcalan v. Turkey*, § 72 et seq. and ECtHR, Grand Chamber, *Öcalan v. Turkey*, § 131 et seqq.

[232] ECtHR, *Winterwerp v. The Netherlands*.

[233] ECtHR, *Bouamar v. Belgium*.

[234] Trechsel (2005), p. 486 f.

[235] ECtHR, *Megyeri v. Germany*, § 23.

[236] Trechsel (2005), p. 487.

[237] ECtHR, *Lamy v. Belgium*, § 29.

[238] Cf. among others ECtHR, *Danov v. Bulgaria*.

[239] In this sense Trechsel (2005), p. 485, who also raised the concerns reported in the text.

[240] ECtHR, *Garcia Alva v. Germany*, § 42. On this important ruling see Trechsel (2005), p. 485 f.

> if the accused is in remand detention or if, in the case of provisional arrest, this has been requested, information of relevance for the assessment of the lawfulness of such deprivation of liberty shall be made available to defence counsel in suitable form.[241]

H. Provisional Conclusions

The main contribution of the European case-law to a participatory understanding of criminal proceedings is of a methodological nature. The analysis carried out in this chapter has highlighted the extreme flexibility of the Strasbourg case-law and the constant attempt of the Court to avoid absolutist solutions. By going far beyond the protection solely of the accused, the European Court promotes a view of criminal proceedings as a complex space in which all the individuals involved should be given the opportunity to make their voice heard and to contribute to a fair decision-making. One might argue that this approach also led to the progressive watering down of fundamental fair trial guarantees and we have seen that this risk exists in some cases.

This conclusion, however, cannot be sustained in general terms. It would probably be no exaggeration to affirm that the European case-law has largely been a faithful interpreter of the main developments that occurred in the European criminal justice in recent years, while paving the way for the adoption of some important solutions by national law. By means of its constant reinterpretation of the fair trial rights acknowledged in the European Convention, the Strasbourg case-law more and more calls for a model of criminal justice based on a balance among conflicting interests.

References

Balsamo A, Lo Piparo A (2008) Principio del contraddittorio, utilizzabilità delle dichiarazioni predibattimentali e nozione di testimone tra giurisprudenza europea e criticità del sistema italiano. In: Balsamo A, Kostoris RE (eds) Giurisprudenza europea e processo penale italiano. Giappichelli, Torino, pp 333–372

Chiavario M (2008) La "lunga marcia" dei diritti dell'uomo nel processo penale. In: Balsamo A, Kostoris RE (eds) Giurisprudenza europea e processo penale italiano. Giappichelli, Torino, pp 11–31

De Matteis L (2008) Diversa qualificazione giuridica dell'accusa e tutela del diritto di difesa. In: Balsamo A, Kostoris RE (eds) Giurisprudenza europea e processo penale italiano. Giappichelli, Torino, pp 215–233

Findlay M (2011) Locating victim communities within global justice and governance. In: Crawford A (ed) International and comparative criminal justice and Urban Governance. Cambridge University Press, Cambridge, pp 109–139

[241] Section 147(2) CCP-Germany.

Giacomolli NJ (2014) O devido processo penal. Abordagem conforme a Constituição Federal e o Pacto de São José da Costa Rica. Atlas S.A., São Paulo

Jackson JD (2005) The effect of human rights on criminal evidentiary processes: towards convergence, divergence or realignment? Mod Law Rev 68:737–764

Jackson J, Johnstone J (2005) The reasonable time requirement: an independent and meaningful right. Crim Law Rev, pp 3 ff.

Jackson JD, Summers SJ (2012) The internationalisation of criminal evidence: beyond the common law and civil law traditions. Cambridge University Press, Cambridge

Kühne H-H (2009) In: Kühne H-H, Miehsler H and Vogler T, Article 6. In: Pabel K, Schmahl S (eds) (2013) Internationaler Kommentar zur Europäischen Menschenrechtskonvention. Carl Heymanns, Köln et al

Lopes A Jr (2017) Direito Processual Penal, 14th edn. Saraiva, São Paulo

Maffei S (2012) The right to confrontation in Europe. Absent, anonymous and vulnerable witnesses. Europa Law Publishing

Maggio P (2012) Judicial reviews against deprivation of liberty. In: Ruggeri S (ed) Liberty and security in Europe. A comparative analysis of pre-trial precautionary measures in criminal proceedings. V&R Unipress (Universitätsverlag Osnabrück), Göttingen, pp 33–44

Marzaduri E (2012) The application of pre-trial precautionary measures. In: Ruggeri S (ed) Liberty and security in Europe. A comparative analysis of pre-trial precautionary measures in criminal proceedings. V&R Unipress (Universitätsverlag Osnabrück), Göttingen, pp 17–32

Negri D (2014) L'imputato presente al processo. Una ricostruzione sistematica. Giappichelli, Torino

Peukert W (2009) Art. 5. In: Frowein J, Peukert W (eds) EMRK-Kommentar. Engel Verlag, Rehl am Rein, pp 70–139

Quattrocolo S (2011) Riqualificazione del fatto nella sentenza penale e tutela del contraddittorio. Jovene, Napoli

Spencer JR (2014) Hearsay evidence in criminal proceedings, II edn. Hart Publishing, Oxford

Stavros S (1993) The guarantees for accused persons under Article 6 of the European convention on human rights. Martinus Nijhoff Publishers, Dortmund et al

Trechsel S (2005) Human rights in criminal proceedings. Oxford University Press, Oxford

Ubertis G (2009) Principi di procedura penale europea, 2nd edn. Raffaello Cortina, Milano

Vogel B (2017) "In camera"-Verfahren als Gewährung effektiven Rechtsschutzes? Neue Entwicklungen im europäischen Sicherheitsrecht. Zeitschrift für die internationale Strafrechtsdogmatik, pp 28–38

Vogler R (2012) England and Wales. In: Ruggeri S (ed) Liberty and security in Europe. A comparative analysis of pre-trial precautionary measures in criminal proceedings. V&R Unipress (Universitätsverlag Osnabrück), Göttingen, pp 87–103

Vogler T (1986) Article 6. In: Golsong H, Karl W, Miehsler H, Petzold H, Rogge K, Vogler T, Wildhaber L (eds) Internationaler Kommentar zur Europäischen Menschenrechtskonvention. Carl Heymanns, Köln

Weigend T (2000) Die Europäische Menschenrechtskonvention als deutsches Recht - Kollisionen und ihre Lösung. Strafverteidiger 2000, pp 384–390

Zacchè F (2008) Gli effetti della giurisprudenza europea in tema di privilegio contro le autoincriminazioni e diritto al silenzio. In: Balsamo A, Kostoris RE (eds) Giurisprudenza europea e processo penale italiano. Giappichelli, Torino, pp 179–195

Chapter 9
Participatory Rights in Criminal Justice Under the American Convention on Human Rights

Contents

A. Premise. The Criminal Trial as a Listening Space with Due Guarantees and the Strong Human Rights Approach of the American Convention 345
B. The Right to Be Fairly Heard and the Overall Assessment of Human Rights Violations 347
C. The Right to Have Personal Access to Court and the Need for Comprehensive Judicial Oversight of Infringements on Human Rights 349
D. Investigative Needs and the Right to Informed Participation in Criminal Proceedings 350
E. Participatory Rights and the Taking of Criminal Evidence 353
I. The Right to Contribute to Evidence-Gathering in the Light of an Overall Human Rights Assessment 353
1. The Defence's Involvement in the Taking of Incriminating Evidence 353
2. Qualitative Conditions of Effective Confrontation, Miscarriage of Justice and Deficiencies of National Law 354
3. Anonymous Witnesses and the Use of Untested Evidence 355
II. The Right to Access to Exculpatory Evidence in Death Penalties 357
F. The Defence's Argumentative Contribution to the Decision-Making 357
G. Restrictions on Freedom, Right to Be Fairly Heard and the Enhanced Need for Overall Human Rights Oversight 359
I. The Broad Protection of Information Rights 359
II. The Right to a Prompt Judicial Hearing and the Protection Against Inhuman Treatment 362
III. *Audi alteram partem* in *habeas corpus* Proceedings 363
H. Provisional Conclusions 364
References 365

A. Premise. The Criminal Trial as a Listening Space with Due Guarantees and the Strong Human Rights Approach of the American Convention

After analysing the Strasbourg system of human rights protection, we shall now examine the developments that have taken place in Inter-American case-law towards a participatory understanding of criminal justice. Like the European Convention, the American Convention of Human Rights does not explicitly enshrine the *audi*

S. Ruggeri, Audi Alteram Partem *in Criminal Proceedings*,
DOI 10.1007/978-3-319-54573-8_9

alteram partem rule as such. Moreover, the Pact of San José also acknowledges the right of 'every person' to a 'hearing [. . .] in the substantiation of any accusation of a criminal nature made against him or for the determination of his rights and obligations of a civil, labor, fiscal, or any other nature'.[1] Unlike other international human rights instruments, the American Convention provides a different linguistic expression—namely, a hearing with 'due guarantees' must be granted. It is not clear whether this lexical choice was due to the proximity to the common law world and especially to ties with the USA.[2] Yet Article 8 ECHR recognised the 'right to a fair trial', so this difference does not seem to be of substantial importance.[3]

One linguistic difference, however, can be observed in comparison to other human rights charters. This difference, which is concerned with the way the right to a hearing with due guarantees was formulated, cannot easily be appreciated in all the official languages of the Convention. Following the linguistic formulation used in the European Convention, the English version of Article 8(1) ACHR acknowledges the right to a fair hearing, whereas the French one refers to the right to have one's lawsuit examined. On the other hand, both the Spanish and Portuguese versions grant the individuals charged with a criminal offence the right to make themselves fairly heard in criminal proceedings. This different formulation cannot be understood as the result of the objective differences among the languages used, revealing a clear shift of the focus to the role of the individuals involved in criminal proceedings. It is noteworthy that under the American Convention the right of defendants who do not speak or understand the language used in court to be assisted without charge by an interpreter or translator stands out at the top of the minimum fair trial rights.[4] As we will see, this acknowledgment highlights the importance attached by the Pact of San José to the right of defendants to personally appear in court and effectively participate in procedural activities.[5]

The Inter-American case-law provides clear examples of the strong human rights orientation of the American Convention. This can mainly be explained by the fact that for several years the Inter-American institutions have mainly dealt with serious human rights violations, such as forced disappearances and torture. As a consequence, the Court was only called upon to address due process issues in relatively recent years.[6] More specifically, the judgements of the Inter-American Court highlight an approach that reflects a comprehensive assessment of fair trial issues in the light of the overall set of the human rights acknowledged in the Pact of San José. In particular, a close overview of the Inter-American jurisprudence reveals a particularly strict link between the right to liberty, the protection against inhuman treatment and the right to a fair hearing. It is also worth observing that this link has

[1]Art. 8(1) ACHR.

[2]In this sense see instead Trechsel (2005), p. 81.

[3]*Ibid.*

[4]Art. 8(3)(a) ACHR.

[5]*Below*, C.

[6]Dondé Matute (2013), p. 42 f.

led to the significant expansion of the scope of the Inter-American protection to complex situations in which the applicant was often victim of serious human rights violations. In this light, one can observe a double role of the person charged with criminal offences in the proceedings before the Inter-American Court, namely as defendant and victim of human rights abuses.

B. The Right to Be Fairly Heard and the Overall Assessment of Human Rights Violations

Against this background, the *audi alteram partem* rule takes on general aims that go beyond the sphere of criminal justice, providing defendants with the guarantee of an independent oversight of fundamental rights. This can also explain the broad scope of the right to a hearing with due guarantees, which applies to any phase of criminal proceedings, from the preliminary enquiry to the executive phase, including interlocutory procedures.[7] It is also noteworthy that this understanding of the right to a fair proceeding has led the Court to redefine the notion of 'victims' in such terms that it encompasses the victim's families, who also hold the right to be heard by a court. As the Inter-American Court has stressed on various occasions,

> it can be inferred from Article 8 of the Convention that the victims of human rights violations, or their next of kin, should have wide-ranging possibilities of being heard and acting in the respective proceedings to clarify the facts and punish those responsible, and to seek due reparation.[8]

This does not entail that the Inter-American Court overlooks the interests of the victim in a strict sense, that is, the person injured by a criminal offence. In particular, the right to a fair hearing not only requires the competent court to examine the accused's viewpoint but also entails positive obligations for the state.[9] These obligations also exist prior to the opening of the trial phase, encompassing, *inter alia*, the duty of the competent authorities to carry out an exhaustive inquiry and later to institute criminal proceedings. The conduct of a proper criminal investigation, therefore, sets the necessary conditions of a fair trial. Doubtless, a complete fact-finding lies at the heart of the interests of the victims and their families, no matter whether human rights violations were committed by the defendants or against them. As the Court put it in *The Serrano-Cruz Sisters v. El Salvador*,

> the next of kin of the alleged victims have the right to expect, and the States the obligation to ensure, that what befell the alleged victims will be investigated effectively by the State authorities; that proceedings will be filed against those allegedly responsible for the

[7]Giacomolli (2014), p. 114 f.

[8]See among others IACtHR, *Garibaldi v. Brazil*, § 116; IACtHR, *Gelmán v. Uruguay*, § 187.

[9]García Ramírez (2011), p. 66 f.

> unlawful acts; and, if applicable, the pertinent penalties will be imposed, and the losses suffered by the next of kin repaired.[10]

From this it follows that the competent authorities, once they learn of the alleged offence, must initiate—*ex officio* and without delay—'a serious, impartial and effective investigation using all available legal means' with a view to 'determining the truth and the pursuit, capture, prosecution and eventual punishment of all the perpetrators of the facts'.[11] Moreover, the Court stressed that, although the conduct of a criminal enquiry is an obligation of means rather than of result,[12] the

> lack of state response is a determinative element when evaluating whether a breach of Article 8(1) [. . .] of the American Convention has occurred, because it is directly related to the principle of effectiveness that should permeate the development of such an investigation.[13]

In general terms, Inter-American case-law attaches great weight to the need to provide the individuals involved in criminal proceedings with a fair opportunity to make their voice heard by an independent authority, with a view to the overall assessment of human rights violations that occurred either during, or by means of, a criminal inquiry.[14] To this end, some qualitative conditions must be met to ensure a fair hearing. In particular, the San José's judges emphasise the need to provide defendants with proper information before their giving their first statement.[15] A peculiarity of the Inter-American system is the strict link between the guarantee of a fair examination and the right to confrontation. We will see that in *Castillo Petruzzi et al. v. Peru* the Court examined the right to be confronted with the incriminating testimony of police officers based on the evidence given by the applicants without legal assistance.[16]

Under the Pact of San José also, the guarantee of a fair hearing undoubtedly holds specific relevance when the individuals concerned are subject to restrictions on freedom.[17] It is noteworthy that the American Convention expressly ensures to the accused persons the right not to incriminate themselves.[18] This guarantee is of such importance that it goes beyond the sphere of criminal proceedings, providing individuals with a protective umbrella also in procedures conducted before or accompanying the judicial proceedings, which can have 'unfavorable and unjustified impact on the juridical status' of the persons concerned.[19]

---

[10]IACtHR, *The Serrano-Cruz Sisters v. El Salvador*, § 64.

[11]IACtHR, *González et al. ("Cotton Field") v. Mexico*, § 290.

[12]IACtHR, *Gomes Lund et al. ("Guerrilha do Araguaia") v. Brazil*, § 138 et seq.

[13]IACtHR, *García Prieto et al. v. El Salvador*, § 115.

[14]García Ramírez (2011), p. 65; Ibáñez Rivas (2014), p. 217.

[15]*Below*, D.

[16]*Below*, E.I.2.

[17]*Below*, G.

[18]Art. 8(2)(g) ACHR.

[19]IACtHR, *Maritza Urrutia v. Guatemala*, § 120.

C. The Right to Have Personal Access to Court and the Need for Comprehensive Judicial Oversight of Infringements on Human Rights

The Pact of San José's approach, markedly oriented towards human rights protection, has led the Court to elaborate a broad jurisprudence, which is strongly based upon the personal involvement of the individuals involved in a criminal law action. To this end, the Inter-American case-law devoted particular attention to the accused's right to personally direct his requests to a court. Even though the American Convention, like other human rights charters, contains no explicit reference to the right to be present at trial, this fundamental guarantee can be deemed acknowledged by the overall system of the accused's fair trial rights.[20] In particular, the fact that defendants can choose to defend themselves[21] not only presupposes their right to personally participate in the proceedings but furthermore requires the national authorities to put them in the best condition to follow the trial hearings and set up a proper defence strategy.

It has also anticipated that under the Convention the right to linguistic assistance lies at the top of the list of fair trial rights, which highlights the importance attached to the direct involvement of the accused in the criminal proceedings initiated against them. Certainly, the reference to a 'court' or 'tribunal' cannot lead to an interpretation that restricts the scope of this provision to the trial phase. It is precisely the prominent position of the right to linguistic assistance that makes it a safeguard potentially applicable to all the phases of criminal proceedings. This explains the lack of further references to linguistic assistance in the provision regarding the right to information on the charge[22] as well as to that concerning the right of the arrested or detained person to be heard by a court, a guarantee often due in the pre-trial phase.[23] The Inter-American case-law has further enhanced this guarantee by strengthening the right to follow the court proceedings in a familiar language in situations characterised by the particular vulnerability of the individuals concerned, especially if detained in a cultural context different from their own one. A particularly interesting case was dealt with in *Tiu Tojín v. Guatemala*, in which the Court stressed the state's obligation to ensure that individuals belonging to rural or indigenous communities be granted the right both to understand the language and to be understood in the proceedings.[24]

The right to be personally involved in court proceedings holds specific importance for the individuals who are suffering or suffered from serious restrictions on human rights. In this respect, the Court enriched the protective scope of the general right to a hearing with due guarantees by requiring the national authorities to check

[20] Giacomolli (2014), p. 115 f.

[21] Art. 8(2)(d) and (e) ACHR.

[22] Art. 8(2)(b) ACHR.

[23] Art. 7(4) ACHR.

[24] IACtHR, *Tiu Tojín v. Guatemala*, § 100.

the physical conditions of the persons concerned. On several occasions, the Inter-American case-law has stressed that forced disappearances put individuals in a condition of extreme vulnerability by depriving them of the ability to defend themselves, especially when constant violations of human rights are tolerated by the State.[25] This confirms that the requirement that the accused personally appear in court and be examined by an independent should not be viewed as a separate guarantee but as the means of assessing (and sometimes avoiding) multiple infringements of the Convention.[26]

To tackle these situations, the state must fulfil positive obligations, starting with the duty to

> provide the relevant authorities with the logistical and scientific resources necessary for gathering and processing the evidence, as well as, specifically, the authority to access the appropriate documents and information for the investigation of the actions denounced and to obtain clues or evidence on the location of the victims.[27]

Against this background, the contracting countries are called upon to grant individuals effective judicial oversight, aimed at a strict assessment of the lawfulness of the measures adopted at the national level. In this respect, the hearing of the detained person provides assurances against large-scale detention for grounds extraneous to the goals of criminal trials. The Inter-American Court dealt with this issue in *Servellón García et al. v. Honduras*, stating that 'programmed and collective arrests, which are not well-founded on the individualization of punishable acts and that lack judicial control, are contrary to the presumption of innocence'.[28] By this means, the granting of a fair judicial hearing can prevent the detention from becoming a 'discriminatory mechanism'.[29]

D. Investigative Needs and the Right to Informed Participation in Criminal Proceedings

Like other human rights charters, the American Convention requires the fulfilment of qualitative conditions to ensure the effectiveness of the accused's participation, starting with the guarantee of information. As noted, there is a strict link between the right to linguistic assistance and the defendants' right to know the charges preferred against them. However, the wording of Article 8(2)(b) ACHR is quite different from that of other international instruments in that it does not contain any reference to the requirement on detailed information. The Inter-American case-law

[25] See among others IACtHR, *Radilla Pacheco v. Mexico*, §§ 138 et seqq.

[26] Casal (2014), p. 197.

[27] IACtHR, *Ibsen Cárdenas and Ibsen Peña v. Bolivia*, § 168.

[28] IACtHR, *Servellón García et al. v. Honduras*, § 96.

[29] *Ibid.*

has considerably contributed to a reconstruction of this guarantee by requiring the accused to be granted proper information

> not only of the charges against him, that is, the crimes or offenses he is charged with, but also of the reasons for them, and the evidence for such charges and the legal definition of the facts.[30]

Expressed in these terms, the right to information clearly expands its scope of protection, imposing upon national authorities a duty of information that not only concerns the accusation but also the grounds and the evidence supporting the decision to charge. This strong interpretation, moreover, has led to the Inter-American Court developing a jurisprudence that largely departs from the formal requirements of national law. According to the Court, the obligation of providing detailed and precise notification concerns 'all the information of the facts in order to fully exercise his right to defense and prove to the judge his version of the facts'.[31]

On the other hand, the American Convention stands out among other international instruments in that it not only refers to the need for prompt information but explicitly requires a 'prior notification' of the charge. The timely fulfilment of the duty of information is of utmost importance in the Inter-American case-law, which considers it an essential element 'for the effective exercise of the right to defense'.[32] Doubtless, this requirement strengthens the guarantee of information, since it not only rules out the lawfulness of any procedure aimed at postponing the information on the charge (like, *e.g.*, penal order procedures existing in some Europe countries) but also burdens the national authorities with the task of providing information on the investigation. In *Tibi v. Ecuador*, the Court found an infringement of Article 8 (2) ACHR, among other reasons, because the alleged victim had not been informed of the court order to investigate.[33] This also confirms the existence of a strict link between the right to informed participation in the proceedings and the right to be fairly heard. As the Court put it,

> for this right to fully operate and satisfy its inherent aims, it is necessary for said notification to take place before the accused renders his first statement. Without this guarantee, his right to adequately prepare his defense would be infringed.[34]

In this way, the Inter-American case-law makes the guarantee of information a general means of ensuring that victims of human rights violations can be put in a realistic position to prepare their defence and make their voice heard in criminal proceedings. Of course, this does not entail that suspects must be granted an absolute right to information on the ongoing investigation. The Court dealt with this issue in *Barreto Leiva v. Venezuela*, acknowledging that

---

[30] IACtHR, *Barreto Leiva v. Venezuela*, § 128.

[31] *Ibid.*

[32] *Ibid.*

[33] IACtHR, *Tibi v. Ecuador*, § 188.

[34] *Ibid.*, § 187.

> it is reasonable that, in certain cases, there is secrecy of the proceedings conducted during the preliminary investigation in a criminal case, in order to guarantee the effectiveness of the administration of justice.[35]

This possibility encounters specific limits, however. On close examination, the Inter-American case-law does not generically stress the need to balance the requirement of secrecy with the 'right to defense of the person being investigated, which entails, *inter alia*, the possibility to learn about the facts attributed to him' but requires, more specifically, the guarantee of information only to be restricted where the risk arises that the criminal inquiry can be 'affected by the elimination or withholding of evidence'.[36] Moreover, a fundamental requirement of congruence must be fulfilled between 'the facts informed to the accused and the indictment and the conviction',[37] even though the Court, as we will see, did not coherently follow this approach while dealing with the information on the legal classification of the offence.

Furthermore, the Inter-American case-law made the right to prior notification of the charge the focal point for granting the accused a general preventive guarantee of information. As the Court stressed it,

> the transition between "person being investigated" and "accused" [...] may occur at any time. It is not possible to wait until the person is formally accused or [...] deprived of liberty to provide him with the information that is essential for the timely exercise of the right to defense.[38]

The comprehensive scope of the duty of information, however, does not mean that the guarantee will always maintain the same features. The Court recognised that 'the content of the notice shall vary according to the progress of the investigation, reaching the highest point [...] with the formal and definitive filing of the charges'. Yet, 'before that and as a minimum requirement, the person under investigation must learn about, in as much detail as possible, the charges against him'.[39]

Against this background, the right to information on the charge takes on more specific features when the accused is subject to a measure of coercion. To this end, the broad scope of protection attached to the prior notification on the charge led to the Court somehow reversing the relationship between the guarantees provided for in Articles 7(4) and 8(2)(b) ACHR, making the general right to information a means of challenging restrictions on further rights acknowledged by the Convention. In the *Barreto Leiva* case, the issue at stake was 'the capacity of Mr. Barreto Leiva by the time he rendered the three statements before the judicial authorities before being subjected to pre-trial detention'.[40] The Court found the postponement of

---

[35]IACtHR, *Barreto Leiva v. Venezuela*, § 45.

[36]*Ibid.*

[37]*Ibid.*, § 47.

[38]*Ibid.*, § 46.

[39]*Ibid.*, § 31.

[40]*Ibid.*, § 32.

information after the enforcement of the coercive measure incompatible with the Convention, thus making it clear that the accused on remand must first be granted proper information of the grounds for the institution of criminal proceedings.

E. Participatory Rights and the Taking of Criminal Evidence

I. The Right to Contribute to Evidence-Gathering in the Light of an Overall Human Rights Assessment

1. The Defence's Involvement in the Taking of Incriminating Evidence

A powerful form of effective participation in criminal proceedings is the possibility of being actively involved in the collection of evidence. This safeguard holds particular relevance in relation to the taking of prosecutorial evidence. Compared to other international charters, the American Convention attaches particular weight to the defence's direct contribution to the obtaining of testimonial evidence by acknowledging the guarantee of confrontation as a 'right of the defense to examine witnesses present in the court'.[41] Thus, the reference to the 'defense' makes it difficult to interpret this guarantee in such a broad way as to allow persons other than the defendants and their lawyer—in particular, an investigative judge—to examine prosecutorial witnesses in favour of the defence.

It would not be an exaggeration to affirm that by this means the Pact of San José also enables defendants to cross-examine incriminating witnesses. Doubtless, the defendant's presence in court strengthens the potential of cross-examination, especially where the contacts with the lawyer were previously restricted.[42] This approach, while confirming the relevance of the accused's right to be present at trial, enhances the role of legal assistance, requiring the contracting countries to ensure free and private communications in court between the defendant and his counsel. Significantly, the right of the defence to examine witnesses present in the court maintains its relevance under the Convention irrespective of the accused's decision to defend himself or to appoint counsel.[43]

Against this background, it is no surprise that the Inter-American institutions adopted a more rigorous approach to the right to challenge incriminating evidence than that followed by other international case-law. The Court has always stressed that 'imposing restrictions on the alleged victim and the defense lawyer' can infringe their right to examine prosecutorial witnesses.[44] This does not entail that the right to confrontation is an absolute guarantee. In its 2002 *Report on Terrorism*

[41] Art. 8(2)(f) ACHR.

[42] Giacomolli (2014), p. 116.

[43] Art. 8(2)(d) ACHR.

[44] IACtHR, *Lori Berenson-Mejía v. Peru*, § 185.

and Human Rights, the Inter-American Commission acknowledged that 'certain limited aspects of the right to due process of law and to a fair trial that might potentially be the subject of derogation in exceptional and *bona fide* emergency situations'. Even in emergency cases, however, 'this is subject to prevailing rules governing derogation'. From this it follows that the suspension of due process guarantees can take place

> only for such time and to the extent strictly required by the exigencies of the situation, that it not entail discrimination of any kind, that it be compatible with all of the state's other obligations under international law, including international humanitarian law where applicable, and that the rule of law and supervision by the judiciary remains intact.

As we will see, the right to examine witnesses present in court can be suspended 'where safety or other circumstances may necessarily require protecting the identity of the witness'. Yet, measures must be adopted 'to ensure a defendant's non-derogable fair trial rights, including the right to challenge the veracity of the witness's evidence by alternative methods'.[45]

2. Qualitative Conditions of Effective Confrontation, Miscarriage of Justice and Deficiencies of National Law

The effective exercise of the right to confrontation presupposes specific conditions to be fulfilled. It is not always easy to ascertain whether and to what extent the lack of proper confrontation depended on miscarriage of justice. In *Castillo Petruzzi et al. v. Peru*, the question at stake was whether defendants had a fair opportunity to challenge the testimony of police officers who had previously gathered their statements during their inquiry. The Court held that depriving the accused persons of the possibility to cross-examine the police and military agents whose testimony had constituted the basis for the charges preferred against them infringed on the American Convention.[46] On close examination, this did not depend on misconduct by the competent authorities but was the result of clear limitations of the Peruvian law, which did not set the necessary conditions for the fulfilment of the Convention's fair trial rights. This deficiency was further aggravated by the fact that the suspects were not granted legal assistance until they gave their statements to the police. Consequently, they had no opportunity to be heard from the time of their detention until they gave evidence before the police,[47] whereas the lawyers, once they were appointed, had no 'means to refute the evidence compiled and on record in the police investigation report'.[48]

A similar question arose in *Palamara Iribarne v. Chile*, a case of a retired Chilean Navy officer prosecuted for disobedience and contempt of authority

[45]IAComHR, *Report on Terrorism and Human Rights*, § 262.

[46]IACtHR, *Castillo Petruzzi et al. v. Peru*, § 153 et seq.

[47]*Ibid.*, § 146.

[48]*Ibid.*, § 153.

because of a book in which he had addressed issues related to military intelligence. The Court was called upon to analyse whether the Naval Prosecutor's dismissal of the lawyer's request, made without access to the case file, for a confrontation between the statements given by the accused and the versions described in the arguments of the military prosecutors infringed upon Article 8(2) ACHR. This case was also peculiar in that the defendant claimed not just to be confronted with prosecutorial witnesses but with the incriminating arguments used by the Military Prosecutors, since 'relevant contradictions' with the accused's statements had to be clarified.[49] The question arose furthermore because Chilean law did not allow for the defence counsel to be present while the accused made a statement. Thus counsel was only involved in the proceedings after the investigation stage had concluded and the case was referred to the military court for trial. As a consequence, while the defendant remained detained, his lawyer had to submit his 'request to the Prosecutor for evidentiary measures to be taken without having had access neither to the investigation procedures nor to the charges brought against the accused'.[50] The Court found that the impossibility for the defence to have 'access to the procedures adopted during the investigation stage and forward evidence prevented Mr. Palamara-Iribarne from defending himself adequately'.[51] Again, this conclusion was due not just to a misconduct of the competent prosecutor but to the legal arrangements set at national level. Remarkably, the Court found the state's responsibility on the basis of both Articles 1 and 2 of the Convention, since Chilean law contained rules that infringed on the guarantees of a fair trial, failing to comply with the general duty to adopt measures aimed to allow for the full exercise of the Convention rights.[52]

3. Anonymous Witnesses and the Use of Untested Evidence

It has been observed that the Inter-American case-law, while considering the right to confrontation non-derogable, does not tighten it to the point that it could undermine other human rights acknowledged by the Convention. In particular, alternative solutions must be found to avoid that the fulfilment of the guarantee of confrontation causes irreparable damages to the fundamental rights of individuals other than the accused. An interesting example of the overall assessments required by the right to confrontation is the recent case *Norín Catrimán et al. v. Chile*. In this complex case, regarding the convictions of some of the leaders and members of the indigenous people *Mapuche*, the Inter-American Court dealt with the right to challenge the testimony of witnesses whose identity had been hidden from the defence. The Court addressed two main questions, i.e., (a) whether means

[49]IACtHR, *Palamara Iribarne v. Chile*, § 176.

[50]*Ibid.*, § 175.

[51]*Ibid.*, § 177.

[52]*Ibid.*, § 181.

acting as counterweight of the lack of direct confrontation were adopted and the defence had the opportunity of challenging the reliability of the witnesses' testimony, and (b) what weight was attached to the witness evidence in the decision-making.

Concerning the first issue, the Court considered the measures adopted against *Norín Catrimán* and *Pichún Paillalao* adequate. Not only could the defence have access to the official records of the statements rendered in the investigative phase but the witnesses were also re-examined in an oral hearing, their identity being made accessible, albeit only to the defendants' counsels.[53] The defence thus had the opportunity to examine the incriminating witnesses, even though they had been placed behind a screen that hid their real face and their voices were distorted while testifying by means of special equipment.

Notwithstanding these arrangements, the decision on whether the witnesses' identity needed to be hidden to the defence, albeit based on national law, lacked however effective judicial oversight. The Court found that the order of *juez de garantía* who authorised these arrangements was not sufficiently reasoned, since it did not explain what grounds made it necessary to hide the witnesses' identity. Based on the Strasbourg case law, the Inter-American Court stressed in very clear terms that contracting countries should adopt means to fulfil the public interest in the ascertainment of events and the need to protect the witnesses' life, physical integrity and security. Despite the great relevance of these rights, however, a proper balance must be struck with the accused's defence rights and the right to confrontation.[54] In particular, there must be a concrete risk either for the witnesses or their relatives, and the onus is on the competent authority to demonstrate that it exists in the case at stake. According to the Court, this test specifically was failed in the *Norín Catrimán et al.* case.[55]

As to the second issue, the Court's reasoning followed in very strict terms the Strasbourg doctrine of sole and decisive evidence, even though the conclusions reached were not the same ones for all the offenders.[56] Thus Inter-American case-law, invoking the European jurisprudence of the *Doorson* and *van Mechelen* cases, pointed out that the adoption of compensating measures does not allow the decision-makers to attach decisive weight for the defendants' conviction to information obtained without the accused having had the opportunity of challenging the testimony of a prosecutorial witness.

---

[53]IACtHR, *Norín Catrimán et al. v. Chile*, § 247.

[54]*Ibid.*, § 242 et seq.

[55]*Ibid.*, § 249.

[56]*Ibid.*, § 251.

II. The Right to Access to Exculpatory Evidence in Death Penalties

Another important aspect of the accused's active participation in the collection of evidence is whether and to what extent the defence can have a fair opportunity to access exculpatory evidence. In this regard, the contracting countries have particularly demanding obligations in cases of mandatory death penalty. In *Dacosta Cadogan v. Barbados*, the Court—dealing with the right to 'obtain the appearance, as witnesses, of experts or other persons who may throw light on the facts', right enshrined in Article 8(2)(f) ACHR—stressed that

> a violation of the due process rights of a defendant in a capital case, such as the failure to provide him or her with [. . .] adequate means for his or her defense [. . .] may result in an arbitrary deprivation of the right to life recognized under Article 4 [ACHR]. The failure to guarantee these rights in a death penalty case could undoubtedly result in a grave and irreversible miscarriage of justice, with the possible outcome being the execution of a person who was not given a fair trial.[57]

In this case, national law allowed the presiding judge to solicit the opinion of an expert to ascertain the existence of a possible alcohol dependency or other 'personality disorders' that could have affected the defendant's capacity at the time of the commission of the alleged offense. Nevertheless, the competent authority failed both to order a psychiatric evaluation and to 'ensure that Mr. Dacosta and his counsel were aware of the availability of a free, voluntary, and detailed mental health evaluation in order to prepare his defense in the trial'.[58] The Court therefore found an infringement of paragraphs 1 and 2 lit. *c* and *f* of Article 8 ACHR, in that the state's passive conduct not only led to the exclusion of evidence possibly relevant to the preparation of the accused's defence but did not also allow the ascertainment by a mental health professional of whether common drunkenness or a disease related to substance dependency existed in the concrete case. As the Court put it, in a death penalty case, this issue can make 'the difference between the defendant's life or death'.[59]

F. The Defence's Argumentative Contribution to the Decision-Making

The Inter-American case-law has never explicitly dealt with the defence's argumentative contribution to decision-making. However, we can draw some conclusions in this regard in two problematic areas, namely (a) the argumentative

[57] IACtHR, *Dacosta Cadogan v. Barbados*, § 85.
[58] *Ibid.*, § 88.
[59] *Ibid.*, § 87.

role of the defence in challenging the charge filed and the legal classification of the offence, and (b) the possibility of challenging the incriminating evidence collected by the investigative bodies.

Concerning the first issue, it has been observed that in the *Barreto Leiva* case, the Inter-American Court stressed the need for congruence between the facts informed to the accused, the indictment and the conviction.[60] This safeguard also entails the accused's right to be kept informed on any change made to the accusation prior to the decision-making, a right of utmost importance to enable the defence to produce new argumentation against the amended charge. The degree and quality of information, moreover, impinges on the effectiveness of this guarantee. In this regard, the Court has not adopted a very consistent approach. As noted, defendants must initially be granted complete information on the indictment, the evidence supporting the charges and the legal definition of the facts. However, as stated in *Fermín Ramírez v. Guatemala*, the lack of information on the changes of legal qualification does not automatically infringe the right to a defence, when 'the facts themselves are maintained invariable and the procedural guarantees included in the law for the change to the new classification are observed'.[61]

This conclusion raises complex questions. What law should lay down the procedural guarantees allowing for changes of legal classification and to what extent can a change of *nomen juris* be unrelated to the factual basis? Even though in the *Fermín Ramírez* case some procedural mistakes were found in the application of national law,[62] the reasoning of the Court reveals that compliance with domestic law does not suffice to ensure the lawfulness of a case in which the change of the indictment led to the trial court handing down a death penalty. By applying Article 374 of the Guatemalan code of criminal procedure, the trial judges limited themselves to warning the defence of a possible modification of the legal classification of the facts without any specification of the features and contents of the new legal classification.[63] Yet the Court stressed the need to interpret national procedural law in line with the American Convention. By relying on the Strasbourg case-law, the judges of San José held that the function of the 'indictment' in a criminal process must be considered *vis-à-vis* the right to a defence.[64] From this it follows that, although national law enables the trial court to change the legal classification of the offence and to impose a more severe sentence than that requested by the public prosecutor, these powers can legitimately be exercised only to the extent that

[60] *Ibid.*, § 47.

[61] IACtHR, *Fermín Ramírez v. Guatemala*, § 67.

[62] *Ibid.*, § 70 et seq. In particular, Guatemalan law allows for evidence to be adduced in the oral trial on new facts or circumstances not included in the indictment. This presupposes, however, that the public prosecutor had previously presented an "Alternative indictment" or the "Extension of the indictment" in order to seek the amendment of the object of the criminal trial.

[63] *Ibid.*, § 73.

[64] *Ibid.*, § 67 et seq.

the accused's right to an effective defence will not be jeopardised.[65] These requirements must be fulfilled especially in a death penalty case, in which the trial must be suspended and the accused must be given the opportunity of adducing new evidence or at least of giving a statement on the new charge.[66]

On the other hand, the Inter-American case-law is well-aware of the risks arising from an uncontrolled use of the *iura novit curia* principle, especially where the change of the legal classification was due to a modification of the factual basis of the accusation without the principle of consistency being observed.[67] In *Fermín Ramírez v. Guatemala*, the trial court considered some facts not included in the indictment (intentional murder produced by asphyxia by strangulation and the possibility of carnal access after death) as proven and re-classified on this basis the offence from aggravated rape to murder.[68] The Court's conclusions, therefore, reveal an approach that not only looks at the formal change of the indictment but also at the reasons for the new legal classification, and particularly on its impact on the fundamental rights of the convicted person.

The second problematic area relates to the defence's argumentative power to challenge prosecutorial evidence. By dealing with *Palamara Iribarne v. Chile*, we have noted that the Inter-American Court examined the Naval Prosecutor's dismissal of the lawyer's request that a confrontation could take place between the statements given by the accused and the versions described in the arguments of the Military Prosecutors. The request was justified by the existence of relevant contradictions that had to be clarified. This highlighted another important feature of the right to an effective defence, that is, the right to challenge incriminating evidence not only with further pieces of evidence but also with exculpatory arguments. It might be assumed that the conclusions reached by the Court as to the state's responsibility for providing rules that opposed the guarantees of a due process can also be understood in the light of the accused's right to challenge the reliability of the prosecutorial information with defensive arguments.

G. Restrictions on Freedom, Right to Be Fairly Heard and the Enhanced Need for Overall Human Rights Oversight

I. The Broad Protection of Information Rights

It has been observed that under the American Convention also, the right to be fairly heard deserves enhanced protection where coercive means are at stake. This is especially apparent in the case of restrictions on freedom.[69] To enable effective

[65]*Ibid.*, § 74 et seq.

[66]*Ibid.*, § 74.

[67]*Ibid.*, § 73 et seq.

[68]*Ibid.*, § 76.

[69]Casal (2014), p. 199.

reaction against coercion and reduce the overall negative impact of deprivation of liberty, the individuals concerned must firstly be provide with proper information. Like other international human rights instruments, the Pact of San José attaches great weight to the need to inform the persons arrested or detained about the grounds for restriction on freedom as well as, if the measure was ordered within criminal proceedings, about the charges filed against them.[70] This double information in turn defines the goals of this guarantee, which aims at protecting the persons concerned against unlawful or arbitrary deprivation of freedom (explicitly prohibited by paragraph 3), while allowing them to set up a proper defence against the charge preferred.[71]

The broader scope of this safeguard than that of the general information due in criminal proceedings under Article 8 ACHR confirms the enhanced protection due to any person arrested or detained. The reference to both arrest and detention[72] ensures a protective umbrella to any situation of deprivation of liberty—no matter how it is defined by national law—carried out by the police or administrative authorities.[73] It is worth observing that the San José judges in turn broadened the subjective scope of the persons who are responsible to inform the individuals arrested or detained. In *Maritza Urrutia v. Guatemala*, the Court, starting with an overall consideration of the judicial guarantees concerned with deprivation of liberty, stressed that the whole set-up of paragraphs 4–6 of Article 7 ACHR establishes

> obligations of a positive nature that impose specific requirements on both State agents and third parties who act with the tolerance and agreement of the former and who are responsible for carrying out detentions.[74]

The competent bodies cannot be released from this responsibility by simply declaring that the detainee became aware of the grounds for coercion. In *Chaparro Álvarez and Lapo Íñiguez v. Ecuador*, the Court confirmed that the right to information entails obligations of 'a positive nature and, thus, susceptible of proof',[75] which therefore offloads onto the state the burden of demonstrating that the victim was provided with the necessary information to set up a proper defence.[76]

The Inter-American case-law has further strengthened the guarantee of information by including the right of the detainee to establish contacts with other persons (especially a next of kin or an attorney) in order to make them aware of the state's

---

[70] Art. 7(4) ACHR.

[71] Casal (2014), p. 193.

[72] It is noteworthy, however, that the English text, unlike the other official versions, restricts the guarantee to the cases of detention.

[73] Casal (2014), p. 193.

[74] IACtHR, *Maritza Urrutia v. Guatemala*, § 71.

[75] IACtHR, *Chaparro Álvarez and Lapo Íñiguez v. Ecuador*, § 73.

[76] Casal (2014), p. 194.

actions and to help them take the appropriate response against the measure adopted. This information pursues different goals depending on the person concerned. As the Court clearly stressed in *Tibi v. Ecuador*,

> Notification to a next of kin or to a close relation is especially significant, for this person to know the whereabouts and the circumstances of the accused and to provide him with the appropriate assistance and protection. In case of notification to an attorney, it is especially important for the detainee to be able to meet privately with him, which is inherent to his right to benefit from a true defense.

Significantly, the guarantee of information in Article 7 ACHR also entails the right to inform a consular official. The consular notification can be of great help, providing the detainee with a number of safeguards. In the 1999 Advisory Opinion '*The Right to Information on Consular Assistance in the Framework of the Guarantees of the due Process of Law*', the Court pointed out that the consul

> may assist the detainee in various acts of defense, such as granting or hiring legal counsel, obtaining evidence in the country of origin, corroborating the conditions under which legal assistance is provided, and observing the situation of the accused while he is in prison.[77]

The proper fulfilment of the aims of this fundamental guarantee requires information to be provided in a simple and understandable language[78] at the very moment in which the coercive measure is enforced.[79] This also applies in the case of arrest *in flagrante delicto*.[80] In this regard, however, the San José case-law somehow softened the protective scope of the guarantee by allowing for information on the reasons for detention to be provided either in writing or orally.[81] In *Chaparro Álvarez and Lapo Íñiguez v. Ecuador*, the Court considered that the failure of national law to require the detainee to be shown the court order excluded the unlawfulness of the State's action under the Convention.[82] The Court, instead, strengthened the formal requirements in relation to the information on the charge, information that must be provided in writing.[83] In the light of the importance of this information, it is debatable whether the Convention can tolerate that under certain circumstances the detainee is not informed on the charge at the time of arrest, provided that information is ensured as promptly as possible.[84] As noted, information must be guaranteed before the first statement of the accused in due advance as to enable the detained person to prepare for the first hearing.[85]

---

[77]IACtHR, *The Right to Information on Consular Assistance in the Framework of the Guarantees of Due Process of Law*, § 86.

[78]Casal (2014), p. 194.

[79]IACtHR, *Palamara Iribarne v. Chile*, § 227; IACtHR, *Cabrera García and Montiel Flores v. Mexico*, § 105.

[80]Casal (2014), p. 194.

[81]*Ibid.*

[82]IACtHR, *Chaparro Álvarez and Lapo Íñiguez v. Ecuador*, § 75.

[83]*Ibid.*, § 74.

[84]In this sense see instead Casal (2014), p. 195.

[85]IACtHR, *The Right to Information on Consular Assistance in the Framework of the Guarantees of Due Process of Law*, § 106.

II. The Right to a Prompt Judicial Hearing and the Protection Against Inhuman Treatment

The granting of proper information sets the necessary condition for the individuals deprived of freedom to make their voice heard and to obtain an impartial examination of the case. This guarantee holds particular relevance under the American Convention in the case of restrictions on freedom carried out without previous judicial order. In particular, arrest *in flagrante delicto* places the individuals concerned in a highly vulnerable position, which requires the judicial authority to promptly give them a fair opportunity to be heard. Therefore, the practice of imprisoning a person who is not afforded a court examination is surely incompatible with the Convention.[86] Of course, the right to a defence plays even greater role in the decision on whether to apply a long-term detention.

Like other human rights charters, the Pact of San José acknowledges the right of any person detained to be promptly brought before a judge or other officer authorized by law to exercise judicial power. It is noteworthy, however, that this fundamental guarantee—in the absence of a list of grounds for arrest or detention laid down at international level—has a general scope of application, not being circumscribed to the cases of arrest and pre-trial detention in criminal proceedings. Thus the Court emphasises the need for a prompt judicial hearing even in cases of deprivation of liberty by administrative or police authorities.[87] In this respect, particular focus was attached to the possibility for foreign people detained for the purpose of expulsion to access a court.[88] In *Vélez Loor v. Panamá*, the Court dealt with a case of liberty that was not related with a criminal offense but with the applicant's irregular migratory status for having entered Panama in an unauthorized area without the necessary documents and in violation of a prior deportation order.[89] In this judgment, the Court highlighted the broader approach of the Pact of San José from that of the European Convention, since the former does not make the application of the guarantee of a fair hearing dependent on 'the reasons or circumstances under which the person has been arrested or detained'.[90] As the Court put it,

> Under the principle *pro persona,* this guarantee must be met whenever the person's detention or arrest is based on his or her migratory status, in accordance with the principles of judicial control and procedural immediacy. In order to establish a true mechanism of control in the face of unlawful and arbitrary detentions, the judicial review must be carried out promptly and in such a way as to guarantee compliance with the law and the detainee's effective enjoyment of his rights, taking into account his special vulnerability.[91]

[86]Giacomolli (2014), p. 115.

[87]IACtHR, *López Álvarez v. Honduras*, §§ 64 ff.

[88]Casal (2014), p. 196 f.

[89]IACtHR, *Vélez Loor v. Panama*, § 106.

[90]*Ibid.*, § 107.

[91]*Ibid.*

On the other hand, we have noted that the vulnerable condition of the person arrested and detained increases the need for an overall check against human rights violations. Therefore, the intervention of an independent body must be as prompt as possible not only to detect but also to prevent further violations of human rights and ill-treatment.[92] In the light of this, the Inter-American case law not only grants the arrested or detained individuals an opportunity to be fairly heard in person but also makes the tool of Article 7(5) ACHR a general means, which enables the competent court to carry out a human rights-oriented assessment of the detention.

In this regard, it can be doubted whether compliance with national law suffices to fulfil the requirement of promptness.[93] In *Durand and Ugarte v. Peru*, the Court shared this view in relation to the Peruvian Anti-Terrorism Law, which allowed the police to keep the arrested persons 15 days before bringing them to the judicial authority.[94] This approach was later abandoned, however, in the *Castillo Petruzzi* case, in which the Court found that this maximum time-limit, alongside the possibility of a prolongation of further 15 days, was unlawful under the Convention.[95] The Inter-American case-law has reiterated this approach in subsequent cases, calling for an autonomous understanding of the guarantee of a prompt judicial hearing especially in areas with significant military presence.[96]

In the light of its systematic importance, judicial examination must fulfil specific qualitative requirements, as it cannot be satisfied by formally bringing the arrested person to the competent court. In order to avoid especially the risk of forced disappearances, the arrested individuals must personally appear in court and have a fair opportunity to be heard.[97] In the *Acosta Calderón* case, the Court found an infringement of the Convention because the police put the detained person at the disposal of the competent judge who, however, did not hear him.[98] The same applies to a case in which the competent judge, despite being present at the moment of the arrest, heard the person concerned only 26 days after the beginning of detention.[99]

III. Audi alteram partem *in* habeas corpus *Proceedings*

Alongside the right to a prompt independent oversight *ex officio*, the American Convention also recognised the right of the individuals deprived of personal

[92]IACtHR, *Villagrán-Morales et al. v. Guatemala*, § 192 ff.

[93]In the same sense Casal (2014), p. 198.

[94]IACtHR, *Durand and Ugarte v. Peru*, § 91.

[95]IACtHR, *Castillo Petruzzi et al. v. Peru*, § 110.

[96]IACtHR, *Cabrera García and Montiel Flores v. Mexico*, 192.

[97]Casal (2014), p. 197.

[98]IACtHR, *Acosta Calderón v. Ecuador*, § 78.

[99]IACtHR, *Chaparro Álvarez and Lapo Íñiguez v. Ecuador*, § 83.

freedom to undertake proceedings in order to have their case heard by a court.[100] Historically, the guarantee of *habeas corpus* has had enormous importance in Latin America, constituting another powerful means of independent assessment not only of the lawfulness of the arrest or detention but also of other human rights violations, concerning the right to physical integrity, the right to life and so on.[101] This explains the weight that the Inter-American case-law here also attached to the requirement that the arrestee or detainee personally appear in court.[102] As the Inter-American Court put it,

> *Habeas corpus* performs a vital role in ensuring that a person's life and physical integrity are respected, in preventing his disappearance or the keeping of his whereabouts secret and in protecting him against torture or other cruel, inhumane, or degrading punishment or treatment.[103]

In the light of the importance of *habeas corpus* proceedings, the Court calls for the highest degree of simplicity in this legal action, while ruling out that the arrested individuals must first lodge their recourse before an administrative authority.[104] Most interestingly, the Inter-American case-law insists on the requirement of accessibility of *habeas corpus* not only for the arrested or detained persons but also for their families, especially in the cases of forced disappearance, which make impossible for them to take proceedings before the judicial authority.[105] The effectiveness of *habeas corpus* presupposes the fulfilment of specific conditions. In particular, the detainee must be provided with legal assistance. Moreover, judicial review must also be carried out as promptly as possible, which helps counter the risk of forced disappearance.[106] The need for anticipated application of this guarantee is of utmost importance in the Inter-American case-law, which prevents the contracting countries from abolishing or even restricting the right to take proceedings before a court in the case of threats of deprivation of freedom.[107]

H. Provisional Conclusions

Notwithstanding the similarities between the American Convention and other international human rights instruments, the Inter-American case-law has developed a complex jurisprudence, which largely reflects most of the social and cultural problems of the countries falling within its jurisdiction. Furthermore, the Inter-

---

[100] Art. 7(6) ACHR.

[101] Casal (2014), p. 203 f.

[102] IACtHR, *Chaparro Álvarez and Lapo Íñiguez v. Ecuador*, § 135.

[103] IACtHR, Adv. Op. OC-8/87, § 35.

[104] IACtHR, *Vélez Loor v. Panama*, § 127.

[105] IACtHR, *Anzualdo Castro v. Peru*, 64.

[106] Casal (2014), p. 205.

[107] Cf. Art. 7(5) ACHR.

American Court has metabolized the experience of other jurisprudences (especially of the Strasbourg case-law), elaborating an autonomous approach to criminal justice, which includes the participatory rights of the individuals involved in criminal proceedings in a general programme of protection of the victims of serious human rights breaches. The acknowledgement of the criminal trial as a listening space with due guarantees links the assessment of fair trial cases with a broader control, extended to the overall system of protection of the human rights enshrined in the Convention. Yet the relatively low number of cases deal with by the Inter-American case-law, compared to the huge number of Strasbourg judgments, does not allow us to draw definitive conclusions.

References

Casal JM (2014) Article 7. In: Steiner and Uribe (eds) Convención Americana sobre Derechos Humanos. Comentario. Konrad Adenauer Stiftung, Berlin, pp 180–206

Dondé Matute J (2013) The Inter-American system of human rights and transnational inquiries. In: Ruggeri S (ed) Transnational inquiries and the protection of fundamental rights in criminal proceedings. A study in memory of Vittorio Grevi and Giovanni Tranchina. Springer, Heidelberg, pp 41–50

García Ramírez S (2011) El debido proceso en la jurisprudencia de la Corte Interamericana de Derechos Humanos. Jornadas Itinerantes del Instituto de la Judicatura Federal del Consejo de la Judicatura del Poder Judicial de la Federación de México. http://www.ijf.cjf.gob.mx/cursosesp/2012/jornadasitinerantes/procesoSGR.pdf

Giacomolli NJ (2014) O devido processo penal. Abordagem conforme a Constituição Federal e o Pacto de São José da Costa Rica. Atlas S.A., São Paulo

Ibáñez Rivas JM (2014) Article 8. In: Steiner and Uribe (eds) Convención Americana sobre Derechos Humanos. Comentario. Konrad Adenauer Stiftung, Berlin, pp 207–254

Trechsel S (2005) Human rights in criminal proceedings. Oxford University Press, Oxford

Chapter 10
Harmonisation of Criminal Justice and Participatory Rights in Criminal Proceedings. New Development in EU Law After the Lisbon Treaty

Contents

A. Harmonisation of Criminal Procedure Law and the Enhancement of Participatory Rights in Criminal Justice After the Lisbon Treaty 368
B. The Right to Be personally Involved in Criminal Proceedings in the EU Area 370
I. The Right to Personal Participation in Criminal Hearings. A Limited Guarantee 370
II. Exceptions to the Right to Personal Participation 372
1. *In absentia* Procedures 372
2. *Inaudito reo* Proceedings 375
a) The *Covaci* Case and the Indications of the European Court of Justice 375
b) The New Safeguards Laid Down by EU Statutory Law 379
III. Towards a Victim's Right to Personally Participate in Criminal Proceedings? 380
C. Conditions of Effective Defence and the Right to Active Participation in Criminal Proceedings 381
I. Language and the Right to Effective Participation in Criminal Proceedings 381
1. Linguistic Guarantees of the Accused 381
2. Linguistic Guarantees of the Victim 383
II. Information Rights and the Guarantee of Effective Defence 386
1. Information Rights of the Accused 386
a) Premise 386
b) Information on the Charge 386
c) Information on the Investigation and the Right to Access the File 388
2. Information Rights of the Victim 389
III. The Right to Be fairly Heard in Criminal Proceedings 390
1. The Voice of the Accused 390
2. The Voice of the Victim 392
IV. The Defence's Contribution to the Gathering of Evidence 393
D. Participatory Rights and Coercive Measures in the Field of Personal Freedom 396
E. Interim Conclusions 398
References 399

S. Ruggeri, Audi Alteram Partem *in Criminal Proceedings*,
DOI 10.1007/978-3-319-54573-8_10

A. Harmonisation of Criminal Procedure Law and the Enhancement of Participatory Rights in Criminal Justice After the Lisbon Treaty

We have anticipated that the development of a broad participatory understanding of criminal proceedings by the Strasbourg case-law has strongly influenced the evolution of EU law in criminal matters over the last two decades. The focus on defence rights as an engine of a fair criminal justice had already followed the harmonisation process of criminal procedure law that occurred under the former Third Pillar in the field of transnational cooperation among member states. Moreover, EU institutions were certainly also aware of the need to strengthen the defence rights in domestic criminal proceedings in the middle of the last decade, as the European Commission launched the proposal of a Framework Decision on certain procedural rights in criminal proceedings throughout the European Union.[1] Alongside specific aspects that constituted the necessary conditions for the active involvement of private parties in criminal proceedings, this proposal, for example, explicitly focused on the right to interpretation, which, in the light of the requirements set forth by the European Convention, must be of such quality as to enable the defendant's effective participation in criminal trials.[2] During the legislative procedure, however, this proposal faced enormous difficulties and was never adopted.

Shortly before the entry into force of the Lisbon Treaty, EU institutions therefore chose a more gradual approach, launching a 'Roadmap' aimed at the enhancement of fair trial rights of the addressee of criminal proceedings.[3] This Roadmap, enacted into the Stockholm Programme,[4] has since 2010 led to the adoption of legislative initiatives of utmost importance in the renewed European scenario not only in light of the unprecedented form of directives in the area of the former Third Pillar but also because of the new goals of harmonisation at the primary law level.

Doubtless, the Lisbon reform brought about significant changes in the process of Europeanization of criminal justice, a process no longer concerned only with international cooperation (surrender procedures, transnational investigations, etc.) but also extended to the harmonisation of the rules concerned with domestic criminal proceedings within the main areas set by Article 82(2) TFEU. To be sure, even the former text of the Treaty of the European Union promoted common actions aimed at ensuring compatibility in the national legislation of the member states with a view to improving judicial cooperation in criminal matters.[5] And even today, harmonisation of criminal procedure law is still allowed to the extent that the

[1] COM(2004) 328 final.

[2] *Ibid.*, § 69.

[3] See 'Roadmap for strengthening the procedural rights of suspected and accused persons in criminal proceedings', Council Resolution of 30 November 2009 (2009/295/01).

[4] The Stockholm Programme—An open and secure Europe serving and protecting citizens (2010/C 115/01), § 2.4.

[5] Art. 31(1)(c) TEU (old text).

EU intervention is necessary to facilitate the application of the principle of mutual recognition of judicial decisions and police and judicial cooperation in transnational cases.[6] In other terms, now, as then, the focus of the EU harmonisation is mainly oriented towards international cooperation, so that the enhancement of individual rights in national proceedings is still anchored to a perspective that still looks primarily on the investigation and prosecution of offences with a transnational character.[7] The method of the EU intervention is however different today and the new legal framework established by the Lisbon Treaty reveals the clear awareness of the need for a harmonisation that, albeit limited to minimum standards, allows full implementation of the mutual recognition principle.

At first glance, the legislative set-up resulting from the Lisbon Treaty does not explicitly acknowledge specific participatory safeguards in criminal proceedings. There is no doubt, however, that the main areas covered by Article 82(2) TFEU, starting with the general provision on the protection of individuals in criminal procedures,[8] allow for EU legislative intervention to strengthen the right to effective participation in criminal trials. Most significantly, this right cannot be limited to the accused, but must also be ensured to other individuals involved in criminal prosecutions. This especially applies to the aggrieved parties, to whom the Lisbon Treaty attached specific attention by promoting legislative initiatives aimed at enhancing the protection of their interests.[9] The EU Charter of fundamental rights goes in the same direction. While providing its own set of individual guarantees concerned with the administration of justice, the Nice-Strasbourg Charter does not follow a self-referential approach but requires an interpretation open to other human rights instruments, especially the European Convention as well as the member states' Constitutions.[10] The legislative initiatives launched after the Lisbon Treaty should be interpreted in this light. This not only applies to the initiatives aimed at implementing the 2009 Roadmap on procedural rights but also to legislative instruments falling outside the scope of this programme, such as the 2012 Directive on the protection of victim's rights. This legislative instrument had the merit of enhancing the participatory rights of the injured party in criminal pro-

---

[6]Art. 82(2) TFEU.

[7]In 2004, the European Commission had already presented the proposal for a Framework Decision on certain procedural rights as 'the necessary complement to the mutual recognition measures that are designed to increase efficiency of prosecution. A set of agreed procedural rights to ensure equivalent treatment of suspected persons throughout the EU should enable judicial cooperation measures to be applied as efficiently as possible, especially those that envisage surrender of persons or of evidence to another Member State'. Cf. COM(2004) 328 final, Explanatory Memorandum, § 52.

[8]Art. 82(2)(b) TFEU.

[9]Art. 82(2)(c) TFEU. On the role of the victim in European criminal justice see Allegrezza (2012), p. 1 ff.

[10]Art. 53 EU FRCh.

ceedings,[11] notwithstanding that most of the guarantees acknowledged were expressed in such terms that the impact of the EU intervention varies considerably depending on the national approach to the role of the victim in criminal justice.[12]

Against this background, the present discussion analyses the evolution that has recently taken place in EU law towards the introduction of a set of autonomous rules aimed at the enhancement of the defence's participatory role in criminal proceedings. In this context, however, it must also be examined whether and to what extent EU law has accumulated the cultural heritage of the Strasbourg case-law, whose flexible approach to criminal justice, as noted, has led to a reconstruction of fair trial guarantees in the light of an overall assessment of conflicting interests.

B. The Right to Be personally Involved in Criminal Proceedings in the EU Area

I. The Right to Personal Participation in Criminal Hearings. A Limited Guarantee

To start with, it is worth observing that under the strong influence of the Strasbourg case-law, the EU institutions have increasingly drawn their focus to the accused's right to personal participation in criminal proceedings. As we will see, one legislative instrument issued in the last year of the Third Pillar—namely, Framework Decision 2009/299/JHA—marked a significant step in the process of indirect harmonisation of criminal procedure law[13] by strengthening the participatory safeguards of individuals tried *in absentia* if subject to an EAW procedure.[14] Notwithstanding the merits of this legislation, it was however unrealistic to think that the new conditions could work properly at the transnational level without previous harmonisation of the rules governing domestic proceedings. In 2013, under the new legislative framework set forth by the Lisbon Treaty, the Commission proposed a Directive aimed at strengthening certain aspects of the presumption of innocence and at laying down minimum standards governing the right to

[11] Directive 2012/29/EU, replacing Framework Decision 2001/220/JHA on the standing of the victim in criminal proceedings, laid down minimum rules on the rights, support and protection of the victim.

[12] Allegrezza (2012), p. 5 f.

[13] See, in this sense, Böse (2011), p. 489 ff.; Siracusano (2011), p. 91 f.

[14] Chapter 13, B.II.2.a.

personal participation in domestic criminal proceedings.[15] After a rather long road, the Directive was approved on 9 March 2016.[16]

This legislative initiative, which was faithfully inspired by the approach of the 2009 Framework Decision, largely departs from the main goal of ensuring the defendant's right to be present at trial.[17] Despite the solemn formulation of Article 8 (1), the scope of the new Directive is not self-evident and it is rather unclear within what limits EU law grants defendants the right to be personally involved in criminal proceedings. Although the English text expressly relates to the 'trial which can result in a decision on the guilt or innocence of a suspect or accused person',[18] significant differences emerge from a comparative analysis of the versions in other languages. While some of them follow the same approach of the English text,[19] others broaden the scope of the guarantee by acknowledging the right to of the accused to take part in any 'proceeding' aimed at a decision on guilt.[20] This issue is of utmost importance and can give rise to serious differences in the implementation of the new rules, especially because various EU countries allow special types of criminal judgments on the merits of the case to be issued prior to the trial phase. It is probable that the question will need the intervention of the European Court of Justice in a near future, which should also define the scope of the new rules in the light of the right to a retrial.[21] At any rate, the right to personal participation has intrinsic limits under this legislative instrument. Whatever the scope of the new regulation is, it does not provide for the accused with certainty a comprehensive

---

[15]COM(2013) 821 final. Although this initiative was not aimed at implementing the 2009 Roadmap for strengthening the procedural rights of suspected or accused persons in criminal proceedings, the European Council, while incorporating the Roadmap into the Stockholm Programme, stressed its non-exhaustive character and called thus for further initiatives on procedural issues, such as the presumption of innocence.

[16]Directive 2016/343/EU.

[17]*Below*, B.II.1.

[18]To be sure, also this formulation is rather unclear as significant differences emerge from a comparative analysis of linguistic versions. Some of them relate solely to the trial phase: see in this sense, alongside the English version (*trial*), the German one that, while mentioning the concept of *Verhandlung*, may seem to concern the *Hauptverhandlung*, that is, the trial hearing. Other linguistic versions broaden the scope of the new rules by relating to any "process" or "proceeding" aimed at a decision on guilt: in this sense cf. the Greek version (*δίκη*) as well as almost all the versions in Romance languages, such as those in Italian (*processo*), French (*procès*), Portuguese (*julgamento*), Romanian (*proces*) and Spanish (*juicio*).

[19]See in this sense, alongside the English version (*trial*), the German one that, while mentioning the concept of *Verhandlung*, may seem to concern the *Hauptverhandlung*, that is, the trial hearing.

[20]In this sense cf. the Greek version (*δίκη*) as well as almost all the versions in Roman languages, such as those in Italian (*processo*), French (*procès*), Portuguese (*julgamento*), Romanian (*proces*) and Spanish (*juicio*).

[21]*Below*, B.II.1.

guarantee with a view to any decision within criminal proceedings. A number of decisions, therefore, fall outside the scope of application of the Directive, which does not ensure participation in phases that, although dealing with the merits of the case, do not aim at a decision on their guilt (*e.g.*, intermediate proceedings). Furthermore, the accused has no right to be personally involved in interlocutory proceedings that can lead to decisions seriously impinging on fundamental rights (*e.g.*, a decision on discontinuance of the proceedings or remand proceedings).

II. Exceptions to the Right to Personal Participation

1. *In absentia* Procedures

Until recently, as noted, EU law had no rules on the requirements that criminal proceedings must fulfil in the case of trials *in absentia*. It was only in 2009 that this delicate issue has increasingly drawn the focus of EU institutions, which amended various legislative instruments and especially the EAW Framework Decision by tightening the conditions upon which defendants can be surrendered to other EU countries in the case of default proceedings. The slowness of member states in implementing this legislation led the EU institutions to launch—under the new legal framework set by the Lisbon Treaty—the proposal for a new legislative instrument intended to harmonise the rules on the right to be present in criminal proceedings. Alongside the limited scope of application of these safeguards, Directive 2016/343/EU provides for specific provisions on *in absentia* proceedings. By following the approach adopted by the Strasbourg case-law, EU law allows for the institution of default proceedings if either the defendants were duly informed of the criminal law action initiated against them or they appointed a lawyer to represent them in court. Where none of these conditions is satisfied, the 2016 Directive does not exclude the conduct of default proceedings, provided, however, that the accused was given the possibility of accessing a retrial or a remedy aimed at a review of the conviction rendered *in absentia*.

On close examination, allowing for the institution of a criminal law action under these conditions entails grave risks for the accused's right to participation in criminal proceedings. Serious concerns arise in relation to information rights. By reproducing the approach of the 2009 legislation, the 2013 proposal required defendants to be summoned to court either in person or by other means received official information of the scheduled trial hearing.[22] These specifications were dropped from the provisions of Article 8 of the Directive, which only required the accused to be 'informed, in due time, of the trial and of the consequences of non-appearance'.[23] The two aforementioned situations, although being inserted into

[22] Art. 8(2)(a)(i) DirPIRPT-proposal.

[23] Paragraph 2(a) DirPIRPT.

Recital no. 36, still provide, however, important interpretative guidelines. Certainly, the reference to 'other means' leaves to the competent authority a great margin of discretion in choosing the information tools in the case at stake, a risk that is scarcely attenuated by the specification that the means used should unequivocally demonstrate that the accused was aware of the scheduled trial.[24] On close examination, even the requirement of a personal summons does not in itself prove that the defendants' absence was due to their unequivocal decision to waive their right to participate in criminal proceedings.[25] Nor does EU law require national authorities to review the grounds that led to the accused not appearing in court.

Furthermore, going beyond the requirement set by the Strasbourg case-law,[26] the 2016 Directive also allows for a trial *in absentia* where a lawyer represents the absent defendant in court. In this regard, a significant change was made from the original proposal that, in line with the 2009 legislation, allowed for the initiation of criminal proceedings where the accused, being aware of the scheduled trial, had given a mandate to a legal counsellor, 'who was either appointed by the person concerned or by the State, to defend him or her at the trial, and was indeed defended by that counsellor at the trial'.[27] Whereas this provision was shifted to Recital no 37, Article 8 of the Directive seems to satisfy itself with the objective fact that 'the suspect or accused person, having been informed of the trial, is represented by a mandated lawyer, who was appointed either by the suspect or accused person or by the State'.[28] Yet the requirement of a mandate given by the accused is not the only possible interpretation of the new provision, which could allow for member states to maintain those legal solutions that require in the case of default proceedings the appointment of a court-appointed lawyer, a result that is clearly far from reflecting the accused's unequivocal decision not to take part in the trial hearing.

It is worth observing, furthermore, that each one of the two conditions laid down by paragraph 2 suffices to justify the enforcement of the judgement. It is true that the appointment of a lawyer should presuppose information of the trial. Moreover, the Directive, following the Strasbourg case-law, draws particular attention 'to the diligence exercised by public authorities in order to inform the person concerned and to the diligence exercised by the person concerned in order to receive information addressed to him or her'.[29] However, the two cases of paragraph 2 reveal disjointed conditions, which legitimises the initiation of a proceeding *in absentia* on the condition that a court-appointed lawyer represents the accused at trial, even though the defendant neither received personal notification nor ever waived the right to personal participation. Despite the efforts made by the competent authorities to make the accused aware of the proceedings, moreover, the requirement of

[24] Art. 8(2)(a)(i) DirPIRPT -proposal.

[25] Recital no. 35 DirPIRPT.

[26] Wahl (2015), p. 74.

[27] Art. 8(2)(b) DirPIRPT -proposal.

[28] Art. 8(2)(b) DirPIRPT.

[29] Recital no. 38 DirPIRPT.

previous information can have different applications according to the national rules on judicial service.

Considerable changes were made to the draft proposal in relation to the possibility of instituting criminal proceedings outside these cases. By following the approach of the 2009 Framework Decision, the 2013 proposal allowed for trials *in absentia*, even though the aforementioned requirements could not be met, provided that the defendants were expressly informed of the possibility of a retrial or a remedy aimed at ensuring a review of the merits of the case and they did not avail themselves of this tool.[30] On close examination, this situation was also highly problematic. In particular, the proposal made the lawfulness of *in absentia* judgments dependent on two rather heterogeneous conditions, namely (a) that the accused expressly decided not to request a retrial or a remedy[31] and (b) that he did not 'request a retrial or appeal within a reasonable time frame'.[32] Equating these two cases, however, was not a good solution, since the failure to request a retrial or a remedy, unlike the case in which the accused expressly decides not to request them, may reflect the objective circumstance that the available tools were not used rather than being the result of the informed decision not to use them.[33]

Although the Directive dropped these arrangements, the new provisions can still give rise to serious human rights concerns. Since the fulfilment of one of the two initial situations allows for the enforcement of the decision rendered *in absentia*,[34] the execution of the conviction does not necessarily depend on the information of subsequent remedies. If none of these conditions were satisfied, the judgement can also be executed, provided that the accused was informed of the possibility of challenging the decision or accessing a retrial. Serious concerns, however, arise as to the way this information should be provided. By transposing the 2009 solutions into the field of national proceedings, the draft proposal required the accused to be 'expressly' informed of the possibility of a retrial or an appeal.[35] By contrast, the final text does not clarify at all how defendants should be made aware of subsequent remedies, whereas Recital no 39 allows for information to be provided either in writing or orally, on the sole condition, in the latter case, that information is noted pursuant to the recording procedure set forth by national law.

---

[30] Art. 8(3) DirPIRPT-proposal.

[31] Art. 8(3)(a) DirPIRPT-proposal.

[32] Art. 8(3)(b) DirPIRPT-proposal.

[33] Critical remarks on this case were also expressed by the CCBE. Cfr. http://www.ccbe.eu/fileadmin/user_upload/NTCdocument/EN_04042014_CCBE_Res1_1399968822.pdf.

[34] Art. 8(3) DirPIRPT.

[35] Art. 8(3) DirPIRPT-proposal.

2. *Inaudito reo* Proceedings

a) The *Covaci* Case and the Indications of the European Court of Justice

The question of whether and to what extent *inaudito reo* proceedings were compatible with the new EU legal framework made little sense until recently. It has been noted that until Directive 2016/343, EU law did not even have a general regulation on the right to personal participation in criminal proceedings, nor were there legal rules on *in absentia* trials in the field of national criminal justice. This issue, however, has arisen in the recent *Covaci* case,[36] which was the first opportunity for the European Court of Justice to examine two of the EU legal instruments issued in the field of criminal justice after the reform of Lisbon Treaty, namely the 2010 Directive on the right to interpretation and translation and the 2012 Directive on the right to information in criminal proceedings.

In this important judgment, the Luxemburg Court examined the case of a Romanian citizen who at a police check in Germany was driving a vehicle for which no valid mandatory motor vehicle civil liability insurance had been taken out, the proof of insurance being determined to be a forgery. Mr. Covaci was thus questioned with the assistance of an interpreter, but since he had no fixed domicile or residence in Germany, he was required to issue an irrevocable written authorisation for three officials of the *Amtsgericht* Laufen to accept service of court documents addressed to him. The competent prosecutor requested a *Strafbefehl*, that is, a judicial decision that under German law, as happens in Italy with penal order proceedings, can be issued through a simplified procedure without trial hearing and against which the convicted person can lodge a challenge. In the latter case, the accused will be tried in court, otherwise the penal order becomes final upon expiry of a period of 2 weeks from its service. The particularities of this case, moreover, were that the public prosecutor requested that the penal order be served on Mr. Covaci through the persons authorised to accept service and above all, that any observation of the person concerned, including an objection lodged against that order, should be written in German.

Against this background, the competent court raised two questions to the Luxembourg Court, i.e., whether EU law should be interpreted as precluding (a) a court order from requiring, under its own law, the accused to lodge an appeal only in the language of the proceedings and (b) the defendants from being required to appoint a person authorised to accept service, where the period for bringing an appeal begins to run upon service on that person. Of the two questions, the former was formulated in such general terms that it could also be applied to ordinary criminal proceedings. The latter, instead, contained a more specific reference to the peculiarities of penal order procedures, in that it raised doubt on whether it is 'irrelevant whether the accused is at all aware of the offence of which he is accused'.

[36] ECJ, *Covaci*.

The order in which the two questions were raised may also appear to be surprising, since the granting of personal information on the conviction is a logical prerequisite for the accused to be able to decide whether to challenge the penal order. However, the Court followed the order established, providing a rather cautious response to the first issue. Despite acknowledging that the broad scope of application of the 2010 Directive certainly covered the situation of Mr. Covaci, the Luxemburg judges, departing from the approach suggested by Advocate General Bot, drew up a clear distinction between the right to interpretation and translation.[37] According to the Court, whereas the former aims at providing defendants unfamiliar with the court's language with the assistance an interpreter with a view to oral statements, the latter entails the state's obligation to translate written documents that are essential to ensure the exercise of the defence rights and the overall fairness of the proceedings. From this it follows that the accused should have the right to the free assistance of an interpreter, if they orally lodge an objection against the penal order. However, EU law does not require the state to provide translation of an objection lodged in written form, nor does this obligation derive from Article 2 DIT, which could be interpreted as entailing the duty of individual countries to take responsibility for the translation of every appeal brought by the persons concerned against a judicial decision issued against them.[38]

The Court, moreover, softened this conclusion by stressing that EU law only aims at establishing minimum standards and does not preclude member states from ensuring the translation of further documents that are essential to guarantee the fairness of criminal proceedings.[39] By this means, the Luxemburg judges offloaded onto the national judicial authorities the responsibility to establish, taking into account the characteristics of both the applicable procedure and the case at stake, whether the challenge lodged in writing against a penal order should be considered an essential document for the purposes of its translation.[40]

Doubtless, this conclusion brought about an innovative interpretation of the provision on the documents of which translation is due, an interpretation that allows broadening the meaning of 'essential documents' by including documents from the accused persons, such as written statements and their appeal against the conviction.[41] However, this approach leaves room for great uncertainty as to way EU law should be applied by the individual national courts, while giving to the defendants no assurance on whether their appeal will be deemed 'essential' in a specific case and whether they can also count on linguistic assistance. Moreover, the distinction between interpretation and translation, despite being in itself logical, cannot lead to the result that defendants must choose to obtain either the free-of-charge assistance

[37] *Ibid.*, § 28 et seqq.

[38] *Ibid.*, § 38.

[39] *Ibid.*, § 49.

[40] *Ibid.*, § 50.

[41] Gialuz (2015), p. 6 f.

of an interpreter or the assistance of a legal counsel 'who will take responsibility for the drafting of the appropriate document, in the language of the proceedings'.[42] Both solutions entail serious risks for the effective exercise of the right to a defence in criminal proceedings, especially in the countries, such as Germany, in which *inaudito reo* procedures do not require mandatory legal assistance.[43] The former provides the accused with the assistance of a person who, albeit equipped with linguistic knowledge, may not be familiar with legal matters. The latter, offloading onto the lawyer the responsibility of the written objection, deprives the defendants, who may be equipped with legal knowledge, of the possibility of making their contribution to the appeal initiative.

The Court's reasoning highlights the effort to reach a balance among conflicting interests without overturning the main features of penal order procedures. This Solomon-like solution, however, does not best fit the specific needs of *inaudito reo* proceduces and particularly does not take into due account the vulnerable condition of the defendants who are convicted without being heard and often without knowing of the existence of a criminal proceeding instituted against them. Yet the Court was certainly aware that service of the penal order 'represents the first opportunity for the accused person to be informed of the accusation against him'[44] and that the objection, far from leading to a second instance, ensures to the convicted individuals a trial hearing at which they can take part.[45]

This approach led the Court to acknowledge the special nature of the service of the penal order, which must satisfy the requirements set out by Article 6 DICP on the right to information in relation to the communication of the accusation.[46] The Luxemburg judges shared the Advocate General's view that EU law allows for a certain leeway in defining the procedure whereby information on the accusation must be provided[47] and can require, therefore, that defendants not residing in that country appoint a person authorised to accept service of a penalty order concerning them. However, this cannot jeopardise their right to have the necessary time to prepare their defence,[48] with the result that the convicted person should in any case be granted the whole prescribed period for challenging the *inaudito reo* decision.

It may seem to be surprising that the Court adopted this two-sided approach, which, on the one hand, softens the EU rules on the guarantee of translation of

[42]ECJ, *Covaci*, § 42.

[43]See § 407 et seqq. CCP-Germany. As noted, the Italian 1988 code introduced the same arrangements, which lasted until 2001 as Law no. 60 amended Article 460 CCP by requiring notice of the penal order to be provided not only to the convicted persons but also to a court-appointed lawyer, if they have not appointed counsel of their own. Cf. Chapter 2, F.III.2.

[44]ECJ, *Covaci*, § 60.

[45]*Ibid.*, § 60.

[46]*Ibid.*, § 61.

[47]*Ibid.*, § 62.

[48]*Ibid.*, § 63.

criminal appeals and, on the other, strengthens the binding force of EU law by requiring the countries, in which *inaudito reo* decisions are allowed, to provide defendants with information on the conviction while granting them the whole period for challenging the decision. Certainly, the latter conclusion reveals the Court's disfavour towards domestic arrangements that allow for penal orders to become final because of the objective circumstance that the decision was not challenged. Moreover, this conclusion was also aimed at avoiding discrimination between defendants with a residence within the jurisdiction concerned and the accused persons whose residence does not fall within that jurisdiction.

Nevertheless, the Court's arrangements may not be sufficient to reduce the distance between the two situations. The requirement of personal information is still of little help for foreign defendants who, despite having the whole period of 2 weeks available, must face alone the delicate decision on whether to challenge the conviction. This risk is highest precisely in those countries that do not grant the accused any legal assistance during the period available to set up the opposition against the penal order. Remarkably, the Court was aware that this period of time could give rise to discrimination between defendants who are resident within the jurisdiction concerned and the individuals whose place of residence does not fall within that jurisdiction. The Luxemburg judges, however, dealt with this issue from the viewpoint of the accused's obligation to appoint a person authorised to accept service of judicial decisions, such obligation lying only with non-resident defendants and that requires, as a form of compensation, the whole prescribed period to be available to them.

On close examination, the main discrimination is between the accused persons who are resident in the trial country and are possibly familiar with that law, and non-resident defendants who are often fully unfamiliar with *lex fori*. The former do not need to appoint a person authorised to accept service of judicial decisions and, after being notified of the penal order, often have the tools to prepare their own defence and assess the convenience of challenging the conviction. The latter are burdened with the obligation to appoint a person authorised to accept service of judicial decisions and, although the period for lodging the challenge begins to run when they are personally served notice of the conviction, must decide alone whether to challenge the penal order without having in most cases the necessary knowledge. In other words, the discrimination will remain untouched if EU law cannot require individual countries to provide non-resident defendants with specific safeguards aimed at assisting them in the decision on whether to challenge a conviction issued in their absence.

For these defendants, the solution adopted by the Court—namely, two free weeks from the moment of personal notification, with the right to have linguistic assistance only if they choose to challenge the penal order—provides a weak guarantee, which can even result in a dangerous boomerang. Whatever decision the accused will made, the granting of personal service of a conviction issued *inaudito reo* leads to the prescribed period beginning to run, with the result that the failure to lodge a challenge renders the 'provisional' conviction inevitably final at the end of the 2 weeks. Further risks arise from the hasty decision to lodge opposition, a decision that, if not based on the full awareness of the consequences of this initiative, can also jeopardise the accused. Surprisingly, the Luxembourg Court did not seem to be concerned about the result of the expiry of the prescribed period, which leads to *res judicata* regardless of whether the accused truly understood the information received and knowingly chose not to oppose the penal order.

b) The New Safeguards Laid Down by EU Statutory Law

More recently, the problem of *inaudito reo* proceedings has taken on further relevance under EU law thanks to the recent Directive 2016/343. It has been observed that the new rules leave member states free to provide for 'proceedings or certain stages thereof' to be conducted not only without involving the accused but even in writing, and that this reference cannot be interpreted as relating to intermediate and interlocutory proceedings, which anyway fall outside the scope of the Directive. Therefore, the meaning of the exceptions should be defined within the scope of the main provision. The most linear interpretation is that member states can discretionarily decide whether to ensure the accused's personal participation not only in interim decisions or phases of the proceedings, which are not aimed at the decision on guilt, but also in special types of proceedings designed for a decision on the merits of the case. This conclusion may seem to support an extensive interpretation of the guarantee of personal participation, which should be related to any procedure aimed at a decision on guilt rather than only the trial hearing.

Against this background, the reference to 'stages' can be interpreted as relating to those decisions on guilt that usually take place in ordinary phases of the criminal proceedings prior to the trial.[49] The reference to 'proceedings' should concern special procedures aimed at an out-of-court decision on the merits. Among these decisions, several European countries provide for bargaining procedures and a small number of them allow for defendants to be convicted by means of a penal order in minor cases. Whereas the former often provide for a hearing *in camera*,[50] the latter constitute typical examples of procedures 'in writing', the accused being convicted through an order that is usually issued in written response to a (written) request of the competent prosecutor. It may be surprising that a legislation aimed at enshrining the right to personal participation in criminal proceedings will also allow for the maintenance of the rather inquisitorial practice of written convictions by means of an *inaudito reo* procedure. Furthermore, Recital no. 41 of the Directive contains a highly worrisome statement:

---

[49] In Italy, this is the case of abbreviated proceedings, which, as noted, take place as a rule in the intermediate phase. Cf. Chapter 2, F.III.3.

[50] In Italy, the competent judge to decide on a plea bargaining can in any time summon the accused persons to check the voluntariness of their consent. Cf. Chapter 2, F.III.3.

> The right to be present at the trial can be exercised only if one or more hearings are held. This means that the right to be present at the trial cannot apply if the relevant national rules of procedure do not provide for a hearing. Such national rules should comply with the Charter and with the ECHR, as interpreted by the Court of Justice and by the European Court of Human Rights, in particular with regard to the right to a fair trial. This is the case, for example, if the proceedings are conducted in a simplified manner following, solely or in part, a written procedure or a procedure in which no hearing is provided for.

This approach leads to the paradoxical conclusion that EU law only grants defendants the right to be present in the criminal proceedings instituted against them if national law provides for one or more hearings for the procedure used in a specific case. From this it follows that the new EU provisions will simply remain inapplicable if national law does not provide for a hearing prior to the decision-making. It is hardly understandable, however, how in such cases national law should be able to satisfy the fair trial requirements set forth by the case-law of both the Luxemburg and the Strasbourg Courts.

III. Towards a Victim's Right to Personally Participate in Criminal Proceedings?

The recent developments occurred in EU law raise the further question of whether victims also have the right to be involved in criminal proceedings and within which terms this right can be exercised. In general terms, Directive 2012/29/EU follows a rather cautious approach also to this delicate issue. The EU legislation stresses that the involvement of the injured party in criminal proceedings depends on several variables, such as the different solutions provided for by national law in relation to the victims' role in criminal proceedings, their formal status, and so on. member states must take into account all these factors while defining the scope of the rights acknowledged to the victim by EU law.[51] The meaning of this provision is somewhat cryptic and, as long as constant reference is made to national law, renders the new EU safeguards by definition inapplicable if member states do not enable the aggrieved parties to play an active role in criminal proceedings or even relegate them to secondary functions.[52]

This does not mean, however, that EU law views the victim's participation in criminal proceedings in neutral terms. On close examination, EU law gives positive consideration to the victims' involvement in criminal proceedings, as is apparent from Recital no. 47 of the 2012 Directive, which stresses that the victim should not be expected to 'incur expenses in relation to their participation in criminal proceedings'. On the other hand, the same Recital highlights an interesting aspect, namely that member states should be required to reimburse the expenses necessary

[51] Recital no. 20 DirVR.

[52] Allegrezza (2012), p. 6.

for the victims' participation in criminal proceedings, to the extent that the competent authority requires their presence and active participation. This statement largely departs from the approach followed in relation to the accused's participation, emphasising the need for victims participating not just effectively but also actively in criminal hearings. To a certain extent, it appears that the protection provided by EU law depends on whether the victim is allowed to play an active role in the proceedings, since in this case only, the injured party can request the reimbursement of the expenses.[53] From the same viewpoint, victims can request translation of documents that are essential for their defence, documents within which, however, there is no right to translation of the passages not relevant for the victim participating actively in the criminal process.[54] Alongside the lack of a clear definition of the requirement of 'active participation', it is clear that the competent authorities must set all the necessary conditions to ensure effectiveness of the participation of the aggrieved parties, starting with the obligation of hearing their version of the events during criminal proceedings.[55]

C. Conditions of Effective Defence and the Right to Active Participation in Criminal Proceedings

I. Language and the Right to Effective Participation in Criminal Proceedings

1. Linguistic Guarantees of the Accused

In the EU area, characterised by a high multilingualism and the co-existence today of 23 official languages, language poses difficult challenges for both national criminal justice systems and the effectiveness of EU criminal policy. Without proper understanding of the language of the process, defendants cannot set up any defence strategy and are deprived of the opportunity of choosing a competent lawyer to deal with the specific case at hand. Furthermore, the institution of criminal proceedings for a charge relating to a criminal law provision that the accused could not know and understand in advance also poses enormous problems for the conduct of a fair prosecution.

It is therefore no surprise that, as the Lisbon Treaty started a new season of legislative initiatives by the EU institutions to strengthen the defence rights in criminal proceedings, with the first Directive issued in the field of criminal justice

[53] Art. 14 DirVR.

[54] Art. 7(5) DirVR.

[55] *Below*, C.III.2.

aimed at setting the necessary conditions to enable the linguistic understanding by the accused.[56] This legislation, moreover, highlights a clear continuity with the Strasbourg case-law and its constant focus on the effectiveness of the defence participation in criminal proceedings. It is worth observing that Directive 2010/64 expressly focuses on the need for full linguistic comprehension to ensure the fairness of the criminal process and to give to the defendants a fair opportunity to understand the charges and to actively participate in criminal hearings.[57]

The strict link between language and the right to effective participation in criminal proceedings makes it necessary to provide these guarantees with the broadest scope of application. It is noteworthy that defendants not only must be granted the assistance of an interpreter in the police questioning and their examination at trial, but furthermore in all the court hearings, including intermediate proceedings.[58] Doubtless, linguistic assistance can be of little use if limited to the hearing activities without the accused having the possibility of preparing a proper defence. In this light, the 2010 Directive further broadens the scope of the guarantee by acknowledging that interpretation must also be available in the communication between the defendants and their counsel with a view to any questioning or hearing during the proceedings.[59]

This solution should certainly be welcomed, even though the effectiveness of the anticipated protection is somewhat blurred by the specification that the guarantee of interpretation must be ensured in the preparatory communications with the lawyer only 'where necessary for purpose of safeguarding the fairness of the proceedings'. It is not clear what this specification exactly means but there it certainly leaves wide room for restrictive implementation by member states. Further concerns arise in relation to the ascertainment of the conditions for the granting of the assistance of an interpreter. Also in this regard, the Directive chooses a rather cautious solution. Although it expressly offloads onto member states the responsibility for ascertaining whether the accused does not speak or understand the language of the proceedings,[60] the exact characteristics of the 'procedure' or 'mechanism' aimed at serving this purpose are unclear. It is also a vague acknowledgement that member states must enable the accused to challenge the decision finding that

---

[56]Directive 2010/64/EU. See, among others, Gialuz (2013), p. 227 ff.; Amalfitano (2014), p. 14 ff.; Vogler (2015), p. 104 ff.

[57]This link is clearly expressed in Article 3(1) DirIT.

[58]It may be surprising that Directive 2010/64 contains no reference to the suspect's examination by the competent prosecutor. This hearing poses difficult challenges especially in the countries where public prosecutors are independent from the judiciary and, despite being an impartial body, autonomously carry out their investigations instituted on the basis of the charge filed against the suspect for the purposes of the future prosecution. On close examination, the legal lacuna is only apparent and can be filled by the provision acknowledging the need for interpretation throughout the proceedings before all the authorities having investigative and judicial tasks. See Art. 2 (1) DirIT.

[59]Art. 2(2) DirIT.

[60]Art. 2(4) DirIT.

there was no need for interpretation or the quality of the interpretation allowed,[61] since EU law does not clarify the minimum features of the tools that must be made available. Moreover, the fact that this acknowledgement was coupled with the usual clause of compliance with national law can lead to the maintenance of domestic solutions that, for instance, postpone the possibility of challenging the decision finding that no interpretation is needed to the conclusion of the first instance.[62]

On the other hand, it is clear that effective participation in the proceedings presupposes the knowledge and understanding of a specific charge. In this regard, the 2010 Directive requires national law to grant the addressee of a criminal law action the translation of essential documents of the proceedings. Although national authorities have a great margin of discretion in defining the essential character of procedural documents, there is no doubt that the charge must be translated to the accused who does not understand the language of the proceedings.[63] Nevertheless, the scope of this fundamental guarantee was not acknowledged in a uniform manner in all the linguistic versions of this Directive.[64] This result can affect the possibility of the suspect challenging in particular the decisions on coercive measures, which presuppose not just a provisional charge but also consistent evidence supporting a strong suspicion of guilt.

2. Linguistic Guarantees of the Victim

The systematic importance of the right to linguistic understanding in criminal proceedings entails that the guarantees of interpretation and translation should not be restricted to the accused. As noted, the Lisbon Treaty specifically focused on the victim's rights in such a broad manner that protection must be ensured both inside and outside the criminal proceedings. Starting with this general acknowledgment, Directive 2012/29 further developed the approach followed in the 2001 Framework Decision, which had limited the reference to language problems to the right to receive information. As a result, the 2012 legislation not only focused on the right to linguistic understanding as a means of following procedural activities but also on the right to be understood in criminal proceedings.[65] The Directive, furthermore,

[61] Art. 2(5) DirIT.

[62] In Italy, for instance, the defence must, as a rule, until the conclusion of the first instance to lodge an appeal against the judgment on the accused's guilt. Cf. Art. 586 CCP-Italy.

[63] Art. 3(3) DirIT.

[64] Both in the English and in the French text, translation not only should be provided in relation to the formal accusation but also to the preliminary charge filed in the investigative phase (the wording of Article 3 relates, respectively, to '*any charge or indictment*' and '*toutes charges ou tout acte d'accusation*'), whereas no distinction was made in other linguistic versions (for instance, the Italian text relates generically to '*gli atti contenenti i capi d'imputazione*'). Finally, there are even linguistic versions that use expressions specifically relating to the indictment (for instance, the Spanish text mentions the '*escrito de acusación*').

[65] Recital no. 21.

stressed the need for individual consideration of the victim's condition, taking into account aspects such as 'the victim's knowledge of the language used to provide information, age, maturity, intellectual and emotional capacity, literacy and any mental or physical impairment'.[66] The strict link between the right to understand and the right to be understood in criminal proceedings lies at the heart of the 2012 Directive. Member states are required to ensure that victims will be granted their right to understand and to be understood by means of linguistic assistance 'from the first contact and during any further necessary interaction they have with a competent authority'[67] as well as for the purposes of lodging a complaint.[68] To ensure the highest degree of effectiveness in the protection of the right to understand and to be understood in criminal proceedings, any communication with the injured party must be granted in a simple and understandable language—again taking into account 'the personal characteristics of the victim'.[69]

Against this background, specific guarantees concern the right to linguistic understanding aimed at ensuring the effective participation of the victim in criminal proceedings. Directive 2012/29 contains a broad provision on the right to interpretation and translation, which largely reproduces the contents of the rules laid down by Directive 2010/64. On close examination, some important features distinguish the two texts, weakening the scope of the safeguards acknowledged to the victim. Again, the legislation on victim's rights reveals a rather cautious approach by laying down guarantees that must be adapted to national legal systems characterised by a very different role of the victim in the criminal process. For instance, the 2012 Directive requires member states to ensure that the injured party who does not understand or speak the language of the criminal proceedings should be granted, upon request, the assistance of an interpreter, free of charge, 'at least during any interviews or questioning [. . .] before investigative and judicial authorities, including during police questioning, and interpretation for their active participation in court hearings and any necessary interim hearings'.[70] Yet this acknowledgment was made conditional on the victim's 'role in the relevant criminal justice system in criminal proceedings'.[71]

Moreover, EU law may not seem to have acknowledged the victim's right to linguistic understanding in absolute terms. The 2012 Directive aimed at striking a balance between conflicting interests by allowing the use of communication technologies, such as videoconferencing, telephone or internet, unless the physical presence of the interpreter is required to enable the victims to 'properly exercise their rights or to understand the proceedings'.[72] This clarification, which is

---

[66] *Ibid.*

[67] Art. 3(1) DirVR.

[68] Art. 5(2) DirVR.

[69] Art. 3(2) DirVR.

[70] Art. 7(1) DirVR.

[71] *Ibid.*

[72] Art. 7(2) DirVR.

preceded by a clause that leaves the defence rights unaffected and relates to the 'rules of judicial discretion', is rather unclear. Depending on the role allowed by national law, the victim not only may not play an active role in the institution of criminal proceedings but can also be coercively brought before the competent authority, while having the obligation to answer all the questions exhaustively. In some cases, however, the sole fact that the victims cannot count on the assistance of an interpreter *in loco*, with whom they can directly communicate and who can immediately answer any request for clarification, appears to be detrimental for the full exercise of the right to a defence. On the other hand, it is unclear with which conflicting interests the right to linguistic understanding should be balanced, not to mention a certain contradiction with the general acknowledgement of the right to be accompanied by a person of the victim's choosing in the first contact with a competent authority.[73]

Further concerns arise in relation to the translation of written information. To be sure, like the accused, the victim who does not understand the language of the process must be granted translation of essential information. This acknowledgement is also weakened, however, by the fact that the guarantee of information must be ensured to the victims 'in accordance with their role in the relevant criminal justice system in criminal proceedings'.[74] Moreover, the Directive, while mentioning information presumptively essential, does not include the charge, unlike what was acknowledged to the defendant by Directive 2010/64. There is not doubt, however, that the knowledge and understanding of the indictment is also necessary for the victim to be able to set up a defence strategy. Should national law deny the translation of the charge, the information about the time and place of the trial, acknowledged by the 2012 Directive,[75] would result in being largely useless.

Last but not least, the rules on the victim's right to linguistic understanding give rise to some methodological criticisms. Thus, the 2012 legislation has adopted a clear functional perspective, which links the right to translation with the essential character of information in order to enable the proper exercise the right to defence. This acknowledgment led to excluding the duty of translation of 'passages of essential documents which are not relevant for the purpose of enabling victims to actively participate in the criminal proceedings'.[76] This provision is rather cryptic and leads to a paradoxical result. If the guarantee of translation only concerns the documents essential to the exercise of the defence rights, how can there be passages that are not relevant to ensure the victim's active participation in the proceedings? A further concern arises from the fact that, unlike the defendants, the victims must be granted linguistic assistance only at their own request. From this it follows that in the absence of the initiative of the interested party, national authorities are not required to verify the linguistic knowledge of the victims or even to appoint an

[73] Art. 3(3) DirVR.

[74] Art. 7(3) DirVR.

[75] Art. 7(4) DirVR.

[76] Art. 7(5) DirVR.

interpreter, when their linguistic difficulties result from the information in the file. Nor is there any duty for the competent authority to scrutinise the voluntariness of the victims' decision to waive linguistic assistance and the awareness of the consequences of the decision made, a result that seems to challenge the proclaimed objective of ensuring the effective participation of the victim in criminal proceedings.

II. Information Rights and the Guarantee of Effective Defence

1. Information Rights of the Accused

a) Premise

Another area in which the EU legislation issued after the Lisbon reform has drawn particular attention from the perspective of the present research concerns the information rights in criminal justice. Directive 2012/13/EU[77] reveals the clear awareness of the EU institutions that proper information plays essential role in enabling effective participation in criminal proceedings. In this respect, the 2012 legislation ensured a double level of information by granting the accused the right both to be informed about the charge and to know the results of the criminal inquiry.

b) Information on the Charge

Following the Strasbourg case-law, EU law construed the guarantee of information on the charge with the broadest scope by granting not only defendants due information on the indictment but also suspects the right to know the preliminary charge.[78] Of course, this does not mean that the same degree of information is due throughout the criminal proceedings. In fact, EU law ensured to suspects and defendants a dual level of information, namely (a) immediate information on the offence under investigation, which must be sufficiently detailed to ensure the exercise of the defence rights and the overall fairness of the procedure,[79] and (b) information on the indictment at a later stage of the proceedings. The latter must be granted the latest after the court procedure has been instituted and must enable the defendant to know the nature and legal classification of the criminal offence, as well as the nature of participation by the accused person.[80] Even though

[77] See among others Quattrocolo (2015), p. 84 ff.

[78] Recital no. 14 DirICP.

[79] Art. 6(1) DirICP.

[80] Art. 6(3) DirICP.

the distinction between these two types of information is not entirely clear,[81] the EU institutions were certainly aware that information rights should be strengthened in the pre-trial phase and that, depending on the development of the investigations, information may reach the standards of completeness provided for in Article 6 (3) DICP. At any rate, it is of utmost importance that information, provided with technical details, will be given in an accessible language in order both to enable defendants to exercise their defence rights properly and to ensure the fairness of the proceedings. To ensure the proper fulfilment of the new rules, the Directive also proposes the adoption of non-legislative means, such as a Letter of rights aimed at providing defendants with information of their rights in a 'simple and even non-technical language so as to be easily understood by a person without specific knowledge of criminal procedural law'.[82]

In a nutshell, the EU legislation, overcoming rigid formalisms, reveals a flexible approach, granting the defendants, by means of a complex notion of 'charge', variable information aimed at enabling them to participate in the proceedings from the pre-trial stage onward. This in turn imposes on the competent authority the obligation to provide the accused with information characterised by different degrees of completeness depending on the stage of the proceedings.[83] Thus the information due after the arrest will inevitably be rather essential, whereas a higher level of detail is required in case of pre-trial detention, since this can usually be ordered only where a strong suspicion of guilt has arisen.[84]

A particularly delicate issue, which clearly impinges on the relationship between the right to information and the accused's active participation in criminal proceedings, concerns the guarantees due in case of a change of the accusation. By using a rather ambiguous formulation, the 2012 Directive only requires the accused to be informed of eventual changes as far as it is necessary to ensure the fairness of criminal proceedings.[85] It is hard to understand when this could not happen. Even in the pre-trial inquiry, unless there are specific investigative needs that prevent the competent body from granting the information under Article 6(1), it is clear that the defence cannot be denied information on the amended charge, especially if this can lead to coercive means being adopted against the suspect. Moreover, the Directive has failed to clarify further issues of utmost importance, *e.g.* under which limits the charge may be amended and which rights the accused must be granted after the amendment of the accusation. In this regard, the EU legislation does not therefore satisfy the need for harmonisation even limited to minimum standards. For

---

[81]On the one hand, one cannot rule out that the qualified information under Article 6(3) is needed, albeit to a different extent, to ensure full exercise of the defence at the pre-trial stage pursuant to paragraph 1. On the other, the information on the accusation can take on different degrees of completeness according to the developments of the court proceedings, as acknowledged in Recital no. 28. On this issue, see for further criticisms Quattrocolo (2015), p. 87 f.

[82]Recital no. 38 DirICP.

[83]Recital no. 29 DirICP.

[84]Art. 6(2) DirICP.

[85]Art. 6(3) DirICP.

instance, it would be appropriate to ensure the translation of the changes of the accusation, while granting the accused—especially where the amendment was the result of prosecutorial evidence—the same rights acknowledged in relation to the original charge by national law.

c) Information on the Investigation and the Right to Access the File

It has been observed that EU ensures a second level of information concerned with the results of the criminal inquiry. Certainly, it is of little use for the defendants to be able to give their contribution to the proceedings if they are denied appropriate information on the evidence gathered by the investigative bodies and can be kept in the dark about the prosecutorial strategy. EU law acknowledges this fundamental guarantee at a double level, namely requiring prompt information to be made available to the arrestee and detainee,[86] while granting the accused the general right to access all the evidence in the possession of the competent authorities.[87]

Notwithstanding the broad scope of the guarantee of information on prosecutorial evidence, this set-up gives rise to the risk of practical abuses, while legitimising the maintenance of some deficient solutions at the national level. The main shortcoming of the EU legislation is that a functional perspective again inspires the granting of information. Although the Directive ensures to defendants very comprehensive information both in favour and against them,[88] the information duty of national authorities seems to be justified solely by the need to safeguard the fairness of the proceedings and the exercise of the defence rights. This in turn raises the question of the stage at which information should be given. Also in this regard, EU law provides for rather vague indications, requiring the relevant information to be granted in due time to enable the exercise of the defence rights and the latest at the time of the submission of the merits of the case to the competent court.[89]

Under EU law, furthermore, information on prosecutorial evidence—no matter whether granted to detained suspects or free defendants—is not an absolute right. Therefore, national authorities have the power to deny access to the file where other interests—especially the right to life and physical integrity of other individuals as well as public interests such as the need to preserve the effectiveness of the ongoing inquiry—conflict with the right to information.[90] Significantly, these derogations not only apply to the pre-trial inquiry but also to the court proceedings, which demonstrates that even the threshold of the opening of the judicial proceedings can be overcome where the competent authority considers that access to the file can jeopardise individual or public interests. This balancing valve may appear to be

---

[86] Art. 7(1) DirICP.

[87] Art. 7(2) DirICP.

[88] Exceptions are provided for in the case of arrest and detention. See *below*, D.

[89] Art. 7(3) DirICP.

[90] Art. 7(4) DirICP.

reasonable in the light of an overall assessment of the procedural fairness. However, it entails the risk that a further postponement of the granting of information can seriously affect the possibility for the defence to effectively take part in criminal proceedings. This result can also depend on the weak provision relating to the means of challenging the decision to deny access to the file. If the judicial authority is competent to issue or review this decision,[91] the 2012 Directive does not require member states to provide for a specific remedy for this purpose.[92]

2. Information Rights of the Victim

An indisputable merit of EU law was to extend to the aggrieved parties the right to information in criminal proceedings. The EU institutions followed a multifaceted approach to this delicate issue, a result that, again, is largely due to the different roles the injured party can play in national criminal justice systems. The first safeguard due to the victims is a form of preparatory information, aimed at providing them, from the first contact with a competent authority, with comprehensive picture of the procedural tools available and the legal assistance to which they can have access.[93] In the field of criminal justice, moreover, the injured party must be granted further information so as to be able to take part actively in the proceedings, if allowed by national law. The duty of detailed information by the competent authority and the respect for the person of the victim are essential conditions for the victim to be able to make 'informed decisions about their participation in proceedings'.[94] There is little doubt that EU law attaches great importance to these guarantees already in the pre-trial phase, where the tension between the information rights and the need not to jeopardise the ongoing inquiry is still high.[95] In this respect, it is of utmost importance for the injured party to obtain the necessary information to obtain a review of the decision not to prosecute.[96] Further information should be ensured to the victim from the initiation of the court proceedings. Thus, the aggrieved parties must be informed of the time and place of the trial resulting from the complaint with regard to the criminal offence suffered[97] and information must also be ensured to enable them to know about the current status of the proceedings.[98]

Notwithstanding these premises, the solutions enacted by EU law still do not provide sufficient protection. If proper information must surely be given after the

[91]*Ibid.*

[92]Recital no. 36 DirICP.

[93]Art. 4 DirVR.

[94]Recital no. 26 DirVR.

[95]Recital no. 28 DirVR.

[96]Recital no. 26 DirVR.

[97]Recital no. 31 DirVR.

[98]Recital no. 26 DirVR.

initiation of a criminal prosecution, no clear indications are provided on the exact contents of the information due in the pre-trial inquiry. The 2012 Directive does not specify the terms within which victims should be notified of the preliminary charge, nor is it clear whether and to what extent they must be kept informed of the developments of the pre-trial investigations. Delicate problems concern the information on the termination of the proceedings. Even though national law provides for a remedy against the decision not to prosecute, victims may not be able to challenge the decision not to institute criminal proceedings, a reaction that presupposes preventive information on the request, rather than on the judicial decision, to discontinue criminal proceedings.

From the victim's viewpoint, another issue is as relevant as the right to receive information on the case, namely the right not to be informed. This right is an important part of the general right to steer away from criminal justice, in order to forget the crime and to be forgotten. The drafters of the 2012 Directive were certainly aware of this issue,[99] to the point that they made the victims' right to information conditional on their explicit request. Although this approach is justified in the light of the right not to be informed, the EU legislative arrangements can lead to counterproductive results, as we saw in relation to the right to linguistic understanding.[100]

III. The Right to Be fairly Heard in Criminal Proceedings

1. The Voice of the Accused

We have seen that a fair criminal trial must grant the individuals concerned a proper opportunity to make their voice heard. Certainly this fundamental requirement cannot be deemed reserved to the accused, but it should also be ensured, albeit with some particularities, to other people involved in criminal proceedings—especially to the victim, and to individuals, such as witnesses, not directly affected by the criminal offence. Although EU law has not yet enacted comprehensive rules on this difficult area, some important indications can be deduced by the existing legislation. Certainly, most of the defensive rights examined above can also be interpreted in the light of the accused's right to be heard in criminal proceedings. In particular, the knowledge and understanding of the charge, as well as the possibility of accessing relevant evidence, constitute essential conditions for the accused to be fairly examined. These safeguards hold specific importance in the pre-trial inquiry because of the vulnerable position of the suspect in the police and prosecutorial questionings. The 2013 Directive on the right to access to a lawyer confirmed this approach by acknowledging legal assistance not only to the accused summoned to

[99] Recital no. 29 DirVR.

[100] *Above*, C.I.2.

appear before a court having jurisdiction in criminal matters[101] but also to the suspect questioned by the police or another law enforcement authority.[102] It is noteworthy that the EU institutions further anticipated these guarantees by ensuring access to a lawyer before the accused appears at either the police station, in the prosecutorial office, or at court. Moreover, defendants must have the possibility of meeting in private—and communicating with—their lawyer before the police questioning and the prosecutorial hearing,[103] and their counsel must be present at the questioning.[104]

Following the Strasbourg case-law, EU legislation emphasises the need for effective participation of the lawyer in the accused's hearing, to the point that, although national law is competent to make the necessary arrangements, these cannot jeopardise 'the effective exercise and essence of the right concerned'.[105] In this light, member states must enable the lawyer, *inter alia*, to 'ask questions, request clarification and make statements, which should be recorded in accordance with national law'.[106] Except for legal assistance, moreover, the EU institutions have failed to enact comprehensive rules on the qualitative requirements of the accused's hearing. In particular, EU law still provides no rules on some important issues, such as the exact information due to suspects and defendants prior to the questioning and especially on the limits of intervention by the competent authority. Furthermore, the recent Directive 2016/343/EU, dealing with some aspects of the presumption of innocence, enacted specific provisions on the privilege against self-incrimination in national criminal proceedings, a issue that had until then been dealt with by EU law in relation to hearings by videoconference in the field of transborder inquiries.[107]

A delicate issue concerns the personal scope of application of these rules, circumscribed to suspects and defendants from the time they are made aware of the institution of criminal proceedings against them.[108] A significant exception relates to the 'persons other than suspects or accused persons who, in the course of questioning by the police or by another law enforcement authority, become suspects or accused persons'.[109] This extension entails serious human rights risks from the perspective of the present discussion. As *Bachmaier Winter* points out, 'there is no precise moment where it can be undoubtedly stated that a witness becomes a suspect',[110] and national countries regulate this delicate change of status in very

[101] Art. 3(2)(d) DirAL.
[102] Art. 3(2)(a) DirAL.
[103] Art. 3(3)(a) DirAL.
[104] Art. 3(3)(b) DirAL.
[105] *Ibid.*
[106] Recital no. 25 DirAL.
[107] Chapter 13, C.II.2.b.
[108] Art. 2(1) DirAL.
[109] Art. 2(3) DirAL.
[110] Bachmaier Winter (2015), p. 114.

different fashions. In this light, the reference to the individuals who become suspects during the police questioning appears to be too restrictive. Certainly, the drafters of the 2013 Directive missed an important opportunity to tackle the practice of police questioning as witnesses persons against whom sufficient evidence of guilt has still arisen.[111] A better solution would probably have been to require also the suspension of the questioning in case of doubts as to the status of the persons examined in order to allow them to appoint a lawyer.[112] The piecemeal approach of EU law, therefore, has left third individuals unprotected, notwithstanding that witnesses are often in a more vulnerable position that defendants, being unable to freely decide whether to appear before the competent authority and which statements to make. The failure to provide them with legal assistance is certainly due to the widespread accused-centred approach to criminal justice. According to this approach, witnesses—even if in a vulnerable position—do not need legal assistance,[113] notwithstanding that it would certainly help avoid the risk of incriminating evidence.

2. The Voice of the Victim

Under EU law also, the right to a fair hearing cannot be deemed a prerogative of the accused. Concerning the victim's side, it is noteworthy that the 2012 Directive structured the right to linguistic assistance with a view to enable the injured party not only to understand but also to be understood in criminal proceedings. The same legislative instrument, further developing this approach, dedicated a specific provision on the victim's right to be heard, while requiring special care where a child victim must be examined.[114] On close examination, EU law has not gone much further than these general acknowledgments. By requiring member states to ensure that the victim 'may provide evidence' in criminal proceedings, the 2012 Directive might legitimise the maintenance of the current solutions by the European countries which impose on the victim the same duties of completeness and truthfulness lying with the witness.[115] Moreover, we have noted that this legislative instrument largely relates to national law with a view to the definition of the procedural rules governing the victim's hearing.[116]

---

[111]*Ibid.*

[112]*Ibid.*

[113]*Ibid.*

[114]Art. 10(1) DVR.

[115]It has been noted that, despite recent reforms, Italian law still lacks a general statute on the victim's questioning by the police and the prosecutor. Cf. Chapter 2, G.II.2. Even at trial, the injured party who could not, or did not choose to, lodge a civil law complaint can be summoned to be examined pursuant the rules governing the testimonial hearing.

[116]Art. 10(2) DVR.

It is not clear from this set-up what relevance EU law attaches exactly to the victim's hearing. On the one hand, specific focus was placed on the use of technologies aimed at allowing the victims' examination without exposing them to the risks and the stress of a criminal trial.[117] On the other, the EU institutions do not seem to consider the victim's physical presence in court as absolutely necessary, since the 2012 Directive stresses that the victim's right to be heard can be fulfilled if the victim is allowed to make written statements or observations.[118] In this light, the 2012 Directive does not go much further than the 2001 Framework Decision on the standing of the victim in criminal proceedings, which required member states to expose the victim to a questioning only insofar as necessary for the purposes of criminal proceedings.[119]

The European Court of Justice followed a similar approach in the *Katz* case,[120] stressing that the 2001 legislation did not entail the obligation, if not provided for by national law, to hear the victim as a witness in the criminal proceedings initiated by a private substitute criminal law action.[121] In the same ruling, however, the Luxemburg judges pointed out that, where national law does not provides for this obligation, the victim must in any case be granted the right to give oral evidence, which should be taken into account in the decision on the merits of the case. Moreover, according to the European judges, while EU law allows for victims to give their contribution to the decision-making, they cannot influence the application of a sentence and the criminal law effects of the judgment.[122] This is apparent from the *Gueye and Sánchez* case, a case of domestic violence in which the Luxemburg case-law interpreted the 2001 Framework Decision as not precluding the imposition of an injunction prohibiting the perpetrator from approaching the victim, notwithstanding the latter had opposed the application of this ancillary penalty.

IV. The Defence's Contribution to the Gathering of Evidence

Over recent years, the EU institutions have increasingly dealt with the collection of overseas evidence within the EU area and the 2014 Directive on a European investigation order has provided rather comprehensive regulations on cross-border investigations.[123] On the contrary, EU law does not still provide for specific provisions on the gathering of evidence in domestic proceedings, nor is there a set of supranational rules governing the defence's contribution in criminal inquiries and

[117] Art. 23(3)(b) DVR.

[118] Recital no. 41 DVR.

[119] Art. 3(2) FDVS.

[120] ECJ, *Katz*. See Rafaraci (2015), p. 218.

[121] *Ibid.*

[122] *Ibid.*

[123] Chapter 13, C.II.2.

the collection of information. Nevertheless, some important indications emerge from the existing legislation.

On the accused's side, Directive 2013/48/EU not only ensured the access to legal assistance during the accused's examination but also the right to have their lawyer attend investigative and evidence-gathering activities, if provided for by national law and insofar as they are allowed or even required to present at these acts.[124] To this end, national law can autonomously define the practical arrangements of legal assistance, provided that these arrangements do not prejudice the effective exercise and essence of the rights concerned. The requirement that the lawyer's attendance at investigative acts be noted using the recording procedure pursuant to national law[125] should be interpreted in this light, that is, as a means of testing not just the counsel's presence in court but furthermore the effectiveness of the defence contribution.

Even though the 2013 Directive makes legal assistance conditional on the provisions of national law, the lawyer must be present at least at three types of investigative acts, i.e. identity parades, confrontations, and the reconstructions of the scene of a crime. Of course, the list is not exhaustive and national legislature can provide for legal assistance in further cases. Yet the exact meaning of these investigations is not very clear, nor does the Directive clarify the role that the suspect should play. Whereas identity parades by definition involve them, this does not always happen in the case of reconstructions of the scene of a crime, which can be held without the suspect's presence. Another rather ambiguous reference concerns confrontations. If confrontation were to be understood as relating solely to the case where suspects are 'brought together with one or more witnesses or victims where there is disagreement between them on important facts or issues',[126] the suspect's presence would be obvious and it would not have been necessary to require a further condition. On close examination, the reference to this type of confrontation cannot be deemed exclusive. Defendants also have the right to be confronted with their accusers, a right of such importance both at the national level and under the European Convention that it also constitutes a principle of EU law.[127] It would be surprising that a legislative instrument which was aimed at enhancing the right to a defence acknowledged legal assistance where a disagreement arises between suspects and other individuals, while leaving the accused unprotected in the delicate confrontation with the accuser. Moreover, if suspects could not count on the assistance of their own counsel when confronted with prosecutorial witnesses or co-defendants, the Directive's requirement that the new rules should be interpreted in the light of the Strasbourg case-law[128] would largely be frustrated.

---

[124]Art. 3(3)(c) DirAL.

[125]Recital no. 26 DirAL.

[126]*Ibid.*

[127]Art. 6(3) TEU.

[128]Recital no. 53 DirAL.

A delicate issue concerned with legal assistance in investigative and evidence-gathering acts is the waiver of the right to be assisted by one's own lawyer. Directive 2013/48/EU enacted a specific provision on this matter,[129] laying down the conditions on which defendants can waive their right to legal assistance. Despite the broad scope of application of this provision that encompasses all the situations listed in Article 3 DirAL, there is no doubt that a waiver should not hold concrete relevance in relation to the accused's examination in court, at least in the countries that require the accused to be in any case assisted by a court-appointed lawyer. Remarkably, the Directive stresses that the new rules cannot affect the mandatory presence or assistance of a lawyer, if provided for by national law. Nevertheless, the new EU rules can also be interpreted as allowing defendants to waive the right to be assisted by their own lawyer. In this light, it is of utmost importance that defendants can be made fully aware of the consequences of their waiver of legal assistance. Doubtless, the 2013 legislation attached great weight to the need for clear and understandable information of the accused. Although it is acknowledged that waiver must be given 'voluntarily and unequivocally', the Directive remains vague as to the authority called upon to provide the accused with the due information and especially the authority before which defendants should waive their right to legal assistance. The only guarantee is that waiver, no matter whether expressed orally or in writing, must be recorded pursuant to national law. It is not an issue of small importance, since the risk of abuses can arise where national law charges with this task the same competent authority for the investigative act at which the accused should be present. A better solution would probably have been to entrust to an impartial body the task of informing the accused about the contents of the right to legal assistance and the consequences of decision to waive it, especially where investigative acts having serious implications on their fundamental rights are at stake.

The legislation on victims' rights also lack consistent rules on evidence-gathering, notwithstanding that Directive 2012/29/EU proclaims that

> justice cannot be effectively achieved unless victims can properly explain the circumstances of the crime and provide their evidence in a manner understandable to the competent authorities.[130]

As noted, the same provision that acknowledges the accused's right to be heard also requires EU countries to ensure that victims are put in a position to produce evidence in criminal proceedings.[131] In this light, some safeguards were laid down in relation to the victim's questioning, such as the right to the assistance of an interpreter at no cost.[132] It is surprising, however, that EU legislation does not attach any relevance to the need for the aggrieved parties to be provided with legal assistance at the delicate moment of their examination. Moreover, no specific

---

[129] Art. 9 DirAL.

[130] Recital no. 34 DirVR.

[131] Art. 10(1) DirVR.

[132] Recital no. 34 DirVR.

provisions govern other investigative acts involving the victims or allowing their presence, since the regulation of these investigations is again entirely relegated to national law.[133] An exception relates to the case of vulnerable victims who suffered from serious crimes, such as rape or sexual assault. In this case, EU law requires specialist support, which may include, *inter alia*, referral to medical and forensic examination for evidence.[134]

D. Participatory Rights and Coercive Measures in the Field of Personal Freedom

Notwithstanding the increasing attention towards coercive measures in the field of international cooperation,[135] EU law still lacks comprehensive rules on the use of measures of coercion in national criminal proceedings. Therefore, no specific rules governing the participation of the defence in the proceedings concerned with interferences with fundamental rights. Nevertheless, some important indications may be deduced by the legislative instruments examined above, indications that reveal the rising focus of EU institutions on participatory rights especially in cases of arrest and remand detention. In particular, Directive 2012/13/EU requires that the arrested and detained persons be given information on 'applicable procedural rights [...] by means of a written Letter of Rights drafted in an easily comprehensible manner so as to assist those persons in understanding their rights'.[136] This information must concern, *inter alia*, the available tools to 'challenge the lawfulness of the arrest, obtaining a review of the detention, or requesting provisional release where, and to the extent that, such a right exists in national law'.[137]

Of course, information on procedural rights may not suffice to ensure their exercise effectively. Significantly, the EU legislation, following the approach of the European Convention, required member states to ensure that the individuals arrested and detained are informed about both the reasons for deprivation of freedom and the offence under investigation. Moreover, we have seen that the 2012 legislation, while granting all defendants a general right to access all the evidence in the possession of the competent authorities, required prompt information on the existing documents to be made available to the arrestee and detainee.[138]

---

[133] Art. 10(2) DirVR.

[134] Recital no. 38 DirVR.

[135] Alongside the means of coercion that can be adopted in EAW proceedings and supervision measures alternative to pre-trial detention, the 2014 Directive on a European investigation order allowed for evidence to be gathered in other member states through coercive means. See Chapter 13, C.II.2.

[136] Recital no. 22 and Art. 4 DirICP.

[137] Recital no. 22 DirICP.

[138] *Above*, C.II.1.c.

Unfortunately, the functional perspective adopted by this legislative instrument has led the EU institutions to circumscribe this right to the 'essential information' necessary to challenge the lawfulness of the arrest or detention. From this it follows that defendants deprived of liberty will not even have access to all the incriminating evidence gathered against them but only to the necessary information to react against the arrest warrant or the detention order. This weak acknowledgment, further dampened by the reference to the standards set by national law, does not clarify who should assess—and especially pursuant to which criteria—the 'essential' character of the information available.

No binding provision of the 2012 Directive, moreover, clarifies at what stage of the proceedings, exactly, information must be provided, although it is apparent that prompt information plays an essential role for the accused to prepare his defence. Some indications, instead, emerge from Recital no. 30, which generically requires, however, that the defence be given access to relevant documents

> at the latest before a competent judicial authority is called to decide upon the lawfulness of the arrest or detention in accordance with Article 5(4) ECHR, and in due time to allow the effective exercise of the right to challenge the lawfulness of the arrest or detention.

Yet the latter is a rather vague indication, while the reference to *habeas corpus* proceedings weakens the EU protection of the accused who may thus not be entitled to know relevant information at the time of the arrest or immediately after the enforcement of coercion.

Surprisingly, there are no specific rules in the existing EU legislation on the need for judicial assessment of the lawfulness of restrictions on freedom, nor on the right of the arrested or detained person to be heard by an independent authority. There is no doubt that these guarantees constitute general principles of EU law and therefore deserve protection at least in the terms in which the European Convention acknowledges them. An important aspect, which has drawn the attention of the EU institutions over recent years, concerns the need to provide individuals in a vulnerable condition, such as those deprived of their freedom, with proper assistance. In this regard, Directive 2013/48/EU, referring to the Letter of Rights provided for in the 2012 legislation,[139] did not generically acknowledge the right to legal assistance but furthermore emphasised the need to inform a third person[140] and especially to allow proper communication between defendants on remand and a person of their confidence.[141] Unfortunately, the clause 'without undue delay' seems to be so vague that it does not provide precise indications on the moment at which these guarantees should be granted. Moreover, the EU institutions failed to specify the role that third persons and especially the lawyer should play in the arrest or remand proceedings.

[139] Recital no. 14 DirAL.

[140] Art. 5 DirAL.

[141] Art. 6 DirAL.

Another criticism that should be raised against the existing legislation is that EU law exclusively focuses on arrest and detention,[142] thus limiting the scope of protection to the cases of deprivation of liberty. There are no specific rules governing the information and the legal assistance due in case of restrictions on personal freedom and interferences with other fundamental rights (property, freedom of telecommunications, etc.). Concerning the right to information, these important cases fall within the scope of Article 7(3) DirCP, with the result that access to the relevant information must be granted in time to enable the exercise of the defence rights and the latest at the time of the submission of the merits of the case to the competent court.

E. Interim Conclusions

The engagement of EU institutions over the last years in strengthening defence rights in criminal proceedings cannot be doubted and considerable steps forward have been made in recent years.[143] Although comprehensive rules do not yet exist, one can clearly observe the characteristics of a participatory understanding of criminal justice, an understanding that goes beyond the sphere of international cooperation in criminal matters.

Notwithstanding these positive developments, EU law is still at the beginning of a long road, in which, however, some methodological shortcomings are already visible. In particular, the EU legislation launched after the entry into force of the Lisbon Treaty, despite its proclaimed intentions, is not always consistent with the Strasbourg case-law and reveals a somewhat piecemeal approach that does not properly fulfil the complex challenges of modern criminal justice. In particular, the current European scenario poses delicate problems, which cannot properly be tackled through an approach that separately looks at the sides of the accused and the victim, requiring, instead, a broad conception of criminal proceedings as a listening space aimed at the settlement of conflicting interests. Furthermore, the examination of the procedural safeguards acknowledged to defendants and victims highlights a significant difference in the method used. Unlike the approach followed to harmonise the defendant's rights, the rules adopted in relation to the aggrieved parties are still far from granting them the rights to participation in a criminal trial,[144] mostly because the effectiveness of most of the guarantees acknowledged to the victim largely depends on national law. Another criticism concerns the lack of consideration by EU law towards participatory guarantees, which should be ensured to third parties and individuals involved in criminal proceedings against their own will.

---

[142]Recital no. 21 DirICP.

[143]For an assessment of the developments occurred in EU law in relation to the right to a defence in criminal proceedings see Rafaraci (2011), p. 119 ff.; Rafaraci (2013), p. 331 ff.

[144]The question was raised in 2001 by *Chiavario*. Cf. Chiavario (2001), p. 938 ff.

References

Allegrezza S (2012) La riscoperta della vittima nella giustizia penale europea. In: Allegrezza S, Belluta H, Gialuz M, Luparia L (eds) Lo scudo e la spada. Giappichelli, Torino, pp 1–31

Amalfitano C (2014) Le prime Direttive europee sul ravvicinamento "processuale": il diritto all'interpretazione, alla traduzione e all'informazione nei procedimenti penali. In: Del Coco R, Pistoia E (eds) Stranieri e giustizia penale. Problemi di perseguibilità e di garanzia nella normativa nazionale ed europea. Cacucci, Bari, pp 1–34

Bachmaier Winter L (2015) The EU directive on the right to access to a lawyer: a critical assessment. In: Ruggeri S (ed) Human rights in european criminal law. New developments in European legislation and case law after the Lisbon treaty. Springer, Heidelberg, pp 111–131

Böse M (2011) Harmonizing procedural rights indirectly: the framework decision on trials in Absentia. N C J Int Law, 489–510

Chiavario M (2001) Il "diritto al processo" delle vittime dei reati e la Corte europea dei diritti dell'uomo. Rivista di diritto processuale, pp 938 ss

Gialuz M (2013) La lingua come diritto: il diritto all'interpretazione e alla traduzione nel processo penale. In: Ruggieri F, Rafaraci T, Di Paolo G, Marcolini S, Belfiore R (eds) Processo penale, lingua e Unione Europea. Cedam, Padova, pp 227ff

Gialuz M (2015) Dalla Corte di Giustizia importanti indicazioni esegetiche in relazione alle prime due Direttive sui diritti dell'imputato. www.penalecontemporaneo.it. Accessed 11 Nov 2015

Quattrocolo S (2015) The right to information in EU legislation. In: Ruggeri S (ed) Human rights in European criminal law. New developments in European legislation and case law after the Lisbon treaty. Springer, Heidelberg, pp 81–93

Rafaraci T (2011) Il diritto di difesa nelle procedure di cooperazione giudiziaria nel contesto dell'Unione europea. In: Rafaraci T (ed) La cooperazione di polizia e giudiziaria in materia penale nell'Unione europea dopo il Trattato di Lisbona. Giuffrè, Milano, pp 119–132

Rafaraci T (2013) The right of defence in EU judicial cooperation in criminal matters. In: Ruggeri S (ed) Transnational inquiries and the protection of fundamental rights in criminal proceedings. A study in memory of Vittorio Grevi and Giovanni Tranchina. Springer, Heidelberg, pp 331–343

Rafaraci T (2015) New perspectives for the protection of the victims in the EU. In: Ruggeri S (ed) Human rights in European criminal law. New developments in European legislation and case law after the Lisbon treaty. Springer, Heidelberg, pp 215–225

Siracusano F (2011) Nuove prospettive in materie di processo *in absentia* e procedure di consegna. In: Rafaraci T (ed) La cooperazione di polizia e giudiziaria in materia penale nell'Unione europea dopo il Trattato di Lisbona. Giuffrè, Milano, pp 85–104

Vogler R (2015) Lost in translation: language rights for defendants in European criminal proceedings. In: Ruggeri S (coord.) Human rights in European criminal law. New developments in European legislation and case law after the Lisbon treaty. Springer, Heidelberg, pp 95–109

Wahl T (2015) Der Rahmenbeschluss zu Abwesenheitsentscheidungen. Brüsseler EU-Justizkooperation als Fall für Straßburg? EuCrim, pp 70–76

Part VI
Developments in International and Supranational Law Towards a Participatory Understanding of Transnational Criminal Justice

Chapter 11
Participatory Rights and Transnational Criminal Justice in the European Convention

Contents

A. Introductory Remarks 403
B. The European Convention and the Protection of Fair Trial Rights in Transnational Cases 405
C. Information and Participatory Safeguards in National Criminal Proceedings Having Transnational Dimension 409
D. Participatory Rights in International Cooperation in Criminal Matters 412
I. Premise 412
II. The Right to Freedom and Participatory Guarantees in Surrender Procedures 412
1. Information Rights in Extradition Proceedings 412
2. Extradition Proceedings and the Right to Be Heard in Person 413
3. The Problem of *in absentia* Trials in the Field of International Surrender 414
III. Participatory Rights in Cross-Border Investigations and the Taking of Overseas Evidence 416
1. Premise 416
2. The Responsibility for Ensuring Confrontation 417
3. The Method of Confrontation 419
4. The Use of Witness Evidence Taken Abroad Without Confrontation 420
E. Provisional Conclusions 422
References 422

A. Introductory Remarks

It is certainly not an easy task to ascertain whether and to what extent the European Convention acknowledges participatory rights to the individuals involved in transnational criminal procedures. Recourse to the European Convention to ensure respect for human rights in transnational cases has been a relatively recent challenge.[1] This is principally due to the general approach of the provisions of this Charter relevant in the field of criminal justice, provisions that were traditionally interpreted as mainly aimed at protecting individuals involved in domestic

[1]Cf. among others Trechsel (1987), p. 69 ff.; van Hoek and Luchtmann (2006), p. 25 ff.; Vogler (2013), p. 27 ff.

S. Ruggeri, Audi Alteram Partem *in Criminal Proceedings*,
DOI 10.1007/978-3-319-54573-8_11

proceedings, except for a few provisions relating to cross-border cases.[2] This approach was in turn the result of a markedly territorial conception of the Convention (and of international human rights law more broadly). The Strasbourg Court has on several occasions confirmed this conception, despite referring to the 'territorial' scope of the States' commitment to 'secur[ing] to everyone within their jurisdiction the rights and freedoms defined'[3] as involving both the acts committed within their territory and the people falling within their jurisdiction.[4]

On the other hand, the fact that the European Court can intervene after domestic remedies have been exhausted[5] has certainly contributed to the development of a case-law that, as noted, aims at the assessment of the overall fairness of proceedings. Yet this jurisprudence hardly fits the specific problems of transborder procedures in which one country is often responsible for a procedure aimed at providing assistance to another country for the purposes of a foreign prosecution. If Protocol No. 16 enters into force, there will be a need to verify whether and to what extent the Court can maintain this approach by ruling in advance by means of advisory opinions to highest national courts.

As far as cross-border cooperation in criminal matters is concerned, a further difficulty in ensuring full respect for fair trial guarantees is due to the widespread understanding of legal assistance in terms of administrative procedures. This concept of international cooperation has long permeated the Strasbourg case law,[6] which has traditionally looked on 'extradition as not so much a criminal prosecution but mere procedural assistance'.[7] It is surprising, however, that at the beginning of the last decade, despite the enhancement of the role of the judiciary in the legal assistance in criminal matters, the Strasbourg Court still denied the application of the fair trial safeguards of Article 6 ECHR in the extradition procedures because the applicant had not been charged under the jurisdiction of the requested country.[8]

---

[2]A significant example is Article 5(1)(f), which allows the arrest or detention of a person against whom action is being taken with a view to deportation or extradition. From this it follows that the provisions of Article 5 (with the sole exception of paragraph 3) should also apply to deportation or extradition procedures. However, we will see that the Strasbourg case-law has somehow softened this conclusion. See *below*, D.II.1.

[3]Art. 1 ECHR.

[4]van Hoek and Luchtmann (2006), p. 31 f.

[5]Art. 35 ECHR.

[6]See already ECtHR, *X v. Netherlands*.

[7]Vogler (2013), p. 37.

[8]ECtHR, *Mamatkulov and Abdrurasulovic v. Turkey*.

B. The European Convention and the Protection of Fair Trial Rights in Transnational Cases

Against this background, we should now analyse the main steps in the long process that has led the Strasbourg case-law to acknowledge fair trial rights specifically in relation to transborder cases. In its earlier jurisprudence, the Strasbourg institutions adopted a rather minimalist approach to this problematic area. This approach changed considerably at the end of the 1980s in the standout decision *Soering v. United Kingdom*, in which the Court found that a contracting state infringed on Article 3 ECHR by extraditing to a non-contracting state an individual who could risk inhuman and degrading treatment or torture in the requesting country.[9] In this important judgment, moreover, the European judges stressed that an extradition procedure can also lead to a violation of the right to a fair hearing, provided, however, that the fugitive suffered or risked suffering a flagrant denial of fair trial guarantees in the requesting country.[10] By this means, therefore, the Strasbourg case-law drew up a clear distinction between human and fundamental rights, in that the latter should only be protected in cases of flagrant violation. Compared to the complex reasoning used to sanction United Kingdom for exposing the applicant to the risk of being held for a long time on death row, the argument used in relation to Article 6 ECHR was somehow laconic. The Court limited itself to acknowledging the exceptional application of fair trial guarantees in one of the most delicate fields of international cooperation.

To be sure, the *Soering* judgement raised strong criticisms in the part concerned with the violation of Article 3 ECHR, mainly because it sought to impose European standards on third countries to avoid future human rights violations.[11] It must be acknowledged that this decision, while anticipating the Convention's protection against the risk of death and inhuman treatment, considerably relaxed the protection of fair trial guarantees in transnational procedures by limiting the Court's intervention to cases of 'flagrant' violations. Alongside the practical difficulty of assessing where and on what basis a violation fits this requirement, the Court's restrictive approach proved rather unjustified.[12] Thus, why should the Convention only cover flagrant cases?

Some years later, the European Court followed a similar approach in *Drozd & Janousek v. France and Spain*,[13] in which the question arose as to whether a contracting country was allowed to provide legal assistance to a non-member State where a criminal process was conducted in violation of Article 6 ECHR.[14]

---

[9]For in-depth reconstruction of this problem area see van Hoek and Luchtmann (2006), p. 31 f.

[10]ECtHR, *Soering v. United Kingdom.*

[11]Vogler (2013), p. 37.

[12]For some criticisms see also Krüßmann (2009), p. 705, who stressed the relativism of fair trial protection in the *Soering* judgment.

[13]ECtHR, *Drozd & Janousek v. France and Spain.*

[14]The applicants claimed that prosecution witnesses had not been isolated and they were not put in a position to follow the proceedings, which were held in Catalan, a language that they did not understand.

Unlike in the *Soering* judgment, the *Drozd* case did not deal with the problem of future infringements of the Convention: here, the issue at stake was whether the judgement should be enforced against a person already tried. This raised the further question of whether contracting states should engage in assessing—albeit only for the purposes of international cooperation—whether the proceedings conducted in a non-member country were in line with the Convention's standards. The Court's response was *trenchant*. Since the Convention

> does not require the Contracting Parties to impose its standards on third States or territories, France was not obliged to verify whether the proceedings which resulted in the conviction were compatible with all the requirements of Article 6 of the Convention.[15]

Here, the Court's self-restraint was clearly justified by the need to avoid any inquiry into the way criminal proceedings had been conducted in a non-contracting country. According to the Strasbourg judges, cooperation should be refused in case of 'a flagrant denial of justice'.[16] The fundamental rights protection was again circumscribed to exceptional cases, in order to avoid the risk that the needs of international cooperation were frustrated. The Court made a further step forward, also justifying this solution in the light of the need to enhance the individual rights protection in transborder cases.

> To require such a review of the manner in which a court not bound by the Convention had applied the principles enshrined in Article 6 would also thwart the current trend towards strengthening international cooperation in the administration of justice, a trend which is in principle in the interests of the persons concerned.[17]

Despite this acknowledgment, the Court's reasoning clearly aimed at preserving the efficiency of international cooperation. On close examination, this restrictive approach raised several human rights concerns. There is no valid reason for restricting the Convention's protection to cases of flagrant human rights violations, which remained undefined in the Strasbourg case-law. Nor can this case-law be deemed the necessary consequence of the logic of non-inquiry. In fact, allowing for refusal of cooperation, albeit only in exceptional cases, challenges the idea that the requested country should abstain from verifying whether another state fulfilled the Convention guarantees, which is the only way to ascertain whether a flagrant denial of justice occurred or not.

Moreover, the conclusions reached in *Drozd* differ from those of the *Soering* case, in that the Court seemed to leave the door open for assessing whether countries bound by Convention had to comply with all the fair trial rights laid down in Article 6 ECHR in the case of international legal assistance. This acknowledgment raises further questions. To what extent should the countries' commitment to the protection of individual rights prevail over the needs of international cooperation? And what consequences derive from full compliance with the Convention

---

[15]ECtHR, *Drozd & Janousek v. France and Spain*, § 110.

[16]*Ibid.*

[17]*Ibid.*

by other countries? The Court said nothing in this respect in the *Drozd* judgment. Alongside the manner in which the question was posed as to whether contracting countries are required to verify the compliance with the Convention in the jurisdiction of third states, the reasoning used by the Court appears to support the conclusion that countries bound by the Convention should inquire into the conduct of other contracting states and can refuse assistance in any case of infringement of fair trial rights acknowledged by the Convention.

Almost 10 years later, *Pellegrini v. Italy* marked a further development in the European case-law.[18] In this judgment, the Court dealt with the problem of whether a contracting state should ascertain—for the purposes of the enforcement of a foreign judgement—whether the proceedings conducted in a non-member country, albeit not of a criminal nature,[19] complied with the requirements of Article 6 ECHR. The Court's response was that the Italian authorities should duly verify the lawfulness of the foreign procedure before authorising the enforcement of the decision annulling the marriage.

This case is of utmost importance not only because for the first time the Court required full compliance with the Convention by non-contracting states beyond the limit of flagrant denial of justice but furthermore for the reasons that led the Strasbourg judges to this conclusion. Beyond the practical implications deriving from the enforcement of the foreign judgment,[20] the solution adopted was mainly justified by the fact that it was not a criminal case. Moreover, *Pellegrini v. Italy* was a domestic case whose extraterritorial features were a consequence of the agreement between Italy and the Holy See, which provides for concurrent jurisdiction in matrimonial matters as to the annulment of the civil effects of the canonical marriage. Besides, both Mr. and Ms. Pellegrini were Italian citizens resident in Italy.[21] The prevailingly domestic features of this case clearly emerged from another important aspect, which distinguished it form the others examined above. On close examination, the *Pellegrini* judgment, far from requiring contracting states to verify the respect for the Convention's rights by non-member countries, made a contracting state (Italy) responsible for the consequences deriving from the enforcement of a judgement pronounced after a procedure held in violation of Convention rights, albeit outside the area of the contracting states (Holy See). This led the Court to charge a contracting country with the task not just of ascertaining past violations by other states but also of assessing whether the enforcement of a foreign unlawful judgement can entail further violations of the Convention.

Transposing these conclusions into the criminal law area leads to the question of whether the European Convention requires contracting states involved in a cross-border procedure also to prevent the risk of future violations. Clearly, this question

[18]ECtHR, *Pellegrini v. Italy*.

[19]In the instant case, the proceedings had been held before the Roman Rota.

[20]ECtHR, *Pellegrini v. Italy*, § 40.

[21]van Hoek and Luchtmann (2006), p. 38 f.

highlights a positive side of the states' obligation towards the European Convention, an obligation that in transborder cases should go beyond the refusal of assistance. It has been observed that the Court dealt with this issue in the *Soering* case, acknowledging the states' commitment (albeit limited to cases of flagrant violation of human rights) to ensuring respect for fair trial guarantees in favour of individuals who suffered or risked suffering from violations of the rights provided for in Article 6 ECHR. Notwithstanding the restrictive conclusions of this case, therefore, the Court had already left the door open for the possibility of indirect responsibility of a state party where the sought assistance exposed individuals to the risk of an infringement of the Convention.

This approach maintains its merits, notwithstanding that the restrictions acknowledged in the *Soering* decision can no longer be sustained. Moreover, we have noted that at the beginning of the last decade, the Strasbourg Court softened its original approach. In *Ilaşcu and Others v. Moldova and Russia*, the European judges called upon a contracting state to preventively enquire into foreign law in order to avoid overseas repercussions on the Convention rights.[22] To be sure, the Court has never sanctioned contracting countries for preventive violations of the right to a fair hearing. In *Mamatkulov and Abdrurasulovic v. Turkey*, however, it came very close to this result by acknowledging that at the relevant time there 'may have been reasons for doubting' that the applicants would receive a fair trial. This confirms the lack of justification of the limit of 'flagrant denial of justice'.[23] As judges *Sir Nicolas Bratz, Bonello, and Hedigan* put it in their partly dissenting opinion on this case, there were 'credible grounds' on the basis of the material available at that time

> for believing that self-incriminating evidence extracted by torture was routinely used to secure guilty verdicts and that suspects were very frequently denied access to a lawyer of their choice, lawyers often being given access to their client by law enforcement officials after the suspect had been held in custody for several days, when the risk of torture was at its greatest.

These grounds also demonstrate how artificial is to draw a rigid distinction between human and fundamental rights. Thus, in *Mamatkulov and Abdrurasulovic v. Turkey*, the practice of maintaining the applicants in custody without access to their lawyer and the use of torture also highlighted severe obstacles to the defendant's right to be fairly heard, which should have sufficed to convict Turkey for the applicants' surrender in light of Article 6 ECHR.

---

[22] ECtHR, *Ilaşcu and Others v Moldova and Russia*.

[23] ECtHR, *Mamatkulov and Abdrurasulovic v. Turkey*, § 91.

C. Information and Participatory Safeguards in National Criminal Proceedings Having Transnational Dimension

Transnational inquiries do not only raise difficult problems in the light of the European Convention in the case of international cooperation; it has been noted that the institution of a criminal law action with transborder features also poses serious human rights challenges. If defendants are not resident in the trial country, practical obstacles make it difficult to inform them of the initiation of criminal proceedings against them. Where the accused is a foreigner or does not in any case understand the language of the proceedings, further problems emerge in ensuring understandable information on the charge.

Since its earlier case-law, the European Court has acknowledged the need to ensure full respect for fair trial rights in the case of criminal proceedings having transnational dimension. In general terms, the Strasbourg case-law has adopted a more rigorous approach to transnational cases than that followed in purely domestic proceedings. As noted, the Court traditionally required the national authorities to fulfil their task of providing defendants with proper information on the institution of criminal proceedings so as to enable them to set up their defence strategy and eventually to waive their right to personal participation. At least in its earlier rulings, the European case-law was rather firm with the need for defendants to be officially informed on the charges preferred against them. Nevertheless, this jurisprudence was considerably softened in the subsequent years, in that the Court increasingly viewed the right to information on the charge in a functional manner, which exempts the national authorities from their obligation to inform the accused, provided that he could in any way achieve proper information. Significantly, the Strasbourg case-law maintained a rigorous approach to domestic cases with transnational dimension. In *Colozza v. Italy*, the Court considered the formalistic approach of the Italian authorities, based on the presumption of knowledge of the proceedings in case of *latitanza*, as

> difficult to reconcile [...] with the diligence which the Contracting States must exercise in order to ensure that the rights guaranteed by Article 6 (art. 6) are enjoyed in an effective manner.[24]

This requirement of diligence was further developed in cases with a transnational dimension. Thus, the European Court adopted a strict interpretation of the right to be informed on the charge in cases in which the element of transnationality consisted in the defendant residing abroad. In *T. v. Italy*, the European judges regarded as insufficient that

> the applicant had learned indirectly that criminal proceedings had been instituted against [the applicant]. To inform someone of a prosecution brought against him is, however, a legal act of such importance that it must be carried out in accordance with procedural and substantive requirements capable of guaranteeing the effective exercise of the accused's

[24] ECtHR, *Colozza v. Italy*, § 28.

rights, as is moreover clear from Article 6(3)(a) of the Convention. Vague and informal knowledge cannot suffice.[25]

An even higher degree of diligence is required where defendants either are not citizen of the trial country or are unfamiliar with its legal culture. In these cases, the further question arises whether the prosecuting authorities fulfilled their task of making the charge and the judicial summons understandable. The Strasbourg case-law examined this question in *Brozicek v. Italy*, in which the competent authority had ignored the express request of Mr. Brozicek that the judicial notification be translated either into his mother language or into one of the international official languages of the United Nations 'in order to avoid from the outset any risk of misunderstanding'.[26] Consequently, the Italian authority sent another judicial notification, asking him to communicate an address in Italy. It remained unclear whether this second notification could reach the defendant, who was convicted in his absence. The Court, interpreting the Italian rules on judicial notification in terms of the Convention's notion of 'accusation', found that the applicant had not been granted his right to know and understand the charge preferred against him and had also been deprived of his right to take part in the proceedings. By carrying out a stricter assessment of the fairness of the proceedings, therefore, the Strasbourg Court considered that the failure by the national authority to use the necessary diligence in providing defendants with a proper knowledge of the proceedings led to a breach of Article 6 ECHR. It cannot be deduced by this decision that this approach left room for any kind of forfeiture of the right to information.

Some years later, in *F.C.B. v. Italy*, the Strasbourg Court did not even engage in ascertaining whether and under which conditions the defendant, who was not reached by an official notification of the process, could waive his right to be present at trial. In this judgment, the Court dealt with the lack of information of the charge in a manner even more oriented towards the right to effective defence. The question at stake, therefore, was whether the defendant, who was resident abroad at the time of the process and then held in prison in another country, had the right to follow the proceedings personally, notwithstanding the assistance of his counsel. Remarkably, the Court found a violation of the right to a fair hearing not only because the Italian authorities had not properly informed the defendant of the proceedings but also because they failed to respond to the explicit request for cooperation made by the Dutch authorities. The Court did not scrutinise whether proper international cooperation would have avoided the infringement of Article 6 ECHR, considering the failure to cooperate by the Italian authorities as lacking the diligence required by the Convention.[27]

On close examination, this judgment allows us to observe an interesting aspect of the right to personal participation in criminal proceedings, that is, the relationship between this right and the guarantee of legal assistance. The conclusions

[25] ECtHR, *T. v. Italy*, § 28.

[26] ECtHR, *Brozicek v. Italy*, § 16.

[27] ECtHR, *F.C.B. v. Italy*, § 33.

reached by the Court reveal that the lack of diligence by the national authorities had serious repercussions on the right to effective defence, affecting the right of a non-resident accused to give his personal contribution to fact-finding. The Italian authorities only showed interest in personally involving the defendant for the purposes of the execution of the judgement pronounced in his absence. Only at that time the Italian authorities requested the cooperation of the Netherlands, which made extradition conditional on the possibility of the defendant being given a retrial.[28]

On this occasion, the European Court said nothing about whether this solution would also satisfy fair trial needs in cases with transnational features. The opportunity to answer the question came about as Mr. Cat Berro, after having returned to Italy in 2004, was arrested and imprisoned for the execution of the conviction rendered in his absence. Mr. Cat Berro therefore lodged a complaint before the enforcement court, claiming the invalidity of the Italian judgment and consequently the unlawfulness of the detention applied in its execution. This question raised two issues of a great interest from the perspective of the mutual relationship among national law and the European Convention, i.e. (a) whether a detention in execution of a judgement declared in breach of the European Convention can still be deemed lawful pursuant to domestic law and, if not, whether and by what means its validity can be challenged at the enforcement stage, and (b) whether the enforcement of a conviction, which was lawful according to national law but was later declared in breach of Article 6 ECHR, can lead to a further infringement of the Convention, rendering the detention based on the conviction unlawful pursuant to both national law and Article 5(1) ECHR.

In its ruling in 2008, the Strasbourg Court did not examine the merits of the complaint but declared the application inadmissible on the ground that the domestic remedies had not been exhausted. The European judges shared the Supreme Court's view that the applicant had had the possibility to lodge an application for suspension of the time limit for appeal against sentence under Article 175 CCP-Italy, as amended by the Italian Law 60/2005. Under these circumstances, the Court considered it impossible to ascertain whether the application for suspension of the time-limit for appeal against the sentence would have ensured to 'the applicant, with a sufficient degree of legal certainty, the opportunity to go before a court and defend himself in a new set of proceedings'. This rather unclear statement seems to mean that, if the defendant had requested to be relieved from the effects of the expiration of time for challenging the conviction rendered *in absentia*, he would have been granted a new trial in which he could have exercised his defence rights. On close examination, this conclusion reflects the diplomatic effort to ease the longstanding tension between the European Court and Italian case-law rather than being the result of an in-depth examination of whether the 2005 rules ensured to the persons convicted *in absentia* a fair compensation for the defence opportunities lost in the first instance. At any rate, the arguments adduced by the Court in the *Cat Berro* case

[28] *Ibid.*, § 23.

confirm the lawfulness of subsequent remedies under the European Convention also in relation to transnational cases.

D. Participatory Rights in International Cooperation in Criminal Matters

I. Premise

Compared to these findings, the European case-law has not followed a straightforward approach to international cooperation in criminal matters. As noted, this situation has diverse causes and is mainly due to the different structure of trans-border procedures, which are coupled with the main proceeding held in the trial country. Modern tools of international cooperation highlight the existence of flexible forms of assistance, which, especially in complex transnational cases, is provided through a number of different procedures aimed at specific goals over the territory of diverse countries. Moreover, it has been noted that the European Court has over almost three decades developed its case-law in two important directions, namely (a) anticipating the Convention's protection to prevent risks of human rights violations and (b) charging the contracting countries with the task of avoiding the infringement of fair trial guarantees by non-member states. Against this background, the present discussion focuses on the specific protection provided by Strasbourg case-law to the participatory rights of individuals involved in two main areas of international cooperation, that is, surrender procedures and the gathering of transnational evidence.

II. The Right to Freedom and Participatory Guarantees in Surrender Procedures

1. Information Rights in Extradition Proceedings

The first problematic issue regarding surrender procedures concerns the information guarantees due to the sought person. In *Caprino v. United Kingdom*, the former European Commission examined whether the information required by Article 5 (2) ECHR was also due in the case of extradition and deportation proceedings. The conclusion was that the individuals concerned must be made aware of the institution of the extradition proceedings against them but not necessarily of the grounds on which the surrender procedure was initiated.[29] Legal scholarship also shared the opinion that the contents and degree of information due in the field of extradition

[29] EComHR, *Caprino v. United Kingdom.*

must be adapted to the circumstances of the case,[30] provided, however, that information is ensured to the necessary extent to enable the arrested person to evaluate the lawfulness of and to challenge the measure adopted.

On close examination, this approach largely frustrates the fundamental requirement of legal certainty by not providing clear indications as to the exact extent of the right to information. Furthermore, this uncertainty weakens the guarantee of information in a field characterised by the particularly vulnerable situation of persons exposed to a surrender procedure for the purpose of a foreign prosecution. Yet it is clear that the more cautious approach of the European case-law in dealing with the right to information in the case of extradition arrest, compared to that followed in the other situations of Article 5(1) ECHR, cannot justify the lowering of the standards of protection of the individuals who are most in need of it.[31] It is true that the scope of the information rights should be adapted to the particular context of the judicial review that can be activated in the case of surrender proceedings under Article 5(4) ECHR,[32] a review which aims at the assessment of the lawfulness not just of the extradition procedure but also of the provisional arrest aimed at extradition.[33] This does not mean, however, that information must only remain circumscribed to formal issues.[34] In the case of extradition sought for the purposes of a foreign prosecution, there is no reason for withholding the right to know the grounds that led to the institution of surrender procedure as well as the evidence that supported the initiation of criminal proceedings abroad.

2. Extradition Proceedings and the Right to Be Heard in Person

The scant information provided to the sought individuals does not set the best conditions for their participation in the surrender procedure. Yet, if reasonable suspicion is necessary to institute an extradition proceeding, the requested person should be presumed innocent pursuant to the fundamental requirement of Article 6 (2) ECHR.[35] From this it also follows that the judicial review of the provisional arrest must be structured in a way that it should ensure to the arrested individuals standards of protection compatible with the condition of innocent persons. Significantly, the European Court has long acknowledged that the judicial review of the arrest ordered with a view to extradition must also satisfy the guarantees of a fair hearing.[36] In *Sanchez-Reisse v. Switzerland*, the Court found a violation of Article 5 (4) ECHR because the Swiss domestic authorities had failed to ensure to the

[30]Trechsel (2005), p. 459.

[31]Renzikowski (2004), p. 227.

[32]*Ibid.*

[33]Trechsel (1987), p. 72.

[34]In this sense see instead Trechsel (1987), p. 72.

[35]Trechsel (2005), p. 154.

[36]Trechsel (1987), p. 72.

arrestee an adversarial procedure. This conclusion is of great systematic importance, confirming that the contracting countries are responsible for the protection of fair trial rights even though a legal action is at stake that aims at a foreign prosecution.

In the *Sanchez-Reisse* case, although the Court recognised (albeit in a rather cryptic way[37]) that, depending on the circumstances, the individuals concerned should be heard in person, it concluded that there was 'no reason to believe that the applicant's presence convinced the Federal Court that he had to be released'.[38] This rather pragmatic argument reflects a clear underestimation of the defence's contribution to decision-making. On close examination, the fact that extradition requests must be supported by a suspicion of guilt makes it difficult to maintain a different approach from that the Court adopted in relation to the detention under Article 5(1)(c) ECHR, acknowledging the need for defendants to be heard prior to the decision on the lawfulness of the measure applied.[39]

3. The Problem of *in absentia* Trials in the Field of International Surrender

A rather different issue is whether the requested country can be deemed responsible for extraditing a person who was not ensured the necessary guarantees in the relevant proceedings carried out in the trial state. In particular, we should examine whether under the European Convention, a proceeding conducted *in absentia* in the requesting country can hinder international cooperation and what guarantees the requested country should ensure to the sought person. The Strasbourg Court examined this issue in the 2006 decision *Battisti v. France*.[40] In this important case, the Court rejected the recourse lodged by Mr. Battisti against the 2005 ruling of the *Conseil d'Etat*, which had deemed the Italian default proceedings compatible with the requirements of a fair trial, thus confirming that the applicant had not unlawfully been deprived of his right to be present at trial. The main argument to support this conclusion was that Mr. Battisti had been duly informed of the criminal proceedings instituted in Italy and that his choice of appointing two lawyers to defend him in court demonstrated his decision to waive his right to participate personally in the court proceedings. In this way, therefore, the European judges confirmed the general approach adopted in relation to domestic cases, according to which defendants can also implicitly waive their right to be present at trial, provided, however, that they were duly informed of the institution of criminal proceedings and the consequences of their decision.

---

[37] Trechsel (2005), p. 482.

[38] ECtHR, *Sanchez-Reisse v. Switzerland*, § 51.

[39] ECtHR, *Wloch v. Poland*, § 126.

[40] ECtHR, *Battisti v. France*. See on this decision Galgani (2013), p. 174 f.

There is little doubt that this conclusion was the result of a careful assessment of the dynamics of such a complex case. However, it would probably be an exaggeration to say that the authorities of a non-member country could not question the worldwide authority of the Strasbourg Court.[41] This especially applies to countries such as Brazil (where Mr. Battisti had fled in the meantime), which must abide by another body of international human rights case-law, namely Inter-American case-law, whose standards of protection, as noted, do not always coincide with those of the European Court. What the Strasbourg judges consider sufficient to infer the implicit waiver of the right to personal participation in criminal proceedings may not be in other human rights case-law. Nor was Brazil required to surrender Mr. Battisti because the extradition treaty between Italy and Brazil excluded the refusal of extradition solely on the grounds that proceedings were conducted *em revelia* in the requesting country.[42] It is true that this clause calls for overall examination of the concrete circumstances of the case at stake.[43] It has been observed, however, that this Treaty, like other bilateral agreements on extradition, was signed at a time in which Brazil still allowed for criminal proceedings to be carried out *em revelia*. Beyond the arguments used by the former President Lula, however, it should be recalled that, when Brazil refused extradition (2010), Brazil not only had long dropped the proceedings *em revelia* but furthermore had already enacted various mechanisms aimed at avoiding the conduct of a criminal law action against defendants unaware of the proceedings.

Of course, this was not the case in the proceeding against Mr. Battisti. However, the defendant's information about the proceedings and his choice to appoint two lawyers to represent him at trial should not necessarily be interpreted in the terms acknowledged by the European judges, for neither the knowledge of criminal proceedings nor the decision to appoint a lawyer of one's own choosing logically demonstrate the waiver of personal participation. This should have required an in-depth reflection on the sustainability of a presumed knowledge of the proceedings in the light of the need, long recognised by the Strasbourg case-law, for unequivocal waiver of personal participation.

---

[41] In this sense see instead *Galgani*, who examined in detail the complex problems arisen in the *Battisti* case. Cf. Galgani (2013), p. 175.

[42] Chapter 5, C.

[43] Galgani (2013), p. 175.

III. Participatory Rights in Cross-Border Investigations and the Taking of Overseas Evidence

1. Premise

The conduct of transborder investigations and the taking of evidence in other countries also pose difficult challenges for the participatory rights of the defence. A delicate issue in view of the examination of the national criminal justice systems selected in this study is whether and to what extent the European Convention grants the accused the right to be confronted with the accuser who lives or is detained abroad. The Commission had already dealt with issue in the 1973 case *X., Y. and Z. v. Austria* in which it examined whether the applicants must be granted their right to confrontation where testimonial evidence is obtained by means of letters rogatory.[44] The Government argued that the national authority was only bound by 'the existing legislation, even if it were at variance with the Convention'. It was a rather unfortunate argument, which highlighted not only a clear underestimation of the relevance that the European Convention already held in Austria law at that time[45] but furthermore a reductive conception of international cooperation as requiring the application of national law to the extent necessary to provide assistance to a foreign prosecution. Starting with this premise, therefore, the Government adopted a restrictive interpretation of Article 6(3)(d) ECHR on the assumption that the European Convention did not entitle the defence to examine prosecutorial witnesses overseas, since the 1959 European Convention on Mutual Assistance had not enabled the accused to confrontation by means of letters rogatory. The Commission rejected these conclusions, acknowledging the need to ensure a guarantee aimed at protecting anyone charged with a criminal offence, even if in another country.

Beyond the solution adopted,[46] this decision revealed a quite modern approach to letters rogatory as a necessary tool for the purposes of transnational inquiries rather than as purely administrative assistance in favour of foreign prosecutions. This approach poses the necessary premises for a discussion on the defence's contribution to the evidence-gathering in the field of transnational criminal justice. From the viewpoint of the right to confrontation, this topic raises three main questions, which respectively concern (a) the responsibility for ensuring confrontation, (b) the method of confrontation and (c) the use of overseas testimonial evidence gathered without confrontation. All the three issues have led the Strasbourg case-law to strike delicate balances between the specific requirements of the cooperating countries and the human rights challenges posed by transnational cases.

---

[44]EComHR, *X., Y. and Z. v. Austria*.

[45]Austria had already ratified in 1958 the European Convention, which thus formed part of the 'existing legislation' in force at that time.

[46]*Below*, D.III.2.

2. The Responsibility for Ensuring Confrontation

The first problematic issue is what country should set the necessary conditions for the accused to be properly confronted with prosecutorial witnesses. At first glance, the fact that the examination must be take place in a country other than the trial state may seem to support the conclusion that the cooperating country should bear the entire responsibility for ensuring confrontation with incriminating witnesses. The Commission sustained this view in *X., Y. and Z. v. Austria*, stating that 'the Austrian authorities were fully responsible for the form and conduct of this hearing on commission including the question of who should participate at the hearing'.

This rather strong argument raises further questions. In particular, what timeframe is available so that the cooperating country can avoid infringements of the Convention? As noted, in national cases the Court usually considers the Convention's requirements to be fulfilled if defendants, despite not being involved in pre-trial questioning of an incriminating witness or a co-accused, had the opportunity to examine them at a later stage of the proceedings. In transborder cases, however, the tasks of the cooperating country are usually exhausted by the execution of specific individual investigative or evidence-gathering activities. Should we assume that the cooperating country can be declared responsible for not granting confrontation during the hearing on commission even though the accused could examine the accuser at a later stage of the proceedings? Notwithstanding that the Commission did not clarify this point, the solution adopted was in line with the approach followed by the European Court in national cases. The application was declared inadmissible in the light of an overall consideration of the 'course of the proceedings and, in particular, to the circumstance that the witness against the applicants was, on their request, re-heard on commission after the applicants had studied the record of his first examination'.

In the field of transnational cooperation, therefore, the Strasbourg case-law seems to broaden the scope of the right to a fair hearing to the extent that the guarantee of confrontation might indistinctly be ensured either during the examination or in a later phase of the proceedings. On close examination, this solution raises even graver human rights concerns than in domestic cases, relieving the cooperating country from its responsibility to comply with the Convention solely on the basis that confrontation will take place at a later stage of the proceedings, no matter whether in the trial state or in another country. This rather vague requirement, however, is linked with future and unpredictable events, such as the decision of the person examined to move to another country, the coercive transfer of a co-accused to the trial state, the practical feasibility of confrontation, and so on. It is not an issue of little importance. In domestic cases, the competent authorities hold responsibility for ensuring full protection of the Convention's safeguards, so that, if confrontation could not take place in the pre-trial phase, a fair opportunity of cross-examination must be ensured in open court. In transborder cases, we cannot overlook that several factors can hinder a future confrontation. Even though modern tools of mutual legal assistance eliminated or largely reduced the decision-making power of governmental authorities, international cooperation can be refused and each case of evidence-gathering puts different authorities and different legal cultures in contact with each other.

Certainly, the prosecuting authority has no jurisdiction in the cooperating country and the tasks of the cooperating authority are limited to the carrying out of the sought investigation. This does not mean that the responsibility for ensuring full respect for the Convention can be split into two separate sides, so that the cooperating country can discretionarily deny confrontation counting on a future opportunity in the trial state. Denying the accused the right to be present at the questioning of prosecutorial witnesses, even though he requested it, does not suffice to satisfy the right to confrontation if the decision can be based unpredictably either on the results of the first or the second hearing. As a consequence, where the defence requests a confrontation on commission, the cooperating country must arrange it unless cogent provisions of its own law prohibit it. The cooperating country cannot invoke the procedures of *lex loci* to exclude the defence's participation. The fact that the cooperating authority holds full responsibility for the 'form' and 'conduct' of the requested hearing does not compel it to conduct the hearing solely on the basis of its own law. It can be assumed that the defence should be involved in the taking of testimonial evidence, if *lex fori* provides it for.

On the other hand, it does not seem that the cooperating authority can be deemed liable for mistakes or omissions depending on the trial country. This issue is of utmost importance, concerning the practical arrangements that are required from the competent authority for the relevant proceedings. The question arose in the case *Solakov v. the Former Yugoslav Republic of Macedonia*, in which the applicant complained that the summons contained 'no detailed information about the venue or exact date of the questioning, the number and names of the witnesses to be heard, or the questions that the investigating judge wished to put to them'.[47] The Court, however, did not address this point, nor did it take into consideration the specific diligence duty lying with the competent authority.

Of course, it may happen that, although the competent authority properly fulfilled its tasks, neither the accused nor the lawyer could take part in the questioning of a prosecutorial witness in the cooperating country for grounds attributable to the foreign authority. As the Commission stressed in *P.V. v. Federal Republic of Germany*,

> assuming that the Turkish law provides for the presence of the accused or his defence counsel at the examination of a witness on commission, the German authorities cannot be held responsible for the non-observance of provisions of the Turkish law by a Turkish court.

This quite obvious acknowledgment can be understood in the sense that any contracting state, should the application be directed against it, holds responsibility for applying its own law in a manner that would avoid infringements of the Convention within its own jurisdiction, even though the consequences might

[47]ECtHR, *Solakov v. the Former Yugoslav Republic of Macedonia*, § 41.

occur in another country. As we will note, the Commission stressed that the trial country can in principle be deemed responsible for the use of untested evidence collected abroad.[48]

3. The Method of Confrontation

International cooperation makes it difficult to always ensure direct confrontation with prosecutorial witnesses. This raises the question of whether and in what form an indirect form of witness examination can take place. It has been observed that the drafters of the Convention allowed for the accused to have prosecutorial witnesses examined, a formulation usually interpreted as enacting indirect confrontation by means of a hearing conducted by an impartial body, such as an investigative magistrate. The Commission confirmed this approach by dealing with a transborder case, the aforementioned *P.V. v. Federal Republic of Germany*:

> this requirement [confrontation] is not only complied with if the accused or his defence counsel have the opportunity of putting questions to the witnesses themselves, but also if they can request that certain questions are put to the witness by the court. Especially, this holds true if witnesses are to be examined on commission.[49]

Of course, this conclusion cannot be interpreted as unconditionally allowing for court examination, while raising the question of the form of the defence's involvement in the taking of testimonial evidence abroad. The solution reached by the European Commission was that the accused must at least be given the possibility of formulating written questions to be addressed to the witness abroad. The European Court also dealt with the accused's participation in the execution of rogatory letters in *Solakov v. the Former Yugoslav Republic of Macedonia*, concluding that the applicant had 'not expressly given any questions that he would have liked to be put to the witnesses'.[50] From this rather unclear statement it can be inferred that the Court confirmed the lawfulness of the solution of written questions in case of transnational evidence-gathering.[51]

This conclusion seems to be rather problematic. In particular, it is hard to imagine how written questions can be defined in advance in international cooperation. It is also questionable whether the defence was put in a position to formulate preventive written questions and who holds responsibility for informing the accused about this possibility and about the circumstances on which the witness will be heard. Furthermore, the *Solakov* judgment casts doubts on the feasibility of this solution. In this case, we have noted that the applicant's lawyers were summoned only one week before the trip and that the court summons contained 'no detailed information about the venue or exact date of the questioning, the number

[48] *Below*, D.III.4.

[49] EComHR, *P.V. v. Federal Republic of Germany*.

[50] ECtHR, *Solakov v. the Former Yugoslav Republic of Macedonia*, § 62.

[51] In this sense Trechsel (2005), p. 311 f.

and names of the witnesses to be heard, or the questions that the investigating judge wished to put to them'. Under these circumstances, it was very unlikely that the applicant or his lawyers could arrange a clear defence strategy. Therefore, the acknowledgment of the possibility for the accused to formulate written questions in advance was rather rhetorical.

To be sure, the Commission had already had the opportunity to examine this issue in *X., Y. and Z. v. Austria*. As noted, the Government argued that neither Austrian law nor the 1959 European Convention on Mutual Legal Assistance allowed for private parties to put questions during testimonial examinations taken through letters rogatory. The defence replied to this argument by proposing an interesting interpretation of Article 6(3)(d) ECHR, according to which, even in case of questioning conducted by the judicial authority, defendants should be put in a position to formulate their own questions. This should entail the defence's presence at the hearing on commission. As the defence rightly stressed,

> it would have been impossible to formulate in advance questions of the defence to be included in the letters rogatory, since this is exclusively feasible if the witness heard was a defence witness, unlike the present one. Questions to a prosecution witness usually emerge, according to the applicants, at the moment when he is heard.[52]

From this approach it follows that even a broad interpretation of Article 6(3)(d) ECHR does not necessarily entail the underestimation of the role of the defence and, on close examination, promotes the accused's direct involvement in the taking of incriminating evidence. As noted, the Commission did not address this point at that time, while declaring the application inadmissible.

4. The Use of Witness Evidence Taken Abroad Without Confrontation

What happens if defendants could not be confronted with their accusers and indirect confrontation has never taken place? Can the untested evidence gathered abroad be admitted at trial and under which conditions can it be used against the accused?

As anticipated, the Commission dealt with this issue in *P.V. v. Federal Republic of Germany* by considering it 'in principle conceivable' that the use of the evidence obtained on commission can infringe the Convention. Starting with this premise, however, the Commission ruled out Germany's responsibility on the assumption that 'the applicant's rights under Article 6(3)(d) were respected with regard to the examination [. . .] on commission'. To support this conclusion, as noted, the Commission argued that the right to confrontation can also be guaranteed by allowing the defence to put indirect questions to the witness. In the case at hand, the Commission found it decisive that the applicant had not complained that it had been impossible for him to request that questions be put to the witness abroad nor was his request rejected. This led the Commission to rule out that the accused's right to confrontation had been impaired abroad and consequently that the use of the

[52]EComHR, *X., Y. and Z. v. Austria*.

untested evidence against him infringed the requirements of a fair trial. This conclusion is surprising taking into account the circumstances of the case. It has been noted that the Commission acknowledged that the law of the cooperating country required the 'presence of the accused or his defence counsel at the examination of a witness on commission', notwithstanding that 'in the present case neither the applicant himself nor his defence counsel were informed of the date of [the witness'] examination'.

In the same case, the Commission also dealt with the problem of the conditions under which the incriminating evidence gathered abroad could be used. The Commission invoked a double argument in this respect. On the one hand, it devaluated the probative value of the overseas testimony on the assumption that the information given by the witness on commission was only 'limited to confirming his previous statements' rendered to the police in Germany. On the other, it stressed that the information given to the police was sufficently reliable in the light of the existence of corroborative elements. One might argue that this further assessment was aimed at demonstrating that the guilty verdict was not mainly based on untested evidence taken overseas—an early manifestation of the sole and decisive evidence doctrine in the field of transnational inquiries. On close examination, this further scrutiny was certainly not required, assuming that defence's right to have prosecutorial witnesses examined had not been impaired. In other words, if the guarantee of confrontation was not infringed, why did the Commission have to examine under which conditions the untested evidence was used against the applicant?

Most significantly, in the *P.V.* case, the Commission engaged in examining whether the competent German authority 'took into account and weighed evidence presented by the defence'. This argument was also of great importance, highlighting the existence of a duty of diligence on the part of the competent authority, which is called upon to hear the viewpoint of the defendant who suffered from sacrifices of his defence rights. Even though the overall reasoning of this decision was rather tortuous, it revealed an approach that somewhat anticipated the solutions reached by the Court in the recent *Al-Khawaja* case. Yet the conclusions adopted by the Commission in *P.V. v. Federal Republic of Germany* were largely unsatisfactory. Unlike in the *Al-Khawaja* case, the Commission did not scrutinise whether other individual rights could justify the lack of confrontation, limiting itself to verifying whether further defensive elements had been taken into consideration. However, the use of corroborating evidence cannot always compensate for the lack of confrontation. Nor can transborder cooperation justify the use of untested evidence on the assumption that it only confirmed information gathered by the police, which in turn did not involve the defence.

E. Provisional Conclusions

The analysis of the approach of the European case-law to transnational criminal justice leads to results that partially differ from those examined in relation to domestic proceedings. By scrutinising national cases with transnational features, the Strasbourg Court did not generally soften the assessment of the fairness of the proceedings. A certain relaxation of the usual qualitative requirements could only be observed in the *F.C.B.* case, although this was mainly due to the Court's attempt to ease the longstanding tensions with the Italian case-law in relation to *in absentia* procedures. Different conclusions apply to international cooperation in criminal matters, in which the individuals concerned were often only ensured a weak version of the ordinary fair trial safeguards—moreover, limited to cases of flagrant violations of such safeguards. It must be acknowledged, however, that the European case-law on the participatory rights in transborder criminal cases is still fragmentary and lacks uniform approach, so it is hard to predict in what direction the Court will go in the near future.

References

Galgani B (2013) Extradition, political offence and the discrimination clause. In: Ruggeri S (ed) Transnational inquiries and the protection of fundamental rights in criminal proceedings. A study in memory of Vittorio Grevi and Giovanni Tranchina. Springer, Heidelberg, pp 167–191

Krüßmann T (2009) Transnationales Strafprozessrecht. Nomos, Baden-Baden

Renzikowski J (2004) Die nachträgliche Sicherungsverwahrung und die Europäische Menschenrechts konvention. Juristische Rundschau, pp 271–275

Trechsel S (1987) Grundrechtsschutz bei der internationalen Zusammenarbeit in Strafsachen. Europäische GRUNDRECHTE-Zeitschrift, pp 69–78

Trechsel S (2005) Human rights in criminal proceedings. Oxford University Press, Oxford

van Hoek A, Luchtmann M (2006) The European convention on human rights and transnational cooperation in criminal matters. In: van Hoek A et al (eds) Multilevel governance in enforcement and adjudication. Intersentia, Antwerp, pp 25–92

Vogler R (2013) Transnational inquiries and the protection of human rights in the case-law of the European court of human rights. In: Ruggeri S (ed) Transnational inquiries and the protection of fundamental rights in criminal proceedings. A study in memory of Vittorio Grevi and Giovanni Tranchina. Springer, Heidelberg, pp 27–40

Chapter 12
Audi alteram partem in Transnational Cases Under the American Convention

Contents

A. Introductory Remarks. The Need for a Systematic Approach to Transnational Cases Under the American Convention 423
B. A Victim-Centred Approach to International Cooperation and the Responsibility of the International Community for Avoiding the Impunity of the Perpetrators of Serious Human Rights Violations 424
C. Participatory Guarantees in International Cooperation Under the American Convention 425
I. Premise 425
II. Extradition Procedures and the Right of the Victims of Serious Human Rights Violations to Examine the Alleged Perpetrators. The Colombian Case of the Justice and Peace Process 426
III. The Right to Obtain Exculpatory Evidence, the Guarantee of Confrontation and the Use of Untested Evidence in Transborder Cases 428
D. Interim Conclusions 430
References 430

A. Introductory Remarks. The Need for a Systematic Approach to Transnational Cases Under the American Convention

Like the European Convention, the Pact of San José does not contain specific provisions explicitly aimed at the protection of due process rights in transnational criminal cases. Perhaps more than in Europe, the recourse to this international Charter to protect the individuals involved in transborder inquiries constitutes a relatively recent achievement, which has been rarely analysed until now.[1] The fact that the Inter-American case-law has only rarely been called upon to examine issues concerned with due process rights in transborder cases has contributed to this situation. Moreover, a few cases were recently raised before the Inter-American institutions, providing a basis for the examination of this problematic area.

[1]For a recent contribution see Dondé Matute (2013), p. 41 ff.

S. Ruggeri, Audi Alteram Partem *in Criminal Proceedings*,
DOI 10.1007/978-3-319-54573-8_12

An interesting aspect which emerges from Inter-American case-law is that the clear attempt to redefine the scope of important guarantees of the Convention in light of other international human rights instruments. The need for a systematic interpretation of Convention rights has been particularly evident in transnational cases. Remarkably, in its 1999 Advisory Opinion '*The Right to Information on Consular Assistance in the Framework of the Guarantees of Due Process of Law*', the Inter-American Court stressed that 'the interpretation of a treaty must take into account not only the agreements and instruments related to the treaty [. . .], but also the system of which it is part'.[2] Starting with this premise, the Court reinterpreted the scope of the due process guarantees concerned with international legal assistance in the light of the standards laid down in the Vienna Convention on Consular Relations, focusing on the need to provide foreigners submitted to grave restrictions on their freedom with proper assistance. In particular, the San José case-law stressed that individuals detained abroad—especially taking into account that 'their most precious juridical rights, perhaps even their lives, hang in the balance'—must be granted a right to consular assistance.[3]

Further case-law confirmed this approach,[4] thus providing a systematic framework for a better understanding of the extent to which the American Convention acknowledged participatory rights of individuals involved in transnational inquiries. As *Dondé Matute* points out, the approach adopted by the Inter-American case-law in 1999 paved the way for a 'progressive interpretation of human rights treaties, meaning that their content can change and expand in accordance with the needs of a particular place and time'.[5] Thus, 'treaties are not isolated legal instruments; they form part of the corpus of international law, which regulates different topics when it is taken as a whole'.[6]

B. A Victim-Centred Approach to International Cooperation and the Responsibility of the International Community for Avoiding the Impunity of the Perpetrators of Serious Human Rights Violations

Proper international cooperation plays a decisive role in the investigation and prosecution of criminal offences having transnational dimension and especially of cases of organised (and often systematic) forms of human rights violations. Delays in requesting legal assistance and the hurdles often imposed by the requested

---

[2]IACtHR, Advisory Opinion '*The Right to Information on Consular Assistance in the Framework of the Guarantees of Due Process of Law*', § 113.

[3]*Ibid.*, § 121 ff.

[4]IACtHR, *Villagrán-Morales et al. v. Guatemala*, § 192 ff.

[5]Dondé Matute (2013), p. 45.

[6]*Ibid.*

country can jeopardise the success of a criminal law action. The Inter-American case-law has shown great sensitivity towards this problem by stressing, in line with its general case-law, that a prompt and effective investigation of serious human rights violations not only is justified by state-related interests but also aims at ensuring the best protection of the victims and their families. The Court stressed this issue in very clear terms in *Goiburú et al. v. Paraguay*, highlighting that the state's obligation to investigate and prosecute human rights abuses also entails the duty of giving a proper criminal law response to the victim's claim for justice, which can lead to the state's responsibility for not requesting extradition 'promptly and with due diligence'.[7]

Most significantly, the Inter-American case-law did not conceive of the responsibility for the proper use of international cooperation tools as limited solely to the requesting country. In the *Goiburú* judgment again, the Court added that 'States Parties to the Convention should cooperate with each other to eliminate the impunity of the violations committed [...] by the prosecution and, if applicable, the punishment of those responsible'.[8] Other countries, therefore, are required to provide wide-ranging cooperation, *e.g.* by not hindering the sought extradition of the alleged perpetrators without justification. This approach also requires contracting countries not just to undertake isolated initiatives but furthermore to provide each other with virtuous cooperation with a view to achieving the most effective criminal law action. In the *Goiburú* judgment, the Court stressed that 'the need to eliminate impunity establishes an obligation for the international community to ensure inter-State cooperation'. This statement is of utmost systematic importance, highlighting the joint responsibility of countries committed to international cooperation for the fulfilment of the Convention's requirements.

C. Participatory Guarantees in International Cooperation Under the American Convention

I. Premise

This victim-centred approach of the Inter-American case-law also to international cooperation in criminal matters entails relevant implications from the perspective of the present discussion, starting with a significant extension of the due process guarantees acknowledged in the Convention. This result can also be observed from the subjective viewpoint of the addressees of the Convention's rights. It is noteworthy that the Pact of San José, unlike the European Convention, enacted into the same paragraph of Article 8 the presumption of innocence and a set of minimum fair rights guarantees. Despite this systematic approach, the due

[7]IACtHR, *Goiburú et al. v. Paraguay*, § 130.
[8]*Ibid.*, § 132.

process rights acknowledged in Article 8(2) ACHR were not reserved to the individuals 'accused of a criminal offense' but to 'every person'. This detail is not of little importance, instead calling for a broad interpretation aimed at extending the due process guarantees to persons other that the accused. In this light, the requirement of full equality also takes on a significance that goes beyond the sphere solely of the defendants, requiring the contracting states to ensure an overall balance among the conflicting interests of different parties involved in criminal proceedings.

There is little doubt that there is an enhanced need for these balances in the field of transnational criminal justice. In this respect, I shall focus on two main topics, i.e. (a) the right of the victims of grave human rights violations to confront the alleged perpetrators in the field of extradition procedures and (b) the right to obtain exculpatory evidence and the guarantee of confrontation of the sought person involved in transnational cases.

II. Extradition Procedures and the Right of the Victims of Serious Human Rights Violations to Examine the Alleged Perpetrators. The Colombian Case of the Justice and Peace Process

Doubtless, extradition is a fundamental tool to enable effective prosecution of transnational offences. Yet extradition procedures can also have negative consequences and can especially entail the risk of hampering justice, while jeopardising the right of the victims of serious crimes to collect evidence and obtain proper investigations of the alleged offences. From the general viewpoint of this discussion, therefore, the question arises of which defence rights the aggrieved parties hold in the extradition procedure.

One of the most delicate issues dealt with by the Inter-American case-law over the recent years was the Process of Justice and Peace Law in Colombia.[9] Certainly, Law 975/2005 was a milestone in solving the domestic conflicts in Colombia, giving rise to an enormous process of demobilization of paramilitary groups and the institution of a huge criminal law action against them. Even though the individuals who accepted demobilization were subject to a reduced punishment of only 8 years, this legislation marked an important step in the ascertainment of serious war crimes and offences against humanity, which aimed at satisfying the victims' right to truth and reparation while entailing the difficult challenge of returning the members of paramilitary groups to civil life.[10] As this process was still ongoing, however, 14 paramilitary leaders were suddenly extradited to US with

[9]Julio Estrada (2013), 125 ff.

[10]*Ibid.*, 127.

the justification by the Colombian Government that, had they remained in Colombia, they would have committed further crimes. On the other hand, this solution impeded the national prosecution of drug trafficking crimes, hindering the legitimate claim for justice of hundreds of Colombian citizens.[11] After initially agreeing to the surrender procedures, the Colombian Supreme Court of Justice, changed its jurisprudence in 2009 by acknowledging the risks that extradition concerned with drug-trafficking offences can entail for the national obligation to investigate and prosecute serious crimes, such as genocide, forced disappearance, torture, and so on.[12]

The Inter-American Commission also monitored the implications of the extradition of paramilitary leaders to US on the basis of the Process of Justice and Peace Law in Colombia, expressing its concerns about the ascertainment of the human rights violations charged and the need to satisfy the victim's claim for justice. After the extradition of the paramilitary leaders, Colombia sought legal assistance to obtain testimonial evidence. Although Colombia stated that it was satisfied with the international cooperation of US authorities, the Inter-American Commission observed that US authorities posed several obstacles to Colombian requests on mutual assistance, obstacles that made almost impossible to achieve the sought testimony, so much so that only one request was answered.[13] Against this background, the Commission viewed the extradition procedure in a rather negative way, that is, as a means that 'undermine[d] the rights of the victims to the truth, justice, and reparation'.[14] A significant consequence of this acknowledgment was the extension to the victims of human rights abuses of important participatory rights that are traditionally considered a prerogative of the accused, such as the right to obtain exculpatory evidence and the right to confrontation. The main concern of the Commission lay in the 'scanty number of victims in the rooms where the voluntary statements were transmitted, due to difficulties in access or in receiving notice of the proceedings',[15] which made it extremely difficult for them to take part in the collection of (spontaneous) testimonial evidence.[16]

The Inter-American Court was even more demanding in the 2009 monitoring of compliance with the judgment *Ituango Massacres v. Colombia*. In this complex case, the Court also examined the implications of the Colombian decision to extradite paramilitary leaders to US during the ongoing process of Peace and Justice. The conclusion was that extradition, despite its relevance 'as an important instrument for the criminal prosecution of cases involving serious human rights violations, [...] cannot be held as a means to favor, seek or ensure impunity in said cases'.[17] In this light, the Inter-American judges acknowledged that the extradition

[11] *Ibid.*, 128.

[12] *Ibid.*, 128.

[13] Dondé Matute (2013), p. 43.

[14] IAComHR, Annual Report (2009), Chapter IV, § 36.

[15] *Ibid.*, Chapter IV, § 40.

[16] Dondé Matute (2013), p. 43.

[17] IACtHR, *Ituango Massacres v. Colombia* (2009), § 19.

to the US 'prevented the victims from having access to the proceedings and requiring a complete confession of the facts'.[18] To be sure, the Court considered that this result was not due to the extradition procedure but to the Colombian Peace and Justice legislation, which allowed the victims' legal representatives neither to question the extradited individuals nor to request complete copies of the preliminary interviews or produce evidence in the proceeding.[19] The Inter-American case-law, therefore, avoided imputing the responsibility for the failure of the victims to be confronted with the alleged perpetrators solely to the lack of proper cooperation by the US authorities, stressing instead that domestic law cannot prevent the trial state from complying with the obligation required by the American Convention to investigate and punish those responsible for serious human rights violations.[20]

By this means, the San José judges redefined the participatory rights of the individuals involved in the extradition procedures, extending the guarantee of confrontation to the victim of serious human rights violations, which must be granted the possibility of being present at the examination of the alleged offenders and obtaining a confession. The Court confirmed this important requirement in the 2013 monitoring of compliance with the *Ituango Massacres* decision, in which it pointed out that, despite the efforts made to satisfy the requirements of the 2006 judgment, there was still a need to ensure to the victims the right to give their own contribution to the examination of the paramilitary leaders extradited.[21]

III. The Right to Obtain Exculpatory Evidence, the Guarantee of Confrontation and the Use of Untested Evidence in Transborder Cases

The second problematic area concerns the right to evidence of the individuals involved in cross-border inquiries. This issue can in turn have various features. Certainly, the accused cannot be deprived of the right not only to obtain exculpatory evidence but also to take part in the taking of incriminating evidence, if the sought information is abroad. Moreover, the right to evidence in transborder cases is not an exclusive prerogative of defendants. It has been noted that the victims of serious human rights violations also hold the right to confront the alleged perpetrators, if extradited to other countries. Moreover, the collection of overseas evidence is also of utmost importance for the best prosecution of complex forms of organised crime having transnational dimension.

On the other hand, it cannot be denied that obtaining pieces of information abroad can also hamper the conduct of the ongoing criminal inquiry, while posing

[18] *Ibid.*, § 18.
[19] *Ibid.*
[20] *Ibid.*, § 18.
[21] IACtHR, *Ituango Massacres v. Colombia* (2013), § 16 et seqq.

difficult challenges for the fulfilment of the rights enshrined in the Convention. Defendants must often face enormous difficulties to prepare their defence and especially to properly participate in the gathering of oral evidence by the accuser, if resident or detained in other countries. It has been observed that the Inter-American Court, dealing with domestic cases, not only ensured to the accused the right to produce exculpatory evidence but also enhanced the right to examine prosecutorial witnesses. Remarkably, the Court has not softened the guarantee of confrontation in cases of organised and terrorism-related crimes, instead confirming the right to question police and military agents whose testimony supported the charges brought against the applicants.

It must now be analysed whether the Inter-American bodies followed the same approach in transborder cases. As far as the right to exculpatory evidence is concerned, one of the main problems is that several international instruments of legal assistance in force in the Americas contain clauses that expressly prevent private parties from using them to obtain evidence situated abroad.[22] This raises the question of whether these instruments in transnational cases can lower the standards laid down by the American Convention. From a human rights perspective, the answer should be negative[23] and consequently, the competent authorities should seek the necessary international cooperation to ensure the widest range of possibilities for the individuals concerned to access exculpatory information.

A different problem is whether and to what extent the accused should be involved in the taking of prosecutorial evidence situated in other countries. It is apparent that the reference by Article 8(2)(f) ACHR to 'witnesses present in the court' cannot be interpreted in the sense that the Convention rules out the fundamental right to confrontation with a witness who, living or being detained abroad or extradited to other countries, cannot appear in court. Clearly, the unavailability of prosecutorial witnesses and the difficulty of ensuring their attendance cannot release the competent authority from its obligation to use all the necessary tools to grant defendants a fair opportunity to be confronted with their accusers, even by means of technical arrangements. Nor can untested evidence be unconditionally used on the ground that the witness cannot appear in court. Certainly, defendants cannot be deprived of the possibility of challenging prosecutorial evidence only because it was taken abroad. Although there is no case-law on the use of untested overseas evidence, there are no reasons for which the Inter-American Court should depart from the approach followed in the *Norín Catrimán* case. This entails the obligation for the competent authority to use the available tools of international cooperation to ensure to the accused a proper opportunity of confrontation.

---

[22]For instance, see Article IV(3)(c) of the Agreement on legal cooperation and mutual assistance between Colombia and the USA.

[23]Dondé Matute (2013), p. 48 f.

D. Interim Conclusions

The approach followed by the Inter-American case-law, despite the scant jurisprudence available, reveals a clear attempt to enhance the protection of vulnerable individuals involved in transborder inquiries. One of the main achievements of Inter-American case-law has been the extension of important due process guarantees to individuals other than the accused, especially the victim. Doubtless, the tools of international cooperation, despite their great potential, entail considerable risks not only for the effective prosecution of serious human rights abuses but also for the victim's claim for truth, justice, and reparation. In this light, the Colombian case of the Justice and Peace Process gives us a clear picture of the repercussions of the extradition of several paramilitary leaders on the victims' right to examine the alleged perpetrators and obtain a confession. On the defendant's side, even though no specific case-law deals with the right to evidence in transborder cases, there are no reasons for departing from the strong approach adopted in relation to the collection of exculpatory evidence and especially to the right to confrontation with incriminating witnesses. This highlights the obligation for the national authorities to use all the available tools to grant the individuals involved in international cooperation the full exercise of their participatory rights in the field of evidence-gathering.

References

Dondé Matute J (2013) The Inter-American system of human rights and transnational inquiries. In: Ruggeri S (ed) Transnational inquiries and the protection of fundamental rights in criminal proceedings. A study in memory of Vittorio Grevi and Giovanni Tranchina. Springer, Heidelberg, pp 41–50

Julio Estrada A (2013) Transnational investigation of criminal procedure and the protection of victims of serious human rights violations in Latin American constitutional jurisprudence. In: Ruggeri S (ed) Transnational inquiries and the protection of fundamental rights in criminal proceedings. A study in memory of Vittorio Grevi and Giovanni Tranchina. Springer, Heidelberg, pp 125–137

Chapter 13
Defence Rights and Participatory Guarantees Acknowledged by EU Law in the International Cooperation Within the Area of Freedom, Security and Justice

Contents

A. Introductory Remarks 432
B. Participatory Guarantees and the Protection of Personal Freedom in International Cooperation Among Member States 432
I. Premise 432
II. The Right to Personal Participation in Criminal Proceedings and Surrender Procedures. The Protection of Absent Defendants in EAW Proceedings 433
1. The Soft Solutions of the 2002 Legislation on the European Arrest Warrant 433
2. Subsequent Developments in EU Law 434
a) The Enhancement of Information and Participatory Rights by the 2009 Legislation 434
b) The Responses of the EU Court of Justice. The '*Melloni* Doctrine' 437
III. Participatory Rights and International Procedures Involving Restrictions on Liberty 438
1. Information Rights and Guarantees of a Fair Hearing in EAW Proceedings 438
2. Defence Rights in the Proceedings on Supervision Measures 443
C. Participatory Rights and Transnational Evidence in the EU Area 445
I. Premise 445
II. Participatory Rights, Transnational Evidence-Gathering and the Developments of Legal Assistance Models 446
1. The Solutions of the Brussels Convention on Transnational Evidence-Gathering 446
2. The Shift from Mutual Legal Assistance to Mutual Recognition and the Defence Rights in the Order Model 447
a) The Combined Methods of Evidence-Gathering in the Order Model and the Weak Protection of Participatory Rights in the EU Legislation on the European Evidence Warrant and the European Investigation Order 447
b) Hearings by Videoconference, Right to Be fairly Heard and the Guarantee of Confrontation in Transnational Cases 452
III. Defence Rights in Joint Criminal Inquiries 454
D. Interim Conclusions 455
References 456

S. Ruggeri, Audi Alteram Partem *in Criminal Proceedings*,
DOI 10.1007/978-3-319-54573-8_13

A. Introductory Remarks

It has been observed that the focus by EU institutions on the defence's contribution to fair criminal justice followed the legislative developments occurred over the last decade in the field of international cooperation within the EU area. Moreover, the evolution of EU legislation did not follow a uniform path. Whereas the main goal pursued in the first legislative season was to strengthen mutual cooperation among member states in core areas of legal assistance, the approach changed considerably within a few years. In particular, the enhancement of mutual trust by means of the EAW procedure resulted in a double-edged sword, exposing the individuals concerned to several risks arising from these new surrender proceedings. The rising awareness of these risks, alongside the failure of the proposal of a legislative tool aimed at defining the main procedural rights in criminal proceedings, led to significant changes in the EU legislative policy in criminal matters. A clear example was the 2009 amendment of the EAW legislation, issued with a view to strengthening the participatory safeguards of absent defendants involved in surrender procedures. Further developments occurred after the entry into force of the Lisbon Treaty. The new legislation launched to implement the 2009 Roadmap was not limited to domestic criminal proceedings but aimed at extending important defence guarantees to the area of transnational criminal justice, albeit only in the field of the EAW proceedings.

Notwithstanding its piecemeal approach, EU law is increasingly developing an autonomous participatory understanding of transnational criminal justice, which is rapidly evolving in relation to the goals of the Union's criminal justice policy, the respect for the diversities of the national criminal justice systems and the heritage of international human rights law.

B. Participatory Guarantees and the Protection of Personal Freedom in International Cooperation Among Member States

I. Premise

Against this background, I shall now analyse the developments that have occurred in EU law in relation to the participatory rights of the individuals involved in international cooperation in criminal matters in the area of freedom, security and justice. The first problem area concerns surrender proceedings. This is a particularly delicate field, in which the tension becomes acute between the need for efficient transnational prosecution, the respect for personal freedom and the protection of the defence rights of the individuals concerned. From the viewpoint of the present discussion, two main problems should now be examined, i.e. (a) the relevance in a surrender procedure of the right to personal participation in criminal proceedings and (b) the fair trial safeguards that the sought person must be ensured in legal assistance procedures involving restrictions on liberty. Concerning the former issue, I shall focus on the guarantees acknowledged to absent defendants in the EAW proceedings. The latter has a broader scope of application, concerning not only the surrender procedures but also the proceedings on supervision measures.

II. The Right to Personal Participation in Criminal Proceedings and Surrender Procedures. The Protection of Absent Defendants in EAW Proceedings

1. The Soft Solutions of the 2002 Legislation on the European Arrest Warrant

Traditionally, international instruments of mutual assistance did not provide specific guarantees for the individuals tried *in absentia* and involved in surrender procedures, nor had the issue of the relevance of *in absentia* judgments in the international cooperation procedures drawn the attention of legal scholarship until recently.[1] In Europe, the 1957 European Convention on Extradition foresaw nothing in this regard and it took more than 20 years before the 1978 Second Additional Protocol enacted the first safeguards. Moreover, the approach followed was still rather minimalist. The requested country could discretionarily reject a request for surrender aimed at the enforcement of a sentence or detention order imposed by a judgment issued *in absentia* only if it considered that the minimum defence rights due to any person charged with a criminal offence had not been satisfied in the relevant proceedings. Furthermore, refusal of surrender was excluded where the requesting state offered sufficient assurance to guarantee to the individuals concerned the right to a retrial aimed at safeguarding their defence rights.[2]

Almost a quarter century after this Protocol, the 2002 Framework Decision on the new European arrest warrant adopted very similar solutions by largely reproducing the approach of the so-called ‘conditional extradition’ at the EU level.[3] Thus this legislation inserted among the guarantees to the sought persons the power of the executing authority to make surrender conditional on the fact that the issuing authority granted them the opportunity to apply for a retrial and to be present at the judgment. Remarkably, there was no reference to the need to preserve ‘minimum defence rights’, whatever this formulation exactly meant. It is also noteworthy that, unlike the 1978 arrangements, the EAW Framework Decision

[1] Wahl (2015), p. 70.

[2] Art. 3(1).

[3] Siracusano (2011), p. 91.

provided for that the person concerned should not have been summoned in person or otherwise informed of the hearing that led to the decision *in absentia*.[4]

This solution reflected the clear attempt to bring the new surrender procedure closer to the Strasbourg case-law, which, as noted, traditionally requires defendants to be given the opportunity of a review of the judgment rendered *in absentia*, unless they unequivocally waived their right to personal participation. It must be taken into consideration, however, that the 2002 Framework Decision inserted this guarantee into an exhaustive list of '*Guarantees to be given by the issuing Member State*' and that the strongly mutual-recognition-based approach of this legislation imposed on the executing authority the general obligation to enforce the warrant issued by a foreign authority. From this it followed that the executing authority could not refuse execution or make it conditional on requirements other than those expressly provided for. Nor could the executing authority call into question the quality of the assurances offered by the issuing country, provided that the possibility for the accused to apply for a retrial was guaranteed. In particular, the requested authority could not further inquiry into whether the sought person could effectively obtain a new opportunity to catch up with the lost opportunities. Moreover, it should be noted that this constituted a mere option for the executing authority, which held, therefore, a considerable margin of discretion in requesting the necessary assurances by the prosecuting authority.

2. Subsequent Developments in EU Law

a) The Enhancement of Information and Participatory Rights by the 2009 Legislation

It has been anticipated that the shortcomings of the 2002 legislation led to a new EU intervention by means of Framework Decision 2009/299/JHA, which, amending some important instruments of legal assistance, inserted a new Article 4a into the EAW Framework Decision.[5] The main goal pursued by this reform was to reduce the margin of discretion of national authorities and to drop the uncertain requirement of assurance, laying down precise conditions under which individuals can be surrendered to other countries for the enforcement of a sentence or a detention order rendered *in absentia*. In particular, a European arrest warrant can be executed where at least one the following situations occur:

- defendants were officially served notice of the scheduled hearing and were informed that a decision on guilt could be issued in their absence
- defendants, after being made aware of the institution of criminal proceedings, appointed a lawyer to defend them at trial and this occurred in a concrete case

[4] Art. 5(1) FD EAW.

[5] For an in-depth analysis of this legal instrument see among others Siracusano (2011), p. 90 ff. For a critical assessment of the 2009 Framework Decision see also Böse (2011), p. 503 ff.

- defendants—after being served with a judgment rendered *in absentia* and after being duly informed of the possibility of requesting a retrial and by this means a re-examination of the merits of their case—have not availed themselves of this right
- defendants, although not being served with the decision issued *in absentia* before their surrender, will personally be notified afterwards, while being duly informed of the possibility of a retrial and the conditions for requesting it.

By means of this legislative reform, the EU institutions clearly aimed at aligning EU law with the protection standards set by the European Convention. An explicit reference to the European jurisprudence can be observed in relation to the conditions required to consider a proceeding held *in absentia* as lawful under EU law. In particular, although EU law allowed the national legislature to lay down the procedures by means of which defendants should be informed of the scheduled hearing, the national rules must fulfil the requirements set by the Convention and the European case-law.[6]

Notwithstanding the merits of this legislative intervention, a close examination reveals that the 2009 reform was not able to achieve a proper balance between the need for efficient transnational prosecution and the protection of the right to personal participation in criminal proceedings. To start with, EU law is far from requiring the defendants to be given personal notice, which is the obvious prerequisite for them to be able to make an informed decision. Even if the accused should preferably be served in person with the court summons, the 2009 Framework Decision also allowed alternative solutions pursuant to the legal arrangements set by national law. Yet the reference to the European case-law may not be sufficient to prevent the risk of a dangerous equivalence between legal knowledge and effective information of criminal proceedings.[7] Furthermore, EU law does not require the executing authority to verify whether the competent authorities of the trial country made the accused aware of the consequences of the decision not to participate personally at trial[8] and especially whether proper safeguards were provided to ensure the voluntariness of the decision to waive personal participation.

The information requirements were further softened in relation to the right to a retrial or a remedy aimed at a review of the judgment rendered *in absentia*. Unlike the information on the institution of criminal proceedings, the individuals convicted *in absentia* must be 'expressly' informed on the possibility of a retrial, which does not mean, however, that they also need to be notified in person. As a consequence, there is nothing to ensure that the failure to request a retrial within the established timeframe was the result of a conscious decision. Furthermore, this result can be caused by the existence of linguistic barriers.[9] Despite the fact that this is certainly

[6] Recital no. 8 of Framework Decision 2009/299/JHA.

[7] Similarly cf. Siracusano (2011), p. 99.

[8] As noted, it suffices that the sought persons were informed that a decision may be handed down if they did not appear at trial.

[9] Heger/Wolter (2015), p. 349.

not an unlikely situation in the multilinguistic EU area, neither the 2009 legislation nor the 2010 Directive on the right to interpretation and translation require the information on a retrial to be provided in a language the accused can understand.

It is also worth observing that EU law appears to consider the obligation of the competent authority to inform the defendants on the institution of criminal proceedings and the accused's waiver of personal participation as fungible requirements. From this it follows that, where it is proven that the sought person chose not to be present at trial, the executing authority should not ascertain whether the national authorities properly fulfilled their task of informing the accused on the institution of criminal proceedings. Yet the 2009 legislation not only did not provide for specific tools to prove the decision to waive but also deemed it sufficient that defendants appointed a lawyer to defend them at trial and this occurred in the concrete case. It is true that it also required the accused to be made aware of the institution of criminal proceedings. Nevertheless, the decision to appoint a lawyer does not necessarily mean that the accused chose not to be present at trial.

Further shortcomings arise where the executing authority decides to surrender the sought individuals notwithstanding that they were not served with the conviction issued *in absentia*, on the sole ground that notification will ensured after the surrender to the issuing country, which must in turn inform them of their right to request a retrial. In this case, the EU institutions considered the assurance of a future notification as sufficient for the accused to be removed from his cultural context and be surrendered to a foreign country with immediate implications on their personal freedom. It is noteworthy that the 2009 legislation, while requiring the accused person awaiting a retrial or appeal to obtain a judicial review of detention, provides that this review must entail, *inter alia*, the suspension or interruption of detention pursuant to national law.[10] Nevertheless, this possibility is dependent on the information on the right to a retrial or appeal, information that, again, does not need to be provided in person.

These observations highlight a more general deficiency of the 2009 legislation, a deficiency that emerges from the very wording of Article 4a, which, far from requiring a progressive order of conditions for surrender, enables the requested authority to execute the arrest warrant where at least one of the aforementioned situations occurs.[11] In other words, each of these situations suffices to justify the accused's surrender, releasing the executing authority from the obligation of inquiring into the others. This result can entail serious human rights risks. On the sole condition that the accused persons were informed of the initiation of criminal proceedings, the requested authority needs not ascertain whether they were also given a fair opportunity to consent to a trial being held in their absence, nor whether the accused's absence was the result of their unequivocal decision to waive the right

[10] Art. 4a(3) FD EAW.

[11] Siracusano (2011), p. 96.

to personal participation.[12] It is even more questionable that the EU legislation considered the right to personal participation at trial and the possibility of a retrial as fungible requirements. In fact, where defendants were served with the decision rendered *in absentia* and provided they could apply for a retrial, the executing authority does not need to scrutinise whether the competent authorities for the relevant proceedings did everything within their power to inform the accused of the institution of criminal proceedings.

b) The Responses of the EU Court of Justice. The '*Melloni* Doctrine'

The opportunity for a practical assessment of the 2009 legislation came about in 2013, as the EU Court of Justice was called upon to rule on the case of Mr. Melloni,[13] an Italian citizen who had been tried in Italy through default proceedings by an Italian court and was later sentenced to 10 years' imprisonment for bankruptcy fraud. Since Mr. Melloni was in Spain at the time of the enforcement of the sentence, the Italian authorities issued a European Arrest Warrant. The Italian authorities argued that Mr. Melloni had been made aware of criminal proceedings since notice was served to the two lawyers whom he had previously appointed. Mr. Melloni claimed before the Spanish authorities that, although he had in the meantime revoked the mandate and appointed another lawyer, notice was still given to the previous two. The applicant also claimed that Italian law in force at that time did not allow for defendants to file an appeal against the judgment *in absentia* if they were defended by counsel appointed by them.

Mr. Melloni filed a *recurso de amparo* before the Spanish Constitutional Tribunal against the order of the *Audiencia Nacional*, which authorised his surrender, by alleging infringement of the right to a fair trial enshrined in Article 24(2) of the Spanish Constitution. The constitutional judges invoked the doctrine of indirect violation of fundamental rights—expressed in a judgment of 2000[14] and later confirmed in relation to the EAW procedures—by stressing that surrender of a person adjudicated *in absentia* for serious offences would lead to an external projection of the infringement of the constitutional right at stake. The Constitutional Tribunal was well aware that the order of *Audiencia Nacional* was based on legislation (namely, the 2002 EAW Framework Decision) subsequently repealed by the Framework Decision 2009/299/JHA. However, it rejected the objection that the 2009 rules could not be applied to the case at hand *ratione temporis*, while focusing on the fact that Framework Decision 2009/299/JHA precluded a refusal of

---

[12]Of a different view cf. *Siracusano*, who considers that the granting of proper information can justify a presumption of waiver in the case of the accused's absence. Cf. Siracusano (2011), p. 97. It can be doubted, however, that mere absence can be interpreted in this manner and, above all, that such a presumption can be in line with the Strasbourg case-law.

[13]ECJ, Grand Chamber, *Melloni v. Ministerio Fiscal*. See among others Böse (2015), p. 139 ff.

[14]STC 91/2000.

surrender where the persons concerned, being aware of the scheduled trial, had given a mandate to counsel (no matter whether appointed by them or by the State) to represent them in court and this happened in a concrete case. As noted, this circumstance suffices and under EU law even requires the surrender of the sought person. This led the Spanish Constitutional Court to request a preliminary ruling by the EU Court of Justice, raising the question of whether the 2009 legislative reform precluded national authorities from making the execution of a European arrest warrant conditional on the conviction being open to review. Furthermore, the Spanish judges requested the Luxembourg Court to ascertain whether this solution satisfies the requirements of an effective judicial remedy and especially whether the national authorities can make surrender dependent on this condition in order to avoid a violation of their own constitutional law whenever it provides a higher level of protection than that deriving from EU law.

As we will note, this case marked a fundamental step for the understanding of the current relationship between constitutional and EU law.[15] The strong defence by the European Court of Justice of the primacy of EU law gave rise to a heated debate, paving the way for a confrontation between domestic courts and EU judges, which is still far from having reached its conclusion. From the viewpoint of the present discussion, it should be noted that the *Melloni* judgment constituted a fundamental resistance test for the EU legislation on EAW proceedings and the consideration under EU law of the accused's participatory rights for the purposes of surrender procedures. The Luxembourg Court invoked the mutual recognition-based logic of the EAW legislation, confirmed by the 2009 reform. The main consequence of this approach is that the national authorities, despite having a certain margin of discretion in deciding whether to surrender a person who did not appear at trial in the relevant proceedings, must enforce the warrant issued by the issuing authority if at least one of the four exceptions set forth by the 2009 Framework Decision is fulfilled. In this way, the Luxembourg case-law implicitly confirmed the self-sufficiency of the mandate given to a counsel without any consideration of the circumstances under which the accused empowered his lawyer.

III. Participatory Rights and International Procedures Involving Restrictions on Liberty

1. Information Rights and Guarantees of a Fair Hearing in EAW Proceedings

A different problem is whether and under which limits the individuals involved in international cooperation tools entailing restrictions on freedom can take part actively in cross-border procedures and have a fair opportunity to make their voice heard. The first field of investigation concerns the EAW procedures.

[15] Chapter 16, C.I.

In this regard also, the EAW Framework Decision provided rather scant guarantees. The 2002 legislation generically ensured to the sought person who did not consent with the surrender to a foreign country the right to be examined by the judicial authority of the executing state. Yet this acknowledgment was weakened by the reference to national law as to the establishment of the practical arrangements.[16] To be sure, the EU institutions did not ignore the need to provide the accused's examination with some safeguards. However, they limited themselves to recognising only minimum rights—namely, the right to be assisted by a lawyer and an interpreter during the hearing—without laying down specific qualitative requirements for the exercise of these guarantees. In particular, it was unclear whether the sought individuals could count on previous communication with their lawyer and interpreter, and how much time they could have to prepare a defence strategy. It is also worth observing that these procedural safeguards had a very limited scope of application, in that EU law required the requested person to be heard solely in case of provisional arrest, whereas no specific guarantees were due where detention was not needed.[17]

A significant issue to which the EU institutions also attached importance in 2002 was the information due to the requested person. At first glance, the strongly mutual-recognition-based inspiration of the EAW legislation may lead us to believe that the EAW Framework Decision limited the information duties of the cooperating authorities towards the requested person to the minimum extent. On close examination, the 2002 legislation did not ignore the need to provide the requested individuals with proper information, requiring the executing authority to inform them of the ongoing procedure and the contents of the arrest warrant as well as of the possibility of consenting with their surrender to the issuing country.[18] The reference to the European arrest warrant in turn enabled the sought person to know some important information, which not only related to the existence of an enforceable judgment or arrest warrant[19] but also to the nature and legal classification of the offence,[20] as well as to the description of the circumstances in which the offence was committed, including the time, place and degree of participation in the offence by the requested person.[21]

Notwithstanding the merits of these rules, the 2002 legislation raised some human rights concerns. Despite the requirement of detailed information on the offence under prosecution in the trial state, no information was due on the grounds that led to a European arrest warrant being issued and especially on the evidence supporting the decision to charge. This issue is of utmost importance when a coercive measure is to be applied in the relevant proceedings. Clearly, the evidence

[16] Art. 14 FD EAW.

[17] Art. 11(1) FD EAW.

[18] Art. 11(1) FD EAW.

[19] Art. 8(1)(c) FD EAW.

[20] Art. 8(1)(d) FD EAW.

[21] Art. 8(1)(e) FD EAW.

on the existence of an arrest warrant provided the sought person with scant information on the justification (especially in terms of suspicion of guilt) of a measure of coercion which led the requesting authority to issue a European arrest warrant. Certainly, the lack of awareness of the grounds for the adoption of a means of coercion cannot enable the accused to set up an effective defence. This risk is multiplied if the accused is serving a sentence or a detention order for another offence abroad, thus suffering from a condition of clear vulnerability that requires clear and detailed information on both the reasons and the consequences of the surrender procedure.[22] However, the EAW legislation was generic also in this regard, providing no clear indications on the implications of the decision not to consent with the requested surrender. Moreover, it must be taken into account that the information required by the executing authority was to be provided pursuant to the rules of *lex loci*, which, therefore, made the protection of the person concerned conditional on the arrangements of national law.

The deficiencies of the original set-up in relation to the effectiveness of the defence rights in EAW proceedings[23] led the EU institutions to extend to the individuals subject to an EAW procedure some of the defensive guarantees acknowledged by means of the legislative initiatives implementing the 2009 Roadmap. In this respect, the first important innovations concern the information rights. Ten years after the EAW legislation, Directive 2012/13/EU enacted some provisions specifically concerned with EAW proceedings, emphasising the need for simple and accessible information, which must promptly be granted to the sought person.[24] Moreover, the comprehensive reference to the 'rights' of the sought individuals should also entail the obligation to insert into the Letters of Rights the information on the right to a judicial hearing if they do not consent to surrender.

In spite of this legislative intervention, it cannot be affirmed that the 2002 standards were considerably improved. To start with, the new safeguards are still only due to the person arrested for the purposes of the execution of a European arrest warrant. In fact, the EU institutions reproduced the approach of the 2002 legislation, making the exercise of information rights dependent on the existence of an ongoing procedure aimed at the application of a measure of coercion in the executing state. Furthermore, if a European arrest warrant was issued to enforce a coercive order in the issuing country, EU law still provides nothing more than the granting of information on the charge and the arrest warrant issued in the relevant proceedings, no information being due on the justification of the decision to apply a coercive measure and the evidence supporting the judicial order.[25]

[22]Bachmaier Winter (2015a), p. 122.

[23]*Ibid.*

[24]Art. 5 DirIT.

[25]The problem was not dealt with by the EU Court of Justice, which has recently pointed out that the information on the existence of an 'arrest warrant' should be interpreted as relating to the national order that led to the European arrest warrant. From this it follows that in the absence of any indication on such 'warrant', the executing authority should deny execution of the European arrest warrant. See ECJ, *Bob-Dogi*.

Doubtless, the lack of proper information can negatively affect the effectiveness of the defence contribution to a procedure that entails high risks for the right to freedom. To be sure, Directive 2013/48/EU also made some steps forward in this direction, requiring the executing authority to inform the requested individuals of their right to appoint a lawyer in the issuing country. The main task of this lawyer is to assist the sought person and the counsel eventually appointed in the executing country, providing them with the necessary information and advice to set up a proper defence strategy in the surrender procedure and especially to enable the requested person to make full use of the rights granted by the EAW legislation.[26] Furthermore, the 2013 legislation did not generically acknowledge the right to legal assistance in the executing country but also laid down some important safeguards. In particular, member states must ensure proper communication between the requested individuals and their lawyers, who must in turn be present and participate during their hearing before a judicial authority in the executing country.[27]

Despite these developments, the effectiveness of the new guarantees depends on several variables. The sought individuals must firstly have the necessary knowledge and economic resources to appoint a lawyer in the trial country with which they possibly have no links.[28] Moreover, the successful role of this lawyer also depends on many factors. Alongside the practical difficulties that can arise in the communication with their colleagues in the executing country, the full exercise of legal assistance clearly presupposes that the lawyer in the issuing country can access the necessary information on the charge and can know the grounds for the surrender procedure, a result that entirely depends on *lex fori*. On close examination, the EU arrangements were rather weak and a much more straightforward solution would have been to require that the trial state provide the accused residing (or detained) in another country with the necessary information.

Furthermore, the assistance of a lawyer in the executing state may also be insufficient to ensure the effective exercise of the defence rights during their judicial hearing. Despite the clear attempt to bring these safeguards closer to those due to the accused in domestic proceedings, the forms of the lawyer's intervention in the judicial hearing of the sought person remain governed by *lex loci*. In the field of domestic criminal justice, however, we have noted that Directive 2013/48/EU emphasised the requirement of effective participation of the defence lawyer and the need that national law does not negatively affects the essence of the right to a defence.[29] Again, the risk arises that the solutions enacted for EAW proceedings can lower the standards acknowledged in relation to the national proceedings.[30]

---

[26] Art. 10(4) DirAL.

[27] Art. 10(2)(b-c) DirAL.

[28] Bachmaier Winter (2015a), p. 123.

[29] Chapter 10, C.III.1.

[30] For similar criticisms see Bachmaier Winter (2015a), p. 123 f.

The distance between domestic and transnational cases was reduced by the EU legislation on the right to interpretation and translation. At first glance, the acknowledgment by Directive 2010/64/EU to the individuals who do not speak or know the language of the executing country[31] appears to simply reproduce the arrangements of the 2002 legislation. On close examination, this requirement cannot be interpreted as a generic reference to *lex loci*, since the sought person must be granted the right to interpretation 'in accordance' with Article 2 DIT, that is, pursuant to the new provisions laid down at the EU level. It is noteworthy that the right to linguistic assistance must be ensured not only in court hearings but also in police questionings, a provision of utmost importance in the field of surrender procedures, which can start with the police arrest based on an alert issued in the Schengen Information System (SIS).[32] To ensure the effectiveness of the accused's participation in the proceedings, moreover, the requested persons must be given linguistic assistance in communications with their lawyer prior to their examination by the executing authority.

Another delicate issue concerns the assessment of the need for linguistic assistance, assessment that—in accordance with the general approach of the 2010 legislation—lies with the competent authorities. Notwithstanding the benefits of this solution, one should not overlook the consequences of an assessment conducted *ex officio*. It has been observed that the 2010 Directive did not clarify what mechanism must be made available at the national law level to ascertain the linguistic knowledge of the individuals concerned.[33] To be sure, EU law requires member states to grant the accused a means of challenging the quality of the interpretation provided or the judicial decision finding that interpretation is not needed. Although this provision is certainly applicable in EAW proceedings, the 2010 legislation failed to specify how this right can be exercised, while stressing that member states are not required to 'provide for a separate mechanism or complaint procedure in which such finding may be challenged'.[34] It is also worrisome that according to Recital 25, the legal action aimed at challenging the decision that found that no interpretation was needed 'should not prejudice the time limits applicable to the execution of a European arrest warrant'. The result is a clear imbalance towards prosecutorial needs and the message is that the sought individuals can claim their right to linguistic understanding in the executing country as long as it does not affect the speediness of the surrender proceeding.

[31] Art. 2(7) DirIT.

[32] Art. 9(2) FdEAW.

[33] Chapter 10, C.I.1.

[34] Recital no. 25 DirIT.

2. Defence Rights in the Proceedings on Supervision Measures

On a second level, we should examine whether and to what extent the individuals involved in international cooperation can participate in a cross-border procedure aimed at the application of alternative measures restricting the right to liberty and free movement. After the enactment of the EAW Framework Decision, EU law long lacked any regulation in this delicate field. This led to the paradoxical result that European arrest warrants were often executed for the purpose of a pre-trial detention in a foreign country even in cases that would have justified the use of alternative measures at national level. This scenario lasted until 2009, as EU institutions launched new legislation aimed at extending the mutual recognition principle to supervision measures alternative to pre-trial detention.[35] The main aim pursued by this legislation was precisely to remedy such discriminatory situations between defendants resident inside and outside the trial country,[36] strengthening by this means the right to liberty and the presumption of innocence.[37] Despite the proclaimed goal of introducing an alternative tool to the surrender procedure, moreover, the 2009 legislation clearly revealed a significant change in the understanding of the principle of mutual recognition in comparison to that of the 2002 legislation. In particular, the 2009 Framework Decision, departing from the traditional approach to the order model, enabled the executing authorities to adapt the contents of the foreign order to the specific needs of their own law, enforcing a supervision measure other than that requested if the latter was incompatible with *lex loci*.[38]

This unprecedented power can entail negative consequences on both participatory rights and the right to liberty of the individuals concerned. Even though EU law prohibits the application of a more intrusive means than that requested by the trial state, the choice of a different measure remains a delicate decision, which requires complex assessments. In particular, the choice of a different measure of coercion presupposes an in-depth examination of its adequacy in relation to specific risks arising for the ongoing inquiry in the issuing country. This assessment may be extremely difficult for the executing authority, which is often unaware of the dynamics of, and the information gathered in, the relevant proceedings. Furthermore, EU law not only does not require the national authorities to hear the addressee of the supervision measure beforehand but also does not impose on national legislatures the duty of providing a subsequent mechanism of reaction. Whereas the issuing authority, duly informed of the other measure, can withdraw the certificate and avoid monitoring,[39] the sought person has no tool to challenge

[35]Framework Decision 2009/829/JHA. On this instrument see among others Belfiore (2011), p. 105 ff.; Rafaraci (2012), p. 67 ff.

[36]Recital no. 4 FdSM.

[37]Hecker (2015), p. 450.

[38]Art. 13 FdSM. Cf. Belfiore (2011), p. 113 f.

[39]Art. 13(3) FDSM.

the decision. These practical difficulties are magnified by the failure to involve both the executing authority and the defence in the choice of another measure, notwithstanding that this decision can have evident repercussions on the sphere of personal freedom. Two coercive means, despite having similar effects in a concrete case, may have a very different legal basis, which can in turn impinge on the overall protection of the right to liberty.[40]

The lack of consideration for the role of the defence, moreover, is not limited only to the case in which another measure should be adopted. The individuals concerned also have no voice in the decision to prolong the supervision measure. Whenever the possibility of continuing monitoring requires confirmation on the necessity of the measure adopted, the executing authority will ask the issuing authority without consulting the defence.[41] It is even more problematic that the sought individuals cannot make their voice heard in the decision by the issuing authority to replace the monitored measure with another more intrusive. This is a very delicate decision, which can entail the shift from a monitoring to a surrender procedure through a European arrest warrant, with grave interferences with the right to freedom. The need for defence intervention is enhanced by the lack of clear statutory indications on the grounds for a more intrusive means, which can be applied not only in the case of a violation of the prescriptions established but also because of more general findings.[42] This leaves an enormous margin of discretion to national authorities. It can be doubted whether this two-sided dialogue between the competent authorities without any involvement of the defence is a direct consequence of the mutual recognition principle and is a necessary step to enhance the mutual trust among European countries. On close examination, the decision to exclude the sought person from the adoption of another supervision measure not only impinges on the exercise of defence rights but also reflects a clear underestimation of the defensive contribution to the decision to apply a measure of coercion that is proportionate to both the alleged offence and the risks of the ongoing inquiry.

---

[40]In Italy, for instance, the obligation to stay at a designated place can entail restrictions very similar to those of house arrest. See Arts. 283(4) and 284(3) CCP-Italy. There are significant differences, however, depending on the measure chosen, with particular regard to the maximum length of coercion. Since Italian law considers house arrest equivalent to pre-trial detention, the former is subjected to the maximum time limits of Article 303 CCP-Italy. By contrast, other pre-trial measures—including the obligation to stay at a designated place—have a maximum duration twice the length of pre-trial detention. Cf. Art. 308(1) CCP-Italy.

[41]Art. 23(3) FDSM.

[42]Art. 19(3) FDSM. To be sure, Recital no. 9 somewhat defined these criteria, providing for a decision to adopt a more serious measure or even a European arrest warrant as a result not only of the breach of supervision measures but also of the failure to comply with a court summons. The fact that these indications are not exhaustive, however, leaves to national legislatures a great margin of discretion. It can be doubted, moreover, whether such a serious consequence can be deemed proportionate in all member states. In Italy, *e.g.*, the application of a more intrusive measure or the application of the same with more intrusive features requires either a violation of the prescriptions concerned with the first measure or the worsening of the risks for the ongoing proceedings. See Arts. 276 and 299(4) CCP-Italy.

C. Participatory Rights and Transnational Evidence in the EU Area

I. Premise

As noted, EU law still has no comprehensive rules on the defence's contribution to the collection of criminal evidence in domestic criminal proceedings. This result is mostly due to the general criminal justice policies of the EU institutions, which left this matter in the hands of national law. By contrast, the collection of overseas evidence and the movement of information among member states have lain at the core of EU agenda for the last two decades. The EU Convention on Mutual Assistance among member states, signed in Brussels in 2000, marked a historic step forward from the old request model to the new order model. The shift of EU law from mutual assistance to mutual recognition, however, was a long process and the EU institutions chose a somewhat cautious approach to enact the new logic of international cooperation into the field of transnational evidence.

Some years after the Brussels Convention, the launching of the EAW legislation raised the question of whether a similar instrument should be adopted to enhance international cooperation in the field of transnational evidence-gathering in the EU area and with a view to facilitating the exchange of information among the competent authorities of the member states. Nevertheless, the extension of the principle of mutual recognition to the area of criminal evidence found strong criticisms on the grounds that evidence law is always strictly linked with the procedures and the characteristics of each criminal justice system and does not allow for information to freely circulate from one country to another. It is therefore no surprise that even a partial goal—namely, the introduction of a European warrant aimed at the taking only of documentary evidence—was achieved more than 5 years after the legislative proposal was presented in 2003.

Significant developments have occurred in this delicate field especially after the entry into force of the Lisbon Treaty, which called for EU legislation aimed at strengthening the mutual admissibility of evidence among member states.[43] A close examination of the results achieved in this long road, however, reveals the persistent backwardness of EU law in the protection of the participatory safeguards of the individuals involved in transborder inquiries, which are more and more characterised by a clear imbalance in favour of investigative needs and the state-related interests concerned with the gathering and movement of evidence among member states.

[43]The reference by Article 82(2) TFEU to the 'admissibility' of evidence requires, moreover, a systematic interpretation. Cf. Ruggeri (2013), p. 287 f.

II. Participatory Rights, Transnational Evidence-Gathering and the Developments of Legal Assistance Models

1. The Solutions of the Brussels Convention on Transnational Evidence-Gathering

It has been observed that the Brussels Convention marked a major step in the EU policy on international cooperation in criminal matters. From the perspective of the present discussion, it is noteworthy that this international instrument had the merit of enacting into the EU area new modes of gathering information in other European countries, decoupled from the intergovernmental logic of traditional legal assistance and aimed at enhancing forms of direct and joint cooperation among the national authorities.

Notwithstanding these innovations, the 2000 Convention lacked coherent rules on the defence's participation in transborder investigations. No specific provisions governed the involvement of private parties in the taking of transnational evidence. To be sure, the Brussels Convention allowed for a combined method of evidence-gathering, whereby *lex loci* could be applied together with specific procedures of *lex loci* requested by the trial authority. In this context, the defence's participation was not necessarily excluded, since the private parties had to be involved in the taking of overseas evidence to the extent that a specific request in this sense was made pursuant to *lex fori*.[44] This solution, however, left great uncertainty about whether the defence could take part in the collection of overseas evidence, the involvement of private parties being conditional on the explicit request of the competent authority or the central administrative authority in the requesting country.[45]

It might be argued that the Brussels Convention aimed at complementing the 1959 Convention of Mutual Assistance of the Council of Europe,[46] which made it still possible for both private parties and the authorities from the trial state to be present at the execution of letters rogatory.[47] Yet this arrangement did not fit the new order model towards which the 2000 Convention clearly moved. Since in the 1959 system the host country ought to consent to the involvement of private parties, the exercise of participatory rights depended on the assessment of governmental authorities. This approach was incompatible with the logic of the mutual recognition of judicial decisions. Moreover, it should be taken into consideration that the 1959 Convention reduced the parties' involvement to a mere presence in the requested action and therefore did not ensure any active participation on the part of the individuals concerned. On close examination, this solution was justified by the general characteristics of the traditional model of letters rogatory, a model

[44] Art. 4(1) EU-CMACM.

[45] Art. 6(2) EU-CMACM.

[46] Art. 1(1) EU-CMACM.

[47] Art. 4 ECMACM.

almost exclusively based on *lex loci* with which both the authorities of the trial state and private parties were often unfamiliar.

Doubtless, the enactment by the 2000 Convention of the combination between *lex loci* and *lex fori* as the main method of evidence-gathering should have entailed an in-depth reflection on the need to ensure a more active role to the defence. In fact, the proper application of the requested formalities, on which the success of the integrated mechanism largely depends, presupposes a high level of knowledge of the foreign law and practice, often unknown to the requested authority. This requirement is of particular importance where the request for assistance aims at executing measures that impinge on the fundamental rights of the parties. Here, the failure to involve private parties or allowing them only a passive role not only can negatively affect the exercise of the defence rights but also entails a clear underestimation of the defensive contribution with a view to a correct application of *lex fori*.

2. The Shift from Mutual Legal Assistance to Mutual Recognition and the Defence Rights in the Order Model

a) The Combined Methods of Evidence-Gathering in the Order Model and the Weak Protection of Participatory Rights in the EU Legislation on the European Evidence Warrant and the European Investigation Order

The shift to the order model did not improve the shortcomings of the old request model. It is worth observing that it took several years before EU institutions launched the first legislative instrument concerned with transnational evidence-gathering, that is, the European evidence warrant. A close examination of the 2008 Framework Decision,[48] however, reveals a more scant attention paid to the participatory rights of the individuals involved in the collection of overseas evidence than that provided by the original draft proposal. In particular, although the EEW legislation left wide room for the limited application of *lex fori*, there was no trace of the possibility of the defence participating in the gathering of documentary evidence abroad. By contrast, EU institutions expressly acknowledged the possibility (albeit linked with the existence of a legal instrument in force) for the issuing authority to be present at the execution of the evidence warrant.[49]

The failure to provide for a clear role of the private parties in the collection of evidence in another member state might be explained by the fact that the defence's involvement was probably considered unnecessary because of the scope of application of the new European evidence warrant, limited to the taking of information already in the possession of the requested authority. This was not always the case,

---

[48] On this legislative instrument see among others Belfiore (2009), p. 1 ff.; Hecker (2013), p. 269 ff.; Gleß (2014), p. 680 ff.

[49] Art. 9(2) FdEEW.

however. In particular, the 2008 legislation allowed for the collection of statements from individuals present at the sought investigation, provided that the issuing authority requested it and the statements were linked with the documentary evidence to be gathered.[50] In such cases, the possibility for the defence to be involved in the evidence-gathering depended on a request of the issuing authority and the provisions of *lex loci*.

It might be argued that the defence's participation was not excluded from the new procedure, since the EAW Framework Decision did not repeal the existing legislation on mutual assistance among member states.[51] This conclusion can be sustained, however, on the condition that legal assistance instruments fall within the scope of application of the EEW legislation. Yet it cannot be denied that, like the solutions of the Brussels Convention, the arrangements of the first mutual recognition-based instrument on gathering overseas evidence were not consistent with the governmental logic of the 1959 Convention and the passive role of private parties in the execution of letters rogatory.

On the other hand, it is worth observing that the EEW Framework Decision set no specific requirements for the effective exercise of the defence rights of the persons examined during the execution of an evidence warrant. In particular, there was no reference to the *nemo tenetur* principle, a guarantee that the representatives of several countries considered to be so deeply rooted in all criminal justice systems that it would have been superfluous to enact it at supranational level.[52] In the light of subsequent developments that occurred in EU law, we cannot affirm that this was a suitable decision. Thus we saw that the recent Directive 2016/343/EU explicitly recognised the privilege against self-incrimination,[53] while structuring this guarantee in such broad terms that it also applies to transborder procedures.

As noted, the EEW legislation was intended to achieve only an intermediate result. The enactment of the mutual recognition principle into the area of transnational evidence fell far short of reaching the goals pursued. It is surprising, however, that shortly after the introduction of the EEW legislation, the European Commission, without waiting for its implementation by EU countries,[54] launched the ambitious challenge of setting up a new legislative tool. This proposal aimed at overcoming the limits of the European evidence warrant and at replacing the old legal assistance instruments with a comprehensive means of collecting overseas evidence in the EU area and securing its admissibility.[55] In its Action Plan Implementing the Stockholm Programme,[56] the Commission confirmed its two-tier approach, thus announcing two (at first sight separate) legislative proposals

[50] Art. 4(6) FdEEW.

[51] Art. 21 FdEAW.

[52] Gleß (2014), p. 689.

[53] Art. 7 DirPIDPT.

[54] Until now, only a few Member States have implemented the EEW Framework Decision.

[55] COM (2009) 262 final.

[56] COM (2010) 171 final.

aimed respectively (a) at establishing a comprehensive regime on obtaining evidence in criminal matters based on the principle of mutual recognition and covering all types of evidence and (b) at introducing common standards for gathering evidence in criminal matters in order to ensure its admissibility. None of these initiatives was even presented, however, as in 2010 eight member states launched a proposal for a Directive concerning a European investigation order (EIO). To be sure, the contents of this proposal were not the same as the initiatives announced by the Commission, focusing initially only on the taking of evidence in other EU countries without any (direct) reference to the movement of information and especially to the problem of securing its admissibility. Like the EEW Framework Decision, this initiative also encountered several hurdles and the legislative process came to its end only in 2014, almost 4 years after the draft proposal was presented.[57]

After this long legislative procedure, one would have expected much more attention to be paid to the balance between the interests of a transnational prosecution and the protection of the rights of individuals involved in cross-border inquiries. The need for proper balancing, moreover, was enhanced by the very broad scope of application of the European investigation order, which, going far beyond the sphere of criminal justice, aimed not only at facilitating the movement of documentary evidence but also at allowing the taking of dynamic evidence in the EU area. Yet all these expectations were largely frustrated by the new legislative instrument, notwithstanding that the EIO Directive solemnly proclaimed the need to protect the fundamental rights of the individuals involved in cross-border inquiries.[58] The weak results of the EIO legislation were mainly due to a methodological shortcoming, for it largely reproduced the approach that the Brussels Convention had adopted 14 years earlier in relation to the method of transnational evidence-gathering. Furthermore, the 2014 Directive revealed a considerable softening of the order model, which moved back to the flexibility of the mutual assistance model, while favouring the combination of *lex loci* with specific formalities of *lex fori*, expressly requested by the issuing authority. There is a significance difference, however, from legal assistance models. Due to the characteristics of the investigation order, the request for the formalities of *lex fori* is in principle binding for the executing authority, which must therefore apply them, unless it would infringe fundamental principles of *lex loci*.[59] From this approach it follows that the possibility for the defence to take part in the sought investigation still largely

[57]Directive 2014/41/EU. On this legislative instrument see from different perspectives Böse (2014), p. 152 ff.; Daniele (2014), Bachmaier Winter (2015b), p. 47 ff.; Caianiello (2015), p. 1 ff. The proposal of this instrument raised heated debate in the criminal law scholarship. See among others Peers (2010), Bachmaier Winter (2010), p. 580ff; Mangiaracina (2014), p. 113 ff. See also the contributions collected in Ruggeri (ed) (2014).

[58]Accompanying Document to the Proposal for a Council Directive regarding a European Investigation Order in criminal matters, Detailed Statement, 9288/10 ADD 2, COPEN 117 EJN 185 CODEC 384 EUROJUST 217, § 1.

[59]Art. 9(2) DirEIO.

depends on two main factors, that is, the provisions of *lex loci* allowing it and the decision of the issuing authority to request their application.

Doubtless, this set-up is highly questionable in the area of freedom, security and justice, in that it exposes the individuals concerned to the risk of unjustified sacrifice of their participatory rights. In particular, defendants prosecuted in the country A are subject to an investigation abroad pursuant to the procedure of country B, with which they are often fully unfamiliar, whereas the application of the law of the trial country (which is in most cases also the law of the accused's own country) is dependent on the discretionary request of the issuing authority. The EIO Directive did not even require the adoption of common practices at the national level, with a view to avoiding the risk of contradictory application of different procedures in individual cases. In other words, EU law did not provide for any mechanism to ensure coherent combination of possibly different procedures.

Although innumerable changes were made to the draft proposal, it is surprising that this issue remained untouched. It is hard to believe that the combined method of evidence-gathering was accepted without any discussion and without almost any consideration as to the severe criticisms of it raised over the last decade. In particular, it is certainly debatable that the promotion of the mutual recognition principle can allow for the national authorities to decide for tactical reasons whether to request the application of certain procedures or, even worse, to select the formalities that are to be applied to the case at stake.[60] This result leaves the individuals concerned fully unaware of the overall applicable law. As *Schünemann* put it clearly, 'the optional forum principle poses a serious threat to legal certainty regarding the applicable procedural law'.[61] Even worse, the general duty of application of foreign procedures, unless fundamental principles of *lex loci* are at risk, gives rise to a forced combination that is far from achieving a proper integration of national procedures, which are possibly an expression of different constitutional requirements.[62] It is also surprising that the drafters of the EIO Directive showed no concern about the limit of non-violation of fundamental principles of *lex loci*, a limit applied by various countries in the field of the assessment of overseas evidence, such as Italy, where it has led to a considerable weakening of the standards of human rights protection.[63]

A close examination of the EIO Directive, moreover, highlights new risks that, in comparison to traditional mutual assistance instruments, reveal a considerable step backward in the protection of participatory rights of the individuals concerned. To start with, the general acknowledgment of the combined method of evidence-gathering was not coupled with any rule allowing for private parties to take part in the execution of the sought investigation. Again, one might invoke the 1959 Convention on Mutual Assistance. It must be taken into account, however, that

[60] Schünemann (2014), p. 171 f.

[61] *Ibid.*, 172.

[62] For a positive consideration of combined method see instead Belfiore (2014), p. 95.

[63] Chapter 4, E.III.4.

the EIO Directive not only takes precedence over other instruments at the Council of Europe level in the relationships between EU countries[64] but furthermore expressly aims at replacing the corresponding provisions of the 1959 Convention.[65]

On close examination, the failure to involve private parties in transborder investigations, alongside the repercussions on the effectiveness of the defence rights,[66] reflects a clear underestimation of the defence's role for the purpose of proper execution of the sought measure. This result is even more questionable when taking into account that the investigation can largely be carried out on the basis of *lex fori*. The EU institutions attached no importance to the contribution that the defence can give to the correct application of their own law. It is hard to see how this result can reflect a new approach aimed at combining the speediness of mutual recognition with the flexibility of traditional mutual assistance. By contrast, this approach reveals a dangerously authoritarian view of the mutual recognition principle. The Directive makes it clear that to achieve an efficient application of the provisions on execution of the investigation order, there is only room for a dialogue between the cooperating authorities.[67]

Under the EIO legislation, moreover, the failure to involve private parties can have unprecedented repercussions on fundamental rights. This is mainly due to the fact that, unlike the European evidence warrant, the European investigation order allows for the use of coercive means as well as of coercive methods of gathering information. It should also be taken into consideration that the EIO Directive, following the EU legislation on supervision measures, allows recourse to another measure if the requested one does not fit the requirements of lawfulness or if the sought measure would not be available in a similar domestic case.[68] In no event, however, the defence is involved in this delicate decision. At first glance, this approach appears to be justified where the different measure was chosen because of the incompatibility of the one requested with *lex loci*, with which the accused especially is often unfamiliar. Furthermore, the recourse to another measure can be due to the decision to obtain the same investigative result through less intrusive measure. This decision entails clear proportionality assessments that must be targeted to the goals of the relevant proceedings and can give rise to the risk of highly discretionary assessments. Surprisingly, neither the issuing authority nor the defence can make their voice heard.

---

[64]Recital no. 35 DirEIO.

[65]Art. 34 DirEIO. To be sure, this argument, already contained in the 2010 proposal, was invoked to support the conclusion contrasted in the text. See Marchetti (2011), p. 163 f. I do not share this opinion because the execution of foreign requests for investigation should be considered as a whole and cannot be governed by a fragmentary combination of rules belonging to different models of international cooperation. At any rate, the reference to the 1959 Convention would not entail a significant step forward in the protection of the defence rights of private parties, allowed, as noted, only to be present at the execution of letters rogatory.

[66]Marchetti (2011), p. 163.

[67]Art. 9(6) DirEIO.

[68]Art. 10(1) DirEIO.

A further imbalance on the defence's account is apparent from the rules on the execution of the sought investigation. The 2010 proposal had already provided for the possibility of authorities of the trial country assisting at the sought investigation with a view to supporting the local authorities.[69] Neither the nature of these authorities nor their relationship with the issuing authority was in any way specified, nor did the draft proposal clarify the exact terms of their assistance. Moreover, the fact that this assistance should not infringe only the fundamental principles of *lex loci* entailed that the executing authority could not easily reject external support. The final text specifies that authorities of the trial country can be involved to the extent they could assist in a similar investigation in a national case.[70] To be sure, the Directive makes it clear that the supporting authorities are in principle bound by *lex loci* and have no law enforcement powers.[71] However, the drafters of the EIO Directive provided for some worrisome exceptions, allowing the exercise of law enforcement powers by a foreign authority on national territory, provided that it is not prohibited by *lex loci* and the cooperating authorities agree with this arrangement.[72] This mechanism introduces an unprecedented system of almost extraterritorial enquiries within the mutual recognition model, which goes beyond the distinctions of models of international assistance drafted so far, while raising many human rights concerns. The lack of any clear specification of the role and position of these 'authorities' can also lead administrative authorities, regardless of their functional relationship with the competent authorities for the criminal proceedings, to carry out investigative means that can severely interfere with the fundamental rights of the addressees of the sought investigation.

b) Hearings by Videoconference, Right to Be fairly Heard and the Guarantee of Confrontation in Transnational Cases

A problematic issue from the viewpoint of the present discussion concerns the right to a fair remote hearing and the possibility of the accused being confronted with incriminating witnesses by videoconference. The 2000 Convention enacted specific rules on the hearing of witnesses or experts by videoconference, while leaving to discretionary choice of Member States whether and to what extent these rules can also be applied to the accused's hearing.[73] These rules, however, provided a rather weak protection of both the accused's right to take part in the gathering of incriminating evidence and the defence rights of the person examined.

Concerning the accused's side, no provision ensured his direct involvement in the hearing of prosecutorial witnesses, which had to be examined 'directly by, or

---

[69] Art. 9(3) DirEIO-proposal.

[70] Art. 9(4) DirEIO.

[71] Art. 9(5) DirEIO.

[72] *Ibid.*

[73] Art. 10 EU-CMACM.

under the direction of, the judicial authority of the requesting member state in accordance with its own laws'.[74] On close examination, this formulation did not rule out cross-examination. Yet the direct involvement of the defence still depended on national law. Furthermore, the 2000 Convention lacked adequate rules aimed at the protection of the defence rights of the person examined. To be sure, witnesses and co-defendants were granted the right to be assisted by an interpreter at their own request or at the request of the trial country.[75] The Convention, however, clarified that the presence of an interpreter was due only 'if necessary' without specifying who should assess – and pursuant to what criteria—the need for linguistic assistance. Even more worryingly, no specific provision ensured legal assistance to the person examined, no matter whether this was a witness or even the accused. Yet it cannot be denied that the assistance of a lawyer is necessary to ensure a fair hearing at least in particularly vulnerable situations. It is surprising that the Convention, despite ensuring to the individuals examined the right not to testify that would accrue to them, failed to grant them legal assistance. Again, the Brussels Convention relied on national law, so that the requested authority was charged with the task of verifying whether a questioning conducted 'directly by, or under the direction of, the judicial authority of the requesting member state' infringed the fundamental principles of its own law.[76] Outside this case, the Convention allowed for the person concerned to be examined by videoconference without the assistance of a lawyer even if it ought to be granted in a national case.

It cannot be affirmed that 14 years later EU law has made significant steps forward. The EIO Directive, reproducing almost literally most of the rules of the Brussels Convention, enacted specific rules on hearings by videoconference not only of witnesses and experts but also of suspects and accused persons.[77] This broad scope of application, which encompasses intermediate situations such as the hearing of co-defendants, also poses two main problems, i.e. (a) the right of the accused to be fairly heard by videoconference and (b) the balance between the right to remote confrontation with prosecutorial witnesses and the safeguards due to the person examined. In both regards, it is surprising that under the EIO Directive, no rules still ensure to the person examined the assistance of a lawyer. One might argue that this is only an apparent lacuna, taking into account that the EIO legislation contains a general reference to the Directive on the right to access to a lawyer[78] and, in more general terms, must be implemented pursuant to the existing EU legislation on procedural rights. On close examination, this is not sufficient to ensure legal assistance, since Directive 2013/48/EU, like the other EU instruments on defence rights in criminal matters, focuses solely on the EAW procedures in the field of international cooperation. Consequently, only the individuals subject to a surrender procedure must be informed that they can appoint a lawyer, whereas there is no

---

[74] Art. 10(5)(c) EU-CMACM.
[75] Art. 10(5)(d) EU-CMACM.
[76] Art. 10(5)(a) EU-CMACM.
[77] Art. 24 DirEIO.
[78] Recital no. 15 DirEIO.

similar provision in the EIO legislation.[79] Yet the solution of a second lawyer in the trial country would be very useful in a hearing by videoconference, protecting the person subject to a remote hearing against the risks of cross-examination. To be sure, we have noted that information on the right to appoint a second lawyer is in any case a weak guarantee for individuals with scant economic recourses. In this regard, one should not expect significant results from the recent Directive 2016/1919/EU, which, as far as international cooperation is concerned, follows the approach of other EU legislation in criminal matters, ensuring the fundamental guarantee of legal aid solely in the case of the EAW proceedings.[80]

The drafters of the EIO Directive also did not show particular concern for the accused's right to confrontation with prosecutorial witnesses or co-defendants when the examination takes place by remote connection. To be sure, the EIO Directive, following the approach of the Brussels Convention, imposed on the competent authority some obligations, such as the duty of informing beforehand the persons to be examined—if the accused, and therefore also a co-defendant, is to be heard by videoconference—of their rights, starting with the right to silence.[81] However, reproducing the approach of the Brussels Convention, the EIO legislation still enables the judicial authority to conduct—or anyway to direct—the hearing by videoconference pursuant to its own law,[82] which confirms the scant attention of EU law towards the defendant's participatory rights.

III. Defence Rights in Joint Criminal Inquiries

It has been noted that the 2000 Convention regulated a new form of cross-border investigation with enormous practical potential, allowing for criminal inquiries to be carried out in joint venture by task forces composed of investigative bodies (as a rule, police officers, investigating magistrates and prosecutors) of two or more countries in order to tackle complex criminal cases having transnational dimension.[83] To be sure, at the time of the Brussels Convention there already existed some international instruments governing the conduct of extraterritorial investigations both outside and inside Europe,[84] notwithstanding that transborder inquiries had strict conditions because of the strong sovereignty approach that traditionally characterised mutual assistance in criminal matters. Among these instruments, the Convention implementing the Schengen Agreement was the first multilateral instrument in

---

[79]Bachmaier Winter (2015a), p. 123.

[80]Art. 5 DirLA.

[81]Art. 24(5)(e) DirEIO.

[82]Art. 24(5)(c) DirEIO.

[83]See among others Vallines García (2006), Zurkinden (2012).

[84]On an in-depth analysis of joint investigations in US transnational cooperation in criminal matters see Thaman (2013), p. 511 ff.

Europe, providing legal basis for the conduct of criminal investigations outside national territory. These forms of transborder investigations, however, were still a part of the request model, and as a result, overseas investigations needed, as a rule, prior authorisation of specific investigative measures (surveillance, hot pursuit) by the cooperating state in response to a request for legal assistance.[85]

The 2000 Convention overcame this approach by introducing 'a new generation of extra-territorial investigations',[86] fully unrelated to the requirement of urgency and aimed at fulfilling the need to enhance horizontal cooperation in fighting specific crimes having cross-border dimensions. These innovations also were not preceded, however, by in-depth reflection on the role of the defence. The Brussels Convention did not enact any specific provisions aimed at ensuring the involvement of private parties—and even the assistance of a lawyer—at the investigative acts carried out by the joint team. The general reference to *lex loci*[87] led to the result that defence contribution could take place only to the extent allowed by the national law of the country in which the team investigates. This approach entailed several shortcomings. Especially in case of complex investigations that require the team to operate in the territory of several countries, a plethora of national rules can be applied even to similar investigative acts[88] without the defence having any certainty whether and under what conditions it can participate.

Subsequent legislation did not amend these defects. In 2002, the very day the EAW Framework Decision was issued (13 June), the EU institutions launched another important instrument[89] aimed at providing a provisional supranational regulation on this type of joint inquiries until the Convention entered into force in all member states.[90] The JIT Framework Decision reproduced integrally the rules of the Brussels Convention on joint investigation teams, thus making the involvement of private parties in the joint inquiries conditional on the law of the country where investigations must be carried out. This instrument is still in force as the Brussels Convention has not yet been ratified by all the EU countries.

D. Interim Conclusions

The analysis of the evolution occurred in EU law in the two main areas of surrender procedures and cross-border investigations gives us a complex picture of transnational criminal justice in the area of freedom, security and justice. After the first legislative phase, based on a strong understanding of the mutual recognition principle, EU institutions softened their approach to international cooperation,

---

[85] See respectively Arts. 40(1) and 41(1) CISA.

[86] Klip (2012), p. 361.

[87] Art. 13(3)(b) EU-CMACM.

[88] Klip (2012), p. 392.

[89] Framework Decision 2002/465/JHA.

[90] Art. 5 FdJIT.

combining the harmonisation goals with the flexibility of the old legal assistance models. The developments occurred over the last years, however, highlight a rather piecemeal approach, which link the new rules on information and defence rights in criminal justice almost exclusively with the EAW procedures, while weakening the fair trial guarantees ensured in domestic cases. Further concerns arise in the field of cross-border investigations and transnational evidence-gathering. In particular, the recent EIO legislation, while allowing for the use of coercive investigations in EU countries other than the trial state, widely ignored the contribution of the defence to the collection of overseas evidence. This raises doubts about whether the path that EU law is following in the field of international cooperation in the EU area is in line with the standards of protection laid down by the European Convention on Human Rights. For the sake of clarity, I will examine this issue while comparing the solutions provided by EU law with those resulting from the Strasbourg case-law.[91]

References

Bachmaier Winter L (2010) European Investigation Order for obtaining evidence in the criminal proceedings. Study of the proposal for a European directive. Zeitschrift für die international Strafrechtsdogmatik, pp 580–589

Bachmaier Winter L (2015a) The EU directive on the right to access to a lawyer: a critical assessment. In: Ruggeri S (ed) Human rights in european criminal law. New developments in European legislation and case law after the Lisbon treaty. Springer, Heidelberg, pp 111–131

Bachmaier Winter L (2015b) Transnational evidence. Towards the Transposition of the Directive 2014/41 Regarding the European Investigation Order in Criminal Matters. Eucrim, pp 47–60

Belfiore R (2009) Movement of evidence in the EU: the present scenario and possible future developments. Eur J Crime Crim Law Crim Justice 17:1–22

Belfiore R (2011) Mutuo riconoscimento delle decisioni sulle misure alternative alla detenzione cautelare. In: Rafaraci T (ed) La cooperazione di polizia e giudiziaria in materia penale nell'Unione europea dopo il Trattato di Lisbona. Giuffrè, Milano, pp 105–117

Belfiore R (2014) Critical remarks on the proposal for a European investigation order and some considerations on the issue of mutual admissibility of evidence. In: Ruggeri S (ed) Transnational evidence and multicultural inquiries in Europe. Developments in EU legislation and new challenges for human rights-oriented criminal investigations in cross-border cases. Springer, Heidelberg, pp 91–105

Böse M (2011) Harmonizing procedural rights indirectly: the framework decision on trials in Absentia. N C J Int Law, 489–510

Böse M (2014) Die Europäische Ermittlungsanordnung–Beweistransfer nach neuen Regeln? Zeitschrift für internationale Strafrechtsdogmatik, pp 152–164

Böse M (2015) Human rights violations and mutual trust: recent case law on the European arrest warrant. In: Ruggeri S (ed) Human rights in European criminal law. New developments in European legislation and case law after the lisbon treaty. Springer, Heidelberg, pp 135–145

Caianiello M (2015) La nuova direttiva UE sull'ordine europeo di indagine penale tra mutuo riconoscimento e ammissione reciproca delle prove. Processo penale e giustizia, pp 1–11

Daniele M (2014) La metamorfosi del diritto delle prove nella Direttiva sull'ordine europeo di indagine penale. www.penalecontemporaneo.it. Accessed 20 Nov 2014

[91]Chapter 15.

Gleß S (2014) Europäisches Beweisrecht. In: Sieber U, Brüner FH, Satzger H, von Heintschell-Heinegg B (eds) Europäisches Strafrecht, 2nd edn. Nomos, Baden-Baden, pp 677–695

Hecker B (2013) Mutual recognition and transfer of evidence. The European Evidence Warrant. In: Ruggeri S (ed) Transnational inquiries and the protection of fundamental rights in criminal proceedings. A study in memory of Vittorio Grevi and Giovanni Tranchina. Springer, Heidelberg, pp 269–278

Hecker B (2015) Europäisches Strafrecht, 5th edn. Springer, Berlin-Heidelberg

Mangiaracina A (2014) A new and controversial scenario in the gathering of evidence at the european level: the proposal for a directive on the European investigation order. Utrecht Law Rev 10(1):113–133

Marchetti MR (2011) Dalla Convenzione di assistenza giudiziaria in materia penale dell'Unione europea al mandato europeo di ricerca delle prove e all'ordine europeo di indagine penale. In: Rafaraci T (ed) La cooperazione di polizia e giudiziaria in material penale nell'Unione europea dopo il Trattato di Lisbona. Giuffrè, Milano, pp 135–167

Peers S (2010) The proposed European Investigation Order: assault on human rights and national sovereignty. www.statewatch.org. Accessed May 2010

Rafaraci T (2012) The application of the principle of mutual recognition to decisions on supervisions measures as an alternative to provisional detention. In: Ruggeri S (ed) Liberty and security. Liberty and security in Europe. A comparative analysis of pre-trial precautionary measures in criminal proceedings. V&R Unipress, Göttingen/Osnabrück, pp 67–83

Ruggeri S (2013) Horizontal cooperation, obtaining evidence overseas and the respect for fundamental rights in the EU. From the European Commission's proposals to the proposal for a directive on a European Investigation Order: Towards a single tool of evidence gathering in the EU? In: Ruggeri S (ed) Transnational inquiries and the protection of fundamental rights in criminal proceedings, A study in memory of Vittorio Grevi and Giovanni Tranchina. Springer, Heidelberg, pp 279–310

Schünemann B (2014) Solution models and principles governing the transnational evidence-gathering in the EU. In: Ruggeri S (ed) Transnational Evidence and Multicultural Inquiries in Europe. Developments in EU legislation and new challenges for human rights-oriented criminal investigations in cross-border cases. Springer, Heidelberg, pp 161–180

Siracusano F (2011) Nuove prospettive in materie di processo *in absentia* e procedure di consegna. In: Rafaraci T (ed) La cooperazione di polizia e giudiziaria in materia penale nell'Unione europea dopo il Trattato di Lisbona. Giuffrè, Milano, pp 85–104

Thaman SC (2013) Report on USA. In: Ruggeri S (ed) Transnational inquiries and the protection of fundamental rights in criminal proceedings. A study in memory of Vittorio Grevi and Giovanni Tranchina. Springer, Heidelberg, pp 509–529

Vallines García E (2006) Los equipos conjuntos de investigación penal. Ed. Colex, Madrid

Wahl T (2015) Der Rahmenbeschluss zu Abwesenheitsentscheidungen. Brüsseler EU-Justizkooperation als Fall für Straßburg? Eucrim, pp 70–76

Zurkinden N (2012) Joint Investigation Teams: Chancen und Grenzen von gemeinsamen Ermittlungsgruppen in der Schweiz, Europa und den USA, Duncker & Humblot, Berlin

Part VII
Solution Models and Principles of a Participatory Approach to Criminal Justice in International Human Rights Law and EU Law

Chapter 14
Principles and Common Requirements of a Participatory Model of Criminal Justice in International Human Rights Law and EU Law

Contents

A. Premise 462
B. The Complex Character of Criminal Proceedings and the Broad Scope of the Right to Be Fairly Heard in International Human Rights Law and EU Law 462
C. The Proactive Role of the Parties in the Exercise of Criminal Prosecution. An Irrelevant Issue Under International Human Rights Law and EU Law? 464
D. The Right to Personal Participation in Criminal Proceedings. The Flexible Approach of International Human Rights Case-Law and the New Findings of EU Law 467
I. The Right to Be personally Involved in Criminal Proceedings and the Assessment of Human Rights Violations Under the European Convention and the Pact of San José 467
II. The Problem of *in absentia* Proceedings. A Comparison Between Strasbourg's Approach and the New Arrangements of EU Law 469
III. Out-of-Court Decisions on the Merits of the Case. The Issue of *inaudito reo* Proceedings Under the European Convention and EU Law 473
IV. The Right of the Aggrieved Parties to Personally Participate in Criminal Proceedings Under the European Convention and EU Law 476
E. Conditions and Qualitative Requirements for Effective Participation in Criminal Proceedings under International and EU Law 477
I. Premise 477
II. Linguistic Guarantees 478
III. Information Safeguards 480
1. Information on the Charge 480
2. Information on the Evidence Available and the Right to Access to the Investigative File 483
F. The Right to a Fair Examination as a General Guarantee of All the Individuals Involved in Criminal Proceedings 484
I. Premise 484
II. The Conditions of a Fair Examination 485
III. *Nemo tenetur* Principle and the Right Not to Be Heard in Criminal Proceedings. The Admissibility of Incriminating Evidence Obtained Coercively 486
IV. The Right to Give Statements in One's Favour 488
G. The Defence's Contribution to Evidence-Gathering 489
I. The Right to Produce Exculpatory Evidence 489
II. The Right to Be Involved in the Taking of Incriminating Evidence. The Complex Challenges of the Right to Confrontation 490

S. Ruggeri, Audi Alteram Partem *in Criminal Proceedings*,
DOI 10.1007/978-3-319-54573-8_14

1. Direct and Indirect Forms of Confrontation 490
2. Context of Confrontation 491
3. Conditions of Effective Confrontation 493
III. A Systematic Understanding of the Right to Confrontation. The Need to Balance the Right to Challenge Incriminating Evidence and the Protection of Other Human Rights 494
H. Participatory Rights and the Requirements of a Fair Decision-Making. The Complex Trade-Offs Among Conflicting Interests Required by International Human Rights Law 496
I. Premise 496
II. The Right to Confrontation and the Proof of Guilt 496
1. The Admissibility of Out-of-Court Evidence in Cases of Subsequent Confrontation and the Problem of Anonymous Testimony 496
2. The Conditions on Use of Untested Evidence 498
III. Argumentative Contribution to the Decision-Making 500
I. *Audi alteram partem* and Restrictions on Freedom. The Requirements of International Human Rights Case-Law and the Developments in the EU Legislation 501
I. Information Rights of Arrested and Detained Individuals 501
II. The Right to a Prompt Independent Review of the Lawfulness of Coercion and the Need for an Overall Human Rights Assessment 504
III. The Defence's Right to Challenge Unlawful Detention. Participatory Rights in *habeas corpus* Proceedings 507
J. Provisional Conclusions 508
References 509

A. Premise

After examining the contribution that international human rights law and EU law have made to the enhancement of participatory safeguards in criminal proceedings, this study provides a second comparative-law analysis. The purpose of the present discussion is to critically compare the models and common principles of a participatory understanding of criminal justice emerging from Strasbourg and Inter-American case-law, as well as from the developments that have taken place in EU law, in order to elaborate some requirements to solve the shortcomings that we have observed in the national criminal justice systems under examination.

B. The Complex Character of Criminal Proceedings and the Broad Scope of the Right to Be Fairly Heard in International Human Rights Law and EU Law

We have seen that one of the most relevant common achievements of both Strasbourg and Inter-American case-law is perhaps the development of a conception of criminal proceedings as a complex listening space. Doubtless, the minimum fair trial rights acknowledged by international human rights instruments to defendants aim at their effective involvement in criminal proceedings, starting with the right to know the charge filed against them and the right to have the necessary time and facilities to prepare their defence. Most of these safeguards emphasise the importance of personal participation of the accused as an essential part of their right to be fairly heard. It is worth observing that both the Rome Convention and the Pact of San José focus on the requirement that information on the accusation be provided not only in a detailed manner but also in a way that the defendant should also be able to understand.

Even more significantly, one could observe the strong contribution of international human rights case-law to the establishment of a model of participatory criminal justice, based on a multisided understanding of the right to a fair hearing. By shifting the focus from the perspective solely of the defendant, both the Strasbourg Court and Inter-American case-law have developed a new understanding of the criminal trial, in which all the individuals concerned, as a rule, must be given a fair opportunity to make their voice heard. In this sense, the *audi alteram partem rule* certainly cuts across the whole set of fair trial rights, calling for a constant balance among conflicting interests. In Europe, the English formulation of the main safeguard of Article 6(1) ECHR[1] has probably contributed to these developments in the Strasbourg case-law, which make the fairness of criminal hearings also dependent on the protection of other individuals involved in a criminal law action.[2] Although the English version of the Pact of San José reproduces the same formulation of the Rome Convention, both the Spanish and Portuguese texts—departing from the French one, which refers to the right to have one's own lawsuit fairly examined[3]—focus on the right of any person charged with a criminal offence to make himself fairly heard.[4] It is therefore no surprise that the Inter-American case-law, going beyond the findings of the European Court, broadened the scope of its assessment of fair trial safeguards by examining complex situations in which the defendant was often victim of serious human rights violations. This has led to the progressive establishment of a strict link between the right to liberty, the protection against inhuman treatment, and the right to a fair hearing, a link that highlights the dual role that the individuals charged with criminal offences often assume in the proceedings before the Inter-American Court, namely as defendants and alleged victims of human rights abuses. In this way, the right to be fairly heard provides the individuals concerned with a general means of achieving an overall scrutiny of the infringement of their most precious rights, allowing them to make their case heard in relation to human rights violations occurred during, and even through, the criminal trial.[5] This does not mean that the Inter-American case-law did not take into due account, like the European Court, the

---

[1]The English text acknowledges the right of any person charged with a criminal offence not just to be heard in court but also to have an overall fair hearing.

[2]Chapter 8, A.

[3]A linguistic comparison may be interesting in this respect. It is worth noting that both the Spanish and Portuguese versions of the European Convention follow the French official text, thus relating to the right to have one's own lawsuit examined by an independent authority.

[4]Chapter 9, A.

[5]Chapter 9, B.

increasing importance of the fair trial rights of victims in a strict sense, namely of the individuals injured by the criminal offence.

The protection of the aggrieved parties lies at the core of the most recent developments of both the Inter-American and the European jurisprudence, which also explains the rising tendency to broaden the very notion of 'victim' beyond the sphere of the individuals directly involved in criminal proceedings or affected by the criminal offence, extending it especially to the next of kin of the individuals injured by serious crimes. Significantly, it is precisely this strongly victim-centred approach that led the San José Court to enrich the scope of the right to be heard with due guarantees by encompassing the state's obligation to institute and carry out proper and complete investigations of the alleged facts, in order to best satisfy the interest of the aggrieved parties in a prompt and reliable criminal law action.[6]

EU law has drawn widely on the cultural heritage of the human rights protection provided by the Strasbourg Court and the European case-law has enriched the scope of the right to a fair hearing, acknowledged by the EU Charter of Fundamental Rights. By focusing on specific defence rights in criminal proceedings, the new EU legislation issued after the entry into force of the Lisbon Treaty reveals the clear emergence of a EU model, which, as noted, is based on the increasing role of private parties in the administration of criminal justice.[7] From the EU Directive on the right to linguistic assistance to the recent legislation on the presumption of innocence and the right to be present at trial, EU institutions have shown increasing attention towards the need to personally involve defendants in criminal proceedings, and as far as international cooperation among member states is concerned, in the EAW proceedings. On the other hand, the scope of the EU intervention was not limited to suspects and accused persons, aiming also to strengthen the participatory safeguards of the victims in criminal proceedings. Notwithstanding these undisputable steps forward, the approach followed by EU law is still incomplete and fragmentary. In its very first ruling on two legislative instruments issued in the field of criminal justice—namely, Directive 2010/64 and Directive 2012/13—the EU Court of Justice has also adopted a rather minimalist approach, which is largely unable to lead to the effective reform of the criminal justice systems of the member states.

C. The Proactive Role of the Parties in the Exercise of Criminal Prosecution. An Irrelevant Issue Under International Human Rights Law and EU Law?

The first problem, in the light of the comparison between the selected countries carried out in this research, relates to the role of private parties in the institution of a criminal law action. It has been observed that the constitutional law of both Brazil

[6] *Ibid.*

[7] Chapter 10, A.

and Italy does not conceive the power to initiate criminal proceedings as an exclusive prerogative of public prosecutors, and despite the dominant state-related conception of criminal prosecution, private parties are increasingly involved in the institution of criminal proceedings. At first glance, international human rights law does not deal with this issue, for there is no specific case-law of either the European Court or the Inter-American Court regarding the contribution of private parties to the initiation of a criminal prosecution. One might also argue that this is the somewhat obvious result of the character of international human rights charters, which traditionally aim at laying down the conditions on which fundamental rights can be restricted and therefore seem to remain neutral on the way prosecutions are instituted and carried out in criminal proceedings. EU law also does not appear to provide clear indications in this regard.[8] In the *Katz* case, the Luxembourg Court only acknowledged that, where national law allows for substitute private prosecution, the victim, despite not being entitled to be heard as a witness, must nevertheless be granted the opportunity to give his testimony.[9]

From these premises it does not follow, however, that international human rights instruments and EU law are indifferent to the manner in which criminal prosecutions are instituted and conducted. On close examination, the case-law of both the Strasbourg Court and the Inter-American Court has on several occasions pointed out important conditions for the fair exercise of the prosecutorial functions. As noted, the strongly victim-centred approach followed by the San José case-law led the Court to emphasise the need for a prompt criminal action. In this light, it is noteworthy that the state's bodies are required to carry out an exhaustive investigation to satisfy the right to truth and reparation of the aggrieved parties and their families.[10] The European Court in turn focused on a core condition for the effective conduct of criminal prosecutions—namely, the principle of equality arms—by requiring both the defence and the prosecutor to be granted the opportunity to know and make observations on the evidence adduced by the other party.[11]

Of course, international human rights law does not express preference for one or another model of criminal prosecution. Furthermore, some of the fundamental safeguards acknowledged by the Strasbourg and Inter-American case-law charge the authorities and the individuals entitled to prosecute with specific human rights obligations. This firstly applies to the right of the individuals accused of a criminal offence to obtain prompt and detailed information on the charges preferred against them. Moreover, it should be taken into account that in the countries characterised by the principle of legality the mandatory character of criminal prosecution is often considered as a clear projection on the procedural plane of the principle *nullum crimen, nulla poena sine lege*, acknowledged by most international human rights

[8]Parlato (2012), p. 389 ff.

[9]Chapter 10, C.III.2.

[10]Chapter 9, B.

[11]Chapter 8, B.

charters.[12] Of course, this does not entail that international human rights law advocates a model of mandatory prosecution. However, the principle *nullum crimen, nulla poena sine lege* not only has considerable implications on the decision-making but also on the possibility of a fair exercise of a criminal prosecution, excluding the accused being brought to court with a charge that exceeds the limits set forth by substantive criminal law. This confirms the need for the investigative bodies to carry out complete inquiries, which is an essential condition for a clear and detailed accusation to be filed against the suspected persons. Most significantly, this fundamental guarantee of substantive criminal law, coupled with the requirements of exhaustive investigations and of detailed information on the accusation, excludes the lawfulness of generic charges. This practice, typical of inquisitorial traditions, not only negatively affects the possibility of effective defence but also frustrates the presumption of innocence, exposing the accused to a court proceeding that might be unjustified.

Doubtless, these findings cannot be deemed to be exclusively concerned with public prosecution, providing methodological indications that apply broadly to any form of criminal prosecution. These results help orient the discussion on the role of private parties in the exercise of criminal prosecutions under international human rights and EU law. In particular, it is clear that, where national law allows for private prosecution, the initiative of the injured parties cannot undermine the obligation of the investigative bodies to exhaustively investigate the alleged offence. Nor can a private prosecution hinder the duty of the prosecutorial authority to scrutinise the need to institute a criminal law action against the suspected persons, which exposes them to a public trial that can be highly detrimental to their image and family life, while entailing the risk of (further) interferences with fundamental rights. From this viewpoint, it is debatable whether international human rights instruments can tolerate forms of private prosecution or of private initiative aimed at ruling out the ordinary exercise of investigative and decision-making powers by the public prosecutor. Furthermore, we have noted that, under the American Convention in particular, the need for a prompt law action of the investigative bodies also holds specific human rights relevance from the perspective of the rights of the aggrieved parties, aiming at the best fulfilment of their right to a proper fact-finding and to the punishment of the perpetrator.

[12]Concerning Italy, see among others Marzaduri (1996), p. 20; Nobili (1998), p. 181 ff. In Germany, criminal law scholarship tends to exclude the principle of legality sharing the same constitutional protection reserved to the *nullum crimen sine lege* principle pursuant to Article 103 (III) Const. However, the strict link between the two principles is not disputed and the mandatory prosecution is even considered to be the downside of *Gesetzlichkeitsprinzip*, in that the latter aims at avoiding the legal limits of criminal law provisions being exceeded, whereas the former prevents them from being lowered and from remaining on paper. Cf. Hassemer (1992), p. 529. For some criticisms on the foundation of this distinction, see Erb (1999), p. 119. Furthermore, the principle of legality shares an essential feature of the *nullum crimen sine lege* principle, that is, the need to respect equality of arms. In this sense see Kühne (2015), p. 210.

All this confirms that the institution of a criminal law action on the part of the victim must be provided with adequate guarantees aimed at reducing the risks for the presumption of innocence and the accused's fair trial rights. There is no doubt that, although the victim has no duty of complete investigation, private prosecution must comply with the requirement of a detailed and understandable charge, to enable the accused persons to set up a proper defence strategy and to make their contribution to evidence-gathering. As noted, moreover, international human rights law calls for mechanisms aimed at avoiding generic charges, which, no matter whether preferred by public or private prosecutors, largely frustrate the possibility of a decision-making in line with the principle *nullum crimen, nulla poena sine lege*.

D. The Right to Personal Participation in Criminal Proceedings. The Flexible Approach of International Human Rights Case-Law and the New Findings of EU Law

I. The Right to Be personally Involved in Criminal Proceedings and the Assessment of Human Rights Violations Under the European Convention and the Pact of San José

As far as the accused is concerned, a particularly delicate issue in international human rights case-law is his personal involvement in criminal proceedings. To be sure, international human rights charters do not generally seem to acknowledge the right to take part personally in criminal proceedings. The International Covenant constitutes an exception, in that it explicitly grants defendants the right to be tried in their own presence—a guarantee significantly enshrined in the same provision that ensures to defendants the right to defend themselves or to obtain the assistance of a lawyer.[13] By contrast, neither the European Convention nor the Pact of San José contains an explicit reference to the right to be present at trial, which does not appear among the general requirements of the right to a fair hearing, nor among the minimum rights of the person charged with a criminal offence. Most of the fair trial safeguards recognised by these charters, however, were structured in such a way that they not only are compatible with, but also promote, the personal involvement of the defendant in criminal proceedings. It is no coincidence that the drafters of the American Convention, as noted, placed the right to linguistic assistance at the top of the accused's fair trial rights, while the Rome Convention emphasises the need for detailed information on the charge in a language the accused can understand. These provisions clearly demonstrate the importance attached to the right of the accused not just to be formally present at trial but furthermore to follow the procedural activities. The fact that the right to understand the charge must also be satisfied in

[13] Art. 14(3)(d) ICCPR.

the pre-trial phase also highlights the need for the competent authorities to enable the accused to actively participate in the whole course of criminal proceedings. Moreover, both charters grant the defendants the right to defend themselves personally or to be assisted by legal counsel of their own choosing; and even though this acknowledgment cannot be interpreted as relating to alternative safeguards, it highlights the clear focus drawn to the personal involvement of the defendants in criminal proceedings even when a lawyer represents them in court.

Starting with these findings, international human rights case-law both in Europe and in Latin America has long conferred to the right to personal participation the broadest scope of application. In this light, it is noteworthy that the Inter-American case-law constantly emphasises the need for a personal hearing of the accused persons in order to ensure ongoing scrutiny of the measures adopted at the national level and the assessment of the physical conditions of the alleged victims of forced disappearances and other human rights infringements.[14]

The European Court has also long recognised the right to be present at trial, charging the national authorities with particular duties of diligence in fulfilling their task of informing the accused persons of the institution of criminal proceedings against them.[15] This approach has two important implications. The first one is that defendants cannot burdened with the task of proving the grounds for which they remained unaware of criminal proceedings as well as with the task of proving that their failure to appear in court was due to *force majeure* or other unforeseeable circumstances. The second consequence is that the competent authorities cannot be relieved from their duty to provide information in the case of conduct by the accused that may have reasons pertaining to administrative law, such as the failure to communicate a change of residence. Unlike the Inter-American case-law, however, the Strasbourg case-law weaken the right to be present at trial in various ways. The European Court tends to soften the guarantee of personal participation in a higher instance, allowing for the proceedings before a higher court to be held in the accused's absence if only legal issues are at stake—a result that is not entirely consistent with the preference expressed for the personal participation of defendants equipped with legal knowledge.[16]

In the following discussion, I shall focus on three problematic areas, which allow us to observe the influence of the Strasbourg case-law on developments in EU law not only in relation to the accused's claim for personal participation but also with regard to other individuals involved in criminal proceedings, namely the victims and their next of kin.

[14] *Ibid.*

[15] Chapter 8, C.II.

[16] Chapter 8, C.I.2.

II. The Problem of **in absentia** *Proceedings. A Comparison Between Strasbourg's Approach and the New Arrangements of EU Law*

The possibility of criminal proceedings being carried out *in absentia*, which is still deeply rooted in the criminal justice tradition of various European countries, can be traced back to very different situations. To be sure, there are no clear provisions in the European Convention against these proceedings and even the International Covenant, although acknowledging the accused's right to be present at trial,[17] does not seem to contain a rigid ban on judgments *in absentia*. A comparison of the Strasbourg case-law and the developments occurred in EU law highlights the need to distinguish two main situations, depending on whether or not the 'absence' was due to a decision of the interested party.

The first situation relates to the case in which the defendant waived personal participation. To be sure, earlier European case-law had not make it entirely clear whether defendants could waive their right to personal participation.[18] Since the 1980s, however, the Court has clearly acknowledged the lawfulness of the waiver of personal involvement, provided that the defendant's conduct unequivocally reveals his decision not to be present at trial.[19] Significantly, the decision to waive participation is allowed even if the competent authorities did not succeed in informing the accused about the institution of criminal proceedings. In this case, the Court does not engage in further inquiry as whether the domestic authority properly fulfilled its duties of diligence. One of the most interesting aspects of the approach adopted by the European case-law is the reconstruction of certain duties of diligence also on the accused's side, an obligation which, as noted, especially concerns defendants with legal knowledge, who should in principle make a contribution to the criminal inquiry. Nevertheless, the flexible jurisprudence on this delicate issue does not allow us to draw a clear picture of the consideration that the accused's presence holds in criminal proceedings under the European Convention, nor of the limits within which defendants can waive their right to take part in criminal proceedings. As anticipated, the Court did not follow a consistent approach in relation to higher instances. Furthermore, there are no clear indications in the European case-law as to the extent to which the national authorities can sanction defendants with legal knowledge who choose not to participate in the court hearings.

Different problems arise in the case of criminal proceedings instituted *in absentia* without any (unequivocal) decision by the defendant, who may in turn have remained fully unaware of the proceedings instituted against him. Even in this

---

[17]Trechsel (2005), p. 254.

[18]As noted, the issue was not dealt with in *Colozza v. Italy*, whereas the *Neumeister* judgment made waiver conditional on specific safeguards. Cf. Chapter 8, C.II.

[19]*Ibid.*

case, conducting a criminal law action is possible according to the Strasbourg case-law, which, however, conditions the lawfulness of the proceedings on the fact that the accused was given the opportunity for a retrial or for a remedy aimed at a review of the judgment made *in absentia*. Furthermore, the Court did not limit itself to acknowledging the right to a subsequent means for obtaining a remedy but also laid down some qualitative requirements that these means must satisfy. In particular, regardless of the solution adopted by national law, the accused must be ensured a mechanism aimed at a fresh determination of the merits of the charge and the competent authority must hear him before ruling again on the case. Beyond these requirements, however, the Strasbourg case-law does not provide for further indications on the exact contents of right to a retrial. The European Court has on several occasions pointed out that the lawfulness of the national arrangements largely depends on the circumstances of the concrete case, which must be assessed by the European Court on the basis of the effectiveness given to the right to a defence in domestic proceedings.[20]

In this way, the Strasbourg Court made itself the ultimate instance for scrutiny of the adequacy of these domestic arrangements. Furthermore, the recourse to a subsequent remedy enabled the European judges to stretch the guarantee of personal participation in criminal proceedings to such a point that it turned out to blur the right to a fair hearing. It is surprising that the Strasbourg Court, despite emphasising the obligation of national authorities to ensure the defendant's knowledge of criminal proceedings, considers his presence at trial to be equivalent to his involvement in a subsequent trial or a higher instance. At any rate, the main weakness of this reasoning is perhaps of a methodological nature. The fact that national authorities applied all the available means to make defendants aware of the institution of criminal proceedings does not make a criminal law action absolutely necessary, especially where the grounds for the accused's absence remained unclear. It is true that especially when serious crimes are at stake, a prompt criminal law action can best satisfy the needs of a social defence policy and can avoid further shortcomings, *e.g.* by reducing the risk that relevant evidence may get lost or that the genuineness of evidence subject to high risk of deterioration may be altered. However, these undisputable advantages are largely outweighed by the risks arising from conducting a criminal law action in the defendant's absence.

In the *Colozza* case, the European Court was already aware that the institution of criminal proceedings in the defendant's absence must satisfy a public interest, in that it held that

> the impossibility of holding a trial by default may paralyse the conduct of criminal proceedings, in that it may lead, for example, to dispersal of the evidence, expiry of the time-limit for prosecution or a miscarriage of justice.[21]

[20]ECtHR, *Öcalan v. Turkey*, § 210.

[21]*Ibid.*

It is surprising, however, the need for a public interest justifying the initiation of a criminal prosecution becomes blurred if defendants are given the opportunity of a retrial or a subsequent remedy. Furthermore, it should not be overlooked that the Strasbourg case-law often weakens the right to personal participation in criminal proceedings in its humanitarian function. Yet it is precisely an overall consideration of the fairness of criminal proceedings that should require an in-depth assessment of the risks arising from a criminal law action, especially when defendants can suffer from severe restrictions on their fundamental rights as a result of coercive means adopted against them *in absentia* (seizure of assets, etc.). Doubtless, there are damages that cannot be erased by means of a remedy or a retrial, even where a 'fresh determination of the merits of the charge' is ensured. Some defensive opportunities are precluded after the end of the first instance, not to mention the adverse effects that the initiation of the criminal trial can produce, due to the tools available in the current phase of the information society, on the image of both the defendants and their families. On the other hand, the functional connection between the right to personal participation and the goals of the criminal trial can be jeopardised by an indiscriminate use of the procedural arrangements inherent in the trials *in absentia*. Allowing for the institution of default proceedings irrespective of whether specific prosecutorial needs require it entails a clear underestimation of the defendants' contribution to fact-finding.

The shortcomings of Strasbourg case-law, moreover, did not remain confined to the sphere of the European Convention, having, as observed, enormous influence on the developments of EU law. As stressed by the Explanatory Memorandum of the draft proposal of Directive 2016/343,[22] the EU intervention was clearly aimed at setting minimum rules in line in the European Convention. Most of the arrangements made by this legislative instrument reveal a clear attempt to enact into the EU area the solutions elaborated by the Strasbourg Court.[23] This especially applies to the requirements of information on the proceedings, information that must be provided to the accused persons, either personally or through other means aimed at ensuring their knowledge of the proceedings instituted against them. Most significantly, the new Directive emphasises the duties of diligence of national authorities in ensuring the proper fulfilment of these responsibilities. The European case-law also clearly inspired the subsequent solutions adopted by the EU legislature, which maintained the lawfulness of criminal proceedings held *in absentia* if the accused was given either a retrial or a legal remedy aimed at a judicial review of the conviction. Whatever mechanism is adopted at the national level, the EU institutions also stressed the need to follow the qualitative requirements set forth by the Strasbourg Court.

To a certain extent, however, the new EU arrangements further weakened the standards of protection of the right to personal participation in criminal proceedings

---

[22]Explanatory Memorandum, § 41.

[23]Chapter 10, B.II.1.

in comparison to those laid down by the European case-law.[24] Notwithstanding the clear preference towards a system of personal notification on the institution of criminal proceedings, EU law shows no interest in the reasons that lead the accused not to appear in court. Further human rights concerns relate to the case in which a lawyer represents the absent defendant in court, the EU institutions allowing for criminal proceedings to be instituted *in absentia* no matter whether the competent authorities fulfilled their task responsibility of informing the accused. Not only does EU law not provide for unequivocal waiver of participation but it does not even seem to require the accused to give a mandate to the lawyer who may have been appointed by the court. To bring this case in line with the European Court's requirement of unequivocal waiver of personal participation, the EU legislation should be reinterpreted in a sense that requires the competent authorities to assess whether the accused knowingly agreed to be represented at trial by the lawyer (even if appointed by the court). Furthermore, the competent authority should also be able to scrutinise whether there was effective communication and a proper exchange of information between counsel and client.[25]

The most serious problems, moreover, arise in relation to cases in which none of these conditions have been met.[26] It is truly surprising that EU law provides for further requirements to ensure the enforcement of a conviction rendered *in absentia* where the defendant neither was informed of the proceedings nor could appoint his own lawyer. Under the new rules, moreover, access to a retrial or a legal remedy aimed at a review of the conviction is far from being effective for at least two reasons. Firstly, EU law does not require national authorities to provide the accused with proper information on the available means of challenging the conviction, which jeopardises the possibility of making the right decision and setting up a proper defensive strategy. Secondly, unlike the draft proposal, Directive 2016/343/EU attached no relevance to the grounds on which subsequent remedies remained unused, the information on a retrial or a legal remedy being by itself a sufficient condition to justify the execution of the conviction.

Under these conditions, there is little doubt that in the EU area, based on the high level of human rights protection, allowing the enforcement of a judgment *in absentia* provided a subsequent remedy is abstractly available weakens the right to personal participation in criminal proceedings to an unacceptable extent. As noted, the alternatives of participation before the decision-making and subsequent solutions can be tolerated as far as such tools can effectively compensate the accused for the loss of the defensive opportunities in the first instance. Nevertheless, this is not always the case at the national level, nor does the 2016 Directive contain clear solutions in this regard. Furthermore, the qualitative requirements that subsequent tools must in any case fulfil—namely, the fresh determination of the merits of the case, including the examination of new evidence, as well as the

[24] *Ibid.*

[25] Wahl (2015), p. 74.

[26] Chapter 10, B.II.1.

reversal of the conviction[27]—may not be enough, *e.g.* where national law limits the right to obtain exculpatory evidence at second instance.[28]

III. Out-of-Court Decisions on the Merits of the Case. The Issue of **inaudito reo** *Proceedings Under the European Convention and EU Law*

The second problematic area concerns the decisions issued out of court through a procedure *inaudito reo.* Until recently, this proceeding certainly did not lie at the core of European criminal law policy, nor did it draw the much attention from the case-law of European courts. In the recent case *Gray v. Germany*, the Strasbourg Court was called upon to examine German penal order procedures, albeit from the particular viewpoint of the participatory rights of the aggrieved party.[29] The Strasbourg judges did not take the opportunity to provide for specific indications on the lawfulness of *inaudito reo* convictions in general, a question that has still remained unanswered under the European Convention. In the present discussion, therefore, I will focus on the new solutions emerging from EU law and the jurisprudence of Luxembourg.

It has been observed that Directive 2016/343 required EU countries to ensure the accused's right to be present in criminal hearings only if domestic law provides for one or more hearings. On the other hand, EU law allowed for member states to maintain special proceedings in writing, aimed at an out-of-court decision on the merits of the case. The drafters of this legislation also did not make any attempt to bring these procedures in line with the fundamental right to a fair hearing. There can be little doubt that by recognising the right to a 'fair and public hearing',[30] the Nice-Strasbourg Charter prevents interpretations aimed at lowering the standards of protection of the European Convention,[31] requiring the scope of its own guarantees to be defined in the same terms acknowledged by this international instrument.[32] Of course, this does not mean that the guarantee of a fair and public hearing is an

[27]Art. 9 DirPIRPT.

[28]In Italy, as noted, the 1988 code enabled defendants tried *in absentia* to request to be relieved from the effects of the expiration of the time limit to appeal a default conviction. Yet the exercise of their right to evidence at second instance depended on the difficult proof that their absence in court had not been their own fault. Significantly, this situation remained unchanged after an important legislative reform, carried out by Law Decree 17/2005, converted in Law 60/2005. Cf. Chapter 2, F.II.1.

[29]Chapter 8, C.III.

[30]Art. 47(2) EU-FRCh.

[31]Art. 53 EU-FRCh.

[32]Art. 52(3) CFR. This provision has led to various reactions and very different suggestions for interpretation. For a strong interpretation of this clause, whereby the EU Charter incorporated the ECHR set-up of human rights protection, see Borowsky (2011), p. 687.

absolute right. However, the EU Charter of fundamental rights does not appear to allow for the accused to be convicted by means of a written procedure, which rules out their contributing to decision-making.

Here also, the question arises whether a person convicted through an *inaudito reo* procedure has the right to obtain a fair compensation mechanism. The question becomes even more relevant in the case of foreign defendants, who are often most in need while deciding whether to apply for a subsequent trial. In this regard, the conclusions reached by the Luxembourg Court in the *Covaci* judgment reveal a scenario in which non-resident defendants must be granted information on the accusation contained in the penal order and must be ensured either legal or linguistic assistance, depending on whether they choose to lodge written or oral opposition—but not both. Furthermore, legal or linguistic assistance is not necessarily due in the period between the service of the decision and the lodging of the objection. This is certainly a debatable result, taking into account that in most cases non-resident defendants are also foreigners who are fully unfamiliar with *lex fori*. Certainly, the main responsibility to ensure this guarantee lies with national law. By dealing with the *Covaci* case, we have noted that German law does not require legal assistance to be provided to the defendant in order to enable him to decide whether to lodge an objection against a penal order, nor does it require the accused to give reasons when challenging a penal order.

A question arises as to whether further EU legislation grants specific safeguards to the accused convicted through an out-of-court decision. The answer is certainly negative in relation to the two legislative instruments examined by the Court in the *Covaci* case. Moreover, no solutions emerge from the Directive on the access to a lawyer,[33] which, despite requiring member states to protect defendants in such time and in such a manner so as to allow them to 'exercise their rights of defence practically and effectively',[34] does not take into account the particular case of a conviction *inaudito reo*. It is true that that 2013 Directive has a very broad scope of application, which includes 'where applicable, sentencing and the resolution of any appeal'.[35] However, this reference only concerns the right to legal assistance within the appeal proceedings, a situation that does not fit the case of a challenge against a penal order, which does not aim at a review of the conviction by a higher court, but a new decision on the merits of the case.

Surprisingly, while this legislation did not deal with the case of penal order procedures, the EU institutions took into consideration the special situation of those member states that enable an authority other than a court having jurisdiction in criminal matters to impose a sanction, which may be appealed or referred to a criminal court. In this particular case, the solution of Directive 2013/48 is somewhat reductive: thus member states can choose not to grant individuals the right to access to a lawyer before administrative authorities, provided that it will be ensured in the

[33] Directive 2013/48/EU. See among others Bachmaier Winter (2015), p. 111 ff.

[34] Art. 3(1) DirAL.

[35] Art. 2(1) DirAL.

proceedings before a criminal court.[36] Again, the case of *inaudito reo* proceedings does not follow this scheme, since a judge having jurisdiction in criminal matters is generally competent to issue penal orders. Clearly, EU law does not cover the case of *inaudito reo* proceedings and applying the same rule would clearly leave foreign individuals unprotected in the time available for lodging the appeal against the (usually single) judge who convicted them. It can be doubted whether this case can be deemed compatible with the Strasbourg case-law's claim that the fair trial guarantees in criminal matters must also be extended to the procedures for administrative offences, where the level of the sanction can be the same as a criminal offence.[37]

It is worth observing, furthermore, that the 2013 Directive requires member states to make the necessary arrangements to ensure that suspects or accused persons who are deprived of liberty are in a position to exercise effectively their right of access to a lawyer, unless they have waived that right. Significantly, this requirement goes beyond the national rules on mandatory legal assistance.[38] Doubtless, individuals convicted without having had the opportunity to be heard and without even knowing of the existence of a criminal law action are in a similar vulnerable condition. Therefore legal assistance should be provided with a view to requesting a criminal trial in which the injured party can participate, unless proof of a waiver exists.

In sum, the overall legislative set-up provided by EU law does not provide for adequate solutions that fit the challenges of the common area of freedom, security and justice in the delicate field of the proceedings *inaudito reo*. It cannot be tolerated that national law allows the institution of criminal proceedings that exclude the defendant's involvement on the basis of a prosecutorial decision, without giving him the possibility to knowingly decide whether to apply for a subsequent trial. Notwithstanding the lack of specific case-law from the Strasbourg Court on this topic, there can be little doubt that this result is not in line with the European jurisprudence. As noted, European case-law has generally recognised the lawfulness of criminal proceedings held without a public hearing, provided, however, that defendants unequivocally waived their right to it and that this waiver does not run counter to any relevant public interest. These findings should make the adoption of simplified written procedures conditional on the fact that the defendants either were given the possibility to waive their right to a court hearing or can access an effective subsequent remedy.

---

[36]Art. 2(4) DirAL.

[37]The question was raised by *Bachmaier Winter*, who, however, considers the EU limitation acceptable. Cf. Bachmaier Winter (2015), p. 117.

[38]Art. 3(4) DirAL.

IV. The Right of the Aggrieved Parties to Personally Participate in Criminal Proceedings Under the European Convention and EU Law

Although the traditional approach to the guarantee of personal participation in criminal proceedings looks at the side of the accused, the complex challenges posed by the *audi alteram partem* rule suggest broadening the focus to other individuals affected by a criminal law action. Doubtless, in a modern view of criminal justice, the guarantee of personal involvement in criminal hearings can no longer be deemed an exclusive prerogative of defendants. The comparative analysis of supranational and international law highlights the problem of whether the individuals most affected by a criminal offence—namely, the victims in the aforementioned broad sense—also hold the right to make their own contribution to the fact-finding.

Under the European Convention, we have noted that in the recent *Gray* judgment, the Strasbourg Court provided some important indications on penal order procedures from the unprecedented perspective of the aggrieved parties. The Court did not raise doubts on German procedural law, which neither grants the aggrieved parties information on a penal order procedure nor enables them to challenge the conviction issued *inaudito reo*. The Court also did not explain why the Convention does not require their involvement, as conversely acknowledged in relation to situations in which the responsibility of state's agents in connection with a victim's death is at stake.

On a more general level, the arguments used by the Court allow us to draw some conclusions on whether the victim has the right to be involved in a criminal inquiry under the Rome Convention. The most interesting aspect is perhaps the reasoning used to justify the obligation to involve the victim's next of kin to safeguard their legitimate interests. According to the Court, this obligation also lies with the state in the case of medical negligence, provided, however, that the interested parties demonstrate the usefulness of their contribution to the criminal inquiry by adducing information aimed at clarifying concrete issues at stake. As noted, this functional perspective is a debatable point of the Court's general approach to several defence rights. It cannot be accepted that the right to be involved in a criminal inquiry is granted only *secondum eventum* or, even worse, that the individuals concerned can be burdened with the task of proving in advance what contribution they could provide in a trial hearing. Even worse, the Court rules out the right to a legal remedy in a procedure that is by definition characterised by the exclusion of private parties prior to the decision-making. Besides, it is surprising that, despite its great sensitivity to the victim's rights, the European case-law showed such scant interest in the direct involvement of the aggrieved parties in criminal inquiries, to the point that the European Convention could even legitimise the solution of making the victim's participation conditional on the prosecutorial choice of the type of proceedings in a concrete case.

Despite its increasing attention towards the victim's rights, EU law provides for very scant indications on his right to directly participate in criminal proceedings. Directive 2012/29/EU, while generally referring to the arrangements of national law as to the role of the injured parties in criminal proceedings, highlights various forms of involvement of the victim, which pursue very diverse aims. The competent authorities can require their presence for investigative purposes, but victims also have the right to participate and make their voice heard in criminal trials. In this context, EU institutions emphasise the need for active participation of the victim, to the extent that some defence rights (*e.g.*, linguistic understanding of essential documents) largely depend on their active role in criminal justice. This approach raises several questions. What should be meant by 'active participation'? Who should decide whether and to what extent the victim's contribution to the fact-finding was truly active? Certainly, the fact that national law is competent to define the terms of the victim's involvement in criminal proceedings largely blurs the effectiveness of the EU acknowledgment. It should be taken into consideration, as noted, that most of the rights ensured by the 2012 legislation can only be claimed at the victim's initiative, without the competent authority having the obligation of promoting their activation in criminal proceedings.

E. Conditions and Qualitative Requirements for Effective Participation in Criminal Proceedings under International and EU Law

I. Premise

International human rights instruments do not recognise fair trial rights solely with a view to the formal involvement of the individuals concerned in criminal proceedings. Both in Europe and in Latin America, the physical presence of the accused does not fully satisfy his right to take part in criminal hearings. It is surely of little use for defendants to be present in court if they are not granted a fair opportunity to be heard and make their contribution to fact-finding. Both the Strasbourg Court and the San José case-law have on several occasions stressed the need to ensure effectiveness to the accused's participation. A clear example was the *Stanford* case, in which, as noted, the European judges pointed out that defendants must be given the right not only to be present but also to hear and follow the proceedings.[39]

Of course, the involvement of private parties in criminal proceedings may assume different features depending on several factors, such as the stage of the proceedings and the individual concerned, not to mention the social background of

[39] Chapter 8, D.I.

the alleged offence. At any rate, some basic conditions must be ensured in any case, setting necessary prerequisites for the active participation of the individuals concerned. EU law has surely inherited from Strasbourg case-law the attention towards the requirement of effective participation. Despite its piecemeal approach, the supranational legislation issued after the Lisbon reform aimed at the harmonisation of a minimum set of core safeguards, which enable the individuals involved in criminal proceedings to take part effectively.

II. Linguistic Guarantees

The comparative examination of international human rights case-law and EU law confirms that the granting of linguistic assistance stands out among the essential conditions for the individuals concerned to be able to follow and effectively participate in criminal proceedings. An emblematic example of the weight attached by international human rights charters to the right to understand procedural activities and to be understood, as noted, is the systematic approach of the Pact of San José to the guarantee of linguistic assistance. The prominent position of this right in the American Convention is not predisposed to reductive interpretations, calling for the extension of the scope of the linguistic guarantees beyond the court proceedings and even in the pre-trial phase, especially where measures of coercion are at stake. Although the European Convention does not follow the same systematic approach, we have seen that it also reserves specific attention to the linguistic safeguards, starting with the information on the accusation and the information due to arrested and detained persons.

Both in Europe and in Latin America, international human rights case-law has further enhanced these safeguards. The Inter-American Court emphasised the importance of the right to understand the language of the proceedings in situations characterised by the particular vulnerability of arrested individuals belonging to rural or indigenous communities detained in a cultural context different from their own one. In this context, linguistic assistance becomes a necessary means for the individuals concerned not only to understand the procedural activities but also to be understood at trial.[40] The Strasbourg Court in turn stressed the need for the accused to be informed of the institution of a criminal law action in a language that, despite not necessarily being his mother language, he must be able to understand. The functional focus on the link between the linguistic understanding of the charge and the right to information holds specific importance in the European case-law for the purposes of the effective exercise of other fair trial rights, starting with the right to be present at trial, the right to appoint a lawyer of one's own choosing, and so on.[41] Furthermore, under the European Convention also, the protection of linguistic

[40] Chapter 9, C.

[41] Chapter 8, D.II.1.

guarantees is enhanced in case of persons in vulnerable situations. This especially applies to the cases of deprivation of freedom, in which the individuals concerned must not only be given proper information on the factual but also on the legal grounds for arrest in a simple and non-technical language.[42]

Despite the lack of specific references to linguistic guarantees in the Nice-Strasbourg Charter, we have seen that the EU institutions also devoted particular attention to linguistic assistance in criminal proceedings. Significantly, the first legislative instrument issued in the field of criminal justice after the Lisbon reform aimed at laying down minimum rules on the right to interpretation and translation in criminal proceedings, as well as in EAW procedures. Clearly, Directive 2010/64/EU was strongly influenced by the Strasbourg case-law, as seen from the way the right to interpretation was conceived as a means of ensuring the effectiveness of the defence participation in criminal proceedings. To this end, EU law requires member states to grant the accused persons the assistance of an interpreter, not only in all court hearings, but also in the previous communications with their lawyers.[43] In this regard, however, EU institutions adopted a somewhat minimalist approach, ensuring to the accused the right to linguistic assistance only to the extent necessary to ensure the fairness of the proceedings.

On the other hand, the assistance of an interpreter may not be enough to ensure active participation in criminal hearings, which largely depends on the understanding of procedural documents. In this respect also, the EU Directive 2010/64 followed a very cautious approach, which, in order not to overload member states with undue costs, limited the guarantee of translation only to the essential documents of the proceedings.[44] Among these documents, the indictment must always be translated for the accused, if they do not speak the language of the proceedings. Nevertheless, the scope of this fundamental safeguard is rather unclear, since the 2010 legislation did not specify whether the pre-trial charge should also be translated. A reductive interpretation of the supranational rules would bring EU law away from the standards of protection set forth by the Strasbourg case-law, leaving suspects unprotected in situations of particular vulnerability and especially in cases of interferences with fundamental rights.

An indisputable merit of EU law, however, was to extend the linguistic safeguards to the victim of a criminal offence. Manifestly, the assistance of an interpreter is a necessary condition for the aggrieved parties also to be able to understand the course of criminal proceedings as well as to be understood and to make their version of the facts heard by the court. Furthermore, Directive 2012/29/EU devoted particular focus on the need for simple and comprehensible communications, which must be adapted to the personal characteristics of the victim in a concrete case.[45] However, EU law did not go so far as to require member states to always ensure the

---

[42] Chapter 8, G.I.

[43] Chapter 10, C.I.1.

[44] *Ibid.*

[45] Chapter 10, C.I.2.

physical presence of an interpreter, thus allowing for technical arrangements aimed at granting remote linguistic assistance, provided, however, that accused persons can properly exercise their defence rights.[46] This approach inevitably leaves a great margin of discretion for the national authorities, which can enhance the vulnerable condition of the victim, depriving him of the precious tool of linguistic assistance *in loco*. Like defendants, the injured party also has the right to translation of procedural documents. Yet EU law allows national authorities not to ensure translation of passages of essential documents that are not relevant with a view to the victim's active involvement in criminal proceedings. In general terms, EU law provides rather scant protection of the participatory rights of the injured parties, who can count on linguistic assistance only at their own request and within the limits laid down by national law.[47]

III. Information Safeguards

1. Information on the Charge

Both in Latin America and in Europe, international human rights case-law holds that the granting of proper information is a core condition for effective participation in criminal proceedings. The forms of this acknowledgment, however, are not identical and the case-law of Strasbourg and San José has in turn developed the information safeguards in rather different fashion. As far as the information on the accusation is concerned, both the European Court and the Inter-American case-law have adopted a broad understanding of this fundamental guarantee, which must not only be provided in a form that can be understood but must also be equipped with the necessary details on the legal and factual grounds for the institution of a criminal law action.

We have noted that the requirement of simple and detailed information is clearly oriented to enable the most effective defence. The European case-law emphasises the link with the right to a defence to such a point that it has often adopted a rather functional approach to the guarantee of information, which individuals can only claim before the Strasbourg Court to the extent they concretely suffered from a restriction on their defence rights.[48] By contrast, the Inter-American case-law has never engaged in assessing whether the lack of proper information caused a concrete damage to the right to a defence or what strategy the defence could have adopted, if the accused had been given better information.[49] On close examination, the functional approach adopted by the European judges does not fit the resources

[46] *Ibid.*

[47] *Ibid.*

[48] Chapter 8, D.II.1.

[49] Chapter 9, D.

available to the international human rights courts, which, as noted, are not equipped to inquire into the concrete restrictions suffered by the lack of information and even less able to scrutinise the hypothetical benefits that would have derived from proper information. Moreover, the impact test on defence rights required by the Strasbourg Court, while weakening the right to information, guarantees to the individuals concerned no certainty about to the extent to which the European Convention protects their information rights. Of course, this doctrine was elaborated in the field of the contentious jurisprudence of Strasbourg and it would not be an easy task for the Court, if requested in a near future to give an advisory opinion, to define in advance limits within which information on the charge should be ensured.

Another aspect that distinguishes the approach followed by the two international courts is the scope of the guarantee of information. Notwithstanding the reference to the 'accusation' in the Rome Convention, the individuals charged with a criminal offence cannot certainly wait until a formal accusation is preferred against them to obtain information on the charge. A literal interpretation of the Convention would frustrate its main goals, depriving the suspects of the ability to set up a proper defence strategy and to challenge the coercive means often ordered against them in the pre-trial phase. The Strasbourg Court has never adopted a rigid interpretation of the right to information on the accusation, instead calling for a flexible approach that looks at the substantial repercussions of criminal investigations on the suspect's fundamental rights. The American Convention does not contain elements that could give rise to formalistic interpretations and the Inter-American Court has on several occasions stressed the need for variable information depending on the stage of the proceedings.

Unlike the European Convention, however, the Pact of San José explicitly recognises the right to 'prior notification' of the charge. This acknowledgment, which is unique among international human rights charters, enhances the link between the guarantee of information and the right to be fairly heard by a court, as highlighted by the San José case-law, which requires defendants to be notified of the charges issued against them even prior to their first statement.[50] In Latin America, moreover, the requirement of prior notification rules out the lawfulness of procedures characterised by the postponement of the involvement of the accused after the decision-making. In the EU area, as noted, the failure of Directive 2012/13 to specify this issue has led the Luxembourg Court to give a rather reductive interpretation of the guarantee of information on the charge. In the *Covaci* case, the Court of Justice confirmed the lawfulness under EU law of the German penal order procedure on the assumption that the notification of the conviction fulfils the task of informing the accused of the accusation.[51]

It has also been observed that the right to information on the charge entails precise obligations for the competent authorities, which are also called upon to inform the accused of any amendment of the charge that make it necessary for the

[50] *Ibid.*

[51] Chapter 10, B.II.2.a.

accused persons to change their defence strategy. The fact that the European Court deemed in some cases the guarantee of Article 6(3)(a) ECHR satisfied, provided that the accused was in any case informed of the institution of criminal proceedings, can probably be seen as another debatable result of the functional approach adopted in relation to this fundamental safeguard.[52] Of course, international human rights law does not conceive of the information rights in absolute terms. Restrictions on the guarantee of information, however, can only be allowed to the extent necessary to prevent specific risks for the proceedings.

EU law has clearly inherited the focus of the Strasbourg case-law on the need to provide defendants with information that is at the same time detailed on both factual and legal questions and is also accessible from a linguistic viewpoint.[53] Furthermore, the 2012 Directive requires the accused person to receive a Letter of Rights including, *inter alia*, information on the accusation, a Letter that must be written in a sufficiently clear manner that all individuals, regardless of their actual knowledge of legal matters, can understand it. Furthermore, EU law also broadened the procedural scope of the guarantee of information, which must be ensured in the pre-trial inquiry especially where restrictions on freedom were ordered against the suspect. The dynamic understanding of the information required by the EU legislation is particularly evident in the cases of amendment of the original charge. The fact that any change must be promptly communicated to the accused not only confirms the existence of precise information duties on the part of the competent authorities but also that the right to information on the accusation cannot be restricted to the time of the initiation of a criminal prosecution, taking on different degrees of completeness during the court proceedings.

At first glance, the approach followed by the EU institutions does not make the granting of information conditional on the scrutiny of a concrete advantage for the defence, as happens under the European Convention. On close examination, a functional perspective deeply inspires the EU law on the guarantee of information. This conclusion especially applies to the information due in the pre-trial phase, whose features were not sufficiently defined at the level of EU law: detailed information on the offence under investigation is only required to the extent that it ensures the effective exercise of defence rights and fairness in the criminal inquiry. Furthermore, amendments of the charge must be communicated only insofar as it is necessary to ensure the fairness of the criminal process. This restrictive approach does not best fit the human rights aims of the EU area. It is difficult to think of a fair criminal proceeding, in which defendants are kept in the dark about changes to the accusation issued against them, forcing them to defend themselves against an outdated charge.

It is worth observing, moreover, that under EU law the information rights—like the linguistic safeguards—do not only concern the accused.[54] The 2012 legislation

[52]Chapter 8, D.II.1.

[53]Chapter 10, C.II.1.b.

[54]Chapter 10, C.II.2.

on victims' rights established a clear link between the guarantee of detailed information and respect for the person of the victim. Thus the injured party must be given information on the procedural tools and legal assistance available, including those necessary to lodge a criminal complaint, prior to the institution of a criminal. Within criminal proceedings, victims must be kept informed of developments in the investigation. In this regard, it is particularly important to inform victims when the decision has been taken not to prosecute the alleged offender. Yet information about the prosecutorial request for termination of the proceedings would be a preferable solution to enable the victim to challenge the prosecutorial initiative before a decision has been issued. Moreover, the right to information holds another important feature from the viewpoint of the victim, who has the right to forget the offence and to be forgotten. Doubtless, the EU institutions devoted attention to the right not to informed on the charge and the institution of criminal proceedings, since information, as noted, is dependent on the explicit request of the victim. Although this arrangement is in principle justified, EU law should have probably required an in-depth scrutiny by an independent body of the voluntariness of the victim's decision not to obtain information, a decision that in turn presupposes awareness of the implications on the participatory rights in criminal proceedings.

2. Information on the Evidence Available and the Right to Access to the Investigative File

Both the Inter-American and the Strasbourg case-law strengthen the information safeguards of the individuals involved in criminal proceedings by also granting them the right to know the evidence collected by the investigative bodies. The Court of San José emphasises the link with the right to prior notification of the charge by giving the accused information on the evidence supporting the charging decision.[55] The European case-law adopted a softer approach in this regard, deeming the right to access prosecutorial evidence to be not necessarily entailed by the information on the accusation.[56] However, defendants hold the right to know the prosecutorial evidence pursuant to Article 6(3)(b) ECHR. Moreover, the Strasbourg Court has also on several occasions pointed out the strict link between the guarantees of lits. (a) and (b) of Article 6(3) ECHR, acknowledging the right to access the incriminating evidence gathered in the pre-trial inquiry.

The focus of the European case-law on this problematic area has certainly contributed to the evolution of EU law. At first sight, Directive 2012/13 emphasised the importance of the information on prosecutorial evidence to the point that, alongside the information due to arrested and detained suspects, defendants have a comprehensive right to access all the evidence in the possession of the competent

[55] Chapter 9, D.

[56] Chapter 8, D.III.

authority, both in favour and against the accused. Again, however, the adoption of a functional approach somehow blurred the broad scope of this right, which must generically be ensured during the pre-trial inquiry in due time to enable the exercise of defence rights.[57]

Under international human rights law, access to prosecutorial and police evidence is not an absolute guarantee, exceptions being allowed so as not to undermine prosecutorial needs. Unlike the notification of the charge, however, evidentiary information not only can be temporarily denied but can also be restricted to certain pieces of evidence. Notwithstanding the findings of *Edwards v. United Kingdom*, both the European Court and the Court of San José acknowledged this possibility, requiring, however, that a concrete risk for the ongoing inquiry justify any restriction on the right to know incriminating evidence. Furthermore, the European case-law broadened—in the light of the *par condicio* principle—the scope of the guarantee of access to the evidence available, access that must also be ensured to the prosecutor in relation to defensive evidence. It is worth observing, moreover, that the Strasbourg Court, dealing especially with serious crimes, recognised the legitimacy of arrangements aimed at limiting access only to a lawyer, provided, however, that the accused is granted a summary of the information gathered. EU law also acknowledges the possibility of restrictions to the right to access to prosecutorial evidence, but such restrictions must be justified by the need either to protect other individual interests or not to undermine the effectiveness of the criminal investigations. Yet the failure to require case-law to provide for a tool to immediately challenge the decision to suspend information can give rise to irreparable damages for the accused person.

F. The Right to a Fair Examination as a General Guarantee of All the Individuals Involved in Criminal Proceedings

I. Premise

It has been observed that, although the right to be fairly heard lies at the heart of the *audi alteram partem* rule, international human rights instruments do not always contain specific provisions on the guarantee of a fair examination. In particular, the Rome Convention, despite enshrining the general right to a fair hearing, does not lay down specific safeguards on the examination of defendants or other people involved in a criminal law action. This does not mean, however, that under this Charter a fair criminal trial can be conducted without the persons concerned being given an opportunity to make themselves heard. Especially in the field of restrictions on liberty, the fact that the arrested or detained individuals must be promptly brought before an independent body does not also aim at an objective scrutiny of the

[57] Chapter 10, C.II.1.c.

justification of the measure applied but furthermore requires the competent authority to grant them the opportunity to be heard. The acknowledgment of the guarantee of a fair examination is more apparent in the American Convention. As noted, at least two of the four official versions of the Pact of San José formulate the right to a fair hearing as the general right of all the individuals charged with a criminal offence to be fairly heard in the proceedings. Furthermore, like the International Covenant, the American Convention expressly acknowledges the right not to be compelled to give evidence against oneself. Under both Conventions, the particular focus attached to personal involvement of the individuals concerned not only aims at enabling them to follow the court procedure but also require the national authorities to hear them. According to the Inter-American case-law, as noted, the examination of the accused provides the court with the opportunity to assess his general conditions and to avoid further human rights violations.

Furthermore, one can also observe the increasing tendency of international human rights case-law to broaden the subjective scope of the right to be fairly heard beyond the sphere of a formal examination. Under the Pact of San José, the institution of a criminal law action—and the conduct of exhaustive criminal investigations—aims to give a voice to the victims and their next of kin. As highlighted by the Court in *'Mapiripán Massacre' v. Colombia*,[58] this obligation links the right to a fair hearing with the protection of the right to life.[59] The Strasbourg case-law on absent and anonymous witnesses—especially in the light of the developments that occurred after the *Al-Khawaja* case—should also be interpreted as an attempt to balance the accused's right to confrontation not only with the prosecutorial need not to waste relevant information but also with the need to give a voice to the injured party and to vulnerable witnesses. Against this background, EU law has also made important steps forward in departing from the traditional accused-centred understanding of criminal justice, providing specific rules on the right of the injured party to be heard and to give evidence in criminal proceedings.

The comparative analysis of international human rights law and EU law allows us to observe three main features of the right to a fair hearing, i.e. (a) the right to be fairly examined, (b) the right not to be examined and (c) the right to give statements in one's favour.

II. The Conditions of a Fair Examination

Certainly, defendants are in their most vulnerable position where they are questioned by the authorities in charge of investigations. Therefore, both international human rights law and EU law set forth some important requirements of fair

58 IACtHR, *'Mapiripán Massacre' v. Colombia*, § 219.

59 Ayala Corao and Rivero (2014), p. 123.

investigative hearings. In particular, the Inter-American Court emphasises the need for proper information before the first statement of the accused, while stressing the importance of legal assistance starting at the police questioning. A peculiarity of the Inter-American system is the strict link between the guarantee of a fair questioning and the right to confrontation in light of an overall consideration of the judicial guarantees in criminal justice. In this respect, the failure to provide the accused with legal assistance in a pre-trial questioning can also lead to an infringement of the right to confrontation, if the accused has not had the opportunity to challenge the prosecutorial arguments deduced by the evidence given at that time.

Since the *John Murray* case, the Strasbourg case-law has also made it clear that suspects must be granted the assistance of a lawyer even at the first police interrogation, a guarantee of such importance that it also entails the right to communicate with the counsel prior to the investigative hearing. EU law has inherited this approach by stressing the need for effective and active participation of the lawyer, who must be enabled to ask questions, make statements, request clarifications, and so on. Nevertheless, the protection ensured by EU law is still far from being fully satisfactory. There are no clear rules on some important issues, such as the information specifically due to the person to be examined and especially the powers of intervention of the competent authority for the hearing. Moreover, the solution of extending the right to access to a lawyer solely to those who become suspects or defendants during a hearing weakens the guarantee of legal assistance. At any rate, the right to access to a lawyer might not be sufficient to ensure legal assistance if the accused persons have no financial means to appoint a lawyer or are in a foreign country, which makes it difficult to find counsel to represent them in court. Following the European case-law, legal aid constitutes a necessary condition for the purposes of ensuring effective participation in criminal proceedings, especially in the case of coercive measures. In this light, it is noteworthy that the guarantee of legal aid in the case of deprivation of liberty stands at the top of the situations provided for by the recent Directive 2016/1919/EU.[60]

III. Nemo tenetur *Principle and the Right Not to Be Heard in Criminal Proceedings. The Admissibility of Incriminating Evidence Obtained Coercively*

Concerning the right not to be compelled to be examined, there is no doubt that, on the accused's side, the privilege against self-incrimination is a clear expression of the presumption of innocence, as pointed out by the Strasbourg Court in the *Saunders* case.[61] EU law has recently followed the same approach by enacting specific rules on the *nemo tenetur* principle into Directive 2016/343 on the

[60] Art. 2(1)(a) DirLA.

[61] Chapter 8, E.III.

presumption of innocence and the right to be present at trial.[62] Furthermore, international human rights case-law reveals a clear tendency to strengthen the right not to incriminate oneself. The Strasbourg case-law makes it a general guarantee not only of defendants but also of individuals not under investigation, providing them with protection against the risk of future prosecution. In this context, the Convention's protection was extended to the extent that the guarantee against self-incrimination can also include the right to silence as well as, under certain circumstances, the right not to go to the witness box.[63] Both the Inter-American Court and the European case-law, moreover, attached particular weight to the privilege against self-incrimination in situations of particular vulnerability for the person examined. Again, especially where interferences with fundamental rights are ongoing, the Strasbourg Court has made it clear that coercion cannot be allowed in order to obtain incriminating evidence from the person concerned—not even if this is justified by the need to protect other human rights acknowledged by the Convention, as compulsion used against vulnerable individuals inevitably results in inhuman treatment.

The increasing tendency to enhance the privilege against self-incrimination can also be observed in relation to the protective scope of this fundamental guarantee and the consequences of its infringement. This phenomenon is apparent from Strasbourg case-law in two ways. On one hand, the European Court—departing from its earlier case-law, which excluded the *nemo tenetur* principle in the case of evidence that could be taken against the will of the person examined—has acknowledged this guarantee in relation to information obtained through measures interfering with the physical integrity.[64] On the other hand, the Strasbourg case-law, while stressing that the authorities competent for administrative investigations are not bound by the same requirements set for criminal proceedings, has progressively abandoned its traditional approach, which made the infringement of Article 6 ECHR conditional on the fact that the information coercively obtained had played an exclusive or decisive role in the accused's conviction. From the *Saunders* judgment it is apparent that a violation of the Convention can arise regardless of the probative relevance attached to the information coercively gathered.[65] Most interestingly, this conclusion contrasts considerably with the Court's traditional approach to the right to confrontation.[66] The Inter-American Court partially departs from this approach, while broadening the protective scope of the guarantee beyond the sphere of criminal proceedings. Moreover, it is noteworthy that the Inter-American

---

[62]Chapter 10, C.III.1.

[63]Chapter 8, E.III.

[64]*Ibid.*

[65]*Ibid.*

[66]Trechsel (2005), p. 345.

case-law, while not giving clear indications on the limits of use of evidence coercively taken, focuses on the impact on the individuals concerned, even if subject to an administrative inquiry.

Another important feature of the right not to be examined can be seen on the victim's side. It has been noted that EU law grants the injured parties the right not only to be kept informed on the proceedings instituted for the offence committed against them but also the right not to be informed. In this context, the right not to be heard is certainly an important expression of the more general right to forget the crime and to be forgotten.

IV. The Right to Give Statements in One's Favour

International human rights instruments do not provide specific indications on the right of individuals involved in criminal proceedings to give evidence in their favour outside a formal questioning by the competent authority. Nevertheless, it lies at the core of the right to a fair hearing that the person charged with a criminal offence should have the opportunity to make his version of the events heard by an independent body. The aforementioned enshrinement by the American Convention of the right of any person accused of a criminal offence not just to obtain a public proceeding, but more specifically to be heard in public by an independent and impartial tribunal, should also be read in this light. On close examination, this fundamental requirement is not extraneous to the system of protection of human rights of the European Convention. It is noteworthy that, despite the great flexibility of the Strasbourg case-law on the right to personal participation in criminal proceedings, the lawfulness of the retrial or the remedy provided by domestic law largely depends on the fact that the competent court gives a voice to the person convicted *in absentia* prior to the decision-making.

At the EU level, the Union's recent legislation has again drawn the focus on the right of the victim to make his voice fairly heard. It has been noted that the indications provided by the Luxembourg Court in the *Katz* case make it clear that, even though national law does not allow victims to give testimonial evidence, EU law must in any case provide them with a proper opportunity to give evidence for the purposes of fact-finding. Following this approach, Directive 2012/29/EU enacted specific rules on the right of the injured party not only to give evidence but also to be heard in criminal proceedings. This acknowledgment is of utmost systematic importance, notwithstanding that it is somewhat blurred by the fact that the Court deemed the right of victims to be heard to have been fulfilled where the injured party was allowed to make statements or explanations in writing.

G. The Defence's Contribution to Evidence-Gathering

I. The Right to Produce Exculpatory Evidence

The comparative examination of the solutions provided by international human rights law in relation to the defence's contribution to the evidence-gathering has highlighted two main safeguards, namely (a) the right to produce exculpatory evidence and (b) the right to challenge the prosecutorial strategy by being involved in the collection of incriminating information. Concerning the former guarantee, both the international human rights charters examined in this study surely protect—in the light of the principle of equality of arms—the defence's right to adduce exculpatory evidence in open court. Instead, it is not self-evident whether and under what conditions the defence can carry out its own investigations. Certainly, private parties have no means of coercion when conducting their own investigations, if allowed by domestic law.[67] However, it can no longer be affirmed that in continental countries defence lawyers cannot formally question witnesses but must forward their request to the bodies in charge of public investigations.[68] Of course, the effective conduct of defensive investigations presupposes some qualitative requirements. In particular, both the Pact of San José and the Rome Convention protect the defence's claim for investigation by granting defendants the right to have sufficient time and facilities to organise their own defence.

The right to adduce exculpatory evidence holds specific relevance where restrictions on liberty or other fundamental rights are at risk. Under both the European Convention and the Pact of San José, the guarantee of *habeas corpus* entails the duty of the competent authorities to disclose adequate information to enable the detained person to produce exculpatory evidence. Moreover, the American Convention imposes on national authorities particularly demanding obligations in the case of a mandatory death penalty. From this it follows that the failure to provide the individuals accused of a capital offence with the necessary means to produce exculpatory evidence can entail an arbitrary deprivation of the right to life recognized under Article 4 ACHR.[69]

---

[67] *Ibid.*, 227.

[68] In this sense see instead Trechsel (2005), p. 227.

[69] Chapter 9, E.II.

II. The Right to Be Involved in the Taking of Incriminating Evidence. The Complex Challenges of the Right to Confrontation

1. Direct and Indirect Forms of Confrontation

More complex problems emerge in relation to the right to challenge prosecutorial evidence and to be involved in the taking of incriminating information. Despite clear similarities with other international human rights instruments, the American Convention gives particular focus on the direct contribution of the defence in obtaining the appearance of prosecutorial witnesses and in the taking of incriminating evidence.[70] The approach followed by the Pact of San José is certainly consistent with the importance reserved to the personal involvement of the accused, especially if communications with a lawyer were restricted prior to the trial hearing.[71] This is the result of the strong human rights approach of the American Convention, which, as noted, promotes the personal appearance of defendants in criminal hearings to enable the court to assess their general conditions and avoid further violations of fundamental rights. The formulation chosen by the drafters of the Rome Convention (and later transposed, albeit with some differences, in the International Covenant) in relation to the right to confrontation does not make it clear who should be entitled to examine prosecutorial witnesses if national law does not enable defendants to question them. Compared to the Pact of San José, the European Convention not only enables defence lawyers to question incriminating witnesses but also allows the judicial authority and even investigating bodies (*e.g.*, an investigating magistrate) to examine incriminating witnesses in the interests of the accused, eventually 'filtrating' the defence's questions.[72]

On close examination, both direct and indirect forms of confrontation give rise to human rights concerns. The clear favour of the American Convention towards the direct involvement of the accused does not mean that he can be left alone in the delicate confrontation with the accuser. We shall see that the effective exercise of the right to confrontation presupposes certain qualitative requirements being met, as highlighted by Inter-American case-law.[73]

The reference to the 'defence' rules out the American Convention tolerating solutions, such as those allowed by the European Convention. In particular, the Pact of San José, calling for direct involvement of the defence, does not allow prosecutorial witnesses to be examined by an investigative judge or a magistrate on behalf of the accused or forwarding his questions to the person examined. It is also questionable whether a hearing conducted in the presence of a special advocate not appointed by the defendant through a closed procedure—as the European Court

[70]Chapter 9, E.I.1.

[71]*Ibid.*

[72]Chapter 8, F.II.2.a.

[73]*Below*, G.II.3.

may seem to allow in the field of security law—fits the requirements of a fair examination. This strong approach of the American Convention in turn enhances the requirements of confrontation where a balance with other interests is required. Thus, even if the right to confrontation is to be limited to protect the life or safety of other individuals, the defence must be granted the opportunity to challenge the veracity of the witness's evidence by alternative methods. By contrast, the approach of the European case-law leads to the result that the examination of a key prosecutorial witness by a lawyer not appointed by the accused does not necessarily infringe on the right to confrontation.

In general terms, it is debatable whether a cross-examination conducted by a lawyer suffices to fulfil the standards established by international human rights law, regardless of the conditions under which the lawyer was appointed. As noted, the Strasbourg case-law makes the convention compatible with the widest range of possibilities. The European Court not only allows for confrontation with the accused but also considers the Convention's requirements to be satisfied where only the lawyer could cross-examine a prosecutorial witness.

This approach, which reveals a clear underestimation of the accused's contribution to evidence-gathering, has in turn impinged on the developments that have occurred in EU law. Far from ensuring to accused persons the right to be present at investigative acts, the 2013 Directive on the right to access to a lawyer provides a rather weak solution, largely referring to national law.[74] Moreover, we have seen that recent Directive 2016/343/EU in turn construed the right to be present in criminal proceedings in such restrictive terms that it excludes the accused having the right to take part in investigative activities[75] and out-of-court decisions. As far as the right to confrontation is concerned, EU law does not apparently acknowledge the right of defendants to examine the accuser, the investigative acts expressly laid down by Directive 2013/48/EU requiring the involvement of the accused as a source of evidence. On close examination, not only can member states provide for legal assistance in further investigative acts but furthermore the 'confrontation' indicated by this legislation can also be interpreted as referring to an investigative act entailing an 'active' role of the accused, namely the confrontation with a prosecutorial witness. However, EU law does not go so far as to require the defendant's personal involvement in the gathering of incriminating evidence, while also not providing for specific indications on the role of the lawyer.

2. Context of Confrontation

The flexible approach of international human rights case-law has also led to a significant expansion of the scope of application of confrontation. This phenomenon is particularly apparent in the European case-law. Notwithstanding the repeated

[74]Chapter 10, C.IV.

[75]*Ibid.*, B.I.

claim that confrontation must ordinarily take place in a public hearing and with the adversarial method, the Strasbourg Court has never gone so far as to circumscribe the scope of confrontation to the trial phase. To be sure, the European case-law has always considered the Rome Convention not to provide binding indications on the stage of the proceedings at which confrontation should take place. An implicit answer to the question of whether the Convention also allows for confrontation in the pre-trial phase was provided by the *Imbrioscia* ruling. Here, the Court even imposed a clear duty of diligence on the defence, which must request to be involved in the procedure aimed at the collection of incriminating evidence.[76] Again, the broad understanding of the scope of this guarantee is probably the result of the systematic approach to the right to confrontation as a part of the more general right to a fair hearing.

The Inter-American Court has never expressly dealt with this issue. However, implicit indications may be deduced from the existing case-law. In particular, it is worth observing that the Court considered the contracting states responsible for providing the accused with legal assistance at the police hearing.[77] The need to anticipate legal assistance should not only be viewed in the light of the accused's right to a fair hearing in the pre-trial phase but is also justified by the risks concerned with the possible confrontation with police evidence at a later stage of the proceedings.

Compared to this case-law, the flexible approach followed by the European Court gives rise to human rights concerns. It can be very dangerous for the accused if, during the pre-trial inquiry, the competent prosecutor or the police can gather incriminating evidence by questioning key witnesses or the victim without the need for a confrontation with the suspect, relying on the fact that he will be given this opportunity at a later stage of the proceedings. Moreover, the Court accepts on the same conditions the admission of evidence taken out of court without the defence's participation, which can then be used to the same extent as information obtained with the involvement of the accused. At first sight, this approach is very different from the exclusionary logic that governs criminal justice in various countries, even of continental Europe, such as Italy. On close examination, the main deficiency of this approach seems to be a rather weak understanding of the *audi alteram partem* rule, which, as observed in relation to *in absentia* trials, cannot be collocated indifferently at the time of the hearing or at later stages without risks for the individuals concerned.

Nevertheless, the European case-law's openness towards out-of-court confrontation must not be interpreted too broadly. As noted, both in the *Imbrioscia* and in the *S.N.* judgment the Court made it clear that the defence must show a concrete interest in participation in the pre-trial questioning of prosecutorial witnesses. This does not entail, however, that the Convention will not be infringed upon if this interest does not arise. In other words, where national law enables the defence to be

---

[76] Chapter 8, F.III.2.

[77] Chapter 9, E.I.2.

present and the interested party has requested it, the competent authority cannot refuse participation, relying on future confrontations at some later stage of the proceedings. In this case, the untested evidence should certainly not be used against the accused. This does not mean that, when national law does not allow suspects to be present at the pre-trial questioning of prosecutorial witnesses, the information gathered can unconditionally be admitted at trial provided a later confrontation took place. Nor can incriminating evidence gathered out of court be used unconditionally against the accused simply due to the fact that the defence did not take any initiative, a result that can also depend on the failure of the competent authorities to inform the defence about this possibility. Although there is no clear case-law from Strasbourg on these cases, it appears that the possibility of using the evidence gathered without the defence's participation should be assessed in the light of the restrictions suffered by the accused and the repercussions of this evidence on the fundamental rights of the individuals concerned.

3. Conditions of Effective Confrontation

Certainly, the effective exercise of the right to confrontation presupposes the fulfilment of certain qualitative requirements. It has been observed that the existence of an undefined charge or the lack of information on previous statements given by the person to be examined do not enable the accused to properly challenge incriminating evidence, even if confrontation has to take place in open court. In such cases, the requirement of adversarial argument can result in a mostly formal guarantee. The problem is aggravated in the case of pre-trial hearings, in which the need to provide the accused with information safeguards is enhanced. In this respect, the European Convention appears to provide rather weak solutions. In the *Isgrò* case, we have noted that the Court, departing from the Commission's approach, ruled out a violation of the right to confrontation solely on the grounds that the accused had to face alone a confrontation with his accuser out of trial. This conclusion—based on the argument that the non-anonymous character of the witness testimony, on one side, and the absence of the prosecutor, on the other, rendered the assistance of the defence lawyer superfluous[78]—did not reflect a correct understanding of the importance of legal assistance for the purpose of effective confrontation.

This conclusion distinguishes the European case-law from the Inter-American case-law, which has never allowed similar limitations to the assistance of a lawyer. Here, legal assistance holds such importance that in the *Castillo Petruzzi* judgment, the Inter-American Court held that the right of the defence to examine prosecutorial witnesses also entails the need to avoid undue restrictions on the victim's lawyers.[79] The need for enhanced defence rights—in terms of effective legal assistance and

[78]ECtHR, *Isgrò v. Italy*, § 35 et seq.

[79]Chapter 9, E.I.2.

access to the prosecutorial file—was also evident in the *Palamara Iribarne* judgment, which confirms the clear attempt of the Inter-American Court to broaden the right to confrontation with an overall consideration of the judicial guarantees in criminal proceedings. Even though the question at stake here was not whether to provide the accused with legal assistance for a confrontation with his accuser, the message left by Inter-American case-law was that effective legal assistance must always be provided in order to permit the accused to challenge any incriminating evidence or arguments brought forward by the prosecutorial authority.

It cannot be excluded that the Strasbourg case-law has influenced the developments in EU law, which, despite ensuring access to a lawyer in investigative acts that require the presence of the accused persons pursuant to national law, provides for rather flexible conditions on the waiver of the right to legal assistance.[80] It is true that here also, clear information must be provided to the accused, who should express his waiver voluntarily and unequivocally. Yet Directive 2013/48/EU does not clarify the authority before which defendants should waive their right to legal assistance. This issue is of utmost importance in the pre-trial phase, especially if one adopts a broad interpretation of the notion of 'confrontation'. At any rate, a close examination of the 2013 legislation clearly reveals the intention of the EU institutions not to burden member states with the task of providing suspects with legal assistance beyond the limits laid down at the domestic level.

III. A Systematic Understanding of the Right to Confrontation. The Need to Balance the Right to Challenge Incriminating Evidence and the Protection of Other Human Rights

Another significant implication of the systematic consideration of the right to confrontation by international human rights case-law is the need to balance the right to challenge incriminating evidence and the protection of other human rights. The analysis of both European and Inter-American case-law highlights the increasing tendency to avoid an absolute interpretation of the right to confrontation, which cannot unconditionally undermine other human rights acknowledged by the two charters.[81] Among the rights to be preserved, the need to protect particular types of 'witnesses' (in the broad sense that this notion has assumed in international human rights law) requires the adoption of alternative methods of confrontation, such as anonymous testimony. The justification for these arrangements varies depending on the interests at stake. In the case of vulnerable witnesses, their examination in open court through the adversarial method not only can negatively affect the person to be heard but can also endanger the reliability of the evidence-gathering. In criminal proceedings for serious organised crimes, a court hearing of undercover informants

[80]Chapter 10, C.IV.

[81]See respectively Chapter 8, F.II.1 and Chapter 9, E.I.1.

and collaborators with justice would frustrate the aim of complex investigations, while entailing great risks for the life, physical integrity and security of the person examined. In the latter cases, the Strasbourg case-law clearly broadens the protective scope of these interests by calling for a balance between the right to confrontation and the rights of the families of prosecutorial witnesses.

An interesting common aspect, however, is that both the European Court and the Inter-American case-law require a proper justification for the means used in lieu of direct confrontation as well as a strict review of whether these measures were adequately adopted in a given case. It is noteworthy that the recent European case-law—while enhancing the probative value of untested evidence used as the main basis for the decision-making—has tightened the duty to provide a justification for the use of this evidence, requiring a concrete risk for the witness to be justified and supported by additional evidence.[82]

Despite these similarities, some significant differences still distinguish the approaches followed by the two Courts. Under the American Convention, the adoption of alternative forms of examination can in no way prejudice the right of the 'defence' to challenge the veracity of the evidence produced by an incriminating witness.[83] The Strasbourg Court does not consider the lawyer's direct involvement in the hearing of a prosecutorial witness to be absolutely necessary. A clear example is the *S.N.* judgment, in which the Court satisfied itself with the fact that the defence lawyer was merely allowed to see the tape and pose indirect questions with a view to a second hearing, notwithstanding that the counsel had actively participated neither in the first nor in the second questioning. Apparently, the solutions adopted by the national authorities in *van Mechelen v. The Netherlands*—both the defendant and his counsel had been placed in an adjacent room and could follow the witness' examination and ask questions—seemed to enhance the right to confrontation. Nevertheless, the European Court rejected this arrangement on the grounds of an incorrect consideration of the tasks of police officers, and after *Sher et al.*, we can also expect a further reduction in the standards of protection set by the Convention in the area of the right to confrontation.

[82]ECtHR, Grand Chamber, *Al-Khawaja and Tahery v. United Kingdom*, § 124. See Vogel (2017), p. 36 f.

[83]Chapter 9, E.I.1.

H. Participatory Rights and the Requirements of a Fair Decision-Making. The Complex Trade-Offs Among Conflicting Interests Required by International Human Rights Law

I. Premise

Along with reconstructing the participatory rights involved in the collection of criminal evidence, international human rights law provides for some important indications with regard to the defence's contribution to fact-finding and the decision on the merits. Two main problems emerge from the examined case-law, which relate to factual and argumentative contributions to decision-making. The former highlights another important implication of the right to confrontation, concerned with the use of out-of-court evidence obtained without the defence's participation, with a view to the decision on the merits of the case. In this respect, two further situations should be distinguished, depending on whether defendants had a fair opportunity for confrontation at a later stage of the proceedings. The latter reveals the importance of the parties' argumentation for the purposes of the decision-making not only on factual but also on legal issues.

II. The Right to Confrontation and the Proof of Guilt

1. The Admissibility of Out-of-Court Evidence in Cases of Subsequent Confrontation and the Problem of Anonymous Testimony

International human rights case-law has progressively set forth different conditions on the use of out-of-court evidence gathered without the defence's participation. It has been observed that as a matter of principle, both the Strasbourg Court and the Inter-American case-law left the door open for the use of out-of-court evidence if confrontation could take place at a later stage of the proceedings. It should also be remembered that the European case-law provided such a broad interpretation of the Convention that it allowed for the use of incriminating evidence gathered not just in a hearing that involved the defence lawyer but by an investigative judge in favour of the accused. From this it follows that under the Rome Convention, subsequent confrontation—no matter whether conducted by the defence or an independent authority—enables full use of the testimonial evidence given in the pre-trial phase.

A delicate problem arises where subsequent confrontation produces evidence inconsistent with that gathered at the pre-trial stage. The problem is enhanced if a contradiction arises between hearsay evidence and the information gathered at trial. The Inter-American Court has never dealt with this issue. By contrast, some important indications may be deduced by the few cases examined by the Strasbourg Court. In particular, the European case-law suggests an informal approach to the admissibility of hearsay evidence by ruling out that out-of-court statements used to counter the evidence given in open court can *a priori* be denied any probative value for the decision-making. The focus on the possibility of the accused examining a prosecutorial witness in court has led the Strasbourg Court to depart from the solutions adopted in relation to untested evidence. The message emerging from European case-law, as noted, is that the negative effects deriving from the use of incriminating evidence collected out of court without the involvement of the defence are attenuated if effective confrontation is ensured at a later stage of the proceedings.[84]

This approach, however, encounters specific limitations where confrontation could only take place by means of an anonymous hearing. Traditionally, the European Court, despite considering anonymous testimony in principle compatible with the Convention, excluded it being the sole or primary basis of a conviction.[85] Recent case-law, however, significantly softened this approach by extending the findings of the *Al-Khawaja* judgment to the field of anonymous testimony. By contrast, the *Norín Catrimán* judgment, although issued in 2014, still followed the sole and decisive evidence doctrine in strict terms. This highlights the cautious approach of the Inter-American case-law to the anonymous testimony gathered through voice distorter and a screen hiding the faces of the witnesses whose identity was only known to the competent judges.

It is questionable why the Inter-American Court maintained this rigorous solution. It is unlikely that the Court ignored the developments that occurred in the European case-law, so the reasons for this approach should lie elsewhere. It is worth observing that in the *Norín Catrimán* case the Inter-American Court did not need to examine the probative value of the untested statements. Even though the measures used in the trials against Norín Catrimán and Pichún Paillalao could have in the abstract safeguarded the defendants' right to examine the prosecutorial witnesses, the Court found that the judicial reasoning was manifestly insufficient. This argument should have sufficed to determine the unfairness of the proceedings. At least in relation to those defendants prosecuted under the 2000 Chilean code of criminal procedure and the Anti-Terrorism Law, the failure to properly justify the decision to hide the witnesses' identity entailed unjustified restriction on the suspect's defence rights.[86] Why should the Court then engage in further argumentation that was not needed and was formulated in such rigorous terms as to demonstrate the unfairness of the conviction of Pichún Paillalao mainly based on untested evidence, whereas it deemed the acquittal Norín Catrimán fair because of the minor weight attached to untested statements?

---

[84]Chapter 8, F.III.2.

[85]*Ibid.*

[86]A different conclusion can be drawn in relation to the proceedings brought against Ancalaf Llaupe, who was prosecuted under the 1906 code, which provided for a pre-trial phase usually held in secret (*sumario*). Cf. IACtHR, *Norín Catrimán et al. v. Chile*, § 235.

On close examination, these conclusions might perhaps be explained in the light of an overall scrutiny of the case at hand, which went beyond the problem of the guarantee of confrontation. The Court found it not fully proved that the defendants' conduct entailed a risk for the life or physical integrity of the witnesses whose identity was protected. It was also relevant that individuals belonging to indigenous people were prosecuted and detained for Anti-Terrorism offences on the basis of a presumption that the acts committed with certain means demonstrated the existence of terroristic goals. The Court stressed the importance of the *nullum poena sine lege* principle in relation to anti-terrorism offences, a principle that requires a clear distinction to be drawn between terroristic and ordinary offences to avoid individuals being investigated and prosecuted on the basis of anti-terrorism law in cases that would satisfy the requirements of ordinary criminal law. This can have severe human rights consequences, as in Chile a prosecution for terroristic offences both justifies the adoption of special restrictions on individual rights during the investigations and entails the risk of more serious sentences and accessory penalties with special disqualifications having a considerable impact on the person convicted.[87]

Starting with these premises, the Inter-American Court found that the presumption of terroristic goals, relying on the fact that the offence was allegedly committed by certain means, laid down by the Chilean Anti-Terrorism Law, infringed on both the *nullum poena sine lege* principle and the presumption of innocence.[88] This in turn affected the fairness of the overall proceedings instituted against the defendants, which put them in the vulnerable condition of victims of an unlawful criminal law action, thus justifying the rigorous approach adopted to safeguard their defence rights and the right to confrontation.

2. The Conditions on Use of Untested Evidence

Different problems relate to cases in which incriminating evidence was gathered out of court without the accused's participation, where confrontation could not take place at any stage of the proceedings. The European Court has traditionally dealt with this issue by examining the use of evidence given by absent witnesses, a situation that can in turn be traced back to different situations. The sole and decisive evidence doctrine, which has characterised the traditional approach of European case-law to untested evidence, has contributed considerably to distinguishing the European law of evidence from the rigid exclusionary rules present in various individual countries. As noted, the developments initiated by the *Al-Khawaja* judgment enabled the Court to enter a territory always considered to exclusively belong to the exclusive competence of national law, namely the territory of admissibility of untested evidence. Yet this process was already underway before *Al-Khawaja*, as the sole and decisive evidence test posed a further condition of use

[87] *Ibid.*, § 164.

[88] *Ibid.*, § 171 et seq.

of incriminating evidence that was not acknowledged everywhere by European countries.

Apparently, the decisiveness test set forth by the Strasbourg case-law, far from being self-sufficient, depended on the solutions adopted by the fact-finders at the national level. As observed, the Court was called upon to ascertain whether national authorities provided defendants with an opportunity for confrontation with the accuser and whether the decision-makers based the convictions solely or mainly on untested evidence. Furthermore, the very notion of 'decisive evidence' is by definition referential, highlighting a link with the national rules of the relevant country, which lay down the degree of proof required to convict the accused. However, the Strasbourg case-law did not always consider itself bound by the assessment made by the national authorities. The Court often reserved the competence to evaluate whether the accused had been granted a proper opportunity of confrontation and whether the measures adopted to compensate the lack of confrontation were adequate to save the overall fairness of the procedure under examination. Moreover, despite its apparent strictness, the concept of 'decisive evidence' is inevitably ambivalent, giving rise to highly discretionary assessments. It is extremely difficult to calculate and exactly measure the weight of a single piece of evidence in the decision-making, a difficult task even in countries traditionally based on the obligation of the judiciary to give reasoned decisions. It is even more demanding to re-construct *ex post facto* the weight attached by another judicial body. Nevertheless, there can be little doubt that the decisiveness test already enabled the Court to re-define the probative value of the information used at the domestic level pursuant to its own criteria.[89]

Against this background, the *Al-Khawaja* doctrine enhanced the decision-making powers of the Court. One of the most significant innovations brought about by this judgment and the subsequent Strasbourg case-law was to shift the focus from the identification of a fair opportunity for confrontation to the assessment of the reliability of untested evidence in the light of the means adopted at the domestic level to compensate the accused for the lack of confrontation. Doubtless, the new reliability test has strengthened the powers of the Court in assessing the suitability of the arrangements made by the national authorities to counterbalance the lack of confrontation. By this means, the European case-law made itself the ultimate judge of the overall fairness of criminal proceedings pursuant to its own criteria. The main problem is that the Court's criteria are still undefined, which does not appear to be in line with the fundamental requirements of legal certainty.

Under the American Convention, there was nothing similar to the developments that occurred in the Strasbourg case-law over the last years. Nevertheless, the conclusions reached in the *Norín Catrimán* judgement allow us to suppose that the Inter-American Court will probably not depart from the rigorous decisiveness test where the individuals concerned—especially if victims of complex human rights violations—had no opportunity to be confronted with their accusers.

---

[89] Jackson and Summers (2012), p. 339.

III. Argumentative Contribution to the Decision-Making

.The second problematic area relates to the argumentative contribution of the defence to the decision-making. In a modern model of fair criminal justice, the private parties should be able to make their own contribution to the decision on the merits not only by means of exculpatory evidence or by participating in the collection of incriminating evidence but also by adducing arguments against the prosecutorial reconstruction of the facts. Both in Europe and Latin America, international human rights case-law attaches great importance to the argumentative contribution of the accused, to the extent that the overall fairness of criminal proceedings is inevitably undermined where defendants are not put in a position to make observations on the prosecutorial allegations. Under the European Convention, this expression of the *audi alteram partem* rule cuts across criminal proceedings and its importance increases in higher instances in which no further evidence can be produced.[90]

One particular aspect of this problem concerns the argumentative contribution of the defence on legal issues. We have noted that the Strasbourg case-law adopts a more rigorous approach to the right to participation in criminal proceedings where the defendant is equipped with legal knowledge. Moreover, the case-law of both the Inter-American Court and the Strasbourg Court emphasises the need to provide the accused with proper information on the charge in relation not only to the factual features of the alleged offence but also to its legal classification. Remarkably, this information duty is not limited to the initial charge but entails the obligation of the competent authorities to inform the accused of eventual changes to the accusation. This should also include information on the amendment of the legal classification. Yet the solutions on this point are not identical in the European and the Inter-American case-law.

Apparently, the Strasbourg case-law emphasises a stricter approach by requiring defendants to be properly informed of the legal classification of the offence under investigation. At least in its earlier jurisprudence, however, the European Court linked the information on the legal classification with the right of effective defence, to the extent that it applied here the same functional approach used in relation to the general right to information on the accusation.[91] The Court departed from this approach in more recent cases, a result that, as noted, can largely be explained by the fact that the decision to change *nomen juris* was issued at a higher instance in which no further evidence could be taken.[92] Consequently, the accused must be put in a position to challenge the new legal classification with exculpatory arguments, especially where no further instance is allowed. There are no indications suggesting that the Court will in the near future follow this approach, especially when the legal classification is amended or integrated at the first instance. In this case, the European Court does not consider the right to information infringed in any situation

[90]Chapter 8, F.IV.

[91]*Ibid.*

[92]*Ibid.*

where defendants had a concrete restriction on their defence rights but tends to save the fairness of the proceedings even though the accusation was amended after the end of the evidence-gathering if the judgment can be reviewed at a higher instance on the accused's initiative.

Compared to these solutions, the Inter-American case-law seems to provide defendants with stronger protection. Especially in death penalty cases, information on any change to legal classification not only should be provided to the extent required by national law but must also comply with the requirements set by the American Convention. From this it follows that under the Pact of San José, unlike what happens under the European Convention, the competent authority, while amending the legal classification of the alleged offence, must give the accused the possibility of producing further evidence and the trial hearing must, if needed, be suspended.[93] These conclusions also apply to the case in which the change of *nomen juris* was due to the taking of evidence as well as to the case in which the competent authority considered some facts as proved.

Beyond these differences, a weak point characterises the case-law of both the European and the Inter-American Court, that is, the maintenance of a rather rigid distinction between factual and legal issues. On this basis, the Inter-American Court accepts certain restrictions on the right to information on the legal classification if the facts remained unchanged.[94] The European case-law, while strengthening the right to information on the amendment of the legal classification made in a higher instance, acknowledged the accused's right to obtain the postponement of the hearing in order to make observations against the new *nomen juris*.[95] Notwithstanding its merits, this arrangement is not the best solution, especially where the accused has no further possibility of producing exculpatory evidence against the amended charge.

I. *Audi alteram partem* and Restrictions on Freedom. The Requirements of International Human Rights Case-Law and the Developments in the EU Legislation

I. Information Rights of Arrested and Detained Individuals

The comparative analysis of international human rights law and EU law reveals the need for enhanced protection of the participatory safeguards of the individuals subjected to measures of coercion. In particular, restrictions on freedom place any person arrested or detained in a highly vulnerable position, which requires

[93] Chapter 9, F.

[94] *Ibid.*

[95] Chapter 8, F.IV.

special protection against arbitrary and unlawful coercion and broad assistance to take all the possible initiatives against the measure applied.

The protection of the individuals deprived of their liberty starts with the information rights, which must be ensured to the extent necessary to enable them to understand the grounds for such drastic measures and to undertake proceedings against the state's action. At the same time, the granting of proper information by the arresting authority constitutes a necessary condition for the fairness of the subsequent procedure. The core importance of the right to information in the field of restrictions on freedom explains the broad scope of application of this guarantee, which in international human rights law goes beyond the sphere of criminal justice. Despite the limited English formulation of Article 7, the other official language versions of the American Convention make it clear that information must be ensured to any person detained or in any way arrested.[96] This broad expression covers even forms of deprivation that, despite being frequent in practice, cannot be classified among the traditional situations of arrest and detention. The reference to the grounds for arrest and 'the charge or charges' filed against the person concerned cannot therefore be used as an argument to restrict the scope of this fundamental guarantee to criminal proceedings.[97] In this regard, the more prudent formulation of the European Convention, which requires to information on 'any charge', clearly indicates the far-reaching scope of the right to information.[98] At the EU level, instead, Directive 2012/13 is expressly focused on criminal justice. However, the protection provided by EU law does not presuppose the formal institution of a criminal inquiry, encompassing also the police arrest enforced before the prosecutor takes charge of investigation, if provided for by national law.[99]

As far as the scope of the guarantee is concerned, the fact that the (at least earlier) case-law of the European Court mainly linked the right to information with the *habeas corpus* proceedings[100] probably influenced the approach followed by EU law. Thus, the 2012 legislation required member states to ensure information on both the grounds for arrest and the offence under investigation, so as to enable the individuals concerned to challenge the measure applied and to request release, if allowed and under the conditions provided for by national law.[101] Moreover, the recourse of *habeas corpus* is certainly not the sole aim of the information due to arrested or detained persons. Remarkably, the European case-law following the *van der Leer* judgment, which called for an autonomous understanding of the guarantees of paragraphs 2 and 4 of Article 5 ECHR,[102] highlights that the right to information should also be interpreted in the light of the obligation of the law

[96] Chapter 9, G.I.

[97] *Ibid.*

[98] Chapter 8, G.I.

[99] Chapter 10, D.

[100] Chapter 8, G.I.

[101] Chapter 10, D.

[102] Chapter 8, G.I.

enforcement authority to promptly bring the arrested person before a judicial or other independent body. It might be argued that the limited approach of the 2012 Directive is due to the failure of EU law to acknowledge this fundamental guarantee. This argument, however, would be misleading, since the right to a prompt independent oversight of the lawfulness of arrest or detention also holds relevance at the EU level since it integrates, at least in the terms acknowledged by the European Convention, the contents of Article 6 of the EU Charter of fundamental rights.

The need for broad interpretation of the aims of the guarantee of information in the field of restrictions on liberty is also clear under the American Convention. In particular, the goal of ensuring an independent scrutiny of arbitrary and unlawful detention lies at the core of the protection provided by the Pact of San José to the right to information, which sets the necessary conditions for the examination of the person concerned, with a view to avoiding further human rights violations.[103]

Concerning the qualitative requirements of the guarantee of information, both international human rights law and EU law emphasise the need for simple and understandable information, in order to make the individuals concerned aware of the situation they are suffering from and to enable them to take possible initiatives against arrest or detention. Also in this regard, the American Convention provides for enhanced protection by requiring information to be also granted to the arrestee's next of kin as well as to a lawyer and even a consular official.[104] EU law follows a similar approach by requiring member states to provide information to third parties and to allow communication between the detained person and a lawyer.[105] However, both the Pact of San José and the Rome Convention provide for vague indications as to the timing of information, only requiring it to be ensured promptly. This imprecise indication led to the European Court allowing for only legal information to be given at the time of the arrest, provided that the person concerned will receive complete information at a later stage.[106] Subsequent case-law further confirmed this approach, which weakened the scope of the guarantee of information by offloading onto individuals the burden of inferring the grounds for arrest or detention from the questioning.[107]

Under the Pact of San José, it is clear that the arresting authority holds responsibility for informing the person concerned, responsibility that the Inter-American Court extended significantly, even to third parties.[108] Moreover, the acknowledgment by the San José case-law that information on the charge, unlike that on the grounds for arrest or detention, must be given in writing is surely not a valid reason

---

[103] Chapter 9, G.I.

[104] *Ibid.*

[105] Chapter 10, D.

[106] Chapter 8, G.I.

[107] *Ibid.*

[108] Chapter 9, G.I.

for delaying the granting of information.[109] Notwithstanding these positive solutions, it is regrettable that the Inter-American Court softened the guarantee in cases of short-term restrictions on liberty, to the point that the arrest order need not necessarily be shown to the person concerned.[110] An interesting solution is the creation of Letters of Rights, such as that required by the 2012 Directive on information rights, even though the effectiveness of this guarantee is also weakened by the strongly functional approach adopted by EU law, according to which, as noted, information aims at enabling the person arrested or detained to challenge the measure applied.[111]

On close examination, the protection granted by both the San José and the Rome Convention is far from being complete and may not be sufficient for the purposes pursued. In particular, no information is due under Article 5(2) ECHR on the evidence collected by the investigative bodies and especially on the pieces of evidence that supported the decision to deprive the accused of his freedom. This seems to contradict the far-reaching approach followed by the Strasbourg Court in relation to *habeas corpus*, an approach that, however, ensures broad information for the purposes of procedures activated by the defence.[112] In this regard, EU law appears to provide greater protection by requiring information also to be granted on existing documents.[113] On the one hand, this solution is significantly weakened by the fact that the individuals arrested or detained must only be given access to the essential information needed to challenge the measure applied. On the other, EU law does not go so far as to require that evidentiary information be necessarily granted at the time of the arrest, provided, however, that it is ensured prior to the competent court ruling on the lawfulness of the coercion enforced pursuant to Article 5(4) ECHR.

II. The Right to a Prompt Independent Review of the Lawfulness of Coercion and the Need for an Overall Human Rights Assessment

Although several Constitutions and almost all international human rights instruments acknowledge the right to a prompt independent scrutiny of arrest and detention, the selected human rights charters provide different models for solutions in relation to the judicial oversight of the lawfulness of the coercion. As noted, this oversight constitutes a guarantee of utmost importance to avoid arbitrary detention, especially where restrictions on liberty are enforced without previous assessment of

[109] *Ibid.*

[110] *Ibid.*

[111] Chapter 10, D.

[112] Chapter 8, G.III.

[113] Chapter 10, D.

its justification and necessity on the part of an independent body. The comparative examination of the Rome Convention and the Pact of San José highlights a considerable difference as to the scope of this fundamental guarantee, which under the former is limited to the arrest or detention in criminal proceedings, whereas the latter ensures a safeguard applicable to any arrest or detention even beyond the sphere of criminal justice. Yet this difference is less stark than it appears. On the one hand, the explicit reference to the situations of Article 3 (c) ECHR cannot lead to the conclusion that the European Convention restricts the right to a prompt court hearing to cases of remand detention, since the guarantee holds even greater importance in the case of police arrest.[114] On the other, the link with criminal justice also lies at the core of the solution enacted by the American Convention,[115] which emphasises the right of the person arrested or detained to be tried within a reasonable time or to be released.[116] However, it would probably be an exaggeration to say that the Inter-American case-law—requiring respect for this guarantee in any case of deprivation of liberty, *e.g.* in relation to a detention for the purpose of an expulsion procedure—departed from the clear intention of the drafters of the Pact of San José.[117]

On close examination, the broader scope of application of the Pact of San José can be explained in the light of the goals of the guarantee. Under the American Convention, a prompt judicial review not only aims at ensuring to the individuals concerned a scrutiny of the lawfulness of the measure applied but also constitutes a general means of avoiding further human rights violations, such as ill-treatment and forced disappearances.[118] Furthermore, this goal corresponds to the general approach of the American Convention to the judicial guarantees, which enable the San José institutions to carry out a complex assessment of the overall respect for the human rights acknowledged. This aspect clearly distinguishes the approach of the Inter-American case-law from that followed by the Strasbourg Court, which, despite not overlooking the need to protect the individuals arrested or detained from the risk of ill-treatment and life-threatening measures, focuses on the aim of ensuring a remedy against arbitrary and unlawful interferences with the right to freedom.[119] Remarkably, the European Court emphasises the guarantee of judicial oversight under Article 5(3) ECHR by requiring the arrestee also to be brought before a judge when restriction on freedom was ordered by the judicial authority and even in the presence of the defendant's lawyer.[120] The Inter-American case-law also enhanced the right to judicial control, finding an infringement of the Pact of San José because the competent judge, despite being present at the moment of the

---

[114] Chapter 8, G.II.

[115] Casal (2014), p. 196.

[116] Art. 7(5) ACHR.

[117] In this sense see instead Casals (2014), p. 196.

[118] Chapter 9, G.II.

[119] Chapter 8, G.II.

[120] *Ibid.*

arrest, heard the person concerned only 26 days after the enforcement of detention.[121]

This case-law raises further questions, which allows us to observe other important safeguards in the solutions provided by international human rights instruments. The first question is whether the competent judge can autonomously decide on the lawfulness of arrest or detention or whether the person arrested also has the right to appear in court and to be heard by the judicial authority. The answer is clearly positive under the American Convention, which does not allows us to interpret the right to a prompt judicial review exclusively as an objective guarantee, for it also entails the right of the individuals concerned to make themselves heard by an independent authority.[122] Moreover, the requirement that the person arrested or detained be not only formally put at the disposal of the judicial authority but also physically brought to court can be explained in the light of the aforementioned broad scope of the guarantee under the Pact of San José. It is not easy to give a positive answer to this question under the European Convention. In the 1984 *McGoff* judgment, the Court had stressed the need for a personal hearing of the arrested person. However, a few years later, the Strasbourg Court—dealing with the *Fox, Campbell and Hartley* case—relaxed this requirement, ruling out a violation of the Convention, although the applicants were first examined by the police and could only infer the necessary information from the police questioning.[123] Of course, granting a court hearing results in a rather weak guarantee if a lawyer cannot assist the individuals concerned. The European Court acknowledged this guarantee in the *John Murray* case for the first time. However, this conclusion was reached in such a Solomon-like manner that the Strasbourg judges left the door open for restrictions on legal assistance due to good cause, a possibility luckily dropped by subsequent case-law.[124]

Furthermore, the effectiveness of this guarantee largely depends on the meaning that can be attached to the adverb 'promptly'. In this regard, the case-law of both the European Court and Inter-American Court has clearly enhanced the protective scope of this requirement, providing a highly dynamic interpretation of the provisions concerned that considerably departs from the understanding of the judicial review of lawfulness of the arrest or detention at the domestic level. This applies, on one hand, to the first contact with the judicial authority. The solution reached in the *Castillo Petruzzi* case makes it clear that the requirement of a prompt judicial hearing cannot be delayed even if the national rules on serious crimes, such as terrorism, allow for the arrested person to remain without judicial review for a long period.[125] On the other, granting a first independent review is not sufficient to guarantee that a long-term restrictive measure, such as remand detention, does not

[121] Chapter 9, G.II.

[122] *Ibid.*

[123] Chapter 8, G.II.

[124] *Ibid.*

[125] Chapter 9, G.II.

exceed the limits set by the principles of necessity and proportionality. In this regard, the European Court redefined the terms of the guarantee of Article 5 (3) ECHR, a rather unfortunate provision, which apparently considers the right to be tried in a reasonable time frame as an alternative to the right to be released during the investigation phase. Following the Court's approach, this provision should be understood as requiring the accused's release whenever custody exceeds the reasonable length on the basis of the concrete information of the case and with regard to the presumption of innocence.[126] Starting with this premise, contracting states must ensure a constant judicial scrutiny of the lawfulness of the ongoing detention.

III. The Defence's Right to Challenge Unlawful Detention. Participatory Rights in habeas corpus *Proceedings*

Habeas corpus as noted, is historically one of the most protective tools against arbitrary deprivation of liberty. Therefore, both the Rome Convention and the Pact of San José enacted specific provisions on this powerful legal action, enabling any person subject to restrictions on freedom to undertake proceedings to obtain an independent oversight of the measure applied. The core importance of *habeas corpus* in both the civil and common law world explains the way this guarantee was laid down by international human rights charters, which shaped it with the broadest scope of application beyond the sphere of criminal justice. At first glance, EU law does not deal with any means of reaction against restrictions on freedom. Yet the EU Directive 2012/13 recognised the right to information due to the individuals arrested or detained, with a view to enabling them to challenge the measure applied and to request to be released, to the extent allowed by national law.

The guarantee of *habeas corpus* complements the right to be brought before an independent authority, providing even more enhanced protection by entrusting the scrutiny solely to the judicial authority. However, neither the focus on the exclusive competence of the judiciary nor a consideration of the origin of *habeas corpus*, aimed at providing a remedy against restrictions on liberty carried by administrative authorities, can lead to a radical exclusion of this guarantee in all the cases of deprivation of freedom ordered by a judicial authority. The European Court followed this approach in its earlier jurisprudence, developing a doctrine know as the 'doctrine of incorporation'. This jurisprudence, however, was significantly attenuated by subsequent case-law.[127]

Furthermore, in the complex scenario of modern criminal justice, characterised by very different forms of restrictions on liberty, the aims of *habeas corpus* cannot be limited to the assessment of the lawfulness of arrest or detention. The Inter-

[126] Maggio (2012), p. 36.

[127] Chapter 8, G.III.

American Court emphasised the multiple goals of *habeas corpus*, extended to the protection of the right to life and the physical integrity of the individuals concerned as well as to the aim of preventing their disappearance or avoiding serious human rights infringements, such torture, ill-treatment, or other cruel, inhumane, or degrading punishment.[128] In particular, the need to counter the risk of forced disappearances led the San José judges also to broaden the scope of the people entitled to the recourse of *habeas corpus*, which can be lodged not only by the individuals arrested or detained but also by their next of kin or other persons related to them.[129] The Inter-American case-law further tightened this protection, allowing them to have recourse to *habeas corpus* even in the case of threat of deprivation of freedom and especially calling for the personal examination of the person concerned, if arrest or detention have already been enforced.[130] To this point, the Strasbourg Court followed a somewhat softer approach. The existing case-law highlights no particular focus on the requirement of personal examination of the person arrested or detained, which must be balanced with the need for a rapid procedure.[131] The European Court even accepts that in some cases the competent court rules on *habeas corpus* without the physical presence of the individuals concerned, provided that some representation is ensured to them.[132] These findings are debatable, even though the European case-law strengthens the requirement of representation to the point that legal assistance must be ensured especially in cases of individuals in a particularly vulnerable situation, such as confinement in a psychiatric institution or minors. Thus, the usual assumption in the Strasbourg case-law that the features of the guarantee of Article 5(4) can vary depending on the circumstances and the type of the deprivation of freedom[133] can lead to a considerable weakening of the participatory rights of the individuals concerned. The need for legal assistance also holds great importance in the Inter-American case-law, especially in cases of people arrested or detained in a foreign country.[134]

J. Provisional Conclusions

The comparative examination of international human rights case-law and EU law provides important indications for the proper understanding of the increasing role of the parties in criminal justice. The developments that have recently taken place especially in the Strasbourg case-law, despite the great flexibility of its

[128] Chapter 9, G.III.

[129] *Ibid.*

[130] *Ibid.*

[131] Chapter 8, G.III.

[132] *Ibid.*

[133] ECtHR, *Bouamar v. Belgium*, § 60.

[134] Chapter 9, G.III.

jurisprudence and the apparent relaxation in the protection of some fundamental rights, reveal a complex approach to criminal proceedings as a listening space and the field of composition of conflicting interests. The approach followed by the Inter-American Court further broadens the assessment of judicial guarantees in criminal proceedings by including it into an overall scrutiny of serious human rights violations. Despite widely drawing on the heritage of the Strasbourg case-law, EU law is increasingly developing an autonomous approach to criminal justice, which in some core areas (*e.g.*, the right to be present at trial), however, can entail serious consequences on the participatory rights of the individuals involved in criminal proceedings.

References

Ayala Corao C, Rivero MD (2014) Article 4. In: Steiner and Uribe (eds) Convención Americana sobre Derechos Humanos. Comentario. Konrad Adenauer Stiftung, Berlin, pp 112–130

Bachmaier Winter L (2015) The EU directive on the right to access to a lawyer: a critical assessment. In: Ruggeri S (ed) Human rights in european criminal law. New developments in European legislation and case law after the Lisbon treaty. Springer, Heidelberg, pp 111–131

Borowsky M (2011) Artikel 52. In: Meyer J (ed) Charta der Grundrechte der Europäischen Union, 3rd edn. Nomos, Baden-Baden

Casal JM (2014) Article 7. In: Steiner and Uribe (eds) Convención Americana sobre Derechos Humanos. Comentario. Konrad Adenauer Stiftung, Berlin, pp 180–206

Erb V (1999) legalität und Opportunität. Duncker & Humblot, Berlin

Hassemer W (1992) Legalität und Opportunität im Strafverfahren – eine Skizze. In: Ostendorf H (ed) Strafverfolgung und Strafverzicht. Festschrift zum 125. Bestehen der Staatsanwaltschaft Schleswig-Holstein. Carl Heymanns, Köln et al

Jackson JD, Summers SJ (2012) The internationalisation of criminal evidence: beyond the common law and civil law traditions. Cambridge University Press, Cambridge

Kühne H-H (2015) Strafprozessrecht. Eine Systematische Darstellung des deutschen und europäischen Strafverfahrensrechts, 9th edn. C.F. Müller, Heidelberg

Maggio P (2012) Judicial reviews against deprivation of liberty. In: Ruggeri S (ed) Liberty and security in Europe. A comparative analysis of pre-trial precautionary measures in criminal proceedings. V&R Unipress (Universitätsverlag Osnabrück), Göttingen, pp 33–44

Marzaduri E (1996) Azione: d) diritto processuale penale. In: Enciclopedia giuridica Treccani, vol V. Treccani, Roma, pp 1–23

Nobili M (1998) Scenari e trasformazioni del processo penale. Cedam, Padova

Parlato L (2012) Il contributo della vittima tra azione e prova. Torri del Vento, Palermo

Trechsel S (2005) Human rights in criminal proceedings. Oxford University Press, Oxford

Vogel B (2017) “In camera”-Verfahren als Gewährung effektiven Rechtsschutzes? Neue Entwicklungen im europäischen Sicherheitsrecht. Zeitschrift für die internationale Strafrechtsdogmatik, pp 28–38

Wahl T (2015) Der Rahmenbeschluss zu Abwesenheitsentscheidungen. Brüsseler EU-Justizkooperation als Fall für Straßburg? EuCrim, pp 70–76

Chapter 15
Solution Models for a Participatory Approach to Transnational Criminal Justice in International and Supranational Law

Contents

A. International Human Rights Law and the Protection of Fair Trial Guarantees. Introductory Remarks 511
B. *Audi alteram partem* and the Specific Human Rights Challenges of Criminal Proceedings with Transnational Features 513
C. *Audi alteram partem* in the Field of Surrender Procedures 515
I. The Right to Personal Participation in the Trial Country and Procedural Guarantees in the Surrender Procedure. The Soft Approach of the Strasbourg Court and the Safeguards Set by EU Law 515
II. Participatory Safeguards and the Right to Evidence in Surrender Procedures. The Qualitative Requirements Set by International Human Rights Case-Law and the Solution Models of EU Law 518
D. Participatory Rights and Transnational Evidence-Gathering 521
I. The Right to Obtain Exculpatory Evidence. A Proactive Right of the Defence in the Field of International Cooperation? 521
II. The Multiple Expressions of the Guarantee of Confrontation in the Field of Transnational Evidence-Gathering 521
1. Responsibility for Ensuring Confrontation 521
2. The Role of the Defence in the Taking of Incriminating Evidence 524
3. The Use of Untested Evidence 525
E. Interim Conclusions 526
References 527

A. International Human Rights Law and the Protection of Fair Trial Guarantees. Introductory Remarks

Despite the general scope of application of international human rights instruments, recourse to international human rights law to protect the individuals involved in transnational inquiries constitutes a relatively recent achievement especially in relation to mutual assistance procedures in criminal matters. The comparative analysis of the European Convention and the Pact of San José has highlighted that this result is due to a number of diverse factors. As far as the Rome Convention is concerned, the traditional approach to international cooperation as a form of administrative assistance has long prevented the European case-law from

S. Ruggeri, Audi Alteram Partem *in Criminal Proceedings*,
DOI 10.1007/978-3-319-54573-8_15

acknowledging the full application of fair trial guarantees.[1] The main factor, moreover, was probably the manner of decision-making of the Strasbourg Court, which led it to develop case-law on several fair trial rights (from the right to be present at trial to the right to confrontation, and so on) that looks at the overall conduct of criminal proceedings. This form of assessment of the state's legal action—aimed at evaluating whether a fundamental right, despite being initially withheld, was ensured at a later stage of the proceedings—does not fit, however, the characteristics of transborder cases, in which each country is often only responsible for a small part of a complex proceeding underway in another country.[2]

The Inter-American Court, while calling for a progressive and systematic understanding of human rights in the light of other international law instruments,[3] pointed out the joint responsibility of the countries involved in transnational criminal cases to provide each other with the widest assistance to ensure the most effective criminal law action against serious human rights violations.[4] Nevertheless, this case-law did not directly aim at granting participatory rights in cross-border procedures, instead reflecting the general victim-centred approach to criminal justice, which makes the conduct of exhaustive investigation the necessary means of ensuring protection to the right to truth and reparation of the victims and their families.

As far as EU law is concerned, we have seen that the enhancement of fair trial rights in transborder criminal cases was not initially at the core of the legislation issued under the former Third Pillar. The main purpose of the legislation launched in the first years of the last decade was to strengthen international cooperation in criminal matters among member states.[5] This was the main basis for the failure of the proposal for a legislative instrument aimed at harmonising some defence rights in criminal proceedings. EU criminal justice policy, however, changed in the midst of the last decade and the progressive softening of the strict logic of mutual recognition was accompanied by the rising interest in some important participatory safeguards,[6] which must be ensured to achieve fair transnational cooperation in criminal matters. The Lisbon reform, while shifting the focus towards fair trial rights in domestic criminal justice, did not diminish the interest of EU institutions in transnational cooperation in criminal matters. Nevertheless, EU law followed a rather piecemeal approach, which extended the new legislation on defence rights only to the EAW procedures, whereas other legislative instruments concerned with different forms of cross-border assistance (*e.g.*, the EIO Directive) ensure very scant guarantees to the participatory rights of the individuals involved. Further

---

[1]Chapter 11, A.

[2]*Ibid.*

[3]Chapter 12, A.

[4]Chapter 12, B.

[5]Chapter 13, A.

[6]One of the most significant legislative innovations was the enhancement of the right to be present at trial for the purpose of various cross-border procedures, starting with the EAW proceedings.

legislation, such as Directive 2016/343/EU, provides safeguards that do not entirely coincide with those acknowledged in the field of international legal assistance, while ignoring the specific challenges concerned with national cases having transnational features.

A delicate question is whether human rights law (at both international law and the EU law level) can be used to counter violations of fair trial rights that occurred in non-contracting countries and what responsibility individual countries hold to ensure compliance with international instruments. The Strasbourg case-law provides some indications on this important issue.[7] The traditional territorial understanding of international human rights charters led to the European Court initially limiting the responsibility of a contracting country requested to provide assistance to a non-member state solely to cases of flagrant infringement of fair trial violations. Neither the *Soering* judgment nor subsequent case-law, which followed this approach, provided clear justification for such self-restraint, which, however, departed from the logic of a rigid non-inquiry for the simple fact that even the denial of assistance in exceptional cases presupposes the possibility of inquiring into the way criminal proceedings were held in other countries. By confirming the restrictive approach of the *Soering* decision, the *Drozd* case suggested that contracting countries are fully responsible for fair trial violations committed in other states-party. The *Pellegrini* judgment, although dealing with the enforceability of a decision issued in a non-criminal proceeding, provided further important indications in the field of transnational criminal justice. By acknowledging an indirect effect of the ECHR safeguards, the Court made it clear that the Convention only apparently imposes its standards on the territory of third countries. Remarkably, the Strasbourg judges broadened the concept of territoriality by calling upon the contracting countries to ensure full protection, pursuant to the European Convention, to all the people falling within their jurisdiction. It is worth observing that responsibility also lies with contracting states with a view to preventing violations of the Convention. In the *Soering* judgment, the Court had already stressed (albeit in a restrictive way) the need to avoid future infringements of the Convention. In this regard, the doctrine of the *Soering* decision is still relevant in the light of the increasing tendency of European case-law to anticipate human rights protections.

B. *Audi alteram partem* and the Specific Human Rights Challenges of Criminal Proceedings with Transnational Features

It is apparent from these preliminary observations that international human rights law surely provides useful solutions in the field of criminal proceedings with a transnational dimension, which solutions, however, pose different challenges from

[7]Chapter 11, B.

those concerned with domestic cases. In particular, enormous difficulties can arise where a criminal law action is to be instituted against foreign defendants or individuals not resident in the trial country. Moreover, particular safeguards are due where coercive means are necessary against a person unfamiliar with the legal culture of the country in which the criminal proceedings are ongoing, as well as against individuals who, despite not having linguistic barriers, are detained abroad. All these cases posed particular difficulties for international human rights case-law, which was called upon to strike a balance between the needs concerned with transnational cooperation and the fulfilment of the human rights requirements set forth in the field of domestic criminal justice, starting with the right to information and effective participation in criminal proceedings.

The comparative examination of the jurisprudence of the European Court and the Inter-American Court reveals the clear attempt by the Strasbourg case-law to tighten the diligence duties by requiring the national authorities to provide detailed and understandable information to foreign defendants and especially to the individuals who do not speak the language of the proceedings.[8] Remarkably, the European Court maintained this approach at a time in which it had already somewhat softened the requirement of diligence in domestic criminal cases. A rigorous approach can also be observed in relation to the cases of national defendants who, being detained abroad, need to be provided with special guarantees. This led the Court to find in the *F.C.B.* case a violation of Article 6 ECHR not only because of the failure by the national authorities to grant the applicant proper information on the criminal proceedings initiated against him but also because of the lack of any arrangement aimed at allowing his participation in criminal proceedings, despite the legal assistance that was ensured to him.[9] The subsequent developments in the Strasbourg case-law regarding this case, as noted, highlight the clear attempt by the European Court to attenuate the tension with Italy in the delicate field of *in absentia* trials. This result can certainly also be viewed as the acknowledgment of the efforts made by the 2005 Italian reform to soften the rigid features of the default proceedings and to enable the accused's participation at least in a higher instance. However, the Court softened its approach to transnational cases, while confirming the lawfulness of the default proceedings if a subsequent remedy is ensured—no matter how it was structured.[10]

Of course, the granting of adequate information and even the possibility of being present at trial may not suffice to ensure effective participation in criminal proceedings, especially if the defendant is a foreigner or is in any case alien to the law of the trial country. It is noteworthy that the Inter-American Court attached particular importance to the need to provide people detained in a foreign country with the broadest safeguards, which should not only include legal assistance but also consular assistance.

[8]Chapter 11, C.

[9]*Ibid.*

[10]*Ibid.*

Compared to these achievements, EU law still reveals considerable backwardness. In particular, Directive 2016/343/EU, while pointing out the need to provide vulnerable defendants with special guarantees,[11] ignored the specific problems concerned with the right to participation in criminal proceedings instituted against foreign defendants or individuals who are resident or even detained in another country. To be sure, a joint examination of Directive 2010/64/EU and Directive 2012/13/EU supports the conclusion that at least individuals who do not speak the language of the trial should be given information on the charge in an accessible and understandable way. The Luxembourg Court confirmed this conclusion in the *Covaci* case, in which, however, it largely overlooked the need to grant foreign defendants the assistance of both an interpreter and a lawyer in the timeframe in which they must decide whether or not to challenge a penal order.

C. *Audi alteram partem* in the Field of Surrender Procedures

I. The Right to Personal Participation in the Trial Country and Procedural Guarantees in the Surrender Procedure. The Soft Approach of the Strasbourg Court and the Safeguards Set by EU Law

Different solution models may be deduced from the comparative examination of international human rights law and EU law in the field of international cooperation in criminal matters. From the perspective of the present discussion, the first problem area relates to the surrender procedures. Here, the comparative analysis of EU law and of the case-law of the Strasbourg Court and of the Inter-American Court highlights two main problems, that is, (a) the procedural safeguards that are due in the requested country in the case of defendants tried *in absentia* in the requesting state and (b) the balance between the right of the sought person to be heard in the surrender procedure and right to evidence of the victim of the alleged offence.

Concerning the first issue, examination of international human rights case-law reveals a considerable weakening of the standards of protection set forth in relation to domestic criminal cases. An enlightening example was the *Battisti* judgment.[12] By dealing with this complex case, the Strasbourg Court satisfied itself with the circumstance that Mr. Battisti had been duly informed about the proceedings instituted against him in Italy and had appointed two lawyers to defend him at trial. The European judges shared the interpretation that this conduct reflected the accused's decision not to be present at trial. Here the Court, while confirming the lawfulness of implicit waiver, departed from its traditional approach to *in absentia*

[11]Recital no. 42 DirPIRPT.

[12]Chapter 11, D.II.3.

trials, according to which the defendant's conduct should unequivocally reflect the decision not to take part personally in the proceedings. It is debatable, however, whether the assistance of a lawyer by itself suffices to satisfy the requirements of the right to defence. It might be argued that the presence in court of one or two lawyers (as happened in the *Battisti* case) was more than sufficient to fulfil the requirement of 'minimum defence rights', set forth by the 1978 Additional Protocol. Nevertheless, it cannot seriously be affirmed that legal assistance ensures effective defence if the defendants were not put in a position to decide whether to personally participate in criminal hearings and especially if they were not duly informed on the consequences of their decision to appoint a lawyer might have upon a future surrender procedure.

On the other hand, the 1978 Protocol, by excluding denial of surrender when the requesting country gives proper assurance that the sought individuals can obtain a retrial aimed at safeguarding their defence rights, favoured a system that releases the requested state from the obligation to assess the respect for the minimum defence rights at the first instance, provided that the accused will (abstractly) have the opportunity of a subsequent remedy. The European case-law confirmed this approach in the field of transnational surrender, giving rise to a further softening of its jurisprudence developed on national trials held *in absentia*. Remarkably, the *F.C.B.* judgment also relied on the mechanism of a retrial without inquiring into whether this solution could allow a fresh determination of the merits on the basis of new evidence—a result that the 2005 Italian reform, as noted, did not ensure in the second instance.

There can be little doubt that this approach affected developments in the EU legislation. A close examination, however, reveals that EU law further departed from the requirements set by the Strasbourg Court on *in absentia* trials.[13] Notwithstanding the merits of Framework Decision 2009/299/JHA, the overall approach followed by this legislation raises serious human rights concerns.[14] The first problematic issue relates to the information that the sought person is to be given on both the institution of criminal proceedings in the trial state and the implications of their decision on whether to take part personally in the court hearings. Unlike the European Court, the EU institutions seemed to be more concerned about the need not to overturn the national rules on judicial service than about the need to provide defendants with proper information on the initiation of a criminal law action against them as well as on the consequences of any decision they will take (in particular, the decision to steer away from the proceedings, the decision to give a mandate to a lawyer, and so on). The scant interest by EU law in an informed decision of the accused reaches its highest point with the rules on the right to a retrial, which allow for the executing authority to surrender the sought person solely on the grounds that a retrial or appeal was not objectively requested.

---

[13]In the same sense Klitsch (2009), p. 19 f. Of a partially different opinion Siracusano (2011), p. 96 fn. 35.

[14]Chapter 13, B.II.2.a.

Moreover, following the *Battisti* doctrine, the 2009 legislation departed from the requirement of an unequivocal waiver, allowing for the surrender of the sought persons on the sole ground that they gave a mandate to a lawyer to defend them at trial. It is certainly a worrisome result that EU law did not attach specific focus to the requirement that the accused be provided with proper safeguards to ensure that he will make the right decision. In this regard, a better solution would probably be to require the competent authority to provide the accused with legal assistance prior to the decision on whether to waive the right to personal participation, as foreseen in relation to the right to translation.[15]

A further aspect that considerably distinguishes the solutions of EU law from the approach adopted by the Strasbourg case-law is the overall consideration that should be given to the waiver decision. It has been observed that the European Court has not always viewed the decision not to be present at trial in in positive terms, considering personal involvement as the best solution when the accused is equipped with legal knowledge—so much so that the Court even called on contracting countries to discourage unjustified absences.[16] In other words, the right to be personally involved in criminal proceedings does not entail that defendants can waive it without justified grounds, especially where they have the necessary knowledge to make a contribution to fact-finding. Instead, EU law reveals a rather neutral consideration of the accused's absence for the purposes of international cooperation. The overall approach of the 2009 legislation—and especially the fact that, outside the situations laid down by Article 4a, the executing authority holds a general ground for refusal of surrender—reveals that under EU law defendants can unconditionally waive their right to personal participation.[17] No room was left for further considerations, such as the legal knowledge of the accused, nor did the 2009 legislation foresee any exception in the field of serious crimes, in which the defendant's participation should in principle be mandatory.[18]

The interpretation of these rules by the EU Court of Justice further softened the understanding of the participatory rights of the person against whom a surrender procedure was initiated.[19] In the *Melloni* case, the Luxembourg judges, ruling out that the Spanish authority could make surrender conditional on the possibility of a retrial, provided a formal interpretation of the requirement that the accused give a mandate to a lawyer. In fact, the Court largely overlooked the need to provide the accused persons with proper information on the consequences of their decision to appoint counsel of their own choosing or to give a mandate to a lawyer appointed by the State. No room was also left for the need to ensure adequate safeguards in particular cases (*e.g.*, in case of defendants who do not speak the language of the

[15] In this sense see Böse (2015), p. 142.

[16] Chapter 8, C.II.

[17] Heger and Wolter (2015), p. 348.

[18] Böse (2015), p. 142.

[19] Chapter 13, B.II.2.b.

proceedings). The message left by this judgment was that national authorities must be satisfied with the objective circumstance that a mandate was given to a lawyer. The executing authority, therefore, does not need to ascertain whether this also reflects the decision to waive the right to personal participation and especially whether defendants were sufficiently provided with proper guarantees when they chose to give a mandate to lawyer.

II. Participatory Safeguards and the Right to Evidence in Surrender Procedures. The Qualitative Requirements Set by International Human Rights Case-Law and the Solution Models of EU Law

The second problematic area concerns the participatory rights of the individuals involved in surrender procedures and other proceedings entailing restrictions on liberty or the right to free movement. In this regard, the first delicate issue relates to the information due to the person against whom a surrender procedure was initiated. The indications emerging from Strasbourg case-law in the *Caprino* ruling highlight a minimalist approach.[20] According to the European judges, although Article 5 ECHR provides a general guarantee applicable to all the situations of detention or arrest, the information that must be provided about provisional arrest within an extradition procedure can vary depending on the circumstances at stake. To be sure, the sought person must in any case be enabled to challenge the lawfulness of the measure applied. However, this generic requirement does not give much certainty as to the exact contents of the information duty provided for by the Convention.

At the EU level, the clear mutual recognition-based inspiration of the EAW Framework Decision did not prevent the EU institutions from laying down some important duties of information on both the cooperating authorities.[21] By issuing a European arrest warrant, the requesting authority must provide detailed information, which includes not only information on an enforceable judgment or a detention order but also the information on the offence under investigation or prosecution in the issuing state. The executing authority must in turn forward to the sought individuals this information together with the information on the ongoing procedure and the possibility of consenting with surrender. Pursuant to the 2012 legislation, all this information must be ensured in clear and accessible terms.

Doubtless, EU law laid down important guarantees to enable the requested person to effectively participate in the surrender procedure. Nevertheless, there are still grave deficiencies especially where the surrender procedure aims at the

[20]Chapter 11, D.II.1.

[21]Chapter 13, B.III.1.

enforcement of pre-trial detention in the issuing country.[22] On close examination, both the information on the existence of a detention order and on the charges preferred in the relevant proceedings give scant indications on the justification of the coercive measure required in the trial state. Furthermore, even though the sought individuals must be informed of the possibility of consenting with the surrender procedure, EU law does not require the executing authority to make them also aware of the exact consequences of this decision.

This raises the problem of the assistance that EU law ensures to the sought person in the surrender procedure before the executing authority. There is no doubt that the granting of proper assistance—especially of linguistic and legal assistance—is of utmost importance to enable the requested person to follow the surrender procedure and to understand the information received. This particularly applies to the information on relevant legal issues, such as the information on the legal classification of the offence under investigation. The correct understanding of the case is in turn a necessary condition to decide whether or not to consent with to surrender procedure.

Both linguistic and legal assistance, moreover, hold specific importance with a view to ensuring a fair examination by a judicial authority in the surrender procedure. In this respect, no clear indications emerge from the European Convention. Although the judicial review of the lawfulness of a provisional arrest issued within an extradition procedure must satisfy the requirements of adversarial proceedings, the Strasbourg Court has not made it clear whether the presence of the sought individuals is necessary and whether they can claim a right to be heard by a judicial authority.[23] In the EU area, the EAW legislation provided clearer rules, requiring a judicial authority in the executing state to hear the sought person who did not consent to the surrender procedure.[24] In the light of this guarantee and with a view to the effective exercise of the information rights, the 2002 legislation ensured to the requested person the assistance of both a lawyer and an interpreter.[25] As to its practical arrangements, however, this acknowledgment was entirely dependent on *lex loci*, which should also govern the hearing of the sought person by the judicial executing authority. In other words, EU law did not provide for any specific indication about the forms of the assistance due to requested individuals as well as about the modes and safeguards required for their judicial examination.

It was only after the Lisbon reform that the EU institutions made some steps forward in this direction.[26] In particular, it is worth observing that Directive 2010/64/EU, linking the right to interpretation in a EAW procedure with the new

[22]*Ibid.*

[23]Chapter 11, D.II.2.

[24]Chapter 13, B.III.1.

[25]*Ibid.*

[26]*Ibid.*

guarantees introduced for domestic criminal proceedings, ensured to the requested person legal assistance not only in the court hearings but also in the police questionings, while charging the executing authority with the task of verifying the conditions for linguistic assistance. Concerning legal assistance, two important innovations were brought about by the 2013 legislation on the right to access to a lawyer. First, the lawyer in the executing country must have the opportunity for private communications with his client and must be present at the judicial hearing. Second, the requested individuals must be given the right to be assisted by another lawyer in the issuing country whose main tasks are to provide them and the lawyer in the executing state with the necessary information and advice.

Although these are certainly positive results, some deficiencies can still be observed.[27] Concerning linguistic assistance, it is noteworthy that, even though the sought person can challenge the decision that found that the conditions do not exist for interpretation, EU law only allows for this possibility to the extent that it does not jeopardise the speediness of the surrender procedure. Furthermore, the successful exercise of the solution of a double legal assistance—namely, in both the issuing and the executing state—largely depends on several factors. Certainly, the lack of EU rules on legal aid still impinges on the effectiveness of the fundamental guarantee of legal assistance. As far as the legal assistance in the executing state is concerned, moreover, it is hard to understand why the EU institutions did not reproduce the same requirements set in the field of national criminal justice and therefore did not limit the competence of national law to establish the conditions of legal assistance by requiring that the effective exercise and the essence of the right to a defence can in no way be jeopardised.

Ultimately, comparison with the Inter-American case-law reveals an unprecedented aspect of the right to a fair hearing in extradition procedures, that is, the right of the victim to examine the alleged perpetrators after extradition has been granted.[28] This is a very delicate issue, which highlights a new balance between the need for efficient international cooperation, the protection of the individuals subject to a surrender procedure and the right to evidence of the victims of serious crimes. By dealing with the Colombian Process of Peace and Justice, the Inter-American Court, despite recognising the importance of extradition for the purposes of a criminal prosecution of grave human rights violations, emphasised the need to avoid surrender procedures frustrating the victims' claim for justice and reparation.[29]

---

[27] *Ibid.*

[28] Chapter 12, C.II.

[29] *Ibid.*

D. Participatory Rights and Transnational Evidence-Gathering

I. The Right to Obtain Exculpatory Evidence. A Proactive Right of the Defence in the Field of International Cooperation?

Complex problems also arise in the field of transnational evidence-gathering. The comparative analysis of EU law and the case-law of the European Court and the Inter-American Court highlights different features of the right to evidence in transborder cases. In the light of the right to effective defence, the first delicate issue regards the possibility for the accused to gather exculpatory evidence situated abroad. In Latin America, various international instruments of legal assistance expressly prevent private parties from using them to obtain evidence situated abroad. It is debatable, however, whether this result can lead to a weakening of the human rights protection provided by the Pact of San José,[30] which entails the positive obligation of the national authorities to use all the available international tools in order to ensure full compliance with the Convention's rights. At the EU level, neither the EEW Framework Decision nor the Commission's proposals acknowledged any proactive role of private parties in the collection of evidence.[31] Regrettably, the recent EIO legislation, despite some criticisms raised in this regard on the draft proposal,[32] did not leave room for the proactive initiative of the defence in the gathering of exculpatory evidence.

II. The Multiple Expressions of the Guarantee of Confrontation in the Field of Transnational Evidence-Gathering

1. Responsibility for Ensuring Confrontation

The need for a re-interpretation of international law instruments in the light of the requirements set forth by human rights charters also emerges in relation to the guarantee of confrontation. In the case *X., Y. and Z. v. Austria*, dealing with the problem of whether the applicants should be granted the guarantee of confrontation by means of letters rogatory, the Commission rejected the argument of the Austrian Government whereby the European Convention did not enable the accused to

[30]Chapter 12, C.III.

[31]This critical point had been addressed by *Allegrezza* in relation to the Commission's Green Paper on obtaining evidence in criminal matters in the EU area. Cf. Allegrezza (2010), p. 576 f.

[32]Ruggeri (2013), p. 305.

examine prosecutorial witnesses overseas because the 1959 European Convention on Mutual Assistance had not addressed the issue of confrontation in the field of letters rogatory. This acknowledgment poses several questions, while setting a good starting point for a comparative discussion on this problematic area.

In 1973, the Commission recognised the 'full responsibility' of the cooperating country for 'the form and conduct' of a testimonial examination on commission, 'including the question of who should participate at the hearing'. This acknowledged seems to be the obvious consequence of the fact that according to the traditional system of mutual assistance, the competent authorities for the relevant proceedings have no jurisdiction in the requested country and that the witness examination should in principle follow the procedures of *lex loci*.[33] The conditions set forth by the Commission in 1973, however, no longer reflect the current requirements of international legal assistance in Europe. At the Council of Europe level, the Second Additional Protocol to the 1959 Convention allows overseas evidence also to be gathered pursuant to specific forms of *lex fori*.[34] Remarkably, although this international instrument specifies that the application of these procedures must be 'necessary under the law of the requesting party', the 2001 Protocol did not attach specific attention to the participatory rights of the individuals concerned. Nor did this international instrument give any relevance to the knowledge of *lex fori* on the part of the requested authority, which is called upon to comply with the requirements set by the requesting authority 'even if unfamiliar to the requested party'.

In the EU area, the EIO Directive, following the approach of the Brussels Convention, also allowed for the combination of *lex loci* and *lex fori*, without providing, however, any qualitative requirement – other than the non-infringement with the general principles of *lex loci* – with a view to ensuring harmonised application of national rules, which could possibly be incompatible with each other.[35] Even more significantly, the EIO legislation, while enabling the executing authority to gather evidence with coercive means, enacted an unprecedented provision that allows for some (undefined) 'authorities' of the issuing country to be present at the execution of the sought investigation and, upon agreement with the executing authority, even to exercise law enforcement powers on foreign territory.[36] The presence of these authorities primarily aims at representing the issuing country in the evidence-gathering procedure, while providing support for the correct understanding and application of the procedures of *lex fori*. However, it is regrettable that private parties were not given a similar opportunity, notwithstanding that the defence can also give its own contribution to the proper application of *lex fori*.[37] At any rate, it cannot be denied that the request of

[33] Chapter 11, D.III.2.

[34] Art. 8 SAP ECMACM.

[35] Chapter 13, C.II.2.a.

[36] *Ibid.*

[37] *Ibid.*

lex fori by the authorities of the trial state nowadays plays a considerable role in the definition of the 'form' of a testimonial hearing abroad.

The evolution that occurred in the law on international legal assistance, moreover, casts doubts on whether the conclusion reached by the Commission in the *X., Y. and Z.* judgment, which excluded Austria's responsibility, is still relevant in Europe. In other words, it should be examined whether the cooperating authority still holds 'full responsibility', even though confrontation will take place at a later state of the proceedings in the trial state.[38] Although there is still no specific European case-law on this point, the solution adopted by the Commission appears to be in line with the usual approach of the Strasbourg Court, which, as noted, broadens the scope of the right to confrontation to the point that it usually rules out the infringement of the Convention if the accused is given a later opportunity to examine a prosecutorial witness. This doctrine, however, was elaborated in relation to domestic criminal proceedings, in which responsibility for ensuring compliance with the Convention's rights lies (if not necessarily with the same body) with the authorities of the same country. In the field of international cooperation, instead, the tasks of the requested authority are by definition circumscribed by the contents of the request, a result that also applies to legal assistance governed by the principle of mutual recognition.

On close examination, in the *X., Y. and Z.* case, the Commission found no violation of the Convention because a second hearing took place on commission after the defence had studied the record of the first hearing. This may seem to indicate that the 'full responsibility' of the cooperating authority ends with the completion of the assistance procedure and that the cooperating country cannot be deemed liable for what happens outside its jurisdiction. Even within these limits, however, it cannot be allowed that, if *lex fori* is applicable in a concrete case and requires the involvement of the defence in the examination of a prosecutorial witness abroad or by remote connection, the cooperating authority is relieved from international responsibility by virtue of counting on a future hearing. More recently, the European case-law confirmed that the contracting states are only fully responsible to the Convention within their own jurisdiction, with the result that the trial country cannot be deemed liable for non-compliance by the requested authorities with *lex loci*, which requires the defence to be present at the testimonial examination.[39]

This conclusion, however, cannot leave the individuals concerned unprotected, nor can entail that national countries should not do as much as possible within their own jurisdiction to enable full compliance with the Convention by other states. Clearly, this approach, which calls for shared responsibility for the protection of human rights, requires a high level of cooperation between the national authorities involved in a cross-border procedure. The Strasbourg Court had the opportunity to examine this important issue in *Solakov v. the Former Yugoslav Republic of*

[38] Chapter 11, D.III.2.

[39] *Ibid.*

Macedonia, in which the applicant complained that the competent judge had not provided him with specific information about the witness examination that was to take place in the US. The European Court did not examine this important issue, however.

2. The Role of the Defence in the Taking of Incriminating Evidence

Against this background, a delicate issue concerns the role of the defence in the taking of incriminating evidence through legal assistance instruments. At first glance, the few responses given by Strasbourg case-law seem to be in line with the general approach followed in domestic cases. In the 1980s, the Commission had already stressed that the guarantee of confrontation can also be satisfied where the defence, despite not having the opportunity of cross-examining prosecutorial witnesses, can request that certain questions be put to the witness by the court through an examination on commission. The solution reached in *P.V. v. Federal Republic of Germany* was that the accused must at least be given the possibility of formulating written questions to be addressed to the witness abroad.[40] The European Court confirmed this approach almost 15 years later in the *Solakov* case, in which, however, it implicitly stressed the existence of a diligence duty on the part of the defendants, who should expressly forward the questions that they would like to be put to the witnesses.[41] This conclusion in turn requires a duty of diligence on the part of the competent authorities, which must put the defendants and their lawyers in a position to know in advance the date and contents of the witness hearing. At any rate, it cannot be denied that the European case-law did not make the slightest attempt to balance the needs of transnational cases with the more rigorous approach adopted in the field of domestic criminal justice, in which it expressly ruled out that written questions can replace a direct confrontation in open court.[42]

International instruments of legal assistance do not specifically deal with the right to confrontation in the overseas examination of witnesses and co-defendants. Not only the 1959 European Convention but also more recent agreements of international cooperation in criminal matters – such as the Brussels Convention and the 2001 Second Additional Protocol to the Council of Europe's Convention—contain no rules governing the participatory role of the accused in the taking of incriminating evidence abroad. This is not in principle excluded, being, however, conditional on the requirements of *lex loci* or *lex fori*, and in the latter case, provided that the requesting authority requests it explicitly.

Moreover, a face-to-face confrontation can be impossible or unfeasible in transborder cases. Remarkably, the aforementioned international instruments, like other recent international law agreements, regulated the possibility of testimonial

[40]Chapter 11, D.III.3.

[41]*Ibid.*

[42]ECtHR, *Windish v. Germany*, § 28.

hearings conducted by videoconference. Doubtless, technological means not only can solve practical problems but furthermore can bring international cooperation closer to the requirements set forth by the Strasbourg case-law especially in relation to vulnerable and anonymous witnesses. On the other hand, hearings by videoconference can also pose delicate human rights problems when ensuring a fair remote confrontation. In this regard, however, the Brussels Convention stated that the hearing by videoconference should be conducted 'directly by, or under the direction of, the judicial authority of the requesting member state'.[43] The EIO legislation reproduced this settlement, making it also conditional on the limit of non-infringement with the fundamental principles of *lex loci*. This raises the question of whether and to what extent the defendants or their lawyer can be involved in the confrontation with prosecutorial witnesses or co-defendants by remote connection[44]—either by means of cross-examination or through the indirect arrangements envisaged by the Strasbourg case-law.

In this regard, it must be acknowledged that there is still no certainty that the defence will be involved in these hearings. The possibility of cross-examination depends on various factors, which are not always predictable: in particular, either *lex loci* or *lex fori* should require direct confrontation and, in the latter case, the issuing authority should request it, provided—in any case—that cross-examination does not infringe fundamental principles of *lex loci*. Furthermore, even if remote cross-examination is allowed and the issuing authority expressly requests it as a specific form of *lex fori*, there is nothing to ensure that a lawyer will assist the accused. At the EU level, despite the express reference by the EIO legislation to Directive 2013/48, it cannot be overlooked that in the field of international cooperation in the EU area, the right to legal assistance was only extended to the EAW proceedings.[45]

As far as the American Convention is concerned, we have noted that the Inter-American case-law broadened the scope of the right to be fairly heard to the point that it extended the right to confrontation to the victims of serious human rights violations. As highlighted by *Ituango Massacres v. Colombia*, the victims' claim for justice and reparation encompasses their right, if not necessarily to obtain the physical presence of the extradited individuals, to have the opportunity to assist with their examination.[46]

3. The Use of Untested Evidence

The last delicate question concerned with the right to confrontation is whether and to what extent untested evidence gathered abroad can be used at trial and whether the requesting state can be deemed responsible for its use under international human

[43]Chapter 13, C.II.2.b.

[44]*Ibid.*

[45]*Ibid.*

[46]Chapter 12, C.II.

rights law. In the *P.V.* case, the European Commission, despite recognising this possibility in abstract terms, ruled out Germany's responsibility for the use of untested evidence on the ground of two main arguments, namely (a) that the applicant did not complain that it had been impossible for him to request that questions be put to the witness abroad, nor was his request rejected, and (b) that the evidence given on commission only confirmed previous statements of the same person and its reliability was corroborated by further information.[47]

These arguments were rather unconvincing, highlighting a dangerous understanding of international cooperation in criminal matters. We have seen that Strasbourg case-law not only imposes clear duties of diligence on the defence but also on the competent authorities, which must duly inform the individuals concerned about the date and the contents of the testimonial hearing. This especially holds true if *lex loci* requires the involvement of the defence in testimonial hearings, which presupposes that the competent authorities must put them in a position to prepare and formulate specific questions. It is also debatable whether the trial court can admit untested evidence on the grounds that it only confirmed other information that was also obtained without any involvement of the accused. The Commission's search for corroborating evidence, despite being apparently in line with the sole and decisive evidence doctrine, highlighted the attempt to compensate for the lack of confrontation through an overall assessment of the evidence produced by the defence. Notwithstanding its limitations, this approach revealed the clear rejection of the idea that the need for efficient transnational prosecution can lead to the unconditional use of untested overseas evidence.

The European Court has not yet dealt with the issue of the conditions of use of untested evidence in transborder cases and it is therefore difficult to predict whether the *Al-Khawaja* doctrine will ever find application in the field of transnational criminal justice. In Latin America, there is also no case-law of the Inter-American Court on this problem, notwithstanding that the strong human rights approach of the Inter-American case-law should not justify departing from the solutions adopted in the *Norín Catrimán* judgment.[48]

E. Interim Conclusions

Despite the increasing spread of crimes with elements of transnationality and cross-border inquiries, there is a limited number of cases in the international human rights jurisprudence concerned with transnational criminal justice. Some of the conclusions in the present discussion were also drawn on the basis of rather old cases, and it is not easy to foresee the road that international courts will walk in a near future. In general terms, the comparative analysis of the jurisprudence of the Strasbourg

[47] Chapter 11, D.III.4.

[48] Chapter 12, C.III.

Court and the Inter-American Court highlights the clear tendency to soften the usual fair trial safeguards. Notwithstanding the strong engagement of the EU institutions in order to strengthen the protection of fundamental rights in the area of freedom, security and justice, it is surprising that the EU legislation issued over the last years has failed to provide comprehensive rules on the participatory rights of the involved in cross-border criminal inquiries, while mainly focusing on surrender proceedings. The recent *Covaci* ruling of the EU Court of Justice, while constituting the first testing ground on the post-Lisbon EU legislation on defence rights in criminal justice, provides a weak interpretation of some of the key participatory safeguards of EU law also in the delicate field of transnational criminal justice.

References

Allegrezza S (2010) Critical remarks on the Green Paper on obtaining evidence from one Member State to another and securing its admissibility. Zeitschrift für die internationale Strafrechtsdogmatik, pp 569–579

Böse M (2015) Human rights violations and mutual trust: recent case law on the European arrest warrant. In: Ruggeri S (ed) Human rights in European criminal law. New developments in European legislation and case law after the lisbon treaty. Springer, Heidelberg, pp 135–145

Heger M, Wolter K (2015) 2. Hauptteil: Auslieferung – 4. Teil. Recht der EG/EU. In: Ambos K, König S, Rackow P (eds) Rechtshilferecht in Strafsachen. Nomos, Baden-Baden, pp 319–495

Klitsch S (2009) Der neue EU-Rahmenbeschluss yu Abwesenheitsverurteilungen – ein Appell zur Revision. Zeitschrift für internationale Strafrechtsdogmatik, pp 1–21

Ruggeri S (2013) Horizontal cooperation, obtaining evidence overseas and the respect for fundamental rights in the EU. From the European Commission's proposals to the proposal for a directive on a European Investigation Order: Towards a single tool of evidence gathering in the EU? In: Ruggeri S (ed) Transnational inquiries and the protection of fundamental rights in criminal proceedings, A study in memory of Vittorio Grevi and Giovanni Tranchina. Springer, Heidelberg, pp 279–310

Siracusano F (2011) Nuove prospettive in materie di processo *in absentia* e procedure di consegna. In: Rafaraci T (ed) La cooperazione di polizia e giudiziaria in materia penale nell'Unione europea dopo il Trattato di Lisbona. Giuffrè, Milano, pp 85–104

Part VIII
De-formalisation of Legal Systems and Reconstruction of a Participatory Model of Criminal Justice

Chapter 16
Mutual Interaction of Systems of Human Rights Protection and the Development of a Participatory Understanding of Criminal Justice Based on Transcultural Dialogue

Contents

A. Introductory Remarks ... 533
B. The Relevance of International Human Rights Law in the Selected Countries and Its Relationship with National Law ... 535
I. The Long Road Towards the Enhancement of International Human Rights Law in Italy ... 535
1. The Traditional Approach to International Human Rights Law and the Weak Formal Status of the European Convention ... 535
2. The Contribution of the Constitutional Case-Law to the Enhancement of International Human Rights Law and the Legislative Reforms of the Constitution ... 536
3. The Shift from the Formal Perspective to the Para-Constitutional Relevance of International Human Rights Law. The Complex Relationship Between Constitutional and Strasbourg Case-Law ... 539
II. The Relevance of the American Convention in the Contracting States and the Relationship with National Law ... 540
1. The Multisided Relevance of International Human Rights Law in Brazil ... 540
2. The Strong Approach of the Inter-American Court to Constitutional Law, Viewed from the Perspective of Brazilian Law ... 542
III. Comparative Remarks ... 544
C. The Relevance of EU Human Rights Law and the Relationship with Constitutional Law ... 546
I. The Approach of the EU Court of Justice and the Reaction of Constitutional Courts in the EU Area ... 546
II. The Approach of the Italian Constitutional Court to EU Law and the 'Counter-Limits Doctrine' ... 550
D. Cross-Fertilisation of Systems of Human Rights Protection and the Enhancement of a Participatory Understanding of National Criminal Justice on the Basis of Transcultural Dialogue ... 553
I. Premise ... 553
II. Personal Participation in Criminal Proceedings and the Lawfulness of Procedures in the Absence of the Individuals Concerned. A Multilevel Approach ... 554
1. Right to Personal Participation, Fairness of Criminal Proceedings and *in absentia* Proceedings ... 554
a) The Impact of International Human Rights Law on the Developments in Criminal Proceedings *in absentia* and the Persistent Lacunas of National Law ... 554
b) New Perspectives of EU Law and the Room for Manoeuvre for Italian Law ... 560

S. Ruggeri, Audi Alteram Partem *in Criminal Proceedings*,
DOI 10.1007/978-3-319-54573-8_16

2. The Problem of *inaudito reo* Proceedings. General Requirements of International Human Rights Law, Developments at the EU Level and the Legal Arrangements of Italian Law 562
III. Conditions of Effective Participation in Criminal Proceedings. The Incidence of International Human Rights Law on the Developments in Brazilian and Italian Criminal Justice and the Evolution of Italian Law Under the Influence of EU Legislation 564
1. Information Rights in Criminal Proceedings 564
a) Information on the Charge. A Human Rights Approach 564
aa) Information Rights and the Need for a Balance Between Conflicting Interests 564
bb) Developments in Italian Criminal Justice Towards EU Law and the Persistent Deficiencies in the Light of the European Convention 567
b) Information on the Evidence Gathered and Interferences with Fundamental Rights. The Safeguards of EU and International Human Rights Law and the Weak National Arrangements 568
2. Linguistic Guarantees in Criminal Proceedings. Developments Towards International Human Rights Law and EU Law and the Shortcomings of National Criminal Justice 570
IV. *Audi alteram partem*, the Right to Be Fairly Examined and the Privilege Against Self-Incrimination 571
1. Procedural Safeguards and Conditions of a Fair Hearing in the Pre-trial Inquiry 571
2. The Right to a Fair Hearing and the Procedural Safeguards Against Coercion. The Increased Enhancement of the *nemo tenetur* Principle 575
3. Private Initiative and the Right to Make Oneself Heard by the Competent Authority 578
V. *Audi alteram partem*, Evidence-Gathering and Qualitative Requirements of a Fair Fact-Finding. The Need for Broad Balance Among Conflicting Interests 580
1. Obtaining Incriminating Evidence. The Need for Systematic Approach to the Right to Confrontation in the Light of the Overall Set of the Human Rights Challenges Posed by Each Concrete Case 580
a) The Requirements Set by International Human Rights Case-Law and the Developments in National Law 580
b) The Risks of an Enlarged View of the Guarantee of Confrontation. The Problems of Indirect Examination and of Subsequent Confrontation 582
c) Right to Confrontation and Inconsistent Evidence. The Need to Avoid an Accused-Centred Understanding of the Principle of *contradictoire* 584
2. Proof of Guilt and the Defence's Contribution to a Fair Decision-Making 586
a) Impossibility of Confrontation and the Use of Untested Evidence. The Need to Avoid Absolutist Interpretations 586
b) Special Forms of Confrontation and the Use of the Information Gathered. The Problem of Anonymous Testimony 590
VI. Participatory Rights and Restrictions on Freedom 591
1. The Right to Be Fairly Heard and the Qualitative Requirements of Effective Participation in Remand Proceedings 591
a) Premise 591
b) The Guarantee of Information in International Human Rights Instruments and EU Law, and the Procedural Safeguards Provided at the Domestic Level 592
c) The Need for Comprehensive Assistance in the Remand Proceedings 594
2. The Guarantee of a Prompt Independent Review of the Deprivation of Liberty and the Voice of the Defence 595

3. Challenging Pre-trial Restrictions on Liberty. The Persistent Distance from the Standards Set Forth by International Human Rights Law and EU Law 598
E. Interaction of Legal Systems and the Strengthening of a Participatory Approach to Transnational Criminal Justice 599
I. Introductory Remarks 599
II. *Audi alteram partem*, Right to Freedom and Procedural Safeguards in the Field of International Surrender. The EU Legislation on the European Arrest Warrant and Its Influence on Italian Law 600
1. *In absentia* Trials and Surrender Procedures with EU Countries 600
2. Participatory Rights in the Executing Country and the Right to Be Fairly Heard in EAW Proceedings 602
3. Coercive Measures and the Right to a Fair Hearing in the Executing Country 604
4. The Enhanced Role of the Judiciary in EAW Proceedings 607
III. Participatory Rights and Transnational Evidence-Gathering 612
1. Responsibility of the Cooperating Countries for the Granting of Participatory Safeguards in Transnational Inquiries. The Feasibility of the Strasbourg Case-Law at the Domestic Level 612
2. The Right to Confrontation, the Participatory Safeguards in the Taking of Incriminating Evidence, and the Use of Untested Evidence 613
F. Conclusions 615
References 615

A. Introductory Remarks

In the light of the analysis conducted hitherto, the present discussion aims at comparing the results emerged from the study of selected countries with the solutions models provided by international human rights and EU law. Therefore, I shall now examine the impact that the solution models provided by the case-law of the Strasbourg Court and the Inter-American Court have had, or may have in the near future, on the development of a participatory understanding of criminal proceedings in both Italy and Brazil. As regards Italy, I shall also focus on the influence that EU law has recently had on the enhancement of participatory rights at the national level. Furthermore, we will also analyse the reasons for which the selected countries still reflect an uneven and even authoritarian view of criminal justice. The examination of this problematic area, however, is far from being unidirectional. As anticipated in Chap. 1, the ultimate purpose of this comparative study is theoretical-reconstructive. In this light, we will also analyse the impact that national arrangements have had on the evolution of international human rights case-law and on the adoption of specific solutions at the EU level.

This process of 'cross-fertilisation'[1] is certainly one of the main products of the increasing dialogue between judges and courts belonging to different legal systems and acting at different levels (international, supranational and national).[2] This

[1]Di Stasi (2014), p. 1ff.

[2]See among others Pollicino (2010); Martinico and Pollicino (2012); Ruggeri (2015), p. 9ff.; Conti (2015), p. 97ff.

phenomenon is highly developed in Europe, where strong contrasts alternate with cyclic re-alignments between national courts and the case-law of both the Strasbourg Court and the Luxembourg Court. In Latin America, despite the relative sparseness of the Inter-American case-law, inter-judicial dialogues have also increased over the last few years and a growing impact can be observed on national criminal justice systems due to two main factors. First, the advisory opinions of the San José Court orient domestic judges towards solutions that were either elaborated in past doctrines or will constitute the basis of future case-law. Second, the Inter-American Court is called upon to do subsequent monitoring for compliance with its judgements. In Europe, there exists no form of subsequent monitoring to determine whether the contracting countries comply with the rulings of the Strasbourg Court. Furthermore, there is no certainty about whether and when the 2013 Additional Protocol No. 16 to the European Convention, which enables the highest courts or tribunals of the contracting states to request the European Court to give advisory opinions, will ever enter into force. Several criticisms have already been raised against this international instrument[3] and it can be doubted whether the conferment of the competence to give advisory opinions to the same body called upon to settle contentious disputes between the individuals and the contracting states under the Convention will improve the relationship between the Strasbourg Court and national courts.[4] It is probable, however, that this international instrument will have an important impact on the decision-making of the European Court, and consequently on the merits of a number of solutions to issues of law which were established with the intervention of the Court after exhausting domestic remedies. For instance, the Strasbourg Court elaborated the sole and decisive evidence doctrine when it was able to assess the probative contribution to convictions of untested evidence, as well as of information collected by alternative means of confrontation. Even more, the *Al-Khawaja* doctrine presupposes that the Court can afterward scrutinise whether adequate counterbalancing measures were adopted at the national level to compensate the accused for the lack of confrontation—a scrutiny that fits a final proceeding.

Against this background, I shall here compare the results of the comparative analysis of national law with the solution models elaborated at the level of international human rights law and EU law. In order to properly carry out this task, however, I will start with some systematic remarks on the relevance of international human rights law in the selected countries. For the purposes of the present discussion, I shall also deal with the development of a human rights law of the European Union in the field of criminal justice and the relationship between EU law and Italian constitutional law in the area under examination.

---

[3]Ruggeri (2014b) and Pollicino (2014).

[4]Pollicino (2014), p. 9ff.

B. The Relevance of International Human Rights Law in the Selected Countries and Its Relationship with National Law

I. The Long Road Towards the Enhancement of International Human Rights Law in Italy

1. The Traditional Approach to International Human Rights Law and the Weak Formal Status of the European Convention

It has been observed that the main modern charters of international human rights were signed in the post-war era, in the same period that Italy enacted its first republican Constitution. The drafters of the Italian Constitution, however, did not provide general clauses governing the relationship between national law and international human rights law. To be sure, the 1947 Constitution introduced a provision allowing for the automatic domestication of the 'international law principles generally acknowledged by the community of States'.[5] However, this formulation was traditionally interpreted as relating solely to international customary law.[6] Moreover, the Constitution provided for the possibility of limitations of sovereignty, limitations, however, allowed only in favour of legal orders aimed at ensuring peace and justice among the nations.[7] From this it followed that international law instruments, whatever their source, were to be relegated to the level of ordinary legislation.[8]

Against this background, it is not surprising that the Italian legislature followed the same approach to international human rights instruments, which were ratified by means of ordinary laws[9] that inevitably conferred them the status of sub-constitutional law. The main consequence was that the 'para-legislative' rank of international human rights charters could not make them resistant against subsequent domestic law. As noted, this formalistic approach became increasingly unsatisfactory as human rights instruments gained relevance in the international scenario.[10] In particular, the enhanced role played by the Strasbourg judiciary in the late 1960s, despite the relatively scant case-law,[11] gave rise to an in-depth reflection

[5]Art. 10(1) Const.-Italy.

[6]In the judgment 238/2014, the Constitutional Court re-interpreted this constitutional provision by deeming a rule of international customary law as inexistent if it infringes on a fundamental principle of domestic law.

[7]Art. 11 Const.-Italy.

[8]Exceptions were provided for in relation to a number of treaties explicitly acknowledged by the Constitution, such as the treaties with the Holy See and the treaties concerned with the status of aliens.

[9]Italy ratified the European Convention through Law 848/1955 and the International Covenant through Law 881/1977.

[10]Chapter 2, B.II.1.

[11]Chiavario (2008), p. 11ff.

on the procedure used to transpose international human rights instruments into national law.

2. The Contribution of the Constitutional Case-Law to the Enhancement of International Human Rights Law and the Legislative Reforms of the Constitution

It took many decades, however, for a change in the traditional understanding of the status of international human rights law and its relevance in the field of criminal justice. In Italy, the constitutional case-law has strongly contributed to the enhancement of international human rights law in various fashions. In the early 1970s, the Constitutional Court had already provided a systematic re-interpretation of the Constitution by acknowledging some of the main fair trial guarantees enshrined in the European Convention (*e.g.*, the right to be tried in a public hearing), although they were not formally laid down by the 1947 Constitution.[12] It was only in the 1990s, however, that the Constitutional Court, dealing with linguistic assistance in criminal proceedings, acknowledged the particular status of the Law ratifying the European Convention and therefore of the European Convention itself. According to the constitutional case-law, this Charter was an 'atypical source of law', which could not therefore be equalised to ordinary domestic legislation.[13] On close examination, this acknowledgement did not confer constitutional status to the European Convention. Nevertheless, it was the first time that the Constitutional Court elevated an international human rights instrument from its para-legislative status by making it immune to the risk of being repealed or amended by subsequent domestic legislation. Most significantly, this approach also required Italian courts to interpret domestic law in the light of the European Convention, broadening the scope especially of the fair trial guarantees with a view to making the protection of the individuals involved in criminal proceedings as effective as possible.[14]

This important ruling, despite not followed up by other rulings, laid the foundations for a more virtuous interaction between domestic and international human rights law. In subsequent decisions, the Constitutional Court confirmed the special status of international human rights charters. In 1999, the constitutional case-law recognised that the human rights provided for in universal or regional conventions ratified by Italy are protected with equal intensity by the Constitution on the ground of the general acknowledgement of the inviolable rights of the person under Article 2 of the Constitution.[15] Starting with this premise, the constitutional judges reached a conclusion of great systematic importance, namely that, beyond individual similarities and differences, the rules on individual rights must be defined by means of

[12]CConst, 12/1971, 17/1981, etc. On this topic see Di Chiara (2009), p. 293ff.

[13]CConst, 10/1993.

[14]*Ibid.*

[15]CConst, 388/1999.

integrated interpretation.[16] Yet this cultural change was not a linear process and it is therefore no surprise that in other rulings issued in the 1990s, the constitutional case-law moved back to the traditional approach based on the formal rank of international human rights law instruments.[17]

At the end of the last century, however, it was already high time that international human rights law was elevated from the formal status of ordinary legislation. In the 1980s, under the increasing influence of the Strasbourg case-law, the drafters of the 1987 Delegation Law for the new code, while calling for a shift towards the adversarial model, had already required the Government to fulfil the obligations deriving from the international conventions on human rights ratified by Italy and relevant in the field of criminal justice.[18] To be sure, this provision also did not prevent the legislature from departing from international law in a future. As a result of this directive, however, the drafters of the 1988 code had to comply with the international requirements to avoid the risk of the unconstitutionality of the new rules for exceeding the limits laid down by the Delegation Law.

The opportunity for the formal enhancement of the European Convention was provided at the end of the 1990s by a controversial ruling of the Constitutional Court. As noted, judgment 361/1998 allowed for the admission at trial of inconsistent and untested evidence given by co-defendants out of court under the conditions laid down by the 1992 anti-mafia legislation for witness testimony. The 1999 fair trial reform, launched as a reaction to this decision, did not aim, however, at constitutionalising the whole European Convention but only enacted into the Constitution a number of 'substantial' fair trial rights of Article 6 ECHR. Compared to the European Convention, moreover, some of these guarantees were laid down with significant differences, whereas other fundamental rights already enshrined in the Italian Constitution, such as the presumption of innocence, remained untouched in their original version. On close examination, the debates on the formal status of the European Convention and the lack of a consistent constitutional case-law can explain the piecemeal approach of the 1999 constitutional reform. Moreover, it was probably because of the urgent need to erase the findings of the ruling 361/1998 that the Italian legislature missed an important opportunity to give coherent solution to the relationship between international human rights instruments and domestic law.

In 2001, another constitutional reform followed a different path to enhance the role of international human rights law. By reforming the constitutional rules on distribution of legislative competences between state and regional government authorities, Constitution Law 3/2001, as noted, amended Article 117 of the Constitution, requiring both the state and the regions to exercise their legislative powers pursuant to the obligations deriving not only from the Constitution but also from EU law and

[16]This judgment, however, followed a somewhat ambiguous approach in that it recognised that constitutional law in any case provided protection not less intensive than that of international charters.

[17]Cf., *inter alia*, CConst, 438/1993, 15/1996, etc.

[18]Art. 1 Law 81/1987.

international law.[19] To be sure, the 2001 reform did not entail the automatic domestication of any international law instrument other than customary international law but only required the national and regional legislatures to abide by international law. Certainly, this reform called for in-depth reflection on the relationship between domestic and international law.

In the subsequent years, significant developments occurred in the constitutional case-law, which entailed a revolutionary change in the understanding of the relationship between domestic law and international human rights charters (particularly the European Convention). Six years after the 2001 constitutional reform, the Constitutional Court issued two important rulings (later known as 'twin judgments'), in which it elucidated with extensive arguments the intermediate rank of the European Convention between the Constitution and ordinary laws.[20] In fact, the 2001 reform did not confer international human rights law constitutional relevance *per se* but through a provision of the Constitution, which therefore still held the highest rank. From this it followed that, if a subsequent domestic law infringed on the European Convention, this would give rise to a violation of the general requirement of Article 117 of the Constitution. In this case, the domestic law should be declared unconstitutional, provided, however, that the international human rights Charter is consistent with constitutional law. Moreover, constitutional case-law required national courts to make every attempt to find an interpretation of domestic law in conformity with the European Convention.

By this means, the Constitutional Court achieved two important results, i.e. (*a*) it converted a review of conformity with the human rights protections of the European Convention into a general review of constitutionality and (*b*) it promoted a centralised system of reviewing conformity with the Convention by proclaiming itself the sole competent court to solve any dispute between domestic law and the European Convention.

The achievements of the twin judgments gave rise to several human rights concerns. The main shortcoming was that the Constitutional Court emphasised the conflicts existing in the relationship between domestic law and international human rights instruments. This did not properly reflect, however, the complex relationship between and the different forms of mutual influence by domestic and international case-law, while also frustrating the role of national courts. Insofar as it has formed part of Italian law since ratification, there can be little doubt that outside conflicted cases, national judges not only are allowed but are furthermore required to apply the European Convention *e.g.* in cases where international human rights law fills a legal gap in domestic law without giving rise to any conflict,[21] or in the case in which a provision of the Rome Convention substantially coincides with a self-executing rule of the Nice-Strasbourg Charter.

---

[19] Art. 117(1) Const.-Italy.

[20] CConst, 348/2007 and 349/2007. On these judgments see, among others, Ruggeri (2007); Pollicino (2008), p. 363ff.

[21] Viganò (2014).

3. The Shift from the Formal Perspective to the Para-Constitutional Relevance of International Human Rights Law. The Complex Relationship Between Constitutional and Strasbourg Case-Law

Subsequent constitutional case-law, while maintaining the foundations of the approach adopted in the twin judgements, progressively enhanced the role of national courts (as well as of the Constitutional Court itself) in terms of the interpretation and application of the European Convention in concrete cases. It is worth observing that in the twins judgments, the Constitutional Court stressed that the special rank of international human rights law is in line with the institutional function of the Strasbourg Court as the official interpreter of the European Convention. According to the constitutional case-law, therefore, super-legislative status should be conferred not just to the European Convention *per se* but to the Strasbourg case-law, in accord with which both domestic law and even constitutional law must always be interpreted.[22] On close examination, these findings were not consistent with the sub-constitutional status acknowledged to the European Convention, shifting the focus from the formal rank of the Rome Convention to the substantial relevance of international human rights law, a relevance that, concurring with constitutional law, must also be para-constitutional.[23]

At any rate, it is noteworthy that in the 2007 judgments, the Constitutional Court emphasised the determinant role of European case-law in continuing to re-define the scope of the Convention's guarantees beyond the minimum standards of human rights protection. Notwithstanding the high cultural value of the openness shown by the Italian constitutional case-law, it cannot be overlooked that this approach poses very difficult challenges for national courts for several reasons. On one hand, the enormous number of European rulings, which are issued in languages foreign to the judges of most contracting countries and provide solutions reached in relation to very different legal systems, do not make it easy for Italian courts to draw clear parallels with the cases at hand. On the other hand, the decision-making of the Strasbourg case-law—despite the increasing tendency to consolidate a number of doctrines beyond the peculiarities of individual legal systems—is still strongly linked with a case-related approach. From this it follows that the arrangements adopted by the European Court can be properly assessed for the purposes of the interpretation of national law only insofar as domestic judges are able to understand the legal context in which the decisions were issued, a difficult task even for constitutional courts. This casts doubt on whether the constant reference to international human rights case-law can truly help redefine the status of the Convention's guarantees in abstract terms. Interpretation cannot by definition give unequivocal responses to formal questions, even in a centralised model such as that envisaged by the Constitutional Court.

---

[22]CConst, 348/2007.

[23]Ruggeri (2007), p. 2.

In this regard, as anticipated, further developments have occurred in the constitutional case-law over last decade. In 2009, the Constitutional Court started strengthening the role of national courts, while circumscribing the general obligation to abide by Strasbourg case-law solely to 'substantial jurisprudence',[24] a formulation that has been deemed to be somewhat ambiguous. More recently, the Court recognised the binding nature of Strasbourg case-law in cases not only of pilot judgments[25] but also of consolidated jurisprudence.[26] This paves the way for a further evolution of the constitutional case-law towards the acknowledgement of new forms of scrutiny of conformity with the Convention, which more directly involve national courts.[27]

II. The Relevance of the American Convention in the Contracting States and the Relationship with National Law

1. The Multisided Relevance of International Human Rights Law in Brazil

At first glance, international human rights law holds a clear status in Brazilian law. Unlike other Constitutions, the 1988 Brazilian Constitution, far from introducing an exhaustive list of fundamental rights and freedoms, acknowledged in advance 'further rights and guarantees' enshrined in the international treaties already in force in Brazil.[28] On close examination, the problem is more complex and it is not an easy task to define the role of international human rights law in Brazilian law or its relationship with constitutional law in particular. Despite this constitutional acknowledgment, international human rights instruments are not automatically domesticated in Brazil. Furthermore, like other international law instruments not concerned with human rights, both the International Covenant and the American Convention were enacted into Brazilian law by means of legislative decrees.[29] Like in Italy, this approach therefore posed the problem of the rank of international human rights charters in national law.

---

[24]CConst, 311/2009.

[25]CConst, 210/2013.

[26]CConst, 49/2015.

[27]Lamarque and Viganò (2014), p. 20ff.; Ruggeri (2015), p. 22 fn. 32.

[28]Art. 5(2) Const.-Brazil. Other countries in Latin America adopted a similar solution. For instance, the Chilean Constitution, as amended in 1989, requires all the bodies of the State to promote the essential rights deriving from human nature, as guaranteed by the Constitution as well as by international treaties in force in Chile. See Art. 5(2) Const.-Chile. See Art. 5(2) Const.-Chile.

[29]Both were enacted and promulgated between 1991 and 1992, that is, respectively, the ICCPR through Legislative Decree 226/1991 and Executive Decree 592/1992, the ACHR though Legislative Decree 27/1992 and Executive Decree 678/1992.

In general terms, the sub-constitutional position of international law treaties is uncontroversial.[30] As far as international human rights law is concerned, however, this formal conclusion turns out to place it at a legislative level, with the result that subsequent domestic legislative changes would frustrate the effects of international human rights instruments on domestic law.[31] This led in 2004 to a constitutional amendment,[32] which enacted a new paragraph 3 into Article 5 of the Federal Constitution. By this means, international human rights instruments, adopted by means of a special quorum, were made equivalent to constitutional amendments.

From this approach it follows that the set of constitutional rights (*bloco de constitucionalidade*) should be integrated with the human rights enacted through constitutional instruments[33] as well as by those provided for by the treaties domesticated through the formal procedure of Article 5(3) of the Constitution.[34] The logical consequence of this approach is a considerable broadening of the scope of the review of constitutionality of domestic law.[35] The main problem, however, still relates to the status of the international human rights instruments, such as the Pact of San José and the International Covenant, which were domesticated before the 2004 constitutional reform.[36] Certainly, the dual regime laid down in Article 5 of the Constitution does not best fit international human rights law.[37] It might be argued that the provision of paragraph 2—opening the constitutional set of fundamental rights and freedoms towards the international treaties in force in Brazil—suffices to acknowledge the constitutional nature of human rights charters, even if adopted before 2004.[38] Although the federal judge Celso de Mello strongly supported this doctrine,[39] the Federal Supreme Tribunal has not yet shared this opinion and the prevailing case-law, according to the decision of the Plenary on 3 December 2008, is that international human rights law has a special, yet intermediate, position between domestic legislation and the Constitution.[40]

Even in these terms, the acknowledgment of the super-legislative (albeit sub-constitutional) rank that international human rights instruments hold as a minimum threshold enables a review of compliance of domestic law with international human rights law (*controle de convencionalidade*).[41] This review can have different features and can be carried out mainly at two different levels. On one

[30]Giacomolli (2014), p. 17.

[31]*Ibid.*, 18.

[32]Constitutional Amendment Law 45/2004.

[33]Mazzuoli (2011), p. 28f.

[34]Giacomolli (2014), p. 16.

[35]Sarlet (2008).

[36]Giacomolli (2014), p. 19.

[37]*Ibid.*

[38]Sarlet (2008); Mazzuoli (2011), p. 25ff.

[39]*HC* 87.585-8, rel. Celso de Mello.

[40]Giacomolli (2014), p. 21f.

[41]Mazzuoli (2011).

hand, Brazilian courts have a general competence to carry out a scrutiny of conformity with the Convention in individual cases (*controle difuso ou concreto*).[42] On the other, the Federal Supreme Tribunal must assess the abstract compatibility of domestic law with international human rights law in force in Brazil (*controle concentrado ou abstracto*) pursuant to the forms laid down by Article 103 of the Constitution.[43]

Against this background, there can be little doubt that Brazilian case-law has played a decisive role in the humanisation of criminal proceedings by carrying out a twofold check on the compliance of national law with both constitutional and international human rights law. Moreover, the American Convention expressly requires that, as far as domestic law does not secure the freedoms and rights acknowledged at the international law level, the contracting states must adopt legislative and any other means to ensure the effective protection of those rights and freedoms.[44] This entails the obligation of the domestic legal order to contribute to the proper fulfilment of international law safeguards, an obligation that does not only lie with the legislature but also with other public bodies.[45]

2. The Strong Approach of the Inter-American Court to Constitutional Law, Viewed from the Perspective of Brazilian Law

As in Italy, one highly delicate problem concerns the relationship between international human rights law and constitutional law. It has been noted that from the perspective of the Brazilian constitutional case-law, this relationship can have different features depending on the formal procedure of enactment of international law instruments. As a minimum, however, international charters which were not domesticated pursuant to the procedure introduced in the 2004 constitutional amendment reform, such as the American Convention, should be ensured an intermediate rank between domestic legislation and constitutional law.

It is also questionable how the Inter-American Court deals with this problematic area. A close examination of the Inter-American case-law highlights a different approach to the constitutional law of the contracting States. In the 2001 *"The Last Temptation of Christ" (Olmedo-Bustos et al.) v. Chile* case, the Inter-American Court had already acknowledged that there is also a risk that constitutional law infringes on the Convention. Therefore, the Court stressed that 'the international responsibility of the State may be engaged by acts or omissions of any power or organ of the State, whatsoever its rank, that violates the American Convention'.[46] In the case at stake, the state's responsibility derived from a provision of the Chilean

[42] Art. 105(III)(a) Const.-Brazil.

[43] See in detail Mazzuoli (2011), p. 73ff.

[44] Art. 2 ACHR.

[45] Giacomolli (2014), p. 26f.

[46] IACtHR, *"The Last Temptation of Christ" (Olmedo-Bustos et al.) v. Chile*, § 72.

Constitution, which provided for previous censorship of cinematographic films. In even more clear terms, judge *Antônio A. Cançado Trindade* pointed out, in his concurring opinion on this case, that

> [A]ny norm of domestic law, irrespective of its rank (constitutional or infra-constitutional), can, by its own existence and applicability, per se engage the responsibility of a State Party to a human rights treaty.[47]

This explains why the Inter-American Court also constantly requires national courts to carry out a concrete scrutiny of consistency of domestic law with the American Convention, a review that, significantly, must be conducted in the light of the Inter-American case-law.[48] The terms in which the scrutiny of conformity with the Convention should be conducted were recently clarified by the *ad hoc* judge *Eduardo Ferrer Mac-Gregor Poisot* in his concurring opinion in the judgment in *Cabrera García and Montiel Flores v. Mexico*.[49] Furthermore, the *ad hoc* judge *Roberto de Figueiredo Caldas* pointed out, in his concurring opinion in the judgment in *Gomes Lund et al. ("Guerrilha do Araguaia") v. Brazil*, that

> all public powers and national spheres, as well as the respective Federal, state and municipal legislatures of all adherent States are under obligation to respect it and conform it.[50]

The fact that national courts must ensure compliance of the state's legal action with international human rights law, however, does not mean that the American Convention holds the status of supranational law, as instead stressed by Roberto de Figueiredo Caldas in the aforementioned concurring opinion.[51] It cannot be ruled out that the application of a human rights treaty can expose the state's law action to the infringement of domestic constitutional requirements in a concrete case. If national bodies must ensure the most effective protection of fundamental rights and can depart from national law where international law provides a higher protection in a concrete case,[52] departure should also logically be allowed from international human rights law where domestic law provides for higher protection. Significantly, the Pact of San José specifies that none of its provisions can be interpreted as 'restricting the enjoyment or exercise of any right or freedom recognized by virtue of the laws of any state party or by virtue of another convention to which one of the said states is a party'.[53] This fundamental provision reveals the awareness by the drafters of the American Convention that domestic law can lead in the concrete case to elevating the standards of human rights protection provided by international law.

---

[47]Para. 40.

[48]IACtHR, *Almonacid Arellano et al. v. Chile*, § 125.

[49]Paras 13 et seqq.

[50]Para. 5.

[51]Para. 5.

[52]Giacomolli (2014), p. 26.

[53]Art. 29(b) ACHR.

The Brazilian Constitution moves in a similar direction by providing for the Federal Republic basing its international relationships on the prevalence of human rights.[54] In this way, the 1988 Constitution highlights the need for an interpretation *pro homine* of the relationship between constitutional and international human rights law, requiring application of the rules that at best protect the individuals concerned in a concrete case.[55] This result should not be viewed, however, as a limitation of sovereignty, since the Constitution itself places human dignity at the heart of the Brazilian Federal Republic.[56]

III. Comparative Remarks

The comparative analysis of Italian and Brazilian law highlights some common lines in the road towards the enhancement of the formal status of international human rights law. In Italy, the 1947 Constitution did not enact specific rules on international human rights law and the provision on the automatic domestication of the international law principles generally acknowledged by the community of states was traditionally interpreted as relating solely to international customary law. The use of the ordinary legislative procedure to ratify both the European Convention and the International Covenant relegated both these Charters to a para-legislative level. Similar problems arose in Brazil. However, it is worth observing that the 1988 Federal Constitution—enacted 40 years later than the Italian Constitution—made it clear that the rights and safeguards laid down at the constitutional level do not exclude further rights enshrined, *inter alia*, in international law instruments in force in Brazil. This fundamental provision should in principle suffice to ensure constitutional status to all the international human rights instruments in force in Brazil. Nevertheless, the constitutional federal case-law has not yet shared this approach on the assumption that under the 2004 constitutional reform, only international instruments adopted by means of a special quorum can be deemed equivalent to constitutional amendments. Whereas this reform certainly broadened the set of constitutional rights, fundamental human rights charters, such as the Pact of San José, should be considered as placed at a legislative level solely on the basis that they were domesticated before 2004.

On close examination, the Brazilian federal case-law has already acknowledged the special rank of international human rights instruments between domestic legislation and the Constitution.[57] This conclusion coincides with the approach

[54]Art. 4(II) Const.-Brazil.

[55]Giacomolli (2014), p. 21.

[56]Art. 1(III) Const.-Brazil. In even more explicit terms, the Chilean Constitution, as amended in 1989, provides for that the exercise of sovereignty is limited by the respect for the essential rights deriving from human nature. Cf. Art. 5(2) Const.-Chile.

[57]Giacomolli (2014), p. 21f.

anticipated in 1993 by the Italian Constitution Court, in which it recognised the atypical nature of the European Convention. In the absence of an explicit acknowledgment of international conventional law by the Constitution at that time, however, this case-law remained isolated, and, except a few rulings, the Constitutional Court maintained its traditional approach throughout the 1990s. A full constitutionalisation of the European Convention was not achieved by the 1999 reform, which only enacted some of the fair trial rights of Article 6 ECHR. The 2001 constitutional reform in turn aimed at binding the national and regional legislatures to the obligations deriving from EU law and international law. This can explain the compromise approach of the 2007 twin judgments, through which the Constitutional Court returned to the doctrine of the intermediate rank of the European Convention between the Constitution and domestic legislation.

The consequences of this common approach, however, were considerably different in the two countries examined. In Italy, the acknowledgment of the atypical status of the European Convention led the constitutional case-law to convert the review of conformity with international human rights law into the general review of constitutionality. The Constitutional Court, therefore, promotes a centralised system of review of conformity with the Convention, which still partially inspires the approach of the constitutional case-law. This leaves limited room for the direct application of the European Convention by Italian courts, while enhancing a conflict-oriented understanding of the relationship between domestic and international human rights law. In Brazil, while the Constitution empowers the Federal Supreme Tribunal to assess the compliance of domestic law with international human rights treaties in force in Brazil, the doctrine of the intermediate rank of the international human rights law does not rule out a further review of conformity with the Convention, which is entrusted to national courts in each concrete case. On close examination, significant developments could also be observed in Italy over recent years, developments that have led to the progressive enhancement of the role of the national judiciary. According to the current constitutional case-law, national courts should abide by the European Convention in cases of 'pilot judgments' and the consolidated case-law of the Strasbourg Court. Here also, however, Italian judges are called upon to scrutinise whether or not the European case-law is in line with the Constitution. In the case of non-compliance with constitutional law, the constitutionality of the Ratification Law of the European Convention could be challenged before the Constitutional Court.

Certainly, the softening of a centralised review of conformity with international human rights law can be explained in the light of the importance attached in both Italy and Brazil to international human rights case-law. In the twin judgments, the Italian Constitutional Court already pointed out that the obligation of compliance with the European Convention must be interpreted in the light of the Strasbourg case-law, an approach maintained notwithstanding that the constitutional judges somewhat curtailed the duty of abiding with Strasbourg jurisprudence. In Brazil also, there can be no doubt that the scrutiny of conformity to the American Convention required from national courts must be conducted in the light of the Inter-American case-law. These findings highlight the widespread awareness that the meaning and the scope of international law safeguards cannot be defined in abstract terms but are to be constantly re-defined by international human rights case-law. In the light of this, it is also apparent that the competent authorities, which are more familiar with the human rights challenges pertaining to the case at hand, can properly assess compliance with international human rights instruments.

The convergence towards flexible decentralised models of scrutiny of conformity with international conventions also demonstrates that the relationship between domestic law and international human rights cannot be characterised as an unconditional duty of compliance with international human rights case-law. In the light of this, it is understandable that the Inter-American Court stressed that any norm of domestic law, even of a constitutional nature, can infringe upon the American Convention. However, if compliance should not be ensured with static safeguards but with dynamic guarantees, as recognised by international human rights case-law in concrete cases, one cannot exclude that the application of international human rights law exposes the state's law action to the risk of violation of constitutional requirements. In Brazil, these legislative antinomies must be solved in the light of the approach of the Federal Constitution, which, basing its international relationships on the prevalence of human rights, calls for an interpretation *pro homine*. It is worth observing that in Italy the constitutional law scholarship has also long proposed a similar approach, calling for a dynamic relationship between domestic and international human rights law in the light of the principle of the highest protection of fundamental rights.[58] Remarkably, this approach also enhances the systematic scope of the constitutional requirements of human dignity and equal treatment,[59] which, therefore, constitute in a sense super-constitutional values.[60] Although the Italian Constitutional Court has on various occasions recognised the principle of the highest protection of fundamental rights, constitutional courts in both countries have until now preferred a somewhat traditional understanding of the relationship between constitutional and international human rights law.

C. The Relevance of EU Human Rights Law and the Relationship with Constitutional Law

I. The Approach of the EU Court of Justice and the Reaction of Constitutional Courts in the EU Area

For the purposes of the present discussion, we shall now focus on the development of EU human rights law and its relationship with constitutional law. From the

[58]See recently Ruggeri (2015), p. 9ff.

[59]Ruggeri (2010), p. 16.

[60]Ruggeri (2015), p. 13.

perspective of transnational criminal justice and the participatory rights in criminal proceedings, this difficult matter took on particular relevance in the *Melloni* case dealt with by the Court of Justice several years ago. As noted, this ruling was issued after Framework Decision 2009/299/JHA had strengthened the defence rights of the person requested through a European arrest warrant, if prosecuted *in absentia* in the trial State.[61] It has been observed that among the questions that the Spanish Constitutional Tribunal referred to the Luxembourg Court, the third one was whether national authorities can make surrender conditional on the possibility of an effective judicial remedy in order to avoid a violation of constitutional law whenever it provides a higher level of protection than that offered by EU law. In other terms, the question was whether EU human rights law can overcome the protection threshold of constitutional law and whether member states can depart from EU law if it endangers inviolable rights acknowledged by constitutional law.

In the *Melloni* case, the Luxembourg Court gave a clear negative response on the assumption that a broad interpretation of the 2009 legislation would frustrate the mutual recognition principle. We have noted that the situations of the new Article 4a were included into an exhaustive list, which requires the executing authority to surrender the sought person. The need not to frustrate the milestone of the judicial cooperation in the EU area led the Luxembourg Court even to adopt a restrictive interpretation of Article 53 of the Fundamental Rights Charter, which rules out national authorities invoking the requirements of their constitutional law to achieve a stronger protection of the individuals rights at stake. The main reason is that it would endanger the need for a uniform application and—at a deeper level still—the primacy of EU law, jeopardising the mutual trust among member states which lies at the core of the principle of mutual recognition.

Whatever views one has of this case, there can be little doubt that it gave rise a contrast between the two courts, which led to a confrontation not just between two legal systems but between two different cultural conceptions of constitutional law as a system of fundamental rights protection.[62] The first one conceives national constitutional law as a source of enrichment of EU law and is furthermore based on the mutual fertilisation of systems of fundamental rights, which can contribute to achieving the best solution in a concrete case. The second looks at national constitutional law as an obstacle to the full realization of EU law, viewed as a self-sufficient system with its own forms of fundamental rights protection. On close examination, separately from the view of the Luxembourg Court, EU law also rejects a self-referential model, while advocating a transcultural understanding of the relationship with national (constitutional) law. This is apparent from various statutory indications at the primary law level. Alongside Article 53 of the Nice-Strasbourg Charter, which reflects the flexible and open approach of EU law towards other legal systems, Article 4 TEU requires the European Union to respect the national identity of member states. There is little doubt that this formulation

[61] Chapter 13, B.II.2.b.

[62] Ruggeri (2015), p. 10ff.

should also be extended to the constitutional identity of EU countries, which in turn not only relates to the state apparatus but also to the overall system of fundamental rights protection.[63] Furthermore, we have seen that the common area of freedom, security and justice can only exist as long as the strongest protection of fundamental rights is ensured. This demonstrates that, where individual safeguards are at stake, there can be no room for rigid forms of respect for single legal systems as traditionally interpreted. Remarkably, the principle of sincere cooperation, enshrined in Article 4 TEU itself, requires the Union and the member states to assist each other in carrying out tasks flowing from the Treaties, tasks that certainly encompass the achievement of the strongest protection of the fundamental rights of the individuals involved in transborder criminal procedures.

The *Melloni* judgment has given rise to different reactions by national courts. The Spanish Constitutional Tribunal, ruling on the *amparo* filed by Mr. Melloni, complied with the judgment of the Luxembourg Court.[64] The constitutional judges invoked the Strasbourg case-law, which enables defendants to waive their right to personal participation in criminal proceedings, while requiring the state to provide them with the assistance of a lawyer in any case—remarkably, even in the case of unjustified absence. In other words, the Spanish Tribunal simply relied on the doctrine, shared by the Luxembourg Court, which allows for unequivocal waiver of the right to personal involvement in criminal proceedings, provided that the accused is ensured legal assistance. Starting with this premise, the constitutional judges, while confirming the doctrine of indirect violation of fundamental rights, revised the conclusions of the 2000 judgment by ruling out the requirement of a retrial being always a necessary condition to save the fairness of a procedure held *in absentia* in the requesting country. To support this conclusion, they relied on the fact that information on the proceedings had been provided to the two lawyers of Mr Melloni, who not only was therefore ensured legal assistance but was also put in a position to take part in the proceedings. The Constitutional Tribunal satisfied itself with this information without examining whether the sought person was truly put in a position to participate in the proceedings held against him and whether his absence could be seen as an unequivocal sign of his desire not to participate. Taking into consideration the self-sufficient nature of the situations listed in Article 4a, this argument released the Spanish Court from the obligation to examine whether the Italian rules on appeal proceedings guaranteed a fresh review of the case, as also required by EU law. It is noteworthy, moreover, that the Spanish judges still relied on the requirement, underlined in the 2000 judgment, that the core contents of the right to a fair trial also be fulfilled in a case of transborder cooperation in order to ensure full respect for the constitutional protection of human dignity.

Remarkably, the focus on human dignity lies at the heart of a decision issued in December 2015 by the German Federal Constitutional Court, which challenged the *Melloni* doctrine.[65] The German constitutional judges ruled out the execution of a European arrest warrant, despite fulfilling the safeguards set by

---

[63]On this argument, which was, however, not taken into consideration by the Luxembourg Court in the *Melloni* judgment, see Ruggeri (2015), p. 23.

[64]STC 26/2014.

[65]BVerfG, order of 15 December 2015, Az. 2 BvR 2735/14.

EU law in relation to proceedings held *in absentia*, being able to infringe on the fundamental requirements of human dignity and the rule of law, which form part of the 'inalienable constitutional identity' under Article 79(3) in conjunction with Article 1(1) of the German Basic Law. The reference to the constitutional identity clearly shifts the focus on the aforementioned limit of EU law actions, as set forth by the Treaty of the European Union. It is also worth observing that the Federal Constitutional Court adopted an unprecedented approach to this problematic area from the viewpoint of substantial criminal law. The constitutional judges started with the premise that German criminal law is strongly based on the principle of individual guilt a part of the inalienable constitutional identity. From this it follows that the possibility of a sanction, which also constitutes a socio-ethical reproach (*sozial-ethischer Vorwurf*), presupposes that the competent court could ascertain the accused's individual blameworthiness (*individuelle Vorwerfbarkeit*), as a rule, in his presence.[66] The German Constitutional Court, therefore, deduced from the principle of individual guilt the procedural-law consequence that defendants must always be ensured minimum defence safeguards. Significantly, these safeguards—and particularly the possibility of contributing to the decision-making by presenting 'circumstances for consideration to the court, circumstances that may be exonerating or relevant for sentencing'[67]—must also be guaranteed in the case of international surrender procedures.

Notwithstanding this strong position, it is worth observing that the German Constitutional Court did not consider it necessary to restrict the principle of primacy of Union law by applying the limit of the inalienable constitutional identity. The constitutional judges stressed that in the case at hand, EU law provided adequate protection of the fundamental rights at stake by enabling the executing authority to enforce a European arrest warrant on the condition that the law of the issuing country ensured a remedy aimed at a fair re-examination of the case. This approach led the German Court to exclude any conflict between domestic and EU law, thus avoiding the path of a preliminary request to the European Court of Justice. It might be argued, furthermore, that the *Melloni* case could also have had a different conclusion, if both the Luxembourg Court and the Spanish Constitutional Court had given another consideration to the notice given to Mr Melloni's lawyers.

[66] 'Protection of Fundamental Rights in Individual Cases is Ensured as Part of Identity Review', Press Release No. 4/2016 of 26 January 2016 on BVerfG, order of 15 December 2015, Az. 2 BvR 2735/14, § 2.a.aa.

[67] *Ibid.*

II. The Approach of the Italian Constitutional Court to EU Law and the 'Counter-Limits Doctrine'

Until now, there has not been a judgement by the Italian Constitutional Court on a case similar to that which led to the *Melloni* judgment and it is therefore difficult to say whether it will ever come. On a first level, this is due to the current features of Italian criminal justice. As noted, despite the 2014 reform on default proceedings, Italian law has not yet departed from its traditional approach, which generally allows a criminal law action to be carried out against absent defendants. It is therefore improbable that Italian courts will invoke limitations to transnational cooperation that they cannot apply in domestic cases. On a second level, it should be examined whether or not EU law has absolute primacy over national law and to what extent limits of constitutional law can be invoked. It has been observed that the 2001 constitutional reform amended Article 117 of the Italian Constitution by requiring both national and regional legislation to respect the obligations deriving from international law instruments and EU law. In both respects, it was the first explicit acknowledgment at the constitutional level. This does not mean, however, that EU law was not previously covered by the Constitution. To be sure, like the European Convention, the Treaties establishing the three Communities were enacted into Italian law through an ordinary Law. However, unlike what happened in relation to international human rights charters, the Constitutional Court has long recognised the constitutional relevance of EU law, albeit in a rather indirect way.[68]

The main reason for this difficult process was that, differently from other (more recent) constitutional Charters, the 1947 Constitution lacked, for obvious chronological reasons, an explicit European clause. As noted, the Italian Constitution, while providing for the automatic enactment of the international law principles generally acknowledged by the community of States, allowed for limitations of sovereignty in favour of legal orders aimed at ensuring peace and justice among nations. As *Martinico* and *Pollicino* put it,

> As a matter of fact, Article 11 was originally conceived to deal with Italian membership of organizations like the United Nations rather than to justify the consequence of supranationalism (a phenomenon that was unknown when the Italian Constitution came into force).[69]

This can explain why in the very first ruling on the relationship between community and Italian law in the midst of the 1960s, the Constitutional Court ruled out Article 11 of the Constitution being able to confer to the Law on execution of a treaty higher rank than that of any other ordinary Law.[70] In this judgment, the constitutional case-law advocated a view of a relationship of equal standing

[68]For in depth analysis of the long road that the Constitutional Court has walked to acknowledge the role of community (and later EU) law in Italy see Ruggeri (2014a), p. 300ff.

[69]Martinico (2012), p. 87.

[70]CConst, 14/1964.

between community and Italian law, with the result that—pursuant to the *lex posterior* principle—self-executing community law should prevail over previous domestic law, although it could also be derogated by subsequent national law. It took almost a decade—and the strong reaction by the European Court of Justice, which defended the unconditional primacy of community law[71]—before the Italian Constitutional Court recognised the constitutional relevance of community law under Article 11 of the Constitution, stressing its resistance to subsequent amendment or derogation by domestic law.[72] Since then, the constitutional case-law has maintained this justification, confirming it even after the 2001 reform of Article 117 of the Constitution.

This does not mean, however, the Italian Constitutional Court has unconditionally accepted the primacy of community law. It is worth observing that in its ruling of 1973, the constitutional judges, while recognising the constitutional protection of community law, for the first time opposed a strong barrier to EU law, that is, the fundamental principles of constitutional law and inalienable human rights. This barrier (known as the 'counter-limits doctrine') has characterised the development of constitutional case-law up to the present day, allowing it to resist the persistent tendency to a monistic view of the relationship between EU law and Italian law by the European Court of Justice. On close examination, the Italian Constitutional Court did not align its jurisprudence to that of the Luxembourg Court. Despite the acknowledgment of the constitutional relevance of community law, this did not confer it a super-constitutional status, since the reference to Article 11 of the Constitution made the impact of community law conditional on the limits inherent in the fundamental principles set forth by constitutional law.

The reaction by the Court of Justice to this mechanism was unavoidable and came a few years later in the *Simmenthal* judgment, which required community law to have immediate effect.[73] It took several years before the Italian Constitutional Court found a way to reconcile the divergence from the Luxembourg case-law. In the midst of the 1980s, the constitutional case-law, while confirming the relevance of community law under Article 11, recognised a different technique to solve legislative antinomies between community and domestic law, which entailed for national judges the obligation of directly applying self-executing community law, while not applying domestic law provisions incompatible with supranational law. In particular, the different scope of community and domestic law led the Court to rule out national rules being declared unconstitutional if incompatible with community law. By this means, the Constitutional Court paved the way for a decentralised judicial review of legislation.

Alongside these findings, significant developments have also occurred in the counter-limits doctrine over the last decades. In the 1973 judgment, the

[71]ECJ, *Costa v. Enel*.

[72]CConst, 183/1973. For several criticisms against this acknowledgment see Ruggeri (2014a), p. 303ff.

[73]ECJ, *Simmenthal*.

Constitutional Court invoked the aforementioned counter-limits as the last defensive barrier of constitutional law and it was intended that overcoming this threshold could potentially have endangered even Italy's adhesion to the Communities. In 1984, this point was not sufficiently clarified. Five years later, the *Fragd* judgment marked a considerable change in the understanding of the counter-limits doctrine by the constitutional case-law,[74] which started conceiving them as a condition of non-applicability of the rules of community law inconsistent with the constitutional identity without jeopardising Italy's membership of the Communities.[75] This important specification in the counter-limits doctrine, however, did not prevent the Court from reiterating its availability to have recourse to this instrument to preserve the constitutional identity, which allowed recovering spaces in favour of a centralised judicial review of legislation.

The reference to the fundamental principles of constitutional law and inalienable human rights seems to put the Italian constitutional case-law in a position close to the doctrine on inalienable constitutional identity of the German Constitutional Court. The main practical difference lies in the fact that the Italian Constitutional Court has until now limited itself to proclaiming the threshold of counter-limits without applying them in any concrete case in relation to EU law.[76] One methodological shortcoming of the 'counter-limits doctrine' is that it establishes a rigid hierarchy between Article 11 and the other constitutional principles.[77] This turns out to deny the nature of Article 11, which, allowing for limitations of sovereignty in favour of a legal order aimed at securing peace and justice among the nations, also recognises fundamental values that surely contribute to defining the constitutional identity.[78] Furthermore, we have noted that Article 4 TEU requires the European Union to respect the national identity of Member States.

On the other hand, it should be noted that the constitutional identity increasingly draws on supranational law with a view to an enhanced protection of the values of peace and justice among nations. Moreover, there is a sort of Europeanization of the constitutional counter-limits, which therefore lose their original nature of exceptional resistance to the growing process of European integration while becoming a fundamental principle of EU law.[79] A clear example of the advanced process of integration is the incidence of the common constitutional traditions on the human rights protection provided by the Luxembourg case-law.[80]

---

[74] CConst, 232/1989.

[75] Martinico (2012), p. 89.

[76] Until now, constitutional case-law has availed itself of counter-limits in relation to international customary law (judgment 238/2014). A few days before the present discussion (January 2017), the Constitutional Court ruled on the *Taricco* case (24 January 2017). Notwithstanding that there were great expectations about this decision, the Constitutional Court did not (immediately) invoke counter-limits but preferred to request a preliminary ruling by the EU Court of Justice. See Amalfitano (2017).

[77] Ruggeri (2014a), p. 317.

[78] *Ibid.*, 317f.

[79] *Ibid.*, 320ff.

[80] Pollicino (2015), p. 242ff.

D. Cross-Fertilisation of Systems of Human Rights Protection and the Enhancement of a Participatory Understanding of National Criminal Justice on the Basis of Transcultural Dialogue

I. Premise

Against this background, we can now examine whether and to what extent international human rights law and, as far as Italy is concerned, EU law affected, or may affect in the near future, the national approach to criminal justice in ways relevant to the present discussion. From the aforementioned observations, however, it is apparent that the incidence of international and supranational patterns on national law constitutes only a part of a much more complex problem. It has been observed that legal systems can no longer be considered to be closed models and that a complex cross-fertilisation increasingly characterises the current relationship between different systems of human rights protection. A close examination of the developments occurred over the last decades both in Europe and in Latin America reveals that this phenomenon not only has strongly contributed to the evolution of national law but furthermore to the establishment of autonomous patterns at the level of international law and EU law.

Certainly, the process of mutual confrontation has achieved even more advanced levels over recent years. Domestic arrangements are increasingly metabolised at the international law level and international human rights case-law provides a prominent platform which spreads new patterns to the contracting countries. From the perspective of the present discussion, a clear example is again provided by the *Al-Khawaja* case, which has not only given rise to a strong confrontation between the UK judiciary and the Strasbourg Court but also to an opportunity for the European Court to be confronted with itself and its own jurisprudence on evidence law. Thus the in-depth review of tempered hearsay evidence by the UK Supreme Court led the Grand Chamber not just to dissent with the lower Chamber but furthermore to depart from one of most constant doctrines of the European case-law, namely the sole and decisive evidence threshold.[81] As noted, moreover, this result has not remained circumscribed to the case at hand and to the problem of absent witnesses but also paved the way for the rapid spread of the new case-law in relation to other criminal justice systems and to different forms of witness testimony. It is difficult to predict, however, to what extent this new jurisprudence will be extended and whether it can provide national authorities with clear models in concrete cases.

This raises two important conclusions. The first one is that, while national criminal justice largely draws on international and EU law, the influence of international and supranational patterns cannot be viewed as a one-way incidence originating from closed and well-defined systems of human rights protection. The

---

[81] Vogler (2014), p. 187.

second is that a rigid and abstract approach to the relationship between national law, international human rights case and EU law becomes less and less sustainable, each system undergoing constant adjustments deriving from a confrontation with the others in relation to concrete judicial cases. In this context, the traditional understanding of the relationship between legal systems has increasingly given way to a more flexible and dynamic phenomenon, that is, a horizontal 'transjudicial dialogue' among judges and courts of different jurisdictions, 'sharing the same great project for the international entrenchment of human rights norms'.[82] In Europe especially, hierarchical conceptions are increasingly replaced with a new view based upon heterarchy, namely an 'open architecture' of human rights law,[83] in which, alongside adaptation to external legal patterns, room should also be left for legitimate dissent and the search for higher standards of fundamental rights protection.[84]

II. Personal Participation in Criminal Proceedings and the Lawfulness of Procedures in the Absence of the Individuals Concerned. A Multilevel Approach

1. Right to Personal Participation, Fairness of Criminal Proceedings and *in absentia* Proceedings

a) The Impact of International Human Rights Law on the Developments in Criminal Proceedings *in absentia* and the Persistent Lacunas of National Law

A clear example of the progressive mutual interaction of legal systems with a view to the enhancement of a participatory approach to criminal justice concerns the personal involvement of private parties in criminal proceedings. In Latin America, we have seen that the need to protect vulnerable individuals belonging to rural or indigenous communities, especially if detained in a cultural context different from their own, has led the Inter-American case-law to enhance their right to be personally involved in and to be put in a condition to understand the proceedings instituted against them. As noted, the requirement of physical presence in court also enables the competent authority to check the general conditions of the detainees and to carry out a general assessment of serious human rights infringements, such as forced disappearances.

This strong position has in turn affected the developments that have occurred at the national level. We have seen that the 1988 Constitution played a decisive role in the reform of Brazilian law, which in 1996 abandoned the old default proceedings.

---

[82] *Ibid.*, 182, developing the approach of Slaughter (1994), p. 99ff.

[83] Krisch (2008), p. 184.

[84] Vogler (2014), p. 187.

The subsequent evolution of federal case-law in relation to the accused's right to be present at trial provides a clear example of the increasing attention attached to international human rights law. In 2009, the Supreme Federal Tribunal invoked both the International Covenant and the American Convention, pointing out that even detained defendants must be granted, on pain of the absolute nullification of the proceedings, the right to be present at trial and take part in obtaining witness testimony. This right is of such importance that the failure to involve the accused cannot be justified on the ground of purely administrative needs.[85] This acknowledgment is also noteworthy since it reveals that the principle of *contradictoire* cannot be sacrificed in the light of the need for reasonable length of the criminal proceedings. If the invalidity entailed by the defendant's absence can jeopardise the length of the procedure, the reasonableness of the overall duration of criminal proceedings must be the result of a fair balance among conflicting interests, a balance in which the right to *contradictoire* must in any case be granted.

In order to reduce the negative impact of nullification on criminal proceedings, the Brazilian federal case-law later relativized the role of the defendant's absence in criminal proceedings, stressing that the failure to immediately contest the nullification should not invalidate the whole proceeding.[86] More recently, however, the Federal Supreme Tribunal has returned to its 2009 jurisprudence, opting for an integrated approach, according to which the guarantee of personal participation in criminal proceedings—as enshrined in international human rights law—integrates the constitutional acknowledgment of the right to full defence.[87] In this light, we can hope for in-depth reflection on the maintenance of some dangerous forms of court summons which still exist in Brazilian law, such as the summons *com hora certa* and *citação por edital*.

In Europe, the Strasbourg case-law on *in absentia* trials also reflects the clear attempt to strike a compromise between the requirement of personal involvement of the accused, typical of common-law countries, and the tradition of continental countries, which have long allowed for the conduct of criminal proceedings without the defendant. It is worth observing that the leading *Colozza* decision was concerned with Italian law. In this judgment, the European Court, after deducing by the general guarantee of a fair trial the right of the accused to take part in criminal hearings, recognised the lawfulness of *in absentia* trials—if allowed by national law—provided that the accused can later obtain a fresh re-determination of the merits of the case. The contrast between these two different approaches was apparent from the clear division line, drawn by the Strasbourg Court, between the case of absence due to the accused's waiver of personal participation and the situations in which criminal proceedings are instituted without any clear indication of the defendant's will. In the former case, the Court, stressing the need to grant the accused the possibility not only of personal but also of effective participation,

[85] *HC* 93.503, rel. Celso de Mello.

[86] *HC* 104.404, rel. Dias Toffoli.

[87] *HC* 98.676, rel. Celso de Mello.

called for unequivocal waiver of the right to personal involvement in criminal proceedings, waiver preceded by due information of the individuals concerned. In the latter, national law must ensure a subsequent tool to enable the accused tried *in absentia* to obtain a retrial or a review of the conviction.

As observed, it took several years before this approach could positively affect Italian law. In 1987, the general requirement of compliance with the European Convention, laid down by the Delegation Law for the new code, did not suffice to orient the new criminal justice towards the indications provided by the Strasbourg case-law. Notwithstanding the *Colozza* case, the 1988 codification reproduced the old default proceedings, without, however, drawing a clear distinction between the two main situations highlighted by the European Court. The intrinsic ambiguity of 'contumacy', which applied both to defendants possibly unaware of the institution of criminal proceedings and to those who chose not to participate in the proceedings, can in turn explain the flexible approach of Strasbourg case-law to the Italian default proceedings. Furthermore, the 1988 code did not comply with the need, set forth by the European Court, to ensure a tool aimed at ensuring the opportunity of a retrial to the defendants convicted *in absentia*. The rules on relief from the effects of the expiration of the time to challenge a conviction *in absentia* did not satisfy this requirement, while offloading onto defendants the burden of proving that they remained unaware of the proceedings without fault.

It took further two decades before the Italian legislature, under the pressure of new convictions by the Strasbourg Court, reformed the rules on relief from the effects of the expiration of the time to challenge an *in absentia* conviction. It must be acknowledged, however, that the European Court further developed its autonomous case-law over the years. On one hand, if waiver of participation presupposes specific information duties on the part of the competent authorities, the Court pointed out that a duty of diligence should also be required from defendants, especially if they are equipped with legal knowledge to give their contribution to the fact-finding. On the other, the Strasbourg case-law has become more and more flexible as to the requirements of subsequent remedies. In the *Öcalan* case, the Court stressed that the suitability of the subsequent remedy largely depends on the circumstances of each concrete case, which should be assessed in the light of the degree of effectiveness of the right to a defence in domestic proceedings.[88] On close examination, the evolution of the European case-law on the right to a retrial turned out to blur the requirement that a public interest justify the conduct of a criminal law action and that the competent authorities comply with their duty of informing the accused about the institution of criminal proceedings.

A clear example was the saga of the decisions issued by the European Court dealing with the Italian default proceedings after the 2005 reform. It has been anticipated that, notwithstanding its merits, this legislation did not satisfy the requirement of a fresh re-determination of the merits of the case. Despite some

[88]In *Mariani v. France*, the Court also seemed to focus solely on whether the defendant was given the opportunity of applying for a retrial.

important achievements, therefore, this important reform could not erase some structural deficiencies of Italian law. Defendants convicted *in absentia* were not ensured the opportunity of a retrial but only had a facilitated access to the second instance, characterised, however, by considerable limitations compared to the first instance. Defendants have no possibility of applying for alternative proceedings in the appeal proceedings. Furthermore, the appeal proceedings maintained the original structure of a scrutiny of the judgment rendered *in absentia*, a scrutiny based mainly on the written records of evidence already collected. Despite opening the door of second instance, moreover, Law 60/2005 failed to amend the conditions for the exercise of the right to evidence in the appeal proceedings. As a consequence, defendants could only have evidence obtained in the second instance by proving that they had been unaware of the initiation of criminal proceedings.[89]

In sum, the solutions provided in 2005 guaranteed in a very weak way the right to effective participation in proceedings[90] and a rigorous application of the original case-law of the European Court would probably have sufficed to find an infringement of the Convention. In the *Sejdovic* case, however, the Grand Chamber, while upholding the conviction of Italy, provided a rather ambiguous response to the 2005 reform,[91] stressing that it was still premature, in the absence of case-law on the new regulation, to draw conclusions on its ability to avoid future infringements of the Convention.[92] Yet the case-law developed after 2005 revealed a rather incoherent picture, highlighting the dangerous shift back towards solutions close to those reached before 2005.[93] Notwithstanding these developments, the *Cat Berro* decision confirmed the adequacy of the 2005 legislative reform to ensure to defendants tried *in absentia* the full satisfaction of their right to a retrial.[94] It would be an oversimplification to say, however, that this result was only due to the aim of reducing inconsistency with Italy in this delicate field. Furthermore, a close examination of the rules on judicial service and on court summons would probably have enabled the European Court to draw different conclusions on the Italian reform of 2005. Indeed, these rules remained unchanged and did not therefore put the accused in a position to waive personal participation.

It took almost another decade before the Italian legislature intervened again in this problematic area. Nevertheless, the new procedure for absent defendants,

[89]Negri (2005), p. 268; Quattrocolo (2014), p. 8.

[90]Carini (2008), p. 283.

[91]Chiavario (2005), p. 256.

[92]ECtHR, Grand Chamber, *Sejdovic v. Italy*.

[93]In some decisions, the Supreme Court offloaded onto the competent authority the task of demonstrating the interruption of any contact between the defendants and their lawyers, if the conviction issued *in absentia* was notified at the law firm chosen by the defendants as their legal domicile. See CCass, *Bidimost*. In other decisions, however, the Supreme Court, while deeming the notification at the law firm equivalent to a personal notification, charged defendants again with the burden of proving the reasons for which they had remained unaware of the notification made at their legal domicile. See CCass, *Ciarlantini*; CCass, *Gherasim*.

[94]ECtHR, *Cat Berro v. Italy*.

despite having largely replaced the old default proceedings, gives rise to further human rights concerns. The examination of the 2014 reform in light of the European Convention reveals that one of the main deficiencies of Law 67/2014 is the high degree of heterogeneity of the situations in which defendants are absent. Certainly, allowing for prosecution to be carried out in the case of defendants who expressly waived their right to be present is in line with the ECHR requirements. The same conclusion, however, does not apply to the case in which the accused was personally summoned to court[95] but did not appear in court for unknown reasons. On close examination, these two situations provide respectively more and less than the requirements traditionally laid down by the European Court. In the former case, the 2014 reform, going beyond the Strasbourg case-law, required defendants to waive their right to participation not only unequivocally but also expressly. In the latter, the fact that the defendants were personally notified of the institution of criminal proceedings demonstrates neither that they waived personal participation nor that they fully understood the exact terms of the court summons and the consequences deriving from their absence at trial.[96] In this case, defendants must be granted the possibility of invoking a legal impediment.[97] However, unlike accidents or *force majeure*, legal impediments must be proven: it does not suffice that they are just probable.[98] The most serious concerns, however, arise in relation to other cases of absence, justified on the ground that the accused was informed about the criminal investigations carried out against them or took part in, during the pre-trial phase, certain initiatives demonstrating their knowledge of the prosecutorial inquiry. As noted, these cases highlight dangerous presumptions of knowledge of the court proceedings or even make the knowledge of criminal proceedings a pure accident.[99] There is little doubt that these situations are scarcely compatible with the European Convention.

Further human rights problems concern the new set of subsequent remedies. It has been observed that, if the accused appears in court, the judicial order allowing the continuation of the proceedings must be revoked and the defendant can either apply for new evidence to be taken or request alternative proceedings.[100] The 2014 reform, however, set forth very restrictive conditions for the exercise of these rights. Again, far from ensuring to defendants a realistic possibility of participation in criminal proceedings, Italian law burdened them with the task of proving the grounds for their absence and the ignorance of the process. Furthermore, the proof of these conditions does not always suffice to grant the accused the same defensive

[95] Art. 420-*bis*(2) CCP-Italy.

[96] It has been noted that the new Article 143 CCP-Italy requires the translation of the court summons and the indictment, provided only, however, that the competent authority finds that the defendant is unable to understand Italian.

[97] Quattrocolo (2014), p. 3.

[98] Art. 420-*bis*(3) CCP-Italy.

[99] Chapter 2, F.II.2.

[100] *Ibid.*

opportunities he would have had at the first instance. In particular, the possibility of requesting new evidence does not affect the validity of the information already gathered without the defence's contribution,[101] evidence that can therefore be used to convict them. A positive result, instead, was dropping the restrictions on the right to apply for the collection of new evidence at second instance, restrictions that still reflected the social stigmatisation of contumacy. As a consequence, non-negligent defendants can request the taking of evidence in the appeal proceedings under the same conditions laid down in the first instance.

Against this background, one should have expected that the Italian legislature in 2014 also allowed for a broad form of retrial for defendants tried *in absentia*—at least when absence was not justified by real knowledge of the proceedings. Nevertheless, the rules on the new form of revocation of final judgments largely disappointed these expectations. Again, as noted, access to this remedy is only allowed if the accused can prove that the unawareness of the proceedings was not due to his negligence. By returning to the logic prior to the 2005 reform, Italian law turned out to charge individuals with the proof of negative circumstances rather than offloading onto the competent authority the burden of proof that the continuation of the criminal process is really needed and is based on the defendant's waiver of participation. This result also raises serious concerns in the light of the European Convention.

There is another point that highlights considerably the methodological distance of both Brazilian and Italian law from the international human rights case-law, namely the understanding of personal participation in terms of an individual right. We have seen that the Strasbourg Court especially has not always given positive consideration to the waiver decision, instead emphasising the importance of the personal involvement in criminal proceedings, especially when the accused is equipped with legal knowledge. This in turn led the Court to require contracting countries to discourage unjustified absences. There is no trace in the selected countries of any duty of collaboration with the administration of criminal justice on the part of the accused, who can freely decide whether to take part personally in criminal proceedings. Nor is there any specific obligation for defendants equipped with legal knowledge.

Ultimately, a delicate question concerns the involvement of the accused in appeal proceedings dealing with points of law. The problem does not relate to the proceedings before the Supreme Court, in which the parties are usually represented by a lawyer specifically entitled to defend them.[102] Yet the proceedings at second instance may also aim at the review of legal questions. Doubtless, even appeals on a point of law can worsen the appellant's position, so that the simple fact that an appeal only deals with legal questions should not be sufficient ground for excluding the accused's participation. In Italy, for instance, although *reformatio in pejus*

---

[101] Art. 420-*bis*(4) CCP-Italy.

[102] In Italy, only the lawyers registered in a special register (*albo*) can represent the parties before the Supreme Court. Cf. 613(1) CCP-Italy.

presupposes a prosecutorial appeal against the first instance decision,[103] the appeal lodged solely by the accused can also entail negative results, even though only the legal basis of the case is at stake. Thus Italian law enables the courts of appeal to re-classify legally the offence,[104] a result that, although it cannot lead to a more severe sentence, can justify the application of more rigorous penitentiary rules.[105] It cannot be affirmed, however, that the lack of specific requirements for the accused equipped with legal knowledge is incompatible with the European Convention. As noted, the European Court has not always been very consistent with its own jurisprudence, since it considered the involvement of the accused derogable in higher instances aimed at the examination of the legal foundation of the case.[106]

b) New Perspectives of EU Law and the Room for Manoeuvre for Italian Law

One would have expected that the recent EU intervention by means of Directive 2016/343/EU would enhance the right to personal participation in criminal proceedings, while reducing the room for manoeuvre of the member states in the maintenance of *in absentia* proceedings. The developments that have occurred in Italian law over the last few years in light of the solutions adopted by the EU institutions, however, do not allow us to look at the potentials of EU law with optimism. This is mainly due to two main factors, namely (*a*) uncertainty as to the exact scope of the new EU rules and (*b*) the weakening of the safeguards provided to the individuals tried *in absentia*.

Doubtless, the cultural heritage of Strasbourg case-law strongly influenced the developments that have recently taken place at the supranational law in Europe. By extending the approach of Framework Decision 2009/299/JHA, the 2016 Directive solemnly granted defendants the right to be personally involved in criminal proceedings. On close examination, EU law is far from acknowledging a comprehensive right to participation with a view to any decision within criminal proceedings. We saw that Directive 2016/343/EU only relates to hearings aimed at a decision on acquittal or conviction.[107] Therefore, member states are still free to exclude the defendant's participation not only in intermediate phases that do not aim at a guilty verdict but also in interim decision on the application of measures interfering with fundamental rights. Furthermore, the exact scope of the new regulation is not at all clear in relation to proceedings aimed at the decision on the merits. This is mainly due to considerable differences in the official languages, which do not make it easy to understand whether defendants must be given the possibility of being present at any procedural hearing aimed at a decision on guilt or only at the trial phase.

[103] Art. 597(2) CCP-Italy.

[104] Art. 597(2) CCP-Italy.

[105] CCass, *Cotugno*.

[106] Chapter 8, C.I.2.

[107] Chapter 10, B.I.

Despite being supported by the Explanatory Memorandum and the discussions in the legislative procedure on the draft proposal, the restrictive interpretation would leave individuals unprotected in criminal hearings that can result in a guilty verdict outside the trial phase. This may in turn lead to a weakening of the existing guarantees in Italy. For instance, the Italian legislature might enable judges to make no allowance for personal summons of the accused in order to scrutinise whether he consents with the request of plea-bargaining lodged by the prosecutor or the lawyer in the pre-trial phase. Moreover, Italian courts may return to the old practice of rejecting a request for abbreviated proceedings lodged by the defence lawyer without the need to hear the accused.

Further complex problems arise in relation to the procedural safeguards that EU law provides to the individuals tried *in absentia*.[108] In particular, the disinterest of the 2016 legislation in the basis for the accused's non-appearance in court may allow the Italian legislature to maintain the high degree of freedom by the competent judge in assessing the reasons that prevent the accused from participating at the scheduled hearing, a freedom confirmed, moreover, by the 2014 legislation.[109] Serious consequences can also derive from the case in which a lawyer represents the absent defendant in court, since Directive 2016/343/EU, unlike the 2009 Framework Decision, does not necessarily require the lawyer to be appointed by the accused. Pursuant to EU law, a criminal trial can be held *in absentia* even if it was a court-appointed lawyer that provided legal assistance, regardless of whether there was any communication between the accused and the counsel representing him in court. The lack of clear indications about the forms of court summons turns out to blur the guarantee that a lawyer must represent the accused, after being informed of the proceedings. The incompleteness of statutory requirements, despite the indications provided by the Recitals of the 2016 legislation, may provide further justification to the new procedure for absent defendants introduced by Italian law. Paradoxically, in the presence of a court-appointed lawyer, EU law might legitimise even the re-introduction of the default proceedings, which traditionally ensured to absent defendants the assistance of a court-appointed lawyer.

On close examination, the main deficiency of this set-up, which also highlights the distance from the Strasbourg case-law, is the persistent disregard for the reasons of non-participation, which under EU law can unconditionally be waived by the individuals concerned. In this context, the EU legislation does certainly not provide clear solution models to Italian law. The same disinterest can be observed in relation to the reasons for which subsequent remedies remained unused. It is true that EU law requires member states to enact a retrial or other remedy to provide the opportunity of a subsequent participation to the defendants tried without the aforementioned conditions being met. Nevertheless, the 2016 Directive makes the enforcement of the conviction held *in absentia* conditional solely on the information on a retrial or legal remedy, information that needs not be provided

---

[108] Chapter 10, B.II.1.

[109] Art. 420-*ter*(2) CCP-Italy.

in person. This approach will surely not be enough to challenge the solution enacted by the 2014 Italian reform, which made the revocation of the judgment and the access to a retrial conditional on the ability of the defendants to demonstrate that they had not negligently remained unaware of the proceedings.[110]

2. The Problem of *inaudito reo* Proceedings. General Requirements of International Human Rights Law, Developments at the EU Level and the Legal Arrangements of Italian Law

In Latin America, we have noted that the specific focus on the need for previous notification of the charge leaves no room for procedures aimed at the involvement of the accused after the decision-making. The European Convention does not provide binding indications on this point, which can explains the soft approach followed by the European judges in the *Gray* case. This does not mean, however, that *inaudito reo* proceedings can unconditionally be tolerated under international human rights law. In particular, it is noteworthy that *inaudito reo* proceedings also affect the right to a public hearing, which under the European Convention also requires unequivocal waiver.

At the EU level, Directive 2016/343 construed the right to personal participation in such a restricted way that it excludes any proceeding other than that aimed at a decision on guilt. Furthermore, the interpretation of the meaning of the main provision, relating to the decisions on acquittal or conviction, impinges on the maintenance of penal order proceedings, characterised by definition by the absence of the accused prior to the decision-making. This approach raises doubt as to whether EU law can help abandon the current *inaudito reo* structure of Italian remand proceedings, in which the individuals concerned are not generally heard prior to the decision-making. On close examination, the approach followed by the 2016 Directive is very conservative. As noted, member states are required to ensure the conditions for the accused to be able to be present in criminal hearings only if national law provides for one or more hearings. In other words, EU countries still have full freedom to maintain special proceedings in writing, aimed at an out-of-court decision on the merits of the case.

The question arises whether EU law grants proper subsequent safeguards to compensate the individuals convicted in Italy through a penal order for the impossibility of being involved in the *inaudito reo* proceedings prior to the decision-making and to enable them to decide whether to lodge an opposition. As noted, the answer is negative, taking into account the findings of the *Covaci* judgment.[111] By dealing with the particular situation of non-resident defendants, the Luxembourg judges stressed that the convicted person must be given information on the accusation contained in the penal order and must be ensured either legal or linguistic

---

[110] Chapter 2, F.II.2.

[111] Chapter 10, B.II.2.a.

assistance depending on whether he chooses to lodge a written or oral opposition. However, the defence or the linguistic guarantee is not necessarily due in the period between the service of the decision and the lodging of the objection.

The question arises whether these conclusions, reached in relation to the German *Strafbefehlsverfahren*, also apply to the Italian penal order proceedings. At first sight, Italian law provides higher protective standards than those required by the EU Court of Justice. To a certain extent, as noted, the penal order proceedings ensure stronger participatory rights than the ordinary proceedings.[112] In particular, a conviction *inaudito reo* is incompatible with the procedure laid down for untraceable defendants. Since Law 60/2001, moreover, defendants not assisted by their own counsel have been ensured the assistance of a lawyer in the period provided to decide whether to lodge an opposition, a lawyer who must also be served notice of the conviction. This does not guarantee, however, that a court-appointed lawyer will always be able to contact the accused, a risk that is particularly high in cases of non-resident defendants. Furthermore, Italian law enables the lawyer, no matter whether appointed by the accused or by the state, to lodge an opposition against the penal order. The consequence is that objection, whenever lodged by the accused's lawyer without a special power or by a court-appointed lawyer, does not reflect a decision of the convicted person. This result should definitively be avoided in the near future. Despite its minimalist approach, the conclusions reached by the Court of Justice in the *Covaci* case provide useful indications for the Italian legislature. By requiring legal or linguistic assistance with a view to assisting the lodging of opposition, EU law calls upon member states to put the accused at least in a position to choose the form of the objection. This in turn presupposes that defendants convicted through an *inaudito reo* procedure must be personally involved in the decision on whether to oppose to a penal order and must be enabled to determine the form of the assistance provided by EU law.

[112] Chapter 2, F.III.2.

III. Conditions of Effective Participation in Criminal Proceedings. The Incidence of International Human Rights Law on the Developments in Brazilian and Italian Criminal Justice and the Evolution of Italian Law Under the Influence of EU Legislation

1. Information Rights in Criminal Proceedings

a) Information on the Charge. A Human Rights Approach

aa) Information Rights and the Need for a Balance Between Conflicting Interests

Doubtless, international human rights law has had strong influence on the enhancement of the information rights in the two countries examined. In Italy, we have seen that the first procedural safeguard specifically concerned with criminal justice among those enacted into the Constitution in 1999—namely, the right of the accused to be confidentially informed on the accusation as soon as possible—was clearly inspired by the European Convention. Furthermore, the substantial perspective adopted by the Strasbourg court, which traditionally looks at the impact of criminal investigations on the individual rights, avoided a restrictive interpretation of the constitutional requirement of prompt and confidential information on the accusation. This calls upon the Italian legislature to strengthen the information rights in the pre-trial phase.

On close examination, the flexible approach of the Strasbourg judges brought the European case-law closer to the past experience of the Italian criminal justice. The Rocco code did not contain an exhaustive list of forms of prosecution and did not even specify the procedural acts through which defendants should be brought to court. Unlike in the current code, the pre-trial inquiry had no time-limits and the fact that prosecutors were in some cases competent to head the investigations in the intermediate phase led to the result that the proceedings were often seamlessly continued without the need for a formal prosecution. From a human rights perspective, this result left great uncertainty as to the exact stage at which the suspect should be treated as 'accused'. In the absence of clear statutory indications, the main opinion was that accusation presupposed that the criminal inquiry had taken on a clear prosecutorial direction against one or more individuals by charging them with a criminal offence. Remarkably, the main case was that of the adoption of restrictive measures, especially pre-trial detention.[113]

This does not mean, however, that international human rights law ignores the requirement of legal certainty, which is inherent in the establishment of a formal system of prosecution. The widespread practice of the Brazilian police investigating individuals without preferring a formal charge, depriving them of the possibility of knowing whether they are being questioned as suspects or witnesses, not only is

[113]Conso (1950), p. 354ff. and 360 fn. 98.

inconsistent with the Federal Constitution but also with the American Convention. In this respect, the arrangements of Italian law better fulfil the requirements of constitutional law and the European Convention, ensuring legal certainty to the individuals concerned.

Furthermore, neither international human rights instruments nor the constitutional law of the two countries require the competent authorities to inform the accused immediately and unconditionally. This point is apparent from the Italian Constitution. It is worth observing that the 1999 constitutional reform, despite reproducing the Italian translation of Article 6(3)(a) ECHR, departed from the requirement of 'promptness' of the English version, enacting a more flexible formulation, which grants the accused the right to receive information 'as soon as possible'. Far from requiring the competent authorities to immediately inform the suspects of the charge filed against them, this expression calls for a balance among conflicting interests.[114] This balance, however, rules out the lawfulness of delays that cannot be justified on the basis of other constitutional interests. In this regard, the arrangements made by the Italian legislature raise several doubts as to its consistency with both the Constitution and the European Convention. In particular, the rules on the information on the prosecutorial charge not only release the competent authority from the duty of information in cases of proceedings for a number of serious crimes, regardless of the existence of conflicting interests, but also allow prosecutors to withdraw information because of specific investigative needs. Even more worryingly, the individuals concerned cannot challenge the prosecutorial decision to withdraw information, a decision that is not subject to any judicial review.

An important difference can be observed between the approach of international human rights law and the arrangements made at the national level. As noted, the Strasbourg Court especially starts with the premise that the use of investigative means interfering with the fundamental rights of the suspects generally requires the competent authority to charge them with a criminal offence. Although the clear inspiration of the formulation used by the Italian Constitution appears to suggest a similar interpretation, Italian law still follows a formalistic approach, which postpones the preferment of formal charges to the end of the prosecutorial inquiry. The registration of the prosecutorial charge at the beginning of the pre-trial phase does not entail in itself any information duty and even the adoption of restrictive measures against the suspect does not oblige the competent prosecutor to prefer a formal charge. The 1988 code did not entirely fulfil the requirements set forth by the 1987 Delegation Law, which expressly required a criminal prosecution to be instituted in case of application of coercive measures. In Brazil also, the use of coercive measures does not entail the obligation to institute the court proceedings. This common approach of the Italian and the Brazilian criminal justice leads to a different balance between information rights and other conflicting interests from that required by international human rights case-law.

[114] Marzaduri (2000), p. 778.

Another delicate question concerns the contents of the information due to the individuals concerned. In Italy, as noted, the contents of the information on the pre-trial charge are still far from satisfying the requirement of preciseness laid down by both the European Convention and the Italian Constitution. Moreover, Italian law does not provide enhanced protection in cases of interferences with fundamental rights. Even more worryingly, the case-law also adopts a rather a minimalist approach to the problem of an undefined accusation even after the institution of the court proceedings. In this regard, Brazilian courts follow a stronger approach, pointing out the need to prefer specific charges and to define the contribution of the individual defendants.

On the other hand, the protective aim of the right to information must avoid the charging decision causing negative effects on the individuals concerned, especially in terms of social stigmatisation. This risk is particularly high in the pre-inquiry, in which even the conditions for the institution of court proceedings are still under examination. Going beyond the requirements of Article 6 ECHR, Italian constitutional law requires information to be given in a confidential way. Moreover, the requirement of respect for private life and the human dignity are also certainly at the core of the European Convention. Despite the lack of explicit reference in the Federal Constitution, Brazilian constitutional case-law also attaches great weight to this issue, restricting the access of defence lawyers to only the information concerned with their clients.

Ultimately, it must be acknowledged that both the European Convention and the Italian Constitution suffer from a somewhat unilateral understanding of right to information on the accusation, which is focused solely on the defendant's side. The lack of explicit provisions cannot lead us to conclude, however, that the right to informed participation in criminal proceedings is an exclusive prerogative solely of the accused. A number of constitutional principles and human rights provisions of the European Convention help avoid an accused-centred approach to the right to information. Certainly, the inviolable right to a defence as well as constitutional requirement that all the parties must be able to take part in the proceedings on an equal footing—as typical expressions of the general protection of human dignity and the acknowledgment of the inviolable rights of any person—also apply to private parties other than the accused. This calls upon national law to ensure them the basic conditions—starting with proper information—to be fairly involved in the proceedings, especially if the individuals concerned suffered, or risk suffering, from restrictions on fundamental rights as a result of a criminal law action.

The arrangements made by the Italian legislature—and especially the requirement of the request of the interested party as a condition for the granting of information to the accused and the suspect—highlight the persistent backwardness of the 1988 code. It is debatable that this common approach fits both defendants and victims, since they hold very different interests in criminal proceedings. The rules governing the restriction on, or the exclusion of, information also reflect an undifferentiated approach. These rules still reveal the inability of Italian law to strike a proper balance between investigative needs and the individual right to information, even though the information to the aggrieved party often does not pose the same risks to the ongoing inquiry. In this respect, Brazilian law provides even weaker protection of the information rights, since the police, instituting investigations on their own initiative, are not required to give information to individuals other than the suspect. Yet this limitation is perhaps even more unjustified under the American Convention, whose judicial guarantees in criminal proceedings must be ensured to any person on an equal footing.[115]

bb) Developments in Italian Criminal Justice Towards EU Law and the Persistent Deficiencies in the Light of the European Convention

A specific problem concerns the developments that have occurred in relation to the issue under examination in the Italian criminal justice as a result of the new EU legislation on information rights in criminal proceedings. As noted, although an extensive interpretation of the constitutional provision of Article 111(2) of the Constitution gained ground, the rules on the information rights remained long unchanged over the following years. It took several years before the Italian legislature reformed this problematic area by fulfilling Italy's obligation to enact the new guarantees introduced by Directive 2012/13/EU.

On close examination, EU law was implemented to a somewhat minimal extent[116] and notwithstanding a number of steps forward,[117] Italian law is still far from the human rights-oriented approach adopted by the Strasbourg Court. This conclusion especially applies to the information on the charge in the pre-trial inquiry. Legislative Decree 101/2014 did not amend the rules on the registration of the prosecutorial charge, rules that still follow the arrangements made by the 1995 legislation. As a result, the competent authority must still only forward information at request of the interested party. Some progress was made in relation to subsequent information. The 2014 legislation enacted a new provision into the rules on the notice of the investigation, in that the prosecutor must inform both suspects and victims that they can obtain information under Article 335(3) CCP.[118] Since the rules on information on the initial charge have remained unchanged, it can however be doubted that this innovation will bring about positive results. The reference solely to paragraph 3 of Article 335 CCP entails that information can still be denied in cases of serious offences and that prosecutors can withhold information on the charge without any judicial oversight. Furthermore, the 2014 Directive also did not modify the general features of the notice of information under Article 369 CCP-Italy, so that there is nothing to ensure that suspects and victims will ever be given information on the charge. The main shortcoming of the current rules is still that the information duty only arises where the investigative authorities decide

[115]Art. 8(2) ACHR.

[116]In the same sense Ciampi (2014).

[117]For an analysis of the influence of this EU legislation on Italian criminal justice see Candito (2015), p. 229ff.

[118]Art. 369(1-*bis*) CCP-Italy.

to carry out investigations at which the lawyer's involvement can be present. Paradoxically, the individuals who are most involved in a criminal inquiry will therefore be granted information depending on the strategy of prosecutors and the police.

In sum, the legislative implementation of the EU law on the right to information in criminal proceedings did not succeed in solving the main deficiencies of Italian criminal justice with regard to information on the charge in the pre-trial inquiry. This raises further doubts as to the consistency with the European Convention, which, despite not entailing an immediate communication of the accusation, does not tolerate that information largely depends on the investigative choices of the prosecutor and the police. Furthermore, Italian law still lacks a clear link between prosecutorial obligations and the use of interferences with fundamental rights. Although this link lies at the heart of the Strasbourg case-law, EU law does not provide any indications in this respect.

b) Information on the Evidence Gathered and Interferences with Fundamental Rights. The Safeguards of EU and International Human Rights Law and the Weak National Arrangements

As noted, international human rights law instruments do not provide explicit statutory indications on whether information is also due on the evidence gathered. Yet both the Inter-American Court and the Strasbourg Court have stressed the strict link between information on the charge and access to the evidence collected. From this it follows that at least the evidence supporting the charging decision should be disclosed to the defence. EU law enhanced this guarantee by granting the accused, alongside the information due in case of arrest or detention, the right to access to all the evidence in the possession of the competent authority. This does not entail, however, that access to prosecutorial evidence is an absolute right. Since court proceedings may not be instituted against all the individuals under investigation, the question arises of how to maintain secrecy on the evidence concerned with the suspects who should not be brought to court. Italian law enables the competent prosecutor, while preferring formal charges, to select the information to be attached to the prosecutorial file, excluding pieces of evidence that either are not concerned with the charges filed or relate to individuals other than those who were brought to court. This power of exclusion, despite being justified by the need to avoid negative repercussions especially on individuals that are still under investigation, leaves a great margin of discretion in the hands of the competent prosecutor. Furthermore, although withholding relevant information clearly jeopardises the possibility of effective defence,[119] Italian courts tend to exclude the invalidity of criminal proceedings, limiting the consequences of unjustified denial of information to the

[119] Scalfati (1999), p. 29.

impermissibility of the evidence that was not attached to the prosecutorial request for proceedings.[120]

The prosecutorial power to withdraw evidentiary information can entail even more serious implications on fundamental rights in the pre-trial phase, especially where coercive measures are adopted. It is noteworthy that Directive 2012/13/EU ensured full access to both incriminating and exculpatory evidence not only to the accused but also to the suspect. As noted, except in the case of arrest or detention, this acknowledgment does not entail an unconditional duty to disclose any piece of evidence, nor must information be immediately forwarded. The first requirement set forth by EU law—namely, that information be granted in due time to enable the exercise of defence rights—allows for national law to deny disclosure where the adoption of coercive means other than restrictions on liberty does not require the previous intervention of the defence. Moreover, the 2012 Directive establishes a maximum time-limit for the granting of information, which must be ensured at the latest at the time of the submission of the merits of the case to the competent court. The postponement of the access to relevant information to the institution of the court proceedings, however, can also be detrimental to the defence, especially where national law provides for a long pre-trial inquiry, as in Italy.

Furthermore, both EU law and international human rights law allow for restrictions to the guarantee of information on prosecutorial evidence. The EU institutions provided for exceptions from the aforementioned rules if the need arises either to protect other individual interests or not to undermine the effectiveness of the criminal investigations. These exceptions are clearly influenced by the Strasbourg case-law, which has traditionally justified limitations to the access to incriminating evidence in order not to frustrate the ongoing investigations. The European Court, however, has generally stressed the need to specify the risks that access to the file entails in a concrete case. The Inter-American case-law seems to go in the same direction. In this respect, Italian law still displays a worrisome picture. Notwithstanding the 1995 arrangements, prosecutors still hold wide discretion in selecting the information to be attached to the request for remand detention or other coercive measures. The situation is even worse in the field of wiretaps, since prosecutors do not even have the obligation to disclose exculpatory evidence. These prosecutorial powers are not consistent with the European Convention and EU law, especially because prosecutors are not required to give reasons on whether concrete risks arise from the disclosure of further pieces of evidence. Even more worryingly, Italian law does not again provide for any judicial oversight of the prosecutor's decision and disclosure not only can be denied to the defence but also to the judge competent to order pre-trial measures.

This important point also highlights the great distance between Italian law and the EU legislation, which explicitly requires member states either to entrust to a judge the decision to withhold certain pieces of evidence or to submit it at least to a judicial review. To be sure, the fact that EU law submitted these guarantees to the

---

[120] CCass, *Abruzzese*.

general requirement of consistency with national law weakens the EU intervention, allowing the maintenance of the current national arrangements. In Italy, this risk is particularly high in relation to the oversight of the prosecutorial selection of the information gathered. It has been noted that during the pre-trial inquiry there is no possibility for the competent judge to scrutinise the prosecutorial choice. Further concerns relate to the selection of the evidence supporting the charging decision. There is no specific provision allowing the defence, after the institution of the court proceedings, to challenge the prosecutorial selection before a higher court. The competent judge or court can at any time declare the inadmissibility of the evidence that was not disclosed to the defence. Yet, the fact that the 2012 Directive does not require member states to provide for a specific remedy for this purpose leads to the result that, where in Italy the question arises at trial, the defence can only challenge intermediate decisions by means of an appeal lodged against the judgement on the merits of the case. The ascertainment of the grounds for denial of information will therefore arrive too late and cannot compensate for the lack of effective *contradictoire* in criminal proceedings.[121]

2. Linguistic Guarantees in Criminal Proceedings. Developments Towards International Human Rights Law and EU Law and the Shortcomings of National Criminal Justice

Over recent decades, considerable steps forwards have been made both in Italy and in Brazil to strengthen the linguistic guarantees in criminal proceedings and to bring them closer to the requirements set forth by international human rights case-law. In Italy, we have seen that in the leading decision 10/1993, the Constitutional Court for the first time invoked the European Convention to enhance the right to translation of the judicial order opening the trial. Some months later, however, the constitutional judges ruled out the need to translate the defendant's summons on the assumption that after first service, foreign suspects must choose their legal domicile in Italy.[122] It was a very unfortunate argument, which highlighted a great cultural distance from the approach adopted by the European Convention to the right to be informed on the accusation in language that can be understood.[123] After the 1999 constitutional reform, the Supreme Court attempted to reduce this distance by requiring the interpretation of the court summons in case of proved ignorance of the Italian language.[124] This approach was misleading, however. The main deficiency lay in the arrangements made at the statutory law level, which still left to the competent authority a great margin of discretion in the assessment of the accused's

[121]For some criticisms of the risks arising from the solution provided for by Recital no. 36 see Candito (2015), p. 235.

[122]CConst, 225/1993.

[123]Similarly Scalfati (1999), p. 38.

[124]CCass, *Jakani*.

knowledge of the Italian language, an assessment that also could not be challenged. By applying this approach, Italian courts ruled out the need to appoint an interpreter whenever the defendants undertook any initiative that revealed their understanding of the charges preferred. This result was clearly unsatisfactory, especially because Italian law offloaded onto the accused the responsibility of making sure the judicial summons could be understood, a responsibility that lay with the competent authority.

By fulfilling Italy's obligation to implement Directive 2010/64/EU, the recent Legislative Decree 32/2014 amended the rules on interpretation and translation in criminal proceedings. As a result, the linguistic assistance can no longer be viewed in terms of an optional procedural arrangement but is a guarantee that must be ensured to all the defendants who are not able to participate in criminal proceedings for linguistic reasons. Although the new Article 143 CCP-Italy requires the translation of the court summons including the indictment, this result, however, still depends on the free assessment of the competent authority; and this legislative reform did not reduce the wide discretion in the assessment of the conditions of legal assistance. The effectiveness of the guarantee of information, therefore, will depend on the practical application of these rules.

A related question is whether the free assessment of the competent judge can be challenged and what the consequences of denial of linguistic assistance are. Although the decision not to appoint an interpreter clearly affects the possibility of effective defence, Italian courts tend to consider the case as a form of intermediate invalidity,[125] which is subject to the time-limits laid down by Article 180 - CCP-Italy. In this regard, Brazilian law has long provided intense protection to non-Portuguese speaking defendants. Over the last years, Brazilian Courts have increasingly enhanced the linguistic safeguards in the light of the American Convention. Moreover, the Federal Supreme Tribunal had already in 1953 declared proceedings void because of the linguistic difficulties of an accused who was questioned in Portuguese.[126]

IV. Audi alteram partem, *the Right to Be Fairly Examined and the Privilege Against Self-Incrimination*

1. Procedural Safeguards and Conditions of a Fair Hearing in the Pre-trial Inquiry

It has been noted that, although the right to a fair examination lies at the heart of the *audi alteram partem* rule, international human rights charters do not generally contain specific provisions on it, nor does the right to a fair hearing appear among the guarantees acknowledged to the person charged with a criminal offence.

[125] *Ibid*. In the same sense CCass, *Zalagaitis*.

[126] STF, *RHC* 32.742. See Giacomolli (2014), p. 117.

Yet the very notion of a fair trial primarily entails the requirement of a fair opportunity to make one's voice heard. More clearly than the European Convention, the Pact of San José focuses on the right to obtain a fair hearing rather than on the right to have one's lawsuit heard fairly. Starting with this general acknowledgment, the Inter-American Court emphasises the importance of a fair hearing as the means of allowing a general assessment of human rights violations that have occurred during, or even through, a criminal law action.

Furthermore, both the European and the Inter-American Court not only have strongly contributed to the definition of this fundamental guarantee but have also laid down the qualitative conditions for a fair hearing. These qualitative requirements are particularly important in the pre-trial inquiry, in which the individuals involved in criminal proceedings are mainly examined by investigative bodies and are exposed to the overwhelming power of the prosecutor and the police. This situation is particularly evident in Brazil, where the police still hold responsibility for the pre-trial inquiry. In this regard, however, we saw that a clear convergence can increasingly be observed in the two countries towards common patterns. In Italy, the centralised model of a prosecutorial inquiry, construed by the drafters of the 1988 code, was soon replaced by a double system, in which the police inquiry can follow the investigations headed (or delegated) by the prosecutor in parallel. As a result, the police can question suspects either autonomously or upon delegation by the prosecutor. Furthermore, the possibility of a judicial hearing is still limited to specific cases, whereas *incidente probatorio* cannot be used to examine the suspects on issues concerned with the facts they are charged with.

Against this background, there is little doubt that the individuals concerned must be granted proper assistance especially in pre-trial questionings. The forms of this assistance differ depending on both the competent authority to conduct the questioning and the person involved. As far as the suspect is concerned, international human rights case-law emphasises the need for proper legal assistance, which in turn entails various procedural safeguards, such as the right to adequate information and the right to previous private communication with the lawyer.[127] EU law further strengthened the guarantee of legal assistance, requiring to set the necessary conditions for the lawyer to be actively involved in the accused's questioning.[128]

In this regard, however, the comparative analysis has highlighted that both Brazil and Italy still provide for weak guarantees. In Brazil, it took several years after the 1988 Constitution before the legislature provided the suspect with legal assistance during the police questioning. Even though suspects today have the right to a previous interview with their counsel, the information due to both the lawyer and the suspect is still scant and does not fulfil the requirements set forth by the Inter-American case-law. Italian law still also has considerable deficiencies. The main problem lies in the fact that pursuant to the current rules, the police can decide whether to question suspects autonomously or to request delegation to the

[127]See respectively Chap. 8, E.I, and Chap. 9, B.

[128]Chapter 10, C.III.

competent prosecutor, although very different rules apply to the two cases. Consequently, there are different safeguards for suspects depending on the solution adopted by law enforcement authorities in a concrete case. In cases of police questioning under Article 350 CCP, no information is due to the lawyer and Italian law satisfies itself if a lawyer who happens to be immediately available is appointed to be present at the questioning. Moreover, there are no statutory indications on the need to give the lawyer enough time to prepare a minimum defence strategy, nor must the suspect be granted a previous interview with the lawyer.

Stronger safeguards are due in cases of prosecutorial interrogation, even if delegated to the police. Even though no information is due on the evidence available, the suspect who is summoned to a prosecutorial interrogation must be granted information on the prosecutorial charge and the defence lawyer must be informed, as a rule, twenty-four hours before the hearing. In exceptional cases, where concrete risks arise for an ongoing inquiry, this time-limit can be waived, provided, however, that the competent authority gives reasons for the waiver and the defence lawyer is informed of the scheduled interrogation in a timely fashion. From the viewpoint of the present discussion, there is little doubt that this result jeopardises the right to legal certainty and does not satisfy the qualitative conditions laid down by the Strasbourg Court. In this respect, the original regulation of 1988 was certainly more protective, laying down a clear dividing line between the police questioning and the prosecutorial interrogation. This result ensured to suspects the safeguards of a prosecutorial hearing after the competent prosecutor had undertaken the direction of the pre-trial inquiry. Furthermore, the current set-up is also debatable in the light of EU law, which grants both defendants and suspects the right for their lawyer not only to be present but also to 'participate effectively when they are questioned by the police or by another law enforcement'.[129] To be sure, the way the lawyer is to be involved should be in accordance with the procedures laid down by national law. Yet the lawyer must be able to make observations, ask questions, and on[130]—all rights that Italian law only acknowledges in the case of a prosecutorial hearing.

On one point, however, Italian law provides for higher protection that that ensured by EU law, which, as noted, acknowledges the right to legal assistance solely to the suspects and defendants as well as to the individuals who have become suspects during the police questioning. This restrictive solution limits the scope of legal protection in the light of the formal status of 'suspect'.[131] By contrast, Italian law adopts a more substantial approach, requiring the competent authority, as noted, to suspend the hearing of individuals other than the suspect or the defendant if their statements can lead to the institution of criminal proceedings against them. Suspension of the hearing also entails the obligation for the competent authority to inform the person examined about the right to be assisted by a lawyer, a guarantee

[129]Recital no. 25 DirAL.

[130]*Ibid.*

[131]Chapter 10, C.III.1.

that does not therefore depend on the fact that he took on the formal status of suspect.[132]

On the other hand, legal assistance may be insufficient to ensure a fair hearing. It can be doubted that the assistance of a court-appointed lawyer constitutes a proper guarantee for the defendants who agree to be questioned by the police or the prosecutor on issued not entirely concerned with their own position, a decision that exposes them to the risk of being summoned again pursuant to the more demanding rules of Article 197-*bis* CCP-Italy. Furthermore, legal assistance is of little help where the accused does not understand the language of the proceedings. In this regard, Legislative Decree 32/2014, implementing Article 2(2) of the Directive 2010/64/EU, broadened the scope of protection, granting the accused the right to be assisted by an interpreter in the interview with counsel prior to an 'interrogation'. This expression must be interpreted in a broad sense, taking also into account that EU law acknowledged the guarantee of linguistic assistance with explicit reference to police questionings.

The need for other types of assistance is enhanced in relation to the hearing of other private parties, especially the individuals injured by serious crimes. In this context, we have noted that the 2012 Italian implementation of the Lanzarote Convention on the Protection of Children against Sexual Exploitation and Sexual Abuse, required prosecutors—while questioning minors in case of particular serious crimes—to provide the assistance of an expert of child psychology or psychiatry. The 2013 reform on gender-based violence later extended this requirement to the police questionings of minors. From the perspective of the present discussion, it is also worth observing that the 2015 implementation of the EU Directive 2012/29 provided a similar assistance to victims (also adults) in a condition of a particular vulnerability, if questioned either by the police or the prosecutor.

Notwithstanding these innovations, there are still no comprehensive provisions in Italy, which are specifically concerned with the police and prosecutorial questionings of the victim and the damaged party at the pre-trial stage. Nor are there consistent rules that grant all vulnerable victims a fair opportunity to be heard by a judge during the pre-trial inquiry. In 2005, however, the EU Court of Justice, while dealing with the problem of minors injured by maltreatment in the *Pupino* case,[133] had already pointed out the limited scope of the Italian rules on *incidente probatorio*. In this important ruling, the Luxembourg judges also highlighted some considerable shortcomings of the domestic law on pre-trial hearings, such as the lack of mechanisms aimed at avoiding unnecessary repetitions of the victim's questioning. The recent Directive 2012/29/EU on victims' rights went in this direction, laying down some important guarantees for the victim during criminal investigations, such as the right to be interviewed without delay and the obligation to reduce the questioning of the victim to the minimum extent necessary for the

[132]Chapter 2, G.II.1.

[133]CJEU, *Pupino*.

purposes of the ongoing investigation.[134] Nevertheless, Italian law does not grant victims a general hearing shortly after the complaint being lodged.

To be sure, some important steps forward were recently made in relation to EU law. One of the most significant innovations, provided by the 2015 Implementation Law, is that repeated questionings of the victim must generally be avoided. However, the Italian legislature did not fully satisfy the requirements set forth by EU law, which requires member states to provide particularly vulnerable victims not only with specialist support but also with legal assistance.[135] Unlike co-defendants, the aggrieved party has still no right to legal assistance if questioned by the police or the prosecutor. The 2015 Italian reform on victims' rights could only partially compensate them for the lack of legal assistance by providing for the general possibility of using *incidente probatorio* to examine highly vulnerable victims. Despite the requirement that the protective means laid down for the trial examination of vulnerable victims are to be applied to *incidente probatorio*,[136] however, Italian law still leaves the injured party without legal protection.

2. The Right to a Fair Hearing and the Procedural Safeguards Against Coercion. The Increased Enhancement of the *nemo tenetur* Principle

The guarantee of a fair hearing also entails the right not to compelled to give evidence against oneself and, to a certain extent, the right not to be examined. In this regard, we have over the last few decades witnessed the widespread tendency to enhance the procedural safeguards against various forms of coercion. This tendency is apparent both from international human rights case-law and from the developments that have occurred in the countries examined.

In Europe, we have noted that the evolution of the Strasbourg case-law following the *Jalloh* judgment highlights the increasing tendency to extend the human rights protections provided by the Rome Convention beyond the sphere of oral evidence, in order to avoid the collection of incriminating evidence through measures interfering with the right to physical integrity carried out against the will of the individuals concerned.[137] In this regard, Italian law does not go in the same direction, conferring new coercive powers to the investigative bodies. By instituting specific rules to counter international terrorism, Law 144/2005 enabled the police to carry out biological sampling of hair or saliva coercively to identify the individuals against whom criminal investigations were initiated, even where they refuse to give their consent.[138] Although this investigation must be previously authorised by the competent prosecutor, Italian law does not still satisfy the requirements set in 1996

[134] Art. 20 DirVR.

[135] Recital no. 38 DirVR.

[136] Art. 398(5-*quater*) CCP-Italy.

[137] Chapter 8, E.III.

[138] Art. 349(2-*bis*) CCP-Italy.

by the Constitutional Court.[139] In this ruling, the constitutional judges declared the regulation on expert evidence unconstitutional on the ground that it allowed for restrictive measures—including the taking of biological samples—without specifying the cases in which, and the forms pursuant to which, these intrusive investigations could be carried out.[140]

A few years later, Law 85/2009, through which Italy adhered to the Prüm Convention and set up a national DNA database, empowered public prosecutors to order compulsory biological sampling in urgent cases.[141] It is questionable whether this power conforms with of the European Convention. To be sure, the sampling must be carried out without endangering human health or physical integrity and respect must in any case be ensured for dignity of the person concerned[142]—all requirements that impinge on the admissibility of the information obtained.[143] Yet the Italian legislature failed to clarify the cases that allow for prosecutorial initiative, and the general reference to the threshold of a maximum of 3 years of detention does not ensure proportionality between the coercion applied and the expected sentence. Compared to these arrangements, Brazilian law adopts a more protective approach, ruling out the possibility of taking blood samples without the consent of the individuals concerned, a strong solution justified by the need to avoid an indirect infringement of the privilege against incrimination. As noted, Brazilian courts have since the 1990s extended this approach to transborder cases.[144]

Moreover, we have seen that there are further forms of obtaining incriminating evidence, which, entailing an indirect (albeit not less intrusive) coercion for the individuals involved in criminal proceedings. As a matter of principle, as far as oral evidence is concerned, indirect coercion will inevitably be exercised on the person examined if he is not free to decide whether and to what extent he can give evidence to the competent authority. In Italy, this does not apply solely to third parties. Whereas the 1988 code ensured to co-defendants the full right to silence, the 2001 reform, introducing the witness testimony of the co-accused, drastically reduced the scope of this guarantee, only preserving the general safeguard against self-incrimination. Despite the intention of this reform, however, we have noted that the application of these rules largely depend on the assessment of the competent authority rather than on the informed decision of the person examined to give evidence against other people. Notwithstanding the duty of information under Article 64(3) CCP-Italy, co-defendants are in their first hearing generally kept in the dark on the evidence available to the investigative bodies. Under these conditions, therefore, they are called upon to decide whether and to what extent they can

[139] In thin sense Zacchè (2008), p. 192f.

[140] CConst, 238/1996.

[141] Art. 359-*bis* CCP-Italy.

[142] Art. 224-*bis* CCP-Italy.

[143] Art. 359-*bis*(3) CCP-Italy.

[144] Chapter 5, E.III.

answer complex questions on issues not entirely concerned with their position, albeit not explicitly directed against other individuals. This situation is highly dangerous where the investigative authorities conduct the first questioning, which entails the risk for the co-accused, who agrees to answer questions, to be summoned to a new examination under 197-*bis* CCP-Italy, governed by the general duty to tell the truth and to give evidence exhaustively. The lack of information and especially the failure to provide co-defendants with safeguards other than just the assistance of a (court-appointed) lawyer makes this set-up also questionable in the light of the general guarantee of a fair hearing. This fundamental safeguard certainly requires the individuals concerned to be put in a position to make informed decisions on whether to give evidence, where this decision can entail negative consequences for the person examined.

In this respect, Brazil's prohibition on examining co-defendants as witnesses appears a more protective solution than that provided for by Italian law, preserving their right to decide whether and to what extent they can give evidence. Here also, it is worth observing that the Federal Supreme Tribunal extended this approach to transnational cases, excluding the possibility of the co-accused being heard as a witness in Brazil for the purposes of a foreign prosecution.[145] This approach seems to satisfy the right not to be compelled to give evidence against oneself, set forth by the American Convention.

At the level of international human rights law, it is also worth observing that both in Europe and in Latin-America, international courts have progressively extended beyond the sphere of criminal justice the scope of the right not to be compelled to give evidence that can entail negative consequences against the person examined. Concerning the American Convention, the explicit acknowledgment of the right not to incriminate oneself led the Inter-American case-law also to ensure this guarantee in a procedure instituted prior to, or conducted parallelly with, the judicial proceedings, if it can have unfavourable and unjustified impact on the juridical status of the individuals concerned. The Strasbourg case-law has for the last few decades followed a less rigorous approach, advocating a clear compromise solution. In particular, the *Saunders* judgment makes it clear that the inspections and administrative inquiries must not necessarily abide by the same safeguards required in criminal proceedings, including the privilege against self-incrimination. Yet the use in criminal proceedings of incriminating evidence obtained in these procedures by a person who must answer the questions of the competent authority can lead to a violation of the general guarantee of a fair hearing.

In this respect, the approach followed by Italian courts, which widely acknowledge the possibility of using information collected in administrative investigations (*e.g.*, tax inspections, liquidation proceedings), is not in line with the Strasbourg case-law.[146] In order to make Italian criminal justice consistent with the European

---

[145] *Ibid.*

[146] Cf. Zacchè (2008), p. 184ff., who also proposes some interesting solutions to bring Italian law closer to the European case-law.

Convention, furthermore, any use of information coercively obtained—following the *Saunders* doctrine—should be avoided irrespective of the probative relevance attached by the fact-finders to the evidence at stake.

In the light of the general enhancement of the right not to give evidence against oneself, it is rather surprising that EU law circumscribes the scope of the right to silence by focusing on formal issues. Similarly to what was provided for in relation to legal assistance, Directive 2013/13/EU extended the privilege against self-incrimination solely to the individuals who become suspects during questioning by the police or by other law enforcement authorities.[147] The recent Directive 2016/343/EU followed the same approach, circumscribing the right to silence to 'questions relating to the criminal offence that a person is suspected or accused of having committed'.[148] In this respect, the Italian rules on the privilege against self-incrimination—as a general guarantee not only of witnesses but also of any person involved in criminal proceedings—reveal the higher protection provided by domestic law.

3. Private Initiative and the Right to Make Oneself Heard by the Competent Authority

The requirements of a fair hearing set forth by international human rights case-law should also lead to a reform of the national solutions on the spontaneous statements that private parties can give to the competent authorities. Again, the initiative of the interested party can entail several risks especially in the pre-trial inquiry. In Italy, the 1988 codification, following the approach of the Rocco code, enabled the suspect to appear at the public prosecutor's office and to give spontaneous statements.[149] Italian law makes it clear that the suspect's conduct does not prevent the application of pre-trial measures.[150] On close examination, this is a rather paternalistic provision, which highlights the clear imbalance between the prosecutor and the suspect. The suspect's initiative can lead to two different situations, depending on whether the prosecutor informs him of the charge filed. If the suspect receives the information under Articles 64, 65 und 364 CCP-Italy, the hearing is equivalent to a prosecutorial examination.[151] The main problem, however, is that the competent prosecutor can discretionarily decide whether to provide this information. In the negative case, suspects are kept in dark on everything and may thus happen to give evidence without any information either on the charge preferred against them or on the evidence available to the investigative bodies. Furthermore, Italian law does not require the suspect to be assisted by a lawyer, and prosecutors can

[147]Recital no. 21 DirAL.

[148]Recital no. 26 DirPIRPT.

[149]Art. 374 CCP-Italy.

[150]Art. 374(3) CCP-Italy.

[151]Art. 374(2) CCP-Italy.

therefore gather statements from a clearly advantageous position without the need to provide the information required in the case of a prosecutorial questioning. Even more worryingly, the statements that the suspect gives to the prosecutor are not only used for the prosecutorial inquiry but can be read out in court to test the reliability of the accused. These negative consequences—alongside the broad discretion of prosecutor in deciding whether to provide suspects with the aforementioned information—are scarcely compatible with the qualitative safeguards of a fair hearing.

Another delicate issue is whether the injured parties have a right to be heard at their own initiative. The solutions provided by the Luxembourg Court in the *Katz* judgment cannot be interpreted in the sense that EU law necessarily requires member states to grant victims the opportunity to give evidence at their own initiative. This solution is only required when national law does not allow victims to give testimonial evidence. The EU Directive 2012/29 was much more explicit in acknowledging the right of the injured party not only to give evidence but also to be heard in criminal proceedings. To be sure, this requirement is also satisfied where the aggrieved parties are only allowed to make statements or explanations in writing, arrangements that can be justified by the need not to expose the victim to personally confront the competent authority. Notwithstanding the recent implementation of this legislation, Italian law still does not enable victims to make their voice heard in the prosecutorial inquiry. There is no comparable provision to that regarding the suspect's spontaneous statements and the judicial examination of the victim through *incidente probatorio* is subjected to the request of either the prosecutor or the accused. The 2015 reform confirmed this approach, and although highly vulnerable victims, as a rule, should be examined by means of this court procedure, the investigative bodies were empowered to question the aggrieved parties at their own initiative and to avoid further hearings, except in cases of absolute necessity for the ongoing investigations. This set-up, therefore, leaves to prosecutors a great margin of discretion in deciding whether to activate a court examination or to hear the victim at their office. In the light of both the European Convention and EU law, however, it is questionable that fundamental fair trial safeguards, such as the information on the charge and the assistance of a lawyer, depend on the prosecutorial discretion.

V. Audi alteram partem, *Evidence-Gathering and Qualitative Requirements of a Fair Fact-Finding. The Need for Broad Balance Among Conflicting Interests*

1. Obtaining Incriminating Evidence. The Need for Systematic Approach to the Right to Confrontation in the Light of the Overall Set of the Human Rights Challenges Posed by Each Concrete Case

a) The Requirements Set by International Human Rights Case-Law and the Developments in National Law

Another problematic area in which a strong mutual influence among different legal systems could be observed over the last few years concerns the contribution of private parties to evidence-gathering and fact-finding. Since international human rights case-law has increasingly dealt with evidence-gathering by laying down conditions on the use of untested evidence and information taken though alternative forms of confrontation, I shall here examine these two issues jointly.

The main methodological indication that may be deduced from international human rights law is perhaps the need for a systematic approach to the accused's participation in the collection of incriminating evidence. The explicit acknowledgment (albeit with some considerable differences) of this fundamental guarantee by international human rights charters does not make it an absolute right. The *Palamara Iribarne* judgment provides a clear example of a systematic understanding of the right to confrontation in the light of the overall set of the judicial guarantees in criminal proceedings, including the right to time and means to prepare an effective defence, the right to legal assistance, the right to be fairly heard and the privilege against self-incrimination. Over recent decades, the Strasbourg Court has also avoided interpretations aimed at emphasizing the importance of this guarantee to the point that it would justify unconditional restrictions on other human rights. The examination of the European case-law allows us to observe the clear tendency to include the defendants' interest in participating in the taking of incriminating evidence into a wider human rights test. Under both Conventions, the right to confrontation, therefore, holds a flexible form depending on the characteristics and the human rights challenges of each case. These challenges mainly vary depending on the interests at hand and especially on the different types of individuals to be examined. Particular care is necessary when the person examined is in a vulnerable position, as in the case of minors. High human rights risks, moreover, arise in the case of undercover informants and collaborators with justice. Here, the need to provide broad protection of fundamental rights such as life, physical integrity, and security, has led international courts to extend the protective scope of the provisions concerned to the families of the individuals examined. In this respect, international human rights case-law has increasingly allowed, albeit not always in consistent terms, the use of alternative arrangements and technical tools to avoid direct confrontation with the accused in open court.

Similar conclusions can also be drawn from the general acknowledgment of the right to *contradictoire* laid down by both the Italian and the Brazilian Constitution. Doubtless, the enshrinement of these constitutional requirements helped strengthen the involvement of private parties—especially of defendants—in the gathering of evidence. In Brazil, albeit with considerably delay, Law 11.690/2008 replaced the old form of judicial questioning of witnesses with the method of cross-examination conducted by the parties, a reform that better satisfied both the constitutional requirements of *contradictoire* and full defence as well as the right to confrontation acknowledged in the American Convention. Italian legislation launched after the 1999 constitutional fair trial reform, despite following a rather accused-centred approach, considerably reduced the widespread use of untested evidence.

More interestingly, we saw that the Italian legislature has over last years engaged in balancing the accused's right to confrontation with other interests of utmost relevance from the perspective of both the Constitution and the European Convention. This has led to the enactment of special forms of confrontation and the provision of specific precautions to avoid human rights risks for the individuals examined as well as for their families. In this context, the 2013 reform on gender-based violence and, more recently, the 2015 legislative implementation of the EU Directive on victims' rights enacted special arrangements to protect vulnerable witnesses and victims from the risks of direct cross-examination. Similar conclusions apply to the trial hearing of undercover officers, including foreign police officers and members of information and security services, as well as auxiliary and third parties involved in undercover investigations under Law 146/2006. The provision of anonymous testimony, alongside the prohibition on revealing the real identification details of the witnesses, not only aims to preserve the ongoing investigation but furthermore—and at a deeper level still—to avoid risks for the physical integrity and the life of the individuals concerned and their next of kin. If the right to an impartial and independent judicial oversight definitively enhances the guarantee of confrontation, there is little doubt that a public hearing increases the pressure of the cross-examination and does not set the best conditions for witnesses (especially if in a vulnerable situation) to give a reliable account of the events.[152]

These legislative solutions, notwithstanding their merits, cannot be deemed to be fully consistent with the Strasbourg case-law, which has long emphasised the need for proper reasoning of the grounds for the adoption of measures in lieu of direct confrontation. Furthermore, the European Court stresses the need for strict oversight of whether these measures were adequately adopted in a concrete case. This doctrine has been further developed over the last few years and, while the approach to the probative value of untested evidence becomes more and more flexible, the recent European case-law has increasingly tightened the obligation to give reasons based on the challenges posed by the case at hand. In some cases, a presumption of risks for the human rights of the person examined is *in re ipsa*, like in the case of

[152] Spencer (2014), p. 15.

undercover agents or collaborators with justice. The same applies to the special precautions provided for in the case of highly vulnerable victims, since the assessment of this requirement justifies the adoption of specific arrangements to avoid risks for the person examined. However, in the proceedings for some serious crimes (ill-treatment in the family, slavery, child prostitution, child pornography, etc.), Italian law allows for different forms of confrontation (including out-of-court confrontation) to be ordered solely on the grounds that these arrangements are necessary or appropriate.[153] These criteria seem to be too generic and it is particularly debatable that the Italian legislature relied on the abstract seriousness of the criminal law provision. In the same cases, the request of the victims or of their lawyers suffices to order shielded testimony with an intercom system,[154] regardless of the human rights challenges posed by the case at hand and without any need for the trial court to justify these measures. This legislation should be adapted to the methodological indications of European case-law.

Remarkably, under the American Convention, alternatives to direct cross-examination can also be adapted, *e.g.* where safety or other circumstances necessarily require protecting the identity of the witness. These arrangements, however, should not undermine the right of the 'defence' to challenge the veracity of the evidence produced by an incriminating witness. From these indications it is not only the need to ensure the core protections of the right to confrontation that emerges, but it is also apparent that departure from direct confrontation in open court must be both necessary and properly reasoned. In this context, Brazilian law requires the competent judge to give a reasoned decision while ordering alternative forms of examination, such as hearing by videoconference or other technological means of transmission of sounds and images in real time.[155]

b) The Risks of an Enlarged View of the Guarantee of Confrontation. The Problems of Indirect Examination and of Subsequent Confrontation

It cannot be denied that the enlarged concept of confrontation adopted by international human rights law entails the risk of a considerable weakening of the participatory safeguards of the accused. This is especially apparent from the approach of the Strasbourg case-law to the forms and the context of confrontation. It has been observed that under the European Convention, the guarantee of confrontation can also be satisfied where an independent authority examines incriminating witnesses. In this respect, the Italian arrangements on the judicial examination of witnesses and co-defendants in the intermediate phase—taking into account that the parties are allowed to be present at the court hearing and can forward questions that arise to the competent judge—can in principle be deemed to be consistent with the Convention. There is

[153] Arts. 398(5-*bis*) and 498(4-*ter*) CCP-Italy.

[154] Art. 498(4-*quater*) CCP-Italy.

[155] Art. 185(2) CCP-Brazil.

little doubt, however, that indirect examination does not grant the defence the same opportunities of direct confrontation. Remarkably, Italian law does not allow for the automatic admission of the testimonial evidence taken in the intermediate phase, evidence that can only be read out at trial against the defendants whose lawyers were present at the hearing *in camera* and only provided, moreover, that the person examined does not refuse confrontation in open court.[156]

As noted, the American Convention follows a more protective approach, promoting the direct involvement of the defence in obtaining the appearance of prosecutorial witnesses and in the taking of incriminating evidence. This does not entail, however, that the Pact of San José requires the contracting states to enable defendants to examine their accusers personally. The explicit reference to the accused by the Italian Constitution also cannot be interpreted in this sense. On close examination, the enactment into the Italian Constitution of the European Convention's provision on the right to have witnesses examined cannot justify the broad interpretation attached to the international text, since confrontation that must take place before a judge clearly cannot be conducted by the same judicial authority.

The entitlement of the defence lawyer to examine incriminating witnesses, however, does not mean that any form of legal assistance can properly serve this purpose. It is debatable whether a court-appointed lawyer, who has never had the opportunity to contact the defendant, can adequately represent him in the examination of the accuser. In this context, it is noteworthy that EU law, following the approach of the Strasbourg case-law, requires member states to allow defendants to have private communications with their lawyers, a fundamental requirement that cannot be restricted solely to the case of the accused's hearing. Italian law provides questionable solutions in this regard, since, as noted, it enables any lawyer immediately available, if neither the accused's counsel nor the court-appointed lawyer are present, to represent the defendant in court and therefore also to cross-examine co-defendants or incriminating witnesses.

The risk of the weakening of the guarantee of confrontation is also apparent from the context of confrontation. Surely, out-of-court examination may better protect certain types of informants. It is worth observing that the European Court has never required confrontation to take place exclusively in a court hearing, provided that defendants had a proper opportunity to examine their accusers. Moreover, Strasbourg case-law has traditionally allowed for confrontation also to take place at a later stage than that at which evidence was given. This subsequent form of confrontation raises a number of human rights concerns. A typical form of subsequent confrontation is when inconsistent statements are read out in court to the witness or co-accused, a situation that, as observed, poses very difficult challenges. Furthermore, it should be noted that the European Court, despite generally considering pre-trial confrontation compatible with the Convention, has always emphasised the

[156] Art. 500(6) CCP-Italy.

need for effective defence at the time in which confrontation with the accuser took place.

The fact that confrontation may take place at a later stage, however, should not unconditionally allow renouncing the necessary involvement of the defence, if provided for by national law. Where national law allows or even requires the involvement of suspects in the police or prosecutorial questioning of a (potentially) incriminating witness or co-defendant, can we seriously maintain that participation at a later stage of the proceedings can compensate them for the lost opportunity? In Italy, for instance, the rules on *incidente probatorio* prevent witnesses and co-defendants from being examined on issues relevant to defendants whose lawyers were not present at the hearing and, if this is possible in timely fashion, the interested parties must be summoned to court. On close examination, denying the addressee of incriminating statements the opportunity for confrontation, on the assumption that he will possibly examine the accuser at a later stage, means ignoring the aim of the right to confrontation. In most cases, furthermore, the accused would be deprived of an opportunity for confrontation that can often be unique, taking place at a time in which the memory of the events is still fresh in the mind of the person examined. In this respect, the risk arises that the European case-law can frustrate the protection ensured by national law.

c) Right to Confrontation and Inconsistent Evidence. The Need to Avoid an Accused-Centred Understanding of the Principle of *contradictoire*

Allowing for subsequent confrontation unconditionally not only raises serious human rights concerns but also often poses the difficulty of dealing with eventual inconsistencies between out-of-court evidence and the information gathered in open court. This case poses different problems from those deriving from the use of alternative forms of confrontation. Thus inconsistencies by definition presuppose defendants having had the opportunity to be confronted with their accuser, with the peculiarity, however, that the person examined in court rendered evidence inconsistent with his previous statements. We saw that among continental countries the 1988 Italian code introduced a quite unique set of rigid exclusionary rules aimed at avoiding the use of inconsistent out-of-court statements for the purposes of the fact-finding. After the controversial decade of the 1990s, the Italian legislature re-adopted an approach strongly oriented towards the protection of the accused's right to confrontation, restoring exclusionary rules with a view to restricting the admission and/or the use at trial of out-of-court testimonial statements. In practice, the scope of some of these exceptions was extended beyond the limits laid down at the statutory law level.

It is debatable, however, whether this approach is fully in line with the European Convention. The Strasbourg case-law provides some useful indications, which again orient the traditional understanding of this problem towards the need for protection of individuals other than the accused. In the few judgments in which this issue was dealt with, the European Court focused on the requirements of an effective confrontation rather than the formal probative value of out-of-court evidence. Furthermore, effective confrontation requires specific conditions to be met, particularly the possibility for defendants to be involved in the evidence-gathering and to access previous statements of the accuser in order to set up a proper defence strategy with regard to the cross-examination. The accused must also be given the opportunity of a previous interview with his counsel. It is hard to imagine how the cross-examination of an incriminating witness—conducted by the first available lawyer who has no possibility of knowing the previous evidence given by the person to be examined—can satisfy the qualitative requirements of the guarantee of confrontation. If these requirements were properly satisfied, the issue of the use of out-of-court statements as evidence of the matters stated would probably no longer be so problematic.

Furthermore, confrontation with incriminating evidence does not only relate to the information rendered by individuals other than the accused, such as prosecutorial witnesses and co-defendants. Serious problems also arise when defendants, while giving evidence in court, are confronted with their previous statements rendered to the investigative bodies in the pre-trial inquiry. In Italy, the risk that investigative questionings lead suspects to give incriminating evidence is high, taking into consideration the scant information and the weak legal assistance provided to them as well as the pressure put on them by the coercive powers of the competent prosecutor. Notwithstanding these evident deficiencies, Italian law still follows a somewhat formalistic approach to this problem, allowing for out-of-court statements rendered by the defendants to the prosecutor, or the police acting upon delegation, to be admitted at trial and to be fully used against them, on the assumption that the prosecutorial hearing provides the accused with legal protection. Legal assistance becomes an even more purely formal guarantee in the case of confrontation with the evidence given in other proceedings, in which defendants may have had a totally different role and may therefore have given evidence according to the different interests they had in the context of the other proceeding. In these cases, allowing the full use of inconsistent statements under the same conditions of Article 503 CCP-Italy, solely on the grounds that a lawyer assisted the accused in another proceeding,[157] clearly constitutes a weak solution and largely overlooks that knowledge of the charge is a necessary prerequisite for effective confrontation.

The constant focus of the European Court on the requirement of effective confrontation should lead to in-depth reflection on this approach. The Inter-American Court also found an infringement of the American Convention in cases in which the defendants were confronted with their past statements given at the pre-trial stage without any legal assistance. This case-law, while implicitly confirming the lawfulness under the Convention of out-of-court confrontation, cannot be interpreted, however, in the sense that any form of legal assistance would be sufficient and no weight should be attached to the qualitative conditions

[157] Art. 238(2-*bis*)&(4) CCP-Italy.

of investigative hearings. As highlighted in the *Castillo Petruzzi* judgment, the right of the defence to examine prosecutorial witnesses also entails the need to avoid undue restrictions for the defence lawyer.

2. Proof of Guilt and the Defence's Contribution to a Fair Decision-Making

a) Impossibility of Confrontation and the Use of Untested Evidence. The Need to Avoid Absolutist Interpretations

The need to avoid a formalistic approach to the *audi alteram partem* rule is enhanced when the use of untested evidence is at stake for the purposes of fact-finding, as well as if relevant information was gathered by special means entailing restrictions on the right to confrontation. The first area largely coincides with the issue of unavailable testimony, following the terminology used by the European Court. In this delicate field, significant developments have taken place worldwide over the last few years in international human rights law, mainly as a result of the rising mutual influence of international and domestic case-law both in Europe and in Latin America. The traditional sole and decisive evidence doctrine elaborated by Strasbourg case-law avoided absolutist interpretations of the right to confrontation, allowing the Strasbourg judges to scrutinise the concrete influence of untested evidence on fact-finding in the light of the overall information gathered. At first glance, this approach may seem to rely on the decision-making at the national level. Yet, as noted, the fuzzy notion of 'decisive evidence'[158] enabled the Strasbourg Court to elaborate its own criteria to evaluate the weight of untested evidence. On close examination, this result is unavoidable. The establishment of the decisive role of a single piece of evidence is not a mechanical task, but leads the European judges to re-define the relevance of the results of the evidence-gathering in light of the overall information available.[159]

There can be little doubt that this doctrine has had a strong impact on Italian criminal justice. It has been noted that in the 1990s, the Constitutional Court had justified the admissibility of evidence given out of court by the accused's next of kin who claim their right not to testify at trial. This arrangement was clearly incompatible with the 1999 constitutional fair trial reform, which allowed derogation from the right to *contradictoire* in cases of impossibility of confrontation due to objective grounds. Even after the constitutional judges departed from their initial approach, the question arose as to whether the admission of unavailable out-of-court evidence pursuant to domestic law sufficed to satisfy the ECHR requirements. Legal scholarship raised doubts about the consistency of Italian law with the European Convention on the assumption that allowing defendants to be convicted

[158] Ferrua (2013), p. 45.

[159] See also Daniele (2008), p. 392.

mainly or exclusively on the basis of untested evidence infringed on the Strasbourg approach.[160] At the end of the last decade, following the increasing number of convictions of Italy by the European Court,[161] the Supreme Court aligned Italian law with the Strasbourg case-law. The Joint Sections re-interpreted Article 526 (1-*bis*) CCP in the light of the European approach by ruling out the exclusive or dominant use of out-of-court testimonial evidence if defendants have never had the opportunity to be confronted with their accuser.[162]

At first sight, this ruling may seem to entail that constitutional law—to be precise, the ban on use of the statements of the accuser who always freely avoided confrontation with the defendant—should also be oriented towards the European standards. This conclusion would be misleading, however. In particular, the requirement of the objective impossibility of involving the parties in the evidence-gathering cannot be overcome by an elusive interpretation, which allows for the joint use of incriminating evidence that has become unavailable because of the will of the accuser, as happens in the case of the defendant's next of kin. In these cases, Italian constitutional law certainly provides a higher standard of protection than that of the sole and decisive evidence test.[163] The question arises whether the European approach should integrate the requirements of constitutional law, limiting the use of testimonial evidence that has become unavailable at trial for grounds unconnected with the accuser's will.[164]

In this respect, it should be acknowledged that the decisiveness doctrine may have a negative impact on domestic law by lowering the probative thresholds required for the fact-finding at the domestic level. This risk is high in Italy, where a greater likelihood of guilt than innocence does not suffice to convict a person, but a high degree of proof of guilt is required in light of the overall information usable at trial. Since the enactment of the BARD rule, doubt on innocence must be unreasonable or simply hypothetical to convict a person. In this context, although the European Court emphasises the need to look at the overall conduct of criminal proceedings and all the information gathered, the decisiveness test focuses on the concrete relevance of individual pieces of evidence, thus aiming to assess the probative weight of each one and to compare it with that of other evidence.[165] This entails the risk of a fragmentary assessment of the information available, which departs from the requirement that the overall evidence must prove the defendant's guilt beyond any reasonable doubt. It might be argued that the sole and decisive evidence doctrine constitutes an empirical rule implied by the provision on the presumption of innocence, interpreted as requiring the defendant's guilt

[160]Ubertis (2007), p. 174f.

[161]See, in particular, ECtHR, *Bracci v. Italy*, *Majadallah v. Italy* and *Kollcaku v. Italy*.

[162]CCass, *D.F.* See Gaeta (2012), p. 35ff.

[163]Ferrua (2013), p. 46f.

[164]In this sense Ferrua (2013), p. 47.

[165]For some criticisms in this respect see Daniele (2008), p. 391, who considers it an impossible undertaking.

to be proved beyond any reasonable doubt.[166] This approach cannot be sustained. It is debatable whether the BARD rule constitutes the only solution compatible with the presumption of innocence enshrined in the European Convention,[167] whose requirements must be applicable to countries with very different probative standards. Remarkably, under the International Covenant, it can also be doubted whether the presumption of innocence requires the defendant's guilt to be proved beyond any reasonable doubt,[168] since there is no clear indication of the probative standards required.[169]

In the case of the objective impossibility of confrontation, moreover, the requirement of corroborative evidence can frustrate the probative value of untested information, which may be intrinsically reliable and fit well with the prosecutorial charge. On close examination, the flexible approach of the European judges leads to the establishment of a rather abstract condition on the use of untested evidence, which can often be fully unrelated with the needs of a concrete case. This point highlights another deficiency of the approach adopted by the Italian Supreme Court, which domesticated the Strasbourg case-law irrespective of the probative value of unavailable evidence. Further risks arise from the combination of the sole and decisive evidence doctrine with the flexible approach of the European Court to subsequent confrontation. Here also, the standards set forth by national law cannot be lowered by the need to achieve a forced alignment with the Strasbourg case-law. One cannot equate the case in which the national authority did not put in place the necessary conditions for a confrontation at the pre-trial stage to that in which, despite the diligent behaviour of the competent authorities, confrontation could not take place because of objective circumstances.

It must be acknowledged, however, that it is not always easy to determine the extent to which the unavailability of evidence at trial must be interpreted. Here also, considerable developments have taken place in Italian law, almost in parallel with the Strasbourg case-law. As noted, the European judges have over recent decades increasingly engaged in protecting special types of informants against the risk of direct confrontation with the alleged perpetrator. On several occasions, the Strasbourg Court acknowledged that under certain conditions the defendant's guilt can be proved on the basis of untested evidence. In *A.H. v. Finland*, the Court made it clear that special arrangements must ensure the reliability of a minor's hearing and that the defendant must be given the opportunity of a subsequent review of the victim's statements, which cannot be the only pieces of evidence supporting the conviction.[170] Remarkably, almost during the same period, the Italian Supreme

[166]In this sense cf. instead Ferrua (2013), p. 42.

[167]Trechsel (2005), p. 163 s. In the sense indicated in the text, from the perspective of Italian law, see Lozzi (2014), p. 491.

[168]Joseph et al. (2004), p. 426.

[169]In this sense Harris et al. (2009), p. 302, who quotes the conclusions that the European Commission of human rights reached in *Austria v. Italy* by requiring for the defendant's conviction a proof 'sufficiently strong in the eyes of the law to establish his guilt'. See EComHR, *Austria v. Italy*.

[170]ECtHR, *A.H. v. Finland*.

Court broadened the scope of the concept of non-repeatability of evidence, which must be seen as encompassing not only the physical unavailability of the source of evidence but also the risks for the psychological integrity of vulnerable individuals.[171]

One might argue that this jurisprudence rendered the principle of *contradictoire* more flexible than in the past. On close examination, the European Court sought a new balance between the defendant's participatory rights and the right of vulnerable individuals not to be exposed to the trauma of a confrontation with the alleged perpetrator.[172] The developments that occurred in Italian case-law are also of utmost importance, relativizing the requirement of *contradictoire* in the evidence-gathering in order to protect further interests of constitutional relevance, such as the right of minors to private life and not to be directly confronted with their alleged assaulter. The search for enhanced balance among conflicting interests, as noted, led the European Court to further relativize the right to confrontation in the *Al-Khawaya* judgment. Whichever criticisms one can direct against this ruling, it aimed at overcoming the incongruence of the ban on (the primary) use of untested evidence that may be intrinsically reliable, while conferring (decisive) relevance to the information rendered by individuals in a particularly vulnerable position whose testimony has become impossible in court. It is difficult to say what Italian courts will do in the near future but it is clear that Italian case-law cannot ignore the developments that have taken place at the European level, especially after the Strasbourg Court recently applied the *Al-Khawaya* doctrine in relation to Italian procedural law in the *Moumen* case.[173]

The developments that occurred in Brazil in relation to the Inter-American case-law only partially coincide with these achievements. Certainly, the enactment of the right to *contradictoire* into the 1988 Federal Constitution paved the way for a reflection on the use of out-of-court evidence, which was long justified in the light of the mostly inquisitorial understanding of the free assessment of evidence. This process, however, was also very slow in Brazil, and it took 20 years before Law 11.690/2008 reformed the rules on the evidence-gathering. By maintaining the principle of free conviction, the Brazilian legislature circumscribed this freedom solely to the evidence lawfully obtained pursuant to the requirements of *contradictoire* and full defence. Although this solution was similar to the general approach of the Italian code, the Brazilian legislature also did not exclude a limited use of untested evidence, prohibiting only its exclusive use for the purposes of the decision on the merits. This arrangement, which lays down at the statutory level a similar solution to that adopted by the Italian Supreme Court, does not seem, however, to be due to the need to fulfil requirements posed by international case-law, reflecting a soft understanding of the constitutional principle of *contradictoire*.

---

[171]CCass, *G.*

[172]Ubertis (2009), p. 4065ff.

[173]ECtHR, *Moumen v. Italy*.

b) Special Forms of Confrontation and the Use of the Information Gathered. The Problem of Anonymous Testimony

As noted, the need to protect particular types of witnesses has increasingly required the adoption of indirect evidence and alternative methods, aimed at avoiding the risks of 'eyeball-to-eyeball' confrontation with the alleged perpetrator. As a matter of principle, the case-law of both the European and the Inter-American Court has not considered anonymous hearings incompatible with international human rights charters. Different developments, however, have occurred in the recent international case-law. The Strasbourg Court, extending the findings of the *Al-Khawaja* judgment, has recently departed from its traditional approach, recognising that the accused can also be convicted on the main or exclusive basis of anonymous testimony where counterbalancing factors were applied to compensate for the lack of confrontation. By contrast, the Inter-American Court maintained the sole and decisive evidence doctrine in the *Norín Catrimán* judgment, thus revealing a cautious approach to the problem of anonymous testimony gathered through voice distorter and a screen hiding the faces of the witnesses whose identity was only known to the competent court. There are no signs suggesting that the Inter-American case-law will in a near future depart from the threshold of the ban on exclusive use of untested evidence, as happened in the Strasbourg case-law.

On close examination, it cannot be said in abstract terms whether anonymous testimony is consistent with international human rights instruments. Certainly, the arrangements made by national authorities—and more generally, the factual background of the case at hand—hold considerable relevance in the assessment of anonymous testimony. This can explain the different solutions adopted by the European Court in the *Doorson* and the *van Mechelen* cases, notwithstanding that in the latter case, both the applicant und his lawyer had been placed in an adjacent room and could follow the witness' examination and ask questions. Similarly, the fact that in the *Norín Catrimán* case individuals belonging to indigenous people were prosecuted and detained for anti-terrorism offences on the basis of the dangerous presumption of terroristic goals, as noted, led the Inter-American Court to restrict the conditions on use of anonymous testimony.

Remarkably, international human rights courts have always attached particular weight to the need for proper justification of anonymity, a requirement that in the European case-law was enhanced in parallel with the developments that followed the *Al-Khawaja* judgment. In this respect, Italian law is not entirely consistent with the standards set by the Strasbourg Court. To be sure, the 2015 legislative implementation of the Directive 2012/29/EU required the adoption of protective means in the case of trial examination of victims in a particularly vulnerable condition, a situation that must by definition be assessed in each concrete case pursuant to the criteria laid down by Article 90-*quater* CCP-Italy.[174] In specific circumstances, however, Italian law does not provide for any justification of the adoption of special

[174] Art. 498(4-*quater*) CCP-Italy.

arrangements. For instance, we have observed that the needs of minors or adults injured by some serious crimes (sexual crimes, stalking, trafficking of human beings, and so on) allow for the recourse of shielded testimony with an intercom system, at the request of the interested individuals or their lawyers. Here, Italian courts are not required to carry out a concrete assessment of the need for such arrangements, which seem to be justified solely on the grounds of the abstract seriousness of the offences at hand.

VI. Participatory Rights and Restrictions on Freedom

1. The Right to Be Fairly Heard and the Qualitative Requirements of Effective Participation in Remand Proceedings

a) Premise

Specific human rights concerns from the perspective of the present discussion arise with regard to the participatory safeguards of the individuals subject to coercive measures. It has been observed that interferences with individual rights are no longer only in the form of coercion measures.[175] Over the last few decades, the progress of science and technology has led to the increasing use of new investigative tools entailing a high degree of interference with fundamental rights without their addressee having any knowledge of the interference and mostly through hidden, non-coercive measures. This result calls for in-depth reflection on the role of the parties concerned both before the application and during the enforcement of investigative coercions in the current era.[176]

Among coercive measures, restrictions on freedom still hold special importance to secure the aims of the criminal process, so that in several Romance-speaking countries pre-trial detention and its alternatives still constitute the stereotype of 'precautionary' measures. Restrictions on freedom and criminal process are so strictly tied with each other that even in the recent past, as noted, countries with an inquisitorial tradition, such as Italy, required the accused to be remanded in custody, as a rule, after the institution of the court proceedings. It is no surprise that the drafters of the Rome Convention, dealing with the right to freedom, enacted specific guarantees for pre-trial restrictions on liberty in criminal proceedings. The more recent American Convention, despite not explicitly relating to criminal justice, construed some important safeguards with a special focus on the restrictions on freedom within criminal proceedings.

---

[175]Chapter 6, J.I.

[176]The need to overcome the traditional concept of interferences with fundamental rights in terms of coercive measures is highlighted by Kühne (2015), p. 248.

In this regard, international human rights instruments provide useful models for solutions especially through the focus attached to the guarantee of independent scrutiny of the justification of deprivation of liberty and of the overall lawfulness of the coercion applied. This guarantee has two main features, namely the assessment conducted *ex officio* by the judicial authority, before which the arrestee or detainee must be brought and a scrutiny activated by the initiative of the interested party. At first glance, international human rights law does not explicitly deal with the involvement of the defence in the decisions on the application of restrictions on freedom. This does not hold true, however. Fundamental safeguards, such as the right to personal information on the grounds for arrest or detention as well as on the eventual charges filed, cannot only be interpreted with a view to *habeas corpus* but also hold importance for the purposes of a prompt judicial hearing. The need for personal participation of the individuals concerned, moreover, holds particular relevance in the Inter-American case-law, which, as noted, makes the judicial scrutiny a general means of assessing the overall conditions of the detainee and of preventing further human rights violations.

Against this background, the question arises of whether and to what extent the countries examined fulfil the safeguards acknowledged by international human rights case-law and whether Italian law satisfies the requirements set forth by the EU legislation.

b) The Guarantee of Information in International Human Rights Instruments and EU Law, and the Procedural Safeguards Provided at the Domestic Level

The highly vulnerable condition produced by coercive measures, along with the general lack of previous hearing of the individuals concerned, makes it necessary for them to understand the grounds for the restriction adopted and to be provided with all the information necessary to set up a proper defence. It has been observed that both in Europe and Latin America, international human rights case-law emphasises the need for personally informing the arrestee and detainee, as highlighted by the requirement that information must be provided in a simple and understandable language. The strict link between information and the right to effective defence has led the American Convention to strengthen the statutory protection by requiring information also to be granted to the next of kin of the arrested or detained person as well as to a lawyer and to a consular official. EU law further developed this approach by requiring the creation of a Letter of Rights, in which, *inter alia*, information must also be provided to a third person and the consular authorities.

Against this background, it can be doubted that the procedural safeguards provided at the domestic level fulfil these qualitative requirements. Brazilian law, despite providing for preventive involvement of the defence in the remand proceedings, does not specify the consequences of the judicial summons, nor does it give clear indications on the 'necessary information' (*peças necessarias*) that must be forwarded to the individuals concerned.[177] By fulfilling its obligation to implement EU law, Italy has made considerable steps forward. Legislative Decree 101/2014 reformed the rules on the administrative obligations on the execution of pre-trial measures by requiring defendants to be provided with information in an understandable language on important issues, such as the right to legal assistance and legal aid, the right to know the charge filed, the right to inform the consular authority and the family, and so on.[178]

At first glance, the comprehensive information provided by the Italian legislation fully satisfies, and even goes beyond, the requirements of EU law. On close examination, Italian legislation is still far from the EU standards and especially from the requirements set by the Strasbourg case-law. In particular, communication on the right to obtain information on the charge does not ensure that the person restricted in their liberty and movement will be informed about the accusation in a concrete case, since this information remains subjected the conditions and limitations laid down by Articles 335 and 369 CCP-Italy. In other words, the Letter of Rights does guarantee information beyond the limits laid down by statutory law. Moreover, Italian law seems to depart from the requirements of EU law since it does not ensure information on all the information available but only on the evidence supporting the measure applied, which, as noted, can still be screened by the competent prosecutor.

Further concerns arise from the time at which the Letter of Rights should be provided. To be sure, international human rights charters provide for vague indications in this respect. Nevertheless, the requirement of 'promptness' does not allow for unjustified delays, which can negatively affect the possibility of setting up effective defence and of a fair hearing of the person concerned. The 2014 Italian legislation introduced some worrisome rules in relation to the case of defendants who do not speak or understand the language of the proceedings. In this regard, EU law also provides for weak safeguards, allowing for national authorities, where a Letter of Rights is not available in the appropriate language, to ensure information orally in a language that defendants understand, provided, however, that a Letter of Rights is given in an understandable language 'without undue delay'.[179] The Italian legislative implementation apparently follows the same approach.[180] Yet there is no clear indication on the time within which full information must be provided. Moreover, the fact that the competent judge before whom the person was brought is called upon to evaluate whether further information is to be provided to the interested person along with the information given by the law enforcement authority under Article 293 CCP-Italy[181] may seem to indicate that full information must

[177] Art. 282(II)(3) CCP-Brazil.

[178] Art. 293 CCP-Italy.

[179] Art. 4(5) DirICP.

[180] Art. 293(1-*bis*) CCP-Italy.

[181] Art. 294(1-*bis*) CCP-Italy.

be ensured at the latest after the judicial hearing. This is a weak result, which can severely impinge on the possibility of preparing adequate defence strategy.

There still exist considerable limitations, furthermore, as to the information rights of individuals other than the accused, especially the injured party. To be sure, EU law enhanced the information safeguards of the victim in the proceedings on the arrest or detention of the alleged offender. The aggrieved parties must be ensured the right to be informed 'when the person remanded in custody, prosecuted or sentenced for criminal offences concerning them is released from or has escaped detention'.[182] Before the Italian legislature implemented this requirement through a new provision that ensures information in these cases,[183] Italian law had already acknowledged the victim's right to information after the ordering of the restrictive measures of coercive removal from the family home and the ban on approaching the areas usually frequented by the victim.[184] Furthermore, the 2013 reform on gender-based violence enabled the victim to be informed of the decision to revoke the coercive measures under Articles 282-*bis* et seqq. CCP-Italy or to replace them with less intrusive measures.[185]

Notwithstanding these steps forward, Directive 2012/29/EU did not provide for any form of participation of the victim in the decision on remand. A different framework can be observed in Brazil, where the complainant has a limited right to request the accused's pre-trial detention. On the contrary, Italian law, despite the increasing tendency to use pre-trial means to protect victims' rights, does not provide for any form of involvement of the aggrieved party in the decision on the application of coercive or control measures. This confirms that Italy is still not culturally prepared for preventive solutions nor especially to give a voice to the aggrieved parties in the decision on the application of coercive measures aimed at protecting them, nor also in proceedings that can lead to the accused's release or the replacement of pre-trial detention with a non-custodial measure.

c) The Need for Comprehensive Assistance in the Remand Proceedings

As noted, the adoption of restrictions on freedom requires the individuals concerned to be provided with comprehensive assistance. In this respect, even proper information does not always suffice to ensure recourse to the assistance acknowledged by the law. Furthermore, the possibility of having effective assistance is a necessary condition of the fairness of the coercion applied. International human rights case-law emphasises the need to provide the individuals restricted in their freedom the main safeguards which are imminent in all judicial proceedings. Because of the highly multilingual nature of the EU area, EU law construed the right to linguistic

[182] Art. 6(5) DirVR.

[183] Art. 90-*ter* CCP-Italy.

[184] Art. 282-*quater* CCP-Italy.

[185] Art. 299(2-*bis*) CCP-Italy.

assistance in very broad terms, requiring the accused persons to be assisted by an interpreter not only in any questioning or court hearing but also in any communication with their lawyer in connection with any questioning or hearing. Moreover, Directive 2013/48/EU stressed the need to provide the individuals restricted in their right to freedom not only with legal assistance 'without undue delay after deprivation of liberty'[186] but also with the assistance of a third person (*e.g.*, a relative)[187] as well as with consular assistance.[188]

Italian law has only partially satisfied these requirements. Although defendants must be given the free-of-charge assistance of an interpreter in communications with their lawyer prior to any questioning,[189] this guarantee is subjected to the eventual derogations of the right to communicate with the lawyer,[190] derogations which have remained unchanged. From this it follows that, if the competent judge suspends communication with the lawyer at request of the prosecutor for exceptional grounds concerned with the ongoing inquiry, linguistic assistance is also not required. Since suspension can be ordered for up to 5 days, which is the time-limit within the judicial hearing must take place in case of remand detention,[191] this entails that defendants may meet both their lawyer and the interpreter at the hearing for the first time.

2. The Guarantee of a Prompt Independent Review of the Deprivation of Liberty and the Voice of the Defence

International human rights law emphasises the need to take the arrestee and detainee from the control of the law enforcement authority and to ensure them an independent assessment of the lawfulness of coercion. As noted, this fundamental guarantee can in turn have two main features, namely (*a*) a scrutiny conducted *ex officio* by the judicial authority before which the arrestee and detainee must be promptly brought and (*b*) an independent assessment promoted by the individuals concerned through *habeas corpus*. Under the European Convention, these two guarantees also have a different scope of application, the former being expressly limited to arrest and pre-trial detention in criminal proceedings. Although no difference can be observed as to the scope of these procedural safeguards under the American Convention, there is little doubt that here also a special focus is drawn towards criminal proceedings in relation to the guarantee of prompt judicial oversight *ex officio*. It has been observed, moreover, that the Inter-American case-law does not limit the aim of the judicial guarantee to the review of the lawfulness of the

186 Art. 3(2)(c) DirAL.

187 Art. 6 DirAL.

188 Art. 7 DirAL.

189 Art. 143 CCP-Italy.

190 Art. 104(4-*bis*) CCP-Italy.

191 Art. 104(3) CCP-Italy.

coercion applied but makes it a general means of checking the overall conditions of the arrested or detained person.

This approach is of utmost importance from the perspective of the present discussion. As noted, the Inter-American Court especially does not conceive of the judicial review in terms of an objective oversight of the lawfulness of deprivation of liberty but requires the assessment of the physical conditions of the individuals concerned, who must thus be personally involved in the judicial procedure. Albeit with some considerable differences, the case-law of both the Inter-American and the European Court attach particular weight to the right of arrested and detained individuals to appear in court and to be heard by the competent judge.

This issue raises the question of the stage at which the judicial hearing must be ensured. We have noted that Brazil and Italy have followed a somewhat different approach over last few decades. The drafters of the 1988 Italian code, despite providing for a prompt judicial scrutiny of arrest, did not depart from the traditional approach to pre-trial detention and further coercive measures, an approach based on the abstract mechanism of decisions issued, as a rule, *inaudito reo*. Surprisingly, the recent 2015 legislation on pre-trial measures, while carrying out a comprehensive reform of this problem area, maintained the same approach, thus missing an important opportunity to enact a previous form of *contradictoire* especially in remand proceedings. The 2011 Brazilian legislature walked a different road, introducing, albeit with some contradictions, the general obligation for the competent judge, before ruling on a request for coercive measures, to summon the 'opposing party'.

These differences may not seem to be censurable under international human rights law, which, requiring a prompt judicial review of arrest and detention, does not necessarily impose on the contracting countries the obligation to provide for previous involvement of the defence. This does not mean, however, equating preventive and subsequent hearing. Remarkably, international human rights case-law stresses that the guarantee of subsequent judicial scrutiny cannot always be excluded where a judge ordered deprivation of freedom. Certainly, if the judicial review also entails the right to be heard by the competent judge, the judicial hearing must satisfy all the requirements of procedural fairness, starting with the guarantees of impartiality of the competent authority and necessary assistance for the individuals concerned.

In this respect, Italian law still raises serious human rights concerns. Italian courts do not exclude the same judge who ordered a restrictive measure later examining the person concerned. Moreover, we have noted that, although a lawyer must assist the defendant during the hearing, the competent prosecutor can obtain suspension of any communication with the counsel, which in turn entails suspension of linguistic assistance. The Italian Supreme Court still considers the postponement of the interview with the lawyer, if lawfully ordered, in line with both the Constitution and the European Convention.[192] Yet there can be little doubt that the

---

[192]CCass, *Agostino*.

failure to provide for postponement of the judicial hearing makes Italian law inconsistent not only with the Strasbourg case-law but also with EU law. Thus, even in the case of justified postponement, lawyers are not put in a position to set up an effective defence strategy, whereas the detained individuals remain unprotected in the judicial questioning. The 2014 reform, transposing the EU Directive 2012/13, eased these adverse effects only to a minimal extent.

Furthermore, international human rights law makes it clear that the guarantee of prompt judicial review does not justify the unlimited maintenance of deprivation of liberty, nor does a system of rigid statutory time limits always suffice to avoid unlawful interferences with the right to freedom. We saw that the European Court especially advocated the need for ongoing judicial oversight of the lawfulness of restrictions on liberty at reasonable intervals. Also in this regard, Italian law is still far from the requirements set forth by the Strasbourg case-law by not providing for any mechanism aimed at ensuring a re-assessment of the justification of coercive measures at the initiative of the competent authority. On close examination, the requirement that the competent judges must at their own initiative revoke or substitute the measure applied while examining the accused, as well as in specific judicial contexts (in particular, *incidente probatorio*, intermediate hearing, trial),[193] does not in itself entail the duty of an ongoing review of the lawfulness of coercion.

Against this background, the guarantee of a subsequent judicial hearing, even if construed in the mandatory terms laid down by Article 294 CCP-Italy, can backfire on the individuals concerned. Not only may the accused be deprived of the necessary assistance to prepare proper defence with regard to the judicial hearing, but furthermore the maintenance of the measure applied potentially suffices to ensure its duration up to the maximum time limit, unless the defence takes the initiative to request its revocation or replacement with a less intrusive measure. Furthermore, Italian law, while requiring the examination of the competent prosecutor prior to the revocation of the ongoing measure or its replacement with a less intrusive one,[194] does not require, as a rule, the hearing of the accused. This is only due in cases of a request made by the defence, based on new elements of information other than that already assessed by the judge.[195] Even more worryingly, defendants do not need to be heard even where the judge, at request of the prosecutor, replaces the ongoing measure with a more intrusive means or applies it with more intrusive arrangements or orders the joint application of another coercive or control measure.[196]

[193] Art. 299(3) CCP-Italy.

[194] Art. 299(3-*bis*) CCP-Italy.

[195] Art. 299(3-*ter*) CCP-Italy.

[196] Art. 299(4) CCP-Italy.

3. Challenging Pre-trial Restrictions on Liberty. The Persistent Distance from the Standards Set Forth by International Human Rights Law and EU Law

Habeas corpus holds core importance under international human rights law in order to enable the individuals subjected to severe restrictions on freedom to obtain an independent review of the measure applied. The importance of this tool, however, cannot be restricted to the aim of taking the arrestee away from the power of the law enforcement authority. Significantly, the European Court has progressively softened the doctrine of incorporation by guaranteeing the right to be brought before a judge even when the restriction on freedom was ordered by the judicial authority, and even in the presence of the defendant's lawyer. At the national level, *habeas corpus* has a long tradition in Brazilian law, and since the first Republican Constitution of 1891, this procedure has been expressly acknowledged by Brazilian constitutional law. Although Italy does not have a similar tradition, the guarantee of Article 5(4) ECHR had a strong influence on developments in criminal justice by leading to the introduction of a special judicial review of the decisions on coercive measures. The consequence is that this guarantee ensures a review on the part of a higher court of coercive measures ordered by a judge rather than by the administrative authority. In this respect, moreover, one can observe some similarities with the Brazilian *habeas corpus*, which, despite maintaining several original features, is also increasingly aimed at protection against unlawful or unreasonably long judicial detention.

Notwithstanding the importance of this procedural tool, international human rights instruments surprisingly do not provide for clear indications as to the participatory rights of the individuals concerned. Brazilian law also lacks coherent rules in this respect, which has led to the higher courts generally adopting a minimalist approach that largely underestimates the need for the applicant to be involved in the *habeas corpus* proceeding and to be provided with proper legal assistance. This approach, however, cannot be deemed consistent with Inter-American case-law. By emphasising the need for a general scrutiny of the conditions of the detainee also by means of *habeas corpus*, with a view to avoiding violations of physical integrity and the right to life, the Court of San José requires the competent judges to involve the individuals concerned.[197] Complainants must in turn be given a fair hearing, starting with effective legal assistance.

As far as Italian law is concerned, notwithstanding the steps forward made by the 1988 code and by subsequent legislation, the judicial review of coercive measures still provides weak safeguards with regard to the effective participation of the complainant in the proceeding. In particular, even though defendants are allowed to appear in court personally,[198] the reference to the general rules on *in camera* hearings[199] leads to the result that the competent authority must only hear them if

[197] Chapter 9, G.III.

[198] Art. 309(6) CCP-Italy.

[199] Art. 309(8) CCP-Italy.

they are present. This result does not seem to be inconsistent with the Strasbourg case-law, which has always recognised the need to satisfy the requirements of a fair hearing in a more cautious way in *habeas corpus* proceedings than in criminal proceedings. In fact, there is no consistent jurisprudence on whether the competent court must also examine the person deprived of freedom.[200] More serious concerns, instead, relate to the information due to the defence. The paternalistic arrangements of the 1995 reform are still in force and extend to the judicial review solely the right to know exculpatory evidence as well as the information attached to the prosecutorial request.[201] This solution, which maintains the prosecutor's wide discretion in the selection of the information produced to support a request for remand detention or other coercive measures, is rarely compatible with the doctrine of the *Garcia Alva* judgment, entailing the risk of the defence suffering 'substantial restrictions on the rights of the defence'.[202]

E. Interaction of Legal Systems and the Strengthening of a Participatory Approach to Transnational Criminal Justice

I. Introductory Remarks

An increasing interaction among different systems of human rights protection can also be observed in the field of transnational criminal justice. As far as Italian international cooperation in the EU area is concerned, the main development that has recently taken place has been the enactment of a new procedure of international surrender by means of the European arrest warrant, a procedure that has largely changed the traditional extradition-based approach. Over the last decades, international human rights case-law has also increasingly dealt with transnational criminal justice. It is not an easy task, however, to evaluate the impact that international human rights law has had (as well as the influence that it will have in a near future) on the selected countries. This is due to a number of factors. On the one hand, the intervention of international courts has helped with adapting some participatory safeguards set for domestic proceedings to the specific needs posed by transnational cases, *e.g.* requiring the suspects to be informed in their own language. On the other, it must be acknowledged that the solutions traditionally provided by the contentious international case-law do not always fit the characteristics of transnational cases, in which the responsibility for human rights protection is often split among two or more countries.

There is also a risk that international human rights standards weaken the defence rights of the individuals involved in legal assistance proceedings. This is especially

[200] Chapter 8, G.III.

[201] Art. 309(5) CCP-Italy.

[202] Chapter 8, G.III.

true in the field of evidence law, in which the sole and decisive evidence doctrine can lead to softening the participatory safeguards concerned with fact-finding in transborder cases.[203] This risk is particularly high in Italy, where the higher courts tend to relax the rules on the use of evidence obtained abroad by requiring compliance only with the fundamental principles of domestic law. Although no explicit reference is generally made to international human rights case-law, this approach often turns out to lower the protection of individual rights to an extent similar to the minimum threshold required by the Strasbourg case-law. The Supreme Court justified this approach in the light of the constitutional model of fair trial by invoking the objective impossibility of obtaining evidence abroad pursuant to the right to *contradictoire* applicable in national cases.[204] Yet this justification is clearly artificial, legitimising Italy's refusal to demand full respect for the domestic rules on evidence-gathering to facilitate the cooperation with foreign countries. The consequence of this approach was a further lowering of the standards of protection of the defence rights, which allows the use of evidence gathered even with full disregard of the essential principles governing the taking of evidence in national proceedings.[205]

The dangerous weakening of the human rights protection in the light of the need not to frustrate international cooperation can also be observed in the EU area. Remarkably, the rigorous enactment of the mutual recognition principle raised several human rights concerns especially in the field of surrender procedures and it is therefore no surprise that EU law (especially the EU legislation recently launched to enhance some defence rights in relation to domestic proceedings) enacted important safeguards in the EAW proceedings particularly. The Italian law on EAW procedures only partially fulfilled the solutions set forth by 2002 EU legislation and, it can largely be doubted whether it has been updated to the new requirements posed by the recent EU legislative instruments.

II. Audi alteram partem, *Right to Freedom and Procedural Safeguards in the Field of International Surrender. The EU Legislation on the European Arrest Warrant and Its Influence on Italian Law*

1. *In absentia* Trials and Surrender Procedures with EU Countries

As far as international surrender is concerned, a clear example of the developments that have occurred in domestic criminal justice as a result of the increasing incidence of supranational law is provided by the enactment into Italian law of

[203] Caprioli (2013), p. 446.

[204] CCass, *Russo*.

[205] Caprioli (2013), p. 447.

the EU legislation on the European arrest warrant. From the viewpoint of the present discussion, a delicate question concerns the relevance of the accused's absence in the trial country for the purposes of the surrender procedure.

At the beginning of the last decade, the new scenario developing in the former Third Pillar provided the opportunity for a different approach to *in absentia* trials in the field of international cooperation. At that time, this delicate issue had caused several problems regarding mutual assistance between Italy and other European countries. It was precisely the need to ease these tensions that led to Italy and Spain signing in 2000 a bilateral treaty on extradition, which anticipated some of the typical characteristics of the future EU policy on mutual assistance, providing an alternative to the ordinary extradition proceedings.[206] This special procedure was strongly based on the principle of mutual recognition, which allowed for refusal of surrender in cases of lack of dual criminality and convictions rendered *in absentia*.[207] Despite some legislative proposals, however, this treaty was never ratified and the adoption of the EAW Framework Decision, less than 2 years later, led to the Italian legislature considerably softening this radical approach by enacting a compromise solution similar to that of the 1978 Protocol.[208]

The implementation of this fundamental tool should have provoked in-depth reflection on the way of dealing with surrender with other EU countries. Nevertheless, Law 69/2005 not only was issued with considerable delay but also provided a regulation that quite literally reproduced the arrangements made at supranational level. International surrender for the purposes of the enforcement of a sentence or a detention order imposed by a decision rendered *in absentia* in Member States, therefore, was submitted to the condition that the issuing authority did not provide adequate assurances of the possibility for the defendants to apply for a retrial in which they could participate. It should be taken into account, furthermore, that the 2005 legislation, departing from the 2002 Framework Decision, did not distinguish between mandatory and discretionary grounds for non-execution, converting all the cases provided for by the EU institutions into mandatory grounds for refusal. This did not entail, however, the lack of discretionary powers on the part of the executing authority, since the assessment of the adequacy of the assurances provided by the foreign country left to the Italian authorities a considerable margin of appreciation.

As noted, Framework Decision 2009/299/JHA largely reformed the 2002 set-up by requiring stricter conditions for the surrender of defendants to other member states.[209] Even though Italy declared that it would avail itself of the further deadline for the implementation provided for by Article 8(3) of the 2009 Framework Decision, the deadline expired on 1 January 2014 without these provisions having

---

[206] Grevi (2000a, b).

[207] De Amicis (2013), p. 21.

[208] The solution enacted at EU level was to a great extent determined by the need to strike a compromise with countries traditionally rooted on *in absentia* procedures, such as Italy. See Chiavario (2013), p. 235.

[209] Chapter 13, B.II.2.a.

been implemented yet. Nor could the domestic rules in force at that time be deemed in line with the new EU legislation.[210] The distance between EU and domestic law was also increased by the formalistic approach of Italian courts, which, far from requiring concrete assurances, allowed for surrender of the accused solely on the condition that foreign law abstractly provided for the possibility of a retrial.[211] We have seen that the 2014 reform, which dropped the default proceedings and introduced a new type of criminal proceedings *in absentia*, raises several human rights concerns and it can be doubted whether it fits the challenges of transborder proceedings.

2. Participatory Rights in the Executing Country and the Right to Be Fairly Heard in EAW Proceedings

Different problems arise in relation to the participatory rights of the sought person in the executing country. In this regard, the EAW Framework Decision adopted a minimalistic approach by generically granting the requested individuals who do not consent to surrender the right to a judicial hearing in the executing state. The effectiveness of this acknowledgment, moreover, was blurred by the reference to the national law of the executing state, who is competent to define the characteristics of the judicial hearing.[212] As a result, the Italian Implementation Law of 2005 reproduced (even at a terminological level) the solutions adopted in the field of extradition. Before ruling on the arrest warrant, the court of appeal must hear both the Attorney General and the defence's lawyer, whereas the sought person and the representative of the foreign country must be examined only if present in court.[213]

On close examination, this solution cannot be deemed consistent with the Framework Decision that, albeit laconically, entitled the requested person to be heard in court. From this it follows that national law, though having a certain margin of discretion in defining the features of this hearing, must provide the sought individuals—not just their lawyers or a court-appointed lawyer—with the opportunity to be personally heard by an independent body. The main problem lies, however, in the lack of proper information on this opportunity. To be sure, Legislative Decree 101/2014, implementing EU Directive 2012/13, amended the 2005 legislation by tightening the requirements of information in EAW proceedings. As a consequence, the sought individuals must be provided with clear and detailed information on their right to consent to the surrender to the issuing country. However, these requirements do not entail the obligation of informing the accused of the consequences of their decision to consent or not with the requested surrender, with the result that in their relationship with other EU countries, the Italian

[210] Savy (2012), p. 12.

[211] CCass, *Prodan*.

[212] Art. 14 FD EAW.

[213] Art. 17(1) Law 69/2005.

authorities are not required to inform the sought individuals on the right to a judicial hearing. This does not seem to be consistent with the 2012 EU legislation, which, by means of a comprehensive reference to the 'rights' of the sought individuals, should also entail the obligation to insert into the Letters of rights the information on the right to a judicial hearing if they do not consent with surrender.

The Supreme Court in turn contributed to the enhancement of the guarantees concerned with the examination of the requested person, requiring the hearing to be postponed where he could not be present because of a legal impediment. Consequently, the decision issued without accounting for the personal impediment would be unlawful.[214] This solution, however, presupposes that the sought individuals have ever expressed their interest in participating in the court hearing and that they were duly informed on the procedure. Yet both the requested person and the defence lawyer must still be notified of the judicial decree setting the date of the hearing through the ordinary means,[215] which cannot ensure that the sought individuals can personally be made aware of the surrender procedure and the consequences of their surrender to a foreign country. Again, Italian law appears to focus on the fulfilment of formal requirements rather than on the effectiveness of individual rights. If the decree is validly served, the lack of personal information remains without legal significance, and the decision on surrender will be issued after hearing a court-appointed lawyer who could be fully unaware of the risks arising from the foreign prosecution. It must be acknowledged, however, the shortcomings of Italian law are again probably the result of rather scant EU regulation, which, focusing on the rights of the requested person solely in the case of arrest, did not recognise any specific guarantees due to the individuals whose detention is not needed.[216]

Further concerns arise in relation to the qualitative requirements of the court hearing. Once again, EU law, while acknowledging the right to be assisted by a lawyer and by an interpreter, required national law to lay down the terms in which these guarantees should be granted in the executing state.[217] In other words, EU institutions offloaded onto national law the responsibility to define all these important arrangements[218] and it is thus no surprise that the lack of clear European parameters led some member states to adopt a rather minimalistic approach. The Italian Implementation Law provided nothing in this regard. In the absence of statutory indications, therefore, the case-law granted individuals who do not understand Italian the right to interpretation pursuant to the code's rules on domestic proceedings. Italian courts also require, however, that the requested individuals should attach a sworn expert appraisal or appoint an interpreter of their confidence, in order to allow the competent Italian authority to follow the hearing without

---

[214] CCass, *Barachini*.

[215] Art. 10(4) Law 69/2005.

[216] Art. 11(1) FD EAW.

[217] Art. 11(2) FD EAW.

[218] Art. 11(2) FD EAW.

undue delay for the ongoing procedure.[219] Doubtless, this solution largely frustrates the guarantee of interpretation, charging individuals with a burden aimed at facilitating the tasks of the judiciary.

It should be ascertained whether this approach can be maintained after the implementation of the 2010 Directive on the right to interpretation and translation in criminal proceedings, which also dealt with the right to interpretation in the EAW procedures. The main problem lies with the fact that Legislative Decree 32/2014 enacted no rules specifically concerned with surrender procedures. This does not mean, however, that the scope of the new guarantees on interpretation and translation should remain limited to domestic proceedings, since Law 69/2005, as noted, contains a general reference to the code rules, where applicable.[220] This has recently led to the Supreme Court acknowledging the right to translation in EAW procedures pursuant to the new provisions of Article 143 CCP, on the condition, however, that the interested party makes a reasoned request.[221] There is little doubt that this arrangement does not fulfil the requirements of the 2010 Directive, which, recognising the right to interpretation pursuant to the provisions laid down in relation to domestic criminal proceedings, required member states to ensure that the competent authorities in every case check the accused's linguistic knowledge. Moreover, there are no statutory indications on the right the challenge the judicial decision not to appoint an interpreter.

3. Coercive Measures and the Right to a Fair Hearing in the Executing Country

More specific challenges concern participatory rights in cases of coercive measures adopted during the surrender procedure. Compared to the ECE rules on provisional arrest, the EAW legislation distinguished in clearer terms the arrest from the detention of the sought person.[222] Moreover, arrest and detention are not the only restrictions on freedom applicable to EAW procedures. Following the approach of the 1957 Convention, the 2002 Framework Decision enabled the national authorities of the executing state to order the provisional release of the sought persons, provided that further measures can be taken according to *lex loci* to prevent the risk of absconding.[223]

By reversing the order of the EU legislation, the Italian Implementation Law firstly laid down rules on the application of coercive measures upon receipt of a European arrest warrant.[224] These measures can be adopted by means of a court

[219] See Chiavario (2013), p. 259.

[220] Art. 39 Law 69/2005.

[221] CCass, *Ivancescu*.

[222] See Arts. 11 and 12 FD EAW.

[223] Art. 12 FD EAW.

[224] Art. 9 Law 69/2005.

procedure, which, moreover, departs from the requirements laid down in the field of passive extradition, since the Ministry plays no role in the application of coercive means that the president of the competent court of appeal can request after hearing the Attorney-General.[225] The conditions for the application of coercive measures largely reproduce the requirements of the extradition procedure and, again, it is questionable that the Italian authorities cannot verify the existence of a strong suspicion of guilt supporting the foreign law action.[226] Although this result is here justified in the light of the mutual trust among EU authorities, it can severely affect the right to freedom of the sought individuals.

Compared to the general solutions adopted in relation to extradition procedures, it must be acknowledged that Italian law grants stronger protection to the individuals subject to coercive measures applied in the field of EAW proceedings. Where the proceedings are initiated on the basis of an alert issued by a foreign authority through the SIS channel, the police must bring the arrested person before the president of the Court of Appeal within twenty-four hours.[227] This procedure, allowing an immediate contact with the judicial authority, differs from the rules on extradition, which, as noted, provide for a time limit twice as long, forty-eight hours. Moreover, the police have further important tasks, such as that of informing the arrested person about the surrender procedure and the contents of the European arrest warrant as well as the task of appointing a lawyer to the sought individuals, if they are without legal assistance.[228] The police must also promptly inform the arrested person's counsel, who can be present in the judicial hearing, which must take place at the latest forty-eight hours after the judicial authority receiving the record of arrest.[229] Even though an interpreter must be present if the arrested person does not understand Italian, the fairness of the court hearing largely depends on the effectiveness of the guarantee of legal assistance. Yet Italian law does not provide for time limits concerning the information due to the lawyer,[230] who may therefore happen to meet the requested person at the hearing for the first time ever. Nor are there clear statutory indications, unlike in domestic cases, where the court hearing cannot take place within the aforementioned time limits,[231] *e.g.* because of a delay in the transmission of the record of arrest. Law 69/2005 provides for only two situations in which the measure should lose its effects and the arrested person must immediately be released, namely (*a*) where the wrong person was arrested and (*b*) if the arrest was performed beyond the limits laid down by the law.[232]

---

[225] Art. 9(4) Law 69/2005. The request of the president cannot be deemed mandatory, as it is the result of the assessment of the need to adopt a coercive means. Of a different opinion Chiavario (2013), p. 284.

[226] Art. 9(5) Law 69/2005.

[227] Art. 11(1) Law 69/2005.

[228] Art. 12(1) Law 69/2005.

[229] Art. 12(2) Law 69/2005.

[230] Chiavario (2013), p. 288.

[231] *Ibid.*, 290.

[232] Art. 13(2) Law 69/2005.

Stronger guarantees apply, instead, where long-term measures of coercion are ordered during an EAW procedure. If the arrest is maintained, the judicial authority can adopt further coercive means of longer duration,[233] such as remand detention. Here also, the sought person has the right to be judicially heard pursuant to the general requirements of Article 14 FD EAW. Compared to cases of extradition, Law 69/2005 laid down detailed rules in this regard. In particular, the President of the Court of Appeal not only must grant the individuals subject to coercive means the assistance of a lawyer and an interpreter but furthermore must provide them with proper information on the surrender procedure, the contents of the European arrest warrant, and especially the consequences of their eventual consent.[234] It is noteworthy that, upon request of the arrested persons, information on the coercive means must also be given to their relatives and, in case of foreign people, to the competent consular authority.[235] Like in extradition procedures, this court hearing is not excluded by the occurrence of a previous hearing after the arrest. This requirement, which distinguishes the surrender procedures from national cases, may seem to be incompatible with the rapidity that should characterise EAW proceedings.[236] However, the risk of duplication of procedural activities is largely compensated for by the need to grant the individuals subjected to long-term coercive means a court hearing, which, unlike that following the arrest, does not aim at their identification but concerns substantial issues. In particular, it aims at assessing whether a concrete risk of absconding exists, which, as noted, is the sole justification for the adoption of measures that deprive the sought person of the right to participate in the surrender procedure as a free man. To this end, the effectiveness of this hearing largely depends on the possibility of a previous communication with the lawyer. The law, however, provides nothing in this regard, only requiring that the lawyer be informed at least twenty-four hours before the hearing.[237] Yet the reference to the code's general provisions allows the application of Article 104 CCP, which grants all the individuals in remand detention the right to communicate with their lawyer from the enforcement of the coercive measure. Doubtless, this is a requirement of utmost importance in the EU legislation after Directive 2013/48/EU, which acknowledged, *inter alia*, the right to legal assistance of the individuals subject to a European arrest warrant without undue delay from the deprivation of their liberty as well as the right to meet and communicate with their counsel.[238]

[233]Unlike in domestic cases, the EAW procedure may seem to link the adoption of further restrictions on freedom solely to the eventuality of the arrest being maintained. On close examination, this interpretation is misleading. Under Article 9 Law 69/2005, the judicial authority can in any case adopt pre-trial means, which have a different justification from that of the arrest. The case-law also rules out further measures of coercion being applied only in case of validation of the arrest. See CCass, *Enciu*.

[234]Art. 10(1) Law 69/2005.

[235]Art. 10(3) Law 69/2005.

[236]Chiavario (2013), p. 292.

[237]Art. 10(2) Law 69/2005.

[238]Art. 10(2)(a-b) DirAL.

4. The Enhanced Role of the Judiciary in EAW Proceedings

As in the field of extradition, the enhancement of the participatory rights of the sought individuals by means of a European arrest warrant was largely due to the strengthening of the role of the judiciary. As noted, the EAW Framework Decision gave rise to a process of strong jurisdictionalization of international cooperation in the EU area. This is apparent from the very definition of the European arrest warrant as a 'judicial decision'.[239] On close examination, the simplicity of this expression disguises a rather ambiguous concept,[240] and it is thus no surprise that the 2002 legislation, in the light of the diversity of national laws, avoided any attempt at further definition,[241] while prudently referring to the national law respectively of the issuing and the executing country.[242] Moreover, it cannot be overlooked that a strong understanding of the order model characterised the first years of mutual recognition-based legislation. This goal would have been largely frustrated if the EU institutions had further delimitated judicial competence in the field of EAW procedures, not to mention the reforms that this option would have entailed at the domestic level in the distribution of powers in criminal proceedings. In second half of the last decade, awareness increasingly grew of the need to strengthen judicial review by circumscribing the plethora of authorities exercising judicial powers at the national level.[243] Notwithstanding these developments, EU institutions have never amended the EAW Framework Decision in this direction.

The 2005 Italian Implementation Law reflected the clear attempt to make the new tool consistent both with the enhanced role of the judiciary provided for in the extradition procedures and with the overall distribution of coercive powers laid down by the code in domestic cases. As a result, the court of appeal was empowered to decide on the execution of arrest warrants issued in another member state.[244] Concerning outgoing requests, instead, the judicial authority is responsible for

[239] Art. 1(1) FdEAW.

[240] Chiavario (2013), p. 198.

[241] Oubiña Barbolla (2012), p. 49.

[242] Art. 1(1) FdEAW.

[243] In 2008, the EEW Framework Decision allowed member states to make a declaration or subsequent notification to the General Secretariat of the Council requiring a validation procedure in all cases where the issuing authority was not a judge, a court, an investigating magistrate, or a public prosecutor, and where the measures necessary to execute the EEW should be ordered or supervised by one of these authorities under the law of the executing state in a similar domestic case [Art. 11(5)]. Almost 6 years later, Directive 2014/41/EU provided for the possibility of investigations being ordered by any competent authority empowered by the issuing country to act in its capacity as an investigating authority in criminal proceedings with competence to order the gathering of evidence in accordance with national law. At the same time, this legislation required the new European investigation order always to be validated in this case, before being transmitted to the executing authority and after examination of its conformity with the conditions laid down in the Directive, by a judge, court, investigating judge, or a public prosecutor in the issuing state [Art. 2(c)(ii)].

[244] Art. 5 Law 69/2005.

addressing to foreign authorities only arrest warrants aimed at the execution of pre-trial detention or house arrest in Italy,[245] while public prosecutors are called upon to issue arrest warrants aimed at carrying out either custodial sentences of at least 1 year or custodial security measures.[246]

In general terms, this distribution of powers is in line with the approach followed in relation to domestic proceedings, an approach that provides for the judicial competence to order coercive measures, while leaving to the prosecutor the power of initiative. Moreover, the enhanced role of the judiciary in the case of incoming requests should be viewed in the light of the human rights implications of the surrender procedure, which require a high level of protection of the right to freedom of the sought person. Yet the 2005 Implementation Law failed in any case to define both the judicial issuing authority and the competent authority that will restrict the liberty of the sought individuals after their surrender. The Supreme Court has in turn ruled out refusal of execution of arrest warrants issued by foreign non-jurisdictional authorities.[247] This approach can lead to problems of compliance with the Strasbourg case-law, according to which, as noted, Article 5(3) ECHR can only be satisfied by means of a review carried out, if not necessarily by the judicial authority, by a body with a high degree of independence and impartiality.[248] Moreover, Law 69/2005 included among the constitutional guarantees of the EAW procedure the fundamental rights enshrined in Articles 5 and 6 of the European Convention.[249]

On the other hand, the 2005 legislation, focusing on the foreign authority which issued the detention order that gave rise to the EAW procedure, rather than on the authority issuing the European arrest warrant, introduced a requirement non-existent in the 2002 Framework Decision. Pursuant to the 2002 EU legislation, the foreign decision must be either a reasoned detention order, signed by a judge, or a final conviction.[250] It can be doubted, however, whether this requirement was due to mandatory constitutional provisions governing the right to freedom, and consequently whether the execution of a European arrest warrant should be denied because a judge had not issued the detention order.[251] On close examination, the need for efficient international cooperation, especially in the EU judicial area, aimed at ensuring the peace and security among states is certainly an interest of constitutional relevance from a human rights perspective as well.[252] From this it follows that legal assistance should be denied, for instance, to avoid discriminatory

[245]Art. 28(1)(a) Law 69/2005.

[246]Art. 28(1)(b-c) Law 69/2005.

[247]CCass, *Piaggio*.

[248]Chiavario (2013), p. 199.

[249]Art. 2 FD EAW. See Marzaduri (2006), p. 88ff.

[250]Art. 1(3) FdEAW.

[251]In this sense see Marzaduri (2006), p. 80ff.

[252]Art. 11 Const.-Italy.

situations[253] entailing a violation of individual rights by either the criminal law system of the foreign country or the procedure carried out abroad.[254]

In this regard, Law 69/2005 reveals a rather formalistic approach to transnational criminal justice, submitting incoming requests to conditions that not only do not aim at satisfying mandatory constitutional requirements, but can also be insufficient to ensure that the detention order was ordered abroad pursuant to a fair procedure. Thus, the fact that a judge must have ordered the detention in the issuing state does not necessarily entail that the judicial authority could review the overall lawfulness of the provisional imprisonment and examine the reasons brought about by the defence.[255] Nor can this result be deemed implied by the requirement of a 'reasoned' judicial order, a requirement that is open to very different solutions depending on whether and to what extent national law requires judges, when remanding defendants in custody, to give reasons on the information attached by the defence. Furthermore, the condition that a judge signed a reasoned detention order reflects an approach that exalts the initial stage of the remand proceedings, while overlooking the need for subsequent judicial oversight of the lawfulness of pre-trial detention. The grounds for this approach probably lie in the Constitution.[256] By ruling out individuals being restricted in their personal freedom without a reasoned judicial order, Article 13 of the Constitution was traditionally interpreted in the sense that a judicial order is only needed to restrict the individuals' liberty. After that moment, instead, the establishment of legal time limits would suffice to keep the duration of pre-trial detention within reasonable boundaries.[257]

In line with this interpretation, Law 69/2005 introduced another provision, which did not exist in the EAW Framework Decision, a provision containing a further basis for refusal, aimed at rejecting the sought surrender to countries which do not provide for fixed time limits laid down at the legislative level.[258] This led the Joint Sections of the Supreme Court to examine the delicate question of whether a European arrest warrant can be executed to surrender individuals to countries whose statutory law does not set maximum time limits for pre-trial detention.[259] The Court's response was that the executing authority should ascertain whether

> the law of the issuing Member State expressly lays down a time-limit for preventive detention until conviction at first instance, or failing this, whether an implicit time-limit can in any case be deduced from other procedural mechanisms that establish, as obligatory and at pre-established intervals, judicial review to confirm the lawful continuance of preventive custody or, alternatively, order release.

[253]CConst, 54/1979.

[254]Marzaduri (2006), p. 83ff.

[255]Similarly Chiavario (2013), p. 227.

[256]Ruggeri (2012), p. 204f.

[257]Art. 13(2) and (5) Const.-Italy.

[258]Art. 18(e) Law 69/2005.

[259]CCass, *Ramoci*. See among others De Amicis (2007); Di Martino (2011), p. 1ff.

This response, although not entirely departing from the constitutional approach, was enlightening from a methodological viewpoint. In the case at stake, the Supreme Court examined the German rules on pre-trial detention (*Untersuchungshaft*), which combine a fixed legal time-limit with a more flexible system of judicial controls.[260] Certainly, Germany is not an exception in the EU area: other European countries entrust exclusively to the judiciary an ongoing oversight of the lawfulness of pre-trial detention without fixed legal time-limits. Although Germany follows a different approach to remand proceedings than that of Italian criminal justice, the Joint Sections considered that such differences cannot be considered to infringe on mandatory constitutional requirements. The Supreme Court also held that refusal of executing an arrest warrant solely on the grounds that another EU country does not provide for the same solutions in force in Italy would unreasonably jeopardise the international cooperation at EU level, which is also, as noted, an interest of constitutional relevance.[261] According to the Supreme Court, however, the executing authority should scrutinise the existence of alternative solutions in the law of the trial country, aimed at ensuring the lawful duration of pre-trial detention, even if not by means of statutory time limits. From this it follows that, where the issuing country provides for maximum time-limits for pre-trial custody, the Italian authorities should not engage in the ascertainment of whether there are further mechanisms aimed at ensuring that provisional imprisonment maintains a valid justification after the initial stage and is restricted to the minimum extent necessary.

The failure of Italian law to enact tools aimed at the ongoing oversight of the lawfulness of the provisional imprisonment can lead to delicate problems. Notwithstanding the rapid course of EAW procedures, it may happen that the decision on the execution of the European warrant can occur long after the initial justification of pre-trial detention was judicially reviewed.[262] Even worse, the Italian authority may happen to decide on a request for surrender even at a stage in which the imprisonment might have already lost its justification. Furthermore, we have noted that the Italian courts are not called upon to verify whether and in which terms the lawfulness of measures ordered was checked abroad and, in particular, whether the defence could be heard and had the opportunity of challenging the prosecutorial requests through exculpatory evidence. Nor can Italian authorities assess whether the sought individuals living in Italy were granted a fair opportunity to communicate with their lawyer abroad and could therefore contribute to challenging the lawfulness of the measure adopted before a higher court.

[260]Also here, it could be argued that the code rules are justified by the Constitution, which requires a judicial review, albeit limited solely to the case of deprivation of liberty, both to order and maintain the individual imprisonment. Cf. Art. 104(2) Const.-Germany. See Sinn (2012), p. 107f.

[261]The Constitutional Court has also moved in this direction. See CConst, 109/2008. For further criticisms see Chiavario (2013), p. 228f.

[262]Art. 17 Law 69/2005.

Yet there should be no doubt that the order model—in an integrated area of freedom, security and justice, strongly rooted on the protection of fundamental rights—cannot justify indifference towards the overall risks arising from transnational cooperation. To this end, the constitutional requirements of the right to liberty must certainly also be complied with in the decision on surrender and the execution procedure.[263] This leads us to analyse whether the proceedings in the executing country can give rise to restrictions on freedom that cannot be tolerated from the viewpoint of national constitutional law, which itself calls for the enhancement of the role on the judiciary at the execution stage.

On close examination, Italian law also watered down the role of the judiciary in relation to the forms of the activation of the execution procedure. By departing from the approach of the 2002 Framework Decision,[264] Italy stands quite unique among other EU countries in that it enhanced the role of the Ministry of Justice to the point that outgoing requests must, as a rule, be transmitted through the central authority.[265] Although the Ministry must immediately involve the Italian judicial authority,[266] this result can largely frustrate the goal of allowing direct contact between judicial authorities. Moreover, Law 69/2005 provides for a special procedure, instituted through an alert for the requested person issued by a foreign authority in the Schengen Information System (SIS). In case of outgoing requests, Italian authorities can use this procedure, instead of issuing an arrest warrant, only where the defendant's place of residence or stay is not known and it is possible that they live in another EU state.[267] By contrast, nothing is foreseen in relation to the case in which Italy receives an alert issued by other member states. In this case, moreover, the peculiarity of the execution procedure is that the judicial authority is not immediately involved but the police intervene first, arresting the sought individuals for the purposes of the EAW procedure and bringing them before the judicial authority.[268]

This set-up should not be deemed incompatible with the EAW Framework Decision, which provides for the provisional arrest of the requested person.[269] Nor does the special procedure through the SIS channel seem to infringe on the European Convention, which allows for the arrest of individuals for the purposes of an extradition or deportation procedure,[270] an arrest that is not necessarily aimed at preventing the risk of flight of the sought person or the risk of committing further offences.[271] Instead, the immediate police arrest after the SIS alert cannot be

[263] Marzaduri (2006), p. 81.

[264] Art. 9 FdEAW.

[265] Art. 4(2) Law 69/2005.

[266] Pursuant to Article 9(1) Law 69/2005 the Ministry of Justice, once it has received the EAW, forwards it without delay to the competent court of appeal.

[267] Art. 29(2) Law 69/2005.

[268] Art. 11(1) Law 69/2005.

[269] Art. 11(1) FdEAW.

[270] Art. 5(1)(f) ECHR.

[271] ECtHR, *Seferovic v. Italy*, § 37. See Gialuz (2012), p. 136.

considered in line with the Italian Constitution, which, albeit enabling the police to restrict the personal freedom of individuals, limits the exercise of this power to exceptional cases of necessity and urgency, strictly defined at statutory level.[272] The grounds for this approach lie in the two main guarantees governing the restrictions on the right to freedom, that is, the need for a law laying down the exact limits of the state's intervention and the need for a reasoned order issued by the judicial authority.[273] There are no binding indications in the Italian constitutional law, which limits the scope of these guarantees to domestic cases, while allowing for derogations in the field of international cooperation. Moreover, as noted, the special procedure through the SIS channel neither submits the police arrest to cases of particular urgency or necessity nor defines in any case the conditions of their intervention. The case-law further increases the distance from constitutional requirements, allowing for police arrest after the SIS alert if the sought person, albeit not untraceable, is not formally resident in Italy.[274] For the same reasons, it might be argued that Italian law also departed from the approach of 1957 Extradition Convention that links the arrest of the sought person solely to the case of urgency.[275]

III. Participatory Rights and Transnational Evidence-Gathering

1. Responsibility of the Cooperating Countries for the Granting of Participatory Safeguards in Transnational Inquiries. The Feasibility of the Strasbourg Case-Law at the Domestic Level

Different human rights problems emerge from legal assistance procedures in the field of transborder investigations and the collection of overseas evidence. In this respect, the first issue concerns the determination of the state's responsibility for human rights violations. The approach followed by the former European Commission in the *X., Y. and Z.* decision, which offloaded onto the requested country the 'full responsibility' for the form of letters rogatory, no longer fits the challenges of a modern transnational evidence-gathering.

In 1988, the Italian code already allowed for the application of foreign procedures where Italian authorities were requested to take evidence for the purposes of a prosecution in the requesting country. This considerably relativized the

---

[272]Art. 13(3) Const.-Italy.

[273]Art. 13(2) Const.-Italy.

[274]CCass, *Franconetti*. On the erroneous terminological choice of Law 69/2005, which converted the supranational expression of 'requested person', applicable in any case of European arrest warrant, into that of 'person sought for the purposes of arrest' (*persona ricercata*), see Lo Voi (2005), p. 242f.

[275]Art. 16 ECE.

assumption that Italy should bear the entire responsibility for the form of the sought legal assistance. A similar conclusion applies to the case of legal assistance requested by Italy, which has since 2001 enabled the national authorities to request the application of Italian procedural law in the taking of evidence abroad. However, not only is this result conditional on the existence of specific rules in an international law instrument in force in Italy but furthermore the 2001 legislation left a great margin of discretion to the domestic authorities in the choice of the formalities to be applied abroad. It is true that the Italian authorities should only request the formalities that are necessary to ensure the use of the information collected at trial. There is no obligation, however, to request the application of further binding procedures, which, despite not affecting the admissibility of overseas evidence, entail the intervention of the defence in the foreign investigation and the collection of the sought information. The consequence is that, except for the rules impinging on the use of overseas evidence, the Italian authorities will determine the extent to which Italy should be responsible for the forms of transnational evidence-gathering under the European Convention. The margin of discretion increases in cases of other modes of legal assistance, *e.g.* in the limited cases in which Italian law allows for the setting-up of a joint investigation team. Here, the direct intervention of the Italian investigative authorities, alongside their involvement in the establishment of specific procedures beyond the requirements of *lex loci*, entails Italy's responsibility for the form of evidence-gathering on foreign territory, without giving the individuals concerned, however, any certainty about the applicable law.

The Inter-American case-law has never addressed the issue of the state's responsibility in the field of transnational evidence-gathering. Over last decades, however, Brazilian law has also increasingly developed more flexible tools of legal assistance and ratified new international law agreements that involve the trial country in the determination of the form of the overseas investigation by requesting the partial application of *lex fori*. This seems to support the conclusion that Brazilian law also allows for shared international responsibility.

2. The Right to Confrontation, the Participatory Safeguards in the Taking of Incriminating Evidence, and the Use of Untested Evidence

The need for enhanced human rights protection emerges where the taking of incriminating evidence is at stake. It has been observed that the Strasbourg case-law strengthened the responsibility of the trial State in this problematic area. This does not of course entail that the trial country can be deemed liable for non-compliance with *lex loci* by the cooperating authorities, but that the competent authorities for the relevant proceedings must put in place all the necessary arrangements to enable the accused to take part in the collection of incriminating evidence. Doubtless, this requirement holds even greater importance under the American Convention, which requires the defence to be directly involved in the confrontation with prosecutorial witnesses. In this regard, Italian law, which has largely maintained the traditional rules on judicial service, does not set the best conditions for defendants to be fairly confronted with their accusers.

Furthermore, the general uncertainty that all the combined methods of evidence-gathering leave about the applicable law inevitably affects the possibility of a fair participation of the defence in transnational inquiries. The imbalance between defence rights and prosecutorial needs further increases at the EU level. As noted, the EIO Directive allows for the active involvement of the authorities of the trial country, without laying down in contrast any provision that ensures the participation of the defence, even where incriminating evidence must be taken abroad. The use of technological means does not entail significant changes in this respect, since the EIO legislation, largely reproducing the solutions of the Brussels Convention, requires witnesses to be examined, as a rule, by the judge of the trial country. Furthermore, we have noted that neither the 2000 Convention nor the EIO Directive ensure legal assistance to the person concerned regardless of whether a witness or the accused must be examined. Yet there is no doubt that the assistance of a lawyer is of utmost importance, especially in cases of vulnerable witnesses. Another delicate situation concerns the hearing of co-defendants who are still under prosecution and therefore deserve specific protection against the risk of self-incriminating statements. In Italy, as noted, co-defendants already must be assisted by a lawyer in the pre-trial phase both during police and prosecutorial hearings, and legal assistance plays an essential role when the co-accused is summoned to give evidence on facts concerned with other individuals, a decision that can lead to a significant change of their procedural status. Although Italy has not yet implemented the EIO Directive, the general set-up provided by this legislative instrument does not pose the best premises for the enhancement of the participatory rights in the case of legal assistance procedures activated with other member states.

A different question is whether the trial state should also be responsible for the violations of the right to confrontation on the part of the cooperating country by allowing for the use of untested evidence gathered abroad. As noted, international human rights courts have not yet dealt with this problem. By focusing on the taking of evidence in response to an investigative order, the EIO legislation also did not enact specific provisions on the admissibility of overseas evidence. In the *P.V.* case, the former European Commission recognised this possibility only in abstract terms. By largely submitting the admissibility of transnational evidence to the ordinary rules applicable to domestic proceedings, both Italy and Brazil converted the question into an issue of national relevance. At first glance, this result highlights a stronger approach than that of the *P.V.* decision, which should lead to the obligation for the competent authorities of trial country to fulfil *lex fori* by admitting information that was gathered pursuant to the domestic rules governing the accused's right to confrontation. This conclusion does however hold true in Italy, since national case-law tends to soften the domestic requirements in transnational cases by only requiring the fulfilment of the general principles of national (evidence) law.

F. Conclusions

Doubtless, an increasing mutual interaction can be observed between international human rights law and domestic law in the field of criminal justice. The increasing influence of international human rights case-law in the selected countries is a part of a more complex phenomenon, which also encompasses the developments that have occurred in international jurisprudence as a result of the diversity of the national systems examined and the increasing tendency of international courts to metabolise national arrangements in order to produce autonomous solution models. In Europe, EU law is clearly involved in this complex process and in turn increasingly contributes to the evolution of Italian criminal justice. The Italian enactment of the EAW legislation, as well as the recent implementation of the EU law on certain defence rights in the field of domestic criminal proceedings, provide clear examples of this phenomenon. These developments in turn reveal significant changes in the way the role of private parties is conceived of in the field of both national and transnational criminal justice. In this regard, however, the comparative-law examination carried out in this Chapter has also shown the persistent resistance in both countries to some solutions provided by international human rights case-law, while highlighting the extent to which Italy is transposing the EU legislative reforms issued after the entry into force of the Lisbon Treaty.

References

Amalfitano C (2017) La vicenda Taricco nuovamente al vaglio della Corte di giustizia: qualche breve riflessione a caldo. http://rivista.eurojus.it. Accessed 29 Jan 2017

Candito GL (2015) The influence of the Directive 2012/13/EU on the Italian system of protection of the right to information in criminal procedures. In: Ruggeri S (ed) Human rights in European criminal law. New developments in European legislation and case law after the lisbon treaty. Springer, Heidelberg, pp 229–260

Caprioli F (2013) Report on Italy. In: Ruggeri S (ed) Transnational inquiries and the protection of fundamental rights in criminal proceedings. A study in memory of Vittorio Grevi and Giovanni Tranchina. Springer, Heidelberg, pp 439–455

Carini C (2008) Errore e rimedi. In: Digesto delle discipline penalistiche. IV Agg. Utet, Torino, pp 258–291

Chiavario M (2005) Una riforma inevitabile: ma basterà? La Legislazione penale pp 253–259

Chiavario M (2008) La "lunga marcia" dei diritti dell'uomo nel processo penale. In: Balsamo A, Kostoris RE (eds) Giurisprudenza europea e processo penale italiano. Giappichelli, Torino, pp 11–31

Chiavario M (2013) Manuale dell'estradizione e del mandato d'arresto europeo. Utet, Torino

Ciampi S (2014) Diritto all'informazione nei procedimenti penali: il recepimento *low profile* della direttiva 2012/13/UE da parte del d.lgs. 1° luglio 2014 n. 101. *Letter of Rights* e *Full Disclosure* nel procedimento penale italiano. www.penalecontemporaneo.it. Accessed 24 Sept 2014

Conso G (1950) Il provvedimento di archiviazione. Rivista italiana di diritto penale, pp 320 ff.

Conti R (2015) La richiesta di "parere consultivo" alla Corte europea delle Alte Corti introdotto dal Protocollo n.16 annesso alla CEDU e il rinvio pregiudiziale alla Corte di Giustizia

UE. Prove d'orchestra per una *nomofilachia europea*. In: Lamarque E (ed) La richiesta di pareri consultivi alla Corte di Strasburgo da parte delle più alte giurisdizioni nazionali. Prime riflessioni in vista della ratifica del Protocollo 16 CEDU. Giappichelli, Torino, pp 97–133

Daniele M (2008) Regole di esclusione della prova e giurisprudenza della Corte europea: profili di potenziale conflitto. In: Balsamo A, Kostoris RE (eds) Giurisprudenza europea e processo penale italiano. Giappichelli, Torino, pp 383–394

De Amicis G (2007) Mandato di arresto europeo e limiti massimi di custodia cautelare: incostituzionalità o "interpretazione costitutionalmente orientatata" del motive di rifiuto alla consegna? Giurisprudenza di merito, pp 1435 ff

De Amicis G (2013) All'incrocio tra diritti fondamentali, mandato d'arresto europeo e decisioni contumaciali: la Corte di Giustizia e il "caso Melloni". Un commento a margine della sentenza Melloni della Corte di Giustizia. www.penalecontemporaneo.it. Accessed 7 June 2013

Di Chiara G (2009) "Against the Administration of Justice in Secret": la pubblicità delle procedure giudiziarie tra Corte europea e assetti del sistema italiano. In: Balsamo A, Kostoris RE (eds) Giurisprudenza europea e processo penale italiano. Giappichelli, Torino, pp 293–308

Di Martino A (2011) Questo limite non è un termine. Tecnicismi «specifici» e «collaterali» nel contesto di un sistema penale internazionalizzato. Archivio penale, pp 1–13

Di Stasi A (2014) La Corte interamericana e la Corte europea dei diritti dell'uomo: da un *trans-regional judicial dialogue* ad una *cross-fertilization*? In: Cassetti L, Di Stasi A, Landa Arroyo L (eds) Diritti e giurisprudenza. La Corte interamericana dei diritti umani e la Corte europea di Strasburgo. Jovene, Napoli, pp 1–25

Ferrua P (2013) La prova nel processo penale: profili generali. In: Ferrua P, Marzaduri E, Spangher G (eds) La prova penale. Giappichelli, Torino, pp 1–56

Gaeta P (2012) Dell'interpretazione conforme alla C.E.D.U.: ovvero, la ricombinazione genica del processo penale. Archivio penale, pp 1–43

Giacomolli NJ (2014) O devido processo penal. Abordagem conforme a Constituição Federal e o Pacto de São José da Costa Rica. Atlas S.A., São Paulo

Gialuz M (2012) Commento all'art. 5 In: Bartole S, De Sena P, Zagrebelsky V (eds) Commentario breve alla Convenzione europea per la salvaguardia dei diritti dell'uomo e dele libertà fondamentali. Cedam, Padova

Grevi V (2000a) Alla ricerca di un processo penale giusto. Giuffrè, Milano

Grevi V (2000b) Giustizia, l'accordo tra Italia e Spagna un modello europeo. In: Correre della Sera (4 December 2000b)

Harris D, O'Boyle M, Warbrick C (2009) Law of the European convention on human rights, 2nd edn. Oxford University Press, Oxford

Joseph S, Schultz J, Castan M (2004) The international covenant on civil and political rights. Cases, materials and commentary, 2nd edn. Oxford University Press, Oxford

Krisch N (2008) The open architecture of European human rights law. Mod Law Rev 71:183–216

Kühne H-H (2015) Strafprozessrecht. Eine systematische Darstellung des deutschen und europäischen Strafverfahrensrechts, 9th edn. C.F. Müller, Heidelberg

Lamarque E, Viganò F (2014) Sulle ricadure interne della sentenza Scoppola. Ovvero: sul gico di squadra tra Cassazione e Corte costituzionale nell'adeguamento del nostro ordinamento alle sentenze di Strasburgo (nota a C. Cost. N. 2010/2013). www.penalecontemporaneo.it. Accessed 31 March 2014

Lo Voi F (2005) Il procedimento davanti alla Corte di appello e i provvedimenti *de libertate*. Il conseno. In: Bargis M, Selvaggi E (eds) Mandato d'arresto europeo. Dall'estradizione alle procedure di consegna. Giappichelli, Torino, pp 241–268

Lozzi G (2014) Lezioni di procedura penale, 9th edn. Giappichelli, Torino

Martinico G (2012) Part 1. In: Martinico G, Pollicino O (eds) The Interaction between Europe's legal systems. Judicial Dialogue and the Creation of Supranation Laws. Edward Elgar, Cheltenham

Martinico G, Pollicino O (2012) The interaction between Europe's legal systems. Judicial dialogue and the creation of supranation laws. Edward Elgar, Cheltenham

Marzaduri E (2000) Commento all'art. 1 legge costituzionale 2/1999. In: La Legislazione penale, pp. 762-804

Marzaduri E (2006) Commento agli artt. 1-2 l. 69/2005. In: Chiavario M, Marzaduri E (eds) Il mandato di arresto europeo. Utet, Torino, pp 58–96

Mazzuoli V d O (2011) O Controle Jurisdictional da Convencionalidade dais Leis, 2nd edn. Revista dos Tribunais, São Paulo

Negri D (2005) Commento all'art. 1 Decreto-legge 17/2005. La Legislazione penale, pp 260–291

Oubiña Barbolla S (2012) The European arrest warrant in law and practice. In: Ruggeri S (ed) Liberty and security in Europe. A comparative analysis of pre-trial precautionary measures in criminal proceedings. V&R Unipress (Universitätsverlag Osnabrück), Göttingen, pp 47–66

Pollicino O (2008) The Constitutional Court at the crossroads between constitutional parochialism and co-operative constitutionalism. Judgments No. 348 and 349 of 22 and 24 October 2007. Eur Const Law Rev, pp 363–382

Pollicino O (2010) Allargamento ad est dello spazio giuridico europeo e rapporto tra Corti costituzionali e Corti europee. Verso una teoria generale dell'impatto interordinamentale del diritto sovranazionale? Giuffrè, Milano

Pollicino O (2014) La Corte costituzionale è una "alta giurisdizione nazionale" ai fini della richiesta di parere alla Corte EDU ex Protocollo 16? www.forumcostituzionale.it

Pollicino O (2015) Corte di giustizia e giudici nazionali: il moto "ascendente", ovverosia l'incidenza delle "tradizioni costituzionali comuni" nella tutela apprestata ai diritti dalla Corte dell'Unione. www.giurcost.org, pp 242–263

Quattrocolo S (2014) Il contumace cede la scena processuale all'assente, mentre l'irreperibile l'abbandona. Riflessioni a prima lettura sulla nuova disciplina del procedimento senza imputato. www.penalecontemporaneo.it. Accessed 30 Apr 2014

Ruggeri A (2007) La CEDU alla ricerca di una nuova identità, tra prospettiva formale-astratta e prospettiva assiologico-sostanziale d'inquadramento sistematico (a prima lettura di Corte cost. nn. 348 e 349 del 2007). www.forumcostituzionale.it

Ruggeri A (2010) Corte costituzionale e Corti europee: il modello, le esperienze, le prospettive. Centro di documentazione europea (Università di Catania), http://www.cde.unict.it/sites/default/files/19_2010.pdf

Ruggeri S (2012) Personal Liberty in Europe. A comparative analysis of pre-trial precautionary measures in criminal proceedings. In: Ruggeri S (ed) Liberty and Security in Europe. A comparative analysis of pre-trial precautionary measures in criminal proceedings. V&R Unipress (Universitätsverlag Osnabrück), Göttingen, pp 185–243

Ruggeri A (2014a) Le fonti del diritto eurounitario ed i loro rapporti con le fonti nazionali. In: Costanzo P, Mezzetti L, Ruggeri A (eds) Lineamenti di diritto costituzionale dell'Unione Europea. Giappichelli, Torino, pp 268–324

Ruggeri A (2014b) Ragionando sui possibili sviluppi dei rapporti tra le Corti europee e i giudici nazionali (con specifico riguardo all'adesione dell'Unione alla CEDU e all'entrata in vigore del Prot. 16). www.forumcostituzionale.it

Ruggeri A (2015) "Dialogue" between European and national courts, in the pursuit of the strongest protection of fundamental rights (with specific regard to criminal and procedural law). In: Ruggeri S (ed) Human rights in European criminal law. New developments in european legislation and case law after the Lisbon treaty. Springer, Heidelberg, pp 9–29

Sarlet IW (2008) A Reforma do Judiciário e os tratados internacionais de direitos humanos: observações sobre o § 3° do art. 5° da Constituição. www.ambito-juridico.com.br

Savy D (2012) La tutela dei diritti fondamentali ed il rispetto dei principi generali del diritto dell'Unione nella disciplina del mandato d'arresto europeo. www.penalecontemporaneo.it

Scalfati A (1999) L'udienza preliminare. Profili di una disciplina in trasformazione. Cedam, Padova

Sinn A (2012) Report on Germany. In: Ruggeri S (ed) Liberty and security in Europe. A comparative analysis of pre-trial precautionary measures in criminal proceedings. V&R Unipress (Universitätsverlag Osnabrück), Göttingen, pp 105–120

Slaughter AM (1994) A typology of transjudicial communication. Univ Richmond Law Rev 29:99–137

Spencer JR (2014) Hearsay evidence in criminal proceedings, II edn. Hart Publishing, Oxford

Trechsel S (2005) Human rights in criminal proceedings. Oxford University Press, Oxford

Ubertis G (2007) Sistema di procedura penale, 2nd edn. Utet, Torino

Ubertis G (2009) La prova dichiarativa debole: problemi e prospettive in materie di assunzione della testimonianza della vittima vulnerabile alla luce della gurisprudenza sovranazionale. Cassazione penale, pp 4058–4067

Viganò F (2014) Convenzione europea dei diritti dell'uomo e resistenze nazionalistiche: Corte costituzionale italiana e Corte di Strasburgo tra "guerra" e "dialogo". Qualche osservazione dall'angolo visuale di un penalista. www.penalecontemporaneo.it

Vogler R (2014) Criminal evidence and respect for fair trial guarantees in the dialogue between the European court of human rights and national courts. In: Ruggeri S (ed) Transnational evidence and multicultural inquiries in Europe. Developments in EU legislation and new challenges for human rights-oriented criminal investigations in cross-border cases. Springer, Heidelberg, pp 181–192

Zacchè F (2008) Gli effetti della giurisprudenza europea in tema di privilegio contro le autoincriminazioni e diritto al silenzio. In: Balsamo A, Kostoris RE (eds) Giurisprudenza europea e processo penale italiano. Giappichelli, Torino, pp 179–195

Chapter 17
Concluding Findings. Proposals and Qualitative Requirements of a Participatory Model of Criminal Justice

Contents

A. *Audi alteram partem*, Fairness of Criminal Proceedings and the Reliability of the Fact-Finding: From the Fragmentary Enhancement of Individual Rights to a Balanced Relationship between Participatory Safeguards 620
B. Participatory Rights, Equality of Arms and the Guarantee of an Independent Review of the Proceedings 623
C. Towards a Participatory Model of Criminal Prosecution? 625
I. The Contribution of Private Parties to the Decision to Initiate a Public Prosecution 625
II. Participatory Safeguards in the Decision Not to Institute or to Drop a Criminal Prosecution 628
D. Personal Participation in Criminal Proceedings and the Problem of the Proceedings Held Without the Involvement of the Individuals Concerned 631
I. The Multifaceted Features of the Guarantee of Personal Participation in a Criminal Law Action. A Human Rights Perspective 631
II. Whether and Under What Conditions the Proceedings Held Without the Involvement of the Accused Can Be Made Compatible with a Participatory Model of Criminal Justice 633
1. The Problem of Trials *in absentia* or *inaudito reo* 633
2. *In absentia* Proceedings and International Surrender Procedures 635
E. Information Safeguards, Prosecutorial Efficiency and Requirements of Effective Participation in Criminal Proceedings 636
I. Decision to Charge, Information Rights and the Need for a Differentiated Approach Depending on the Role of Private Parties in Criminal Proceedings 636
II. Access to Relevant Evidence, Coercive Measures, and Defence Rights 639
F. Criminal Proceedings as a Listening Space 640
I. Premise. Right to a Fair Examination, Right to Make Oneself Heard, Right Not to Be Heard 640
II. Procedural Safeguards of a Fair Questioning and the Need for Differentiated Assistance Depending on the Person to Be Examined 640
III. Whether and How Private Parties Can Make Themselves Heard in Criminal Proceedings Without Being Questioned by the Competent Authorities 644
IV. Right Not to Be Questioned, Right Not to Give Evidence Against Oneself and Right to Be Forgotten 645
G. Active Involvement of Private Parties in Evidence-Gathering and the Defence's Contribution to Decision-Making. A Multifaceted Approach to Evidence Law 647

S. Ruggeri, Audi Alteram Partem *in Criminal Proceedings*,
DOI 10.1007/978-3-319-54573-8_17

I. Different Forms of Confrontation and the Need to Balance the Accused's Right to Participate in the Taking of Incriminating Evidence with the Protection of the Human Rights of Other Individuals Involved in Criminal Proceedings ... 647
II. Qualitative Requirements of a Fair Confrontation ... 648
III. Decision-Making Process in a Participatory Model of Criminal Justice ... 649
1. The Contribution of Private Parties to the Fact-Finding ... 649
a) The Need to Scrutinise the Probative Relevance in a Concrete Case Beyond the Rigid Conditions of Use of Out-of-Court Evidence. The Argumentative Role of the Parties in the Fact-Finding ... 649
b) Untested Evidence and the Proof of Guilt. The Progressive Erosion of the Sole and Decisive Evidence Doctrine ... 652
c) Variations of the Right to Confrontation and the Factual Background for the Use of Indirect Evidence. The Need for Justification *in concreto* ... 654
2. Argumentation and the Legal Contribution of the Defence to Decision-Making ... 655
H. Restrictions on Freedom and the Need for Enhanced Participatory Safeguards ... 658
I. Decision-Making on Restrictions on Liberty and the Right to a Fair Hearing by an Independent Authority ... 658
1. The Perspective of Domestic Proceedings. The Need to Involve the Individuals Against Whom Pre-Trial Measures Are Requested in the Decision-Making and to Enable Them to Contribute to Further Decisions on the Measure Applied ... 658
2. The Perspective of International Surrender Procedures. The Need to Strengthen the Oversight of Participatory Safeguards in the Trial Country and the Right to a Fair Hearing in the Host State ... 660
II. Qualitative Requirements of Effective Participation in the Decision on Coercive Measures. Information Safeguards and the Right to Comprehensive Assistance for the Individuals Concerned ... 661
III. Proportionality of Restrictions on Freedom and the Guarantee of Regular Judicial Oversight ... 664
I. Concluding Remarks ... 665
References ... 665

A. *Audi alteram partem*, Fairness of Criminal Proceedings and the Reliability of the Fact-Finding: From the Fragmentary Enhancement of Individual Rights to a Balanced Relationship between Participatory Safeguards

In the light of the analysis conducted in this study, there is no doubt that the *audi alteram partem* rule increasingly permeates—with its multiple expressions—both the national and the transnational criminal justice in Europe and Latin America. It would be oversimplifying, however, to consider the participatory safeguards of the individuals involved in criminal proceedings solely in terms of expressions of defence rights. Even though the right to a defence highlights important features of this problematic area, this focus cannot be deemed to be exhaustive.

On the first level, the individual character of some defence rights should not lead us to overlook the existence of clear duties of diligence on the side of private parties. The Strasbourg case-law emphasised this issue especially in relation to the right to personal participation in criminal proceedings. Although defendants can unequivocally waive their right to be present at trial, waiver cannot be tolerated unconditionally. If the competent authority must make all the necessary arrangements to ensure personal information to the individuals concerned, a duty of diligence also lies with the accused, who cannot elude judicial service and should in principle attend the judicial hearings if equipped with knowledge in legal matters.[1] Both Italy and Brazil conceive of personal involvement in criminal proceedings as an individual right, which can be waived by the interested party. This does not mean, however, that defendants can first escape from notification and later invoke their right to be present at trial. An interpretation of the Brazilian notification *com hora certa* in the light of the constitutional requirements of *contradictoire* and full defence—through a strict scrutiny by the judiciary—should aim at countering the risk of absconding.[2]

In Italy, the wide range of presumptions of knowledge, maintained by Law 67/2014, demonstrates the scant consideration by the legislature of the need to provide the individuals concerned with personal information on the institution of a criminal law action and therefore to set the necessary conditions for them to be involved in criminal proceedings. Not even defendants equipped with legal knowledge have the obligation to contribute to fact-finding, so it would be difficult to conceive of any form of sanction for the choice of avoiding the proceedings, as envisaged by the European Court. Yet some procedural tools highlight the growing tendency by Italian law to encourage responsibility not only in the public prosecutor but also in the private parties, *e.g.* promoting the adoption of initiatives aimed at enabling the collection of evidence through a court procedure. For instance, the inadmissibility of evidence gathered through autonomous investigations of either the prosecutor or defence's lawyers, notwithstanding the circumstances that made it unavailable at trial were known or predictable in the pre-trial stage, constitutes a sort of sanction for the party that did not request *incidente probatorio*. This reveals a clear preference for a procedural model that promotes the contribution of the interested parties (albeit in a hearing *in camera*) to evidence-gathering.[3]

These observations may seem to support the conclusion that the effective involvement of the parties not only strengthens the fairness of the proceedings but also the reliability of fact-finding.[4] Remarkably, the principle of *contradictoire* is widely considered as the best method of reliable fact-finding, and in this sense Italian law enshrines it at the constitutional level.[5] This conclusion, however, cannot be sustained in absolute terms. For instance, it is clear that compelling (both in a direct and indirect way) the person to be examined to appear in court and

---

[1] Chapter 8, F.IV.

[2] Chapter 3, E.II.

[3] Chapter 2, I.II.2.

[4] On the requirements of reliable evidence and reliable evidence-gathering in the field of transnational criminal justice, see Gleß (2006), p. 230 ff.

[5] See recently among others Mazza (2014), p. 250 ff.

to answer the questions does not with certainty pose the best premises for obtaining reliable findings, especially if confrontation takes place in a public hearing. Furthermore, the analysis of the domestic law of the selected countries in the light of the requirements set by international human rights case-law displays a much more complex relationship between participatory safeguards, the requirement of fairness and the reliability of fact-finding. In the modern era, this relationship goes beyond the enhancement of defence guarantees in relation to specific prosecutorial needs, calling for a comprehensive balance between different interests. This approach calls for a restriction on individual participatory rights not just with a view to ensure a more efficient prosecution but in order not to jeopardise fundamental rights of other people involved in criminal proceedings or to give them a voice outside a public hearing.

On close examination, in countries such as Italy in which there is not a comprehensive statute on the hearing of the aggrieved parties, who are subjected to the same obligations laid down for the witness testimony, direct confrontation with the alleged perpetrator not only entails serious risks for the person examined but also raises doubts as to the reliability of fact-finding. Significantly, Italian courts tend to broaden the requirements of hearsay evidence to avoid undue risks for vulnerable victims and new technological means have progressively been introduced to prevent the shortcomings of 'face-to-face' confrontation. The Strasbourg case-law has always attached particular weight to the protection of vulnerable witnesses, a broad concept that also encompasses the injured party. Since the *Al-Khawaja* judgment, moreover, the European judges have also removed the limit of the ban on use of the untested evidence as the main basis of the accused's conviction, provided, however, that counterbalancing measures are applied at the national level and further elements confirm the reliability of the evidence at hand.

Far from 'watering down' the right to confrontation under Article 6(3)(d) ECHR,[6] the *Al-Khawaja* doctrine makes it clear that the probative value of testimonial evidence must always be defined in a specific case and untested evidence should not necessarily be accorded lower status. At a deeper level still, despite the softening of the guarantee of confrontation, these developments in the European case-law highlight a broader understanding of the participatory rights of the individuals involved in criminal proceedings than that emerging from statutory international law. In this context, the accused's right to be involved in the gathering of incriminating evidence must always be balanced with other conflicting interests, especially with the right of vulnerable informants not to be exposed to the risk of direct confrontation. Ultimately, national courts are called upon to provide the necessary balance among conflicting interests by not excluding *a priori* the use of the testimony of the injured party who is no longer physically available at trial. Remarkably, EU law also attaches particular weight to the right of the victim not to

[6]Gearty C (2012) UK Constitutional Group, 9 January 2012, Al-Khawaja and Tahery v the United Kingdom, http://ukconstitutionallaw.org/2012/01/09/conor-gearty-al-khawaja-and-tahery-v-united-kingdom/.

be heard and even to be forgotten, so that any future EU regulation specifically concerned with evidence-gathering will surely need to balance the right to confrontation with the protection of these interests.

On the other hand, the *Al-Khawaja* judgment confirms that direct confrontation is not always necessary to achieve the most reliable ascertainment of the facts and consequently that a reliable fact-finding can, under certain circumstances, be based on untested evidence. It cannot be affirmed, therefore, that the European Court weakened the safeguard of confrontation to the extent that it accepted the eventuality of a lower standard of trustworthiness of the decision-making in light of a broader notion of fairness of criminal proceedings. In the *Al-Khawaja* judgment, the counterbalancing factors that should allow for the use of untested evidence aim at saving both the reliability of fact-finding and the overall fairness of the proceedings. Certainly, the requirement of reliability is only one of the components of a fair fact-finding, which confirms that fairness remains the overriding principle when balancing interests.[7] On close examination, there is complex relationship between reliability and procedural fairness. In some cases, a less reliable result must be tolerated to save the overall fairness of the proceedings and therefore also the social acceptability of decision-making. In other cases, as highlighted by the further developments of the *Al-Khawaja* doctrine, a certain softening of the participatory safeguards of individual parties does not necessarily affect the reliability of fact-finding, which is enhanced by properly balancing the accused's right to *contradictoire* not only with prosecutorial needs but also with the interest of other individuals involved in criminal proceedings either not to be heard or to be examined through particular arrangements. This strengthens the responsibility of the judiciary, while revealing the need to define the qualitative requirements that, in the light of the solution models set by EU law and international human rights law, should guide the conduct of a criminal law action and the decision-making in the countries examined.

B. Participatory Rights, Equality of Arms and the Guarantee of an Independent Review of the Proceedings

Doubtless, equality of arms constitutes the first requirement of a participatory understanding of criminal justice based upon the principle of procedural fairness. Furthermore, the *par condicio* principle does not satisfy itself with the acknowledgment of a formal equality of rights and procedural powers, *e.g.* by conferring to the defence similar powers to those acknowledged to the investigative bodies. The example of the Italian law on defensive investigations is enlightening, demonstrating that the extension of investigative powers to the defence lawyer, similar to those tailored to the prosecutorial authority, leads to a formal equality of arms, while weakening the principle of *contradictoire*.

[7] Gleß (2006), p. 198.

On close examination, criminal proceedings are often characterised by strong imbalances not only between the accused and the public prosecutor but also among the private parties. The need for effective trade-offs increases in the field of transnational criminal justice, in which, on the one hand, the interests of two or more countries must be taken into consideration and, on the other, the individuals concerned must often face great difficulties to be heard or to participate in investigative activities in foreign countries. In this light, the failure to define the exact role of private parties in the execution of a European investigation order can negatively affect their effective participation.[8] *De lege ferenda*, the EIO Directive should be amended through a reform that enables the private parties to take part in the investigative activities in the executing country, while defining the role of the defence in the investigations concerned. In the field of domestic criminal justice, inevitable imbalances can also arise from social and economic differences among the parties, a problem that can have serious consequences in countries with a large territorial extent, such as Brazil. The search for a constant balance between the interests at hand, however, does not necessarily entail the unilateral enhancement of the safeguards of the defence. As noted, the acknowledgment by the Italian Constitution of the accused's right to have exculpatory evidence obtained cannot be interpreted in absolute terms. Remarkably, the European Court has also emphasised the need to ensure that both the person charged with a criminal offence and the public prosecutor have a fair opportunity to know, and make observations on, the relevant evidence produced by the other parties.

This approach confirms the existence of complex balancing tasks by the judiciary, as highlighted by the strict link, set by international human rights law, between the right to a fair hearing and the guarantee of an independent scrutiny of criminal proceedings. This does not legitimise the return to the old investigative magistrates, a concrete risk that arises from the active role acknowledged by Brazilian law to the competent judges in the gathering of evidence during the police inquiry. The Italian Constitution also emphasises the strict link between the right to *contradictoire*, the principle of equality of arms and the guarantee of an independent and impartial scrutiny. This link, however, has not yet been exploited properly. *De lege ferenda*, the use in the pre-trial phase of interferences with fundamental rights, which still lie in the hands of the competent prosecutor (*e.g.*, search), should require the previous independent assessment of their justification, at least where no grounds for urgency exist in a specific case. Moreover, even coercive measures that can only be ordered by the judicial authority (*e.g.*, pre-trial detention and alternatives to custody) necessitate a constant independent oversight of the lawfulness of the measure applied. Of course, these reforms presuppose that the competent judges are provided with the necessary information to carry out their tasks properly. To ensure effective *par condicio*, moreover, the proactive role of the defence should be strengthened especially in the pre-trial inquiry by enabling the individuals concerned to lodge their requests before the competent judge. In this

[8]Chapter 13, C.II.2.a.

context, suspects and victims especially should be granted the right to be heard by a judge at their own initiative and to request the carrying out of investigations in their favour. The weak *jus postulandi* in the prosecutorial and police inquiries is a clear sign of the inquisitorial tradition that still exists by and large in the countries examined.

C. Towards a Participatory Model of Criminal Prosecution?

I. The Contribution of Private Parties to the Decision to Initiate a Public Prosecution

Before dealing with the participatory safeguards of private parties in criminal proceedings, the analysis conducted in this study leads us to define the conditions under which private parties can contribute to the initiation of a criminal prosecution according to a modern view of criminal justice. Despite their differences, the selected countries not only are more and more open towards forms of private prosecution but furthermore are increasingly developing a participatory model of public prosecution. It is noteworthy that in the same year in which the Brazilian Federal Constitution enshrined the victim's right to institute criminal proceedings in the absence of the prosecutor's initiative, the Italian legislature introduced a model of criminal justice characterised not only by a state-centred system of criminal prosecution but also by the strong centralisation of the pre-trial investigations. This model, as noted, did not last long and a few years later the Italian legislature decentralised again the structure of the pre-trial inquiry by enabling the police to carry out autonomous investigations in parallel to those delegated by the competent prosecutor. From the perspective of the present discussion, it is even more significant that the legislative reforms issued at the end of the 1990s strengthened the role of private parties in the institution of criminal proceedings.

This further development of the model of public prosecution can be observed from two viewpoints, which are respectively concerned with the contribution that defendants and the aggrieved parties can make to the initiation of a public criminal prosecution. Both issues should now be examined in light of the requirement of exhaustive criminal investigations, stressed by international human rights case-law, as well as in relation to the constitutional requirement of *contradictoire* and the mandatory character of public prosecution.

As far as the defendant is concerned, the 1988 Italian code already provided an important exception to the dominant model of prosecutorial initiative as the result of the assessment of the sole public prosecutor. Thus the public prosecutor, before lodging a request for immediate proceedings, had to promote a preventive confrontation with the suspect on the issues supported by consistent evidence.[9] By further developing this model, the tool of Article 415-*bis* CCP-Italy, along with ensuring

[9] Art. 453(1) CCP-Italy.

information on the results of the pre-trial inquiry, aims to involve the suspects in the decision to charge by providing them with the opportunity of avoiding an unfounded prosecution. The importance of this mechanism for the purposes of a re-definition of a participatory view of public prosecution, however, has largely been overlooked. Still today, the implementing rules of the Italian code display a model in which the decision on the sustainability of the future charge (and of a criminal trial) should be made on the basis of the information gathered during the pre-trial inquiry.[10] Italian courts have in turn contributed to weakening the potential of this mechanism by ruling out with various arguments its applicability in the field of alternative proceedings. Yet the systematic value of this tool is unquestionable. The preventive involvement of the defendant prevents the risk of solitary prosecutorial decisions, typical of the inquisitorial tradition.

However, some qualitative requirements must be satisfied to give effectiveness to the private initiative. First of all, defendants must be personally informed of the prosecutorial intention to institute criminal proceedings, so that they can make their contribution along with that of their defence lawyer. Furthermore, confrontation with the defendant makes no sense if the prosecutor can unconditionally dismiss any request. If defendants cannot charge the investigative bodies with the task of carrying out unfounded inquiries in their favour, this should also entail the obligation of prosecutors to give reasons if they decide to withdraw dilatory or irrelevant requests. Ultimately, the possibility of effective *contradictoire* taking place in advance on the need to institute criminal proceedings requires the defendant to be informed not only about the prosecutor's decision to initiate a criminal prosecution but also about the specific form pursuant to which prosecution will be initiated. This problem has not yet drawn the attention that it certainly deserves, a result that is mainly due to the widespread opinion that notice under Article 415-*bis* CCP-Italy is not required in the case of alternative proceedings. It has been observed, however, that this opinion cannot be sustained in absolute terms, which therefore poses the need to ensure to the addressee of the notice the necessary information on the type of criminal proceedings that the competent prosecutor decides to institute.[11]

Different problems concern the possibility of the injured party being involved in the decision to charge. In this respect, the victim may also have interest in knowing in advance the form of the prosecution that the competent authority decides to initiate. As noted, Italian law recently recognised, albeit only in a limited number of cases, the right of the victim to be preventively informed of the prosecutorial initiative.[12] Outside these limits, moreover, the Italian legislature should examine whether and to what extent the injured party must also be put in a position to challenge the institution of an alternative procedure that may frustrate their participation in criminal proceedings.

Another delicate question is whether and under what conditions the aggrieved parties can contribute to the initiation of a public prosecution and how their

---

[10] Article 125 RICCP.

[11] Chapter 2, E.II.2.

[12] *Ibid.*

initiative can affect the prosecutor's power to institute criminal proceedings. As far as Italy in concerned, it has been noted that the victim's *ricorso* before the justice of the peace raises the question of whether a private prosecution can be exercised without frustrating the powers of the competent prosecutor.[13] On close examination, the way the drafters of the 2000 reform structured this procedure should also have posed another question, namely how the injured party, alternatively to the means of complaint, can contribute to a prosecution that remains of a public character. In fact, although the victim's *ricorso* is directly forwarded to the judge, the public prosecutor must be served thereof, and according to the constitutional case-law, the absence of any initiative of the prosecutor prevents the justice of the peace from instituting the criminal proceedings. The compromise solution found by the Constitutional Court is based on the mechanism of Article 409(5) CCP-Italy, a tool that, however, does not seem to fit this case. Thus, unlike in an ordinary case of request for termination of the proceedings, the justice of the peace should require the prosecutor to prefer charges that may not be supported by sufficient evidence, the prosecutor having (if formally the power) not enough time to verify the sustainability of the victim's proposal for charge by means of autonomous investigations. It may be argued that the prosecutor is not called upon to scrutinise the extent to which the victim' proposal is founded, but must initiate a prosecution in any case other than that of manifestly unfounded charges. This conclusion, however, affects the ordinary rules governing the initiation of a public prosecution by satisfying the principle of legality only to a formal extent. On the contrary, requiring the public prosecutor to institute criminal proceedings without any investigation and without any assessment of the merits of the charge not only frustrates the general duty to carry out exhaustive criminal investigations but also the requirement of a founded criminal prosecution, while exposing defendants to the risks of an unjustified trial. On close examination, the form of this particular initiative of the victim renders the role of the public prosecutor so weak that one might conclude that this proceeding is in a sort of cobweb, which turns out to undermine the constitutional doctrine of a parallel public prosecution.

All these concerns should lead to an in-depth reflection on the lawfulness of a procedure that, moreover, makes the prosecutorial powers dependent on the victim's decision to lodge a complaint or to file a *ricorso*. In this respect, Brazilian law provides a much more straightforward model, in which, in cases of offences requiring unconditional public prosecution, the possibility for the victim to initiate a subsidiary legal action is justified by the inactivity of the public prosecutor and the private initiative maintains a public character.[14] Unlike in Italy, therefore, the public prosecutor is not involved in a procedure activated by the victim and maintains in any time the power to initiate a public prosecution under the ordinary conditions.[15]

[13]Chapter 2, D.I.

[14]Lopes Jr (2017), p. 213.

[15]*Ibid.*, 222 f.

II. Participatory Safeguards in the Decision Not to Institute or to Drop a Criminal Prosecution

Doubtless, the legal systems of countries based on the principle of legality, such as those of Italy and Brazil, also need provide private parties with a fair opportunity to contribute to the decision not to institute criminal proceedings. In fact, a modern understanding of the principle of mandatory prosecution not only rejects the idea that the decision to charge can be result of the solitary assessment of the public prosecutor but also does not satisfy itself with a procedure that involves just two public bodies, namely the public prosecutor and the competent judge for the oversight.

In this respect, we saw that Brazilian law still reflects an out-dated model of termination of the proceedings. The decision not to initiate a criminal prosecution is left entirely to the competent judge, to whom the prosecutor must forward the request for discontinuance of the proceedings. Furthermore, the judge, when not agreeing with the prosecutorial request, must forward the case to the General Prosecutor, who can either prefer charges against the suspect, forward the case to another public prosecutor, or reiterate the request for discontinuance of the proceedings, by which request the competent judge should now abide.[16] As a result, the decision not to initiate a prosecution does not presuppose the hearing of private parties, and the termination of the proceedings ultimately depends on the assessment of the prosecutorial authority. A positive model, instead, can be observed at the federal level. As noted, the Federal Public Prosecutor's High Council requires prosecutors, in cases of proceedings in which the public prosecution depends on a private *representação*, to address their application for termination of the proceedings to any interested person, who can attach documents or arguments with a view to a new assessment of the case.[17] This solution, however, has its limitations due to the vagueness of the notion of 'interested person' as well as because of the failure to define the exact powers of the individuals involved in the decision on termination of the proceedings. *De jure condendo*, a proper solution should be also to involve both the suspect and the victim in the judicial procedure on dropping criminal proceedings in the cases falling within the jurisdiction of the courts of provincial states.[18]

Of course, national law must set forth the necessary conditions to ensure the effective involvement of these parties. The solution of Italian law, which requires the judge only to hear the victim if he appears in court,[19] can be maintained on the condition that the aggrieved party is ensured personal notification of the judicial summons. Moreover, both the suspect and the victim must be provided not only

[16]Chapter 3, D.II.

[17]*Ibid.*

[18]Lopes Jr (2017), p. 148 f. fn. 22.

[19]Chapter 2, D.II.1.

with legal but also with linguistic assistance. Ultimately, the legislature should clarify the conditions under which the victims can challenge before a higher instance the decision to discontinue the proceedings without giving them the necessary time to lodge their opposition, and the competent judge should be required to give reasons for which the victim's challenge is unfounded.

There is an enhanced need to fulfil the participatory safeguards of private parties in the case of diversion. In Italy, we have noted that Legislative Decree 274/2000 adopted a procedural mechanism to drop a prosecution because of the low severity of the deed, in the context of criminal proceedings before the justice of the peace, particularly with a view to strengthening the involvement of the injured party in the decision on dropping the prosecution. As to the situation in which the pre-trial inquiry should be terminated, however, Italian law does not provide clear indications about whether the absence of a prosecutorial interest by the aggrieved parties also entails the duty of the prosecutor to hear them. In the light of the general aim of this form of diversion, the statutory solution needs re-interpretation so as to require the competent prosecutor, after deciding to request discontinuance of the proceedings on the grounds of the low severity of the offence, to examine the victims about their interest in the initiation of a criminal prosecution. Thus the aggrieved parties can only show their interest in the initiation of a criminal prosecution after a situation that could lead to a termination of the proceedings.[20]

In the field of proceedings before the justice of the peace, moreover, Italian law also allows dropping a prosecution because of the low severity of the deed after the institution of the court proceedings. This situation enhances the role of the accused, who is entitled to challenge the decision to drop the proceedings. Furthermore, the assessment of the damage that the institution of a criminal trial would cause to personal interests (such as work, family, or health) highlights the need to examine the interested parties. On close examination, Italian law may seem to satisfy itself with the lack of opposition by the victim and the defendant, which should not necessarily entail the duty to hear them. In this regard, the Joint Sections, on the assumption that the injured party must expressly challenge the proposal for diversion, has recently clarified that the failure of the victim who was regularly summoned to appear in court does not prevent the justice of the peace from dropping criminal proceedings because of the low severity of the deed.[21] By this means, the formal validity of the judicial service prevails over the right to participation of the aggrieved party, whose non-appearance, following the Supreme Court, is irrelevant for the purposes of the diversion procedure. This logic is debatable and the legislature should intervene to avoid in the future similar forms of presumption of consent by the aggrieved parties in a decision that can affect their interest in the prosecution of the alleged offence.

Of course, the fulfilment of the participatory safeguards of private parties does not entail that the decision to terminate the proceedings can be opposed without

---

[20]Marzaduri (2016), p. 1135 f.

[21]CCass., *P.g. in proc. Steger*.

justification. This particularly applies to the victim, who should not be able to challenge the proposal for diversion without valid reasons. In this respect, it is debatable that in the field of restorative justice, Italian law, despite requiring the judge to hear the parties, does not enable the victim to challenge the decision to extinguish the offence in the case of rectifying measures. The legal solution does not appear to be justified by the judicial assessment of the adequacy of the rectifying measures,[22] since the victim should be put in a position to challenge the properness of the accused's proposal. Like in the case of the termination of the proceedings for the low severity of the deed, therefore, the aggrieved parties should be entitled to challenge beforehand a decision that frustrates their interest in a criminal prosecution. The competent authority, however, should be able to scrutinise the merits of the victim's challenge and thus to assess the existence of a justified basis on which to (further) prosecute the accused as well as the adequacy of the rectifying measures proposed. From this viewpoint, the Italian legislature made a step forward in the recent reform carried out by Law 28/2015, which, as noted, introduced a general tool of termination of the proceedings for low severity of the deed, provided, moreover, that the accused has not repeated the same behaviour. Although this mechanism, unlike that existing in the proceedings before the justice of the peace, aims at not punishing the accused for the offence, Italian law has strengthened the role of both the victim and the suspect, granting them the right to be notified of the prosecutorial request for discontinuance of the proceedings irrespective of a specific application on their side.[23] On the other hand, it is noteworthy that the individuals bear the burden of giving reasons of their decision to challenge the prosecutorial request for discontinuance of the proceedings for the low severity of the deed, on pain of inadmissibility of the challenge lodged.[24]

These forms of discontinuance of the proceedings pose another important question, which relates to the phase (and the procedural context) in which the procedure should best be terminated. The question is particularly relevant in the case of diversion for low severity of the offence, a conclusion of the proceedings that, presupposing the ascertainment of the commission of the deed and the criminal law relevance of the alleged offence, can affect the defendant's image. It has been observed that the solution of the 2015 reform, which has provided for a mandatory form of *contradictoire* with the suspect and victim, entails several human rights risks, which highlight the inadequacy of the discontinuance of the proceedings for these purposes. This does not mean, however, that dropping the prosecution after the accused has been brought to court with a formal accusation is a proper solution, especially for vulnerable individuals and minor defendants, who are exposed to the risk of a public trial. *De lege ferenda*, one should consider the possibility of introducing a special hearing *in camera* for these purposes prior to the initiation of court proceedings. Furthermore, not only should the interested parties be

---

[22]In this sense instead Marzaduri (2016), p. 1139.

[23]Art. 411(1-*bis*) CCP-Italy.

[24]*Ibid.*

summoned but the legislature should also enhance their right to evidence and to challenge the prosecutorial initiative. Like the intermediate phase, this hearing should follow the end of the preliminary investigation. As an alternative to this solution, the tool of Article 415-*bis* CCP-Italy could also allow for the proceedings to be discontinued when the competent prosecutor has already decided to prefer a formal charge against the defendants without exposing them to the shortcoming of a criminal prosecution.

D. Personal Participation in Criminal Proceedings and the Problem of the Proceedings Held Without the Involvement of the Individuals Concerned

I. The Multifaceted Features of the Guarantee of Personal Participation in a Criminal Law Action. A Human Rights Perspective

The comparative-law examination of the selected countries in the light of the requirements set by international and supranational law highlights that personal participation of the individuals involved in criminal proceedings should not be viewed as a separate right. A human rights-oriented view of criminal proceedings calls for in-depth analysis of the repercussions that a criminal law action may entail on the sphere of fundamental rights. The right to be personally involved in criminal proceedings has a clear human rights foundation, aiming both to prevent the negative implications of a criminal law action and to ensure the fairness of the procedure. Furthermore, there is also a strict link with the reliability of decison-making, since, depending on their knowledge, defendants can make essential contribution to fact-finding as well as to the decision on legal issues in the case at hand. This fundamental requirement also applies to those countries, such as Italy and Brazil, which provide for mandatory assistance of the lawyer without imposing on defendants the duty to be present, and without allowing them to waive legal assistance. Even in these countries, the possibility for the accused to participate in procedural activities—viewed not just in terms of a passive presence but in terms of active involvement in criminal proceedings—can be of utmost importance for enhancing the effectiveness of legal assistance.

Furthermore, there is also a strict link between personal participation and the tasks of the judiciary. Significantly, this also occurred in inquisitorial systems, in which the detention of the person concerned often aimed at obtaining forced confessions and therefore constituted a necessary step of a fruitful inquiry. In a human rights-oriented model of criminal justice, instead, the free and informed involvement of the individuals involved in criminal proceedings is a necessary condition of a fair fact-finding, enabling the competent authorities to carry out their tasks properly. For instance, we have noted that in Italy the competent judge for a plea-bargaining can summon the accused to scrutinise the willingness of his request. *De lege ferenda*, the same logic should apply to the evidentiary agreements that the defence lawyer can propose or join in the court proceedings: thus the lawyer's initiative should presuppose the involvement of the person who will undergo the consequences of the admission of out-of-court evidence. From this perspective, the recent reform carried out by the Italian Law 67/2014 does not go in the right direction. There can be little doubt that in the cases in which the institution of a criminal prosecution is not based on the unequivocal decision to avoid the proceedings, the judicial authority should bear full responsibility for verifying whether all the individuals concerned personally received the necessary information about the proceedings. In Brazil, the continued use of judicial service by edict is also highly problematic. The link between personal participation and the fair decision-making is enhanced where coercive measures have been enforced. As highlighted by the Inter-American case-law, the personal involvement of the individuals concerned allows for the competent authority not only to scrutinise the abstract justification of the measure applied but also the physical conditions of the individuals concerned.

Against this background, it is clear that the right to personal involvement in criminal proceedings cannot be balanced with the requirement of reasonable length of the procedure. The Italian Constitution should be interpreted in this manner, in that the general acknowledgment of the principle of reasonable duration of judicial proceedings presupposes that the procedure satisfies all the constitutional requirements, namely that the parties are granted effective participation in the proceedings on an equal footing before an independent and impartial judge. As noted, the guarantee of personal participation holds particular importance in the case of restrictions on freedom and, as highlighted by the Brazilian case-law, it cannot be unconditionally denied for administrative grounds to the accused who wishes to be present at the hearings.

In order to promote the effective involvement in the proceedings, information on the legal action instituted must personally be provided to the individuals concerned. The decision on whether and how to take part in the proceedings requires clear and detailed information on the prosecution. To this end, an in-depth reform of the rules on judicial service is necessary both in Brazil and in Italy so as to remove any kind of dangerous presumption of knowledge of the person involved in the proceedings. Delicate problems also relate to the rules on the judicial service to the defence lawyer, not only in case of court-appointed lawyer, but also where defendants appoint a counsel of their own confidence and chose the law firm as their legal domicile. In a number of cases, the personal appointment of a defence lawyer does not guarantee that information will personally reach the accused. Difficult challenges arise in the case of foreign defendants or individuals who do not speak the language of the proceedings. It cannot be tolerated that the validity of criminal proceedings is saved on the assumption that the suspect appointed a lawyer in the pre-trial inquiry without proper information on the implications of this choice. In general terms, it must be avoided that a criminal law action can be instituted on the sole ground that information was provided to the lawyer. In the light of this, the proof should lie with the competent authority that the accused was personally notified of the proceedings and put in a condition to participate. In this respect also, the Italian 2014 reform did not go in the right direction. As noted, despite ensuring an unprecedented tool of retrial, the new revocation of *in absentia* convictions again offload onto the accused the burden of proving the grounds for the ignorance of the proceedings. This result must soon be corrected in order to prevent future infringements of the European Convention.

The need to personally involve the individuals concerned is enhanced in the field of transnational criminal justice and especially in the case of surrender procedures. Pursuant to Italian law, there is no obligation for the competent authority to rule on a request for extradition to involve the sought person, who, unlike the Attorney-General and the defence lawyer, must only be heard if he appears in court. This result can be very detrimental, taking into account the scant safeguards provided to the person sought for international surrender. *De lege ferenda*, the rules on trans-border investigations should also provide the interested parties with more certainty as to whether they can take part in the evidence-gathering procedure. Allowing for participation solely pursuant to the arrangements made by the cooperating authorities is surely not a proper solution.

II. Whether and Under What Conditions the Proceedings Held Without the Involvement of the Accused Can Be Made Compatible with a Participatory Model of Criminal Justice

1. The Problem of Trials *in absentia* or *inaudito reo*

Against this background, it must be examined whether and to what extent a participatory model of criminal justice can tolerate that individuals are convicted by means of proceedings held either *in absentia* or without in any case giving them a fair hearing prior to the decision-making. As far as *in absentia* trials are concerned, different conclusions should in principle be drawn, pursuant to the European case-law, depending on whether or not the accused's absence was the result of a free and informed decision. On close examination, this distinction can be misleading. It has been observed that Strasbourg case-law does not allow for defendants to unconditionally waive their right to personal participation. One of the most interesting aspects emerging from the European case-law was to relativize the individual value of the decision to avoid the proceedings. This methodological approach can be very useful even in the countries examined, notwithstanding that, as noted, they do not charge the accused with the obligation of contributing to the fact-finding either personally or through their defence lawyer. In the light of the current developments that have occurred in the two criminal justice systems, the person who freely decides not to take part in the proceedings can surely not be denied fundamental safeguards, such as legal assistance or the assistance of an interpreter (*e.g.*, in the communications with a lawyer or with a view to challenging specific decisions). However, it might be acceptable that a legislature adopts other arrangements to enhance the responsibility of the accused's decisions. For instance, if defendants equipped with legal knowledge refuses to appear in court, they may be restricted in their right to claim personal participation in a higher instance aimed at the scrutiny of the legal classification of the alleged offence or they may be restricted in their right to challenge the conviction for the same grounds.

It has been noted, moreover, that waiver can only be tolerated if the individuals concerned were provided with clear information as to the consequences of their decision. If there is not enough evidence that the accused ever received this information, the criminal proceedings should in principle not be initiated. *De lege ferenda*, a proper solution may be to provide for a preliminary hearing in which the competent judge informs the accused of the contents of the charges preferred and the implications of the decision not to take part personally in criminal hearings. Waiver should therefore be made before the judicial authority.

Even more complex problems arise if it is not proven whether the accused ever received information on the proceedings. Certainly, the institution of a criminal law action in the absence of the accused entails serious risks to both the fairness of the procedure and the reliability of fact-finding, and it should therefore only be allowed under strict conditions. The first one is the existence of such a significant public interest as to justify the institution of criminal proceedings by bearing the risk of excluding the accused's contribution. The public interest can also have relevance from a human rights perspective, *e.g.* in the light of the particular social impact of the alleged offence and the need to give prompt satisfaction to the victims. Secondly, it must be demonstrated that the competent authorities made every effort to ensure proper information to the person concerned. Thirdly, a procedural mechanism should be set up in order not just to guarantee a retrial aimed at a fresh re-determination of the merits but the same defensive opportunities lost in the proceedings held *in absentia*. Access to this tool should be granted without any burden of proof being offloaded onto the accused. In the absence of these minimum requirements, the possibility of a criminal law action being held *in absentia* should be excluded. The only justification to initiate criminal proceedings should be to gather urgent evidence and especially to collect oral evidence from victims and vulnerable witnesses. Afterwards, criminal proceedings should be suspended. A good alternative, however, could perhaps be the introduction of a separate procedure to avoid that criminal proceedings are initiated with a view to being suspended after the fulfilment of urgent aims. Furthermore, if there is no evidence that the accused eluded information on the proceedings, it seems that coupling the suspension of the proceedings with a further suspension of the time limit to prosecute the alleged offence (as provided for in both countries) gives rise to an unjustified sanction for the individuals concerned.

As long as subsequent remedies do not satisfy the basic requirements of the *audi alteram partem* rule, furthermore, it cannot be tolerated that a criminal conviction can be issued through a procedure, such as the penal order proceedings, which releases the competent authorities from their general obligation to inform the accused about the prosecution instituted prior to decision-making. This result clearly deprives defendants of a fair opportunity to decide whether and how to participate in criminal proceedings. As noted, the need to involve the accused prior to the decision-making is apparent from the American Convention, and if the guarantee of a previous information on the charge had also been acknowledged in the European human rights Charters, the Luxembourg Court possibly could not have advocated the lawfulness of the penal order proceedings by interpreting the notification of the conviction in terms of a subsequent information on the charge. On close examination, the European Convention placing the information on the accusation at the top of the fair trial rights of any person charged with an offence makes it the prerequisite for the exercise of all the subsequent safeguards acknowledged. Moreover, the fact that the Strasbourg Court calls for the unequivocal waiver of the right to a fair hearing requires the national authorities to set all the necessary conditions for the accused to able to make an informed decision. Ultimately, as noted, the European case-law allows us to observe another deficiency of the penal order procedure, which not only affects the accused's right to be informed on the charge prior to the decision-making but also the interest of the aggrieved parties in a proper investigation of the case. From a human rights perspective, this type of proceeding should no longer exist under the current conditions.

2. *In absentia* Proceedings and International Surrender Procedures

The need to fulfil these minimum requirements should lead to an in-depth reflection on the compromise solutions adopted by several extradition agreements, which leave to the cooperating authority a great margin of discretion in establishing the conditions of surrender in cases of proceedings held *in absentia* in the requesting country. As noted, the international law instruments in force in both Italy and Brazil highlight a number of different legal solutions, some of them showing indifference towards the fact that the accused was tried *in absentia*, while others rely instead on generic assurances that provide the sought individuals with scant certainty about whether they will be surrendered to the requesting country. Notwithstanding the steps forward made by Framework Decision 2009/299/JHA, EU law provides for alternative solutions, which, however, do not always ensure to the sought person prosecuted *in absentia* the right to a retrial or a further instance in the issuing state. The new form of revocation of final judgments introduced by the 2004 Italian reform—despite the clear intention to allow for a remedy to unlawful convictions under the European Convention and to fulfil the obligations towards EU law—does not make it easy for the accused to obtain a retrial. The extradition instruments in force in Brazil also entail considerable limitations for the assessment of the host country and, although some of them enable the requested authority to scrutinise the fulfilment of individual safeguards in the relevant proceedings, this assessment is circumscribed to the minimum defence rights.

This situation calls for in-depth reform. If a soft approach to the problem of *in absentia* trials, which allows for the conduct of a criminal law action in the requesting country on the condition that the accused was given the possibility of a retrial or of access to a further instance, is debatable in domestic proceedings, even more serious concerns arise in the field of international cooperation. Here, the competent authorities surely hold the enhanced duty to ensure personal information on the proceedings instituted and cannot be relieved of this obligation on the assumption that defendants will be granted a subsequent remedy, of which they may also be unaware. *De jure condendo*, the 2009 EU legislation should be reformed by requiring the executing authority to scrutinise the ability of the retrial not only to provide a fresh re-determination of the merits of the case but also to compensate the accused for the defensive opportunities lost. Yet the possibility of a retrial or remedy provided by *lex fori* should not be a further disjoined condition, but the cooperating authority should in any case verify where a cogent public interest justified the institution of a proceeding *in absentia* and whether the competent authorities made their best effort to ensure personal information to the accused.

E. Information Safeguards, Prosecutorial Efficiency and Requirements of Effective Participation in Criminal Proceedings

I. Decision to Charge, Information Rights and the Need for a Differentiated Approach Depending on the Role of Private Parties in Criminal Proceedings

A human rights-oriented model of criminal justice does not satisfy itself with the passive involvement of private parties, but pursues the most effective participation in criminal proceedings. The comparative analysis conducted in this study reveals that specific conditions must be fulfilled to achieve this result properly. As noted, the first one is surely the granting of adequate information. If notice of the institution of criminal proceedings enables the accused to choose whether to participate personally, the decision on the defence strategy largely depends on proper information about the contents and the scope of the prosecution filed. Furthermore, the effective involvement of private parties in investigative activities presupposes that the defence is made aware of relevant evidence produced by other parties and especially by the competent prosecutor. Otherwise, the guarantee of *contradictoire* is satisfied only at a formal level.

The great importance of the information safeguards from the viewpoint of constitutional law, as well as under international human rights law and EU law, calls for in-depth reforms in the criminal justice of both the selected countries. Although this process of reform has already partially been initiated, it is still far from being completed. As far as the information on the charge is concerned, the explicit acknowledgment of this right by both the European Convention and the Pact of San José, as well as by the Italian Constitution, should guide the balance between information guarantees and other conflicting interests. Certainly, the right to information cannot be seen in absolute terms, as highlighted by the flexible approach of the Italian Constitution to the requirement of 'promptness'. The fact that the guarantee of information encompasses precise duties for the competent authorities entails clear consequences from a human rights perspective. The first one is that restrictions on the obligation to inform the accused on the accusation presupposes that a formal charge must be preferred against any person against whom suspicion of guilt has arisen. The practice of the police questioning suspects without a formal charge, as still happens in Brazil, must therefore be banned[25] and should have drastic implications on the admissibility of the information obtained, as provided for by Italian law. Moreover, the existence of a duty of information on the side of the competent authorities entails that in the pre-trial inquiry, especially where interferences with fundamental rights are necessary, the individuals concerned must be made personally aware of the scope and the contents of the charge filed without the need for explicit request by the interested party. This calls for a reform of the solution provided for by the Italian code as to the information on the prosecutorial charge, which must only be provided if requested by either the suspect or the victim.[26]

Another relevant implication relates to the obligations lying with the competent authority, namely that derogations from the duty of information can only be allowed if other fundamental rights or further interests of constitutional relevance are at risk. Even in such cases, however, the proof lies with the competent authority to demonstrate that a risk arises in the situation at hand. In the light of this, any abstract presumption of danger for the ongoing inquiry, such as that provided by Italian law in relation to a number of serious crimes,[27] should be avoided in the near future. The requirement of a concrete risk for the criminal inquiry has two further important consequences. On the one hand, it confirms the inadequacy of an undifferentiated approach, such as that adopted by the Italian code, which submits to the same conditions the information to the accused and the victim. Where the victim's knowledge of the charge does not jeopardise the investigative efficiency, information cannot be denied or made conditional on unjustified requirements, such as the explicit request of the interested party. On the other, it is clear that even the existence of risks for the inquiry does not in itself suffice to limit the right to be informed on the charge as a condition of effective defence in criminal proceedings, if justification can be provided by the same body in charge of the investigations, as happens in both the countries examined. *De lege ferenda*, Italian law should enable the competent judge to scrutinise the registration of the prosecutorial charge. This scrutiny should not only aim at ascertaining the existence of concrete grounds for restricting the information rights but could also reduce the risk of mistakes in the

[25] In the same sense cf. Lopes Jr and Jakobsen Glockner (2013), p. 448.

[26] Art. 335(3) CCP-Italy.

[27] *Ibid.*

legal classification of the offence, which can in turn entail grave consequences from a human rights perspective.

An in-depth reflection on this problematic area in the light of the indications provided by constitutional law and international human rights law, moreover, should call for a considerable improvement of the qualitative requirements of the information due to private parties, so as to satisfy the need for 'detailed' and 'understandable' information. There is strict link in the pre-trial inquiry between the obligation to inform the individuals concerned of the charge preferred, the possibility of setting up an effective defence strategy, and the need for a fair investigation. *De lege ferenda*, this link should lead to a reform of the Italian rules on the information of the prosecutorial charge, rules that, despite the 2014 implementation of the EU Directive on the right to information in criminal proceedings, still satisfy themselves with the notification of formal aspects of the alleged offence. After the institution of the court proceedings, a strict link can be observed between the guarantee of detailed information on the indictment and the requirements of a fair prosecution. It is clear that regardless of the system adopted, the prosecutorial authority or the person who initiated a criminal prosecution is responsible for providing a well-defined accusation, and that the preferment of undefined charges inevitably affects the validity of the prosecution, leaving no room for compromise solutions, such as that provided by the Italian case-law.[28]

Alongside the requirement of preciseness, the need for simple and understandable information is enhanced in transnational cases, especially where criminal charges are preferred against non-resident defendants or defendants who do not speak the language of the trial State. In this respect, the Italian implementation of the EU Directive 2010/64 was certainly too restrictive, since translation must only be provided for specific procedural acts and, as far as the decision to charge is concerned, the law only requires the indictment to be translated; translation of further acts (or parts of further acts) is at the judge's discretion.[29] A reform of the Italian rules is therefore necessary both to broaden the scope of the linguistic guarantees and to ensure the ability to understand the prosecutorial charge (especially if interference with fundamental rights other than pre-trial measures are stake), as required by some of the versions in other languages of Directive 2010/64/EU.[30] Of course, the requirement of a charge that can be understood holds greater relevance where a non-resident accused can suffer from restrictions on fundamental rights because of the institution of a procedure of international cooperation. The need for simple and accessible information on substantial issues, such as the nature and legal classification of the offence, as well as the circumstances in which the offence was committed, as required by EU law in relation to EAW proceedings,[31] should also be fulfilled in the field of extradition procedures with non-EU countries.

---

[28]Chapter 2, E.II.3.

[29]Art. 143(1-2) CCP-Italy, as reformed by Legislative Decree 32/2014.

[30]Chapter 10, C.I.1.

[31]Chapter 13, B.III.1.

II. Access to Relevant Evidence, Coercive Measures, and Defence Rights

As emerged from the examination of domestic and international human rights law, information on the charge is not enough to enable the effective contribution of the defence if the individuals concerned cannot know the grounds that led to, and cannot access the information that supports, the decision to charge. In this respect, the comparative analysis conducted in this study has revealed some persistent deficiencies of national law in relation to the requirements set by international human rights law and by EU law. In the light of these findings, we can here draw several conclusions.

As far as the information supporting the indictment is concerned, it is quite obvious that the public prosecutor holds the power to withhold information on the results of the ongoing investigation, especially where evidence concerns individuals whom the prosecutor decides not to bring to court with a formal charge. Moreover, where national law (like in Brazil) acknowledges private prosecution, it is clear that it is not the responsibility of private prosecutors to fully disclose all the information available, as they are free to decide which pieces of evidence are to be produced. However, we have seen that the decision to withhold relevant information entails serious human rights concerns. In the light of the strict link between the guarantee of information on the charge and the right to have the necessary facilities to set up a proper defence strategy, it appears that the defence cannot be denied access to relevant information concerned with the charges preferred against them. This entails that information can only be withheld if it is not at all concerned with the charges preferred and the individuals accused. *De jure condendo*, a judicial review should help avoid abuses.

The need for independent scrutiny is enhanced in relation to the information supporting the decision to adopt measures of coercion in the pre-trial inquiry. Although serious interferences with fundamental rights (such as wiretaps, remand detention, etc.) presuppose a strong suspicion of guilt, we saw that Italian law not only does not require the preferment of a provisional charge but also leaves to the competent prosecutor broad discretion in the selection of the evidence supporting the decision to adopt a coercive measure.[32] This result should be improved in a near future. Because of the intrusiveness of interferences with fundamental rights, the decision to apply for the adoption of restrictions on freedom should entail the obligation to disclose to the individuals concerned all the relevant evidence, any distinction between exculpatory and incriminating evidence leading to unsatisfactory results. The only legitimate selection should concern information relevant to other individuals or charges. The lawfulness of the decision to withhold relevant evidence also diminishes in the case of wiretapping, taking into account the requirement of necessity, which the European Convention lays down in relation to measures that affect the right to private and family life.

---

[32]Chapter 2, E.III.

The need to provide information on the evidence supporting the decision to apply coercive measures increases in transborder cases. In this regard, we have observed that even at the EU level, the legislation on EAW proceedings has not made significant steps forward, largely following the conservative approach of several extradition agreements.[33] *De lege ferenda*, the information rights in the case of surrender procedures should certainly be strengthened in the EU area of freedom, security and justice by granting the individuals concerned comprehensive information not only about the existence of the national order that led to the European arrest warrant in the issuing State but furthermore about the justification of the decision to apply a coercive measure and the evidence supporting the judicial order.

F. Criminal Proceedings as a Listening Space

I. Premise. Right to a Fair Examination, Right to Make Oneself Heard, Right Not to Be Heard

A human rights-oriented criminal law action requires that the individuals concerned be granted a fair opportunity to make their voice heard. This fundamental guarantee has different features and poses various challenges depending on various factors, such as the role of the person to be examined in criminal proceedings, whether the competent authority or the individuals concerned take the initiative, and so on. Different problems also arise in the field of domestic and transnational criminal justice. The comparative analysis of the selected countries in the light of the requirements set by the international human rights case-law and by EU law highlights the increasing characterisation of criminal proceedings as a listening space. Against this common background, three main safeguards must be ensured in a participatory model of criminal justice, i.e. (a) the right to a fair examination, (b) the right to make one's own voice fairly heard without a formal questioning by the competent authorities and (c) the right not to be questioned and even to be forgotten.

II. Procedural Safeguards of a Fair Questioning and the Need for Differentiated Assistance Depending on the Person to Be Examined

Concerning the first issue, we have noted that one of the main difficulties in the selected countries is to ensure to private parties a fair questioning in the investigative phase. In this respect, specific conditions must be satisfied for the individuals

[33]Chapter 13, B.III.1.

concerned to have a fair opportunity to be heard. The first condition is, once again, the granting of proper information. It has been observed that a fair hearing cannot take place if the suspect is questioned without a formal charge. Information on the charge, however, does not suffice to compensate the individuals examined for the imbalance with the competent authority if they cannot access the relevant evidence gathered by the investigative bodies. On close examination, the need for information in the case of a pre-trial questioning is not so far from that arising in the field of coercive measures. Certainly, the police or the prosecutorial questionings cannot be equated to restrictive measures. Yet they cannot be deemed to be measures neutral to fundamental rights. Both in Brazil and in Italy, the pre-trial hearings can entail coercing the suspect to appear at the prosecutor's office or the police station. Furthermore, there is little doubt that the prosecutorial and the police questionings can interfere with various fundamental rights of the individuals examined, who should therefore be put in a position to give evidence after receiving proper information. This holds true especially if the statements rendered can later be used against them at trial, as allowed by Italian law in relation to the evidence given by the suspect with legal assistance at the pre-trial stages.[34] *De lege ferenda*, the Italian rules on prosecutorial hearings should enhance the disclosure of relevant evidence beyond the case of immediate proceedings,[35] both when suspects are interrogated by the prosecutor or questioned by the police upon delegation. In this regard, the legislative set-up provided by the 1988 Italian code, which ruled out the possibility of delegating the interrogation of the suspect, was probably more adequate than the current one. In the near future, it should be avoided that the fulfilment of the information rights depends on the investigative strategy of the police after the prosecutor has taken over the leadership of the pre-trial inquiry.

The granting of information, however, is also insufficient to ensure a fair examination if the person concerned is to be confronted alone with the authority in charge of the investigations. In this regard, legal assistance constitutes the first guarantee that must be given to any person examined. Yet it is not enough that mandatory legal assistance is ensured to the suspect in the police questioning, as provided for by both Italian and Brazilian law, if some qualitative conditions are not fulfilled. In particular, legal assistance turns out to be a merely formal guarantee if a court-appointed lawyer (or even a lawyer who is only appointed for a specific procedural act) is required to be present but had no opportunity to set up a defence strategy and to communicate with the person examined in advance. Even more, the assistance of an unprepared lawyer without any contact with the suspect can backfire, justifying the admissibility at trial of the statements rendered by this formal means, as allowed by Italian law. In the light of this, the requirement of effectiveness of legal assistance must be improved. This also applies to the pre-trial hearings conducted by a judge. Especially where the hearing of a person subject to a restrictive measure is at stake, it should be avoided that the person concerned can be

[34] Arts. 503(5) and 513 CCP-Italy.

[35] Chapter 2, G.II.2.

examined by the competent authority without having had the opportunity of previous communication with the lawyer, as can still occur under Italian law.[36] Both the individuals summoned to be examined and their lawyer must surely be given the necessary time to prepare an adequate defence strategy.

Along with legal assistance, further forms of assistance may be necessary to ensure a fair questioning of the individuals concerned. Thus, the assistance of an interpreter is required if the person to be examined does not speak or understand the language of the proceedings, assistance that should also be granted to allow effective communication with the lawyer, as required by EU law. Moreover, national law must provide for adequate mechanisms of oversight of the decision not to provide linguistic assistance as well as of the quality of the linguistic assistance so as to enable the effective participation of the accused in criminal hearings pursuant to the requirements set forth by the Strasbourg case-law[37] and, more recently, by the Luxembourg Court.[38] In this regard, Italian law still needs a reform aimed not only at establishing the criteria pursuant to which the competent authority should scrutinise the need for linguistic assistance[39] but also at ensuring to the accused a mechanism to challenge the quality of the assistance provided. A good solution to ensure the quality of interpretation is to provide for a professional register of interpreters and translators, access to which should presuppose a previous test of the preparedness of the applicants. The absence in Italy of a general register, such as that of experts, along with the lack of obligation of courts and prosecutors even to appoint people who appear in the (often informal) register existing in some tribunals, does not set the best conditions for a professional linguistic assistance.[40] Moreover, interpretation is not a mechanical task and can give rise to advantages or disadvantages for the one or the other party. Therefore, it is essential that interpreters maintain their impartiality. To this end, it should be prevented that that the same person who provided assistance to the competent authority during the prosecutorial inquiry or at trial can later be appointed to the accused who does not understand the language of the proceedings, as is still possible under Italian law, notwithstanding the implementation of the EU Directive 2010/64.[41]

Even these types of assistance can turn out to be purely formal guarantees in particular situations, especially in the case of the questioning of co-defendants by the investigative bodies. The analysis of Italian law led us to observe the limitations of legal assistance where co-defendants are called upon to decide whether to give evidence on issues not exclusively concerned with their position without receiving clear information on the addressee of their statements. *De lege ferenda*, along with

[36]Chapter 2, J.III.1.

[37]See among others ECtHR, Grand Chamber, *Hermi v. Italy*.

[38]Chapter 10, C.I.1.

[39]In this regard cf. Curtotti Nappi (2014), p. 129 ff.

[40]*Ibid*., 130.

[41]*Ibid*.

legal assistance, the co-accused should be properly informed before deciding whether to take on the role of special witnesses under Article 197-*bis* CCP-Italy. In particular, the change of the procedural status—and the drastic limitation of the right to silence—should be the consequence of the informed decision to answer questions directly concerned with other individuals rather than being the result of a future and unpredictable assessment of the competent authorities. To ensure this result, co-defendants should waive their right to silence before a judge.[42]

Further assistance is due to other informants as well as to the injured party. In this regard, both Brazil and Italy have undoubtedly made considerable steps forward especially under the influence of international law. EU law has also increasingly engaged in strengthening the participatory rights of vulnerable victims. Notwithstanding the merits of recent reforms, Italian law should enact specific rules especially on the pre-trial questioning of the aggrieved party, which are still governed by the generic regulation on informants and potential witnesses. In particular, the rules governing testimonial hearings, including the obligation to appear in court and to answer exhaustively all the questions, do not fit the vulnerable condition of victims in most cases. On the other hand, the fact that the injured party is often called upon to make important decisions during their questioning (*e.g.*, whether to withdraw a complaint or to accept a proposal for conciliation) should require the assistance of a lawyer.

In transnational cases, these problems are magnified by the linguistic difficulties and the lack of familiarity of the individuals concerned with the legal culture of one of the cooperating states. The particular vulnerability of the person involved in transborder procedures enhances the need not to weaken the guarantees of a fair hearing. As far as extradition procedures are concerned, Italian law should strengthen the safeguards regarding the interrogation of the sought person by the Attorney-General.[43] The requested individuals should be provided with the assistance of an interpreter and especially with proper information on the consequences of the decisions that they will make. In this respect, a good solution might be *de lege ferenda* to entrust the first hearing to the competent court or a delegated judge. Judicial scrutiny will certainly ensure the opportunity for an overall assessment of the conflicting interests at stake, including those concerned with the prosecution carried out in the requesting state.[44] It is worth observing that, where the extension of extradition is requested to further acts committed prior to the surrender, Italian law requires the judicial authority to hear the extradited person and the evidence gathered will be attached to the request for extension.[45]

In this respect, however, considerable changes are still necessary. The personal contribution of the sought person cannot be underestimated solely on the grounds that legal assistance is provided. Therefore the rules on extradition procedures

---

[42]Tonini (2001), p. 272.

[43]Chapter 7, C.III.1.a.

[44]Chiavario (2013), p. 108.

[45]Art. 710 CCP-Italy.

should be amended by providing for the mandatory interrogation of the requested person, as required by Brazilian law, although only after the trial country has forwarded its request for extradition. From the same perspective, the Italian legislation on EAW procedures should also entail the obligation for the competent court to examine the sought person. It is rather contradictory that despite the clear enhancement of the role of the judicial authority in the EU area of freedom, security and justice, the judicial hearing of the person against whom a procedure of international surrender was initiated still is merely a possibility. Of course, even the guarantee of a judicial hearing may not be enough if it is not provided with enhanced procedural safeguards. Especially if the sought person is subject to restrictive measures,[46] both legal and linguistic assistance are required for the individuals examined, who should be put in a position to obtain a previous communication with their lawyer and should be informed of the hearing in due time.

III. Whether and How Private Parties Can Make Themselves Heard in Criminal Proceedings Without Being Questioned by the Competent Authorities

A different question is whether and how private parties can make their voice heard in criminal proceedings without a formal questioning by the competent authority. The examination of the spontaneous statements that the accused can at any time give to the competent prosecutor under Italian law allows us to draw some conclusions on this fundamental safeguard. In the pre-trial phase, the fact that suspects take the initiative to give evidence to the competent authority for the investigations should ensure them at least the information on the charge preferred. In countries, such as Italy and Brazil, in which the competent judge for the pre-trial inquiry is not in charge of the investigations but has the task of protecting the individuals concerned for specific investigative purposes, the suspect should also be able to give statements to the judicial authority. The rules on *incidente probatorio* may be adapted to this end.

From a similar perspective, the victim should also be granted the opportunity to give evidence before an independent authority. In this respect, the Luxembourg Court provided in the *Katz* judgment a clear compromise solution, requiring EU countries to ensure to the victims a fear hearing only if national law does not provide for a testimonial examination. Although Italian law has recently brought about various positive innovations in relation to the victim's rights, a new tool should be introduced to enable the aggrieved parties to make themselves heard by an independent body without a formal questioning. In Italy, the problem also arises in court proceedings in which the victim, if they did not lodge a civil-law complaint, cannot request to be examined. This result, based upon the assumption that the

---

[46]Chapter 7, C.III.1.b.

victim does not hold the status of formal 'party' under Italian law, is questionable from a human rights perspective and should be reviewed. The most straightforward solution is certainly to enact a specific statute on the court examination of the injured party, providing for particular safeguards aimed at satisfying the specific needs of the victim in criminal proceedings.

IV. Right Not to Be Questioned, Right Not to Give Evidence Against Oneself and Right to Be Forgotten

A fair hearing, moreover, will not take place as long as the individuals concerned can coercively be questioned. It has been observed that, despite the wide scope of the right to silence acknowledged to both defendants in the pre-trial phase, both Italy and Brazil allow for the investigative bodies to compel them to be questioned, a result that the accused cannot avoid by appearing at the prosecutor's office to render spontaneous statements. The freedom of the accused to decide whether to appear in court to be examined in the judicial proceedings is more apparent than what one would expect. By deciding not to appear in court or by refusing the court examination, defendants can in Italy be convicted on the basis of the information that they rendered either to the prosecutor or the competent judge in the pre-trial inquiry or in other proceedings.[47] As noted, the possibility of refusing the questioning by the competent authority diminishes in relation to other private parties. As far as co-defendants are concerned, the decision to give evidence on issues not exclusively concerned with their position enables the police and the prosecutor to re-examine them as informants pursuant to the rules governing the witness testimony of Article 197-*bis* CCP-Italy, which drastically reduce the scope of the right to silence. Moreover, the Italian code submits the victim to the same obligations lying with the witness, such as the duty both to appear before the competent authority and to answer exhaustively all questions, without, however, the assistance of a lawyer.

We have already exposed the reasons for which the solutions provided by Italian law are largely unsatisfactory, which allows us to draw now some methodological conclusions. A human rights-oriented model of criminal justice cannot tolerate that suspects serve the purposes of a criminal investigation to the point that they can coercively be questioned, especially in the phase in which they can mostly suffer from interferences with fundamental rights and their information rights are often reduced to the minimum extent. This approach, which reflects the persistent understanding of the accused as the object of a criminal inquiry rather than the holder of individual rights, can no longer be sustained. Remarkably, Italian law shows respect for the free will of the defendants, who are to be informed that they can either appear at the prosecutor's office to give spontaneous statements or

[47] Art. 513 CCP-Italy.

request to be questioned.[48] *De lege ferenda*, this solution should be extended to the pre-trial inquiry, to the extent that the investigative bodies should only be enabled to question the suspect if specifically requested. A similar approach should also apply to the co-accused, as long as he is called upon to give evidence against himself. The use of direct coercion to obtain the physical presence of the person examined and of indirect coercion to obtain the sought evidence can only be accepted if the co-accused is questioned on issues exclusively concerned with other individuals, which confirms the need to provide co-defendants with proper information prior to the questioning.

The application of coercive means, furthermore, should be avoided in obtaining oral evidence from the victim. In this regard, Brazilian law provides an interesting model. By excluding the application of the rules governing the witness testimony, as noted, the victim is not required to tell the truth nor can be prosecuted for false statements.[49] Here also, the use of coercion is allowed to obtain the appearance of the aggrieved parties and indirect coercion is exercised in that victim cannot claim the right to silence. This solution, however, can only be justified where the victim's initiative led to the institution of the police inquiry. Where criminal investigations are initiated *ex officio*, as can happen under Italian law,[50] there is no valid justification for the use of coercion on the injured party, taking into account the rising attention paid by the international law and EU law towards the protection of vulnerable victims.

On the other hand, the general prohibition on the use of coercive means to obtain incriminating evidence against the will of the individuals concerned raises serious doubts on the lawfulness of investigative measures such as biological sampling. It has been observed that, whereas Brazil still rules out the use of these investigations both in domestic and transborder cases, Italy has recently enabled criminal courts to order coercive biological sampling, while progressively enhancing the powers of the investigative bodies in this sense.[51] The condition of respect for the dignity as well as for the health or physical integrity of the person concerned satisfies only partially the requirements laid down by the Strasbourg Court, which since the *Jalloh* judgment, as noted, has shifted the focus also to the implications of the *nemo tenetur* principle. In order to save the lawfulness of this investigation, it is necessary in the light of the indications provided by the European case-law[52] that not only does the law specify the cases in which it is allowed but furthermore a strict scrutiny is carried of the public interest justifying this measure and on its proportionality in relation to the expected sentence. Moreover, the individuals submitted to a coercive means aimed at obtaining incriminating evidence against their will—

[48] Art. 415-*bis* CCP-Italy.

[49] Chapter 3, G.I.

[50] Art. 330 CCP-Italy.

[51] Chapter 16, D.IV.2.

[52] ECtHR, *Jalloh v. Germany*, § 118 et seqq.

especially if not charged with the offence at hand—must be provided with specific safeguards, *e.g.* the assistance of a lawyer and of an interpreter.

G. Active Involvement of Private Parties in Evidence-Gathering and the Defence's Contribution to Decision-Making. A Multifaceted Approach to Evidence Law

I. Different Forms of Confrontation and the Need to Balance the Accused's Right to Participate in the Taking of Incriminating Evidence with the Protection of the Human Rights of Other Individuals Involved in Criminal Proceedings

A participatory model of criminal justice requires setting the necessary conditions for private parties to be actively involved in evidence-gathering. In the light of this comparative analysis, we shall now focus on the taking of incriminating evidence. International human rights law, although having strongly contributed to the enhancement of the accused's right to be confronted with incriminating witnesses, has increasingly shaped the right to confrontation as a multisided guarantee, which calls for balance among conflicting interests. In this respect, international human rights instruments also leave a different margin of manoeuvre to the contracting States. Unlike the Pact of San José, the European Convention does not require the defence to be directly involved in the examination of incriminating witnesses nor does it grant the accused the right to obtain the appearance of incriminating witnesses. Of course, this does not mean that any form of confrontation is allowed under the Rome Convention, whereas the American Convention does not allow alternatives to direct confrontation in a public hearing.

The complex human rights challenges of modern criminal justice go far beyond the sphere of the participatory safeguards of the accused, highlighting the need for alternatives to the traditional confrontation in open court. These alternatives firstly aim at ensuring a high degree of protection for the human rights of the person examined, who can suffer from considerable damages as a result of cross-examination in open court. Moreover, both the European Court and the Inter-American case-law have broadened the scope of human rights scrutiny to protection of the fundamental rights of individuals who are indirectly involved in collecting criminal evidence, such as the next of kin and the victim. Over relatively recent times, both the selected countries have enacted new alternatives to the court examination. The situations that led to these developments are different in the two countries, however. Brazil has only recently enabled the parties to cross-examine witnesses, which, strengthening the participatory rights of the defence, has also called for enhanced protection of the person examined by means of remote hearing. The developments that occurred in Italian law in the 1990s resulted in the progressive weakening of the right to confrontation of the accused and the 2001 fair trial reform aimed to restore important participatory safeguards of the accused in the evidence-gathering. The enactment in the late 1990s of special arrangements to protect minors injured by serious crimes has led to further reforms, which have strengthened the forms of out-of-court examination in relation to other particular types of informants (undercover agents, victims in a vulnerable condition, etc.).

Despite the merits of these reforms, there is a need for comprehensive rules, which should specify the necessary forms of examination depending on the needs of particular types of witnesses or victims, while laying down the interests justifying the adoption of protective means. If the commitments of international law and of EU law increasingly require the adoption of protective means to avoid the risk of human rights violations deriving from criminal law hearings, the application of these means should follow a strict scrutiny of necessity and proportionality, and defendants should be put in a position to know the grounds that justify their use.

II. Qualitative Requirements of a Fair Confrontation

Irrespective of the form of testimonial hearings, some qualitative requirements must be satisfied in any case to ensure a fair evidence-gathering. These requirements firstly relate to the accused's side. The assistance of a lawyer in the cross-examination of incriminating witnesses ensures only a first level of guarantee for the defendant. Also in this respect, the rules on judicial service must be reformed to enable the accused to be directly involved in the evidence-gathering. Even in countries that do not allow for defendants to cross-examine victims and witnesses, they must be in a position to make their own contribution (also through technical means) to the taking of incriminating evidence, a requirement of utmost importance also in transnational cases. Moreover, the personal involvement of the accused constitutes a necessary condition of a qualitative legal assistance. Even a court-appointed lawyer will often need a previous communication with the accused to properly cross-examine core witnesses. Furthermore, effective confrontation presupposes a high degree of information, a condition that also holds great relevance where confrontation takes place through a judicial examination, as provided for in the intermediate phase by Italian law. In these cases, defence lawyers, if allowed to put supplementary questions to witnesses or co-defendants, should obtain sufficient information on the evidence supporting the charges filed. The need for proper assistance is also apparent on the side of the person examined, particularly if a minor or a vulnerable witness is to be heard. To this end, both Italy and Brazil recently enhanced the possibility of the victim being provided with psychological support during their hearing. As noted, clear and detailed information must be ensured to co-defendants in order to enable them to make informed decisions on the evidence that they will render to the competent authority.

These requirements must certainly be satisfied in the trial hearings and can help handle specific situations, such as inconsistencies between the results of the court examination and the evidence obtained out of court. Moreover, the fulfilment of qualitative conditions is also necessary where pre-trial hearings are at stake. It has been observed that the flexible approach of the Strasbourg case-law, which allows for subsequent confrontation, cannot be sustained in absolute terms. If national law requires *contradictoire* also to be satisfied in the pre-trial inquiry, the competent authorities must put in place all the necessary arrangements to ensure confrontation at this stage of the proceedings. In this respect, the Italian rules on *incidente probatorio*, which require summoning the lawyers of other individuals who might be affected by the evidence that is to be gathered, provide a positive example. Here also, however, legal assistance may not be enough. *De lege ferenda*, information rights should be enhanced in the Italian law on *incidente probatorio*, especially since the evidence taken by this means will later be included in any case in the trial file.

Furthermore, there is also a need to strengthen the qualitative requirements of a fair confrontation where the accused is to be questioned in the pre-trial stage. The analysis of the Inter-American case-law has highlighted the risks that can fall on the defendants from the use of statements that they rendered out of trial to law enforcement authorities. If the accused can be used as an accuser of himself, the enhancement of participatory safeguards in the out-of-court hearing is also justified from the viewpoint of the right to confrontation. In this regard, we have seen that in Italy, the questioning of the suspect by the investigative bodies entails mandatory legal assistance. In Brazil, a similar result was achieved by the 2003 reform. Yet the investigative hearings still provide scant information to the defence, which is therefore not able properly to face the confrontation with the competent authority. *De jure condendo*, the information rights should be strengthened also in this respect, since at trial, all the parties can request the reading out of the information obtained by the suspects both in cases of inconsistencies and if they simply fail to appear in court. To be sure, we saw that in Brazil legal scholarship raised strong criticisms on the unconditional maintenance of the investigative secrecy and it is increasingly recognised that the defence lawyer can access relevant evidence, at least where the investigations were completed, as also acknowledged by the Federal Supreme Tribunal in its *Súmula Vinculante* No. 14.[53]

III. Decision-Making Process in a Participatory Model of Criminal Justice

1. The Contribution of Private Parties to the Fact-Finding

a) The Need to Scrutinise the Probative Relevance in a Concrete Case Beyond the Rigid Conditions of Use of Out-of-Court Evidence. The Argumentative Role of the Parties in the Fact-Finding

The enhancement of the participatory safeguards concerned with the evidence-gathering is strictly linked with the rising importance of the contribution of private parties to decision-making. This contribution can in turn have different features. As

[53] Lopes Jr and Jakobsen Glockner (2013), p. 205.

far as the fact-finding is concerned, both Italy and Brazil, reacting to their inquisitorial tradition, have increasingly introduced various procedural tools to exclude or hinder the use of untested evidence and imposed a number of conditions for admitting information obtained out of court with the defence's contribution. This approach enhanced the participatory safeguards of the defence only to a minimal extent. On the one hand, the ban on using untested evidence gives rise to an artificial reduction of the information available, while frustrating *a priori* the fact-finding on the assumption of the unreliability of information collected out of court. On the other, the exceptions which allow for admissibility of out-of-court evidence gathered with the defence's contribution is often justified on the basis of purely formal guarantees.

Also in this difficult area, modern criminal justice requires the achievement of a much more complex approach to the set of conflicting interests at stake. Doubtless, international human rights case-law has contributed to overcoming an understanding of criminal justice characterised by rigid exclusionary rules,[54] which do not fit the difficult challenges posed by criminal proceedings. From a human rights perspective, exclusionary rules are often unable to give a voice to individuals, such as vulnerable witnesses or the injured party, who may suffer from considerable damages if summoned to be examined in open court or may have suffered from restrictive measures to render statements out of court. Further risks can also arise for the defendant from the exceptions to some exclusionary rules, as observed in relation to the statements rendered by the accused to the investigative bodies under Italian law. On a deeper level still, it can today be doubted whether exclusionary rules can always be justified by the unreliability of the information whose admissibility they aim to ban and therefore by the inability to obtain a reliable decision-making.[55] The sole and decisive evidence doctrine, adopted by the Strasbourg Court and followed by the Inter-American Court, already revealed the need for a more flexible approach, which shifts the focus from abstract admissibility to the probative relevance of out-of-court evidence.[56] The case-law developed on the basis of the *Al-Khawaja* judgment has further developed this focus. From this viewpoint, one might argue that the European Court has remained consistent with its own jurisprudence. The maintenance of rigid barriers on the use of out-of-court of evidence, furthermore, has become more and more debatable even in the countries traditionally based on systems of unreasoned verdicts. Even with some significant exceptions, considerable developments have occurred in the conception of oral evidence, which has led to an in-depth reflection on the admissibility of evidence that, as noted, is largely becoming 'a function of probative value, rather than being dictated by any peremptory legal definition'.[57]

[54]In this respect see Daniele (2008), p. 392 ff., who warns, however, about the risks of replacing the exclusionary rules with flexible rules on the assessment of criminal evidence.

[55]Ferrua (2013), p. 5.

[56]Balsamo and Lo Piparo (2008), p. 336 ff.

[57]Roberts and Zuckerman (2010), p. 26.

One of the most significant consequences of this approach is the strengthening of the contribution of the parties in a field that was traditionally considered to be a 'forbidden garden' even for the legislature, namely the assessment of criminal evidence.[58] In several continental countries, whereas the acknowledgment of the principle of *contradictoire* led to the establishment of rigid exclusionary rules, which largely allowed for a formal participation of the individuals involved in criminal proceedings, the assessment of the evidence gathered still remained in the exclusive competence of the decision-makers. In this sense, the principle of free judicial conviction, after being relieved from the inquisitorial tendency to allow the unconditional use of out-of-court evidence, confirmed the autonomous powers of the decision-makers and the need to free them from any external influence on the fact-finding—no matter whether of the legislature or of the parties.

Doubtless, the widespread softening of exclusionary rules calls for the enhancement of the argumentative role of the parties in the decision-making process. This especially entails clear demonstrative duties for the parties interested in the use of untested evidence, which should explain the grounds that made confrontation impossible by sustaining the reliability of the evidence-gathering procedure and the probative value of the information at stake. These developments should be accompanied by the enhancement of the duty to give reasons on the arguments of the defence. Remarkably, the European Court attached such importance to the argument made by the defence that the failure by the decision-makers to consider a memorandum from the defence would entail an infringement of Article 6 ECHR.[59] At the national level, one could also observe the progressive enhancement of the argumentative contribution of the parties over recent years. Italian law provides a clear example. The 1988 code did not required the fact-finders to provide a reasoned assessment of the arguments brought about by the parties. Criminal judgments must only 'indicate' the arguments of the parties in their concluding remarks.[60] Moreover, although both the prosecutor and the defence have the right to obtain evidence in rebuttal,[61] the failure by the decision-makers to assess it cannot be challenged before the Supreme Court.[62] The right to obtain a critical assessment on evidence in rebuttal,[63] therefore, was a rather rhetorical acknowledgment, which can be particularly detrimental in the case of defendants convicted for the first time in the second instance. Although these limitations are still formally in force, the Italian case-law has progressively empowered the Supreme Court to scrutinise the fulfilment by the decision-makers of the duty to give reasons in relation to the arguments made by the defence. In 2006, the Italian legislature reformed the rules on the appeal proceedings by allowing the Supreme Court to scrutinise the case of

---

[58]Ferrua (1998), p. 597 ff.

[59]Chapter 8, F.IV.

[60]Art. 546(1)(d) CCP-Italy.

[61]Art. 495(2) CCP-Italy.

[62]Art. 606(1)(d) CCP-Italy.

[63]Illuminati (2016), p. 758.

misunderstood assessment of evidence as well as the case in which the decision-makers failed to assess decisive evidence already obtained in court.[64]

b) Untested Evidence and the Proof of Guilt. The Progressive Erosion of the Sole and Decisive Evidence Doctrine

Against this background, an enhanced argumentative duty should lie with the party who requests the admission of untested evidence, whereas the decision-makers who decide to use it should have an enhanced duty to give reasons. It has been observed that, notwithstanding the clear acknowledgment of the principle of *contradictoire*, Italian law does not rule out any use of untested evidence gathered out of court. Since 2008, Brazilian law has also strengthened the relevance of the guarantee of *contradictoire* for the purposes of the proof of guilt, to the extent, however, that it only rules out the exclusive use of out-of-court evidence.[65] This approach has some limitations, however. By excluding the possibility for the accused to be convicted on the basis of the evidence rendered by a person who freely refused confrontation, the Italian Constitution also rules out the use of information in relation to which no confrontation could take place because of the free decision of the accuser. The constitutional derogation regarding the impossibility of *contradictoire* for objective grounds confirms this conclusion, thus leaving no room, *e.g.*, for a limited use of the statements given by relatives of the accused who decide not to testify at trial.[66]

The approach followed by the Italian Constitution entails another important consequence, namely that the investigative authority which gathered oral evidence at the pre-trial stage cannot freely avoid (a procedure that provides for) the involvement of private parties. This requires re-defining the limits of use of urgent investigations in the pre-trial inquiry by the parties and especially by the public prosecutor, who should prefer a procedure open to the *contradictoire* of other parties, unless it jeopardises the taking of the sought information. The use of untested (oral) evidence that can no longer be taken at trial, therefore, should presuppose the proof that the competent authority made its best effort to enable the participation of the defence.

Where these conditions are met, there is no need to make the use of untested evidence dependent on further requirements, such as the existence of external corroboration, nor should it be necessary to demonstrate the non-decisiveness of its evidentiary contribution, as required by the European case-law. The *Al-Khawaja* doctrine reveals the shortcomings of abstract limits of use of untested evidence, whose reliability must be demonstrated in a concrete case either intrinsically or extrinsically. As Lord Phillips stressed, giving the judgment of the Supreme Court in the *Al-Khawaja* case,

---

[64] Art. 606(1)(e) CCP-Italy, as reformed by Law 47/2006. See Bargis (2016), p. 884 ff.

[65] Chapter 3, I.

[66] Chapter 16, D.5.II.a.

> The sole or decisive test produces a paradox. It permits the court to have regard to evidence if the support that it gives to the prosecution case is peripheral, but not where it is decisive. The more cogent the evidence the less it can be relied upon.

On close examination, these arguments can also apply to the case in which testimonial evidence has become unavailable at trial because of circumstances of which the investigative authorities were aware in the pre-trial inquiry. If the prosecutor, despite knowing the precarious health conditions of a core witness or of the victim, decides to examine them instead of requesting the anticipated evidence-gathering in a court procedure, this is not a sufficient reason for excluding *a priori* the information obtained by a person who died before the trial, nor is there any valid argument to make the use of this information conditional on abstract limits, such as those posed by the decisiveness test.

The need for a review by Italian law of its current approach to the use of unavailable evidence, as noted, was recently enhanced by the *Moumen* judgment.[67] In this case, the Strasbourg Court confirmed the existence of an enhanced duty of information on the part of the national authorities, which must make all the possible efforts to obtain the appearance of absent witnesses. The failure by the competent authority to properly fulfil this obligation, however, does not in itself entail an infringement of the Convention. By invoking the *Al-Khawaja* doctrine, the *Moumen* judgment scrutinised the application of compensating tools aimed at allowing for a fair assessment of the reliability of the untested evidence. It may be surprising that the European Court engaged in the evaluation of counterbalancing measures after having recognised that the testimony of the absent witness B did not have decisive influence on decision-making.[68] On close examination, the Court stressed that the adoption of compensating measures by the domestic authorities not only aims at saving the overall fairness of the procedure but also at ensuring the reliability of fact-finding. This highlights a further evolution in the Strasbourg case-law towards a model in which, in cases of lack confrontation, the probative relevance of any piece of evidence—regardless of its decisiveness—must be demonstrated in each concrete case. It is difficult to predict the consequences of this new approach, which may seem, however, to produce a further erosion of the sole and decisive evidence doctrine. In this context, the demonstrative tasks of the private parties—and consequently their contribution for the purposes of decision-making—have proportionally been enhanced in that the defence must be granted the opportunity to provide its version of the events and to challenge the reliability of the absent witness.

[67] ECtHR, *Moumen v. Italy*.

[68] *Ibid.*, §§ 53–55.

c) Variations of the Right to Confrontation and the Factual Background for the Use of Indirect Evidence. The Need for Justification *in concreto*

The need for flexible solutions is enhanced where *contradictoire* is in itself feasible, although human rights concerns or state-related interests do not allow for defendants to be directly confronted with their accuser in a public hearing. It has been observed that the factual background of the concrete cases plays enormous importance in the international human rights case-law, which not only led both the Strasbourg Court and the Inter-American Court to provide different solutions but also led the European judges to rule in a different way in relation to anonymous testimony depending on the interests at stake.[69] In Europe, in the light of the general tendency to soften not only the exclusionary rules but also rigid conditions of use of criminal evidence, the Strasbourg Court has extended the findings of the *Al-Khawaja* doctrine to the cases of anonymous testimony and of testimonial evidence given by vulnerable witnesses.

We can agree or not with this development, which however undoubtedly entails two important consequences. The first is that it strengthens the duty of the competent authorities to justify the decision to apply (and the choice of) special arrangements aimed at an indirect form of confrontation with the accused, as a part of their general obligation to adopt measures in order to counterbalance the restriction on the right to examine the accuser. The need for enhanced justification of alternatives to direct confrontation is enhanced under the American Convention, which, as noted, recognises the right of the defence to examine prosecutorial witnesses and obtain their appearance in court. Irrespective of the decisive weight attached to indirect evidence by the decision-makers, there is little doubt that this formulation, despite not excluding indirect forms of confrontation, requires the competent authorities to justify the reasons for which special arrangements are due in a concrete case. The second consequence is the enhancement of the argumentative contribution of the parties for the purposes of decision-making. It has been noted that the shift of the focus towards the assessment of evidence obtained without direct confrontation strengthens the demonstrative relevance of criminal evidence and therefore the need for a careful proof of its reliability.[70] In this context, the party interested in the use of the indirect evidence or the results of an anonymous testimony (especially the public prosecutor) should demonstrate the adequacy of the arrangements made both to save the fairness of the proceedings and to ensure the reliability of the information obtained. The defence must in turn be granted wide latitude to challenge the measures adopted especially in terms of the necessary information. And here also, the softening of the ordinary requirements of confrontation enhances the duty of the decision-makers to provide reasoned analysis on the arguments brought by the accused on the evidence-gathering procedure.

[69] Chapter 16, D.5.II.b.

[70] On the proof of evidence see Gascón Inchausti (1999).

In this respect, some reforms are due at the national level. In some particular cases, a presumption of dangerousness of cross-examination can be accepted in exceptional circumstances. This is the case for undercover officers, including foreign police officers, members of information and security services. As noted, Italian Law 146/2006 allowed for these individuals not to give their personal information but instead to give the identifying details used for the purposes of the undercover inquiry.[71] Such cases, therefore, highlight situations in which testimony is ordinarily taken in anonymous form and the real identity of the person examined is hidden not only to the defence but even to the competent court. Outside these limits, however, we have seen that reasons must be provided on the interests justifying the use of special forms of confrontation and the adequacy of the arrangements made. To this end, a justification based on the abstract seriousness of the prosecuted crime is not enough and the party which requests derogation from the ordinary rules on the court examination should adduce the reasons and the interests at stake.

2. Argumentation and the Legal Contribution of the Defence to Decision-Making

The contribution of the private parties is not only limited to fact-finding. The analysis of the developments that have occurred in the Strasbourg case-law over the last decades has also revealed the need to grant defendants the opportunity to give their contribution to the decision-making on legal matters and especially to the decision on the legal classification of the offence under prosecution.[72] One of the main results achieved by the European Court in this respect, moreover, was to link the right to be involved in the decision-making on legal issues with two fair trial safeguards acknowledged by the Convention, namely the right to be informed of the accusation, which also entails the legal characterisation of the charge preferred, and the right to set up effective defence.[73]

Despite some inconsistencies, the Strasbourg case-law provides the basis for drawing some conclusions on this important issue from the viewpoint of the selected countries. In particular, the European jurisprudence allows us to distinguish between two main situations, i.e. (a) the case in which the decision-makers provide a new legal classification of the offence shortly prior to the pronouncement of the judgement or even convicts the accused for offences not clearly provided for in the indictment, and (b) the case in which a higher court re-defines *nomen juris*. As far as the former situation is concerned, Italian law still reveals considerable backwardness. In particular, it is noteworthy that the 1988 code acknowledged specific safeguards to the parties in case of amendment of the charge during the

[71] Art. 497(2-*bis*) CCP-Italy.

[72] Chapter 8, F.IV. On this topic see among others De Matteis (2008), p. 215 ff.

[73] Chapter 8, F.IV.

trial, especially the possibility for the accused to request a period to arrange a defence strategy on the basis of the amended charge and to request the collection of new evidence if necessary for the decision-making.[74] Further safeguards concern other private parties: the victim must also be summoned to court,[75] and the Constitutional Court extended to parties other than the accused the right to request additional evidence.[76] However, it is worth observing that these guarantees are only due if the public prosecutor amends or integrates the factual issues of the indictment either by re-defining the charge or by charging the accused with (further or new) aggravating circumstances or with another charge. On the contrary, no defensive safeguards are provided for if the trial court amends *nomen juris* in the judgment, a power that under Italian law the decision-makers can always exercise *ex officio* on the basis of the principle *jura novit curia*.

This result, which was already criticised shortly after the entry into force of the 1988 code,[77] became even more questionable from a human rights after the constitutionalisation of the principle of *contradictoire* as the milestone of the new model of a fair (criminal) justice, in parallel with the enactment of the Convention's right of the accused to be informed on the charge.[78] Neither this constitutional reform nor the 2001 amendment of Article 117 of the Italian Constitution, however, led to any change of this legal set-up, nor did the 2007 twin judgments of the Constitutional Court give rise to a reflection on the approach adopted by Italian law. In the light of the developments that in the same years occurred in the Strasbourg case-law, however, there is little doubt that convicting a person for an offence provided with a new legal classification without giving him any opportunity to arrange a proper defence frustrates the fair trial guarantees laid down by the Rome Convention and by the Italian Constitution, also taking into account that the amendment of *nomen juris* often entails a hidden form of amendment of the factual characteristics of the offence. This conclusion is not contradicted by the compromise approach followed by the Strasbourg Court, which looks at the possibility of the defence challenging the new legal classification in a higher instance.[79] Thus, the procedural safeguards provided by the Italian code for the second instance cannot effectively compensate the accused for the opportunities lost in the first instance, taking into consideration the limitations to the right to evidence existent in the second instance.[80] Moreover, Italian courts still tend to require the proof of a concrete damage that the defence suffered from the conviction for another *nomen juris*.[81] This result—despite being consistent with the approach followed by the

[74] Art. 521(1-2) CCP-Italy.

[75] Art. 521(3) CCP-Italy.

[76] CConst, 241/1992 and 50/1995.

[77] Ferrua (1990), p. 24 f.

[78] In these terms see Quattrocolo (2011), p. 71 f.

[79] Chapter 8, F.IV.

[80] In this regard cf. Ubertis (2009), p. 57. Of a different opinion Quattrocolo (2011), p. 146 f.

[81] Quattrocolo (2011), p. 144 f.

Strasbourg case-law in the *Pélissier and Sassi* judgment—cannot be sustained, since it burdens the defence with the task of proving a damage instead of charging the trial judges with the task of giving the parties the necessary time and facilities to adapt their defence strategy prior to the decision-making.

Similar shortcomings can be observed in Brazil. Notwithstanding the reform carried out by Law 11.719/2008, Brazilian law still allows for the trial court to provide *emendatio libelli* while maintaining the facts charged.[82] Before the 2008 reform, the Federal Supreme Tribunal had already stressed that decision-makers can amend the legal classification of the offence without any previous formality.[83] This approach raises several human rights concerns from the perspective of the constitutional requirement of *contradictoire*,[84] and it is questionable whether it fits the conditions of a fair trial.[85] Therefore, the general power of Article 383 - CCP-Brazil should be reinterpreted by enhancing the *contradictoire* of the parties in the case of *emendatio libelli*, especially taking into account the risks that arise from the institution of a public prosecution (if the offence is subject to public prosecution) as a result of the new classification of the offence.[86] *De lege ferenda*, the possibility of a person being convicted for an offence provided with another *nomen juris* without the parties having the opportunity to adjust their defence should also be avoided in Italy, and some defensive tools, such as a period to arrange a new defence, should be put at their disposal, irrespective of eventual compensating mechanisms in a higher instance. The fact that the trial court can provide *emendatio libelli* after the completion of the collection of evidence requested by the parties no longer justifies the autonomous exercise of this power in a model of criminal justice strongly based upon the contribution of the parties.

Further concerns arise in the case in which a higher court redefines *nomen juris* for the first time. Here, in the case of appeal lodged solely by the accused, the possibility of a re-definition of the legal classification of the offence can give rise to delicate problems in the light of the prohibition of *reformatio in pejus*.[87] Furthermore, *emendatio libelli* in the second instance poses the problem of the possibility of the accused effectively challenging the conviction issued for another *nomen juris*, if provided for by national law. In this regard, the structure of the proceedings before the Supreme Court often does not satisfy this requirement. This can explain why the European Court tightened the conditions of *emendatio libelli* in a higher instance by requiring the competent court to amend the legal classification of the charge after granting the accused the opportunity to provide defensive arguments

[82]Art. 383 CCP-Brazil.

[83]STJ, HC 84.489/DF, rel. Jane Silva.

[84]Lopes Jr (2017), p. 893.

[85]Giacomolli (2008), p. 107.

[86]Lopes Jr (2017), p. 895 f.

[87]Quattrocolo (2011), p. 220 ff.

on the new legal classification of the charge.[88] This point highlights another deficiency of Italian law, which requires prompt legislative intervention.

H. Restrictions on Freedom and the Need for Enhanced Participatory Safeguards

I. Decision-Making on Restrictions on Liberty and the Right to a Fair Hearing by an Independent Authority

1. The Perspective of Domestic Proceedings. The Need to Involve the Individuals Against Whom Pre-Trial Measures Are Requested in the Decision-Making and to Enable Them to Contribute to Further Decisions on the Measure Applied

The comparative analysis has highlighted that the application of coercive measures enhances the need for specific participatory safeguards for the individuals concerned. It has been observed that international human rights case-law has attached particular weight to the personal involvement of any person deprived of freedom in the proceedings on judicial review of the lawfulness of arrest and detention. This guarantee surely goes beyond the sphere of criminal proceedings, enabling the competent authorities (as well as international human rights courts, if called upon to scrutinise it) to carry out an in-depth examination of the overall conditions of the arrested or detained person and to detect or even prevent further human rights violations. Yet, as far as the European case-law is concerned, it must be acknowledged that it does not provide for clear indications on whether the judicial review activated by the individuals concerned also entails the obligation of the competent authority to examine them in *habeas corpus* proceedings.[89]

At the domestic level, we saw that the selected countries have recently made some important steps forward in this regard. In particular, Brazilian courts have increasingly recognised the right of the detainee to appear in court personally, a right that cannot be restricted on the grounds of administrative or organisatorial problems. In Italy, the 1995 reform, overruling the approach of 1988 code, strengthened the right to a judicial hearing by ruling out the possibility for the individuals subjected to pre-trial measures other than arrest to be questioned by the prosecutor before being heard by the judge. Despite the importance of this judicial hearing, however, Italian law does not ensure further opportunities to be personally involved in subsequent decisions that can be issued especially during the remand proceedings and therefore to make their voice heard before an independent authority. As noted, there is still no certainty that the accused will be examined by the competent judge,

[88]Chapter 8, F.IV.

[89]Chapter 16, D.VI.3.

even if the prosecutor requests the replacement of the coercive means applied with a more intrusive measure. Even more worryingly, there is also no certainty of being heard in the case of the judicial review activated by the defence under Article 309 CCP-Italy, since suspects need only be heard if they appear in court.

In the light of the criminal law character of both remand proceedings and the judicial review of coercive measures, there is little doubt that the individuals subject to restrictions on liberty should be granted not only the right to a first judicial hearing but also the opportunity to take part in further phases of the proceedings, especially where decisions are at stake which can (further) affect their fundamental rights. In this regard, the possibility for the public prosecutor to request a more intrusive measure at any stage, alongside the possibility of the competent court for the judicial review activated by the defence confirming the coercive measure applied, should entail the obligation to adopt all necessary means to grant the individuals concerned the opportunity for a judicial hearing.

This leads to the further question of the time at which the person subjected to a pre-trial measure should be involved in the procedure. Both Brazil and Italy traditionally followed the doctrine of *inaudito reo* proceedings and it was only recently that the former enacted a soft form of preventive involvement of the defence prior to the decision-making. By contrast, Italy has always been faithful to its traditional approach and even the 2015 reform on pre-trial measures missed an important opportunity to introduce a preventive hearing of the person against whom a remand detention or another coercive measure was requested. Furthermore, Italian law (unlike Brazilian law) not only does not grant any proactive role to the aggrieved parties but also still does not give them a voice in the decision the application of coercive measures—the victim has no right to be examined either before or after the decision-making. On the other hand, we have noted that international human rights law does not require the preventive participation of the person deprived of freedom in criminal proceedings. Moreover, the acknowledgment of the right to be promptly brought before a judicial authority, which appears in both the European Convention and the Pact of San José, entails by definition the possibility of subsequent judicial intervention. However, international human rights courts have always emphasised the need for the fundamental fair trial safeguards to be fulfilled in the judicial hearing.

This entails the need for an in-depth reform of the current legal solutions adopted by the countries examined. As long as Italian courts allow for the accused subject to a pre-trial measure to be heard by the same judge who ordered the means already enforced, a preventive hearing constitutes the only solution to ensure an impartial hearing. Furthermore, it seems that the postponement of the hearing should be justified by conflicting interests with which the right to contribute to the decision-making should be balanced. In the absence of cogent reasons contrasting the previous intervention of the defence, the individuals concerned should be granted the opportunity to make their voice heard beforehand. Of course, the preventive hearing must provide an effective opportunity of exercise of the defence rights, which entails the need for a reform of the solution enacted by the Brazilian legislation in order to specify the consequences of the preventive summons of the defendants and especially the procedural safeguards that should be given to them while the decision is being made on the application of pre-trial measures. Ultimately, there is no valid reason for excluding the hearing of the victim. Doubtless, the examination of the aggrieved parties, preferably by protective means, can make a relevant contribution to the decision on the application of pre-trial measures that are intended to protect them.

2. The Perspective of International Surrender Procedures. The Need to Strengthen the Oversight of Participatory Safeguards in the Trial Country and the Right to a Fair Hearing in the Host State

Transnational inquiries require specific safeguards where interferences with fundamental rights are at stake. In the field of international cooperation, surrender procedures can have direct implications on the right to freedom. Notwithstanding the clear repercussions on the right to liberty, however, international surrender procedures did not traditionally attach particular relevance to the participatory rights of the sought person. This is confirmed by the scant attention paid to the relevance on the surrender procedure of the failure to involve the accused in the trial country. Even today, the mere fact that the defendants were tried *in absentia* is not generally considered to impede their surrender and even the most protective international instruments limit themselves to requiring respect for the minimum defence rights in the requesting state. A similar approach can be observed as to the involvement of the accused in the proceedings that led to a detention order in the trial country. In the light of the mutual recognition principle, Italian law has adopted a formalistic approach in this respect, relying on merely the issuing of an arrest warrant by a foreign judicial authority and thus overlooking the need to scrutinise whether the sought person has had the opportunity of a fair hearing before an impartial authority in the issuing country. It has been noted, however, that the principle of mutual recognition cannot be invoked to justify the non-inquiry by the host state into the conditions that led to the issuing of the detention order.[90] On close examination, the requested authority should not satisfy itself with the formal circumstance of a judge issuing a detention order in the trial country but should be able to inquire into whether the accused was granted an effective opportunity for a fair judicial hearing (*e.g.*, by means of a remote hearing) in the proceedings that led to the detention order in the trial country.

Further problems arise in relation to participatory safeguards in the cooperation procedure in the host country. It has been observed that even the EAW Framework Decision, despite the proclaimed goal of ensuring a standard of fundamental rights protection not lower than that provided by Article 6 TEU, limited itself to the generic acknowledgment of the right of the sought person to obtain a judicial hearing. This led the Italian legislature to reproduce the minimalistic solutions enacted in the field of extradition, which, while requiring the competent authority to hear their lawyer, does not provide a mandatory examination of the sought

[90]Chapter 16, E.II.4.

person, who will only be heard if he does not consent to the surrender procedure. Surprisingly, the recent Italian legislation, while implementing the EU instruments on some defence rights in criminal proceedings, did not enhance the standards of human rights protection. Still today, since the requested person may remain unaware of the exact implications of consent to the European arrest warrant and may therefore not be in a position to make an informed decision.

As noted, this approach does not fit the requirements of a human rights-oriented model of criminal justice. *De lege ferenda*, procedural mechanisms should be enacted to ensure to the sought person a judicial hearing in any case and the opportunity to decide before an independent authority whether or not to consent to the surrender procedure. In this regard, the solution of the Brazilian *Estatuto do Estrangeiro* appears to go in the right direction, in that the competent court must always hear the sought individuals, although only after the trial country has forwarded its request for extradition.[91] The Italian legislation on the EAW proceedings also provides a proper solution model in relation to cases in which measures of coercion are ordered against the requested person. Here, the judicial authority (the president of the competent court of appeal) is responsible for informing the sought person of the European arrest warrant as well as of the possibility of consenting to the surrender procedure and particularly on the implications of this decision.[92] A similar arrangement should be applied to all cases of the surrender procedure. There is no valid reason for maintaining the judicial hearing as an alternative to the decision to consent to the surrender procedure, especially if this decision is to be made before the prosecutorial authority, without proper information on its consequences.

II. Qualitative Requirements of Effective Participation in the Decision on Coercive Measures. Information Safeguards and the Right to Comprehensive Assistance for the Individuals Concerned

Even an independent hearing does not suffice to enable the private parties to fairly participate in the decision on the application of coercive measures. As noted, international human rights law ensures to any person deprived of liberty the right to adequate information. Compared to the European Convention, the Pact of San José broadens the scope of this information, which must also be provided to the next of kin of the arrested or detained person as well as to a lawyer and to a consular official. EU law further extended the scope of the information safeguards by recognising the right to have a third person informed of the reasons of deprivation of freedom. The guarantee of information, moreover, is strictly linked with the

[91] Chapter 7, C.III.1.a.

[92] Chapter 16, E.II.3.

assistance due to the arrestee or detainee. In the light of the particularly vulnerable condition deriving from restrictions on freedom, this not only includes the assistance of a lawyer and an interpreter but also the assistance of a third person (*e.g.*, a family member) and of a consular official. To strengthen both the rights to information and to proper assistance, the 2014 Italian implementation of the EU legislation reformed the rules on the administrative obligations on the execution of pre-trial measures by requiring defendants to be provided with information in an understandable language on important issues, such as the right to legal assistance and legal aid, the right to know the charge filed, the right to inform their consular authority and the family, and so on.

Notwithstanding these important steps forward, some qualitative requirements must be fulfilled to ensure to the individuals concerned a fair participation in the decision on the application of coercive measures. On one level, the strict link between the two guarantees of information and assistance require information to be provided in a complete manner and in due time to allow for effective defence especially with a view to the judicial hearing. As noted, Italian law does not seem to provide a proper solution by requiring the judicial authority to integrate the information given by the law enforcement authority, as long as the judicial hearing can follow the adoption of pre-trial measures. In this respect also, the anticipation of the judicial hearing would therefore enhance the participatory rights of the accused. A delicate question concerns the information on relevant evidence. On close examination, there is no valid justification for hiding relevant information on the available evidence to both the individuals concerned as well as to the other persons and bodies called upon to provide them with assistance; and it is even more debatable that information is also hidden from the authority that is competent to order and maintain the sought measure of coercion. Allowing the prosecutor who requested a pre-trial measure to withdraw information with the only exception of exculpatory evidence is a somewhat paternalistic approach, since the defence must also be put in a position to challenge the prosecutorial request by calling into question the incriminating evidence collected.[93] Of course, a given limited selection of the information available may aim at not jeopardising the ongoing inquiry or may serve other interests, such as the protection of the victim. Furthermore, it can be detrimental to disclose information concerned with other individuals, especially if no measure of coercion was adopted against them. This does not entail, however, that the ability to select particular information must be uncontrolled. It is precisely the need for a balance among conflicting interests that requires the introduction of independent review of the selection made by the prosecutor. *De lege ferenda*, a different body than the competent authority to order or maintain the sought measure of coercion should carry out this review.

Of course, information remains a scant guarantee if the basic requirements are not satisfied to ensure effective assistance of the person against whom pre-trial measures were requested or a restrictive measure has already been enforced. As noted, it is

[93]Chapter 16, D.III.1.b.

highly debatable that communication with the lawyer can be suspended until the judicial hearing and that suspects can therefore meet their lawyer and the interpreter at the hearing for the first time ever, a solution that Italian law has maintained, despite the implementation of the EU legislation on both the right to information and the right to access to a lawyer in criminal proceedings.[94] *De jure condendo*, this result should be avoided and the individuals against whom a request of restriction on freedom was made should be granted the necessary time to prepare their defence through the assistance provided by the law. Special arrangements are necessary in the case of remote hearing of persons already in remand detention, a vulnerable situation that requires enhanced assistance (*e.g.*, by means of legal assistance both in prison and in court), as highlighted by Brazilian legal scholarship.[95]

Transnational cases pose more specific challenges and require enhanced protection of the individuals involved. It has been observed that the Italian law on the EAW proceedings strengthens the right of the person subjected to coercive measures to a judicial hearing in comparison to domestic cases by providing for a court examination irrespective of a previous judicial hearing after provisional arrest. This guarantee is also strictly linked with the provision of enhanced information rights, which in the case of coercive measures the judicial authority must provide to the individuals concerned as well as to their relatives and a consular official.[96] Notwithstanding these positive solutions, Italian law lacks clear safeguards in relation to the rights to legal and linguistic assistance, which, despite being acknowledged, are still subject to the existing limits found in domestic cases. Notwithstanding the provision that the lawyer must be informed at least 24 h prior to the hearing, the general applicability of the ordinary code rules governing the national proceedings allows for the suspension of previous communications between the sought individuals and their counsel, which in turn entails suspension of the assistance of an interpreter. Of course, meeting the lawyer (especially a court-appointed lawyer) at the hearing for the first time ever is highly detrimental to the sought person. Therefore, suspension of previous communications with the lawyer should not be allowed beyond the time necessary to prepare the defence, as provided for by Brazilian law, which requires the judicial hearing to take place at the earliest 10 days after the appointment of a lawyer to the requested individuals, if they are not represented by their own counsel.[97] Moreover, it should be ensured that the competent authority scrutinises the need for linguistic assistance regardless of a request by the sought person, who should also be granted a procedural tool to challenge the decision not to appoint an interpreter as well as to challenge the quality of the interpretation provided.

---

[94] Chapter 2, J.III.1.

[95] Chapter 16, D.VI.1.c.

[96] *Ibid.*

[97] Chapter 5, D.II.

III. Proportionality of Restrictions on Freedom and the Guarantee of Regular Judicial Oversight

The proportionality of restrictions on freedom cannot exclusively be assessed prior to their application but must be viewed in dynamic terms, that is, in relation to the overall duration of the measure applied. In this respect, both Italian and Brazilian law reveal considerable backwardness. It has been observed that Italian law not only does not generally ensure to the person against whom coercive measures were requested the opportunity to preventively contribute to the decision-making but furthermore does not provide for subsequent hearings, even in case of substitution of the measure applied with another more intrusive measure. Neither Brazil nor Italy, moreover, require regular review of the measure enforced, nor do they provide for fixed opportunities for the person concerned to be heard by an independent authority. Notwithstanding the recent reforms on pre-trial measures, this result has remained unchanged in both countries and the proposals aimed at introducing regular review of pre-trial detention, such as that launched in Brazil, which required judges to re-examine the justification of the coercive measure at most every 60 days, has never been enacted into legislation.

In Europe, the extensive case-law of the Strasbourg Court in this sense has constituted the basis for non-binding initiatives, such as Recommendation Rec (2006)13 of the Committee of Ministers of the Council of Europe and the EU Green Paper on the application of EU criminal justice legislation in the field of detention,[98] which more and more call for a constant monitoring of pre-trial detention. In particular, Recommendation Rec (2006)13 reflected a model in which short-term periodical reviews (at intervals normally no longer than a month) must be carried out at the initiative of the prosecuting authority or investigating judicial authority on pain of the automatic release of the person concerned.[99] This approach provides proper models of solutions for the criminal justice systems examined in this study, in which the absence of regular reviews leads to the result that the ordinary length of custodial measures often reaches the maximum time limits laid down at the statutory law level. The need for periodic review of the proportionality of pre-trial detention is further enhanced in the field of international cooperation, in which the decision on surrender may be issued when the foreign detention order has already lost its justification. The *Ramoci* judgment of the Italian Supreme Court, alongside the possibility of judicially-based tools to control the length of pre-trial detention, may seem to show a preference—in the delicate field of transnational procedures—towards a flexible system of monitoring of coercive measures in comparison to maximum time-limits at the statutory law level. This approach cannot remain confined to the area of international cooperation in criminal matters.

---

[98] COM(2011) 327 final, § 4.2.

[99] Recommendation (2006)13, § 17.

In Brazil also, both constitutional law and the requirements set forth by international law call for the introduction of a mechanism aimed at ensuring a constant independent oversight of coercive measures. In this respect, as noted, the 2011 reform of pre-trial measures missed an important opportunity, failing to enact not only a system of periodic review but also maximum time-limits of remand detention especially. The frequent recourse to coercive measures for the purposes of social defence and the reliability of criminal justice certainly do not constitute valid reasons for maintaining the indefinite duration of coercive measures.[100] Alongside fixed stages of the proceedings, which can already be used for these purposes (*e.g.*, conclusion of the police inquiry, preferment of the indictment, and so on), it would be desirable for the Brazilian legislature, following the experience of other countries in Latin America, also to introduce a system of periodic reviews (*e.g.*, at the latest, after 30 days) of coercive measures.[101]

I. Concluding Remarks

At the end of this study, we can conclude that the *audi alteram partem* rule in the field of domestic and transnational criminal justice reveals highly complex problems, which go far beyond the enhancement of the defence rights of individual parties. The fulfilment of participatory safeguards of private parties requires constant trade-offs among conflicting interests. The need for such trade-offs, however, is not always external but often requires a re-definition of fair trial rights in the light of an overall assessment of the human rights challenges posed by the case at hand. In this context, the aforementioned qualitative requirements only set some minimum conditions for the enhancement of a participatory model of criminal justice, which conditions will hopefully provide the basis for further discussion in a near future.

References

Balsamo A, Lo Piparo A (2008) Principio del contraddittorio, utilizzabilità delle dichiarazioni predibattimentali e nozione di testimone tra giurisprudenza europea e criticità del sistema italiano. In: Balsamo A, Kostoris RE (eds) Giurisprudenza europea e processo penale italiano. Giappichelli, Torino, pp 333–372

Bargis M (2016) Impugnazioni. In: Conso G, Grevi V, Bargis M (eds) Compendio di procedura penale, 8th edn. Wolters Kluwer/Cedam, Padova, pp 801–948

Chiavario M (2013) Manuale dell'estradizione e del mandato d'arresto europeo. Utet, Torino

[100] Giacomolli (2013), p. 92.

[101] *Ibid.*, 93.

Curtotti Nappi D (2014) La normativa in tema di assistenza linguistica tra direttiva europea e nuove prassi applicative. Diritto penle e giustizia pp 115–132

Daniele M (2008) Regole di esclusione della prova e giurisprudenza della Corte europea: profili di potenziale conflitto. In: Balsamo A, Kostoris RE (eds) Giurisprudenza europea e processo penale italiano. Giappichelli, Torino, pp 383–394

De Matteis L (2008) Diversa qualificazione giuridica dell'accusa e tutela del diritto di difesa. In: Balsamo A, Kostoris RE (eds) Giurisprudenza europea e processo penale italiano. Giappichelli, Torino, pp 215–233

Ferrua P (1990) La difesa nel processo penale: profilo di una funzione. In: in Id., Studi sul processo penale, vol I. Giappichelli, Torino, pp 15–35

Ferrua P (1998) Un giardino proibito per il legislatore: la valutazione delle prove. Questione giustizia, pp 597ff

Ferrua P (2013) La prova nel processo penale: profili generali. In: Ferrua P, Marzaduri E, Spangher G (eds) La prova penale. Giappichelli, Torino, pp 1–56

Gascón Inchausti F (1999) El control de la fiabilidad probatoria: "prueba sobre la prueba" en el proceso penal. Tirant Lo Banch, Valencia

Giacomolli NJ (2008) Reformas(?) do Processo Penal. Lumen Juris, Rio de Janeiro

Giacomolli NJ (2013) Prisão, liberdade e as cautelares alternativas ao cárcere. Marcial Pons, São Paulo

Gleß S (2006) Beweisrechtsgrundsätze einer grenzüberschreitenden Strafverfolgung. Nomos, Baden-Baden

Illuminati G (2016) Giudizio. In: Conso G, Grevi V, Bargis M (eds) Compendio di procedura penale, 8th edn. Wolters Kluwer/Cedam, Padova, pp 689–760

Lopes A Jr (2017) Direito Processual Penal, 14th edn. Saraiva, São Paulo

Lopes A Jr, Jakobsen Glockner R (2013) Investigação preliminar no processo penal. Saraiva, São Paulo

Marzaduri E (2016) Procedimento penale davanti al giudice di pace. In: Conso G, Grevi V, Bargis M (eds) Compendio di procedura penale, 8th edn. Wolters Kluwer Italia/Cedam, Padova, pp 1099–1147

Mazza O (2014) Contraddittorio (principio del) (diritto processuale penale). In: Enciclopedia del diritto, Annali VII. Giuffrè, Milano, pp. 247–274

Quattrocolo S (2011) Riqualificazione del fatto nella sentenza penale e tutela del contraddittorio. Jovene, Napoli

Roberts P, Zuckerman A (2010) Criminal evidence, 2nd edn. Oxford University Press, Oxford

Tonini P (2001) Riforma del sistema probatorio: un'attuazione parziale del "giusto processo". Diritto penale e processo, pp 269–273

Ubertis G (2009) Principi di procedura penale europea, 2nd edn. Raffaello Cortina, Milano

Appendix A: Format for the Comparative-Law Examination of Domestic Criminal Justice

A. Introductory remarks on national criminal justice and on the role of private parties in criminal proceedings
B. *Audi alteram partem* in constitutional law
C. Principle of *contradictoire* and equality of arms
D. The role of private parties in the decisions to charge
E. *Audi alteram partem* and information rights
F. Participatory safeguards in criminal proceedings. Right to personal participation and *in absentia* trials
G. Procedural safeguards of a fair hearing. Right to be fairly examined, right not to be heard and right to be forgotten
H. *Audi alteram partem* and the evidence-gathering
I. Right to *contradictoire* and the decision-making. The contribution of private parties to fact-finding and the argumentative role of the defence in the decision on legal issues
J. Right to *contradictoire* and measures of coercion with specific regard to restrictions on freedom

S. Ruggeri, Audi Alteram Partem *in Criminal Proceedings*,
DOI 10.1007/978-3-319-54573-8

Appendix B: Format for the Comparative-Law Examination of Transnational Criminal Justice

A. General rules governing transnational cases
B. Human rights in international cooperation
C. Information rights in transborder cases
D. Participatory rights in surrender procedures
E. *Contradictoire* and transnational evidence-gathering

S. Ruggeri, Audi Alteram Partem *in Criminal Proceedings*,
DOI 10.1007/978-3-319-54573-8

References

Literature

Abade D (2013) Direitos fundamentais na cooperação juridical internacional. Saraiva, São Paulo

Allegrezza S (2010) Critical remarks on the Green Paper on obtaining evidence from one Member State to another and securing its admissibility. Zeitschrift für die internationale Strafrechtsdogmatik, pp 569–579

Allegrezza S (2012) La riscoperta della vittima nella giustizia penale europea. In: Allegrezza S, Belluta H, Gialuz M, Luparia L (eds) Lo scudo e la spada. Giappichelli, Torino, pp 1–31

Amalfitano C (2014) Le prime Direttive europee sul ravvicinamento "processuale": il diritto all'interpretazione, alla traduzione e all'informazione nei procedimenti penali. In: Del Coco R, Pistoia E (eds) Stranieri e giustizia penale. Problemi di perseguibilità e di garanzia nella normativa nazionale ed europea. Cacucci, Bari, pp 1–34

Amalfitano C (2017) La vicenda Taricco nuovamente al vaglio della Corte di giustizia: qualche breve riflessione a caldo. http://rivista.eurojus.it. Accessed 29 Jan 2017

Amodio E (2001) Giusto processo, diritto al silenzio e obblighi di verità dell'imputato sul fatto altrui. Cassazione penale, pp 3592 ff

Ashworth A, Redmayne M (2010) The criminal process, 4th edn. Oxford University Press, Oxford

Ayala Corao C, Rivero MD (2014) Article 4. In: Steiner and Uribe (eds) Convención Americana sobre Derechos Humanos. Comentario. Konrad Adenauer Stiftung, Berlin, pp 112–130

Bachmaier Winter L (2010) European Investigation Order for obtaining evidence in the criminal proceedings. Study of the proposal for a European directive. Zeitschrift für die international Strafrechtsdogmatik, pp 580–589

Bachmaier Winter L (2015a) The EU directive on the right to access to a lawyer: a critical assessment. In: Ruggeri S (ed) Human rights in european criminal law. New developments in European legislation and case law after the Lisbon treaty. Springer, Heidelberg, pp 111–131

Bachmaier Winter L (2015b) Transnational evidence. Towards the Transposition of the Directive 2014/41 Regarding the European Investigation Order in Criminal Matters. Eucrim, pp 47–60

Balsamo A, Lo Piparo A (2004) La prova "per sentito dire". La testimonianza indiretta tra teoria e prassi applicativa. Giuffrè, Milano

Balsamo A, Lo Piparo A (2008) Principio del contraddittorio, utilizzabilità delle dichiarazioni predibattimentali e nozione di testimone tra giurisprudenza europea e criticità del sistema italiano. In: Balsamo A, Kostoris RE (eds) Giurisprudenza europea e processo penale italiano. Giappichelli, Torino, pp 333–372

Bargis M (1996) Commento all'art. 13 legge 66/1996. La Legislazione penale, pp 498ff

S. Ruggeri, Audi Alteram Partem *in Criminal Proceedings*,
DOI 10.1007/978-3-319-54573-8

Bargis M (2016) Impugnazioni. In: Conso G, Grevi V, Bargis M (eds) Compendio di procedura penale, 8th edn. Wolters Kluwer/Cedam, Padova, pp 801–948
Belfiore R (2009) Movement of evidence in the EU: the present scenario and possible future developments. Eur J Crime Crim Law Crim Justice 17:1–22
Belfiore R (2011) Mutuo riconoscimento delle decisioni sulle misure alternative alla detenzione cautelare. In: Rafaraci T (ed) La cooperazione di polizia e giudiziaria in materia penale nell'Unione europea dopo il Trattato di Lisbona. Giuffrè, Milano, pp 105–117
Belfiore R (2014) Critical remarks on the proposal for a European investigation order and some considerations on the issue of mutual admissibility of evidence. In: Ruggeri S (ed) Transnational evidence and multicultural inquiries in Europe. Developments in EU legislation and new challenges for human rights-oriented criminal investigations in cross-border cases. Springer, Heidelberg, pp 91–105
Bellavista G (1952) Il processo penale monitorio, 2nd edn. Giuffrè, Milano
Bene T (2004) L'avviso di conclusione delle indagini. ESI, Napoli
Bene T (2013) La persona offesa tra diritto di difesa e diritto alla giurisdizione: le nuove tendenze legislative. Archivio penale, pp 9–30
Borowsky M (2011) Artikel 52. In: Meyer J (ed) Charta der Grundrechte der Europäischen Union, 3rd edn. Nomos, Baden-Baden
Böse M (2007) Der Grundsatz der Verfügbarkeit von Informationen in der strafrechtlichen Zusammenarbeit der Europäischen Union. Bonn University Press, V&R Unipress
Böse M (2011) Harmonizing procedural rights indirectly: the framework decision on trials in Absentia. N C J Int Law, 489–510
Böse M (2014) Die Europäische Ermittlungsanordnung–Beweistransfer nach neuen Regeln? Zeitschrift für internationale Strafrechtsdogmatik, pp 152–164
Böse M (2015) Human rights violations and mutual trust: recent case law on the European arrest warrant. In: Ruggeri S (ed) Human rights in European criminal law. New developments in European legislation and case law after the lisbon treaty. Springer, Heidelberg, pp 135–145
Busetto ML (2009) Il contraddittorio inquinato. Cedam, Padova
Caianiello M (2003) Poteri dei privati nell'esercizio dell'azione penale. Giappichelli, Torino
Caianiello M (2015) La nuova direttiva UE sull'ordine europeo di indagine penale tra mutuo riconoscimento e ammissione reciproca delle prove. Processo penale e giustizia, pp 1–11
Calamandrei P (1926) Il procedimento monitorio nella legislazione italiana. Unitas, Milano
Campo A (1993) Sulla legittimazione della persona offesa a ricorrere per cassazione ex art. 409 comma 6 c.p.p. avverso il provvedimento di archiviazione emesso in violazione del contraddittorio. Cassazione penale, pp 1496–1500
Candito GL (2015) The influence of the Directive 2012/13/EU on the Italian system of protection of the right to information in criminal procedures. In: Ruggeri S (ed) Human rights in European criminal law. New developments in European legislation and case law after the lisbon treaty. Springer, Heidelberg, pp 229–260
Caprioli F (1994) L'archiviazione. Jovene, Napoli
Caprioli F (2000) Nuovi epiloghi della fase investigativa: procedimenti contro ignoti e avviso di conclusione delle indagini preliminari. In: Peroni F (ed) Il processo penale dopo la riforma del giudice unico. Cedam, Padova, pp 245–285
Caprioli F (2002) Palingenesi di un divieto probatorio. La testimonianza del funzionario di polizia nel rinnovato assetto processuale. In: Kostoris RE (ed) Il giusto processo tra contraddittorio e diritto al silenzio. Giappichelli, Torino, pp 59–91
Caprioli F (2004) "Giusto processo" e rito degli irreperibili. In: La Legislazione penale, pp 586 ff
Caprioli F (2013) Report on Italy. In: Ruggeri S (ed) Transnational inquiries and the protection of fundamental rights in criminal proceedings. A study in memory of Vittorio Grevi and Giovanni Tranchina. Springer, Heidelberg, pp 439–455
Caprioli F (2014) Indagini preliminari e udienza preliminare. In: Conso G, Grevi V, Bargis M (eds) Compendio di procedura penale, 7th edn. Wolters Kluwer Italia/Cedam, Padova, pp 512–686
Caprioli F (2015) Prime considerazioni sul proscioglimento per particolare tenuità del fatto. Diritto penale contemporaneo (rivista trimestrale 2/2015), pp 82–105

Carcano D, Manzione D (2001) Il giusto processo. Commento alla legge 1 marzo 2001, n. 63. Giuffrè, Milano
Carini C (2008) Errore e rimedi. In: Digesto delle discipline penalistiche. IV Agg. Utet, Torino, pp 258–291
Carnelutti F (1924) Nota intorno alla natura del processo monitorio. Rivista di diritto processuale civile, pp 270 ff
Carnelutti F (1947) Lezioni sul processo penale. II vol. Ed. dell'Ateneo, Roma
Carnelutti F (1949) Processo contro ignoti. Rivista italiana di diritto processuale, II, pp 257 ff
Carnelutti F (1963) Verso la riforma del processo penale. Morano, Napoli
Carrara F (1875) Azione penale. Rivista penale, pp 4 ff
Cartabia M (2008) La Convenzione europea dei diritti dell'uomo e l'ordinamento italiano. In: Balsamo A, Kostoris RE (eds) Giurisprudenza europea e processo penale italiano. Giappichelli, Torino, pp 67–79
Casal JM (2014) Article 7. In: Steiner and Uribe (eds) Convención Americana sobre Derechos Humanos. Comentario. Konrad Adenauer Stiftung, Berlin, pp 180–206
Casara R, Melchior AP (2013) Teoría do Processo Penal Brasileiro. Vol. I, Dogmática e Crítica: Conceitos Fundamentais. Lumen Juris, Rio de Janeiro
Catalano EM (2002) L'accertamento dei fatti processuali. Indice penale, pp 521–570
Cervini R (2000) Princípios de cooperação judicial penal internacional consagrados no Projeto de Protocolo de Assistência Jurídica Mútua em assuntos penais do Mercosul. In: Cervini R, Tavares J (eds) Princípios de Cooperação Judicial Penal Internacional no Protocolo do Mercosul. Revista dos Tribunais, São Paulo, pp 25–162
Cesari C (2001) "Giusto processo", contraddittorio ed irripetibilità degli atti di indagine. Rivista italiana di diritto e procedura penale, pp 56–87
Cesari C (2006) Le clausole di irrilevanza del fatto nel sistema processuale penale. Giappichelli, Torino
Chiavario M (1969) La Convenzione europea dei diritti dell'uomo nel sistema delle fonti normative in materia penale. Giuffrè, Milano
Chiavario M (1971) Il pubblico ministero organo di giustizia? Rivista italiana di diritto e procedura penale, pp 714–743
Chiavario M (1975) Appunti sulla problematica dell'"azione" nel processo penale italiano: incertezze, prospettive e limiti. Rivista trimestrale di diritto e procedura civile, pp 864 ff
Chiavario M (1984) Processo penale e garanzie della persona, II, Le garanzie fondamentali, 3rd edn. Giuffrè, Milano
Chiavario M (1991) Cooperazione internazionale ed obiettivi di garanzia e di efficienza nella nuova disciplina dei rapporti con autorità giudiziarie straniere. In: Chiavario M (ed) Commento al nuovo codice di procedura penale, vol VI. Utet, Torino, pp 661–678
Chiavario M (2001) Il "diritto al processo" delle vittime dei reati e la Corte europea dei diritti dell'uomo. Rivista di diritto processuale, pp 938 ss
Chiavario M (2005) Una riforma inevitabile: ma basterà? La Legislazione penale pp 253–259
Chiavario M (2008) La "lunga marcia" dei diritti dell'uomo nel processo penale. In: Balsamo A, Kostoris RE (eds) Giurisprudenza europea e processo penale italiano. Giappichelli, Torino, pp 11–31
Chiavario M (2013) Manuale dell'estradizione e del mandato d'arresto europeo. Utet, Torino
Chiavario M (2015) Diritto processuale penale, 6th edn. Utet, Torino
Ciampi S (2014) Diritto all'informazione nei procedimenti penali: il recepimento *low profile* della direttiva 2012/13/UE da parte del d.lgs. 1° luglio 2014 n. 101. *Letter of Rights* e *Full Disclosure* nel procedimento penale italiano. www.penalecontemporaneo.it. Accessed 24 Sept 2014
Confalonieri A (1996) Il controllo giurisdizionale sulla custodia cautelare: esperienza italiana e francese a confront. Cedam, Padova
Conso G (1950) Il provvedimento di archiviazione. Rivista italiana di diritto penale, pp 320 ff.
Conso G (1969) Costituzione e processo penale. Giuffrè, Milano
Conti C (2000) Le due anime del contraddittorio. Diritto penale e processo, pp 197–202
Conti C (2001a) Principio del contraddittorio e utilizzabilità delle precedenti dichiarazioni. Diritto penale e processo, pp 592–607

Conti C (2001b) Giusto processo (diritto processuale penale). In: Enciclopedia del diritto, vol V Agg. Giuffrè, Milano, pp 627–649

Conti C (2003) L'imputato nel procedimento connesso. Diritto al silenzio e obbligo di verità. Cedam, Padova

Conti C (2013) Contraddittorio. In: Digesto delle discipline penalistiche, vol VII Agg. Utet, Torino, pp 103–122

Conti R (2015) La richiesta di "parere consultivo" alla Corte europea delle Alte Corti introdotto dal Protocollo n.16 annesso alla CEDU e il rinvio pregiudiziale alla Corte di Giustizia UE. Prove d'orchestra per una *nomofilachia europea*. In: Lamarque E (ed) La richiesta di pareri consultivi alla Corte di Strasburgo da parte delle più alte giurisdizioni nazionali. Prime riflessioni in vista della ratifica del Protocollo 16 CEDU. Giappichelli, Torino, pp 97–133

Cordero F (1958) Archiviazione. In Enciclopedia del diritto, vol II. Giuffrè, Milano, pp 1025–1035

Cordero F (1963) Tre studi sulle prove penali. Giuffrè, Milano

Cordero F (1966) Ideologie del processo penale. Giuffrè, Milano

Cordero F (1987a) Procedura penale, 9th edn. Giuffrè, Milano

Cordero F (1987b) Procedura penale, 9th edn. Giuffrè, Milano

Cordero F (1991) Procedura penale, 1st edn. Giuffrè, Milano

Cordero F (1992) Codice commentato, 2nd edn. Utet, Torino

Cordero F (2012) Procedura penale, 9th edn. Giuffrè, Milano

Curtotti Nappi D (2007) I nuovi orizzonti investigativi del difensore: le informazioni assunte all'estero. Osservatorio del processo penale 2:14 ff

Curtotti Nappi D (2014) La normativa in tema di assistenza linguistica tra direttiva europea e nuove prassi applicative. Diritto penle e giustizia pp 115–132

Daniele M (2008) Regole di esclusione della prova e giurisprudenza della Corte europea: profili di potenziale conflitto. In: Balsamo A, Kostoris RE (eds) Giurisprudenza europea e processo penale italiano. Giappichelli, Torino, pp 383–394

Daniele M (2014) La metamorfosi del diritto delle prove nella Direttiva sull'ordine europeo di indagine penale. www.penalecontemporaneo.it. Accessed 20 Nov 2014

De Amicis G (2007) Mandato di arresto europeo e limiti massimi di custodia cautelare: incostituzionalità o "interpretazione costitutionalmente orientatata" del motive di rifiuto alla consegna? Giurisprudenza di merito, pp 1435 ff

De Amicis G (2013) All'incrocio tra diritti fondamentali, mandato d'arresto europeo e decisioni contumaciali: la Corte di Giustizia e il "caso Melloni". Un commento a margine della sentenza Melloni della Corte di Giustizia. www.penalecontemporaneo.it. Accessed 7 June 2013

De Matteis L (2008) Diversa qualificazione giuridica dell'accusa e tutela del diritto di difesa. In: Balsamo A, Kostoris RE (eds) Giurisprudenza europea e processo penale italiano. Giappichelli, Torino, pp 215–233

De Salvia M (2008) L'obbligo degli Stati di conformarsi alle decisioni della Corte europea e del Comitato dei Ministri del Consiglio d'Europa. In: Balsamo A, Kostoris RE (eds) Giurisprudenza europea e processo penale italiano. Giappichelli, Torino, pp 67–79

Delmanto R Jr (2004) Inatividade no Processo Penal Brasileiro. Revista dos Tribunais, São Paulo

Di Bitonto ML (2004) Profili dispositivi dell'accertamento penale. Giappichelli, Torino

Di Chiara G (1994a) Il contraddittorio nei riti camerali. Giuffrè, Milano

Di Chiara G (1994b) Cooperazione tra Stati ed assunzione della rpova in territorio straniero. Trasferte giudiziarie e recenti esperienze: il processo c.d. *Big John*. In: Di Federico G, Di Chiara G (eds) Cooperazione tra Stati ed assunzione della rpova in territorio straniero. Lo Scarabeo, Bologna, pp 1ff

Di Chiara G (1997) Testimonianza dei "soggetti deboli" e limiti all'esame incrociato. Giurisprudenza costituzionale pp 2564 ff

Di Chiara G (2002) Incidente probatorio. In: Enciclopedia del diritto, VI Agg. Giuffrè, Milano, pp 546–565

Di Chiara G (2003) Diritto processuale penale. In: Fiandaca G, Di Chiara G (eds) Una introduzione al sistema penale. Per una lettura costituzionalmente orientata. Jovene, Napoli, pp 189–365

Di Chiara G (2009a) "Against the Administration of Justice in Secret": la pubblicità delle procedure giudiziarie tra Corte europea e assetti del sistema italiano. In: Balsamo A, Kostoris RE (eds) Giurisprudenza europea e processo penale italiano. Giappichelli, Torino, pp 293–308

Di Chiara G (ed) (2009b) Eccezioni al contraddittorio e giusto processo. Un itinerario attraverso la giurisprudenza. Giappichelli, Torino

Di Chiara G (2012) Report on Italy. In: Ruggeri S (ed) Liberty and Security in Europe. A comparative analysis of pre-trial precautionary measures in criminal proceedings. V&R Unipress (Universitätsverlag Osnabrück), Göttingen, pp 121–139

Di Martino A (2011) Questo limite non è un termine. Tecnicismi «specifici» e «collaterali» nel contesto di un sistema penale internazionalizzato. Archivio penale, pp 1–13

Di Stasi A (2014) La Corte interamericana e la Corte europea dei diritti dell'uomo: da un *trans-regional judicial dialogue* ad una *cross-fertilization*? In: Cassetti L, Di Stasi A, Landa Arroyo L (eds) Diritti e giurisprudenza. La Corte interamericana dei diritti umani e la Corte europea di Strasburgo. Jovene, Napoli, pp 1–25

Dondé Matute J (2013) The Inter-American system of human rights and transnational inquiries. In: Ruggeri S (ed) Transnational inquiries and the protection of fundamental rights in criminal proceedings. A study in memory of Vittorio Grevi and Giovanni Tranchina. Springer, Heidelberg, pp 41–50

Ebert A (2000) Der Tatverdacht im Strafverfahren unter spezieller Berücksichtigung des Tatnachweises im Strafbefehlsverfahren. Peter Lang, Frankfurt am Main

Erb V (1999) legalität und Opportunität. Duncker & Humblot, Berlin

Ferrua P (1990) La difesa nel processo penale: profilo di una funzione. In: in Id., Studi sul processo penale, vol I. Giappichelli, Torino, pp 15–35

Ferrua P (1992) La sentenza costituzionale n. 255 del 1992: declino del processo accusatorio. Rivista italiana di diritto e procedura penale, pp 1455ff

Ferrua P (1998) Un giardino proibito per il legislatore: la valutazione delle prove. Questione giustizia, pp 597ff

Ferrua P (2009) La dialettica regola-eccezioni nell'impianto dell'art. 111 Cost.: il quadro sistematico. In: Di Chiara G (ed) Eccezioni al contraddittorio e giusto processo. Un itinerario attraverso la giurisprudenza. Giappichelli, Torino, pp 3–40

Ferrua P (2012) Il 'giusto processo', 3rd edn. Zanichelli, Bologna

Ferrua P (2013) La prova nel processo penale: profili generali. In: Ferrua P, Marzaduri E, Spangher G (eds) La prova penale. Giappichelli, Torino, pp 1–56

Findlay M (2011) Locating victim communities within global justice and governance. In: Crawford A (ed) International and comparative criminal justice and Urban Governance. Cambridge University Press, Cambridge, pp 109–139

Fiorio C (2008) La nuova prova nel processo penale. Giappichelli, Torino

Fraga M (1985) O Novo Estatuto do Estrangeiro Comentado. Forense, Rio de Janeiro

Gaeta P (2001) Le modifiche alla disciplina delle informazioni assunte dal pubblico ministero e dalla polizia giudiziaria. In: Tonini P (ed) Giusto processo. Nuove norme sulla formazione e valutazione della prova. Cedam, Padova, pp 431–443

Gaeta P (2012) Dell'interpretazione conforme alla C.E.D.U.: ovvero, la ricombinazione genica del processo penale. Archivio penale, pp 1–43

Gaito A (1987) Commento all'art. 663. In: Conso G, Grevi V (eds) Commentario breve al codice di procedura penale. Cedam, Padova

Galantini N (1992) L'inutilizzabilità della prova nel processo penale. Cedam, Padova

Galgani B (2013) Extradition, political offence and the discrimination clause. In: Ruggeri S (ed) Transnational inquiries and the protection of fundamental rights in criminal proceedings. A study in memory of Vittorio Grevi and Giovanni Tranchina. Springer, Heidelberg, pp 167–191

García Ramírez S (2011) El debido proceso en la jurisprudencia de la Corte Interamericana de Derechos Humanos. Jornadas Itinerantes del Instituto de la Judicatura Federal del Consejo de la Judicatura del Poder Judicial de la Federación de México. http://www.ijf.cjf.gob.mx/cursosesp/2012/jornadasitinerantes/procesoSGR.pdf

Garlati L (ed) (2010) L'inconscio inquisitorio. L'eredità del Codice Rocco nella cultura processualpenalistica italiana. Giuffrè, Milano

Gascón Inchausti F (1999) El control de la fiabilidad probatoria: "prueba sobre la prueba" en el proceso penal. Tirant Lo Banch, Valencia

Giacomolli NJ (2008) Reformas(?) do Processo Penal. Lumen Juris, Rio de Janeiro

Giacomolli NJ (2013) Prisão, liberdade e as cautelares alternativas ao cárcere. Marcial Pons, São Paulo

Giacomolli NJ (2014) O devido processo penal. Abordagem conforme a Constituição Federal e o Pacto de São José da Costa Rica. Atlas S.A., São Paulo

Gialuz M (2008) Applicazione della pena su richiesta delle parti. In: Enciclopedia del diritto, Annali II-1. Giuffrè, Milano, pp 13–47

Gialuz M (2012) Commento all'art. 5 In: Bartole S, De Sena P, Zagrebelsky V (eds) Commentario breve alla Convenzione europea per la salvaguardia dei diritti dell'uomo e dele libertà fondamentali. Cedam, Padova

Gialuz M (2013) La lingua come diritto: il diritto all'interpretazione e alla traduzione nel processo penale. In: Ruggieri F, Rafaraci T, Di Paolo G, Marcolini S, Belfiore R (eds) Processo penale, lingua e Unione Europea. Cedam, Padova, pp 227ff

Gialuz M (2015) Dalla Corte di Giustizia importanti indicazioni esegetiche in relazione alle prime due Direttive sui diritti dell'imputato. www.penalecontemporaneo.it. Accessed 11 Nov 2015

Gimeno Sendra V (2007) Derecho procesal penal, 2nd edn. Colex, Majadahonda

Giostra G (1994) L'archiviazione. Lineamenti sistematici e questioni interpretative, 2nd edn. Giappichelli, Torino

Giostra G (2001) Contraddittorio (principio del): II) Diritto processuale penale. In: Enciclopedia giuridica Treccani, vol VIII. Treccani, Roma, pp 1–13

Giostra G (2002) Prova e contraddittorio. Note a margine di una garbata polemica. Cassazione penale, pp 3288–3292

Giuliani L (2016) Indagini preliminari e udienza preliminare. In: Conso G, Grevi V, Bargis M (eds) Compendio di procedura penale, 8th edn. Wolters Kluwer/Cedam, Padova, pp 457–591

Gleß S (2006) Beweisrechtsgrundsätze einer grenzüberschreitenden Strafverfolgung. Nomos, Baden-Baden

Gleß S (2014) Europäisches Beweisrecht. In: Sieber U, Brüner FH, Satzger H, von Heintschell-Heinegg B (eds) Europäisches Strafrecht, 2nd edn. Nomos, Baden-Baden, pp 677–695

Gomes LF, Mazzuoli V d O (2010) Comentários à convenção americana sobre direitos humanos: Pacto de San José da Costa Rica, 3rd edn. Revista dos Tribunais, São Paulo

Grevi V (2000a) Alla ricerca di un processo penale giusto. Giuffrè, Milano

Grevi V (2000b) Giustizia, l'accordo tra Italia e Spagna un modello europeo. In: Correre della Sera (4 December 2000)

Grifantini FM (2007) Utilizzabilità in dibattimento degli atti provenienti dale fasi anteriori. In: Ferrua P, Grifantini FM, Illuminati G, Orlandi R (eds) La prova nel dibattimento penale, 3rd edn. Giappichelli, Torino, pp 167–313

Grilli L (1990) Le notificazioni penali. Giuffrè, Milano

Gusy C (2010). Article 104. In: von Mangoldt H, Klein F, Starck C (eds) Kommentar zum Grundgesetz, III vol. (Arts. 83–146), 6th edn. Vahlen Verlag, München, paras. 1–78

Harris D, O'Boyle M, Warbrick C (2009) Law of the European convention on human rights, 2nd edn. Oxford University Press, Oxford

Hassan Choukr F (1995) Garantias constitucionais na investigação criminal. Revista dos Tribunais, São Paulo

Hassan Choukr F (2011) Código de Processo Penal. Comentários Consolidados e Crítica Jurisprudencial, 5th edn. Lumen Juris, Rio de Janeiro

Hassemer W (1992) Legalität und Opportunität im Strafverfahren – eine Skizze. In: Ostendorf H (ed) Strafverfolgung und Strafverzicht. Festschrift zum 125. Bestehen der Staatsanwaltschaft Schleswig-Holstein. Carl Heymanns, Köln et al

Hauck P (2014) Heimliche Strafverfolgung und Schutz der Privatheit. Mohr Siebeck, Tübingen

Hecker B (2013) Mutual recognition and transfer of evidence. The European Evidence Warrant. In: Ruggeri S (ed) Transnational inquiries and the protection of fundamental rights in criminal

proceedings. A study in memory of Vittorio Grevi and Giovanni Tranchina. Springer, Heidelberg, pp 269–278
Hecker B (2015) Europäisches Strafrecht, 5th edn. Springer, Berlin-Heidelberg
Heger M, Wolter K (2015) 2. Hauptteil: Auslieferung – 4. Teil. Recht der EG/EU. In: Ambos K, König S, Rackow P (eds) Rechtshilferecht in Strafsachen. Nomos, Baden-Baden, pp 319–495
Iasevoli C (2007) Persona offesa dal reato. In: Enciclopedia giuridica Treccani, vol XXIII. Treccani, Roma, pp 1–8
Ibáñez Rivas JM (2014) Article 8. In: Steiner and Uribe (eds) Convención Americana sobre Derechos Humanos. Comentario. Konrad Adenauer Stiftung, Berlin, pp 207–254
Illuminati G (1997) Relazione. In: G.I.P. e libertà personale. Verso un contraddittorio anticipato? Jovene, Napoli, pp 31 ff
Illuminati G (2003) Il giudizio senza oralità. In: Verso la scoperta di un modello processuale. Giuffrè, Milano, pp 67 ff
Illuminati G (2016) Giudizio. In: Conso G, Grevi V, Bargis M (eds) Compendio di procedura penale, 8th edn. Wolters Kluwer/Cedam, Padova, pp 689–760
Jackson JD (2005) The effect of human rights on criminal evidentiary processes: towards convergence, divergence or realignment? Mod Law Rev 68:737–764
Jackson J, Johnstone J (2005) The reasonable time requirement: an independent and meaningful right. Crim Law Rev, pp 3 ff.
Jackson JD, Summers SJ (2012) The internationalisation of criminal evidence: beyond the common law and civil law traditions. Cambridge University Press, Cambridge
Jescheck H-H (1955) Entwicklung, Aufgaben und Methoden der Strafrechtsvergleichung. Mohr Siebeck, Tübingen
Joseph S, Schultz J, Castan M (2004) The international covenant on civil and political rights. Cases, materials and commentary, 2nd edn. Oxford University Press, Oxford
Julio Estrada A (2013) Transnational investigation of criminal procedure and the protection of victims of serious human rights violations in Latin American constitutional jurisprudence. In: Ruggeri S (ed) Transnational inquiries and the protection of fundamental rights in criminal proceedings. A study in memory of Vittorio Grevi and Giovanni Tranchina. Springer, Heidelberg, pp 125–137
Klitsch S (2009) Der neue EU-Rahmenbeschluss yu Abwesenheitsverurteilungen – ein Appell zur Revision. Zeitschrift für internationale Strafrechtsdogmatik, pp 1–21
Kostoris RE (1993) I consulenti tecnici nel processo penale. Giuffrè, Milano
Kostoris RE (2008) Verso un processo penale non più statocentrico. In: Balsamo A, Kostoris RE (eds) Giurisprudenza europea e processo penale italiano. Giappichelli, Torino, pp 3–10
Krisch N (2008) The open architecture of European human rights law. Mod Law Rev 71:183–216
Krüßmann T (2009) Transnationales Strafprozessrecht. Nomos, Baden-Baden
Kühne H-H (2009) In: Kühne H-H, Miehsler H and Vogler T, Article 6. In: Pabel K, Schmahl S (eds) (2013) Internationaler Kommentar zur Europäischen Menschenrechtskonvention. Carl Heymanns, Köln et al
Kühne H-H (2015) Strafprozessrecht. Eine Systematische Darstellung des deutschen und europäischen Strafverfahrensrechts, 9th edn. C.F. Müller, Heidelberg
Lamarque E, Viganò F (2014) Sulle ricadute interne della sentenza Scoppola. Ovvero: sul gioco di squadra tra Cassazione e Corte costituzionale nell'adeguamento del nostro ordinamento alle sentenze di Strasburgo (nota a C. cost. n. 210/2013). www.penalecontemporaneo.it. Accessed 31 Mar 2014
Lauria Tucci R (2004) Direitos e garantias individuais no processo penal brasileiro. Saraiva, São Paulo
Lauria Tucci R, Cruz e Tucci JR (1993) Devido Processo Legal e Tutela Jurisdicional. Revista dos Tribunais, São Paulo
Leone G (1961) Trattato di diritto processuale penale, vol II. Jovene, Napoli
Lo Voi F (2005) Il procedimento davanti alla Corte di appello e i provvedimenti *de libertate*. Il conseno. In: Bargis M, Selvaggi E (eds) Mandato d'arresto europeo. Dall'estradizione alle procedure di consegna. Giappichelli, Torino, pp 241–268

Lopes A Jr (2001) Sistemas de Investigação Preliminar no Processo Penal. Lumen Juris, Rio de Janeiro
Lopes A Jr (2011) O Novo Regime Jurídico da Prisão Processual, Liberdade Provisória e Medidas Cautelares Diversas. Lumen Juris, Rio de Janeiro
Lopes A Jr (2013) Direito Processual Penal, 10th edn. Saraiva, São Paulo
Lopes A Jr (2017) Direito Processual Penal, 14th edn. Saraiva, São Paulo
Lopes A Jr, Badaró GH (2009) Direito ao Processo Penal no Prazo Razoável, 2nd edn. Lumen Juris, Rio de Janeiro
Lopes A Jr, Jakobsen Glockner R (2013) Investigação preliminar no processo penal. Saraiva, São Paulo
Lorusso S (2008) Una scelta di efficienza processuale che non legittima forzature o abusi. Guida al diritto 11:67ff
Lozzi G (1997) I princìpi di oralità e del contraddittorio nel processo penale. Rivista italiana di diritto e procedura penale, pp 669–693
Lozzi G (2014) Lezioni di procedura penale, 9th edn. Giappichelli, Torino
Luiso FP (1981) Principio del contraddittorio ed efficacia della sentenza verso terzi. Giuffrè, Milano
Maffei S (2012) The right to confrontation in Europe. Absent, anonymous and vulnerable witnesses. Europa Law Publishing
Maggio P (2010) Prova e valutazione giudiziale dei comportamenti mafiosi: i risvolti processuali. In: Fiandaca G, Visconti C (eds) Scenari di Mafia. Orizzonti criminologici e innovazioni normative. Giappichelli, Torino, pp 491–519
Maggio P (2012) Judicial reviews against deprivation of liberty. In: Ruggeri S (ed) Liberty and security in Europe. A comparative analysis of pre-trial precautionary measures in criminal proceedings. V&R Unipress (Universitätsverlag Osnabrück), Göttingen, pp 33–44
Mangiaracina A (2010) Garanzie partecipative e giudizio in absentia. Giappichelli, Torino
Mangiaracina A (2014) A new and controversial scenario in the gathering of evidence at the european level: the proposal for a directive on the European investigation order. Utrecht Law Rev 10(1):113–133
Marchetti MR (1990) L'estradizione: profili processuali e principio di specialità. Cedam, Padova
Marchetti MR (1993) Commento all'art. 714. In: Chiavario M (ed) Commento al nuovo codice di procedura penale. 1st Agg. Utet, Torino, pp 456ff
Marchetti MR (2005) L'assistenza giudiziaria internazionale. Giuffrè, Milano
Marchetti MR (2008) Rogatoria (dir. proc. pen.) In: Enciclopedia del diritto, Annali II-1. Giuffrè, Milano, pp 1035–1074
Marchetti MR (2011) Dalla Convenzione di assistenza giudiziaria in materia penale dell'Unione europea al mandato europeo di ricerca delle prove e all'ordine europeo di indagine penale. In: Rafaraci T (ed) La cooperazione di polizia e giudiziaria in material penale nell'Unione europea dopo il Trattato di Lisbona. Giuffrè, Milano, pp 135–167
Marchetti MR (2016) Rapporti giurisdizionali con autorità straniere. In: Conso G, Grevi V, Bargis M (eds) Compendio di procedura penale, 8th edn. Wolters Kluwer Italia/Cedam, Padova, pp 989–1072
Marques da Silva IL (2008) Reforma Processual Penal de 2008. Revista dos Tribunais, São Paulo
Martinico G (2012) Part 1. In: Martinico G, Pollicino O (eds) The Interaction between Europe's legal systems. Judicial Dialogue and the Creation of Supranation Laws. Edward Elgar, Cheltenham
Martinico G, Pollicino O (2012) The interaction between Europe's legal systems. Judicial dialogue and the creation of supranation laws. Edward Elgar, Cheltenham
Marzaduri E (1983) Autorità giudiziaria ed autorità amministrativa nel procedimento di estradizione passiva. Rivista italiana di diritto e procedura penale, pp 611–644
Marzaduri E (1986) Riesame dei provevdimenti restrittivi della libertà personale. In: Novissimo digesto italiano, Appendice. Utet, Torino, pp 771–787
Marzaduri E (1989) Imputato e imputazione. In: Digesto delle discipline penalistiche, vol VI. Utet, Torino, pp 278ff
Marzaduri E (1990) Brevi considerazioni sui poteri del giudice nell'applicazione della pena su richiesta delle parti. Cassazione penale, pp 729–733

Marzaduri E (1993) Libertà personale e garanzie giurisdizionali nel procedimento di estradizione passiva. Giuffrè, Milano

Marzaduri E (1994) Misure cautelari personali (princìpi generali e disciplina). In: Digesto delle discipline penalistiche, vol VIII. Utet, Torino, pp 59 ff

Marzaduri E (1996) Azione: d) diritto processuale penale. In: Enciclopedia giuridica Treccani, vol V. Treccani, Roma, pp 1–23

Marzaduri E (1997) Commento agli artt. 2-3 legge 234/1997. La Legislazione penale, pp 750–765

Marzaduri E (1998) Commento all'art. 275. In: Chiavario M (ed) Commento al nuovo codice di procedura penale, vol III Agg. Utet, Torino, pp 162–192

Marzaduri E (2000) Commento all'art. 1 legge costituzionale 2/1999. In: La Legislazione penale, pp. 762-804

Marzaduri E (2002a) Giusto processo e misure cautelari. In: Kostoris RE (ed) Il giusto processo, tra contraddittorio e diritto al silenzio. Giappichelli, Torino, pp. 261ff.

Marzaduri E (2002b) Commento all'art. 3 l. 63/2001. La Legislazione penale, pp 164–172

Marzaduri E (2004a) Note minime in tema di giusto processo penale. In: Various Authors, Nuove forme di tutela delle situazioni soggettive. Aspetti pubblicistici. Giuffrè, Milano, pp 283–298

Marzaduri E (2004b) Indagini preliminari e modello processuale: profili di incoerenza originaria del codice Vassalli. In: Verso la riscoperta di un modello processuale. Giuffrè, Milano, pp 223–226

Marzaduri E (2004c) Commento agli artt. 1-3 legge 134/2003. La Legislazione penale, pp 241–258

Marzaduri E (2006) Commento agli artt. 1-2 l. 69/2005. In: Chiavario M, Marzaduri E (eds) Il mandato di arresto europeo. Utet, Torino, pp 58–96

Marzaduri E (2007) Commento agli artt. 1–2. In: Chiavario M, De Francesco G, Manzione D, Marzaduri E (eds) Il mandato di arresto europeo. Commento alla legge 22 aprile 2005 n. 69. Utet, Torino, pp 57–96

Marzaduri E (2008) Spunti per una riflessione sui presupposti applicativi delle intercettazioni telefoniche a fini probatori. Cassazione penale, pp 4833–4853

Marzaduri E (2009) La prova negoziata e l'art. 111 Cost.: tra deroga al contraddittorio e valorizzazione dei profili dispositivi dell'accertamento penale. In: Di Chiara G (ed) Eccezioni al contraddittorio e giusto processo. Un itinerario attraverso la giurisprudenza. Giappichelli, Torino, pp 189–224

Marzaduri E (2012) The application of pre-trial precautionary measures. In: Ruggeri S (ed) Liberty and security in Europe. A comparative analysis of pre-trial precautionary measures in criminal proceedings. V&R Unipress (Universitätsverlag Osnabrück), Göttingen, pp 17–32

Marzaduri E (2016a) Procedimento davanti al tribunale in composizione monocratica. In: Conso G, Grevi V, Bargis M (eds), Compendio di procedura penale, 8th edn. Wolters Kluwer Italia/Cedam, Padova, pp 761–800

Marzaduri E (2016b) Procedimento penale davanti al giudice di pace. In: Conso G, Grevi V, Bargis M (eds) Compendio di procedura penale, 8th edn. Wolters Kluwer Italia/Cedam, Padova, pp 1099–1147

Mazza O (2014) Contraddittorio (principio del) (diritto processuale penale). In: Enciclopedia del diritto, Annali VII. Giuffrè, Milano, pp. 247–274

Mazzuoli V d O (2011) O Controle Jurisdictional da Convencionalidade dais Leis, 2nd edn. Revista dos Tribunais, São Paulo

Melillo G (2009) Tecniche investigative speciali e squadre investigative comuni. In: Illuminati G (ed) Prova penale e Unione Europea. Bononia University Press, Bologna, pp 93–111

Montagna M (2010) Art. 294. In: Giarda A, Spangher G (eds), Codice di procedura penale commentato. I Tomo, 4th edn. Ipsoa, Milano

Moraes Pitombo SM (1983) O indiciamento como Ato de Polícia Judiciária. Revista dos Tribunais 577:313–316

Morosini PG (2009) Provata condotta illecita e processo per fatti di criminalità organizzata. In: Di Chiara G (ed) Eccezioni al contraddittorio e giusto processo. Un itinerario attraverso la giurisprudenza. Giappichelli, Torino, pp 387–411

Müller-Franken S (2010) Art. 104. In: Stern K, Becker F (eds) Grundrechte-Kommentar, Carl Heymanns Verlag, Köln, paras. 1–129

Negri D (2004) *Fumus commissi delicti*. La prova per le fattispecie cautelari. Giappichelli, Torino

Negri D (2005) Commento all'art. 1 Decreto-legge 17/2005. La Legislazione penale, pp 260–291

Negri D (2014) L'imputato presente al processo. Una ricostruzione sistematica. Giappichelli, Torino

Nobili M (1998) Scenari e trasformazioni del processo penale. Cedam, Padova

Nobili M (2001) Giusto processo e indagini difensive: verso una nuova procedura penale? Diritto penale e processo, pp 5–14

G de Souza N (2014) Código de Processo Penal Comentado, 13th edn. Forense, Rio de Janeiro

Orlandi R (1992) Atti e informazioni dell'autorità amministrativa nel processo penale. Giuffrè, Milano

Orlandi R (2009) Il giudizio immediato cosiddetto custodiale. In: Amato G, Santorello C (eds) Misure urgenti di sicurezza pubblica. Utet, Torino, pp 85–89

Orlandi R (2010) L'attività argomentativa delle parti nel dibattimento penale. In: Ferrua P, Grifantini FM, Illuminati G, Orlandi R (eds) La prova nel dibattimento penale, 4th edn. Giappichelli, Torino, pp 3 ff.

Oubiña Barbolla S (2012) The European arrest warrant in law and practice. In: Ruggeri S (ed) Liberty and security in Europe. A comparative analysis of pre-trial precautionary measures in criminal proceedings. V&R Unipress (Universitätsverlag Osnabrück), Göttingen, pp 47–66

Pacelli E (2012) Curso de Processo Penal, 16th edn. Atlas, São Paulo

Paeffgen H-U (1986) Vorüberlegungen zu einer Dogmatik des Untersuchungshaftsrechts. Carl Heymann, Mainz

Paolozzi G (1988) Il procedimento alternativo per decreto penale. Giuffrè, Milano

Parlato L (2012) Il contributo della vittima tra azione e prova. Torri del Vento, Palermo

Peers S (2010) The proposed European Investigation Order: assault on human rights and national sovereignty. www.statewatch.org. Accessed May 2010

Pellegrini Grinover A (1990) As garantias constitucionais do processo. In: Pellegrini Grinover A (ed) Novas tendências do direito processual. Forense Universitária, Rio de Janeiro, pp 1–119

Pellegrini Grinover A (1996) Influência do Código-Modelo de Processo Penal para Ibero-América na legislação latino-americana. Convergências e dissonâncias comos os sistemas italiano e brasileiro. In: Pellegrini Grinover A (ed) O Processo em Evolução. Forense Universitária, Rio de Janeiro, pp 218–241

Pellegrini Grinover A, Scarance Fernandes A, Magalhães Gomes Filho A (2001) As nulidades no processo penal, 7th edn. Revista dos Tribunais, São Paulo

Pereira AC, Ambos K (eds) (2006) Mercosul e União Europeia. Lumen Juris, Rio de Janeiro

Peukert W (2009) Art. 5. In: Frowein J, Peukert W (eds) EMRK-Kommentar. Engel Verlag, Rehl am Rein, pp 70–139

Pieth M (2012) Schweizerisches Strafprozessrecht, 2nd edn. Helbing Lichtenhahn Verlag, Basel

Pimenta Lopes MV (2013) A paridade de armas no processo penal. www.conteudojuridico.com.br

Pisani M (2001) In tema di assunzione all'estero delle prove da oarte dell'autorità giudiziaria italiana. Rivista italiana di diritto e procedura penale, pp 557–573

Polastri Lima M (2002) A Prova Penal. Lumen Juris, Rio de Janeiro

Pollicino O (2008) The Constitutional Court at the crossroads between constitutional parochialism and co-operative constitutionalism. Judgments No. 348 and 349 of 22 and 24 October 2007. Eur Const Law Rev, pp 363–382

Pollicino O (2010) Allargamento ad est dello spazio giuridico europeo e rapporto tra Corti costituzionali e Corti europee. Verso una teoria generale dell'impatto interordinamentale del diritto sovranazionale? Giuffrè, Milano

Pollicino O (2014) La Corte costituzionale è una "alta giurisdizione nazionale" ai fini della richiesta di parere alla Corte EDU ex Protocollo 16? www.forumcostituzionale.it

Pollicino O (2015) Corte di giustizia e giudici nazionali: il moto "ascendente", ovverosia l'incidenza delle "tradizioni costituzionali comuni" nella tutela apprestata ai diritti dalla Corte dell'Unione. www.giurcost.org, pp 242–263

Pontes de Miranda FC (1979) História e Prática do Habeas Corpus, 8th edn. Saraiva, São Paulo

Quattrocolo S (2004) Esiguità del fatto e regole per l'esercizio dell'azione penale. Jovene, Napoli

Quattrocolo S (2011) Riqualificazione del fatto nella sentenza penale e tutela del contraddittorio. Jovene, Napoli

Quattrocolo S (2014) Il contumace cede la scena processuale all'assente, mentre l'irreperibile l'abbandona. Riflessioni a prima lettura sulla nuova disciplina del procedimento senza imputato. www.penalecontemporaneo.it. Accessed 30 Apr 2014

Quattrocolo S (2015) The right to information in EU legislation. In: Ruggeri S (ed) Human rights in European criminal law. New developments in European legislation and case law after the Lisbon treaty. Springer, Heidelberg, pp 81–93

Rafaraci T (2011) Il diritto di difesa nelle procedure di cooperazione giudiziaria nel contesto dell'Unione europea. In: Rafaraci T (ed) La cooperazione di polizia e giudiziaria in materia penale nell'Unione europea dopo il Trattato di Lisbona. Giuffrè, Milano, pp 119–132

Rafaraci T (2012) The application of the principle of mutual recognition to decisions on supervisions measures as an alternative to provisional detention. In: Ruggeri S (ed) Liberty and security. Liberty and security in Europe. A comparative analysis of pre-trial precautionary measures in criminal proceedings. V&R Unipress, Göttingen/Osnabrück, pp 67–83

Rafaraci T (2013) The right of defence in EU judicial cooperation in criminal matters. In: Ruggeri S (ed) Transnational inquiries and the protection of fundamental rights in criminal proceedings. A study in memory of Vittorio Grevi and Giovanni Tranchina. Springer, Heidelberg, pp 331–343

Rafaraci T (2015) New perspectives for the protection of the victims in the EU. In: Ruggeri S (ed) Human rights in European criminal law. New developments in European legislation and case law after the Lisbon treaty. Springer, Heidelberg, pp 215–225

Randazzo B (2011) Il giudizio dinanzi alla Corte europea dei diritti: un nuovo processo costituzionale. www.rivistaaic.it

Renzikowski J (2004) Die nachträgliche Sicherungsverwahrung und die Europäische Menschenrechts - konvention. Juristische Rundschau, pp 271–275

Rivello PP (1993) Commento all'art. 7 Decreto-legge 306/1992. La Legislazione penale, pp 92–103

Roberts P, Zuckerman A (2010) Criminal evidence, 2nd edn. Oxford University Press, Oxford

Ruggeri S (2002) Esercizio dell'azione penale, pubblico ministero e persona offesa nella prospettiva del procedimento davanti al giudice di pace. Giurisorudenza italiana, pp 655–660

Ruggeri A (2007) La CEDU alla ricerca di una nuova identità, tra prospettiva formale-astratta e prospettiva assiologico-sostanziale d'inquadramento sistematico (a prima lettura di Corte cost. nn. 348 e 349 del 2007). www.forumcostituzionale.it

Ruggeri S (2008) Il procedimento per decreto penale. Dalla logica dell'accertamento sommario alla dinamica del giudizio. Giappichelli, Torino

Ruggeri S (2009) Il procedimento per decreto penale. In: Di Chiara G (ed) Eccezioni al contraddittorio e giusto processo. Un itinerario attraverso la giurisprudenza. Giappichelli, Torino, pp 133–188

Ruggeri A (2010) Corte costituzionale e Corti europee: il modello, le esperienze, le prospettive. Centro di documentazione europea (Università di Catania), http://www.cde.unict.it/sites/default/files/19_2010.pdf

Ruggeri S (2012) Personal Liberty in Europe. A comparative analysis of pre-trial precautionary measures in criminal proceedings. In: Ruggeri S (ed) Liberty and Security in Europe. A comparative analysis of pre-trial precautionary measures in criminal proceedings. V&R Unipress (Universitätsverlag Osnabrück), Göttingen, pp 185–243

Ruggeri S (2013a) Horizontal cooperation, obtaining evidence overseas and the respect for fundamental rights in the EU. From the European Commission's proposals to the proposal for a directive on a European Investigation Order: Towards a single tool of evidence gathering in the EU? In: Ruggeri S (ed) Transnational inquiries and the protection of fundamental rights in criminal proceedings, A study in memory of Vittorio Grevi and Giovanni Tranchina. Springer, Heidelberg, pp 279–310

Ruggeri S (2013b) Transnational inquiries and the protection of fundamental rights in comparative law. Models of gathering overseas evidence in criminal matters. In: Ruggeri S (ed) Transnational inquiries and the protection of fundamental rights in criminal proceedings, A study in memory of Vittorio Grevi and Giovanni Tranchina. Springer, Heidelberg, pp 533–573

Ruggeri S (ed) (2014a) Transnational evidence and multicultural inquiries in Europe. Developments in EU legislation and new challenges for human rights-oriented criminal investigations in cross-border cases. Springer, Heidelberg

Ruggeri A (2014b) Le fonti del diritto eurounitario ed i loro rapporti con le fonti nazionali. In: Costanzo P, Mezzetti L, Ruggeri A (eds) Lineamenti di diritto costituzionale dell'Unione Europea. Giappichelli, Torino, pp 268–324

Ruggeri A (2014c) Ragionando sui possibili sviluppi dei rapporti tra le Corti europee e i giudici nazionali (con specifico riguardo all'adesione dell'Unione alla CEDU e all'entrata in vigore del Prot. 16). www.forumcostituzionale.it

Ruggeri A (2015a) "Dialogue" between European and national courts, in the pursuit of the strongest protection of fundamental rights (with specific regard to criminal and procedural law). In: Ruggeri S (ed) Human rights in European criminal law. New developments in european legislation and case law after the Lisbon treaty. Springer, Heidelberg, pp 9–29

Ruggeri S (2015b) Investigative and prosecutorial discretion in criminal matters: the contribution of the Italian experience. In: Caianiello M, Hodgson J (eds), Discretionary criminal justice in a comparative context. Carolina Academic Press, Durham (North Carolina), pp 59–85

Ruggeri S (5/2015c) Procedimento per decreto penale e opposizione preventiva del querelante. Linee-guida per un modello partecipativo di giustizia penale monitoria. Processo penale e giustizia, pp 58–65

Sabatini G (1956) Trattato dei procedimenti speciali e complementari nel processo penale. Utet, Torino

Sarlet IW (2008) A Reforma do Judiciário e os tratados internacionais de direitos humanos: observações sobre o § 3° do art. 5° da Constituição. www.ambito-juridico.com.br

Savy D (2012) La tutela dei diritti fondamentali ed il rispetto dei principi generali del diritto dell'Unione nella disciplina del mandato d'arresto europeo. www.penalecontemporaneo.it

Scalfati A (1999) L'udienza preliminare. Profili di una disciplina in trasformazione. Cedam, Padova

Scalfati A (2000) Le nuove prospettive del decreto penale. In: Peroni F (ed) Il processo penale dopo la riforma del giudice unico. Cedam, Padova, pp 521 ff

Scarance Fernandes A (1995) O papel da vítima no processo criminal. Malheiros, São Paulo

Scarance Fernandes A (2010) Processo penal constitucional, 6th edn. Revista dos Tribunais, São Paulo

Scella A (2002) Tutela del contraddittorio e utilizzazione di prove formate in altri procedimenti. In: Kostoris RE (ed) Il giusto processo tra contraddittorio e diritto al silenzio. Giappichelli, Torino, pp 92 ff

Scella A (2011) Verso le squadre investigative comuni: lo scenario italiano. In: Rafaraci T (ed) La cooperazione di polizia e giudiziaria in materia penale nell'Unione europea dopo il Trattato di Lisbona. Giuffrè, Milano, pp 215–229

Schünemann B (2014) Solution models and principles governing the transnational evidence-gathering in the EU. In: Ruggeri S (ed) Transnational Evidence and Multicultural Inquiries in Europe. Developments in EU legislation and new challenges for human rights-oriented criminal investigations in cross-border cases. Springer, Heidelberg, pp 161–180

Sieber U (2006) Strafrechtsvergleichung im Wandel – Aufgaben, Methoden und Theoriensätze der vergleichenden Strafrechtswissenschaft. In: Sieber U, Albrecht H-J (eds) Strafrecht und Kriminologie unter einem Dach. Duncker & Humblot, Berlin, pp 78 ff.

Sinn A (2012) Report on Germany. In: Ruggeri S (ed) Liberty and security in Europe. A comparative analysis of pre-trial precautionary measures in criminal proceedings. V&R Unipress (Universitätsverlag Osnabrück), Göttingen, pp 105–120

Siracusano D (1973) Istruzione del processo penale. In: Enciclopedia del diritto, vol XXIII. Giuffrè, Milano, pp 166–204

Siracusano F (2008) Investigazioni difensive. In: Enciclopedia del diritto, Annali II-1. Giuffrè, Milano, pp 496–518

Siracusano F (2010) Giudizio immediato. In: Digesto delle discipline penalistiche. Agg., vol V. Utet, Torino, pp 399 ff

Siracusano F (2011) Nuove prospettive in materie di processo *in absentia* e procedure di consegna. In: Rafaraci T (ed) La cooperazione di polizia e giudiziaria in materia penale nell'Unione europea dopo il Trattato di Lisbona. Giuffrè, Milano, pp 85–104

Slaughter AM (1994) A typology of transjudicial communication. Univ Richmond Law Rev 29:99–137

Spangher G (1997) Relazione. In: G.I.P. e libertà personale. Verso un contraddittorio anticipato? Jovene, Napoli, pp 46 ff

Spencer JR (2014) Hearsay evidence in criminal proceedings, II edn. Hart Publishing, Oxford

Stavros S (1993) The guarantees for accused persons under Article 6 of the European convention on human rights. Martinus Nijhoff Publishers, Dortmund et al

Thaman SC (2013) Report on USA. In: Ruggeri S (ed) Transnational inquiries and the protection of fundamental rights in criminal proceedings. A study in memory of Vittorio Grevi and Giovanni Tranchina. Springer, Heidelberg, pp 509–529

Többens HW (1979) Der Freibeweis und die Prozessvoraussetzungen im Strafprozess. Freiburg i. Br

Tonini P (2001) Riforma del sistema probatorio: un'attuazione parziale del "giusto processo". Diritto penale e processo, pp 269–273

Tourinho Filho F da Costa (2010) Código de Processo Penal Comentado, vol I–II, 10th edn. Saraiva, São Paulo

Tranchina G (1961) Il procedimento per decreto penale e l'art. 24 della Costituzione. Rivista di diritto processuale, pp 516 ff

Tranchina G (1989) Persona offesa dal reato. In: Enciclopedia giuridica Treccani, vol XXIII. Treccani, Roma, pp 1 ff

Trechsel S (1987) Grundrechtsschutz bei der internationalen Zusammenarbeit in Strafsachen. Europäische GRUNDRECHTE-Zeitschrift, pp 69–78

Trechsel S (2005) Human rights in criminal proceedings. Oxford University Press, Oxford

Ubertis G (1995) Prova (in generale). In: Digesto delle discipline penalistiche, vol X. Utet, Torino, pp 296–338

Ubertis G (2002) Prova e contraddittorio. Cassazione penale, pp 1182–1184

Ubertis G (2003) Prova e contraddittorio. In: Verso la riscoperta di un nuovo modello processuale. Convegno in memoria di Antonino Galati. Giuffrè, Milano, pp 197–202

Ubertis G (2007) Sistema di procedura penale, 2nd edn. Utet, Torino

Ubertis G (2009a) Principi di procedura penale europea, 2nd edn. Raffaello Cortina, Milano

Ubertis G (2009b) La prova dichiarativa debole: problemi e prospettive in materie di assunzione della testimonianza della vittima vulnerabile alla luce della gurisprudenza sovranazionale. Cassazione penale, pp 4058–4067

Ubertis G (2013) Sistema di procedura penale, Principi generali, vol I, 3rd edn. Utet, Torino

van Hoek A, Luchtmann M (2006) The European convention on human rights and transnational cooperation in criminal matters. In: van Hoek A et al (eds) Multilevel governance in enforcement and adjudication. Intersentia, Antwerp, pp 25–92

Vallines García E (2006) Los equipos conjuntos de investigación penal. Ed. Colex, Madrid

Viganò F (2014) Convenzione europea dei diritti dell'uomo e resistenze nazionalistiche: Corte costituzionale italiana e Corte di Strasburgo tra "guerra" e "dialogo". Qualche osservazione dall'angolo visuale di un penalista. www.penalecontemporaneo.it

Vogel J (2010) Transkulturelles Strafrecht. Goltdammer's Archiv für Strafrecht 157:1–13

Vogel B (2017) "In camera"-Verfahren als Gewährung effektiven Rechtsschutzes? Neue Entwicklungen im europäischen Sicherheitsrecht. Zeitschrift für die internationale Strafrechtsdogmatik, pp 28–38

Vogler R (2012) England and Wales. In: Ruggeri S (ed) Liberty and security in Europe. A comparative analysis of pre-trial precautionary measures in criminal proceedings. V&R Unipress (Universitätsverlag Osnabrück), Göttingen, pp 87–103

Vogler R (2013) Transnational inquiries and the protection of human rights in the case-law of the European court of human rights. In: Ruggeri S (ed) Transnational inquiries and the protection of fundamental rights in criminal proceedings. A study in memory of Vittorio Grevi and Giovanni Tranchina. Springer, Heidelberg, pp 27–40

Vogler R (2014) Criminal evidence and respect for fair trial guarantees in the dialogue between the European court of human rights and national courts. In: Ruggeri S (ed) Transnational evidence and multicultural inquiries in Europe. Developments in EU legislation and new challenges for human rights-oriented criminal investigations in cross-border cases. Springer, Heidelberg, pp 181–192

Vogler R (2015) Lost in translation: language rights for defendants in European criminal proceedings. In: Ruggeri S (coord.) Human rights in European criminal law. New developments in European legislation and case law after the Lisbon treaty. Springer, Heidelberg, pp 95–109

Vogler T (1986) Article 6. In: Golsong H, Karl W, Miehsler H, Petzold H, Rogge K, Vogler T, Wildhaber L (eds) Internationaler Kommentar zur Europäischen Menschenrechtskonvention. Carl Heymanns, Köln

Vogliotti M (1998) La logica *floue* della Corte europea dei diritti dell'uomo tra tutela del testimone e salvaguardia del contraddittorio: il caso delle «testimonianze anonime». La Giurisprudenza italiana, cc. 851–860

Volk K (1978) Prozeßvoraussetzungen im Strafrecht. Zum Verhältniss von materiellem Recht und Prozeßrecht. Ebelsbach am Main

Wahl T (2015) Der Rahmenbeschluss zu Abwesenheitsentscheidungen. Brüsseler EU-Justizkooperation als Fall für Straßburg? EuCrim, pp 70–76

Weigend T (2000) Die Europäische Menschenrechtskonvention als deutsches Recht - Kollisionen und ihre Lösung. Strafverteidiger 2000, pp 384–390

Zacchè F (2008) Gli effetti della giurisprudenza europea in tema di privilegio contro le autoincriminazioni e diritto al silenzio. In: Balsamo A, Kostoris RE (eds) Giurisprudenza europea e processo penale italiano. Giappichelli, Torino, pp 179–195

Zumpano MA (2000) Rapporti tra processo civile e processo penale. Giappichelli, Torino

Zurkinden N (2012) Joint Investigation Teams: Chancen und Grenzen von gemeinsamen Ermittlungsgruppen in der Schweiz, Europa und den USA, Duncker & Humblot, Berlin

International Case-Law

European Court of Human Rights

A. et al. v. United Kingdom, Grand Chamber, judgment of 19 february 2009, Appl. No. 3455/05

A.H. v. Finland, judgment of 7 May 2007, Appl. No. 46602/99

Al-Khawaja and Tahery v. United Kingdom, Grand Chamber, judgment of 15 December 2011, Appl. No. 26766/05 and 22228/06

A.S. v. Finland, judgment of 28 September 2010, Appl. No. 40156/07

Asch v. Austria, judgment of 26 April 1991, Appl. No. 12398/86

Battisti v. France, decision of 12 December 2006, Appl. No. 28796/05

Bocos-Cuesta v. The Netherlands, judgment of 10 November 2005, Appl. No. 54789/00

Bouamar v. Belgium, judgment of 29 February 1988, Appl. No. 9106/80

Bracci v. Italy, judgment of 13 October 2005, Appl. No. 36822/02

Brandstetter v. Austria, judgment of 28 August 1991, Appl. No. 11170/84 12876/87 13468/87

Brozicek v. Italy, judgment of 19 December 1989, Appl. No. 10964/84

Brusco v. France, judgment of 14 October 2010, Appl. No. 1466/07

Camilleri v. Malta, decision of 16 March 2000, Appl. No. 51760/99

Cat Berro v. Italy, decision of 25 November 2008, Appl. No. 34192/07

Colozza v. Italy, judgment of 12 February 1985, Appl. No. 9024/80

Condron v. United Kingdom, judgment of 2 May 2000, Appl. No. 35718/97
Constantinescu v. Romania, judgment of 27 June 2000, Appl. No. 28871/95
Corigliano v. Italy, judgment of 10 December 1982, Appl. No. 8304/78
Craxi v. Italy, judgment of 5 December 2002, Appl. No. 34896/97
Danov v. Bulgaria, judgment of 26 October 2006, Appl. No. 56796/00
De Cubber v. Belgium, judgment of 26 October 1984, Appl. No. 9186/80
Deweer v. Belgium, judgment of 27 February 1980, Appl. No. 6903/75
De Wilde, Ooms and Versyp ('Vagrancy') v. Belgium, judgment of 18 November 1970, Appl. No. 2832/66, 2835/66 and 2899/66 hereas
D.M.T. and D.K.I. v. Bulgaria, judgment of 24 July 2012, Appl. No. 29476/06
Doorson v. The Netherlands, judgment of 26 March 1996, Appl. No. 20524/92
Döry v. Sweden, judgment of 11 November 2002, Appl. No. 28394/95
Drassich v. Italy, judgment of 11 December 2007, Appl. No. 25575/04
Drozd & Janousek v. France and Spain, judgment of 26 June 1992, Appl. No. 12747/87
Eckle v. Germany, judgment of 15 July 1982, Appl. No. 8130/78
Edwards v. United Kingdom, judgment of 16 February 1992, Appl. No. 13071/87
Ellis and Simms v. United Kingdom, judgment of 10 April 2012, Appl. No. 46099/06 and 46699/06
F.C.B. v. Italy, judgment of 28 August 1991, Appl. No. 12151/86
Fodale v. Italy, judgment of 1 June 2006, Appl. No. 70148/01
Foti et al. v. Italy, judgment of 10 December 1982, Appl. No. 7604/76, 7719/76, 7781/77 and 7913/77
Foucher v. France, judgment of 18 March 1997, Appl. No. 22209/93
Fox, Campbell and Hartley v. United Kingdom, judgment of 30 August 1990, Appl. No. 12244/86 12245/86 12383/86
Franquesa Freixas v. Spain, decision of 21 November 2000, Appl. No. 53590/99
Funke v. France, judgment of 25 February 1993, Appl. No. 10828/84
Gäfgen v. Germany, Grand Chamber, judgment of 1 June 2010, Appl. No. 22978/05
Garcia Alva v. Germany, judgment of 13 February 2001, Appl. No. 23541/94
Gray v. Germany, judgment of 22 May 2014, Appl. No. 49278/09
Haxhia v. Albania, judgment of 8 October 2013, Appl. No. 29861/03
Hermi v. Italy, Grand Chamber, judgment of 18 October 2006, Appl. No. 18114/02
Hugh Jordan v. United Kingdom, judgment of 4 May 2001, Appl. No. 24746/94
I.H. and others v. Austria, judgment of 20 April 2006, Appl. No. 42780/98
Ilaşcu and Others v Moldova and Russia, judgment of 8 July 2004, Appl. No. 48787/99.
Imbrioscia v. Switzerland, judgment of 24 November 1993, Appl. No. 13972/88
Isgrò v. Italy, judgment of 19 February 1991, Appl. No. 11339/85
Jalloh v. Germany, Grand Chamber, judgment of 11 June 2006, Appl. No. 54810/00
Jasper v. United Kingdom, judgment of 16 February 2000, Appl. No. 27052/95
John Murray v. United Kingdom, Grand Chamber, judgment of 8 February 1996, Appl. No. 18731/91
Keus v. The Netherlands, judgment of 25 October 1990, Appl. No. 12228/86
Kurt v. Turkey, judgment of 25 may 1998, Appl. No. 24276/94
Lamy v. Belgium, judgment of 30 March 1989, Appl. No. 10444/83
Liebreich v. Germany, judgment of 8 January 2008, Appl. No. 30443/03
Lucà v. Italy, judgment of 27 February 2001, Appl. No. 33354/96
Lückhof and Spanner v. Austria, judgment of 10 January 2008, Appl. No. 58452/00 and 61920/00
Kollcaku v. Italy, judgment of 8 February 2007, Appl. No. 25701/03
Kremzow v. Austria, judgment of 21 September 1993, Appl. No. 12350/86
Lala v. The Netherlands, judgment of 22 September 1994, Appl. No. 14861/89
Laukkanen and Manninen v. Finland, 3 February 2004, Appl. No. 50230/99
Magee v. United Kingdom, judgment of 6 June 2000, Appl. No. 28135/95
Majadallah v. Italy, judgment of 19 October 2006, Appl. No. 62094/00
Mamatkulov and Abdrurasulovic v. Turkey, judgment of 6 February 2003, Appl. No. 46827/99 46951/99
Mariani v. France, judgment of 31 March 2005, Appl. No. 43640/98
Mattoccia v. Italy, judgment of 25 July 2000, Appl. No. 23969/94

McGoff v. Sweden, judgment of 26 October 1984, Appl. No. 9017/80
Megyeri v. Germany, judgment of 12 May 1992, Appl. No. 13770/88
Moumen v. Italy, judgment of 6 June 2016, Appl. No. 3977/13
Neumeister v. Austria, judgment of 27 June 1968, Appl. No. 1936/63
O'Halloran and Francis v. United Kingdom, Grand Chamber, judgment of 29 June 2007, Appl. No. 15809/02 and 25624/02
Öcalan v. Turkey, 1st Chamber, judgment of 12 March 2003, Appl. No. 46221/99
Öcalan v. Turkey, Grand Chamber, judgment of 12 May 2005, Appl. No. 46221/99
Pélissier and Sassi v. France, Grand Chamber, judgment of 25 March 1999, Appl. No. 25444/94
Pellegrini v. Italy, judgment of 10 July 2001, Appl. No. 30882/96
Pello v. Estonia, judgment of 12 April 2007, Appl. No. 11423/03
Pesukic v. Switzerland, judgment of 6 December 2012, Appl. No. 25088/07
P.G. and J.H. v. United Kingdom, judgment of 25 September 2001, Appl. No. 44787/98
Piersack v. Belgium, judgment of 1 October 1982, Appl. No. 8692/79
Poitrimol v. France, judgment of 23 November 1993, Appl. No. 14032/88
Quadrelli v. Italy, judgment of 11 January 2000, Appl. No. 28168/95
Rowe and Davis v. United Kingdom, 16 February 2000, Appl. No. 28901/95
Sanchez-Reisse v. Switzerland, judgment of 21 October 1986, Appl. No. 9862/82
Saunders v. United Kingdom, Grand Chamber, judgment of 17 December 1996, Appl. No. 19187/91
Schatschaschwili v. Germany, judgment of 17 April 2014, Appl. No. 9154/10
Schiesser v. Switzerland, judgment of 4 December 1979, Appl. No. 7710/76
Seferovic v. Italy, judgment of 8 February 2011, Appl. No. 12921/04
Sejdovic v. Italy, 1st Chamber, judgment of 10 November 2004, Appl. No. 56581/00
Sejdovic v. Italy, Grand Chamber, judgment of 1 March 2006, Appl. No. 56581/00
Serves v. Italy, judgment of 20 October 1997, Appl. No. 20225/92
Shannon v. United Kingdom, judgment of 4 October 2005, Appl. No. 6563/03
Sher et al. v. United Kingdom, judgment of 20 October 2015, Appl. No. 5201/11
Sipavicius v. Lithuania, judgment of 21 February 2002, Appl. No. 49093/99
S.N. v. Sweden, judgment of 2 July 2002, Appl. No. 34209/96
Soering v. United Kingdom, judgment of 7 July 1989, Appl. No. 14038/88
Solakov v. the Former Yugoslav Republic of Macedonia, judgment of 21 October 2001, Appl. No. 47023/99
Somogyi v. Italy, judgment of 18 May 2004, Appl. No. 67972/01
Stanford v. United Kingdom, judgment of 23 February 1994, Appl. No. 16757/90
T. v. Italy, judgment of 12 October 1992, Appl. No. 14104/88
Tomasi v. France, judgment of 27 August 1992, Appl. No. 12850/87
van Mechelen v. The Netherlands, judgment of 23 April 1997, Appl. No. 21363/93, 21364/93, 21427/93 and 22056/93
van der Leer v. The Netherlands, judgment of 21 February 1990, Appl. No. 11509/85
Varbanov v. Bulgaria, judgment of 5 October 2000, Appl. No. 31365/96
X v. Netherlands, decision of 6 July 1976, Appl. No. 7512/76
X. v. United Kingdom, judgment of 5 November 1981, Appl. No. 7215/75
Winterwerp v. The Netherlands, judgment of 27 November 1981, Appl. No. 6301/73
Windisch v. Austria, judgment of 27 September 1990, Appl. No. 12489/86
Wloch v. Poland, judgment of 19 October 2000, Appl. No.27785/95

European Commission of Human Rights

Austria v. Italy, decision of 11 January 1961, Appl. No. 788/60

Bonazzi v. Italy, decision of 19 march 1981, Appl. 7955/77
Caprino v. United Kingdom, decision of 3 March 1978, Appl. No. 6871/75
P.V. v. Federal Republic of Germany, decision of 13 July 1987, Appl. No. 11853/85
X. v. United Kingdom, report of 16 July 1980, Appl. No. 6998/75
X., Y. and Z. v. Austria, decision of 5 February 1973, Appl. No. 5049/71

Inter-American Court of Human Rights

Judgments and Monitoring Compliance

Acosta Calderón v. Ecuador, judgment of 24 June 2005, Serie C No. 129
Almonacid Arellano et al. v. Chile, judgment of 26 September 2006, Serie C No. 154
Anzualdo Castro v. Peru, judgment of 22 September 2009, Series C No. 202
Barreto Leiva v. Venezuela, judgment of 17 November 2009, Serie C No. 206
Cabrera García and Montiel Flores v. Mexico, judgment of 26 November 2010, Serie C No. 220
Castillo Petruzzi et al. v. Peru, judgment of 30 May 1999, Serie C No. 52
Chaparro Álvarez and Lapo Íñiguez v. Ecuador, judgment of 21 November 2007, Serie C No. 170
Dacosta Cadogan v. Barbados, judgment of 24 September 2009, Serie C No. 204
Durand and Ugarte v. Peru, judgment of 16 August 2000, Series C No. 68
Fermín Ramírez v. Guatemala, judgment of 20 June 2005, Serie C No. 126
García Prieto et al. v. El Salvador, judgment 20 November 2007, Serie C No. 168
Garibaldi v. Brazil, judgment of 23 September 2009, Serie C No. 203
Gelman v. Uruguay, judgment of 24 February 2011, Serie C No. 221
Goiburú et al. v. Paraguay, judgment of 22 September 2006, Serie C No. 153
Gomes Lund et al. ("Guerrilha do Araguaia") v. Brazil, judgment of 24 November 2010, Serie C No. 219
González et al. ("Cotton Field") v. Mexico, judgment of 16 November 2009, Serie C No. 205
Ibsen Cárdenas and Ibsen Peña v. Bolivia, judgment of 1 September 2010, Serie C No. 217
Ituango Massacres v. Colombia, monitoring compliance with judgment. Court's Order of 7 July 2009
Ituango Massacres v. Colombia, monitoring compliance with judgment. Court's Order of 21 May 2013
Lori Berenson-Mejía v. Peru, judgment of 25 November 2004, Serie C No. 119
López Álvarez v. Honduras, judgment of 1 February 2006, Serie C No. 141
'Mapiripán Massacre' v. Colombia, judgment of 15 September 2005, Series C No. 134
Maritza Urrutia v. Guatemala, judgment of 27 November 2003, Series C No. 103
Norín Catrimán et al. v. Chile, judgment of 29 May 2014, Series C No. 279
Palamara Iribarne v. Chile, judgment of 22 November 2005, Serie C No. 135
Radilla Pacheco v. Mexico, judgment of 23 November 2009, Serie C No. 209
Servellón García et al. v. Honduras, judgment of 21 September 2006, Serie C No. 152
The Last Temptation of Christ (Olmedo Bustos at al.) v. Chile, judgment of 5 February 2001, Series C No. 73
The Serrano-Cruz Sisters v. El Salvador, judgment of 1 March 2005, Serie C No. 120
Tibi v. Ecuador, judgment of 7 September 2004, Serie C No. 114
Tiu Tojín v. Guatemala, judgment of 26 November 2008, Serie C No. 190
Vélez Loor v. Panama, judgment of 23 November 2010, Serie C No. 218
Villagrán-Morales et al. v. Guatemala, judgment of19 November 1999, Series C No. 63

Advisory Opinions

Habeas Corpus *in emergency situations (Arts. 27(2), 25(1) and 7(7) ACHR)*, Advisory Opinions OC-8/87 of 30 January 1987, Serie A No. 8
The Right to Information on Consular Assistance in the Framework of the Guarantees of Due Process of Law, Advisory Opinion OC-16/99 of 1 October 1999, Series A No. 16

Inter-American Commission on Human Rights

Annual Report (2009), OEA/Ser.L/V/II, Doc. 51 corr. 1, 30 December 2009

European Court of Justice

Bob-Dogi, judgment of 1 June 2016, C-241/15
Costa v. Enel, judgment of 15 July 1964, C-6/64
Covaci, judgment of 15 October 2015, C-216/14
Gueye and Sánchez, judgment of 15 Septemeber 2011, C-483/09 and C-1/110
Katz, judgment of 9 September 2008, C-404/07
Pupino, Grand Chamber, judgment of 16 June 2005, C-105/03
Simmenthal, judgment of 9 March 1978, C-106/77

National Case-Law

Italian case-law

Constitutional Court

Judgment of 7 March 1964 No. 14
Judgment of 24 May 1967 No. 61
Judgment of 2 February 1971 No. 12
Judgment of 27 December 1973 No. 183
Judgment of 21 June 1979 No. 54
Judgment of 27 July 1979 No. 84
Judgment of 22 December 1980 No. 184
Judgment of 10 February 1981 No. 17
Judgment of 8 March 1984 No. 170
Judgment of 21 April 1989 No. 232
Judgment of 2 July 1990 No. 313
Judgment of 12 October 1990 No. 443
Judgment of 11 February 1991 No. 74
Judgment of 15 February 1991 No. 81
Judgment of 15 February 1991 No. 88

Judgment of 5 April 1991 No. 145
Judgment of 25 May 1991 No. 221
Judgment of 16 July 1991 No. 353
Judgment of 31 January 1992 No. 23
Judgment of 31 January 1992 No. 24
Judgment of 3 June 1992 No. 241
Judgment of 19 January 1993 No. 10
Judgment of 25 November 1993 No. 418
Judgment of 14 December 1993 No. 438
Judgment of 30 December 1993 No. 474
Judgment 10 March 1994 No. 77
Judgment of 20 February 1995 No. 50
Judgment of 16 May 1995 No. 179
Decision of 14 April 1995 No. 131
Judgment of 25 July 1995 No. 379
Judgment of 29 January 1996 No. 15
Judgment of 9 July 1996 No. 238
Judgment of 1 October 1996 No. 384
Judgment of 30 July 1997 No. 283
Judgment of 9 July 1998 No. 262
Judgment of 11 February 1998 No. 361
Decision of 23 December 1998 No. 432
Decision of 16 April 1999 No. 124
Judgment of 22 October 1999 No. 388
Judgment of 25 October 2000 No. 440
Judgment of 18 November 2000 No. 504
Decision of 8 June 2001 No. 182
Decision of 21 December 2001 No. 426
Judgment of 26 February 2002 No. 32
Decision of 26 February 2002 No. 36
Decision of 16 May 2002 No. 203
Judgment of 19 November 2001 No. 460
Decision of 15 January 2003 No. 8
Judgment of 29 January 2005 No. 63
Decision of 4 October 2005 No. 361
Judgment 21 November 2006 No. 381
Decision of 24 July 2007 No. 323
Judgment of 24 October 2007 No. 348
Judgment of 24 October 2007 No. 349
Decision of 18 April 2008 No. 109
Judgment of 30 July 2008 No. 305
Decision of 30 July 2008 No. 321
Decision of 10 October 2008 No. 339
Judgment of 26 June 2009 No. 184
Judgment of 26 November 2009 No. 311
Judgment of 4 December 2009 No. 317
Judgment of 18 Decembre 2009 No. 333
Judgment of 7 April 2011 No. 113
Judgment of 18 July 2013 No. 210
Judgment of 22 October 2014 No. 238
Judgment of 26 March 2015 No. 49
Judgment 26 January 2017 No. 21

Supreme Court

Abruzzese, 5th Section, 22 April 2009, CED 243899
Agostino, 1st Section, 6 February 1995, CED 200224
Amato et al., 2nd Section, 7 July 2006, CED 234968
Askin, 6th Section, 26 April 1995, CED 201143
Baldan, Joint Sections, 9 July 1997, Cassazione penale 1998, p. 64
Ballinari et al., 1st Section, 30 May 1982, Giurisprudenza italiana (1982)(II), p. 16
Barachini, 6th Section, 12 December 2008, CED 241926
Bardi, 6th Section, 16 of April 2003, Cassazione penale 2004, p. 2455 f.
Barillà, 5th Section, 17 October 2002, CED 223240
Barlettelli, 6th Section, 10 January 2003, CED 224219
Battistella, Joint Sections, 20 December 2007, CED 238239-240
Bidimost, 1st Section, 1 March 2006, CED 233614
Bosio, 4th Section, 22 June 2000, CED 217276
Capozza, 5th Section, 22 September 2004, CED 230215
Capri, 2nd Section, 18 March 2008, CED 239739
Carboni, Joint Sections, 19 May 1984, Cassazione penale (1984), p. 1611
Cardoni, Joint Sections, 9 June 1995, Cassazione penale (1996), p. 473 ff.
Caruso, 3rd Section, 4 December 2002, CED 223737
Ciarlantini, 1st Section, 12 December 2007, CED 239207
Cotugno, 5th Section, 20 April 2005, Cassazione penale (2007), p. 4240
De Falco, 1 December 2010, CED 248963
D.F., Joint Sections, 25 Novemeber 2010, CED 250197
Di Costanzo, 6st Section, 18 February 1993, CED 194541
Enciu, 6th Section, 6 May 2008, CED 241256
Fà, 1st Section, 17 June 2004, CED 229850
Ferrara, 2nd Section 27 January 2005, CED 231106
Franconetti, 6th Section, 4 April 2007, CED 237667
G., 3rd Section, 25 November 2000, Foro italiano (II), 20
Gherasim, 5th Section, 10 May 2006, Rivista penale (2007), p. 234
Gorduna, 6th Section, 19 April 2003, Cassazione penale (2005), p. 114
Gradi, 4th Section, 7 November 2003, Cassazione penale (2004), p. 3266 f.
Greco, 1st Section, 21 October 2003, CED 227641
Huzuneanu, Joint Sections, 31 January 2008, CED 238472
Iamundo, 6th Section, 9 October 2008, CED 241864
Iuzzolini, 6th Section, 24 May 1995, Diritto penale e processo (1995), p. 822
Ivancescu, Sez. VI, 13 January 2015, No. 1190
Jakani, Joint Sections, 23 June 2000, Guida al diritto (2000)(26), p. 73
Kaneva, 1st Section, 29 May 2007, Rivista di diritto e procedura penale 2008, p. 1382
Kusi Kwaben, 4th Section, 29 November 2000, Archivio della nuova procedura penale (2002), p. 226
Lodigiani et al., 6th Section, 30 January 2003, CED 224145
Mariano, Joint Sections, 23 February 2000, Cassazione penale (2000), p. 2228
Mariottini, 1st Section, 22 May 2003, CED 225488
Maksymenko, 6th Section, 22 January 2010, CED 246173
Morandi, 6th Section, 16 November 1999, Archivio della nuova procedura penale 2000, p. 423
Morini, Joint Sections, 31 January 2008, CED 238680
Muscas, 1st Section, 28 November 2001, Archivio della nuova procedura penale 2002, p. 714
Neroni, 5th Section, 29 July 2005, CED 232297
Noschese, 6th Section, 7 June 1994, CED 198737
Odigie Obeide, 6th Section, 3 March 2000, CED 215851
Papia et al., 6th Section, 3 March 2004, CED 228471

Perri, 1st Section, 22 September 2005, CED 232088
Piaggio, 6th Section, 14 February 2007, CED 235560
Pizzata, 1st Section, 22 January 2009, CED 243796
Plaku, 1st Section, 17 June 2005, CED 232105
P.g. in proc. Steger, Joint Sections, 16 july 2015, www.penalecontemporaneo.it
Poporogu, 6th Section, 7 April 1999, Archivio della nuova procedura penale (1999), p. 669
Pozzi, 2nd Section, 8 March 2002, CED 222025
P.o. in proc. Mercuri, 4th Section, 16 April 2008, CED 240227
Prodan, 6th Section, 26 November 2009, CED 245452
Rabei Osman, 6th Section, 1 December 2004, CED 230499
Ramoci, Joint Sections, 30 January 2007, Cassazione penale (2007), p. 911
Remling, 3rd Section, 23 April 2009, CED 243956
Rossi, 6th Section, 10 April 2003, Guida al diritto (2004)(5), p. 92
Russo, 28 April 2009, CED 243938
Sanna, 1st Section, 9 June 1995, CED 202460
Sava, 6th Section, 2 October 2006, CED 235298
Scardaccione, 3rd Section, 24 June 1998, Guida al diritto (1998)(37), p. 88
S.L., Joint Sections, 28 June 2006, CED 234214
Tammaro, Joint Sections, 21 June 2000, CED 216246
Torcasio, Joint Sections, 28 May 2003, Cassazione penale (2003), p. 21
Torresan, 17 August 1989, Cassazione penale (2003), p. 1955
Venezia, 6th Section, 12 October 1995, Rivista penale (1995), p. 662
Von Pinoci, 6th Section, 2 December 2004, CED rv. 230229
XY, 5th Section, 12 November 2001, Guida al diritto (2002)(5), p. 88
Zaccaria, 2nd Section, 17 March 2009, CED 244253
Zalagaitis, Joint Sections, 24 September 2003, Cassazione penale (2004), 1563
Zita, 2nd Section, 19 October 2005, Guida al diritto (2006)(14), p. 97

Brazilian Case-Law

Federal Supreme Tribunal

RHC 32.742, DJ de 4 Junly 1955, rel. Min. Barros Barreto
Ext. 426, dec. of 1 July 1985, rel. Min. Rafael Mayer
Ext. 541, dec. of 7 November 1992, rel. original Min. Néri da Silveira, rel. para o Acórdão min. Sepúlveda Pertence
Ext. 663, dec. of 28 August 1996, rel. Min. Celso de Mello
Ext. 669, DJ of 29 March 1996, rel. Min. Celso de Mello
Carta Rog. 8.443, dec. of 3 September 1998, rel. Min. Celso de Mello
Carta Rog. 10.920, dec. of 29 September 2003, rel. Min. Maurício Corrêa
HC 83.588, DJ of 15 December 2006, rel. Min. Marco Aurélio
RE 460.971, dec. of 13 February 2007, rel. Min. Sepúlveda Pertence
HC 90.485/SP, dec. of 10 April 2007, rel. Min. Cezar Peluso
HC 84.489/DF, dec. of 8 November 2007, rel. Min. Jane Silva
HC 87.759/DF, dec. of 26 February 2008, rel. Min. Marco Aurélio
Ext. 1.098, DJ of 11 April 2008, rel. Min. Cezar Peluso
RE 554.410-ED, dec. of 19 August 2008, rel. Min. Joaquim Barbosa
HC 87.585-8, DJ of 25 June 2009, rel. Min. Celso de Mello
HC 93.503, DJ of 7 August 2009, rel. Min. Celso de Mello
HC 84.580-1/SP, DJ of 18 September 2009, rel. Min. Celso de Mello

HC 153.140, DJ of 12 August 2010, rel. Min. Felix Fischer
HC 104.404, DJ of 30 November 2010, rel. Min. Dias Toffoli
HC 110.623, DJ of 13 March 2012, rel. Min. Ricardo Lewandowski
HC 98.676, DJ of 8 August 2012, rel. Min. Celso de Mello

Superior Court of Justice

HC 19.506, dec. of 5 December 2006, rel. Min. Felix Fischer
AgRg 2484, dec. 29 June 2007, rel. Min. Barros Monteiro
HC 93.557, dec. of 19 February 2008, rel. Min. Arnaldo Esteves Lima
HC 151.357, dec. of 21 October 2010, rel. Min. Og Fernandes
REsp 1.259.482, 27 October 2011, rel. Min. Marco Aurélio Bellize

Spanish Case-Law

Constitutional Court

Judgment of 30 March 2000 No. 91
Judgment of 13 february 2014 No. 26

German Case-Law

Constitutional Court

Order of 15 December 2015, Az. 2 BvR 2735/14

MIX
Papier aus verantwortungsvollen Quellen
Paper from responsible sources
FSC® C105338

If you have any concerns about our products,
you can contact us on
ProductSafety@springernature.com

In case Publisher is established outside the EU,
the EU authorized representative is:
Springer Nature Customer Service Center GmbH
Europaplatz 3, 69115 Heidelberg, Germany

Printed by Libri Plureos GmbH
in Hamburg, Germany